Fodor's Road Guide USA

Minnesota
Nebraska
North Dakota
South Dakota

First Edition

Fodor's Travel Publications
New York Toronto London Sydney Auckland
www.fodors.com

Fodor's Road Guide USA: Minnesota, Nebraska, North Dakota, South Dakota

President: Bonnie Ammer
Publisher: Kris Kliemann
Executive Managing Editor: Denise DeGennaro
Editorial Director: Karen Cure
Director of Marketing Development: Jeanne Kramer
Associate Managing Editor: Linda Schmidt
Senior Editor: Constance Jones
Director of Production and Manufacturing: Chuck Bloodgood
Creative Director: Fabrizio La Rocca

Contributors

Editing: Kathy Astor (South Dakota), Natalie Kusz (Minnesota), Linda Downs (Nebraska), and Pat Hadley-Miller (North Dakota), with Kim Anderson, Nuha Ansari, Michele Bloom, Richard Brunelli, Nancy Condry, Steve Crohn, Sarah Cupp, Michael de Zayas, Karen Deaver, Hannah Fons, Anna Halasz, Amy Hegarty, Jay Hyams, Richard Koss, Fran Levine, Elizabeth Minyard, Sidharth Murdeshwar, Eric Reymond, Barbara Stewart, Daniel Taras, Susan Walton, and Ethan Young

Writing: Sue Berg (North Dakota), Tom and Nyla Griffith (South Dakota), Dave Kenney (Minnesota), and Candy Moulton and Mike Whye (Nebraska), with Sarah Gil, Keisha Hutchins, LaKeisha Light, Melanie Mize, Tina Ross, Alan Ryan, Frances Schamberg, Margo Waite, and Kirsten Weisenberger

Research: Alex Bajoris, Ephen Colter, Doug Hirlinger, Janue Johnson, Eric Joseph, Tenisha Light, Mary Ann O'Grady, and Jordana Rosenberg

Black-and-White Maps: Rebecca Baer, Robert Blake, David Lindroth, Todd Pasini

Production/Manufacturing: Robert B. Shields

Cover: Melanie Acevedo/Photonica (background photo), Bart Nagel (photo, illustration)

Interior Photos: Corbis (Minnesota and North Dakota), Nebraska Division of Travel and Tourism/Department of Economic Development (Nebraska), South Dakota Tourism (South Dakota)

Copyright

First Edition
ISBN 0-679-00498-X
ISSN 1528-1531

Special Sales

PRINTED IN THE UNITED STATES OF AMERICA
10 9 8 7 6 5 4 3 2 1

CONTENTS

Great Road Trips

Of all the things that went wrong with Clark Griswold's vacation, one stands out: The theme park he had driven across the country to visit was closed when he got there. Clark, the suburban bumbler played by Chevy Chase in 1983's hilarious *National Lampoon's Vacation,* is fictional, of course. But his story is poignantly true. Although most Americans get only two precious weeks of vacation a year, many set off on their journeys with surprisingly little guidance. Many travelers find out about their destination from friends and family or wait to get travel information until they arrive in their hotel, where racks of brochures dispense the "facts," along with free city magazines. But it's hard to distinguish the truth from hype in these sources. And it makes no sense to spend priceless vacation time in a hotel room reading about a place when you could be out seeing it up close and personal.

Congratulate yourself on picking up this guide. Studying it—before you leave home—is the best possible first step toward making sure your vacation fulfills your every dream.

Inside you'll find all the tools you need to plan a perfect road trip. In the hundreds of towns we describe, you'll find thousands of places to explore. So you'll always know what's around the next bend. And with the practical information we provide, you can easily call to confirm the details that matter and study up on what you'll want to see and do, before you leave home.

By all means, when you plan your trip, allow yourself time to make a few detours. Because as wonderful as it is to visit sights you've read about, it's the serendipitous experiences that often prove the most memorable: the hole-in-the-wall diner that serves a transcendent tomato soup, the historical society gallery stuffed with dusty local curiosities of days gone by. As you whiz down the highway, use the book to find out more about the towns announced by roadside signs. Consider turning off at the next exit. And always remember: In this great country of ours, there's an adventure around every corner.

HOW TO USE THIS BOOK

Alphabetical organization should make it a snap to navigate through this book. Still, in putting it together, we've made certain decisions and used certain terms you need to know about.

LOCATIONS AND CATEGORIZATIONS

Color map coordinates are given for every town in the guide.

Attractions, restaurants, and lodging places are listed under the nearest town covered in the guide.

Parks and forests are sometimes listed under the main access point.

Exact street addresses are provided whenever possible; when they were not available or applicable, directions and/or cross-streets are indicated.

CITIES

For state capitals and larger cities, attractions are alphabetized by category. Shopping sections focus on good shopping areas where you'll find a concentration of interesting shops. We include malls only if they're unusual in some way and individual stores only when they're community institutions. Restaurants and hotels are grouped by price category then arranged alphabetically.

RESTAURANTS

All are air-conditioned unless otherwise noted, and all permit smoking unless they're identified as "no-smoking."

Dress: Assume that no jackets or ties are required for men unless otherwise noted.

Family-style service: Restaurants characterized this way serve food communally, out of serving dishes as you might at home.

Meals and hours: Assume that restaurants are open for lunch and dinner unless otherwise noted. We always specify days closed and meals not available.

Prices: The price ranges listed are for dinner entrées (or lunch entrées if no dinner is served).

Reservations: They are always a good idea. We don't mention them unless they're essential or are not accepted.

Fodor's Choice: Stars denote restaurants that are Fodor's Choices—our editors' picks of the state's very best in a given price category.

LODGINGS

All are air-conditioned unless otherwise noted, and all permit smoking unless they're identified as "no-smoking."

AP: This designation means that a hostelry operates on the American Plan (AP)—-that is, rates include all meals. AP may be an option or it may be the only meal plan available; be sure to find out.

Baths: You'll find private bathrooms with bathtubs unless noted otherwise.

Business services: If we tell you they're there, you can expect a variety on the premises.

Exercising: We note if there's "exercise equipment" even when there's no designated area; if you want a dedicated facility, look for "gym."

Facilities: We list what's available but don't note charges to use them. When pricing accommodations, always ask what's included.

Hot tub: This term denotes hot tubs, Jacuzzis, and whirlpools.

MAP: Rates at these properties include two meals.

No smoking: Properties with this designation prohibit smoking.

Opening and closing: Assume that hostelries are open year-round unless otherwise noted.

Pets: We note whether or not they're welcome and whether there's a charge.

Pools: Assume they're outdoors with fresh water; indoor pools are noted.

Prices: The price ranges listed are for a high-season double room for two, excluding tax and service charge.

Telephone and TV: Assume that you'll find them unless otherwise noted.

Fodor's Choice: Stars denote hostelries that are Fodor's Choices—our editors' picks of the state's very best in a given price category.

NATIONAL PARKS

National parks protect and preserve the treasures of America's heritage, and they're always worth visiting whenever you're in the area. Many are worth a long detour. If you will travel to many national parks, consider purchasing the National Parks Pass ($50), which gets you and your companions free admission to all parks for one year. (Camping and parking are extra.) A percentage of the proceeds from sales of the pass helps to fund important projects in the parks. Both the Golden Age Passport ($10), for those 62 and older, and the Golden Access Passport (free), for travelers with disabilities, entitle holders to free entry to all national parks, plus 50% off fees for the use of many park facilities and services. You must show proof of age and of U.S. citizenship or permanent residency (such as a U.S. passport, driver's license, or birth certificate) and, if requesting Golden Access, proof of your disability. You must get your Golden Access or Golden Age passport in person; the former is available at all federal recreation areas, the latter at federal recreation areas that charge fees. You may purchase the National Parks Pass by mail or through the Internet. For information, contact the National Park Service (Department of the Interior, 1849 C St. NW, Washington, DC 20240-0001, 202/208—4747, *www.nps.gov*). To buy the National Parks Pass, write to 27540 Ave. Mentry, Valencia, CA 91355, call 888/GO—PARKS, or visit www.national-parks.org.

IMPORTANT TIP

Although all prices, opening times, and other details in this book are based on information supplied to us at press time, changes occur all the time in the travel world, and Fodor's cannot accept responsibility for facts that become outdated or for inadvertent errors or omissions. So always confirm information when it matters, especially if you're making a detour to visit a specific place.

Let Us Hear from You

Keeping a travel guide fresh and up-to-date is a big job, and we welcome any and all comments. We'd love to have your thoughts on places we've listed, and we're interested in hearing about your own special finds, even the ones in your own back yard. Our guides are thoroughly updated for each new edition, and we're always adding new information, so your feedback is vital. Contact us via e-mail in care of roadnotes@fodors.com (specifying the name of the book on the subject line) or via snail mail in care of Road Guides at Fodor's, 280 Park Avenue, New York, NY 10017. We look forward to hearing from you. And in the meantime, have a wonderful road trip.

THE EDITORS

Important Numbers and On-Line Info

LODGINGS

Adam's Mark	800/444—2326	www.adamsmark.com
Baymont Inns	800/428—3438	www.baymontinns.com
Best Western	800/528—1234	www.bestwestern.com
	TDD 800/528—2222	
Budget Host	800/283—4678	www.budgethost.com
Clarion	800/252—7466	www.clarioninn.com
Comfort	800/228—5150	www.comfortinn.com
Courtyard by Marriott	800/321—2211	www.courtyard.com
Days Inn	800/325—2525	www.daysinn.com
Doubletree	800/222—8733	www.doubletreehotels.com
Drury Inns	800/325—8300	www.druryinn.com
Econo Lodge	800/555—2666	www.hotelchoice.com
Embassy Suites	800/362—2779	www.embassysuites.com
Exel Inns of America	800/356—8013	www.exelinns.com
Fairfield Inn by Marriott	800/228—2800	www.fairfieldinn.com
Fairmont Hotels	800/527—4727	www.fairmont.com
Forte	800/225—5843	www.forte-hotels.com
Four Seasons	800/332—3442	www.fourseasons.com
Friendship Inns	800/453—4511	www.hotelchoice.com
Hampton Inn	800/426—7866	www.hampton-inn.com
Hilton	800/445—8667	www.hilton.com
	TDD 800/368—1133	
Holiday Inn	800/465—4329	www.holiday-inn.com
	TDD 800/238—5544	
Howard Johnson	800/446—4656	www.hojo.com
	TDD 800/654—8442	
Hyatt & Resorts	800/233—1234	www.hyatt.com
Inns of America	800/826—0778	www.innsofamerica.com
Inter-Continental	800/327—0200	www.interconti.com
La Quinta	800/531—5900	www.laquinta.com
	TDD 800/426—3101	
Loews	800/235—6397	www.loewshotels.com
Marriott	800/228—9290	www.marriott.com
Master Hosts Inns	800/251—1962	www.reservahost.com
Le Meridien	800/225—5843	www.lemeridien.com
Motel 6	800/466—8356	www.motel6.com
Omni	800/843—6664	www.omnihotels.com
Quality Inn	800/228—5151	www.qualityinn.com
Radisson	800/333—3333	www.radisson.com
Ramada	800/228—2828	www.ramada.com
	TDD 800/533—6634	
Red Carpet/Scottish Inns	800/251—1962	www.reservahost.com
Red Lion	800/547—8010	www.redlion.com
Red Roof Inn	800/843—7663	www.redroof.com
Renaissance	800/468—3571	www.renaissancehotels.com
Residence Inn by Marriott	800/331—3131	www.residenceinn.com
Ritz-Carlton	800/241—3333	www.ritzcarlton.com
Rodeway	800/228—2000	www.rodeway.com

Sheraton	800/325—3535	www.sheraton.com
Shilo Inn	800/222—2244	www.shiloinns.com
Signature Inns	800/822—5252	www.signature-inns.com
Sleep Inn	800/221—2222	www.sleepinn.com
Super 8	800/848—8888	www.super8.com
Susse Chalet	800/258—1980	www.sussechalet.com
Travelodge/Viscount	800/255—3050	www.travelodge.com
Vagabond	800/522—1555	www.vagabondinns.com
Westin Hotels & Resorts	800/937—8461	www.westin.com
Wyndham Hotels & Resorts	800/996—3426	www.wyndham.com

AIRLINES

Air Canada	888/247—2262	www.aircanada.ca
Alaska	800/426—0333	www.alaska-air.com
American	800/433—7300	www.aa.com
America West	800/235—9292	www.americawest.com
British Airways	800/247—9297	www.british-airways.com
Canadian	800/426—7000	www.cdnair.ca
Continental Airlines	800/525—0280	www.continental.com
Delta	800/221—1212	www.delta.com
Midway Airlines	800/446—4392	www.midwayair.com
Northwest	800/225—2525	www.nwa.com
SkyWest	800/453—9417	www.delta.com
Southwest	800/435—9792	www.southwest.com
TWA	800/221—2000	www.twa.com
United	800/241—6522	www.ual.com
USAir	800/428—4322	www.usair.com

BUSES AND TRAINS

Amtrak	800/872—7245	www.amtrak.com
Greyhound	800/231—2222	www.greyhound.com
Trailways	800/343—9999	www.trailways.com

CAR RENTALS

Advantage	800/777—5500	www.arac.com
Alamo	800/327—9633	www.goalamo.com
Allstate	800/634—6186	www.bnm.com/as.htm
Avis	800/331—1212	www.avis.com
Budget	800/527—0700	www.budget.com
Dollar	800/800—4000	www.dollar.com
Enterprise	800/325—8007	www.pickenterprise.com
Hertz	800/654—3131	www.hertz.com
National	800/328—4567	www.nationalcar.com
Payless	800/237—2804	www.paylesscarrental.com
Rent-A-Wreck	800/535—1391	www.rent-a-wreck.com
Thrifty	800/367—2277	www.thrifty.com

Note: Area codes are changing all over the United States as this book goes to press. For the latest updates, check www.areacode-info.com.

Fodor's Road Guide USA

Minnesota
Nebraska
North Dakota
South Dakota

Minnesota

Minnesota's nickname, the "Land of 10,000 Lakes," is an understatement. Its 11,842 lakes (just counting those larger than 10 acres) offer more shoreline than Florida, California, and Hawaii combined. It also is the starting place for the world's third-longest river, the Mississippi. Its name comes from the Dakota word meaning "sky-tinted water."

Minnesota's identity is closely linked to its wealth of water. The sport of waterskiing was invented in 1922 by a young Minnesotan who'd become bored with fishing on Lake Pepin. One out of every six people in the state owns a boat, the highest ratio in the country. Minnesota also ranks as number one in the per-capita rate of fishing license purchases. And fishing isn't just a warm-weather activity, either. Every winter, little heated shacks pop up on thousands of lakes. Inside, you'll find anglers huddling over holes in the ice, hoping to hook a lunker.

That's not to say that Minnesota is one big puddle. Far from it.

While the state's outdoor attractions lure all sorts of visitors including boaters, hikers, cross-country skiers, and snowmobilers, it also has plenty to offer those who don't consider themselves outdoor types. In particular, the Twin Cities of Minneapolis and St. Paul feature a wide variety of entertainment opportunities, including theater, music, shopping, and spectator sports.

Minnesota spans 406 miles from Canada to Iowa, and if you travel all of them, you'll see three distinct kinds of terrain. To the west and south you'll find grassland plains and prairies. Much of this land has been converted to agricultural use since the arrival of white settlers 150 years ago, but some still remains in its native state. Northern Minnesota is home to coniferous forest. The eastern part of the state, once known as the "Big Woods," is the natural home of hardwood forests, but most of the trees were cut down for lumber long ago.

Agriculture, timber, and eventually iron mining formed the backbone of Minnesota's early economy. Farming is still a major cog in the state's economic machine. With its more than 92,000 farms, Minnesota ranks high in the production of corn, sugar beets,

CAPITAL: ST. PAUL	POPULATION: 4,375,099	AREA: 79,548 SQUARE MI
BORDERS: ND, SD, IA, WI, CANADA, LAKE SUPERIOR		TIME ZONE: CENTRAL
POSTAL ABBREVIATION: MN	WEB SITE: WWW.EXPLOREMINNESOTA.COM.	

soybeans, wheat, peas, hogs, and turkeys. Other industries such as manufacturing (this is the birthplace of Scotch tape and the snowmobile), transportation, banking, and retail round out a well-diversified economic mix.

History

About 10,000 years ago, most of the area now known as Minnesota was covered by glaciers more than a mile thick. As the glaciers melted, they left behind thousands of lakes and rivers. At about this time, the first humans arrived in the area following herds of large game. Some of the earlier inhabitants left behind rock carvings and ceremonial earth mounds that can still be seen today.

The Dakota people were Minnesota's most established residents when French fur traders began arriving in the 1600s. Eventually, the Ojibway people moved in from the east and pushed the Dakota southward. In the early 1800s, the Dakota signed a treaty allowing the U.S. government to build what became known as Fort Snelling at the confluence of the Mississippi and Minnesota rivers. In the years that followed, the government forced the Dakota and Ojibway to cede more and more land. Settlers began arriving by the thousands. In 1858, Minnesota became the nation's 32nd state. Four years later, hundreds of people died when the Dakota, frustrated over the government's broken promises, launched a series of attacks against white settlers. As a result of these attacks, 38 Dakota were hanged and many others were sent to prison. Nearly all the remaining Dakota were expelled from Minnesota and forced to live under horrible conditions in North and South Dakota.

Over the next several decades, thousands of immigrants arrived in Minnesota to work in lumbering and farming. By 1900, nearly half of all Minnesotans were of German ancestry, but Scandinavians from Norway, Sweden, and Denmark outnumbered settlers from any single country. The state's Scandinavian heritage has resulted in a disproportionate number of blond, blue-eyed people named Larsen, Peterson, Johnson, and Andersen. In later years, as the cities and new industries grew, people from eastern and southern Europe began arriving in large numbers. Finland, Yugoslavia, and Italy sent many workers to Minnesota mines and factories. A few people of African ancestry had come to Minnesota with the first white explorers. Their numbers increased following the Civil War. In the 1920s, Mexican migrant workers began arriving, establishing a base population of Spanish speakers. In the 1980s, Minnesota became home to many refugees from Vietnam, Cambodia, and Laos. Minneapolis, St. Paul, and Duluth have always had the largest African-American, Hispanic, and Asian communities in the state. But recently, smaller cities such as Willmar and Hutchinson have seen their minority populations grow dramatically thanks in large part to jobs in the meat-packing industry.

Regions

1. TWIN CITIES

These twins are not identical, but it's not stretching the analogy too far to say they're fraternal. Taken together, Minneapolis and St. Paul form a single metropolitan area

MN Timeline

Late 1600s	1679	1736	1783
French explorers (voyageurs) begin arriving.	Frenchman Daniel Greysolon Sieur Duluth claims the region for King Louis XIV.	War breaks out between the Dakota and Ojibway. Fighting lasts for more than 100 years and results in the Ojibway pushing the Dakota to the west and south.	The Treaty of Paris cedes much of Minnesota territory to the United States.

INTRODUCTION
HISTORY
REGIONS
WHEN TO VISIT
STATE'S GREATS
RULES OF THE ROAD
DRIVING TOURS

with two distinct personalities. St. Paul is the older, more sedate city, known for its architectural landmarks and Irish immigrant heritage. Minneapolis is the younger, hipper sibling with a thriving downtown and more than a dozen lakes within the city limits. Both cities cling to their own identities, but they can never completely separate. They share a public transportation system, for example. The international airport is just as convenient to St. Paul as it is to Minneapolis.

The confluence of the Mississippi and Minnesota rivers is the focus of the seven-county Twin Cities metropolitan area, which spreads into suburbs and eventually farmland. Wisconsin provides the easternmost border.

Towns listed: Anoka, Bloomington, Elk River, Hastings, Lakeville, Minneapolis, St. Paul, Shakopee, Stillwater, Taylors Falls

2. IRON RANGE

The rich iron ore that first attracted miners to this region of northern Minnesota is gone now, but there's still iron to be found in the range's hard taconite bedrock. The communities that grew up around the mines—towns like Virginia, Eveleth, Chisholm, and Hibbing—are now trying to diversify their economies and market themselves as vacation destinations or gateways. The region is a gold mine, so to speak, of iron-age industrial history. It actually includes three separate ranges. The northernmost Vermilion Range begins near the Canadian border and stretches west toward Tower. The Mesabi Range is the largest of the three, snaking southwest from the Arrowhead. The smaller Cuyuna Range is farther south and west, near Aitkin.

Towns listed: Babbitt, Baudette, Chisholm, Cook, Eveleth, Grand Rapids, Hibbing, Roseau, Virginia

3. ARROWHEAD

Some of Minnesota's most scenic country lies in the northeast, known as the Arrowhead. It includes part of the Iron Range, but it also encompasses the North Shore area between Duluth and Grand Portage and the wilderness areas in the far north. This is where you'll find the untouched beauty of Superior National Forest and the Boundary Waters Canoe Area Wilderness. Farther west is Voyageurs National Park.

Towns listed: Cloquet, Crane Lake, Duluth, Ely, Grand Marais, Grand Portage, International Falls, Lutsen, Tower, Two Harbors, Voyageurs National Park

4. CENTRAL LAKES AREA

When people talk about the best fishing spots in Minnesota, they often bring up the Central Lakes Area, which stretches from Lake Mille Lacs north into the Chippewa National

1803	1818	1820	1823	1837
The western part of Minnesota is included in the Louisiana Purchase.	Britain cedes the northern strip of Minnesota bordering Canada.	Fort St. Anthony (later Fort Snelling) is established at the confluence of the Mississippi and Minnesota rivers.	The first steamboats begin arriving at developing settlements along the Mississippi River. A gristmill is established at St. Anthony Falls.	Dakota sign treaty ceding all land east of the Mississippi to the United States.

Forest. Some of the state's biggest and most popular fishing lakes are here, lakes with memorable names like Mille Lacs, Leech, and Winnibigoshish. In winter, ice houses pop up on the frozen lakes. Snowmobiles and cross-country skiers spread out along hundreds of miles of marked trails.

Towns listed: Aitkin, Bemidji, Brainerd, Cross Lake, Deer River, Deerwood, Hinkley, Litchfield, Little Falls, Mora, Onamia, Park Rapids, Pine River, St. Cloud, Sauk Centre, Walker.

5. RED RIVER VALLEY

The Red River Valley is one of the flattest land surfaces in North America. What now is land was once the floor of Lake Agassiz, a vast glacier-dammed lake that developed at the end of the last ice age. About 9,300 years ago, the waters of Lake Agassiz drained away, leaving behind the rich, fertile farmland and a host of smaller lakes including Red Lake and Lake of the Woods. Agriculture is the big draw here, but the presence of Moorhead and its sister city, Fargo, North Dakota (the largest metropolitan area between Minneapolis-St. Paul and Spokane, Washington), ensures plenty of entertainment and dining choices as well. As its name suggests, this region follows the Red River and hugs the North Dakota border.

Towns listed: Alexandria, Crookston, Detroit Lakes, Fergus Falls, Glenwood, Moorhead, Thief River Falls

6. BLUFFS REGION

This was the main passageway for early white settlement in Minnesota. It's not hard to imagine immigrant farmers, timber-cutters, and their families traveling by steamboat toward their homes, gazing up at the tall limestone bluffs lining the Mississippi River. The river communities, from Red Wing to La Crescent, are some of the oldest in the state. Most of them still retain much of their 19th-century charm, making them popular day-trip destinations for tourists and residents in the Twin Cities.

Towns listed: Lake City, Preston, Red Wing, Wabasha, Winona.

7. SOUTHERN PRAIRIE

At one time, most of the southern quarter of Minnesota was covered with prairie grasslands. Now fewer than 150,000 acres remain. Early settlers turned Minnesota's southern prairies into farms, and today agriculture remains the most important sector of the region's economy. This area was the scene of a defining moment in Minnesota's history: the Dakota conflict of 1862. Many communities feature markers, monuments, and history centers that will help visitors understand the significance of the event. The region stretches north from the Iowa border and curves up toward the point on the map where Minnesota, South Dakota, and North Dakota meet.

Towns listed: Albert Lea, Austin, Blue Earth, Fairmont, Faribault, Granite Falls, Hutchinson, Jackson, Le Sueur, Luverne, Mankato, Mantorville, Marshall, Morris, New Prague,

1849	**1851**	**1851**	**1853**	**1855**
Congress passes legislation creating the Minnesota Territory.	Dakota sign two more treaties ceding all of their remaining lands (most of southern Minnesota).	The University of Minnesota is established.	Completion of the Soo Ship Canal at Sault Ste. Marie opens a Great Lakes water route to Duluth and the surrounding area.	Ojibway sign a final treaty ceding most of their land to the United States.

New Ulm, Northfield, Owatonna, Pipestone, Redwood Falls, Rochester, St. Peter, Spring Valley, Tracy, Willmar.

When to Visit

Minnesota's weather tends toward extremes. It's gained a well-deserved reputation for bone-chilling temperatures in winter. Not as well known is the fact that sauna-like conditions with high temperatures and high humidity are common during July and August. The record high temperature of 114°F has been recorded twice, once in Beardsley in 1917 and again in Moorhead in 1936. The town of Tower lays claim to the state's lowest low: -60°F in 1996. Still, those are the extremes. Many visitors find that Minnesota's climate is quite easy to take, provided they're dressed correctly.

Winter sports enthusiasts want ice and snow, and Minnesota usually delivers. Lakes often freeze over before Thanksgiving and don't clear until early April. Snowfall can be more erratic. Blizzards have whitewashed the state as early as Halloween, but most residents have also seen a few brown Christmases as well. In 1991, 29 inches of snow fell on the town of Cook in a 24-hour period. That set a state record. The record for total snowfall during a winter season was set in Lutsen in 1995–96: 153.9 inches—nearly 13 feet.

The theater of seasons puts on a whole different kind of show during the warmer months. Mild temperatures melt the ice in March and April, revealing the thousands of lakes for which the state is famous. Most Minnesotans wait until at least Memorial Day to take their first dip, but there are plenty of others who jump in before then. The water usually remains comfortable for swimming into early September. If there's a downside to summer amid all these lakes, it's the mosquito. The Minnesota "state bird," as some people call it, can be a real pest during years of heavy rain.

CLIMATE CHART
Average High/Low Temperatures (°F) and Monthly Precipitation (in inches).

	JAN.	FEB.	MAR.	APR.	MAY	JUNE
MINNEAPOLIS/	21/3	27/9	39/23	57/36	69/48	79/58
ST. PAUL	1.0	0.9	1.9	2.4	3.4	4.1
	JULY	AUG.	SEPT.	OCT.	NOV.	DEC.
	84/63	81/60	71/50	59/39	41/25	26/10
	3.5	3.6	2.7	2.2	1.6	1.1
	JAN.	FEB.	MAR.	APR.	MAY	JUNE
DULUTH	16/-2	22/3	33/16	48/28	62/39	71/48
	1.2	0.8	1.9	2.3	3.0	3.8
	JULY	AUG.	SEPT.	OCT.	NOV.	DEC.
	77/55	74/54	64/45	53/36	35/22	20/5
	3.6	4.0	3.8	2.5	1.8	1.2

1858
Minnesota becomes the nation's 32nd state.

1860
First telegraph line reaches St. Paul.

1862
Frustrated by broken U.S. promises, the Dakota wage war on white farmers and towns. Hundreds of people die in six weeks of fighting.

1873
The first of five straight summers of insect plagues devastates farms in western Minnesota.

1876
The Jesse James gang is thwarted in its attempt to rob the First National Bank of Northfield.

ROCHESTER	JAN.	FEB.	MAR.	APR.	MAY	JUNE
	20/3	28/8	38/21	55/35	68/45	78/55
	0.8	.0.7	1.8	2.7	3.4	3.7
	JULY	AUG.	SEPT.	OCT.	NOV.	DEC.
	82/60	79/58	70/49	58/38	41/24	25/9
	4.2	3.9	3.5	2.3	1.6	1.0

INTERNATIONAL FALLS	JAN.	FEB.	MAR.	APR.	MAY	JUNE
	12/-10	19/-4	33/11	50/28	65/40	73/50
	0.9	0.7	1.1	1.6	2.5	3.9
	JULY	AUG.	SEPT.	OCT.	NOV.	DEC.
	79/55	76/52	64/43	52/33	33/17	17/-2
	3.6	3.1	3.2	2.0	1.2	0.9

FESTIVALS AND SEASONAL EVENTS
WINTER

Jan. **Icefest.** Radar runs, human bowling, sleigh rides, ice dances, and other cold-weather activities help the people of Brainerd get through winter with smiles on their faces. | 218/562–7811.

John Beargrease Sled Dog Marathon. Dogs pull mushers 330 miles up the North Shore Trail from Duluth to Grand Portage in this race. | 218/722–7631.

Jan.–Feb. **St. Paul Winter Carnival.** This is the nation's oldest and largest winter festival. | 651/223–4700.

Feb. **Polar Bear Days.** This 10-day festival in Chisholm is designed to help the people of the Northland beat winter blues. Among the popular events are dog weight pulls, in which single dogs lug sleds weighted down with dog food around an ice track. | 218/254–3600.

SPRING

Apr. **Last Chance Curling Bonspiel.** The world's best curlers gather in Hibbing to compete on 14 sheets of ice. | 218/262–3895.

May **Ole Ope Fest.** This citywide festival celebrates Alexandria's Scandinavian heritage and its association with the controversial Kensington Runestone, which some say is proof that the Vikings beat Columbus to the New World. | 800/235–9441.

June **Grandma's Marathon.** The footrace starts in Two Harbors, parallels Lake Superior, and ends at Duluth's Canal Park. | 218/727–0947.

1880	1884	1890	1894	1905
The first telephone communication between Minneapolis and St. Paul is established.	The first iron mine opens in Tower on the Vermilion Range.	U.S. Census establishes Minneapolis as the most populous city in Minnesota.	A huge fire destroys Hinckley and six nearby towns, killing 400 people.	Legislature convenes for the first time at the new Capitol in St. Paul.

Judy Garland Festival. This Grand Rapids festival is a celebration of the entertainer's life featuring a musical program, films, and appearances of some Munchkins. | 218/327–9276.

INTRODUCTION
HISTORY
REGIONS
WHEN TO VISIT
STATE'S GREATS
RULES OF THE ROAD
DRIVING TOURS

SUMMER

July

Riverboat Heritage Days. Each year Aitkin celebrates its riverboat-era heritage with events including melodrama, riverboat exhibits, a heritage tour, a carnival, street dances, and a parade. | 218/927–2316 or 800/526–8342.

Minneapolis Aquatennial. A 10-day, citywide carnival featuring milk-carton boat races, sand castle competitions, and Minnesota's largest parade. | 612/331–8371.

Austin's SPAM Town USA Festival/SPAM Jam. At this festival you can watch or participate in a series of events somehow connected to the town's most famous product. Among them is the 5-mi SPAM Hog Jog. | 800/444–5713.

Aug.

Song of Hiawatha Pageant. Gather at the amphitheater north of Pipestone to see and hear townspeople perform Longfellow's poem "Hiawatha." | 507/825–3316.

River City Days. This citywide shindig in Red Wing includes a food festival, country music, dragon-boat races, a car show, a parade, and fireworks. | 800/498–3444.

Sept.

Defeat of Jesse James Days. In Northfield, visitors can watch a live reenactment of the James-Younger gang's failed bank robbery in 1876. The four-day festival also includes a rodeo, a tractor pull, a midway, and a parade. | 507/645–5604.

Faribault Area Balloon Rally and Air Fest. Watch the skies over Faribault fill with the colorful nylon of hot-air balloons during this popular autumn festival. | 800/658–2354.

AUTUMN

Oct.

Big Island Rendezvous and Festival. Visit re-created scenes from the fur-trade era, listen to bluegrass music, and sample the ethnic delicacies at this festival in Albert Lea's Bancroft Park. | 507/373–3938 or 800/658–2526.

Nov.

Fairmont Glows. Fairmont's homes, businesses, and city parks light up for the holiday season, drawing visitors from all over the region. | 507/235–5547.

1915	1917	1918	1920	1929
Agrarian discontent leads to the founding of the Nonpartisan League.	Legislature establishes Commission of Public Safety, with sweeping powers to suppress activities deemed contrary to the war effort.	In a replay of the Great Hinckley Fire, another fire sweeps through Moose Lake, Cloquet, and Carlton, killing 453 people.	Farmers and laborers join forces to form the Farmer-Labor party.	Minneapolis's Foshay Tower is completed and remains Minnesota's tallest building for more than 40 years.

Dec.   **Winterfest.** This three-day event, which takes place in Luverne early in the month, includes a Christmas Light Parade, hockey tournaments, craft show, a snow sculpture contest, a radar run, a parade of homes, and a live nativity musical. | 507/283–4061.

State's Greats

Any discussion of the top attractions in Minnesota almost has to begin with the state's lakes. They're what make Minnesota unique. If your travel plans keep you within the Twin Cities metro area, don't fret. There are quite a few lakes within the city limits, and even more in the suburbs. Once you leave the Twin Cities, your choices expand exponentially. There are the hundreds of resort lakes that draw anglers and snowmobilers from all over, the pristine Canadian border lakes that are explorable only by canoe, and, of course, that inland sea called Lake Superior.

But don't get the impression that the state is blessed with outdoor beauty and nothing else. After all, even winter-hardened Minnesotans can't spend all their time communing with nature. That's one big reason that this is the home of the nation's largest shopping mall. Bloomington's Mall of America is probably the ultimate example of how Minnesotans have adapted to their state's sometimes harsh climate.

Beaches, Forests, and Parks

Winter is about the only thing that will prevent you from finding a beach in Minnesota. No matter where you are, you'll find one without much effort. If you're looking for urban sand, you may want to try the Minneapolis chain of lakes (**Calhoun, Cedar,** and **Harriet**) or **Como Lake** and **Lake Phalen** in St. Paul. If you're traveling outside the Twin Cities, you'll find that most lakes have at least one public beach. Most lake resorts feature their own private beaches. You'll also find plenty of places to stop along **Lake Superior.** Just don't expect to dig your toes into soft sand. The beaches there are made mostly of little rounded stones.

If there's anything Minnesota has more of than lakes, it's trees. In fact, forests cover a third of the state. There are 55 state forests in Minnesota and two national forests: **Superior,** in the northeast tip, and **Chippewa,** between Grand Rapids and Bemidji.

Minnesota has one of the top park systems in the nation, with 66 state parks. It also is home to **Voyageurs National Park,** the only water-based national park in the United States.

Culture, History, and the Arts

Minnesota history is on display in ready-to-absorb formulas at sites throughout the state. Just pick a topic that interests you. Perhaps you want to learn more about the people who lived in Minnesota before white settlement. **Pipestone National Monument** encompasses a quarry where Native Americans extracted reddish stone for ceremo-

1939	1944	1959	1973	1974
Republicans return to power with the election of Gov. Harold Stassen.	The Farmer-Labor party and the Democrats merge to form the Democratic Farmer Labor party (DFL), the political incubator of Hubert Humphrey and Walter Mondale.	St. Lawrence Seaway is completed, making Duluth a world port.	A *Time* magazine cover story touts "The Good Life in Minnesota."	In Minnesota's most famous environmental case, Reserve Mining in Silver Bay is ordered to stop dumping taconite tailings into Lake Superior.

INTRODUCTION
HISTORY
REGIONS
WHEN TO VISIT
STATE'S GREATS
RULES OF THE ROAD
DRIVING TOURS

nial pipes. The **Site of Fond du Lac,** on the St. Louis River near Duluth, was a Native American village before turning into a trading post for fur trappers. Historic **Fort Snelling** in St. Paul is a good place to learn about early white settlement in Minnesota. The history of the 1862 Dakota conflict is told at several sites in southern Minnesota including the **Lower Sioux Agency and History Center** in Redwood Falls and the **Treaty Site History Center** in St. Peter. Step into a re-created turn-of-the-20th-century logging camp at the **Forest History Center** in Grand Rapids or find out what it takes to be an iron miner at **Ironworld USA** in Chisholm. If you're looking for something a little more refined, St. Paul's **James J. Hill House** provides a glimpse of railroad-baron luxury. **The American Swedish Institute** in Minneapolis showcases the Swedish heritage in a mansion setting.

The Twin Cities combined form the culture capital of Minnesota. Many visitors are surprised to find such a large menu of cultural offerings in what they assumed was a not-quite-cutting-edge Midwestern metropolis. The **Guthrie Theater** headlines an impressive and diverse collection of theatrical outlets. The **Minnesota Orchestra** and the **St. Paul Chamber Orchestra** are both world class. **The Science Museum of Minnesota** and the **Minnesota Children's Museum** in St. Paul offer innovative hands-on learning for children and adults. **The Minneapolis Institute of Arts,** the **Walker Art Center,** and the **Frederick R. Weisman Art Museum** feature masterpieces from nearly every age and culture.

Sports

For obvious reasons, water sports are among the most popular activities in Minnesota. It would be hard to go anywhere in the state where someone wasn't dropping a line in nearby water, hoping to snag a walleye, northern, or muskie. **Lake Mille Lacs, Leech Lake, Lake Winnibigoshish,** and **Lake of the Woods** are among the most popular fishing destinations in the state. Canoeing is also a major attraction. The **Boundary Waters Canoe Area Wilderness** in Superior National Forest offers some of the finest paddling in the world. For a different kind of canoeing experience, try putting in at one of the many launching spots along the Mississippi River.

When the lakes start freezing and the snow starts falling, Minnesota shifts into winter sports mode. While they don't compare to the slopes out west, Minnesota's ski resorts do feature surprisingly good snow and facilities. **Lutsen Mountains Ski Area** along the North Shore has plenty of slopes and panoramic views of Lake Superior. **Afton Alps** near Hastings is one of the biggest and most popular ski destinations in the Twin Cities area. Opportunities for cross-country skiing and snowmobiling abound with thousands of miles of groomed trails throughout the state.

Minnesota is home to more than 450 golf courses, many of which take advantage of the state's wooded areas and lakes. Resorts such as **Madden's** on Gull Lake in Brainerd and **Izaty's Golf and Yacht Club** in Onamia feature championship courses that rank among the state's best. In the Twin Cities area, your many choices include St. Paul's **Keller Golf Course,** which has hosted more professional tournaments than any other in Minnesota, and the challenging **Majestic Oaks Golf Course** in Ham Lake, north of Minneapolis.

1992
Mall of America, the nation's largest shopping center, opens in Bloomington.

Other Points of Interest

Minnesotans as a group like to think of themselves as a bit eccentric, so if you want to get an accurate reading on the Minnesota psyche, you should visit at least a few eyebrow-raisers along the way. The **Museum of Questionable Medical Devices** in Minneapolis is a shrine to medical quackery. Litchfield is home to the **Largest Ball of Twine** ever wound by one person. And in a state that claims to be home to Paul Bunyan, you'll have no problem finding Bunyanesque figures of all kinds. The most famous are the **statues of Paul Bunyan and Babe the Blue Ox** in Bemidji, but they're just the beginning. Baudette proudly displays **Willie the Walleye,** the world's largest cloudy-eyed fish. Mora is home to the **Largest Dala Horse in North America.** Virginia's **Floating Loon** is in the Guinness Book of Records. A 55-ft-tall **Jolly Green Giant** stands guard over Blue Earth.

Rules of the Road

License Requirements: To drive in Minnesota, you must be at least 16 years old and have a valid driver's license. Visitors to the state may drive in Minnesota as long as they have a valid driver's license from their home state or country.

Right Turn on Red: Unless you see a sign telling you not to, you may make a right turn after stopping for a red light if you are in the correct turn lane and your path is clear.

Seat Belt and Helmet Laws: All drivers, front-seat passengers, and any other passengers aged 4 to 10 must wear seat belts. Children younger than four must ride in a federally approved safety seat. Motorcyclists must wear helmets.

Speed Limits: 65 mph is the speed limit on all interstate highways inside urban areas and on non-interstate freeways and expressways. The limit rises to 70 mph on interstates outside urban areas. In most other locations, the limit remains 55 mph.

For More Information: Contact the Minnesota Department of Public Safety at 651/282–6565.

Iron Range Discovery Driving Tour
FROM HIBBING TO ELY

Distance: 80 mi   Time: 1–2 days
Breaks: Virginia is a good place to stop if you're not in a rush. It's one of the Iron Range's largest cities, with plenty of places to dine and shop.

This tour immerses you in the colorful past and present of Minnesota's iron ore country. You'll start on the Mesabi Range, site of the largest concentration of iron ore deposits in the world. As you head east, you'll cross over into the Vermilion Range, where the first Minnesota iron deposits were discovered in 1865. The scenery is not always pretty. Huge gaping holes where ore was once extracted pockmark the landscape. New-growth forests of poplar and aspen are sure signs that the land has been disturbed. Still, the sights you'll see are impressive nonetheless, evidence of Minnesotans' grit and determination. Make this trip during the warmer months. While you'll be traveling primarily on major roads, you probably won't want to chance getting caught in a snowstorm.

❶ Begin your tour in **Hibbing** (U.S. 169 takes you right into downtown). The town has been a center of Iron Range lore almost from the beginning. The **Hibbing Historical**

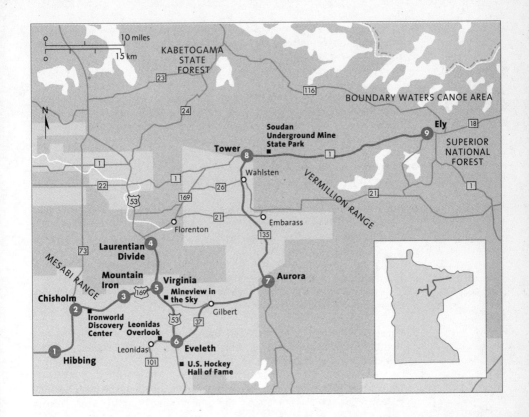

Society Museum is a good place to learn about the evolution of Minnesota iron mining. The now inactive **Hull-Rust Mahoning Mine** is the world's largest open-pit mine and the first of its kind on the Mesabi Range. Visit the mine exhibits and let your jaw drop as you survey the massive man-made hole.

➋ After you've toured Hibbing, head 6 mi north on U.S. 169 until you hit **Chisholm.** This is another major site in Minnesota's iron-mining history. It is the home of the **Iron-world Discovery Center,** south of town on U.S. 169. The 85-ft-tall **Iron Ore Miner Statue** (across from Ironworld on U.S. 169) is the third-largest structural memorial in the United States. The **Minnesota Museum of Mining,** beneath the water tower in Mining Memorial Park, displays iron mining equipment including mining trucks, a steam locomotive, a 1910 Atlantic steam shovel, and early diamond drills.

➌ Head 3 mi east on U.S. 169 and you'll find **Mountain Iron.** Feast your eyes on the huge **Steam Locomotive,** on the north end of town, that once hauled ore out of the Mountain Iron pit. There are two mine-viewing sites here, too: the Minntac Site (north end of Mountain Ave.) and the Wacootah Overlook (on Route 102). The Minntac ore-taconite operation of U.S. Steel offers Friday tours on a first come, first served basis.

➍ When you're ready, head 4 mi east on U.S. 169, turn north onto U.S. 53 and travel another 4 mi to the **Laurentian Divide,** a rolling crest dividing the Lake Superior and Hudson Bay watersheds. There's a picnic area here with hiking trails and a half-mile fitness trail.

⑤ Now backtrack a little traveling 4 mi south on U.S. 53. You'll find yourself in **Virginia,** which is home to another good iron-mining vantage point. **Mineview in the Sky,** south of town on U.S. 53, sits on a 20-story pile of rock overlooking Virginia and the Rouchleau mine group.

⑥ Five miles south of Virginia on U.S. 53 is the town of **Eveleth.** From **Leonidas Overlook,** the highest man-made point on the Mesabi Range, you'll get a bird's-eye view of the mining world. At the **U.S. Hockey Hall of Fame** you can have your picture taken next to the World's Largest Hockey Stick (on Grant Ave.).

⑦ The next stop is **Aurora,** 10 mi east of Eveleth on Route 37. Huge mining trucks pass right by you while you're standing at the **LTV Mine Overlook.**

⑧ Now it's time for the older Vermilion Range. Travel 20 mi north on Route 135 and you'll hit **Tower.** The **Steam Locomotive** at the west end of Main Street once hauled ore for the Duluth and Iron Range Railroad. There's a museum and interpretive center here.

From Tower, it's a quick 2 mi east on Route 1 to **Soudan Underground Mine State Park.** This is the home of Minnesota's first underground mine. The 1½-hour tour includes a ½-mi elevator ride and an electric train ride, as well as some stair climbing and walking over uneven terrain.

⑨ When you've finished exploring the park, travel 22 mi east on Route 1 to **Ely,** your final stop. Here you can learn about the history and culture of the Vermilion Range at the **Vermilion Interpretive Center** (1900 E. Camp St.).

The trip back to Hibbing is easy. Follow Route 1 until it splits and becomes U.S. 169 4 mi west of Tower. Follow U.S. 169 past Virginia and Chisholm until you reach Hibbing.

Great River Road Along U.S. 61 Driving Tour
FROM RED WING TO LA CRESCENT

Distance: 107 miles   Time: 1–2 days
Breaks: Although Wabasha isn't quite the halfway point, it's a good place to stop. There are a number of places to stay here, including the state's oldest operating hotel.

This tour follows the bluffs that hug the Mississippi River between Red Wing and La Crescent; some of Minnesota's oldest communities are here, river towns that came into their own during the steamboat era. Much of their 19th-century architecture survives. The ancient landscape was created more than a million years ago and escaped the glacial scouring that marked much of the rest of the state. This is a year-round tour, but the sights are especially beautiful in fall. In late winter you can see bald eagles.

❶ Begin in downtown **Red Wing,** near the intersection of U.S. 61 and U.S. 63. The town's most distinctive feature is **Barn Bluff,** a huge sandstone and dolomite formation that towers above town. You can park at the end of E. 5th Street and climb trails to the top. Well-preserved Victorian architecture is one of Red Wing's biggest attractions. The **St. James Hotel** was built in 1875. You can also catch a play or musical at the ornate **T. B. Sheldon Auditorium.** The **Pottery District** (north of downtown off U.S. 61) surrounds

INTRODUCTION
HISTORY
REGIONS
WHEN TO VISIT
STATE'S GREATS
RULES OF THE ROAD
DRIVING TOURS

the old Red Wing Stoneware Company factory and is now home to outlet stores, specialty shops, and galleries of local artisans.

❷ Your next stop is **Frontenac,** about 10 mi southeast of Red Wing on U.S. 61. Actually, Frontenac consists of two unincorporated communities: Old Frontenac and Frontenac Station. Old Frontenac was founded in 1839 and is a historic district. It includes the **Lakeside Hotel,** which is now part of a larger resort complex. In **Frontenac State Park** more than 200 species pass through during the spring and fall. In winter there's cross-country skiing on 6 mi of trails and snowmobiling on 8 mi of trails.

❸ Leaving Frontenac State Park, head 5 mi southeast on U.S. 61 into **Lake City.** The Great River Road follows the Mississippi shoreline closely here and provides panoramic views of Lake Pepin, which is actually a bulge in the river created by sediment downstream. The town's 2½-mile Riverwalk is a great place to enjoy the lake's scenery. This is the birthplace of waterskiing.

❹ After you've explored Lake City, head southeast on U.S. 61 for approximately 11 mi to **Reads Landing.** It's hard to believe this was once a bustling staging area for rafts of sawmill-bound northern pine. One of the few reminders of Reads Landing's glory days is the 1870 brick schoolhouse that now houses the **Wabasha County Historical Society** and displays of Mississippi River artifacts and Laura Ingalls Wilder memorabilia. Reads Landing also marks the northern boundary of the **Upper Mississippi River National Wildlife and Fish Refuge,** a huge, protected floodplain stretching south to Rock Island, Illinois.

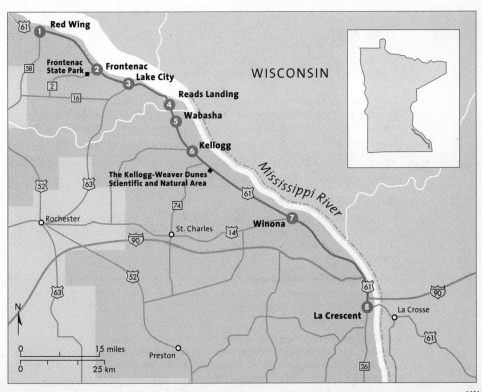

❺ **Wabasha** is 3 mi southeast of Reads Landing on U.S. 61. Here people boast that their home is both the oldest town in Minnesota and the setting for the movie *Grumpy Old Men* and its sequel. The **Anderson House,** built in 1856, is the oldest operating hotel in the state. Life in Wabasha is so tranquil that bald eagles build their nests along the river, sometimes within the city limits. The people at the **Eagle Watch Observatory** can help you spot the great birds.

❻ Continue southeast out of Wabasha on U.S. 61 for 5 mi and you'll come to **Kellogg.** Try as you might, you'll find few signs that this was a turn-of-the-20th-century transportation hub. Among the remaining attractions is the **L.A.R.K. Toy Factory,** where woodcarvers create toys and carousel animals. **The Kellogg-Weaver Dunes Scientific and Natural Area** is home to one of the largest populations of the rare Blanding's turtle.

❼ The mighty Mississippi goes in and out of view as you leave Kellogg and wind 31 mi southeast on U.S. 61 to **Winona.** Once there, your gaze will immediately rise to **Sugar Loaf Bluff,** a huge chunk of limestone overlooking town that is reflected in **Lake Winona,** 500 feet below. More than two dozen downtown structures are listed on the National Register of Historic Places. Among them are the **Church of Saint Stanislaus Kostka** and the Egyptian Revival–style **Winona National and Savings Bank.**

❽ Leaving Winona, travel another 22 mi southeast on U.S. 61 to **La Crescent,** the self-proclaimed apple capital of Minnesota. Harvest time is a great time to follow **Apple Blossom Drive** (Route 29). From there you can enjoy a panoramic view of the Mississippi and choose from among the two dozen or so varieties of apples available at the orchards along the way. You can munch on them as you retrace your route along U.S. 61 back to Red Wing.

AITKIN

MAP 3, E5

(Nearby towns also listed: Cross Lake, Deerwood, Onamia)

Deep in water and woods country, this quiet Northwoods outpost lies between the busier urban centers of Brainerd, Grand Rapids, and Duluth. The area around Aitkin was home to the Dakota and Ojibway, and later became a center for the fur trade, the Mississippi riverboat trade, and logging.

Information: Aitkin Chamber of Commerce | 12 2nd St. NW, Aitkin, 56431 | 218/927–2316 or 800/526–8342 | upnorth@aitkin.com | www.aitkin.com.

Attractions

Berglund Park. Ten miles north of Aitkin, in Palisade, this park, with picnic tables, campsites, and boat ramp, sits aside the Mississippi River. Canoeing and boating are favorite pastimes on the winding river. | Junction of Hwy. 232 and County Rd. 69, Palisade | 218/927–2316 | Free.

Rice Lake National Wildlife Refuge. Waterfowl migrating up and down the Mississippi River flyway stop here to rest and nest; walking trails allow you to watch them. The 18,281-acre refuge is 5 mi south of McGregor. | Rte. 65 | 218/768–2402 | www.fws.gov/r3pao/rice_lk | Free | Daily.

Savanna Portage State Park. The Continental Divide splits this 15,800-acre park: water to the west of the divide flows into the Mississippi River, water to the east into Lake Superior. Dakota and Ojibway tribespeople, as well as fur traders and Canadian *voyageurs,* once carried their canoes along a rugged path between Lake Superior and the Mississippi, six mi through marsh, swamp, and forest; today, the Savanna Portage Trail is well maintained, and you can traverse it in much less than the five days it took the canoemen. Canoes, boats (with electric motors only), and snowmobiles are allowed on the park's trails and waterways. To get there, take Rte. 65 to Aitkin County Rd. 14, and follow for 11 mi. | County Rd. 14 | 218/426–3271 | www.dnr.state.mn.us/parks_and_recreation/state_parks/savanna_portage | Park permit required | Daily.

ON THE CALENDAR

JULY: *Riverboat Heritage Days.* During the third weekend of the month, Aitkin celebrates its riverboat-era heritage with special events, including melodrama, riverboat exhibits, a heritage tour, a carnival, street dances, and a parade. | 218/927–2316 or 800/526–8342.

NOV.: *Fish House Parade.* Wacky floats, dressed-up ice-fishing houses, and celebrity guests help kick off winter the day after Thanksgiving every year. | 218/927–2316.

NOV. *Chamber Craft Sale.* Held on the day after Thanksgiving, this fair draws many to the West Side Calvary Church to sell or buy items such as Christmas decorations and winter clothing. | 218/927–2316.

Dining

Birchwood Cafe. American. The specialty of the house at this diner is the Birchwood pancake breakfast, made from a special house recipe and featuring pancakes larger than a dinner plate. | 120 Minnesota Ave. N | 218/927–6400 | Breakfast also available. No dinner | $4–$7 | No credit cards.

40 Club Restaurant. American. Prime rib is the specialty on Friday and Saturday nights at this bar and restaurant, just off the highway. Walleye, steaks, and chicken dishes fill out the menu. | 950 2nd St. NW | 218/927–7090 | $7–$14 | AE, D, MC, V.

Manhattan Beach Lodge. American. A fireplace and lots of stone and wood—tables, chairs, and paneling—give this lodge a cozy touch. Steak and fish are dependable here. Kids' menu. | 39051 Rte. 66, Manhattan Beach | 218/692–3381 | Closed Oct.–Apr. and Mon. No lunch. No dinner Sun. | $12–$19 | D, MC, V.

Lodging

40 Club Inn. A restaurant is next door to this country-style motor inn, a mile west of Aitkin on Route 210. Complimentary Continental breakfast. Indoor pool. Some hot tubs, sauna. | 44440 Hwy. 218 W | 218/927–2903 or 800/682–8152 | 39 rooms, 2 suites | $45–$75, $104–$125 suites | AE, D, MC, V.

Manhattan Beach Resort. Big Trout Lake can be seen from every guest room at this resort, 25 mi northwest of Aitkin. Pine furnishings and handmade quilts give the rooms a rustic appeal, complemented in suites by fireplaces. Complimentary Continental breakfast. Some microwaves, some refrigerators. Cable TV. Hot tub, sauna. Exercise equipment. Beach, dock, boating, fishing. Business services. No pets. No smoking. | 39051 Rte. 66, Manhattan Beach | 218/692–3381 or 800/399–4360 | fax 218/692–2774 | info@mblodge.com | www.mblodge.com | 18 rooms | $79–$99 | AE, D, MC, V.

Red Door Resort and Motel. Made up of a motel, cabins, and a campground, this resort is on Rte. 1, on the north shore of Lake Mille Lacs, 20 mi southwest of Aitkin. Lake. Beach, boating, fishing. Snowmobiling. Playground. Laundry facilities. | Rte. 1, Box 359 | 218/678–3686 | 10 rooms, 4 cabins | $45–$80, $65–$90 cabins | AE, D, MC, V.

Ripple River Motel and RV Park. The Ripple River flows just north of this motel, which sits on the southern edge of town. It is 10 mi from Lake Mille Lacs. Room access is via outside corridors. Complimentary Continental breakfast. Microwaves, refrigerators. Cable TV. Cross-country skiing, snowmobiling. Business services. Some pets allowed. | 701 Minnesota Ave. S | 218/927–3734 or 800/258–3734 | fax 218/927–3540 | jfkeimig@msn.com | www.ripplerivermotel.com | 29 rooms | $42–$75, $20 full RV hook-up | AE, D, MC, V.

ALBERT LEA

MAP 3, E10

(Nearby towns also listed: Austin, Blue Earth, Owatonna)

Named after the man who originally surveyed this part of southern Minnesota, Albert Lea stands at the busy intersection of I–90 and I–35. This city of 18,000 encompasses six lakes, 38 parks, and (in winter) 250 miles of groomed snowmobile trails. It's an important agricultural, manufacturing, and distribution center for southern Minnesota.

Information: Albert Lea Convention and Visitors Bureau | 202 N. Broadway, Albert Lea, 56007 | 800/345–8414 | www.albertlea.com.

Attractions

Fountain Lake. Here, you can fish, waterski, and sail the day away in the heart of Albert Lea, Freeborn County, north of downtown. Parks and picnic areas are available. | Rte. 65N | 507/377–4370 | Free | Daily.

Freeborn County Historical Museum, Library, and Village. The historical village here has 14 buildings, including a schoolhouse, a general store, and a jail. The library offers extensive genealogical information. | 1031 N. Bridge Ave. | 507/373–8003 | www.smig.net/fchm | $5 | Museum and library hours: May 1–Sept., Tues.–Fri. 10–5, weekends 1–5; Oct.–May 1, Tues.–Fri. 10–5, closed weekends. Village hours: May–Dec., Tues.–Fri. 10–5, weekends 1–5.

Myre-Big Island State Park. You can enjoy hiking, biking, wildlife watching, snowshoeing, and canoeing on these 1,600 acres of parkland, which include 16 mi of trails. It's at the junction of I–35 and I–90. | 507/379–3403 | www.dnr.state.mn.us/parks_and_recreation/state_parks/myre_big_island | Park permit required | Daily.

Pelican Breeze Cruise Boat. Narrated cruises of Albert Lea Lake detail the history of the area. The tours leave from Frank Hall Park Dock on the northern shore of the lake. On Friday nights (at 6), you can take a pizza cruise. | Frank Hall Dr. | 507/377–5076 | $8 | June–Sept., weekends 2 PM.

Story Lady Doll and Toy Museum. The museum's core collection includes 400 storybook dolls, and others including designer Barbies. Local collectors exhibit their collections here every month. | 131 N. Broadway Ave. | 507/377–1820 | $2 | Apr.–Dec., Tues.–Sun. 10–5; closed Mon.

ON THE CALENDAR

JULY: *Doc Evans Jazz Festival.* Dixieland jazz is played at Fountain Lake Park on the first Saturday of the month in honor of the Minnesota native and jazz musician. | 800/345–8414.

AUG.: *Freeborn County Fair.* The fairgrounds, at 1029 Bridge St., are the site of live entertainment, livestock exhibits, and a midway, from late July to early August. | 507/373–6965.

OCT.: *Big Island Rendezvous and Festival.* During the first weekend of the month, in Bancroft Park, you can watch a reenactment of the fur-trade era, listen to bluegrass music, and sample ethnic delicacies. | 507/373–3938 or 800/658–2526.

Dining

Casa Zamora Restaurant. Mexican. Since 1969, this family-owned restaurant has been serving such traditional favorites as enchiladas, tacos, and burritos from its expansive menu. | 2006 E. Main St. | 507/373–6475 | $6–$9 | MC, V.

Elbow Room. American. The moniker reflects the small size of this restaurant, which has six booths and one table. Burgers, barbecue ribs, and hot beef top lunch orders. | 310 E. 8th St. | 507/373–1836 | Breakfast also available, no dinner | $3–$5 | No credit cards.

Lodging

AmericInn of Albert Lea. A fireplace warms the spacious lobby of this hotel, which is less than 1 mi north of the Albert Lea Municipal Airport and just south of I–90 off exit 157. Complimentary Continental breakfast. Some microwaves, some refrigerators. Cable TV. Indoor pool. Spa. Video games. Laundry facilities, laundry service. No pets. | 811 E. Plaza St. | 507/373–4324 or 800/634–3444 | fax 507/373–4048 | www.AmericInn.com/minnesota/albertlea.html | 42 rooms, 18 suites | $55–$70, $69–$119 suites | AE, V, MC.

Bel Aire. Standing across the street from a shopping mall, this hotel is 1½ mi south of Albert Lea. Complimentary Continental breakfast. Cable TV. Pool. Playground. Some pets allowed. | 700 U.S. 69S | 507/373–3983 or 800/373–4073 | fax 507/373–5161 | 46 rooms | $35–$65 | D, MC, V.

Budget Host Albert Lea Inn. This budget inn is on the east edge of town, near several other accommodations. Restaurant, bar. Cable TV. Indoor pool. Hot tub. Video games. Laundry facilities. Business services. Some pets allowed. | 2301 E. Main St. | 507/373–8291 | fax 507/373–4043 | www.budgethost.com | 124 rooms | $59–$69 | AE, D, DC, MC, V.

Days Inn. The intersection of I–35 and I–90 is 1 mi north of this hotel. Restaurant, bar. In-room data ports. Cable TV. Indoor pool. Laundry facilities. Business services. Some pets allowed. | 2306 E. Main St. | 507/373–6471 | fax 507/373–7517 | 129 rooms | $59–$79 | AE, D, DC, MC, V.

Super 8. On the east edge of town, this hostelry stands among several restaurants and other accommodations. Some microwaves. Cable TV, in-room VCRs. Cross-country skiing. Business services. Pets allowed. | 2019 East Main St. | 507/377–0591 | www.super8hotels.com | 60 rooms | $37–$58 | AE, D, DC, MC, V.

ALEXANDRIA

MAP 3, C6

(Nearby towns also listed: Fergus Falls, Glenwood)

The people of Alexandria are quick to point out that their city is a regional center for tourism, health care, manufacturing, and retail. But they've also built a civic identity around their Scandinavian heritage. Just try counting all the businesses that have "Viking" in their names. Alexandria's best-known tourist attraction, the Runestone Museum, celebrates the 1898 discovery of a carved stone that supposedly proves that Vikings arrived in the North American interior long before anyone heard of Christopher Columbus.

Information: **Alexandria Lakes Area Chamber of Commerce** | 206 Broadway, Alexandria, 56308 | 320/763–3161 or 800/235–9441 | www.alexandriamn.org.

Attractions

Big Ole. This 28-ft-tall Norseman was originally built for display at the 1965 World's Fair in New York. Now he greets visitors to Alexandria at the north end of Broadway and informs them that they're in the "Birthplace of America."

Lake Carlos State Park. Outdoor activities abound at this preserve 10 mi north of town: swimming, fishing, boating, and snowmobiling are among the many. | Rte. 29 | 320/852–7200 | www.dnr.state.mn.us/parks_and_recreation/state_parks/lake_carlos | Park permit required | Daily.

Runestone Museum. Find out why some Minnesotans believe Viking explorers arrived deep in North America long before Columbus "discovered" the new world. The carvings on the runestone include the date 1362. Is it a historical treasure or an elaborate hoax? | 206 Broadway | 320/763–3160 | www.atc.tec.mn.us/runestone | $5 | Closed Mid-May–mid-Oct.: Mon.–Sat. 9–5, Sun. 11–4. Mid-Oct.–mid-May: Mon.–Fri. 9–4, Sat 9–3; closed Sunday.

ON THE CALENDAR

SEPT.: *Grape Stomp Fall Festival.* Tours of wineries, live entertainment, food vendors, and craft booths are the main attractions at this celebration held at the Carlos Creek Winery. | 320/846–5443.

MAY: *Ole Ope Fest.* This citywide festival, late in the month, celebrates Alexandria's Scandinavian heritage and its association with the controversial Kensington Runestone. | 800/235–9441.

JUNE: *Vikingland Drum Corps Classic.* Nationally ranked drum and bugle corps compete against each other at this annual event, held the last Saturday of the month. | 800/235–9441.

JUNE: *Vikingland Band Festival.* Minnesota's finest marching bands gather for competition on the last Sunday of the month. | 800/235–9441.

Dining

Brass Lantern. American. Homemade soups, pies, and cinnamon and caramel rolls are some of the favorites here, along with dinner entrées such as roast beef, walleye, and prime rib. The restaurant is in the Viking Plaza Mall. | 3109 Hwy. 29S | 320/763–4818 | Breakfast also available | $5–$9 | AE, D, MC, V.

Heartland Sirloin Buffet. American. This all-buffet restaurant sits on the south end of the Viking Plaza Mall. Fried chicken, sirloin steak, ham, shrimp, and hashbrowns are on the menu. Tuesday and Friday nights are kids' nights, meaning lots of pizza and french fries. | 3313 Rte. 29S | 320/763–7866 | $7–$8 | MC, V.

Lake Cafe. American. You can take in views of Lake Darling from the large windows at this restaurant in the Radisson Arrowwood. Prime rib, walleye, and hamburgers are dinner staples. | 2100 Arrowwood La. | 320/762–1124 | Closed weekends. Breakfast also available | $10–$25 | AE, D, DC, MC, V.

Luigi's. Pizza. Video games and televisions provide entertainment while you wait for your homemade pizza and ice cream at this family-friendly eatery at the Radisson Arrowwood. | 2100 Arrowwood La. | 320/762–1124 | Closed weekdays | $3–$10 | AE, D, DC, MC, V.

Traveler's Inn. American. High pressed-tin ceilings, oak paneling, and etched-glass windows are original details of this 1924 inn. The menu is similar to that of the Brass Lantern (*above*), which is owned by the same family. Roast beef, prime rib, and sandwiches are some examples. Hearty breakfasts include homemade cinnamon and caramel rolls. | 511 Broadway St. | 320/763–4000 | Breakfast also available | $6–$9 | AE, D, MC, V.

CAR RENTAL TIPS

- ❑ Review auto insurance policy to find out what it covers when you're away from home.
- ❑ Know the local traffic laws.
- ❑ Jot down make, model, color, and license plate number of rental car and carry the information with you.
- ❑ Locate gas tank—make sure gas cap is on and can be opened.
- ❑ Check trunk for spare and jack.
- ❑ Test the ignition—make sure you know how to remove the key.
- ❑ Test the horn, headlights, blinkers, and windshield wipers.

*Excerpted from *Fodor's: How to Pack: Experts Share Their Secrets*
© 1997, by Fodor's Travel Publications

Lodging

AmericInn. Next door to a popular department store, this hotel is 2 mi from town. Complimentary Continental breakfast. Cable TV. Indoor pool. Hot tub. Business services. | 4520 Rte. 29S | 320/763–6808 | fax 320/763–6808 | www.AmericInn.com/minnesota/alexandria.html | 53 rooms, 17 suites | $69–$91, $84–$127 suites | AE, D, DC, MC, V.

Best Inn. Right on Hwy 29, you'll find a no-surprises motel equipped for business travelers, with shopping next door. Complimentary Continental breakfast. In-room data ports. Cable TV. Indoor pool. Hot tub. Business services. | 507 50th Ave. W | 320/762–5161 | fax 320/762–5337 | manager@bestinnalexandria.com | www.bestinnalexandria.com | 46 rooms | $45–$75 | AE, D, DC, MC, V.

Big Foot Resort. At the southwest corner of Lake Mary, this 19-acre resort has close to 1,000 ft of lakefront. Cabins sleep six and their patios and decks have lake views. No air-conditioning. Kitchenettes, refrigerators. No room phones. Basketball, volleyball. Beach, dock, boating. Playground. Some pets allowed. | 8231 State Hwy. 114 SW | 320/283–5533 or 888/239–2512 | fax 320/283–5040 | www.bigfootresort.com | 6 cabins | $90–$100 | MC, V.

Cedar Rose Inn. High gabled roofs, a wraparound porch, and stained-glass windows distinguish this 1900 home in a residential area. Inside, antiques and chandeliers complement the polished maple floors underfoot and exposed beams overhead. One room has a fireplace. Complimentary breakfast. Some in-room hot tubs. Bicycles. No pets. | 422 7th Ave. | 320/762–8430 or 888/203–5333 | cedarose@gctel.com | 4 rooms | $75–$130 | MC, V.

Days Inn. Visible from I–94, on Hwy. 29 S, this motor hotel is good for a road-trip rest. Complimentary Continental breakfast. Cable TV. Business services. Pool. Hot tub. | 4810 Rte. 29S | 320/762–1171, ext. 234 | fax 320/762–1171 | www.daysinn.com | 59 rooms | $58–$73 | AE, D, DC, MC, V.

Holiday Inn. The parking lot of this hotel, 1 mi west of downtown, leads directly to a snowmobile trail. Restaurant, bar (with entertainment), room service. In-room data ports. Cable TV. Indoor pool, wading pool. Hot tub, sauna. Laundry facilities. Business services. | 5637 Rte. 29S | 320/763–6577 | fax 320/762–2092 | www.holiday-inn.com | 149 rooms | $95–$110 | AE, D, DC, MC, V.

Radisson Arrowwood. Directly on the shores of Lake Darling, 4 mi northwest of Alexandria, this rustic-but-modern resort hotel on 250 acres has lake-view balconies on most of its rooms. Bar, dining room, room service. In-room data ports, some microwaves, some refrigerators. Cable TV. 2 pools (1 indoor). Hot tub. 18-hole golf course, tennis. Health club. Beach, water sports, boating, bicycles. Ice-skating, cross-country skiing, sleigh rides, snowmobiling, tobogganing. Video games. Children's programs (5–12 yrs.), playground. Business services, airport shuttle. Pets allowed. | 2100 Arrowwood La. | 320/762–1124 or 800/333–3333 | fax 320/762–0133 | resort@rea-alp.com | www.radisson.com | 200 rooms, 24 suites | $149–$199, $225–$250 suites | AE, D, DC, MC, V.

Super 8. One mi west of downtown, this hostelry is within a block of snowmobile trails. Cable TV. Video games. Business services. | 4620 Rte. 29S | 320/763–6552 | www.super8hotels.com | 57 rooms | $52–$80 | AE, D, DC, MC, V.

ANOKA

MAP 3, E7

(Nearby towns also listed: Elk River, Minneapolis, St. Paul)

The Rum River flows through the middle of Anoka, while the Mississippi forms the city's southern border. Anoka's location, about 20 mi northwest of the Twin Cities, has made it a natural for development—its farmland quickly turning into residential communities. It is now the residential and commercial focal point of one of the state's fastest-growing counties.

Information: Anoka Area Chamber of Commerce | 222 E. Main St., Suite 108, Anoka, 55303 | 612/421–7130 | www.anokaareachamber.com.

Attractions

Anoka County Historical Society Museum. Photographs, artifacts, and documents illustrate the history of area towns and hamlets. | 1900 3rd Ave. S | 763/421–0600 | fax 763/421–0601 | www.anokahistorical@yahoo.com | $2.50 | Tues.–Fri. 12:30–4.

Father Hennepin Stone. Lying in the town's Mississippi Point Park, this is either an historical artifact or the work of a clever graffiti artist. The inscription reads "Father Louis Hennepin—1680." Hennepin was an early Franciscan explorer. | Hwy. 169 | 763/421–0600 | Free | Daily.

Jonathan Emerson Monument. Emerson was an old settler who decided to carve his philosophy of life in stone. The monument is in the Hill Forest Cemetery on West Main Street. | 612/421–7130 | http://www.ci.anoka.mn.us/parksandrec/cemeteries.html | Free | Daily.

ON THE CALENDAR

JULY: *Anoka County Suburban Fair*. Late in the month, you can take in tractor and truck pulls, a bull fight, motorcross racing, demolition derbies, and live entertainment. | 612/427–4070.
OCT.: *Halloween Celebration*. Haunted houses, block parties, wine tastings, and a foot race make up this month-long festival, punctuated by a parade on the last Saturday of the month. | 612/421–7130.

Dining

Seasons. Continental. The dining room here, painted in mauve to soothing effect, overlooks a golf course. It's known for its baked cod *au fromage*. Kids' menu. Sun. brunch. | 12800 Bunker Prairie NW | 612/755–4444 | $10–$20 | AE, D, DC, MC, V.

Vineyard Restaurant. American. A trellis and wine rack hold plants and wine bottles above your head at this casual eatery at the intersection of Thurston Avenue and Rte. 10. Slow-roasted prime rib, served with a bacon-cauliflower salad is the specialty. There are also seafood, lobster, and chicken dishes. | 1125 W. Hwy. 10 | 612/427–0959 | No lunch Sat. | $10–$20 | AE, D, MC, V.

Lodging

Anoka Super 8. This two-story motel, built in 1990, is on the city's western edge, 1 mi from downtown. Complimentary Continental breakfast. Cable TV. Laundry services. Business services. Pets allowed. | 1129 W. Hwy. 10 | 612/422–8000 or 800/800–8000 | fax 612/422–4892 | www.super8.com | 56 rooms | $67–$120 | AE, D, DC, MC, V.

Ticknor Hill. Rooms are antiques-filled at this 1867 Queen Anne B&B on the National Register of Historic Places. There are also peaceful porches and a billiard room. The Mississippi and Rum rivers are two blocks to the north. Some in-room hot tubs. No pets. | 1625 3rd Ave. S | 763/421–9687 or 800/484–3954 ext. 6391 | 4 rooms | $110–$135 | AE, D, DC, MC, V.

AUSTIN

MAP 3, F10

(Nearby towns also listed: Albert Lea, Mantorville, Owatonna, Preston, Spring Valley)

Austin is the home of SPAM luncheon meat, which was introduced to the nation in 1937 by the local Hormel Foods Corporation. The city is proud of its connection with the often-maligned canned-meat product and bills itself as SPAM Town USA. Its meat- and food-processing plants make it a regional agricultural hub.

Information: Austin Convention and Visitors Bureau | 329 Main St. N, Austin, 55912 | 507/437–4563 or 800/444–5713 | www.spamtownusa.com.

Attractions

Austin Area Arts Center. You can take workshops in several artistic media, or view an exhibit by a local artist, at this center in the Oak Park mall. | 1301 18th Ave. NW | 507/433–8451 | Free | Wed.–Fri. 11:30–5, Sat. 10:30–5, Sun. 12:30–4:30.

J. C. Hormel Nature Center. The initial 185 acres for this 278-acre nature center were pur- chased from the Hormel family by local citizens who raised the donations and grant money themselves. The grounds include more than 200,000 trees, 10 mi of trails and prairie, and an interpretive center. | 1304 NE 21st St. | 507/437–7519 | Free | Mon.–Sat. 9–5, Sun. 1–5.

Mower County Historical Center. The attractions here include a carriage museum, a rural school, and a Native American display. The train exhibit features a vintage locomotive, caboose, passenger car, baggage car, and depot. | 1303 S.W. 6th Ave. | 507/437–6082 | $2 | Mon.–Fri. 10–4.

New SPAM Museum. Video exhibits, kiosks, and displays illustrate the history of Hormel Foods and its products, including SPAM. | 1101 North Main St. | 507/437–5611 | Free | Call for hours.

CANNED CUISINE

Minnesota is not particularly well known for its cuisine. Its largely Scandinavian heritage has contributed a few notable dishes including *lutefisk* (codfish soaked in lye), but this is hot dish (casserole) country. Home of vegetables in white sauce. If you really must know what Minnesota's most significant culinary contribution is . . .

It's SPAM.

In the mid-1930s, the George A. Hormel Company in Austin was looking for a new product to help it weather the depression. It settled on a luncheon meat, a concoc- tion of spiced ham, pork shoulder, and sodium nitrate. Hormel packed its new prod- uct in a funny-looking, rectangular can and gave it an easy-to-remember name: SPAM. It was an instant hit. Almost immediately, dozens of competitors came out with similar products, but none could match the popularity of SPAM. Today it remains one of the most recognizable brand names in the world.

That's not to say that SPAM is universally admired. Ever since World War II, SPAM has grated on the American consciousness. The war produced countless jokes about the underappreciated luncheon meat (SPAM is ham that didn't pass its physical), but the dubious reputation that SPAM earned during the war was a bit unfair. The canned meat included in the soldiers' rations was not SPAM at all. It was a govern- ment-issued imitation that by all accounts was much less tasty than the Hormel original. But it didn't matter. As *Yank* magazine put it: "That which we call SPAM by any other name would taste as lousy."

© Corbis

ON THE CALENDAR

FEB.: *Stories from the Heartland.* During the last weekend of the month, storytellers from across the country come to the 1929 Paramount Theater to share music, humor, folktales, and life experiences with audiences young and old. | 800/444–5713.

JULY: *SPAM Town USA Festival/SPAM Jam.* Here's where you can watch or participate in a series of events somehow connected to the town's most famous product—among them, the 5-mi SPAM Hog Jog. | 1st weekend in July | 800/444–5713.

AUG.: *Mower County Fair.* Live entertainment, 4-H and FFA displays, fine arts demonstrations, a children's farmyard, and a carnival are a few of the attractions here. | 2nd week in Aug. | 800/444–5713.

SEPT.: *National Barrow Show.* Held at Austin's Mower County Fairgrounds, this event draws people from around the world to see the exhibition, judging, and sale of eight major breeds of swine. | 800/444–5713.

Dining

Windrift Restaurant and Lounge. American. Steaks and sandwiches are the specialty of this restaurant, decorated with prints. Other dinner options include the seafood, chicken, and burgers. | 2505 11th St. NE | 507/437–7132 | No lunch | $8–$15 | MC, V.

Lodging

AmericInn and Suites. Built in 1999, this hotel sits on the northern end of town just north of I–90, exit 178A (4th Street), off U.S. 63. Some rooms have fireplaces. Complimentary Continental breakfast. Some microwaves, some refrigerators. Cable TV. Indoor pool. Sauna. Business services. No pets. | 1700 8th St. NW | 507/437–7337 or 800/634–3444 | fax 507/437–7337 | www.americinn.com | 54 rooms | $79–$160 | AE, D, DC, MC, V.

Holiday Inn. Both businesspeople and families enjoy this full-service hotel, right off I–90 (exit 178A), northwest of town. The main attraction is the Holidome, an indoor recreation area with three pools, a putting green, games, and a health club, among other diversions. 4 restaurants, bar (with entertainment), room service. In-room data ports, some refrigerators. Cable TV. 3 indoor pools, wading pool. Sauna. Putting green. Health club. Video games. Laundry facilities. Business services, airport shuttle. Some pets allowed. | 1701 4th St. NW | 507/433–1000 or 800/985–8850 | fax 507/433–8749 | hiata@clear.lakes.com | www.holiday-inn.com | 121 rooms, 11 suites | $89–$99, $119–$159 suites | AE, D, DC, MC, V.

BABBITT

MAP 3, F3

(Nearby towns also listed: Ely, Tower)

A company town in the truest sense, Babbitt is a product of the Reserve Mining Company, which constructed a big taconite plant here in 1951 and immediately afterward built streets, public utilities, and commercial buildings. The company turned all the facilities over to the Village of Babbitt after the town was incorporated in 1956; today its population is 1200. The Boundary Waters Canoe Area Wilderness is 20 mi away.

Information: **City of Babbitt** | 71 South Dr., Babbitt, 55706 | 218/827–3464 | www.babbitt-mn.com.

Attractions

Babbitt Beach. On Birch Lake, 2 mi northeast of Babbitt, this beach has a playground, fishing dock, hiking/biking trails, and picnic tables. | CR 70 | 218/827–3464 | Free | Daily.

JUNE: *Peter Mitchell Days.* Carnival rides, fireworks, soft ball tournaments are held in honor of Peter Mitchell, the man who first discovered taconite (a flintlike rock containing iron ore) in Babbitt. | 218/827–3476.

Dining

Babbitt Diner. American. Trophies and country hats cover the walls at this family restaurant where breakfast favorites include biscuits and gravy and omelets. Liver and onions, burgers, sandwiches, 8-oz steaks, soups, and salads are lunch favorites. | 9 Commerce Rd. | 218/827–3470 | Breakfast also available | $7–$9 | No credit cards.

Lodging

Alder Place Inn. Built in the 1950s, this single-story inn sits on 2 acres, next to snowmobile, bicycle, and cross-country skiing trails. Rooms are done in gingham and prints with pine furnishings. The common area is a sunroom with a fireplace. Picnic area. Cable TV. Pets allowed (fee). | 13 Alder Rd. | 218/827–2220 | fax 218/827–2220 | 10 rooms | $34–$45 | AE, D, MC, V.

Timber Bay Lodge and Houseboats. A resort deep in the Superior National Forest, this hostelry has log-sided cabins with fireplaces, decks and views of Birch Lake. You can also rent houseboats. Cabin rates are based on a one-week stay, houseboat rates on a three-day rental. No air-conditioning, kitchenettes, some microwaves. Cable TV. Beach, marina, boating. Kids' programs. Some pets allowed. | 8347 Timber Bay Rd. | 218/827–3682 or 800/846–6821 | timber@uslink.net | www.timberbay.com | 12 cabins, 5 houseboats | $710–$1,185 cabins (1–wk rental), $160–$320 houseboats (3–day rental) | Closed Oct.–mid-May | D, MC, V.

BAUDETTE

MAP 3, D2

(Nearby towns also listed: International Falls, Roseau)

You can't get much farther north in the state, without stepping into Canada. Baudette and its surrounding area are serious fishing country, with more than 40 resorts accommodating anglers of all levels and travelers looking for a quiet respite on a lakefront beach. The local economy depends not only on tourism but on manufacturing, agriculture, and timber as well.

Information: Lake of the Woods Tourism | Box 518, Baudette, 56623 | 218/634–1174 or 800/382–FISH | www.lakeofthewoodsmn.com.

Attractions

Baudette Tourist Park. You can see Canada across the Rainy River at this park, 1 mi east of Baudette. The five wooded acres contain a picnic shelter, grills, a playground, and tennis courts. | Rte. 11 | 800/382–FISH(3474) | Free | Open spring–fall.

Lake of the Woods. With more than 65,000 mi of shoreline, this body of water in the northernmost portion of the state, partly in the United States and partly in Canada, is one of the largest in the world. Because of its size, it freezes much later in the year than other area lakes, and stays frozen much longer; in spring you can hear the ice groaning and cracking. More than 14,000 islands dot its waters, which are famous for big walleye pike and muskies. | Rtes. 11 and 313 | www.dnr.state.mn.us/parks_and_recreation/state_parks/zippel_bay/index.html | Free | Daily.

Although he's not real, **Willie Walleye**—weighing in at two tons and measuring 40 ft in length—claims to be the world's largest walleye. | Intersection of International Dr. and Hwy.11 | 800/382–FISH (3474).

Abutting Lake of the Woods, 3,000-acre **Zippel Bay State Park** is 10 mi north of Baudette, on County Road 8. Swimming, fishing, boating, snowmobiling, and many other outdoor activities are available, and in summer you can discover wild strawberries, chokecherries, cranberries, blueberries, and edible mushrooms. There's a 2-mi white-sand beach. | 218/783–6252 | www.dnr.state.mn.us/parks_and_recreation/state_parks/zippel_bay/index.html | State Park Permit fee $4 daily, $20 annually | Daily.

Lake of the Woods County Museum. Exhibits in this museum, in the county courthouse, cover a variety of subjects, among which are the Lake of the Woods, regional geology, natural history, and the great forest fire of 1910. | 119 8th Ave. SE | 218/634–1200 | Free. | May–Sept., Tues.–Sat. 10–4, Sun. 1–4.

Northwest Angle and Islands. Separated from the rest of Minnesota by Lake of the Woods, and dotted with resorts, this peninsula is partly in Canada, and has a vast network of snowmobile trails. The area is accessible by car or by a 40-mi boat ride from Angle Inlet on the mainland. | Accessible via Rte. 11 or Rte. 313 | 800/434–853 | www.ccco.net/nwa/edgeangle.html.

Rainy River. This stream travels northbound from Rainy Lake to Lake of the Woods. There's whitewater at Manitou Rapids and Clementson Rapids. To get there, take Rte. 11, which parallels the Rainy River for about 70 mi between International Falls and Baudette. | 800/382–FISH.

Red Lake Wildlife Management Area and Norris Camp. Built by the Civilian Conservation Corps in the 1930s, the camp stands in the natural habitat of bald eagles, bear, moose, and other wildlife. | Faunce Butterfield Rd. | 218/783–6861 | Free | Daily.

Dining
Ranch House. American. Works by local artists hang from the walls at this family restaurant, where burgers, steaks, walleye, and breakfast selections fill the menu. | 203 W. Main St. | 218/634–2420 | $7–$13 | AE, MC, V.

Lodging
Sportsman's Lodge. The lodge is really a full-service, year-round resort, on 18½ acres at the south end of Lake of the Woods. Bar, dining room, picnic area. Some kitchenettes. Cable TV. Indoor pool. Hot tub. Dock, water sports. snowmobiling. Business services. | 3244 Bur Oak Rd. NW | 218/634–1342 or 800/862–8602 | northern@wiktel.com | www.sportsmanslodgelow.com | 30 rooms, 4 suites, 20 cabins | $79, $79–$130 suites, $128–$256 cabins | AE, D, MC, V.

Walleye Inn. Directly off the highway on the western edge of Baudette. Complimentary Continental breakfast. Cable TV. Business services. | Rte. 11 | 218/634–1550 | 39 rooms | $46–$80 | MC, V.

Wigwam Resort. This resort fills a large wooded property along the Lake of the Woods at the mouth of the Rainy River. Wood paneling mixes with Native American motifs in the lodge rooms and cabins. Restaurant, 3 bars (live entertainment), picnic area. Some kitchenettes, some microwaves, some refrigerators, some in-room hot tubs. Cable TV, no room phones. Dock, boating, fishing. Pets allowed (fee). | 3502 Four Mile Bay Dr. NW | 218/634–2168 or 800/448–9260 | wigwam@wiktel.com | www.fishandgame.com/wigwam | 14 rooms, 12 cabins | $60–$75 rooms, $75 cabins | AE, D, MC, V.

BEMIDJI

MAP 3, C4

(Nearby town also listed: Walker)

The name of this city comes from an Ojibway word meaning "lake with crossed waters," referring to the Mississippi River, which crosses Lake Bemidji. The area was settled by Shay-now-ish-kun, an Ojibway man referred to by whites as "Chief Bemidji." You may already have heard of the city's giant statues of Paul Bunyan and Babe the Blue Ox, but they're just part of the Bemidji story. Living up to its billing as the "First City on the Mississippi River," the town hosts shopping centers, medical facilities, and Bemidji State University, making it a regional hub. If residents had an "official" garment, it would be a red-and-black-plaid flannel shirt, just like the one a certain oversized lumberjack supposedly wore.

Information: Bemidji Visitors and Convention Bureau | Box 66, Bemidji, 56619 | 218/759–0164 | www.visitbemidji.com.

Attractions
Bemidji State University. BSU is largely known for its music programs, environmental studies, and peat research. | 1500 Birchmont Dr. NE | 218/755–2040 | www.bemidji.msus.edu | Daily.

Bemidji Tourist Information Center. Make sure your tongue is firmly in cheek as you survey the collection of Paul Bunyan's tools and artifacts. The fireplace here consists of stones from every U.S. state and Canadian province. | 300 Bemidji Ave. | 800/458–2223 | Free. | Weekdays 8–4:30, Sat. 12–4; closed Sun.
Standing next to the visitor center, **Paul Bunyan and Babe the Blue Ox** have been local landmarks since they were constructed in 1937—Paul for a Paul Bunyan carnival and Babe as a traveling exhibit for parades and shows. Both are truly Bunyan-size. Paul, modeled after the then-city mayor Earl Bucklan, weighs 2½ tons and is 18 ft tall; Babe is three times life-size, has his eyes light up and smoke pours out of his nostrils, suggesting that he's breathing frigid air. | 300 Bemidji Ave. | www.visitbemidji.com/bemidji/PaulBabe.html.

Itasca State Park. The mighty Mississippi begins from Lake Itasca at this park 30 mi south of Bemidji, where there are more than 6,000 acres of old-growth forest. | U.S. 71 | 218/266–2100 or 800/458–2223 | Free | Daily.

Lake Bemidji State Park. This 1,688-acre state park is in the pine-moraine region of Minnesota. Hikers can explore the beauty of a tamarack bog carpeted with lady's slippers, dragon's mouth, grass pink, and insect-eating sundews and pitcher plants. Stop by the visitors center before you go fishing, bird-watching, hiking, or cross-country skiing. | 3401 State Park Rd. NE | 218/755–3843 | www.dnr.state.mn.us/parks_and_recreation/state_parks/lake_bemidji | Park permit required | Daily.

ON THE CALENDAR
FEB.: *Minnesota Finlandia.* Amateur and professional skiiers come from across the globe to partake in this cross-country race at the Buena Vista Ski Area, 12 mi north of Bemidji. | 218/751–0041 | www.minnesotafinlandia.com.
JUNE–OCT.: *Paul Bunyan Playhouse.* It's not Broadway, but it'll do. Professional casts perform rotating plays and musicals. | 218/751–7270.
JULY: *Beltrami County Fair.* Head to the fairgrounds, at 7300 Frontage Rd. NW, for agricultural exhibits, carnival rides, and live entertainment. | 800/458–2223.
JULY: *Paul Bunyan Water Carnival.* A beard-growing contest adds extra interest to this carnival, which also has a water show, a parade, and fireworks. | 800/458–2223.

Dining
Back Yard. American. Latticework, mirrors, and plants ornament the walls of this restaurant with a grand piano in the middle. Walleye and prime rib are the specialties, complemented by chicken and shrimp dishes. Piano music Fri.–Sat. | 2450 Paul Bunyan Dr./U.S. 2W | 218/444–7242 | $13–$20 | AE, D, DC, MC, V.

Country Kitchen. American. Home of the Paul Bunyan roll, a caramel or glazed roll, this chain restaurant about a mile north of downtown serves a wide range of dishes, including pancakes, omelettes, sandwiches, soups, hamburgers, smothered chicken, pasta Alfredo, and whitefish filet. | 710 Paul Bunyan Dr. NW | 218/444–8963 | No reservations accepted | Open 24 hours | $5–$7 | MC, V.

Cyber Bugs Cafe. American. You can surf the Web while sipping your espresso and munching on a sandwich. | 311 3rd St. NW | 218/444–2927 | $1–$3 | No credit cards.

Gangelhoff's. Contemporary. Wooden chairs and tables and a big aquarium give this casual place flair. The seafood, steak, and pasta are popular. Kids' menu. | 3600 Moberg Dr. | 218/751–9500 | $10–$35 | AE, D, DC, MC, V.

Lodging

AmericInn. The lobby here has a fireplace, and is 1 mi northwest of the university. Complimentary Continental breakfast. In-room data ports, some refrigerators, some in-room hot tubs. Cable TV. Indoor pool. Hot tub, sauna. Laundry facilities. | 1200 Paul Bunyan Dr. NW | 218/751–3000 | fax 218/751–3000 | www.AmericInn.com/minnesota/bemidji.html | 59 rooms | $58–$69 | AE, D, DC, MC, V.

Best Western. On the northwest edge of town, this hotel is next door to two restaurants, 1 mi from both a shopping mall and cross-country or downhill skiing. Complimentary Continental breakfast. Cable TV. Indoor pool. Hot tub. Business services. | 2420 Paul Bunyan Dr. NW | 218/751–0390 | fax 218/751–2887 | 60 rooms | $49–$70 | AE, D, DC, MC, V.

Comfort Inn. This hotel is about as close as you can get to the Beltrami County Airport, which is ½ mi away. Complimentary Continental breakfast. In-room data ports, some refrigerators, some in-room hot tubs. Cable TV. Indoor pool. Hot tub, sauna. Business services, airport shuttle. | 3500 Comfort Dr. | 218/751–7700 | fax 218/444–8742 | www.comfortinn.com | 61 rooms, 18 suites | $54–$69, $69–$99 suites | AE, D, DC, MC, V.

Finn 'n Feather Resort. On Lake Andrusia, 10 mi east of town, this resort has a private beach. Picnic area. No air-conditioning. Pool. Hot tub. Tennis. Beach, boating. Video games. Laundry facilities. | Rte. 3, Box 870 | 218/335–6598 or 800/776–3466 | fax 218/335–6151 | tfallis@paulbunyan.net | www.finn-n-feather.com | 19 apartments | $600–$1,400 (7–day minimum stay) | Closed Labor Day–mid-June | MC, V.

Holiday Inn Express. Next to the Paul Bunyan Mall, this hotel, built in 1996, sits 1½ mi east of U.S. 71. In-room data ports, in-room hot tubs. Cable TV. Indoor pool. Hot tub, sauna. Video games. Laundry facilities. Business services. Pets allowed. | 2422 Ridgeway Ave. NW | 218/751–2487 or 800/617–4379 | fax 218/751–0771 | bjiex@paulbunyan.net | www.basshotels.com | 69 rooms | $63–$109 | AE, D, MC, V.

Kohl's Resort. This resort sits on Big Turtle Lake, in Buena Vista State Forest, 10 mi north of Bemidji. Many cabins have fireplaces and knotty pine paneling; they have between one and five bedrooms. As an alternative, you can stay in one of the poolside rooms. Kitchenettes, microwaves, refrigerators. Cable TV, no room phones. Indoor pool. Outdoor hot tub, sauna. Hiking. Beach, boating, fishing. Cross-country skiing, snowmobiling. Shops. Playground. Laundry facilities. Business services. No pets. | 15707 Big Turtle Dr. NE | 218/243–2131 or 800/336–4384 | fax 218/243–3464 | www.kohlsresort.com | 4 rooms, 18 cabins | $75–$95 rooms, $725–$1,350 cabins (weekly rate in season) | MC, V.

Northern Inn. Bemidji's only full-service hotel has the largest indoor recreational facility in northern Minnesota. Bemidji State Park is 5 mi away. Restaurant, bar, room service. In-room data ports. Cable TV. Indoor pool. Beauty salon, hot tub. Putting green. Exercise equipment. Laundry facilities. Business services, airport shuttle. Some pets allowed. | 3600 Moberg Dr. | 218/751–9500 | www.gphotels.com/northerninn | 123 rooms, 4 suites | $74–$79, $130 suites | AE, D, DC, MC, V.

Place in the Woods Resort. You can see Turtle River Lake between the pines, spruce, and maple from the private deck of the log cabins at this resort. Each cabin contains a full kitchen and wood-burning stove. Nine miles of trails lace the 45 wooded acres. Kitchenettes, microwaves, refrigerators, some in-room hot tubs. No room phones, no TV. Hiking. Beach,

dock, water sports, boating, fishing. Cross-country skiing, snowmobiling. No pets. | 11380
Turtle River Lake Rd. NE | 218/586–2345 or 800/676–4547 | apitw@paulbunyan.net |
www.aplaceinthewoodsresort.com | 12 cabins | $140–$320 | D, MC, V.

Ruttger's Birchmont Lodge. Five generations of the same family have owned and operated this lodge, on 22 acres, including 1,700 ft of sandy beach on Lake Bemidji. Sports and
recreation directors can help you choose between activities from waterskiing to movies.
Bar, dining room. No air-conditioning in some rooms, in-room data ports, some kitchenettes,
refrigerators. Cable TV. 2 pools (1 indoor). Hot tub. Tennis. Gym. Beach, dock, water sports,
boating. Cross-country skiing. Children's programs (ages 4–12). Laundry facilities. Business
services, airport shuttle. Some pets allowed. | 530 Birchmont Beach Rd. NE | 218/751–1630
or 888/788–8437 | rruttger@paulbunyan.net | www.ruttger.com | 28 rooms, 40 cottages |
$62–$148, $152–$309 cottages | AE, D, MC, V.

Super 8. This motel is on the fringe of the Minnesota woods, between a mall and the air-
port. Complimentary Continental breakfast. Cable TV. Hot tub, sauna. Business services. |
1815 Paul Bunyan Dr. NW | 218/751–8481 | fax 218/751–8870 | www.super8motels.com | 101
rooms | $46–$60 | AE, D, DC, MC, V.

BLOOMINGTON

MAP 3, E8

(Nearby towns also listed: Lakeville, Minneapolis, New Prague, St. Paul, Shakopee)

Bloomington is the home of Mall of America, the nation's largest shopping and entertainment complex, and Minnesota's most popular tourist attraction. The town is a southern Minneapolis suburb that ranks as the third-largest city in the state. It is also home
to the Minneapolis/St. Paul International Airport.

Information: Bloomington Convention and Visitors Bureau | 7900 International Dr.,
Ste. 990, Bloomington, 55425 | 612/858–8500 or 800/346–4289 | www.blooming-
tonmn.org.

Attractions
Hyland Hills Ski and Snowboard Area. Part of the 1,000-acre Hyland Park Reserve, this ski
area is 5 mi west of the Mall of America, just south of Route 100 and I–494. Hyland has 14
runs, three chair lifts, three rope tows, and a 300-ft vertical drop. | E. Bush Lake Rd., Bloom-
ington | www.hylandski.com | 952/835–4250 | Closed Apr.–Thanksgiving.

Mall of America. Just try seeing everything there is to see here in one day. This megamall
contains more than 500 stores and restaurants, an indoor theme park, a movie complex,
a mini-golf course, an interactive "Lego-Land" shop, and a walk-through aquarium. And
that's not even a complete list. | 60 E. Broadway | 612/883–8800 | www.mallofamerica.com
| Free | Daily.

Minnesota Valley National Wildlife Refuge. Among other wildlife red foxes, eagles, great
blue herons, and beavers find safe haven here. | 3815 E. 80th St. | 952/854–5900 | Free | Daily.

ON THE CALENDAR
FEB.: *Bloomington Loves Its Kids Month Kickoff.* This month-long celebration kicks off
at Knott's Camp Snoopy and the Mall of America. Opening ceremonies honor outstanding community members, and there's a community carnival and kids programming
throughout the month. | 952/948–8877.

Dining
Asia Grille. Pan-Asian. Asian delicacies can be ordered here at the ornate bar. The dining
room has terrazzo floors and plenty of wood. Repeat customers like the sashimi-style

tuna spring rolls and the "make your own noodle-dish." | 549 Prairie Center Dr., Eden Prairie | 612/944–4095 | $8–$15 | AE, D, DC, MC, V.

Big Bowl. Pan-Asian. The stenciled Chinese wall lettering and colorful lamps give this restaurant a glamorous lift, despite its mall setting. It's known for its Chinese noodles and Vietnamese noodle soup. | 3669 Galleria, Edina | 612/928–7888 | Reservations not accepted | $8–$15 | AE, D, DC, MC, V.

Biscayne Bay. Seafood. The candlelit tables are a soft touch at this suburban restaurant in the Hilton Airport hotel (*see* Hilton Airport, *below*), where lobster bisque and crab-and-smoked-trout cakes rule. | 3800 E. 80th St. | 952/854–2100 | No lunch. Closed Sun. | $15–$30 | AE, D, DC, MC, V.

Da Afghan. Middle Eastern. Afghan rugs serve as tablecloths and exotic music plays in the background at this eatery, known for an assortment of lamb dishes, from lamb kabobs to curried lamb, and for a garlic-marinated Afghan filet mignon. Kids' menu. Beer and wine only. | 929 W. 80th St. | 952/888–5824 | No lunch Sun.–Wed. | $10–$20 | AE, MC, V.

David Fong's. Chinese. A bustling lounge adds excitement to this Asian restaurant where steak kow (stir-fried filet mignon) and various other meat specialties are on the menu. Kids' menu. | 9392 Lyndale Ave. S | 612/888–9294 | Closed Sun. | $12–$22 | AE, DC, MC, V.

Kincaid's. Contemporary. At this restaurant on the water you can take in the view of Lake Normandy while surrounded by dark mahogany and brass, a plate of rock salt–roasted prime rib or garlic- and vermouth-grilled salmon with king crab legs before you. Kids' menu.

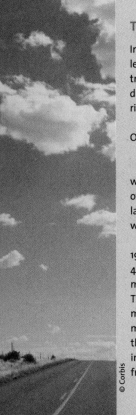

THE BIG MALL

In 1982, major league baseball's Minnesota Twins and the NFL's Minnesota Vikings left Metropolitan Stadium in Bloomington for their new home in the climate-controlled comfort of Minneapolis's Hubert H. Humphrey Metrodome. Old Met Stadium was leveled and Bloomington was left with a huge empty lot. What would rise in its place?

Some pushed for office buildings.

Others wanted condominiums.

Still others argued for a new convention center.

But in the end, Bloomington gave its okay to a mall. And not just any mall. This would be the nation's largest retail and entertainment complex. There were plenty of naysayers. The local news media were especially skeptical. Why build the nation's largest mall in Minnesota? Who would want to travel here to shop, especially in winter?

As it turned out, a lot of people want to shop here. Since its grand opening in 1992, Mall of America has averaged at least 35 million visits a year. Between 30 and 40% of those visitors are tourists who've traveled from outside the Twin Cities metro area.

There appear to be several reasons behind the mall's success. For one thing, the mall is less than 2 mi from the Minneapolis-St. Paul International Airport and that's made marketing to tourists much easier. Climate is another big factor. Weather in the Twin Cities tends toward extremes—hot and cold—and, for many people, an indoor mall with a seven-acre amusement park offers an attractive alternative to freezing or sweating.

© Corbis

Sun. brunch. | 8400 Normandale Lake Blvd. | 612/921–2255 | No lunch weekends | $16–$28 | AE, D, DC, MC, V.

La Fougasse. French. Floor-to-ceiling windows and a sidewalk café create a bright atmosphere in this hotel bistro (*see* Hotel Sofitel, *below*), where you can sup on onion soup and crêpes à la Reine. Sun. brunch. | 5601 W. 78th St. | 612/835–1900 | $7–$15 | AE, DC, MC, V.

Mandarin Kitchen. Chinese. Mandarin fare is the specialty of this house decorated with Chinese pastoral art. Lobster, crab, and whole fish dishes are also popular. | 8766 Lyndale Ave. S | 612/884–5356 | $9–$15 | AE, D, DC, MC, V.

Olive Garden. Italian. The France Ave. exit off of I-494 brings you to this Italian chain restaurant, known for its bottomless soup kettle, salad bowl, and bread basket. The menu includes multitudes of old favorites and a range of pastas. | 4701 West 80th St. | 612/831–4044 | fax 612/831–0476 | $10–$17 | AE, D, MC, V.

Oriental Jade Chinese Restaurant. Chinese. The weekday lunch buffet is your chance to load up on classic American/Chinese dishes. The dinner menu is à la carte. | 8907 Penn Ave. S | 612/884–3295 | No lunch Sun. | $7–$10 | No credit cards.

Planet Hollywood. American. A long escalator takes you to Hollywood-style glitz at the top of the Mall of America. Try the ribs, burgers, pasta, little pizzas, or fajitas. | 402 South Ave. | 612/854–7827 | $8–$18 | AE, D, DC, MC, V.

Rainforest Cafe. Caribbean. Within the Mall of America, you can dine on dishes such as chicken Bombay (marinated in turmeric, curry, and coconut milk), while seated in a mock rain forest complete with fake monkeys and fake thunderstorms. Kids' menu. | 102 South Ave. | 612/854–7500 | $10–$18 | AE, D, DC, MC, V.

Ruby Tuesday. American. The menu is incredibly diverse at this chain restaurant, on the second floor of the Mall of America, near the north entrance. Try the Ultimate Tuesday platter, which features ribs, steak, chicken, shrimp, cole slaw, and fries, or the 7-oz chicken barbecue sandwich, topped with ham, bacon, and the works. | 234 N. Garden | 952/854–8282 | $6–$16 | AE, D, MC, V.

Tejas. Southwestern. Adorned with southwestern paintings, pottery, and desert plants, the restaurant serves similar-themed foods, such as the popular grilled chicken and wild rice burrito with mango habanero sauce. | 3910 W. 50th St. | 952/926–0800 | Closed Sun. | $10–$20 | AE, DC, MC, V.

TGI Friday's. American. This popular, lively, kitschy chain restaurant is in the shadow of the Radisson. The menu ranges from steaks to salad to flaming fajitas. Kids' menu. | 7730 Normandale Blvd. | 612/831–6553 | $8.99–$16.99 | AE, D, DC, MC, V.

Tony Roma's. Barbecue. In the Mall of America, next to Macy's, on the third floor, is this barbecue chain, famed for its spicy baby back ribs. You'll also find hearty sandwiches and salads. Pictures of the original 1952 restaurant hang on the walls. | 346 South Blvd. | 612/854–7940 | $7–$17 | AE, D, DC, MC, V.

Lodging

Baymont Inn. Its location, about 2 mi from the Mall of America, makes this hotel an easy home base for shopping and dining excursions. Complimentary Continental breakfast. In-room data ports. Cable TV. Video games. Business services, airport shuttle. Some pets allowed. | 7815 Nicollet Ave. S | 612/881–7311 | fax 612/881–0604 | 190 rooms | $60–$74 | AE, D, DC, MC, V.

Best Western Thunderbird. A Native American theme extends throughout the hotel, with sculptures, paintings, draperies, and carpeting all reflecting the culture. The Mall of America is next door and you're at I-494, exit 2A. Restaurant, bar (with entertainment), room service. Microwaves, refrigerators. Cable TV. 2 pools (1 indoor). Hot tub. Exercise equipment. Business services, airport shuttle. Some pets allowed. | 2201 E. 78th St. | 952/854–3411 | fax 952/854–1183 | 263 rooms | $110–$115 | AE, D, DC, MC, V.

Clarion Hotel. Each room has a forest or lake view here, 7 mi west of the Mall of America. There are free shuttles to the mall, to a casino, and to the airport. Restaurant, bar. In-room data ports. Cable TV. Indoor pool. Hot tub, sauna. Video games. Business services, airport shuttle, free parking. | 8151 Bridge Rd. | 612/830–1300 | fax 612/830–1535 | www.clarion-minneapolis.com | 252 rooms | $75–$100 | AE, D, DC, MC, V.

Comfort Inn. Four blocks from the Mall of America, to which there is a free shuttle, this hotel is off I–494, exit 2A. Restaurant, bar, complimentary Continental breakfast. In-room data ports, some in-room hot tubs. Cable TV. Indoor pool. Exercise equipment. Business services, airport shuttle, free parking. | 1321 E. 78th St. | 952/854–3400 | fax 952/854–2234 | www.resobase.com/destinations/minneapolis/comfort-bloomington | 272 rooms | $79–$99 | AE, D, DC, MC, V.

Country Inn and Suites. A free shuttle will take you to the Mall of America, or to the airport which is 5 mi to the east. Complimentary Continental breakfast. Some refrigerators. Cable TV. 2 Indoor pools. Hot tub. Exercise equipment. Business services, airport shuttle. | 2221 Killebrew Dr. | 952/854–5555 | fax 952/854–5564 | 70 rooms, 164 suites | $118–$128, $135–$145 suites | AE, D, DC, MC, V.

Days Inn–Airport. Five mi west of the airport, this hotel is directly off Route 77, ¼ mi south of I–494, at the Killbrew Dr. exit. Restaurant, bar. Cable TV. Pool. Hot tub, sauna. Video games. Airport shuttle. | 1901 Killebrew Dr. | 952/854–8400 | fax 952/854–3331 | 207 rooms | $119–$139 | AE, D, DC, MC, V.

Days Inn Bloomington West Business. This six-story chain provides free shuttles to and from the Mall of America, 4 mi away. The hotel sits in a business district off I–494, exit 68 and Rte. 100. Complimentary Continental breakfast. In-room data ports, some microwaves, some refrigerators. Cable TV. Laundry facilities, laundry service. Airport shuttle. | 8000 Bridge Rd. | 952/831–9595 | fax 952/835–5909 | www.daysinn.com | 167 rooms | $60–$85 | AE, D, MC, V.

Doubletree Grand Hotel–Mall of America. Step out the lobby door of this hotel and behold the Mall of America. Restaurant, bar, room service. In-room data ports. Cable TV. Indoor pool. Hot tub. Exercise equipment. Business services, airport shuttle. | 7901 24th Ave. S | 952/854–2244 | fax 952/854–4421 | www.doubletreehotels.com | 321 rooms | $99–$129 | AE, D, DC, MC, V.

Embassy Suites. This atrium-style hotel is 11 mi from Minneapolis, 15 mi from St. Paul, and has a free shuttle to the Mall of America and to the airport. Restaurant, bar. In-room data ports, microwaves, refrigerators. Cable TV. Indoor pool. Hot tub. Exercise equipment. Video games. Laundry facilities. Business services, airport shuttle. | 2800 W. 80th St. | 952/884–4811 | fax 952/884–8137 | 219 rooms | $119–$159 | AE, D, DC, MC, V.

Embassy Suites–Airport. This property has a 10-story garden with tropical plants, trees, and bubbling brooks. There's a free shuttle to both the Mall of America and the airport, which is 4 mi east. Restaurant, bar, complimentary breakfast. In-room data ports, microwaves. Cable TV. Indoor pool. Hot tub. Exercise equipment. Business services, airport shuttle. | 7901 34th Ave. S | 612/854–1000 or 888/287–3390 | fax 612/854–6557 | www.resobase.com/destinations/minneapolis/embassy-airport | 310 rooms | $129–$159 | AE, D, DC, MC, V.

Exel Inn. You can catch a free shuttle from this hotel to the Mall of America—three blocks to the south—and to the airport. Complimentary Continental breakfast. In-room data ports. Cable TV. Exercise equipment. Business services, airport shuttle. | 2701 E. 78th St. | 612/854–7200 | fax 612/854–8652 | www.exelinns.com | 203 rooms | $64–$73 | AE, D, DC, MC, V.

Fairfield Inn by Marriott. This is one of the more convenient hotels to the Mall of America, which is directly across the street. If you want to save your energy for shopping, a free shuttle is available to take you there, as well as to the airport. Complimentary Continental breakfast. Some refrigerators. Cable TV. Indoor pool. Hot tub. Business services, airport shuttle. | 2401 E. 80th St. | 952/858–8475 | fax 952/858–8475 | www.fairfieldinn.com/MSPBL | 134 rooms | $90–$135 | AE, D, DC, MC, V.

Friendly Host Inn. This two-building complex is at 12th Street off I–494, exit 3 (Portland Ave), 4 mi west of the airport and eight blocks west of the Metropolitan Sports Center and Mall of America. Complimentary Continental breakfast. Some kitchenettes, some microwaves, some refrigerators. Indoor pool, whirlpool. Free parking. | 1225 E. 78th St. | 952/854–3322 or 800/341–8000 | fax 952/854–3322 | www.bestvalueinn.com/Lodges/W056.htm | 47 rooms | $59–$79 | AE, D, DC, MC, V.

Hampton Inn. This hotel is in the heart of Bloomington's business district. Complimentary Continental breakfast. In-room data ports. Cable TV. Business services, airport shuttle, free parking. | 4201 W. 80th St. | 612/835–6643 | fax 612/835–7217 | www.hamptoninn.com | 135 rooms | $84–$99 | AE, D, DC, MC, V.

Hampton Inn. Eight miles east of Mall of America, this hostelry caters to business travelers. Complimentary Continental breakfast. In-room data ports. Cable TV. Business services. | 7740 Flying Cloud Dr., Eden Prairie | 952/942–9000 | fax 952/942–0725 | www.hamptoninn.com | 122 rooms | $74–$84 | AE, D, DC, MC, V.

Hawthorn Suites. With an attached 2½-acre indoor park containing an Olympic-size pool, a fitness center, a jogging track, a skating rink, and a playground, this hotel is a destination in itself. It's two blocks south of I–494 (France Ave. exit). Complimentary breakfast. In-room data ports, kitchenettes, microwaves. Cable TV, in-room VCRs (and movies). Indoor pool. Playground. Laundry facilities. Business services, airport shuttle. | 3400 Edinborough Way, Edina | 612/893–9300 | fax 612/893–9885 | www.hawthorn.com/suites/hotels/minn.html | 141 suites | $129–$149 | AE, D, DC, MC, V.

Hilton Airport. Overlooking the Minnesota River Valley, this is the closest full-service hotel to the Minneapolis/St. Paul International Airport, which is 1½ mi east on I–494. There's a free shuttle to both the airport and the Mall of America. Restaurant (*see* Biscayne Bay, *above*), bar, room service. In-room data ports. Cable TV. Indoor pool. Hot tub, sauna. Exercise equipment. Video games. Laundry facilities. Business services, airport shuttle. | 3800 E. 80th St. | 952/854–2100 | fax 952/854–8002 | www.hilton.com/hotels/MSPAHHF | 288 rooms, 12 suites | $90–$120, $135–$160 suites | AE, D, DC, MC, V.

Holiday Inn Central. Standing on the edge of Bloomington's business district, this hotel has a free shuttle to the Mall of America and to the airport. Restaurant, bar, room service. In-room data ports. Cable TV. Indoor pool. Hot tub. Exercise equipment. Video games. Laundry facilities. Business services, airport shuttle. | 1201 W. 94th St. | 952/884–8211 | fax 952/881–5574 | www.khconline.com/bloom.htm | 171 rooms | $85–$105 | AE, D, DC, MC, V.

Holiday Inn Express. Less than one block south of the Mall of America, the hotel nonetheless has a free shuttle to take you there. Complimentary Continental breakfast. In-room data ports, some refrigerators. Cable TV. Business services, airport shuttle. | 814 E. 79th St. | 952/854–5558 | fax 952/854–4623 | 142 rooms | $79–$109 | AE, D, DC, MC, V.

Holiday Inn Select–International Airport. From this hotel you have views of the Twin Cities' skylines and the Minnesota River valley. The Mall of America is 1 mi west. Restaurant, bar. In-room data ports, some refrigerators. Cable TV. Indoor pool. Hot tub, massage. Gym. Business services, airport shuttle. | 3 Apple Tree Sq., | 952/854–9000 | fax 952/854–9000 | 430 rooms, 130 suites | $100–$120, $120–$260 suites | AE, D, DC, MC, V.

Hotel Sofitel. At Bloomington's business crossroads, this European-style hotel has 24-hour concierge service and interpreters in four languages. There's also a free shuttle to the Mall of America and the airport. Restaurant (*see* La Fougasse, *above*), bar. In-room data ports. Cable TV. Indoor pool. Massage. Exercise equipment. Business services, airport shuttle. | 5601 W. 78th St. | 952/835–1900 or 800/876–6303 (outside MN) | fax 952/835–2696 | 282 rooms | $130–$299 | AE, D, DC, MC, V.

Homewood Suites Hotel. In the heart of Bloomington, across from Mall of America, sits this seven-story, all-suites hotel, constructed in 1998. To get there, take I–494 (24th Ave. exit). Complimentary Continental breakfast. In-room data ports, kitchenettes. Cable TV. Indoor

pool. Exercise equipment. Laundry facilities. Business services, airport shuttle. | 2261 Killebrew Dr. | 952/854–0900 | fax 952/854–9571 | www.homewoodsuites.com | 144 rooms | $129–$144 | AE, D, DC, MC, V.

Marriott. A garden courtyard and a gazebo courtyard enhance this hotel, which is 1 block south of the Mall of America. Free shuttles take you to the mall or to the airport. Restaurant, bar, room service. In-room data ports. Cable TV. Indoor pool. Hot tub. Exercise equipment. Business services, airport shuttle. No pets. | 2020 E. 79th St. | 952/854–7441 | fax 952/854–7671 | www.marriotthotels.com/MSPMN | 478 rooms | $119–$179 | AE, D, DC, MC, V.

Park Inn Suite. This hotel designed for business travelers is in Bloomington's corporate business hub. There are free shuttles to the Mall of America and the airport. Complimentary breakfast. In-room data ports, refrigerators. Cable TV. Business services, airport shuttle. | 7770 Johnson Ave. | 952/893–9999 | fax 952/893–1316 | mail@parkinnbloomington.com | www.parkinnbloomington.com | 163 rooms | $94–$124 | AE, D, DC, MC, V.

Radisson-South. This towering hotel is 9 mi from the airport, and 7 mi from the Mall of America. Restaurant, bar. In-room data ports. Cable TV. Indoor pool. Hot tub. Exercise equipment. Business services, airport shuttle. | 7800 Normandale Blvd. | 612/835–7800 | fax 612/893–8419 | www.radisson.com | 580 rooms | $155–$169 | AE, D, DC, MC, V.

Ramada Inn Ltd.–Burnsville. Each suite has a unique fantasy theme at this FantaSuite hotel. You can try out your alter egos in the Space Odyssey Suite, the Casino Royale Suite, or the Arabian Nights Suite. Standard rooms are also available. It's at the junction of Route 13 and I–35, exit 3A, 15 mi from Bloomington. Complimentary Continental breakfast. Cable TV. Indoor-outdoor pool. Hot tub. Business services. | 250 N. River Ridge Cir., Burnsville | 612/890–9550 | fax 612/890–5161 | www.ramada.com | 59 rooms, 30 suites | $69–$85, $140–$225 suites | AE, D, DC, MC, V.

Residence Inn Bloomington. Each of the 128 spacious suites here offers separate living and sleeping areas. It's ½ mi from the Mall of America. Complimentary breakfast. In-room data ports, kitchenettes, refrigerators. Cable TV, in-room VCRs (and movies). Pool. Hot tub. Exercise equipment. Laundry facilities. Business services, airport shuttle, free parking. Some pets allowed (fee). | 7850 Bloomington Avenue S, Minneapolis | 612/876–0900 | fax 612/876–0592 | www.residenceinn.com/MSPLL | 126 suites | $99–$179 | AE, D, DC, MC, V.

Select Inn. This hotel is along Bloomington's strip off I–494, exit 7A. Free shuttles take you to the Mall of America. Complimentary Continental breakfast. Cable TV. Indoor pool. Exercise equipment. Laundry facilities. Business services, airport shuttle. Some pets allowed (fee). | 7851 Normandale Blvd. | 952/835–7400 or 800/641–1000 | fax 952/835–4124 | 142 rooms | $52–$67 | AE, D, DC, MC, V.

Sheraton-Airport. This full-service hotel is 4 blocks from the Mall of America. Restaurant, bar, room service. Cable TV. Indoor pool. Hot tub. Exercise equipment. Business services, airport shuttle, free parking. | 2500 E. 79th St. | 612/854–1771 | fax 612/854–5898 | 250 rooms | $99–$109 | AE, D, DC, MC, V.

Super 8. Standing about 15 mi west of Bloomington, this chain hotel is off of Hwy. 212, next door to the Eden Prairie shopping center. Complimentary Continental breakfast. Cable TV. Laundry facilities. Business services. | 11500 W. 78th St., Eden Prairie | 952/829–0888 | fax 952/829–0854 | 61 rooms | $56–$68 | AE, D, DC, MC, V.

Wyndham Garden. Warm your toes by the fireplace lobby in this hotel in Bloomington's corporate business center. Free shuttles run to the Mall of America and to the airport. Restaurant, bar, room service. In-room data ports. Cable TV. Indoor pool. Hot tub. Exercise equipment. Business services, airport shuttle, free parking. | 4460 W. 78th St., Circle | 952/831–3131 | fax 952/831–6372 | 209 rooms | $95–$115 | AE, D, DC, MC, V.

BLUE EARTH

(Nearby towns also listed: Albert Lea, Fairmont)

Blue Earth has several things going for it that other small cities do not. It's the center point on the nation's longest highway, I–90; it's the home of Minnesota's first stained-glass window (in the Good Shepherd Episcopal Church); and it's the birthplace, they say, of the ice-cream sandwich. And don't forget, the world's largest Jolly Green Giant statue is here, standing guard over some of the state's richest farmland. The town gets its name from the Blue Earth River that encircles it. The river was given the Indian name "Mahkota" (meaning Blue Earth) for the blue-black clay found in the high river banks.

Information: Blue Earth Chamber of Commerce | 118 E. 6th St., Blue Earth, 56013 | 507/526–2916 | www.chamber.blue-earth.mn.us.

Attractions

Faribault County Historical Society. Wakefield House, which houses the society, was built in 1868 by one of Blue Earth's founders. On the grounds you'll also find a 19th-century rural school, a log house, and an Episcopal church. | 405 E. 6th St. | 507/526–5421 | Free | Mon.–Fri. 9–2 or by appointment.

The Woodland School and Krosch Log House. looks much as it most likely did when students learned their lessons there back in the 1870s. Originally, the log house sheltered a family with 11 children. | 405 E. 6th St. | 507/526–5421 | Free | Mon.–Fri. 9–2 or by appointment.

Green Giant Statue Park. A 55-ft image of the green goliath (who wears a size 78 shoe), erected in 1979 to celebrate the region's agriculture, grins over picnic tables and a tourist information center. | Rte. 169 and Green Giant Ave.

ON THE CALENDAR

JULY: *Faribault County Fair.* Celebrate the peak of summer the fourth week of the month with carnival rides, agricultural exhibits, and live entertainment. | 507/854–3374.
AUG.: *Upper Midwest Woodcarvers and Quilters Expo.* People come from all over to admire the juried and non-juried exhibitions of woodcarvings and quilts. | 507/526–2916.
SEPT.: *Faribault Area Balloon Rally and Air Fest.* A popular hot-air balloon display brightens the skies of Faribault. | 800/658–2354.

Dining

Hamilton Hall. American. Memorabilia of Blue Earth adorns the walls of this family restaurant, which is known for homemade soups, particularly the vegetable beef soup and the chili. There's always a daily soup special as well. | 202 S. Moore St., | 507/526–2000 | No dinner Sun., breakfast served daily | $6–$12 | D, MC, V.

Lodging

AmericInn. North of town, at I–90, exit 119 this hotel is surrounded by restaurants. Complimentary Continental breakfast. Some in-room hot tubs. Cable TV. Indoor pool. | 1495 Domes Dr. (U.S. 169N) | 507/526–4215 | fax 507/526–4615 | www.AmericInn.com/minnesota/blueearth.html | 38 rooms | $66–$135 | AE, MC, V.

Budget Inn. Parking is in front of the rooms at this two-story motel 1 mi south of I–90, exit 119. Kitchenettes, microwaves, refrigerators. Cable TV. Laundry facilities. Free Parking. Small pets allowed. | Rte. 169 and 5thSt. | 507/526–2706 | $35–$55 | MC, V.

Super 8. A warm, craft- and antiques-filled lobby welcomes you to this motel, two blocks north of Green Giant Park. Complimentary Continental breakfast. Cable TV. Hot tub. Busi-

ness services. | 1420 Giant Dr. | 507/526–7376 | fax 507/526–2246 | 38 rooms, 2 suites | $45–
$55, $60–$75 suites | AE, D, DC, MC, V.

BRAINERD

MAP 3, D6

(Nearby towns also listed: Cross Lake, Deerwood, Little Falls, Onamia, Pine River)

Brainerd sits on the Mississippi River at the geographical center of the state. It once
was part of a dense forest used by the Ojibway as a hunting ground and blueberry
patch. You'll find nearly 500 lakes and dozens of resorts and campgrounds within a
25-mi radius of the town. Like Bemidji to the north, Brainerd is steeped in Paul Bunyan
lore. A popular amusement park here features a 26-ft-tall talking Paul.

Information: **Brainerd/Crosslakes Area Chambers of Commerce** | 124 N. 6th St., Brain-
erd, 56401 | 218/829–2838 or 800/450–2838 | www.brainerdchamber.com.

Attractions

Crow Wing County Historical Society Museum. The collection here includes Native Amer-
ican artifacts as well as logging, railroad, and farming tools. | 320 Laurel St. | 218/829–3268
| $3 suggested donation | Memorial Day–Labor Day, weekdays 9–5, Sat. 10–2; Labor Day–
Memorial Day, weekdays 1–5, Sat. 10–2.

Madden's Golf Courses. Madden's features four courses for golfers of various skill levels.
The Classic, Pine Beach East, and Pine Beach West are all 18-hole courses. For less demand-
ing golfers, there's the par-three Social 9. | 11266 Pine Beach Peninsula | 800/642–5363 |
$85–$100, The Classic; $35, Pine Beach East and West; $12, Social 9 | April–Oct., sunrise to
sunset.

Paul Bunyan Amusement Center. After being greeted by a giant Paul Bunyan, ride the rides,
take in the logging exhibits, or putt your way around the miniature golf course. | 1900 Fairview
Rd. N | 218/829–6342 (summer only) | www.paulbunyancenter.com | $8 | Memorial Day–
Labor Day, daily 10–8.

Paul Bunyan Trail. *See* Cross Lake, *below.*

The Pines. You can pick and choose between three championship 9-hole courses here, where
each hole features four or more tees. Natural hazards make the courses both challenging
and scenic. | 23521 Nokomis Ave. S, Nisswa | 888/437–4637 | $40–$45, 9 holes; $70–$80, 18
holes (includes carts) | April–Oct., sunrise to sunset.

Recreational Areas. Dozens of lakes with such names as Bertha, Fishtrap, Horseshoe, and
Nokay surround Brainerd. They're home to some of the state's most popular resorts. |
800/450–2838.

ON THE CALENDAR

JAN.: *Icefest.* Radar runs, human bowling, sleigh rides, ice dances, and other cold-
weather activities, occurring at Breezy Point Resort, help the people of Brainerd get
through winter with smiles on their faces. | 218/562–7811.
JAN.: *Ancient Runner V Antique Snowmobile Rendezvous.* Trail riding, obstacles, and
snowmobile rallies are the highlights of this celebration, which takes place annually
the last weekend in the month. Many of the snowmobile races are along the Paul Bun-
yon Trail. There are a bonfire and a parade. | 218/568–8911 or 800/950–0291.
APR.–OCT.: *Brainerd International Raceway.* Watch the cars whip by at Minnesota's
largest motor-sports arena, on a 400-acre site near North Long Lake. | 218/824–7220.
AUG.: *Crow Wing County Fair.* Come for the amusement rides, livestock exhibitions,
and live entertainment. | 218/764–3165.

Dining

Bar Harbor Supper Club. Contemporary. Travel by car or boat to this family-owned restaurant where you can sink your teeth into barbecued pork ribs and a large selection of seafood. Kids' menu. Sun. brunch. | 6512 Interlachen Rd., Lakeshore | 218/963–2568 | $9–$26 | AE, D, DC, MC, V.

Boathouse Eatery. American. Tall ceilings and Northwoods decor at this eatery at Quarterdeck Resort bring to mind a lumber baron's boathouse. Try the barbecue ribs and the walleye pike. Kids' menu. Buffet lunch. Sun. brunch. | 1588 Quarterdeck Rd. W, Nisswa | 218/963–7537 | $10–$20 | AE, D, DC, MC, V.

Diamond House Chinese Restaurant. Chinese. You can order from the menu or opt for the all-you-can-eat buffet where there's fried shrimp, pork, or rice; garlic chicken; beef with broccoli; and sweet and sour chicken. | 520 Washington St. | 218/828–8782 | $5–$7 | MC, V.

Iven's on the Bay. Seafood. This New England–style seafood house is known for its pan-fried walleye pike. Kids' menu. Sun. brunch in summer. | 5195 N. Rte. 371 | 218/829–9872 | No lunch | $12–$20 | AE, DC, MC, V.

Kavanaugh's Restaurant. Eclectic. Just 4 mi north of Brainerd on Route 371, this restaurant has breathtaking views of Sylvan Lake and the surrounding gardens. Each entrée comes with the house-special garlic bread. Try the boneless herb-crusted pork chop, served with rosemary-apple demiglace. Save room for the famous walnut caramel ice cream pie. | 1685 Kavanaugh Dr. | 218/829–5226 or 800/562–7061 | Closed Labor Day–Memorial Day and Sun. | $16–$25 | AE, D, MC, V.

Lost Lake Lodge Restaurant. American. This lodge full of lakeland charm celebrates the Northwoods in food and spirits. The menu touts Minnesota beers; breads are made from flour ground at the grist mill on site. The five entrées on the menu change daily and may include French country chicken marinated in olive oil, garlic, parsley, basil, and rosemary and cooked outdoors over a charcoal grill, or a top sirloin with a Gorgonzola sauce. Reservations are essential between May and October. | 6415 Lost Lake Rd., Lake Shore | 218/963–2681 or 800/450–2681 | $13–$26 | MC, V.

Lodging

AmericInn–Baxter. In the heart of the Brainerd Lakes area, this hotel is next to restaurants and the Paul Bunyan Amusement Center. Complimentary Continental breakfast. Some microwaves, refrigerators, in-room hot tubs. Cable TV. Indoor pool. Hot tub. Laundry facilities. Business services. Free parking. | 600 Dellwood Dr., Baxter | 218/829–3080 or 800/634–3444 | fax 218/829–9715 | www.AmericInn.com/minnesota/brainerd.html | 59 rooms, 6 suites | $64–$74, $95–$105 suites | AE, D, DC, MC, V.

Breezy Point. This 1920s resort on Pelican Lake stands out for its family activities and kids' programs. 2 restaurants, 1 bar, dining room. Some kitchenettes, refrigerators. Cable TV. 5 pools (2 indoor). Hot tubs. 2 18-hole golf courses, tennis. Exercise equipment. Beach, dock, water sports, boating. Ice-skating, cross-country skiing. Video games. Children's programs (ages 5–12), playground. Business services. | 9252 Breezy Point Dr. | 218/562–7811 or 800/432–3777 | fax 218/562–4510 | www.breezypt.com | 69 rooms, 132 apartments | $109–$145, $150–$410 apartments | AE, D, DC, MC, V.

Comfort Suites. The only outdoor water park in Brainerd is at this chain hotel 10 mi west of downtown; you'll find a 250-ft tube slide and a 150-ft body slide. Some rooms have fireplaces. Complimentary Continental breakfast. Some in-room hot tubs. Cable TV. Hot tub, sauna. Exercise equipment. Video games. | 1221 Edgewood Dr. N, Baxter | 218/825–7234 or 877/5–GETWET | fax 218/829–3738 | getwet@brainerd.net | www.comfortinn.com | 67 rooms | $99–$200 | AE, D, MC, V.

Country Inn. Downtown Brainerd is 1 mi east of this 2-story 1995 hotel, which has a fireplaced lobby with comfortable couches and high-backed chairs. Complimentary Continental breakfast. In-room data ports, microwaves, refrigerators, some in-room hot tubs. Cable TV.

Indoor pool. Hot tub, sauna. Business services, free parking. Some pets allowed. | 1220 Dellwood Dr. N, Baxter | 218/828–2161 | fax 218/825–8419 | 56 rooms, 12 suites | 56 rooms, 12 suites | $79–$89, $99–119 suites | AE, D, DC, MC, V.

Cragun's Conference and Golf Resort. Treat yourself to this resort and conference center with two private beaches on Gull Lake, 8 mi north of Brainerd. Restaurant, bar (with entertainment), dining room. Cable TV. 2 pools. Hot tubs. Golf privileges, 8 tennis courts. Exercise equipment, 2 beaches, boating. Cross-country skiing, snowmobiling. Children's and teens' programs (ages 4–12, and ages 13–19). Laundry facilities. Business services, airport shuttle. | 11000 Cragun's Dr. | 218/829–3591 or 800/272–4867 | fax 218/829–9188 | info@craguns.com | www.craguns.com | 155 rooms, 21 suites, 6 apartments, 43 cabins | $72–$182, $112–$198 suites, $162–$261, apartments, $129–$702 cabins | AE, D, MC, V.

Days Inn. This hotel rests nearly in the shadows of the amusement park landmarks Paul Bunyan and Babe the Blue Ox. Complimentary Continental breakfast. Cable TV. Business services. Some pets allowed. | 1630 Fairview Rd. | 218/829–0391 | fax 218/828–0749. | 59 rooms | $44–$79 | AE, D, DC, MC, V.

Days Inn–Nisswa. Convenient to golfers, this chain is ½ mi from The Pines, one of the state's finest championship golf courses. Complimentary Continental breakfast. Cable TV. Indoor pool. Hot tub. Laundry facilities. Some pets allowed (deposit). | 24186 N. Smiley Rd., Nisswa | 218/963–3500 | fax 218/963–4936 | 46 rooms | $60–$95 | AE, D, MC, V.

Grand View Lodge. This four-season lodge on Gull Lake, 8 mi north of Brainerd, has plenty of outdoor attractions, including a 1,500-ft natural sand beach and a garden walk. The lodge houses a 110-ft indoor water slide. Bar, dining room. Refrigerators. Cable TV. Pool. Hot tub. Driving range, 2 golf courses. Beach, water sports, boating. Video games. Children's programs (ages 3–12). Business services, airport shuttle. | 23521 Nokomis Rd. S, Nisswa | 218/963–2234 or 800/432–3788 | fax 218/963–2269 | vacation@grandviewlodge.com | www.grandviewlodge.com | 12 rooms, 17 suites, 17 town homes, 9 cabins, 60 cottages | $250–$975 rooms and cottages, $225–$425 suites, $175–$480 town homes, $195–$350 cabins | AE, D, MC, V.

Lost Lake Lodge. Nestled between the private Lost Lake and the Upper Gull Lake Narrows is this cluster of cabins, with access to both waterways and a slew of nature trails. The resort sits on 81 acres and rates include two meals a day and boating equipment at your disposal. Most cabins cozy right to the shoreline. Restaurant, complimentary breakfast. Some kitchenettes, refrigerators. No room phones, no TV. Lake. Beach, dock, water sports, boating, fishing. Children's programs (ages 3–12). | 6415 Lost Lake Rd., Lake Shore | 218/963–2681 or 800/450–2681 | fax 218/963–0509 | vacation@lostlake.com | www.lostlake.com | 14 rooms | $285–$585 | AE, MC, V.

Madden's on Gull Lake. Minnesota's largest resort, this luxury resort stretches for a mile along the coast of Gull Lake and encompasses 1,000 acres. Rooms are built to feel like cabins, with lots of wood and a rustic flavor. 3 restaurants, 2 bars. Some microwaves, some refrigerators. Cable TV. 3 indoor pools, 2 outdoor pools, lake. 4 golf courses. Beach, dock, water sports, boating. Shops, video games. Children's programs (ages 4–12). Laundry facilities. Business services. | 11266 Pine Beach Peninsula | 218/829–2811 or 800/642–5363 | www.maddens.com | 287 rooms | $150–$200 | AE, MC, V.

Paul Bunyan Inn. Surrounded by pines, this Northwoods inn, ¼ mi from Brainerd, also has a courtyard with a gazebo. Picnic area, complimentary Continental breakfast. Some microwaves. Cable TV. Indoor pool. Hot tub, sauna. Business services. | 1800 Fairview Dr. N, Baxter | 218/829–3571 | fax 218/829–3571 | pbmotel@brainerd.com | 34 rooms, 10 suites | $55–$70, $92–$115 suites | AE, D, DC, MC, V.

Quarterdeck Resort. County Road 77 encircles Gull Lake, 18 mi northwest of Brainerd in the town of Nisswa, where you'll find this hostelry. Each room has a gas fireplace and a pull-out sofa; most come with cooking utensils, so you can make your own meals. Restaurant. Some kitchenettes, some microwaves, some refrigerators, some in-room hot tubs. Cable

TV, in-room VCR. Volleyball, fishing, bicycles. Video games. Children's programs (ages 4–14). | 9820 Birch Bay Dr. SW, Nisswa | 218/963–2482 or 800/950–5596 | fax 218/963–7984 | quarterdeckresort.com | 44 rooms, 8 suites) | $128–$228 | Open year-round | D, MC, V.

Ramada Inn. This full-service hotel is ½ mi south of town. Restaurant, bar, room service. In-room data ports. Cable TV. Indoor pool. Hot tub, sauna. Tennis. Laundry facilities. Business services, airport shuttle, free parking. Some pets allowed. | 2115 6th St. S (Rte. 371) | 218/829–1441 | fax 218/829–1444 | www.northernhospitality.com/ramadainn | 150 rooms | $73–$91 | AE, D, DC, MC, V.

Super 8. One mi north of Paul Bunyan Amusement Center, this motel stands next to a Wall-Mart. Complimentary Continental breakfast. Cable TV. Video games. Laundry service. Business services. | Rte. 371N, Baxter | 218/828–4288 | fax 218/828–4288, ext. 200 | 62 rooms | $52–$62 | AE, D, DC, MC, V.

CHISHOLM

MAP 3, F4

(Nearby towns also listed: Cook, Crane Lake, Ely, Eveleth, Hibbing, Virginia)

Although it's in the center of Minnesota's Iron Range, this town of 6,000 emerged first as a timber town. Then, in the 1880s, iron mining took over. In 1908, a huge fire destroyed the town, and the village council passed an ordinance requiring that all Main Street buildings be constructed of brick. Today, Chisholm serves as a retreat for vacationers and a reservations center for Northwest Airlines.

Information: Chisholm Chamber of Commerce | 10 2nd Ave. W, Chisholm, 55719 | 218/254–3600 or 800/422–0806 | www.chisholmmnchamber.com.

Attractions

Iron Man. This 81-ft-high, 150-ton statue is a tribute to the iron-ore miners of the Mesabi, Cuyuna, and Vermilion Iron Ranges. It's the third-largest freestanding statue in the nation, following the Statue of Liberty and St. Louis, Missouri's, Gateway to the West arch. | Rte. 169 on the west side of Chisholm (across from Ironworld) | 800/422–0806.

Ironworld Discovery Center. Find out what it took (and takes) to be a miner on Minnesota's Iron Range. The attractions here include audiovisual presentations, ethnic craft demonstrations, and scenic train rides. | Highway 169 on the west side of Chisholm | 218/254–7959 or 800/372–6437 | www.ironworld.com | $8 | Mid-June–mid-Sept., daily 8–4:30.

Minnesota Museum of Mining. Iron-mining equipment, a steam engine, ore cars, trucks, and a Greyhound bus are among the exhibits on display here. | Memorial Park Complex, W. Lake St. | 218/254–5543 | www.fnbchisholm.com/mining | $3 | May–Sept., daily 9–6.

ON THE CALENDAR

FEB.: *Polar Bear Days.* This 10-day festival is designed to help the people of the Northwoods beat winter blues. Among the popular events are the dog weight pulls, in which single dogs lug sleds weighted down with dog food around an ice track. | 800/422–0806.

JULY–SEPT.: *Minnesota Ethnic Days.* For three months, the Iron World Discovery Center in Chisholm hosts a run of ethnic festivals. Past events have included a Polka Fest, Festival Finlandia, All Slav Days, Grape Festival, and an International Button Box Festival. | 218/254–7959 or 800/372–6437.

AUG.: *St. Louis County Fair.* This annual hoe-down at the Iron World Discovery Center in Chisholm has lots to see and do, including auto races, carnival rides, livestock shows, and geology exhibits. | 218/254–7959 or 800/372–6437.

Dining

Iron Kettle Family Restaurant. American. This country kitchen serves breakfast all day and is known for its omelets, prime rib, and Friday fish fry. | Hwy. 169 and 3rd St. S | 218/254–3339 | Breakfast also served | $5–$10 | AE, D, MC, V.

Lodging

McNair's Bed and Breakfast. Surrounded by manicured grounds and adjacent to Superior National Forest, this B&B is an elegant Northwoods stop 18 miles from Chisholm. Dining room. Kitchenettes, in-room hot tubs. Hiking, bicycles. | 7694 Rte. 5, Side Lake | 218/254–5878 | 2 rooms | $140–$150 | Credit cards not accepted.

CLOQUET

MAP 3, F5

(Nearby towns also listed: Duluth, Two Harbors)

Home of the only gas station ever designed by Frank Lloyd Wright, Cloquet was originally the home of Dakota Sioux and Ojibway Native Americans. The area saw its first European settlers in the 17th century, when French explorers arrived. An 1878 sawmill, constructed at Knife Falls on the St. Louis River, blossomed into an entire community: Cloquet, "The Wood City." A 1918 fire destroyed the town, which rebuilt itself and carried on its lumber-related activities, which are still the area's economic base.

Information: **Cloquet Area Chamber of Commerce** | 225 Sunnyside Dr., Cloquet, 55720-0426 | 218/879–1551 or 800/554–4350 | www.cloquetmn.com/chamber.

Attractions

Lindholm Service Station. This 1956 structure is the only gas station ever designed by celebrated architect Frank Lloyd Wright. | Rte. 45 at Rte. 43 | 800/554–4350.

ON THE CALENDAR

FEB.: *Business Expo.* Local businesses meet at this event to show off their goods. The event is open to the public. | 218/993–2901 or 800/362–7405.
JULY: *Lumberjack Days.* Live music, bed races, games, arts and crafts, and a big parade give this citywide celebration its spark. | 218/879–1551.

Dining

Perkins Restaurant & Bakery. American. This chain restaurant is open 24 hours a day and breakfast is available all day long. The on-premises bakery is famous for its mammoth muffins. A variety of substantial dinner salads are served in bowls made of bread and a kids' menu is available. | 109 Big Lake Rd. | 218/879–8380 | Open 24 hours. Breakfast also served | $6–$11 | AE, D, DC, MC, V.

Lodging

AmericInn. The Black Bear Casino and the popular Jay Cooke State Park (*see* Duluth) are each within 10 mi of this hotel. Complimentary Continental breakfast. Some refrigerators. Cable TV. Indoor pool. Hot tub, sauna. Business services. Some pets allowed. | 111 Big Lake Rd. | 218/879–1231 or 800/634–3444 | fax 218/879–2237 | www.AmericInn.com/minnesota/cloquet.html | 51 rooms | $55–$90 | AE, D, DC, MC, V.

Golden Gate Motel. Only 15 minutes from Duluth and within 3 mi of Black Bear Casino and Jay Cooke State Park, this motel is one block off of I-35, exit 239 (Scanlon). The hotel provides a free shuttle to local casinos. Microwaves, refrigerators. Cable TV. | 3202 River Gate Ave. | 218/879–6752 or 800/732–4241 | 25 rooms | $45–$59 | AE, D, MC, V.

Sunnyside Motel. Here's a no-frills option for budget-conscious travelers; a campground is also on-site. | 807 Sunnyside Dr. (Highway 33N) | 218/879–4655 | fax 218/879–5232 | 9 rooms | $30–$50 | AE, D, MC, V.

COOK

MAP 3, F3

(Nearby towns also listed: Chisholm, Crane Lake, Ely, Tower, Virginia)

Until 1910, Cook was known as Ashawa. When the U.S. Postal Service proposed that the name be changed to avoid confusion with a similarly named town in southern Minnesota, Ashawa was renamed Cook in honor of a local lumber dealer and railroad official. Cook still serves the lumber industry and is the western gateway to Superior National Forest. Many of Cook's residents still work for companies that produce wood and building products.

Information: Lake Vermilion Resort Association | Box 159, Cook, 55723 | 218/666–5850 or 800/648–5897 | www.lakevermilionresorts.com.

Attractions

Elbow Lake. There's enough walleye to go around in this popular lake. In addition to being an angler's paradise, it's also a good place for swimming, water sports, and sunbathing. | 10 mi east of Cook, on Hwy. 24 | 800/648–5897 | Free | Daily.

Lake Vermilion. *See* Tower, *below.*

Pelican Lake. Swimmers and sunbathers share this lake's 54 miles of shoreline with big northern pike and those who fish for them. | 20 mi northwest of Cook off Hwy. 53 | 800/648–5897 | Free | Daily.

Superior National Forest. Cook is a western gateway to Superior National Forest, which stretches 150 mi along the U.S.–Canadian border. Its 3 million acres encourage an almost limitless variety of outdoor activities, including camping, picnicking, boating, canoeing, fishing, hiking, backpacking, and biking. The Boundary Water Canoe Area Wilderness, which may be the best canoe country in the United States, is part of the forest. | U.S. Hwy. 53 | 218/626–4300 | www.fs.fed.us/r9/superior | Free | Daily.

ON THE CALENDAR
OCT.: *Community Variety Show.* This evening showcase for local talent, sponsored by Cook Community Education, benefits a local charity. | 218/666–5221.

Dining

Montana. American. This local hangout is an essential pit stop. For lunch try the hot beef sandwich and for dinner the juicy pork chops or the shrimp basket. | 29 River St. | 218/666–2074 | No dinner Sunday. Breakfast served daily | $6.95–$8.50 | No credit cards.

Lodging

Head-O-Lake Resort. Each lakeside cottage at this resort is decorated with knotty pine interiors and has room to sleep at least six. Cabins have full kitchens, Weber grills, and screened porches, and linens are provided. The cabins rent weekly. Microwaves, refrigerators. Cable TV, in-room VCRs. Beach, dock, water sports, boating, fishing. | 3084 Vermilion Dr. | 218/666–5612 or 800/321–9340 | hot@rangenet.com | www.headolakesresort.com. rooms | 9 | $710 weekly | MC, V.

Ludlow's Island Lodge. A shuttle boat takes you to this family-owned resort spread across two shores on a private island on Lake Vermilion. The cottages are rustic-looking with knotty pine interiors but they are quite modern. No air-conditioning, microwaves, some in-room hot tubs. No TV in some cabins. Tennis. Exercise equipment, racquetball. Beach, dock, water sports, boating. Children's programs, playground. Laundry facilities. Business services, airport shuttle. | 8166 Ludlow Dr. | 218/666–5407 | fax 218/666–2488 | info@ludlowsresort.com | www.ludlowsresort.com | 18 cabins | $275–$400 | Closed Oct.–Apr. | AE, MC, V.

CRANE LAKE

MAP 3, F2

(Nearby towns also listed: Chisholm, Cook, Ely, International Falls, Tower, Virginia, Voyageurs National Park)

The road literally ends at this isolated outpost, which anchors the northwest corner of Voyageurs National Park. Glaciers have left behind a gorgeous landscape of lakes, forests, and jagged white and pink granite. Most of the surrounding wilderness remains untouched. The local economy depends largely on tourism, which thrives in both summer and winter.

Information: **Crane Lake Visitor and Tourism Bureau** | 7238 Handberg Rd., Crane Lake, 55725 | 218/993–2901 or 800/362–7405 | www.visitcranelake.com.

Attractions

Vermilion Gorge. Vermilion Gorge on the west end of Crane Lake in Voyageurs National Park is ideal for picnics and fishing trips. There are two different routes to choose from; one requires a boat. The trailhead is in Voyageurs National Park, just past the main office. | 218/283–9821.

Dining

Borderland Lodge. American. An angling theme prevails at this dining room decorated with fishing artifacts. Sit back and enjoy the bay views while you savor a handcut trim steak. Breakfast is served. | 7480 Crane Lake Rd. | 218/993–2233 or 800/777–8392 | fax 218/993–2495 | www.visitcranelake.com | $4–$17 | AE, D, MC, V.

Nelson's Resort Restaurant. American. The views of Crane Lake are spectacular here, and there's a Thursday night Swedish buffet. The buffet contains over 15 items, including hearty main dishes like turkey and roast beef. | 7632 Nelsons Rd. | 218/993–2295 or 800/433–0743 | fax 218/993–2242 | Closed Oct.–Apr. | $12–$23 | D, MC, V.

Lodging

Borderland Lodge. Outdoor enthusiasts flock here for its central location: 2 mi from Voyageurs National Park, 3 mi from the Canadian border, and 1 mi from the Boundary Water Canoe Area Wilderness. Restaurant, bar. Pool, lake, wading pool. Hiking. Boating, fishing. Snowmobiling. Baby-sitting. Laundry facilities. Some pets allowed. | 7480 Crane Lake Rd. | 218/993–2233 or 800/777–8392 | fax 218/993–2495 | www.borderlandlodge.com | 14 cabins | $78–$480 | AE, D, MC, V.

Nelson's Resort. In operation since 1931, this resort is on the Minnesota–Ontario border waters of Crane Lake. Bar, 2 dining rooms. No air-conditioning, some kitchenettes, microwaves. No TV in rooms, TV in common area. Sauna. Dock, water sports, boating, bicycles. Playground. Laundry facilities. Business services, airport shuttle. | 7632 Nelson Rd. | 218/993–2295 or 800/433–0743 | fax 218/993–2242 | www.nelsonsresort.com | 28 cabins | $100–$115 per person | Closed Oct.–Apr. | D, MC, V.

Pine Point Lodge. This resort sits on a 12-acre private peninsula with a half mile of shoreline and is accessible only by boat. The lodge provides a shuttle from the end of County Road 24. Take Highway 53 north to Orr, turn east on County Road 23, which becomes County Road 24 at Buyck. Follow it until you reach the "end of the road." If you need a pontoon shuttle, enter the Voyageurs office to inform the receptionist that you are a Pine Point guest, and he or she will call for one. Kitchenettes, microwaves, refrigerators. Lake. Hiking. Beach, dock, boating, fishing. Playground. | 218/993–2311 or 800/628–4446 | fax 218/993–2311 | www.pinepointlodge.com | 9 cabins | $90–$140 | AE, D, DC, MC, V.

Sand Point Lodge. Four pine-panelled cabins line up side by side on the shores of Sand Point Lake, 8 mi north of Crane Lake. All have an outdoor grill and a deck and are rented by the week. Boat departure for the lodge is from Hanberg Marina on Crane Lake; the resort is accessible only via water. Microwaves, refrigerators. No TV. Lake. Beach, dock, water sports, boating, fishing. | Rt. 3 | 218/374–3891 | splodge@blackduck.net | www.visit-cranelake.com/link_outs/sandpoint.html | 4 cabins, 1 apartment | $700–$1,100, cabin or apartment | Sept.–Apr. | AE, D, MC, V.

Scott's Resort and Seaplane Base. The waters of Crane Lake nearly cascade across the front door of your cabin at this resort on the southwest corner of the lake. The two-bedroom cabin is cedar; others are pine-panelled. Boats are for rent on the premises. Restaurant, bar. Microwaves, refrigerators. No TV. Lake. Beach, dock, water sports, boating, fishing. Shops. | 7546 Gold Coast Rd. | 218/993–2341 or 800/993–8576 | 4 cabins | $495–$750 per week, $95 per night | Sept.–Apr. | D, MC, V.

CROOKSTON

MAP 3, B3

(Nearby town also listed: Thief River Falls)

Crookston's history is closely linked to the development of river and rail transportation in the region. Its growth, largely in 1871, followed that of the railroad, which crossed the Red Lake River on its way to North Dakota. Now it's home to many agriculture-related industries as well as a campus of the University of Minnesota.

Information: Crookston Area Chamber of Commerce | Box 115, Crookston, 56716 | 218/281–4320 or 800/809–5997.

Attractions

Central Park. In summer you can picnic, swim, fish, canoe, and even roller-skate in an indoor arena. When cold weather arrives, the roller rink becomes an ice rink. | Ash and E. 2nd Sts. | 218/281–1232 | Daily.

Polk County Historical Museum. The exhibits here include an original log cabin, a one-room schoolhouse, a chapel, and a miniature train collection. | Off Hwy. 2 east of Crookston | 218/281–1038 | Free | May–Sept., daily.

ON THE CALENDAR
AUG.: *Ox Cart Days.* The oxen and the carts take back seat to a parade, dance, stage shows, stagecoach rides, and fun runs through Central Park, the third weekend of the month. | 800/809–5997.

Dining
China Moon Restaurant. Chinese. This restaurant is best known for seafood dishes, such as shrimp with vegetables, shrimp with almonds, and lobster with mushrooms. | 114 S. Broadway | 218/281–3136 | $6–$11 | No credit cards.

Lodging
Golf Terrace Motel. Standing next to a family-style restaurant and across the street from a bowling alley, the motel is on the north side of town on Rte. 2 (also called University Avenue), and one block from a nine-hole golf course, which offers guest privileges. Cable TV. Pets allowed. | 1731 University Ave. | 218/281–2626. rooms | 17 | $30–$40 | AE, D, MC, V.

Northland Inn. Directly off of Rte. 2, this hotel is on the north end of town. Restaurant, bar. In-room data ports. Cable TV. Indoor pool. Hot tub. Video Games. Business services. | 2200 University Ave. | 218/281–5210 or 800/423–7541 | 74 rooms | $55–$60 | AE, D, DC, MC, V.

CROSS LAKE

MAP 3, D5

(Nearby towns also listed: Aitkin, Brainerd, Deerwood, Pine River)

Cross Lake is surrounded by miles upon miles of connecting waterways known as the Whitefish Chain of Lakes. Logging began here in the 1890s and soon established itself as the economic backbone of the area. In the 1920s, the area became a favorite vacation spot for some of the country's most notorious gangsters. Now, recreation is the biggest industry, and thousands of visitors come here year-round to enjoy the great outdoors.

Information: Brainerd/Crosslakes Area Chambers of Commerce | 124 N. 6th St., Brainerd, 56401 | 218/829–2838 or 800/450–2838 | www.brainerdchamber.com.

Attractions

Paul Bunyan Trail. One hundred miles of trail link 16 communities between the southern trailhead at Brainerd and the northern entrance at Lake Bemidji State Park. Between Brainerd and Hackensack, for 48 mi, the path is paved; the rest is gravel, except for 5 mi at Lake Bemidji State Park. You can bike, hike, or skate on the path; the only motorized activity allowed is snowmobiling. | Excelsior Rd., Baxter | 218/829–2838 or 800/450–2838 | www.dnr.state.mn.us.com | Free | Daily.

ON THE CALENDAR

APR.: *Commerce and Industry Show.* Central Minnesota businesses of all sizes and types showcase their products and services to the public at the Brainerd Civic Center during the third weekend of every April. | 502 Jackson St. | 218/829–2838 | www.Brainerdchamber.com.

Dining

Moonlite Bay Family Restaurant. American. The summer boating crowd comes here to enjoy burgers on the spacious lakeside deck; in winter, snowmobilers favor the house specialty, steak sandwiches. Live bands play on weekends year-round. | Intersection of Rtes. 16 and 66 | 218/692–3575 | Memorial Day–Labor Day, 11–1 AM; Closed Sept.–May and Tues. | $5–$12 | MC, V.

Lodging

Bay View Lodge. Pine-paneled, carpeted cabins are on Rush Lake in the Whitefish Chain. Paddle bikes, kayaks, and canoes are available. Picnic area. Microwaves. Lake. Sauna. Beach, dock, water sports, boating. Laundry facilities. | HC 83, Box 1000 | 218/543–4182 | 12 cabins | $350–1,300 weekly | June–Apr. | D, MC, V.

Beacon Shores Resort. This is a small, quiet, and heavily wooded lake resort 5 mi from town. Cable TV. Lake. Beach, dock, boating. Baby-sitting. Laundry facilities. | 36859 Silver Peak Rd. | 218/543–4166 or 800/950–5907 | fax 218/543–6415 | www.beaconshores.com | 8 cabins, 2 town homes | $505–$1,100/wk. cabins, $800–1535/wk. town homes | AE, D, MC, V.

Boyd Lodge. For six decades, the same family has owned and operated this 200-acre resort on Big Whitefish Lake. The cottages each have a deck, kitchen, living room, dining room, and one bedroom. Kitchenettes. Cable TV. 2 pools, wading pool. 2 hot tubs, 2 saunas. Tennis. Beach, boating. Cross-country skiing. Children's programs, playground. Laundry facilities. Business services. | 36653 Silver Peak Rd. | 218/543–4125 | www.boydlodge.com | 36 cottages | $1,150–$1,300 cottages/wk. (7–day minimum stay in summer), $1,450–$2,640 loft cottages (7–day minimum stay in summer) | MC, V.

Lovelands Resort. Lakefront cabins with one to four bedrooms are privately situated on ten acres around Rush Lake, one of 14 in the Whitefish Chain. Fishing for bass and walleye is especially popular; a fish cleaning house is on the grounds. Cabins have tongue and groove pine interiors, decks, and private docks with 14-ft fishing boats. Kitchenettes, refrigerators. Lake. Beach, fishing. Playground. | 13710 Rte. 16 | 218/692–2511 | fax 218/692–2511 | rlmax@crosslake.net | sceniclodging.com | 12 cabins | $550–$1,400 (7–day minimum stay) | Closed Nov.–Apr. | MC, V.

Pine Terrace Resort. The knotty-pine interiors of these lakeside or hillside log cabins on Star Lake remind you of the woods outside. Kitchenettes. Lake. Hiking, volleyball. Beach, dock, boating, fishing. Laundry facilities. | 35101 Pine Terrace Rd. | 218/543–4606 or 800/950–1986 | fax 218/543–4216 | www.pineterrace.com | 12 cabins | $424–$1,071/wk | AE, D, DC, MC, V.

DEER RIVER

(Nearby towns also listed: Grand Rapids, Hibbing)

This small town on the edge of the Chippewa National Forest serves as a harvesting point for loggers as well as a hub for agriculture and recreation. Deer River is among the main gateways for anglers in search of game fish on Lake Winnibigoshish.

Information: Lake Winnibigoshish Area Resort Association | HCR 3, Box 772, Deer River, 56636 | 218/246–2560 | www.lakewinnie.net.

Attractions
Chippewa National Forest. This is the United States' oldest national forest and encompasses 1.6 million acres of timber and more than 1,300 lakes. Camp (with a permit), fish, swim, or hike. A 28-mi scenic highway leads through the forest. | Rte. 38 | 218/335–8600 | www.fs.fed.us/r9/chippewa | Free | Daily.
"Big Winnie," as locals call **Lake Winnibigoshish**, is in the Chippewa National Forest and offers 141 miles of unspoiled shoreline dotted with good boat access and lodges. The Lake Winnie Dam, built in 1884, created the sprawling body of water that in turn made way for two more of Minnesota's best fishing lakes, Cut Foot Sioux and Little Winnie. | Off U.S. Hwy. 2 | 218/246–2560 | www.lakewinnie.net | Free.

ON THE CALENDAR
JULY: *Deep River Wild Rice Festival.* The food specialties at this Fourth-of-July-weekend event include turtle stew and wild rice hot dish (casserole). Be on hand for the baking contests, parade, and wild rice medallion hunt. | 218/246–2560.

Dining
Shay's Family Restaurant. American. A collection of 19th-century antiques and collectible bottles in the bar are real conversation pieces at this local hangout, which rarely closes. The menu includes prime rib and shrimp, and all-you-can-eat fish fry on Fridays. | 220 Hwy. 2E | 218/246–8307 | No lunch | $5–$16 | D, DC, MC, V.

Lodging
Bowen Lodge. The pine cabins here have decks that face west, overlooking Lake Winnibigoshish. The marina and beach hug Cutfoot Sioux Lake. Bar. Kitchenettes. Lake. Hiking. Beach, dock, boating, fishing, bicycles. Baby-sitting, children's programs (ages 3–12),

playground. Laundry facilities. Business services. | 58485 Bowens Rd. | 218/246–8707 or 800/331–8925 | fax 218/246–2360 | www.bowenlodge.com | 16 cabins | $95–$350 | AE, MC, V.

Cutfoot Sioux Inn. The cabins at this resort in the Chippewa National Forest are close to the water, with no steep bank or steps to climb. Kitchenettes. Lake. Hiking. Beach, boating, fishing, bicycles. Snowmobiling. Baby-sitting, playground. Laundry facilities. Some pets allowed. | 44394 Rte. 46 | 218/246–8706 or 800/752–7357 | fax 218/246–8706 | www.cutfoot.com | 14 cabins | $65–$160 | D, MC, V.

Nelson's Lakewood Lodge Resort. "North of the Stress Zone" says a lot about how people feel about this place on Sandy Lake, deep in the Chippewa National Forest. Cabins have bay views, and some have porches. There are also three full-hook-up RV sites. Picnic area. Kitchenettes, microwaves. Lake. Sauna. Beach, dock. Shops. Playground. | 52856 Rte. 35 | 218/659–2839 or 800/495–8437 | fax 218/798–2604 | www.northofthestresszone.com | 8 cabins | Cabins $585 weekly, RV sites $20 nightly | Closed Nov.–May | D, MC, V.

THE NAMING OF LAKES

The naming of lakes—with a nod to T. S. Eliot and Andrew Lloyd Webber—is a difficult matter. And it's especially difficult in Minnesota, which bills itself as "The Land of 10,000 Lakes" but actually has half again as many.

Among those 15,000 lakes and names, you'll find one of your own if your name is Alexander, Andrew, Ann, Carlos, Carrie, Dora, Edward, Ethel, George, Grace, Harriet, Howard, Ida, Jasper, Jeanette, Jennie, Jessie, Joe, Leif, Lewis, Lida, Lizzie, Louise, Marion, Mary, Maud, Melissa, Mitchell, Rebecca, Sarah, Stuart, Susan, or Winnie. Even if you're known simply as Darling, or if you prefer to be just Woman, there's a lake for you.

Many lakes, of course, are named for local birds, beasts, and fish, so you'll find Bass, Bear, Beaver, Crane, Eagle, Elk, Fox, Goose, Moose, Trout, Turtle, and, for ballet fans, Swan. Seven Beavers has a nice family feel to it, and Tame Fish sounds nice, but Leech and Serpent are definitely worrisome. Compared to those, Big Cormorant sounds inviting.

Shapes often provide names, so you'll find Crescent, Crooked, Elbow, Fish Hook, Heart, Horseshoe, Kettle, and Round. Colors are handy as names, too, so there's Blue, Clear, Green, Silver, Red, Vermilion, and the more humble Brown.

But some other names are more troubling. How did Bad Medicine get its name, or East Battle, Gunflint, Cut Foot Sioux, Devil Track, Dead, Ice Cracking, Juggler, and Stalker? And maybe we don't really want to know the origin of Mantrap. We can be fairly certain that Pokegama has nothing to do with Japanese cartoons, but we can only wonder what Lac Qui Parle is saying.

Some names strain to identify a location, like Island Lake South or Lake of the Woods, but none strain as much as Upper South Long Lake. Then, for good measure, Minnesota also has Little Lake, Long Lake, Little Long Lake, Lost Lake, and Long Lost Lake. More confusing is East Lost Lake; if everybody knows it's east, how lost can it be?

You can bet all these names are real at Reno Lake, but if you still don't believe, Minnesota even has a Pig's Eye Lake for you.

© Corbis

DEERWOOD

(Nearby towns also listed: Aitkin, Brainerd, Cross Lake)

Deerwood is the first and oldest town on Minnesota's Cuyuna Iron Range. Recreation is the big draw these days. The city is surrounded by lakes, large and small, and has seven of them within its limits.

Information: Deerwood Civic and Commerce | Box 422, Deerwood, 56444 | 218/534–3163.

Attractions

Grand Casino Mille Lacs. *See* Onamia, *below.*

Mille Lacs Lake. *See* Onamia, *below.*

Kart Kountry. This is a one-stop family fun park with go-carts, bumper boats, bumper carts, miniature golf, batting cages, arcade, water wars, and monster truck rides. | 11419 Gull Lake Dr. SW | 218/829–4963 | $5 | Memorial Day–Labor Day 10–10 daily; May and Sept., weekends 10–10.

ON THE CALENDAR
AUG.: *Deerwood Summerfest.* A two-day event with craft fair, bake sale, beer garden, and bingo, the festivities conclude with a big street dance in the evening. | 218/546–8131 | www.cuyunarange.com.

Dining

Ruttger's Bay Lake Lodge Restaurant. American. This family-owned and -operated dining room, housed in a large log cabin a half-hour east of Brainerd, has been in business since 1898. Large bay windows frame Ruttger's Bay, and menu selections include pan-fried walleye (served with a house special remoulade sauce) and champagne scallops in maple syrup cream. | Rte. 2 | 800/450–4545 | Closed Nov.–Apr. | $8–$15 | AE, D, DC, MC, V.

White Hawk Supper Club. American. This is the place for casual dining on Bay Lake, especially if you're hungry for barbecued ribs, fried chicken, or homemade pizza. | 3200 County Rd. 10 NE | 218/678–2419 | Daily 4–1 AM. Closed Mar. | $5–$15 | MC, V.

Lodging

Country Inn by Carlson. This inn is close to fishing on Lake Mille Lacs (15 mi) and Grand Casino Mille Lacs (18 mi). Complimentary Continental breakfast. Some refrigerators. Cable TV. Indoor pool. Hot tub, sauna. Laundry facilities. | 23884 E. Front St. | 218/534–3101 or 800/456–4000 | fax 218/534–3685 | 38 rooms | $65–$88 | AE, D, DC, MC, V.

Deerwood Motel. Built during the early 1980s, this motel is in downtown Deerwood. Two levels give you a choice of inside or outside room entrances. Microwaves, refrigerators. Cable TV. | Rte. 210 at Rte. 6 | 218/534–3163 | 16 rooms | $40–$65.

Ruttger's Bay Lake Lodge. The 400-acres of Bay Lake shoreline here contribute to the country-club feel of this lodge, which is 18 mi. from Brainerd. Bar, dining room. Cable TV. 3 pools (1 indoor). Hot tub. 27-hole golf course, putting green. Exercise equipment. Beach, water sports, boating. Children's programs (ages 4–12). Laundry facilities. Business services. | Rte. 2, Box 400 | 218/678–2885 or 800/450–4545 | fax 218/678–2864 | www.ruttgers.com | 30 rooms, 88 apartments, 37 cottages | $318, $318–$954 apartments and cottages | D, MC, V.

DETROIT LAKES

MAP 3, B5

(Nearby towns also listed: Fergus Falls, Moorhead, Park Rapids)

More than 200 years ago, a French missionary admired the beautiful *détroit* (strait) here, for which the town was named. At first it was called simply Detroit. But "Lakes" was added in 1926 to avoid confusion with Detroit, Michigan. The new name made sense, as no fewer than 412 lakes lie within a 25-mile radius of the town. The town has two swimming beaches, one of which is a mile long. Tourism and agriculture are major sources of income.

Information: **Detroit Lakes Regional Chamber of Commerce** | 700 Washington Ave., Detroit Lakes, 56501 | 800/542–3992 | www.visitdetroitlakes.com.

Attractions

Becker County Historical Society Museum. The purpose of the historical society is to collect, preserve, and disseminate the history of Becker County, as well as the county's place and role in the history of Minnesota and the United States. There's also a genealogical library here. | 714 Summit St. | 218/847–2938 | Free | Memorial Day–Labor Day, Mon.–Fri. 10–5.

Detroit Lakes City Park. This is a good place to picnic and play. Lifeguards are on hand in summer to patrol the mile-long beach. | S. Washington Ave., by Detroit Lake | 800/542–3992 | June–Labor Day, daily.

Tamarac National Wildlife Refuge. Eagles, swans, and deer are among the critters that make this refuge their home. Bird-watchers flock to see almost 200 different birds, including highly sought-after black-backed woodpeckers and Connecticut warblers. Rolling, forested hills, 18 mi northeast of Detroit Lakes, are interspersed with lakes, rivers, marshes, and shrub swamp. | County Rd. 29, at County Rd. 26 | 218/847–2641 | http://www.fws.gov/r3pao/tamarac/ | Free | Daily.

Winter Wonderland Trail System. More than 66 kilometers of groomed and ungroomed cross-country ski trails, and 200 mi of groomed snowmobile trails interconnect with other trail systems, such as those at Itasca State Park. The trailhead is on Detroit lake at the Holiday Inn. | 800/542–3992 | Free | Daily.

ON THE CALENDAR

MAY: *Detroit Lakes Festival of Birds.* For three days, bird-watchers participate in workshops, lectures, a banquet, and a trade show. There are also children's programs. | 800/542–3992.

JUNE: *White Earth Powwow.* You're welcome to join in the celebration marking the treaty between the Sioux and the Chippewa peoples. | 218/983–3285.

JULY: *Northwest Water Carnival.* This event includes ten days of family activities, including beach games, contests, dances, and the largest parade in the region. | 800/542–3992.

AUG.: *WE Country Music Fest.* The nation's largest outdoor country music and camping festival happens the first week of the month on local Soopass Ranch. | 218/847–1681.

AUG.: *Becker County Fair.* Animals, arts and crafts, rides, and live music make this the place to close out summer in Becker County. | 218/847–3141.

Dining

Country Kitchen. American. Homemade buttermilk pancakes, grilled steaks, and smothered chicken are favorites at this family-oriented spot. | 705 Highway 10E | 218/847–0472 | Breakfast also available | $5–$8 | AE, D, DC, MC, V.

Fireside. Continental. Panelled, oak-trimmed walls warm you while you partake of ribs, beef, or the local favorite, walleye pike. | 1462 E. Shore Dr. | 218/847–8192 | Closed late Nov.–Mar. No lunch | $8–$18 | AE, D, DC, MC, V.

Lakeside. American. Antiques, from toy cars to vintage dresses, adorn the walls of this dining room, which serves very popular ribs and walleye dinners. A dining deck, open in good weather, overlooks Detroit Lake. Kids' menu. Sun. brunch. | 200 W. Lake Dr. | 218/847–7887 | Closed Labor Day–Memorial Day | $10–$18 | MC, V.

Lodging

Best Western Holland House and Suites. Standing 1 mi from town, this hotel has the distinction of being the first in Minnesota to install an indoor water slide. Complimentary Continental breakfast. In-room data ports, refrigerators, in-room hot tubs. Cable TV. Indoor pool, wading pool. Hot tub, sauna. Laundry facilities. Business services. | 615 U.S. 10E | 218/847–4483 | fax 218/847–1770 | www.bestwestern.com/hollandhouse | 56 rooms | $79–$129 | AE, D, DC, MC, V.

Budget Host Inn. The 1950s-style motel is 1 mi from Sand Beach and 1½ mi from Detroit Lakes. Microwaves, refrigerators. Cable TV. Pets allowed. | 895 Hwy. E | 218/847–4454 | thiel@tekstar.com | www.BudgetHost.com | 24 rooms | $27–$64 | AE, D, MC, V.

Country Inn and Suites. Built in 1995, this hotel is 2½ mi from Detroit Lakes on East Shore Drive. Complimentary breakfast. Microwaves, refrigerators. Cable TV. 2 pools. Hot tub. | 1330 Hwy. 10E | 734/529–8822 | 46 rooms | $59–$89 | AE, D, DC, MC, V.

Fair Hills. Evening hootenannies and talent shows add to the summer-camp atmosphere at this Pelican Lake resort. The cottages are all beside the water. Dining room, picnic area. Some kitchenettes. Pool, wading pool. Hot tub. Golf course, tennis. Beach, water sports, dock, boating. Children's programs (ages 4–14). Laundry facilities. Business services, airport shuttle. | 24270 County Rd. 20 | 218/532–2222 | www.fairhillsresort.com | 18 rooms in lodge, 86 cottages | $115, $604 cottages (7–day minimum stay) | Closed Oct.–Apr. | AE, D, MC, V.

Holiday Inn. Paddleboat, canoe, kayak, and bike rentals are available at this lakeside hotel, which is 1 mi from town. Restaurant, bar (with entertainment), room service. In-room data ports, some minibars. Cable TV. Indoor pool. Hot tub, sauna. Health club. Laundry facilities. Business services. Free parking. | 1155 Highway 10E | 218/847–2121 | fax 218/847–2121, ext. 142 | www.detroitlakes.com/holidayinn | 103 rooms | $80–$120 | AE, D, DC, MC, V.

DULUTH

MAP 3, F5

(Nearby towns also listed: Cloquet, Two Harbors)

Truly an international city, Duluth is Minnesota's gateway to the sea. The Duluth-Superior Harbor is the largest inland fresh-water port in the world, and flags of many countries fly above the huge vessels that come here via the St. Lawrence Seaway to deliver and pick up their cargo. Grain, iron ore, coal, wood, and many other products from throughout the Midwest are shipped across the globe from here.

Duluth hugs a 600-ft bluff overlooking Lake Superior and was originally home to Dakota and Ojibway natives. White explorers began arriving in the 1600s, and in 1679 a French voyageur named Sieur Daniel Greysolon Duluth claimed the area for King Louis XIV. Settlers moved in and established themselves as fur traders, loggers, fishermen, farmers, and miners. Duluth's waterfront became a harboring place for lake shipping vessels and, eventually, a railroad terminal.

Tourism emerged as an important industry in the 1960s, thanks in part to the completion of the city's arena and auditorium complex. Now, with the opening of many more attractions, including Canal Park and its Marine Museum, the St. Louis County Heritage and Arts Center (The Depot), and Spirit Mountain Ski Area, Duluth has become one of the most popular tourist destinations in Minnesota.

Information: Duluth Convention and Visitors Bureau | 100 Lake Place Dr., Duluth, 55802 | 218/722–4011 or 800/438–5884 | www.visitduluth.com.

Attractions

Aerial Lift Bridge. This Duluth landmark spans 336 ft and stands 138 ft tall. It takes less than a minute to lift out of the way of passing ships. | Lake Ave. S, near Canal Park | Free | Daily.

Canal Park Marine Museum. Take in displays, historic artifacts, and programs that explain both Duluth-Superior Harbor's role in Great Lakes shipping and how the U.S. Army Corps of Engineers maintains the nation's waterways. | 600 Lake Ave. S | 218/727–2497 | Free | Apr.–mid-Dec., daily 10–4:30; mid-Dec.–Mar., Fri.–Sun. 10–4:30.

The Depot, St. Louis County Heritage and Arts Center. The city's old Union Depot has been transformed into a cultural center that's home to three museums, an arts institute, and four performing arts groups. | 506 W. Michigan St. | 218/727–8025 | www.visitduluth.com/Depot | $8 | Mon.–Sat. 9:30–6; Sun 1–5.
Cobblestone streets create a 1910 street scene at **Depot Square.** Prices at the old-time ice-cream parlor and gift shops are strictly 21st century. | 218/727–8025 | Daily 9:30–6.
Kids enjoy the **Duluth Children's Museum,** where a giant walk-through tree is among the most popular exhibits. | 218/733–2543 | $8 | Daily 9:30–6.
If trains and cable cars interest you, don't miss the displays of railroad and trolley memorabilia at the **Lake Superior Railroad Museum.** | 218/727–8025 | Free | Daily 9:30–6.
Exhibits at the **St. Louis County Historical Society** tell the stories of Minnesota's early logging and fur trades. | 218/727–8025 | Free | Daily 9:30–6.

Duluth OMNIMAX Theater. Films shown on the huge dome screen here give you a three-dimensional multimedia experience. | 301 Harbor Dr. | 218/727–0022 or 218/722–5573 | fax 218/722–5573 | www.decc.ort/attractions/omi.htm | $6.50 | Daily.

Duluth-Superior Excursions. Ride the Vista Cruiser $1/2$ mi into the harbor and enjoy the view. Special lunch and dinner cruises are available. | 323 Harbor Dr. | 218/722–6218 | www.visitduluth.com/vista | $9 | May–Oct.

Enger Tower. In a park along Skyline Drive, this landmark offers a superior view of Duluth and the lake. | Daily.

Fitger's Brewery Complex. This is what you get when you turn an old brewery into a shopping center. More than 25 specialty shops and restaurants reside here. | 600 E. Superior St. | 218/722–8826 | www.fitgers.com | Daily.
Get close to the world's largest lake as you stroll down the **Duluth Lakewalk,** which runs between Fitzger's Brewery Complex and Duluth Canal Park. | 800/4–DULUTH.

Fond-du-Luth Casino. Over 500 slot machines (including poker and keno), 12 blackjack tables, and bingo games are available. | 129 E. Superior St. | 218/722–0280 or 877/873–0280 | fax 218/722–7505 | www.fondduluthcasino.com | Free | Daily.

Glensheen. Here's a great place to take a tour and get a feel for Duluth's past. This estate, built around 1905, sits on the shore of Lake Superior. | 3300 London Rd. | 218/724–8864 or 218/724–8863 (recording) | $9 | www.d.umn.edu/glen | May–Oct., daily 9:30–4; Nov.–Apr., Fri.–Sun. 11–2.

Grand Slam Family Fun Center. The largest indoor multiple-activity center in the Upper Midwest, it includes Fun USA, Rock City Pizza, Grand Slam, Eagle Amusements, and Castle of Terror. | 395 Lake Ave. S (Canal Park) | 218/727–3837 | fax 218/722–0157 | www.funusa.net | Free | Daily.

Great Lakes Aquarium. America's only all-freshwater aquarium is on the harbor at the foot of Fifth Ave. West. The 62,382-square-ft building houses a natural history center, science center, and cultural exhibits, and has classroom space, a café, and gift shop. | 353 Harbor Dr. | 218/740–FISH (3474) or 877/866–3474 | fax 218/740–2020 | www.glaquarium.org | $11 | Daily.

Jay Cooke State Park. Hikers have a lot of rough terrain to choose from here. Campers and picnickers find plenty of places to settle down. | 500 Hwy. 210 E, Carlton | 218/384–4610 | www.dnr.state.mn.us/parks_and_recreation/state_parks/jay_cooke | Park permit required | Daily.

Karpeles Manuscript Library Museum. The collection here shares space with quarterly rotating exhibits. | 902 E. 1st St. | 218/728–0630 | Free | June–Aug., daily 12–4; Sept.–May, Tues.–Sun. 12–4.

Lake Superior Zoological Gardens. More than 500 animals make their homes at this zoo. | 72nd Ave. W. and Grand Ave. | 218/733–3777 | $5 | Daily 10–4.

Leif Erikson Park. Fans of the famous Norwegian explorer get a kick out of the statue and the replica of the ship in which he sailed to North America more than a millennium ago. | London Rd. and 11th Ave. E | 800/438–5884 | Free | May–mid-Sept., daily dawn–dusk.

North Shore Scenic Railroad. The main sightseeing trip offered here lasts 90 minutes and runs from Duluth to Lester River. Other, longer excursions to Two Harbors are available. | 506 W. Michigan St. | 218/722–1273 or 800/423–1273 | $9–$17 | Apr.–Oct., Fri.–Sun. 9–6:30.

Park Point Recreation Center. Picnic, swim, or launch your boat at this popular family destination. | 500 Minnesota Ave. | 800/438–5884 | Free | June–Labor Day, daily.

S.S. *William A. Irvin*. The *Irvin* had a long and distinguished career as the flagship of U.S. Steel's Great Lakes Fleet. Now this 610-ft ore carrier stays in port and welcomes aboard visitors who want to see its engine room, staterooms, and pilot-house. | 350 Harbor Dr. | 218/722–5573 or 218/722–7876 | $6.50 | Memorial Day–Labor Day, Sun.–Thurs. 9–6, Fri.–Sat. 9–8; Labor Day–mid-Oct., Sun.–Thurs. 10–4, Fri.–Sat. 10–6.

Scenic North Shore Drive. The word "scenic" may be an understatement. On one side there's the gray majesty of Lake Superior; on the other, green forests that stretch beyond view. | Hwy. 61, from Duluth to Two Harbors.

Skyline Parkway Drive. If you don't have time for an excursion up North Shore Drive, consider this instead. The road winds along the city bluffs and provides panoramic views. It begins at I–35, exit 249, and stretches to the eastern end of the city.

Spirit Mountain Ski Area. Ski down 24 runs within sight of Duluth, 10 mi away. There are five chairlifts here, and a vertical drop of 700 ft. | 10 mi south of Duluth, on I–35 | 218/628–2891 or 800/642–6377 | www.spiritmt.com | Daily.

University of Minnesota, Duluth. This is the second-largest piece of the University of Minnesota puzzle after the Twin Cities campus. Nearly 8,000 students attend. | 10 University Dr. | 218/726–8000 | www.d.umn.edu | Daily.
The programs at the UM Duluth's **Marshall W. Alworth Planetarium** cover topics ranging from stargazing and planets to recent scientific discoveries. All shows are live, and the staff encourages audience participation. | 10 University Dr. | 218/726–7129 | www.d.umn.edu/~planet | Free | Wed. 7 PM, planetarium show.
On the University of Minnesota, Duluth, campus is the **Tweed Museum of Art.** The museum's extensive holdings of European and North American art include a unique collection of paintings and illustrations of Canadian Mounted Police. | 10 University Dr. | 218/726–8222 | www.d.umn.edu/tma | Free | Tues. 9–8, Wed.–Fri. 9–4:30, weekends 1–5; closed Mon.

Vista Fleet Harbor Cruises and Dining Experience. During fully narrated sightseeing, lunch, dinner, or late evening moonlight cruises, you can get a close view of bustling harbor commerce with its busy grain elevators, freighters, and saltwater ships from around the world. | 323 Harbor Dr. | 218/722–6218 | fax 218/727–2919 | www.visitduluth.com/vista | $9 | May–Oct.

ON THE CALENDAR

JAN.: *John Beargrease Sled Dog Marathon.* Dogs pull mushers 330 mi up the North Shore Trail from Duluth to Grand Portage. | 218/722–7631.

JUNE: *Grandma's Marathon.* The marathon and its supporting events, the Garry Bjorklund Half Marathon and the William A. Irvin 5K, draw more than 14,000 entrants and tens of thousands of spectators each year. It starts in Two Harbors, parallels Lake Superior, and ends at Duluth's Canal Park. | 218/727–0947.

AUG.: *International Folk Festival.* The first Saturday of the month, head to the park to bask in the sounds of folk music from around the world. | 218/722–7425.

AUG.: *Bayfront Blues Festival.* International, national, and regional acts perform on two stages at this outdoor festival, held the second weekend of the month. | 715/392–1857.

Dining

Bennett's on the Lake. Contemporary. Some of Duluth's most imaginative cuisine comes with a close-up view of Lake Superior here. Try the seafood tower, with shrimp, scallops, and lobster piled atop spinach pasta. | 600 E. Superior St. | 218/722–2829 | No lunch weekends | $12–$25 | AE, D, MC, V.

Buffalo House. American. Since 1972, this has been the place get hearty buffalo burgers and steaks, barbecued ribs, and extra large shrimp. | 2590 Guss Rd. | 218/624–9901 | $6–$19 | AE, D, MC, V.

Fitger's Brewhouse. American. Known for sandwiches and quesadillas, this brew pub and restaurant was created at the site of Fitger's Brewery, which closed in 1972 after 115 years of brewing on the Lake Superior shore. Kids' menu. | 600 E. Superior St. | 218/726–1392 | $6–$12 | AE, D, MC, V.

Grandma's Canal Park. American. Old photographs, signs, and other memorabilia cover the walls of this historic building under the Aerial Lift Bridge. Try the chicken tetrazzini and Grandma's marathon spaghetti. Kids' menu. | 522 Lake Ave. S | 218/727–4192 | $8–$20 | AE, D, DC, MC, V.

New Scenic Cafe. Eclectic. Locals have been going to this lakeside restaurant since the 1950s. There's something for everyone—fresh lake salmon, trout, red beans and rice, Indian dishes, and pistashio-crusted Walleye, as well as vegetarian and vegan entrées. Local artists display their works here, 8 mi north of Duluth. | 546 North Shore Scenic Dr. | 218/525–6274 | $10–$18 | MC, V.

Pickwick. American. Dark wood and antique beer steins create an old-time pub atmosphere. The char-broiled steaks and peppered cheeseburgers are popular. Kids' menu. | 508 E. Superior St. | 218/727–8901 | Closed Sun. | $10–$24 | AE, D, DC, MC, V.

Top of the Harbor. American. The city, the harbor, and Lake Superior provide the main attraction from this 16th-floor revolving restaurant at the top of the Radisson (*see* Radisson, *below*) as it makes its 72-minute rotation. Photographs identify what you're seeing. Try the filet mignon and pasta carbonara. Kids' menu, early-bird suppers. Sun. brunch. | 505 W. Superior St. | 218/727–8981 | $12–$22 | AE, D, DC, MC, V.

Lodging

Allyndale. The woodsy setting of this hotel, standing on 5 acres, features a children's playground. Picnic area. Microwaves, refrigerators. Cable TV. Snowmobiling. Playground. Some pets allowed. | 510 N. 66th Ave. W | 218/628–1061 or 800/806–1061 | 18 rooms, 3 suites | $38–$58, suites $70–$80 | AE, D, DC, MC, V.

Best Western Edgewater. Standing next to an outdoor recreation area with playground, miniature golf, and shuffleboard, this hotel is 2 mi from downtown Duluth. Complimentary Continental breakfast. In-room data ports, refrigerators. Cable TV. Indoor pool. Hot tub, sauna. Miniature golf. Video games. Playground. Business services, free parking. Some pets allowed. | 2400 London Rd. | 218/728–3601 or 800/777–7925 | fax 218/728–3727 | www.zmchotels.com | 281 rooms | $109–$139 | AE, D, DC, MC, V.

Comfort Inn. A 24-hour restaurant is next door to this motel, off I–35 at exit 253B (40th Ave). Complimentary Continental breakfast. Some kitchenettes. Cable TV. Indoor pool. Hot tub, sauna. Laundry facilities. Business services. | 3900 W. Superior St. | 218/628–1464 | fax 218/624–7263 | 81 rooms | $69–$114 | AE, D, DC, MC, V.

Comfort Suites. Directly on Lake Superior, this hotel has direct access to the popular Lakewalk. Complimentary Continental breakfast. In-room data ports, refrigerators, some in-room hot tubs. Cable TV. Indoor pool. 2 Hot tubs. Laundry facilities. Business services. | 408 Canal Park Dr. | 218/727–1378 | fax 218/727–1947 | 82 rooms | $79–$249 | AE, D, DC, MC, V.

Country Inn and Suites This 3-story structure, built in 1997, is 3 mi south of town at I–35, exit 249, beneath Spirit Mountain Ski Hill. Complimentary Continental breakfast. Microwaves. Cable TV. Pool. Hot tub. | 9330 Skyline Pkwy. | 218/628–0668 or 800/456–4000 | 70 | $70–$150 | AE, D, DC, MC, V.

Days Inn. This is one of the most convenient hotels to the international airport, which is 5 mi away. Complimentary Continental breakfast. Cable TV. Business services. Some pets allowed. | 909 Cottonwood Ave. | 218/727–3110 | fax 218/727–3110, ext. 301 | 86 rooms | $59–$99 | AE, D, DC, MC, V.

Firelight Inn on Oregon Creek. In the heart of the oldest district downtown, this house was built in 1910. Complimentary breakfast. | 2211 E. 3rd St. | 218/724–0272 or 888/724–0273 | www.firelightinn.duluth.com | 10 rooms | $115–$135 | MC, V.

Fitger's Inn. Lake Superior is visible from some rooms at this hostelry, which is 5 mi from downtown. Restaurant, bar (with entertainment), room service. In-room data ports, some in-room hot tubs. Cable TV. Exercise equipment. Business services. Some pets allowed. | 600 E. Superior St. | 218/722–8826 or 800/726–2982 | www.fitgers.com | 62 rooms, 20 suites | $80–$110, $135–$200 suites | AE, D, DC, MC, V.

Holiday Inn. A skywalk system connects this property to a 40-store shopping center and other downtown businesses. Restaurant, bar. In-room data ports, microwaves, refrigerators. Cable TV. Indoor pool. Hot tub. Exercise equipment. | 200 W. 1st St. | 218/722–1202 or 800/477–7089 | fax 218/722–0233 | holidayinn@duluth.com | www.duluth.com/holidayinn | 353 rooms, 56 suites | $90–$110, $120–$160 suites | AE, D, DC, MC, V.

Mansion Bed & Breakfast Inn. A historic landmark and Duluth's only B&B on the water, the English Tudor house was built in 1929. You can explore seven acres of manicured lawns and gardens, or relax in its living room or screened porch. Complimentary breakfast. Lake. Hot tub. Beach. Library. | 3600 London Rd. | 218/724–0739 | www.mansion.duluth.com | 25 | $159–$199 | AE, DC, MC, V.

Radisson. This unusual circular tower hotel is 5 blocks from the waterfront, and is topped with a revolving restaurant (*see* Top of the Harbor, *above*). Restaurant, bar. Cable TV. Indoor pool. Hot tub, sauna. Business services. Some pets allowed. | 505 W. Superior St. | 218/727–8981 | fax 218/727–0162 | www.radisson.com | 268 rooms | $80–$115 | AE, D, DC, MC, V.

Spirit Mountain Lodge. Seven miles north of town, this rustic three-story lodge overlooks Spirit Valley and the St. Louis River. It's right on I–35, at exit 249. Complimentary Continental breakfast. Cable TV. Pool. Hot tub, sauna. Video games. Laundry service. | 9315 Westgate Blvd. | 218/628–3691 or 800/777–8530 | fax 218/628–3691 | www.travelodge.com | 100 rooms | $49–$129 | MC, V.

Super 8. Canal Park and the Aerial Lift Bridge are less than 5 mi from this hotel. Complimentary Continental breakfast. Cable TV. Hot tub, sauna. Laundry facilities. Business services. | 4100 W. Superior St. | 218/628–2241 | www.super8motels.com | 59 rooms | $63–$73 | AE, D, DC, MC, V.

ELK RIVER

MAP 3, E7

(Nearby towns also listed: Anoka, Minneapolis, St. Cloud, St. Paul)

In 1849, settlers found the confluence of the Mississippi and Elk rivers the perfect setting for a trading post. They began bartering at a log cabin, the first structure in the soon-to-be town of Elk River. About the same time, a farmer named Oliver H. Kelley set down roots in the area and went on to establish a successful farmers' movement called The Grange. Agriculture remains the bedrock of the local economy, but a more cosmopolitan life is in the tide as increasing numbers of residents commute to work in the Twin Cities.

Information: **Elk River Area Chamber of Commerce** | 509 U.S. 10, Elk River, 55330 | 612/441–3110 | www.elkriver-mn.com.

Attractions

Lake Orono. The lake covers 281 acres, and has a public park with sheltered picnic areas and playground equipment, a beach with swimming area, boating, and fishing. | Gary St. and Rte. 10 | 763/441–7420 | Free | Daily.

Oliver H. Kelley Farm. Pick heirloom vegetables from the garden, visit farmhands and animals in the barn, or churn your own butter at this working 1860s farm. | 15788 Kelley Farm Rd. | 612/441–6896 | www.mnhs.org/places/sites/ohkf | Free | May–Oct., Mon.–Sat. 10–5, Sun. noon–5; Nov.–Apr., Sat.–Sun. noon–4.

Sherburne National Wildlife Refuge. The 30,000 acres of tall-grass prairie, oak forests, and wetland habitat make this refuge popular with birds, animals, and the people who come to see them. It's 12 mi north of Elk River. | 17076 293rd Ave., Zimmerman | 612/389–3323 | Free | Daily.

ON THE CALENDAR

JULY: *4th of July Celebration*. A day-long celebration in the city park with amusements, rides, a water skiing show, and fireworks display over Lake Orono. | 612/441–3110.
JULY: *Sherburne County Fair*. With a carnival, tractor pulls, demolition derby, rodeo, 4-H exhibits, and plenty of food, this traditional county fair, established in 1915, draws folks from afar to the Sherburne County Fairgrounds. | 612/441–3722.

Dining

Bridgemans Restaurant. American. Eye-catching yellow, black, and white tile counters and bright lighting create a casual spot for burgers and fries, prime rib, or just an ice cream treat. | 17323 Hwy. 10 | 612/441–2777 | $4–$9 | AE, MC, V.

Lodging

AmericInn. This two-story, L-shape motel is one block from the Mississippi River. Complimentary Continental breakfast. Cable TV, in-room VCRs, TV in common area. Indoor pool. Hot tub, sauna. Some pets allowed ($10). | 17432 U.S. 10 | 612/441–8554 or 800/634–3444 | fax 612/441–8554 | www.AmericInn.com/minnesota/elkriver | 42 rooms | $70–$75 | AE, D, DC, MC, V.

Country Inn & Suites. Route 169 and Elk Hills Drive are near this three-story hostelry, and a restaurant is next door. Complimentary Continental breakfast. In-room data ports, some microwaves, some refrigerators. Cable TV. Pool. Hot tub. Laundry service. | 18894 Dodge St. NW | 763/241–6990 | fax 763/241–7301 | www.countryinns.com | 79 rooms | $60–$90 | MC, V.

Red Carpet Inn. Though not the most modern place in town, this two-building inn has helpful staff and a big back yard, is on the southern edge of the business district, and has a Chinese restaurant attached. Restaurant, complimentary Continental breakfast. Microwaves, refrigerators. Cable TV. Pool. Pets allowed ($5). | 17291 U.S. 10NW | 612/441–2424 | fax 612/241–9720 | www.redcarpetinn.com | 43 rooms | $45–59 | AE, D, DC, MC, V.

ELY

MAP 3, G3

(Nearby towns also listed: Babbitt, Chisholm, Cook, Crane Lake, Grand Marais, Tower)

In the heart of the Superior National Forest lies the town of Ely, the primary gateway to the Boundary Waters Canoe Area Wilderness (BWCAW). Thousands of campers, canoeists, and other visitors flock to the area each year in search the outdoors and this unique ecosystem that stretches into Canada. Ely is a good place to arrange for trips and pick up last minute supplies.

Information: Ely Chamber of Commerce | 1600 E. Sheridan St., Ely, 55731 | 218/365–6123 or 800/777–7281 | www.ely.org.

Attractions

★ **Boundary Waters Canoe Area Wilderness.** The wildlands in the northwestern part of Superior National Forest have over 1 million acres free of roads, resorts, or private cabins and 1,200 mi of canoe routes. Except for a half dozen lakes that allow limited use of motorboats, the Boundary Waters are off limits to anything but canoes and kayaks (and feet). Admission to the BWCAW is limited and based on a lottery drawing held in late January. All applications must be submitted between November 1 and January 15 for the best chance of a permit, though late applications are accepted. Groups size is limited to 9. Contact the central reservations center or one of the local outfitters for details. | 218/626–4300 or 877/550–6777 | www.bwcaw.org | $22 | Daily.

Canoe Country Outfitters. This local wilderness supply shop is a complete canoe outfitter with a choice of boats, food, and all camping equipment. The staff will not only help you map out a trip but will also guide you through the BWCAW permit application process. | 629 E. Sheridan St. | 218/365–4046 | www.northernnet.com/cco | May–mid-Oct., daily.

Greenstone Outcropping at Pillow Rock. This is the only place in the United States where you'll find surface ellipsoidal greenstone, which is some of the earth's oldest rock, formed over 3 billion years ago. Greenstones are ancient, underwater lava flows which have solidified, and been worn away over time. | 12th Ave. | 218/365–6123.

International Wolf Center. Observe the resident gray wolf pack in its forest habitat and learn about issues involving human contact with wolves. | 1396 Rte. 169 | 800/ELY–WOLF | www.wolf.org | $2.50 | May–mid-Oct., daily; mid-Oct.–Apr., Fri.–Sun.

Native American Pictographs. It's an easy day's paddle from Ely to these cliff paintings on South Hegman Lake. Inquire at the Ely Chamber or local canoe shops for maps and directions. | 800/777–7281.

Superior National Forest. The Superior National Forest is a 3-million-acre wilderness with camping, picnicking, canoeing, fishing, hiking, backpacking, and biking. It stretches for 150 mi along the U.S.–Canadian border and includes the Boundary Water Canoe Area Wilderness, which may be the best canoeing in the United States. Camping fees are $10 per person, which covers trips of any duration. | Hwy. 169, off U.S. Hwy. 53 | 218/626–4300 | www.fs.fed.us/r9/superior/ | Free | Daily.

Tom and Woods' Moose Lake Wilderness Canoe Trips. Right on Moose Lake, 20 mi east of Ely, spare you the hassle and expense of hauling equipment to the starting point. | Moose Lake | 800/322–5837 | www.tomandwoods.com | May–Sept., daily.

Vermilion Interpretive Center. Covering 12,000 years of local history, this information center has exhibits on such topics as Indians, voyageurs, mines, logging, and immigrants. | 1900 E. Camp St. | 218/365–3226 | Free | May.–Sept., daily 10–4; Oct.–Apr., Wed.–Sat. 1–4.

ON THE CALENDAR

FEB.: *Voyageur Winter Festival.* Fight winter blues at this 10-day snow-sculpture festival, where you can participate in an amateur sculpting contest. There are music jams, spaghetti dinners, and ski races. | 800/777–7281.

JULY: *Blueberry Art Festival.* Head to Whiteside Park for arts and crafts demonstrations, live entertainment, and ethnic food. Most years, this is when blueberries are ready for harvest. | 218/365–6123.

SEPT.: *Harvest Moon Festival.* Over 120 arts and crafts booths display the works of local artisans at the fair. Ethnic foods and entertainment are also available. | 218/365–6123.

Dining

Cranberry's. Eclectic. You can choose from traditional American foods as well as authentic Mexican dishes while enjoying the ski and snow memorabilia on the walls. | 47 E. Sheridan St. | 218/365–4301 | $6–$12 | AE, D, DC, MC, V.

Evergreen Restaurant. American. Inside the Hilton, the dining room and its outdoor deck overlook Shagawa Lake. | 400 N. Pioneer Rd. | 218/ 365–6565 | $9–$13 | AE, D, MC, V.

Minglewood Cafe. Café. This local landmark is a cozy café known for big breakfasts, scones, and sandwiches. A block away from Whiteside Park, it's a great place to pick up a picnic box lunch or settle in among magazines, journals, and newspapers from around the region. Kids' menu. | 528 E. Sheridan St. | 218/365–3398 | www.minglewood.com | No dinner | $4–$8 | AE, D, DC, MC, V.

Lodging

Budget Host. Standing in Superior National Forest, this hostelry is a main departure point for the Boundary Waters Canoe Area. Wood plank walls line the common areas and mounted fish and moose keep an eye on you. A snowmobile trail runs right by the motel, and the hotel's owner does guided fishing tours. Cable TV. Sauna. Business services, airport shuttle. Some pets allowed ($5). | 1047 E. Sheridan St. | 218/365–3237 | fax 218/365–3099 | stay@ely-motels.com | www.ely-motels.com | 17 rooms | $50–$65 | AE, D, DC, MC, V.

Holiday Inn Sunspree Resort. Fishing and paddle boats are available at this resort hotel, as well as canoes and kayaks. Restaurant, room service. Refrigerators. Pool, lake, wading pool. Sauna. Health club. Dock, boating, fishing. Shops. Laundry service. Business services. | 400 North Pioneer Rd. | 218/365–6565 or 800/365–5070 | fax 218/365–2840 | www.ely-holidayinn.com | 61 rooms | $119–$139 | AE, MC, V.

Olson Bay Resort. The main lodge building at this Shagawa Lake resort was originally a community hall for Finnish immigrants. Accommodations are in mostly lakefront cabins with decks and outdoor furniture. The naturalist program is geared to kids, with minnow races, fishing, and the like. Rates are based on a six-night stay. Bar, dining room, picnic area. Kitchenettes, microwaves, TV. Sauna. Hiking. Beach, boating, playground. Laundry facilities. Airport shuttle. | 2279 Grant McMahan Blvd. | 218/365–4876 or 800/777–4419 | fax 218/ 365–3431 | olsonbay@northernnet.com | www.criterionwebs.com/olsonbay | 7 cottages | $450–$700 (6 nights) | Closed Oct.–Apr. | D, MC, V.

VACATION COUNTDOWN Your checklist for a perfect journey

Way Ahead

- ❏ Devise a trip budget.
- ❏ Write down the five things you want most from this trip. Keep this list handy before and during your trip.
- ❏ Book lodging and transportation.
- ❏ Arrange for pet care.
- ❏ Photocopy any important documentation (passport, driver's license, vehicle registration, and so on) you'll carry with you on your trip. Store the copies in a safe place at home.
- ❏ Review health and home-owners insurance policies to find out what they cover when you're away from home.

A Month Before

- ❏ Make restaurant reservations and buy theater and concert tickets. Visit fodors.com for links to local events and news.
- ❏ Familiarize yourself with the local language or lingo.
- ❏ Schedule a tune-up for your car.

Two Weeks Before

- ❏ Create your itinerary.
- ❏ Enjoy a book or movie set in your destination to get you in the mood.
- ❏ Prepare a packing list.
- ❏ Shop for missing essentials.
- ❏ Repair, launder, or dry-clean the clothes you will take with you.
- ❏ Replenish your supply of prescription drugs and contact lenses if necessary.

A Week Before

- ❏ Stop newspaper and mail deliveries.
- ❏ Pay bills.
- ❏ Stock up on film and batteries.
- ❏ Label your luggage.
- ❏ Finalize your packing list—always take less than you think you need.
- ❏ Pack a toiletries kit filled with travel-size essentials.
- ❏ Check tire treads.
- ❏ Write down your insurance agent's number and any other emergency numbers and take them with you.
- ❏ Get lots of sleep. You want to be well-rested and healthy for your impending trip.

A Day Before

- ❏ Collect passport, driver's license, insurance card, vehicle registration, and other documents.
- ❏ Check travel documents.
- ❏ Give a copy of your itinerary to a family member or friend.
- ❏ Check your car's fluids, lights, tire inflation, and wiper blades.
- ❏ Get packing!

During Your Trip

- ❏ Keep a journal/scrapbook as a personal souvenir.
- ❏ Spend time with locals.
- ❏ Take time to explore. Don't plan too much. Let yourself get lost and use your Fodor's guide to get back on track.

River Point Resort and Outfitting Co. Wildwood Lodge, 8½ mi southeast of town on Highway 1, overlooks 2,500 feet of wilderness shoreline. The knotty-pine lodge has a beamed, vaulted ceiling and a floor-to-ceiling stone fireplace. You can choose one of 13 vacation homes or villas, some with woodburning stoves. Paddle boats, pontoon boats, and sailboats are available. Picnic area. Kitchenettes, microwaves, refrigerators, in-room hot tubs. No room phones, TV in common area. Lake. Sauna. Beach, boating. Shops, library. Playground. Laundry facilities. Airport shuttle. No pets. | 12007 River Point Rd. | 800/456–5580 | fax 218/365–6139; Oct.–Apr. 763/559–8976 | info@riverpointresort.com | www.riverpointresort.com | 13 cabins and villas | $95–$300 | Closed Oct.–Apr. | MC, V.

Super 8. This modern 2-story facility is right in the middle of town. Cable TV. Hot tub, sauna. Business services. | 1605 E. Sheridan St. | 218/365–2873 | fax 218/365–5632 | 30 rooms, 2 suites | $60–$95 | AE, D, DC, MC, V.

Timber Bay Lodge and Houseboats. *See* Babbitt, *above.*

Westgate. This 2-story, chalet-style motel bills itself as a prime location on "the quiet side of town." It's very popular with snowmobilers—the trail leads right up to the lodge—so it can be pretty noisy anyway. Complimentary Continental breakfast. Cable TV. Business services, airport shuttle. | 110 N. 2nd Ave. W | 218/365–4513 or 800/806–4979 | fax 218/365–5364 | www.northernnet.com/westgate | 17 rooms | $40–$60 | AE, D, DC, MC, V.

EVELETH

MAP 3, F4

(Nearby towns also listed: Chisholm, Hibbing, Tower, Virginia)

Founded in 1892, Eveleth is on the Mesabi Iron Range and best known for two things: iron ore and hockey. Area mines produce a large percentage of the nation's iron ore, and the town is home to the U.S. Hockey Hall of Fame; it's also the birthplace of six former U.S. Olympic Hockey Team members.

Information: **Eveleth Chamber of Commerce** | 801 Hat Trick Dr., Eveleth, 55734 | 218/744–1940 | www.evelethmn.com.

Attractions

Northside Park. The city's largest park, bordered by Grant, Adams, and Shackelton Aves., has a pine-shaded stream flowing through it. There's ice skating in winter. | 218/744–1940 | Free | Daily.

U.S. Hockey Hall of Fame. Great American hockey players are enshrined here. The Canadians have their own hall of fame, so some of your favorites might be absent. | 801 Hat Trick Ave. | 218/744–5167 or 800/443–7825 | www.ushockeyhall.com | $6 | Mon.–Sat. 9–5, Sun. 10–3.

ON THE CALENDAR

JULY: *4th of July Celebration.* The biggest and best fireworks display in the Iron Range is the highlight of this city's signature event, which also has music, food, crafts and more. | 218/744–1940.

Dining

K&K and B Drive-In. American. You can have a 1950s eat-in-your-car experience, complete with car-hop service, year-round, just 2 mi south of town on Hwy. 53. Inside as well as open-air dining are also available. Homemade pastries and ice-cream treats have been added to a traditional burger menu. | Rte. 53 at Cedar Island Dr. | 218/744–2772 | $4–$7 | No credit cards.

Lord Stanleys' Restaurant. American. Locals vie with tourists for a table and the chance to have a great steak or prime rib at this hotel dining room. | 701 Hat Trick Ave. (next to Hockey Hall of Fame) | 218/744–2703 | Breakfast also available. No lunch | $9–$15 | AE, D, MC, V.

Lodging
Eveleth Inn. The Hockey Hall of Fame is right next door to this facility. Restaurant, bar, room service. Some microwaves, some refrigerators. Cable TV. Indoor pool. Sauna. Laundry facilities. Business services. Some pets allowed. | Hat Trick Ave./U.S. 53 | 218/744–2703 | fax 218/744–5865 | 145 rooms | $62–$95 | AE, D, DC, MC, V.

Kokes Downtown Motel. Rooms in this two-level, 1950s-style motel have indoor or outdoor entrances. It's two blocks from the business district, 3 mi from the Laurentian Trail and Iron Trail system, and ½ mi from the U.S. Hockey Hall of Fame. Cable TV, room phones. Pets allowed. | 714 Fayal Rd. | 218/744–4500 or 800/892–5107 | fax 218/744–4500 | gkoke@yahoo.com | www.evelethmn.com/chamber/kokes | 14 rooms | $38–$48 | MC, V.

Super 8. Backwoods furniture and a fireplace warm the lobby of this two-story motel, which stands 1 mi from town. The two suites have hot tubs. Complimentary Continental breakfast. Cable TV. Indoor pool. Hot tub, sauna. Game room. Laundry facilities. Business services. | 1080 Industrial Park Dr. | 218/744–1661 | fax 218/744–4343 | www.super8.com | 53 rooms, 2 suites | $60–$65, $58–$90 suites | AE, D, DC, MC, V.

FAIRMONT

MAP 3, D10

(Nearby towns also listed: Blue Earth, Jackson)

Fairmont bills itself as a city of lakes and a convenient stop for road-weary travelers. A chain of five lakes with public beaches and parks runs through the city. Its location on I–90, about halfway between Chicago and the Black Hills of South Dakota, does make it a good place to get some rest. A group of English farmers who arrived here in the 1870s, known as the "Fairmont sportsmen," introduced fox hunting into southern Minnesota.

Information: **Fairmont Convention and Visitors Bureau** | Box 976, Torgerson Dr., Fairmont, 56031 | 800/657–3280 | www.fairmont.org.

Attractions
Fairmont Opera House. Take in a tour or show at this 1901 theater. Off-hours tours by appointment. | 45 Downtown Plaza | 507/238–4900 or 800/657–3280 | www.fairmont.org/docs/opera.htm | Tours Mon.–Fri. 11–5.

Martin County Historical Society and Pioneer Museum. Replicas of 19th-century buildings, such as a school house, a doctor's and dentist's office, and a pioneer home, depict the period along with Indian artifacts and and war memorabilia. | 304 E. Blue Earth Ave. | 507/235–5178 | www.fairmont.org/docs/fmtsites.htm | Free | May–Sept., Tues.–Sat. 1:30–4:30, Mon. 6:30–8:30.

ON THE CALENDAR
NOV.: *Fairmont Glows.* Homes, businesses, and city parks light up for the holiday season, drawing visitors from all over the region. The lights are up from mid-month through New Year's Day. | 507/235–5547.

Dining
The Ranch. American. One of the big draws to this large, open dining room is the 40-item salad bar, though the place is equally well known for steaks, seafood, and the boneless pork. Kids' menu. | 1330 N. State St. | 507/235–3044 | $7–$12 | D, MC, V.

Shenanigan's. American. Homemade pizza, shrimp, chicken, and bacon cheese burgers are specialties that attract families as well as a casual chic crowd. | 115 E. 3rd Ave. | 507/238–2911 | $7–$13 | AE, D, MC, V.

Lodging

Budget Inn. This basic, single-story inn was built in the 1960s. Its big draw is the indoor heated pool and convenient location—about ½ mi from town and from I–90, exit 102. Cable TV. Indoor pool. Hot tub, sauna. | 1122 N. State St. | 507/235–3373 | fax 507/235–3286 | 43 rooms | $26–$49 | AE, D, DC, MC, V.

Comfort Inn. Only 2 mi from downtown, this two-story hotel is at Route 15 and I–90, exit 102, next to Torge's Bar and Grill. Complimentary Continental breakfast. Cable TV. Pool. | 2225 N. State St. | 507/238–5444 | www.comfortinn.com/fairmont | 40 | $58–$87 | AE, D, DC, MC, V.

Holiday Inn of Fairmont. Renovated in 1998, all rooms have inside entrances. The property is 3½ mi from the airport at Route 15 and I–90, exit 102. A Torge's restaurant is on the premises. 2 restaurants, bar. In-room data ports. Cable TV. Pool, wading pool. Hot tub, sauna. Putting green. Health club. Video games. Laundry service. Airport shuttle. Pets allowed. | I-90 at Hwy. 15, Fairmont | 507/238–4771 | fax 507/238–9371 | mntorges@frontiernet.com | www.torgersonproperties.com | 105 rooms, 2 suites | $84–$94, $99–$159 suites | AE, D, DC, MC, V.

Super 8. The motel is half a block from I–90, exit 102, within a block of restaurants. Complimentary Continental breakfast. Cable TV. Business services, airport shuttle. Pets allowed. | 1200 Torgerson Dr. | 507/238–9444 | fax 507/238–9371 | www.super8.com | 47 rooms | $45–$54 | AE, D, DC, MC, V.

FARIBAULT

MAP 3, E9

(Nearby towns also listed: Le Sueur, Mankato, Mantorville, New Prague, Northfield, Owatonna, St. Peter)

Named after French-Canadian fur trader Alexander Faribault, who built a large trading post here in 1826, this is a pleasant residential city with a historic downtown, 25 minutes south of the Twin Cities. Two major companies are headquartered here: Faribault Woolen Mills, producing Faribo wool blankets, and Sellner Manufacturing, which makes the Tilt-A-Whirl and other amusement rides.

Information: Faribault Chamber of Commerce | 530 Wilson Ave., Faribault, 55021 | 507/334–4381 or 800/658–2354 | www.faribaultmn.org.

Attractions

Alexander Faribault House. The home of the town's fur-trader namesake has been restored and filled with period antiques. Also on the site is a museum of Native American artifacts. | 12 1st Ave. NE | 507/334–7913 | $2 | May–Oct., daily.

Faribault Woolen Mill. Wool blankets and throws have been produced here since 1865. A tour lets you view the processes that transform raw wool into blankets. | 1819 2nd Ave. | 507/334–1644 or 800/448–9665 | fax 507/334–9431 | www.faribowool.com | Free | Mon.–Fri. 10–2.

Rice County Historical Society Museum. Slide and video presentations, exhibits, and pioneer artifacts tell the story of local Native American and county history. | 1814 2nd Ave. NW | 507/332–2121 | Free | Sept.–May, Tues.–Fri. 9–4; June–Aug., Mon.–Fri. 1–4.

River Bend Nature Center. With 700 acres of woodlands, this is a great place for kids and adults to learn about nature. Stop in at the interpretive center for maps, area history, and species facts. | Rustead Rd. | 507/332–7151 | www.rbnc.org | Free | Daily.

ON THE CALENDAR
SEPT.: *Faribault Area Balloon Rally.* Antique aircraft go on display and ultra-lights putter overhead, as the skies over Faribault Municipal Airport become speckled with the colorful nylon of hot-air balloons. | 800/658–2354.

Dining
Depot Bar & Grill. American. You'll dine casually on everything from burgers and steaks to pasta and southwestern dishes. | 311 Heritage Pl. | 507/332–2825 | $6–$18 | AE, D, DC, MC, V.

Lavender. American. Paintings, prints, jewelry, and even grandfather clocks are displayed and sold at this restaurant, which is known for its steaks, seafood, and prime rib. Kids' menu. | 2424 N. Lyndale Ave. | 507/334–3500 | $6–$12 | AE, D, DC, MC, V.

Lodging
AmericInn. You can relax in style here after a day cruising the region. Complimentary breakfast. Microwaves, refrigerators, some in-room hot tubs. Cable TV. Pool. Sauna. Laundry service. Pets allowed. | 1801 Lavender Dr. | 507/334–9464 or 800/634–3444 | www.americinnfaribault.com | 61 rooms | $64–$69 | AE, D, DC, MC, V.

Galaxie. Built in 1965, this 2-floor inn has a breakfast area and a cozy wall-papered lobby. It stands two blocks from I–35, exit 56. Complimentary Continental breakfast, room service. In-room data ports. Cable TV. Indoor pool. Hot tub, sauna. Business services. | 1401 Rte. 60W | 507/334–5508 | fax 507/334–2165 | 59 rooms | $39–$56 | AE, D, DC, MC, V.

Select Inn. Proud of its no-frills style, this inn is right off I–35, at exit 56, with restaurants next door. The Sakatah Singing Hills State Bike Trail is behind the motel. Cable TV, in-room VCRs (and movies). Indoor pool. Business services. | 4040 Rte. 60W | 507/334–2051 | www.selectinn.com/faribault/frb.html | 67 rooms | $43–$58 | AE, D, DC, MC, V.

FERGUS FALLS

MAP 3, B6

(Nearby towns also listed: Alexandria, Detroit Lakes, Moorhead)

Agriculture is the leading industry in Fergus Falls. You'll see plenty of crop, dairy, and pig farms, and some bison ranches as well. Tourism is also big business. Surrounding Otter Tail County is home to 1,048 lakes and more than 100 resorts.

Information: **Fergus Falls Convention and Visitors Bureau** | Box 686, City Hall, Fergus Falls, 56538 | 218/736–6979 or 800/726–8959 | www.visitfergusfalls.com.

Attractions
Otter Tail County Historical Society Museum. Dioramas, period rooms, and other historical displays cover local history. A large section is devoted to agriculture's role in the county's development. | 1110 W. Lincoln Ave. | 218/736–6038 | www.fergusfalls.com/tourism/museum.html | Free | Mon.–Fri. 9–5, Sat. 1–4, Sun 1–4; closed Sun. from Sept.–June only.

Pebble Lake City Park. This 152-acre municipal park has an 18-hole golf course, a clubhouse, a beach, a playground, and biking trails. | County Rd. 88 | 218/739–3205 | Free | Apr.–Sept., daily.

The Riverwalk. The path stretches along the south bank of the Otter Tail River, from Union Avenue to Veteran's Park and downtown on the Eastside, and passes architectural treasures such as the 1903 Renaissance Revival Post Office, the 1928 Colonial Revival City Hall, and the 1929 Medieval Revival Inn. | Union Ave. to Veterans Pk. | 218/736–6979 | Free.

ON THE CALENDAR
JUNE: *Summerfest.* This city-wide celebration includes children's programs, a parade, an arts and crafts show and sale, and street dance. | 218/736–6979.

Dining
Legion Restaurant. American. Popular dishes include the extra-jumbo-sized shrimp, pork tenderloin, fried chicken, and walleye. On Wednesdays, Mexican food is added to the menu, on Thursdays Italian food, and on Fridays all-you-can-eat barbecued ribs. | 2010 Pebble Lake Rd. | 218/739–5643 | $10–$14 | D, MC, V.

Mabel Murphy's. American. From outside, you'll think this is a cozy old cottage; and once inside, you'll have a hard time deciding in which fireside nook to sit. House specials include prime rib or walleye (fried or broiled), with your choice of a vegetable, a trip to the salad bar, or the pub stew with chunks of beef and vegetables. There's outdoor dining in summer, overlooking the woods. Don't be surprised if a deer comes looking for a snack. Kids' menu. | Rte. 210 W | 218/739–4406 | No lunch Sun. | $9–$24 | AE, D, MC, V.

Lodging
AmericInn Motel. Standing off I–94, at exit 54, this facility is also 1 mi from Otter Tail County trails. Some suites have microwaves, refrigerators, and hot tubs. Complimentary Continental breakfast. In-room data ports. Cable TV. Pool. Hot tub, sauna. Laundry service. Business services. Pets allowed. | 526 Western Ave. N | 218/739–3900 or 800/634–3444 | fax 218/739–3900 | www.americinn.com | 60 rooms, 9 suites | $56–$115, $74–$116 suites | AE, D, MC, V.

Bakketopp Hus Bed & Breakfast. You can have breakfast overlooking the mountainside lake, and enjoy the serenity of country life, 8 mi north of town on Rte. 27. Common areas have high vaulted ceilings and American oak antiques. One suite has a private sunken garden and an in-room hot tub. Complementary breakfast. Cable TV. Lake. No smoking. | 20571 Hillcrest Rd. | 218/739–2915 or 800/739–2915 | ddn@prtel.com | www.bbonline.com/mn/bakketopp | 3 rooms | $70–$105 | D, MC, V.

Comfort Inn. This small, 2-story member of the chain is at exit 54 (SR 210 W), off I–94. Several restaurants are within walking distance. The three suites have hot tubs. Complimentary Continental breakfast. Some microwaves, some refrigerators, some in–room hot tubs. Cable TV. Laundry facilities. Business services. | 425 Western Ave. | 218/736–5787 | fax 218/736–5787 | 35 rooms, 3 suites | $44–$49, $71–$111 suites | AE, D, DC, MC, V.

Days Inn. The town's main hotel strip is the setting for this two-story motel with a spacious parking lot. Complimentary Continental breakfast. Cable TV. Indoor pool. Hot tub. Business services. | 610 Western Ave. | 218/739–3311 | 57 rooms | $49–$75 | AE, D, DC, MC, V.

Super 8. This 2-story hotel is on the edge of town directly off I–94, at exit 54. Cable TV. Business services. | 2454 College Way | 218/739–3261 | 32 rooms | $50–$55 | AE, D, DC, MC, V.

GLENWOOD

MAP 3, C7

(Nearby towns also listed: Alexandria, Morris, Sauk Centre)

Glenwood lies on the eastern shore of Lake Minnewaska, the 13th largest lake in Minnesota. It's a popular vacation area with seven resorts and campgrounds. More than 30 industrial businesses also call Glenwood home.

Information: Glenwood Area Chamber of Commerce | 200 North Franklin St., Glenwood, 56334 | 800/304–5666 | www.members.tripod.com/~glenwoodmn.

Attractions

Chalet Campsite. This is a convenient place to launch a boat, go for a swim, or set up a tent (the camping fee is $15–$20). Rest rooms and showers are available. | Rte. 104 | 320/634–5433 | Free | Daily.

Department of Natural Resources, Area Fisheries Headquarters. Walleye, trout, and other fish eggs are hatched, then grown to maturity in ponds for the purpose of stocking the lake with fish. Tours are given in the Spring during hatching season. | 23070 N. Lakeshore Dr. | 320/634–4576 | Free | Mon.–Fri. 9–4.

Pope County Historical Museum. The exhibits here include a gallery of Native American arts and crafts, a country store, and a furnished log cabin. | 809 S. Lakeshore Dr. | 320/634–3293 | Free | Memorial Day–Labor Day, Tues.–Sat. 10–5, Sun. 1–4; Labor Day–Memorial Day, Tues.–Sat. 10–5; closed Mon.

ON THE CALENDAR

JUNE: *Terrace Mill Heritage Festival.* Learn rosemaling, woodcarving, and other traditional crafts at the Historic Terrace Mill, on County Road 104. | 320/278–3289.
JULY: *Waterama.* A queen is crowned during this annual event, which includes parades, boat races, sport tournaments, 10K and 5K races, and a play. | 800/304–5666.

Dining

Minnewaska House Supper Club. Steak. Known for steak, chops, and seafood, this local landmark has an open grill in the middle of the dining room, so you can watch them prepare your food. The house special is the Erickson pork chop. | Intersection of Hwys. 28 and 29 | 320/634–4566 | No lunch Sun. | $10–$30 | AE, MC, V.

Torges on the Lake. American. People come to enjoy the chicken baskets, soup and salad bar, fish-n-chips, seafood, and steaks, as well as great views of the lake. Open-air dining is also available. | 1860 Lake Shore Dr. | 320/634–4311 | $5–$8 | AE, D, MC, V.

Lodging

Green Valley Resort. Each bring-your-own-linens cabin has a picnic table on either a deck or a lawn. Campfire rings are available. Picnic area. Kitchenettes, no TV. Lake. Basketball. Beach, dock, boating. Playground. Laundry facilities. Pets allowed (fee). | 17632 N. Pelican Lake Rd. (3 mi west of Glenwood, Rte. 28 and N. Pelican Lake Rd.) | 320/634–4010 or 800/834–4010 | www.minnewaskamn.com/greenvalley | 12 cabins | $81–$160 | Oct. 15–May 1 | D, MC, V.

Peters' Sunset Beach Resort. Owned consecutively by four generations of the Peters family, this full-service golf resort is on Lake Minnewaska, and has accommodations just steps away from the first tee. The 2-, 3-, and 4-bedroom cottages and townhouses are fully furnished and great for families. The 18-hole course measures 6,400 yards, has eight water holes, and has an MGA rating of 70.7. Dining room. Kitchenettes Cable TV, some room phones. Sauna. 18-hole golf course, putting green, tennis. Beach, boating. Bicycles. Business services. | 20040 S. Lakeshore Dr. | 320/634–4501 or 800/356–8654 | fax 320/634–5606 | golfpsb@runestone.net | www.petersresort.com | 20 cottages | $129–$272 | Closed Nov.–mid-May | MAP | MC, V.

Scotwood Motel. If you're in need of a quick place to bed down and not overly concerned with newness, then this local landmark at the junction of routes 55 and 28 should do the trick. It's about a mile uphill from town and has two stories and inside corridors. Complimentary Continental breakfast. Cable TV. Indoor pool. Hot tub. Game room. | Jct. Rte. 55 and Rte. 28 | 320/634–5105 | 46 rooms | $36–$46 | AE, D, MC, V.

GRAND MARAIS

MAP 3, H3

(Nearby towns also listed: Ely, Grand Portage, Lutsen, Voyageurs National Park)

Grand Marais is an outdoorsy kind of town. Perched on the shore of Lake Superior, it is close to the Boundary Water Canoe Area Wilderness and Superior National Forest, with easy access to nature-based adventures. The historic Gunflint Trail starts at the edge of town. Canada is a 40-minute drive away.

Information: **Grand Marais Chamber of Commerce** | Box 1048, Grand Marais, 55604 | 218/387–2524 or 800/622–4014 | www.grandmaraismn.com.

Attractions

Canoeing. Grand Marais is a good place to load up on everything you'll need for multi-day canoe journeys in the Boundary Waters Canoe Area Wilderness. You can pick up maps and lists of outfitters from the Grand Marais Information Center (218/387–2524 or 800/622–4014) or Gunflint Trail Association Outfitters (800/338–6932). | www.gunflint-trail.com/canoetrips.

Grand Portage National Monument. In the late 18th century, the 8½-mi Grand Portage (a land link between Lake Superior and area rivers) was a major gateway into the interior of North America for explorers, fur traders, and indigenous peoples. In summer it served as headquarters for the Northwest Company. The reconstructed headquarters includes a

© Corbis

BOUNDARY WATERS CANOE AREA WILDERNESS

In a state with thousands of lakes, it's hard to choose one area that rises above the others in terms of outdoor adventure. Still, the Boundary Waters Canoe Area Wilderness (BWCAW) offers a vacation experience unlike any other, anywhere.

The BWCAW and Canada's Quetico Provincial Park combine to form the largest canoe wilderness in the world. There's no logging. No mining. No development. It's a unique area and an extremely popular destination. If you're thinking about a trip to the BWCAW, it helps to plan ahead.

The BWCAW and Quetico Park operate on a reservation system to control the number of visitors and protect the wilderness from overuse. Because there are a limited numbers of permits, it's a good idea to make reservations early. The most popular routes fill up first and holiday weekends are especially busy. The U.S. Forest Service begins issuing permits in December for the following summer. You can almost always get a permit without advance notice, but you may not be able to get the route you were hoping for.

Motorized vehicles and equipment are not allowed in the BWCAW. Groups of more than nine people are prohibited. So are cans and bottles.

The main entry points to the BWCAW are near Crane Lake, Ely, Grand Marais, and the Lutsen-Tofte area. Unless you're an experienced canoeist, you probably will want to prepare for your trip and plan your route with the help of one of the many outfitters in the area. If you do use an outfitter, you won't have to bring much with you. Keep it simple: minimal clothing, sturdy footwear, a few personal items, and maybe some simple fishing equipment. Your outfitter will supply the rest.

Towns listed: Crane Lake, Ely, Grand Marais, Lutsen

stockade, great hall, kitchen, and canoe warehouse. | Mile Creek Rd. | 218/475–2202 | www.nps.gov/grpo | Free | Daily.

Gunflint Trail. Along this 60-mi road surrounded by the Boundary Waters Canoe Area Wilderness (BWCAW) and Superior National Forest, you can rough it or pamper yourself at resorts, campgrounds, and B&Bs. The Trail starts in Grand Marais and ends at Saganaga Lake at the Ontario border. | 218/387–1750.

Judge C. R. Magney State Park. Peace, quiet, and the Devil's Kettle waterfall are the big draws here. The most popular hike leads from the trailhead upstream, along the Brule River, to Devil's Kettle, where the river splits around a mass of volcanic rock. | 4051 Rte. 1E | 218/387–3039 | www.dnr.state.mn.us | $4 | Daily.

North Shore Drive. *See* Duluth.

ON THE CALENDAR

AUG.: *Fisherman's Picnic.* Something's fishy here including the fishing contests and fishburgers. Don't forget the not-so-fishy attractions like the crafts exhibits, a parade, and fireworks. | 800/622–4014.

NOV.: *Grand Marais Chamber of Commerce Christmas Parade.* The "come as you are" festivities include a parade with floats, bands, fire trucks, and photo opportunities with Santa. | 218/387–2524.

Dining

Angry Trout Café. American. At the harborside, this restaurant is known for fresh Northwoods fare and for organic salads. In summer, there is open-air dining with views of the harbor. Beer and wine only. No smoking. | 408 Rte. 61W | 218/387–1265 | Closed late Oct.–Apr. | $12–$20 | MC, V.

Birch Terrace Supper Club. American. This rustic 1898 log mansion has views overlooking Native American burial grounds and Lake Superior. Fireplaces and stuffed deer and moose give it a hunting-lodge flavor, and the kitchen serves fresh Lake Superior trout, ribs, and steak. The cocktail lounge has a fireplace, a deck overlooking the lake, and a menu of lighter fare. Kids' menu. | 601 W. 6th Ave. | 218/387–2215 | No lunch | $10–$23 | D, MC, V.

Blue Water Cafe. American. With its harbor view and massive Lake Superior map on the wall, this is a good place to plot your next move while dining on local walleye, trout, or homemade meatloaf. | 20 W. Wisconsin St. | 218/387–1597 | $7–$12 | D, MC, V.

Leng's Fountain. American. In business since 1938, Leng's has the last original working soda fountain in Minnesota. Old-fashioned malts and banana splits are specialties, in addition to homemade soups, pork tenderloin burgers marinated in hot spices, and the Route 61 burger that's served with wild rice, mushrooms, two cheeses, and onions. | 5 W. Wisconsin St. | 218/387–2648 | $5–$8 | No credit cards.

Naniboujou Lodge and Restaurant. American. Built in the 1920s, the dining room has a painted ceiling and fieldstone fireplace, and is decorated with Cree Indian designs. Walleye trout, salmon, steak, and pasta are popular dishes. | 20 Naniboujou Tr. | 218/387–2688 | $5–$17 | D, MC, V.

Lodging

Aspen Lodge. One block off of Lake Superior, this three-story hotel has a view of the lake from the lobby and from many rooms. Complimentary Continental breakfast. Some in-room hot tubs. Cable TV, room phones. Pool. Hot tub, sauna. Laundry facilities. Business services. | 330 Rte. 61E | 218/387–2500 or 800/247–6020 | fax 218/387–2647 | www.grand-maraismn.com/aspenlodge.html | 51 rooms | $59–$130 | AE, D, DC, MC, V.

Bearskin Lodge. In a secluded setting on East Bearskin Lake, the lodge has rooms with fireplaces and screened porches. Lodgepole pine, Norway pine, and spruce log cabins are in private lakeside nooks, and also have fireplaces. Dining room. No air-conditioning, kitchenettes, microwaves. Hot tub, sauna. Hiking. Beach, docks, boating, bicycles. Children's programs (ages 3–15), playground. Laundry facilities. Business services. | 124 E. Bearskin Rd. | 218/388–2292 or 800/338–4170 | fax 218/388–4410 | stay@bearskin.com | www.bearskin.com | 4 rooms, 11 cottages | $102–$169 rooms, $90–$306 cottages | D, MC, V.

Best Western Superior Inn and Suites. Directly on Lake Superior, this hotel has rooms with your choice of lake-view balconies or outdoor, ground-floor access. The North Shore Corridor snowmobile trail system is right beside the property. Complimentary Continental breakfast. Refrigerators. Cable TV. Hot tub. Snowmobiling. Laundry facilities. Business services. Some pets allowed. | 1st Ave. E | 218/387–2240 or 800/842–8439 | fax 218/387–2244 | bwsuperiorinn@lakesnet.net | www.bestwestern.com/superiorinn | 56 rooms, 10 suites | $79–$129 rooms, $109–$179 suites | AE, D, DC, MC, V.

Clearwater Canoe Outfitters and Lodge. Built in 1926, the log structure is a great starting-off point for canoe trips. Lakeside cabin, B&B, or suite accommodations are available. There is also a bunkhouse for 14, a tepee that sleeps six, or rustic Wyoming screenhouses for the intrepid. Canoe outfitter services are the focus and mainstay of the lodge. Cabin rates are based on a seven-day stay. Picnic area. No air-conditioning, microwaves. Sauna. Hiking. Beach, docks, boating. Bicycles. Playground. Some pets allowed. | 355 Old Rail La. | 218/388–2254 or 800/527–0554 | clearwater@canoe-bwca.com | www.canoe-bwca.com | 5 rooms, 6 cabins | $68–$100 rooms, $730–$770 cabins | Closed Oct.–May | D, MC, V.

Devil Track Lodge. Opened in 1999, the lodge has a café and lounge with a cobblestone gas fireplace. Lake. Hot tub, sauna. Beach, dock. Playground. | 205 Fireweed La. | 218/387–9414 or 877/387–9414 | fax 218/387–2432 | www.deviltrack.com | 6 rooms | $80–$100 | D, MC, V.

Golden Eagle Lodge. These fully equipped modern cabins, the only buildings on Flour Lake, are nestled in the woods and have fireplaces, wraparound decks, and great possibilities for moose and deer sightings. To get there, travel 27 mi on the Gunflint Trail (Route 12), then 3 mi on Rte. 66. Kitchenettes, microwaves. No room phones, no TV. Lake. Beach, dock, boating. Cross-country skiing. No pets. | 468 Clearwater Rd. | 218/388–2203 or 800/346–2203 | fax 218/388–9417 | www.golden-eagle.com | 12 cabins | $730–$1,300 weekly | AE, DC, MC, V.

Moosehorn Lodge. On a peninsula overlooking Gunflint Lake, this home gives you the choice of a lakefront cottage or B&B accommodations in the main house. Cottages have pine paneling, fireplaces, are fully furnished, and require a one-week minimum stay. B&B rooms are frilly and bright, with four-poster beds, lace curtains, and antiques. Picnic area, dining room. Kitchenettes, microwaves. Sauna. Hiking. Beach, boating, bicycles. Cross-country skiing. Playground. | 194 N. Gunflint Lake Rd. | 218/388–2233 | fax 218/388–9476 | www.moosehorn.com | 3 rooms, 3 cottages | $95–$200 rooms, $650–$950 cottages | Closed Oct.–Apr. | MC, V.

Naniboujou Lodge. This Lake Superior lodge was built in the 1920s as an exclusive resort getaway. In fact, Babe Ruth and Jack Dempsey were founding members. It's gone through many incarnations since then, but still stands today in splendor, with Minnesota's largest native rock fireplace (200 tons), a Great Hall dining room decorated with Cree Indian designs, and simple guest rooms, some with fireplaces. Restaurant. No air-conditioning, no room phones. Cross-country skiing. No smoking. Business services. | 20 Naniboujou Tr | 218/387–2688 | info@naniboujou.com | www.naniboujou.com | 24 rooms | $59–$89 | D, MC, V.

Nor'wester Lodge. Operated by the same family who built the lodge in 1931, this small resort sits on the north shore of Poplar Lake, 30 mi up the Gunflint Trail from Grand Marais. Cabins are private, have decks and docks, are fully equipped, and can accommodate between two and ten people. You can also arrange for canoe expeditions, or short day trips. Rates are based on a one-week stay. Picnic area. No air-conditioning, kitchenettes, microwaves. TV in common area. Sauna. Beach, dock, water sports, boating. Cross-country skiing. Playground. Laundry facilities. Some pets allowed. | 7778 Gunflint Tr | 218/388–2252 or 800/992–4386 | www.boreal.org/norwester | 7 cottages | $774–$1,134 | D, MC, V.

Rockwood Lodge. Built in the 1920s of native Norway red pine, this Poplar Lake lodge is 4 mi from the Canadian border. Cabin accommodations range from a modern A-frame log cabin and small pine home to some older, more typical summer cabins, all with porches. Rates are based on a one-week stay. It's 35 mi north of Grand Marais, on the Gunflint Trail. Bar, dining room. No air-conditioning, kitchenettes, microwaves. Sauna. Hiking. Beaches, boating. Playground. Laundry facilities. Business services. No pets. | 625 Gunflint Tr | 218/388–2242 or 800/942–2922 | rockwood@boreal.org | www.boreal.org/rockwood | 9 cottages | $700–$1,800 | AE, D, MC, V.

The Shoreline. Convenience is key at this hotel in the middle of downtown. The building is right on the lake; you can request a room with a view. There's a lobby with a fireplace and two family suites—one with four single beds and one with two queen-size beds. Complimentary Continental breakfast. No air-conditioning, in-room data ports, refrigerators. Cable TV. Business services. No pets. No smoking. | 20 S. Broadway | 218/387-2633 or 800/247–6020 | fax 218/387-2499 | gmhotel@worldnet.att.com | 30 rooms | $39–$99 | AE, D, DC, MC, V.

Snuggle Inn. You will be downtown and only one block from the harbor at this B&B. Paintings and crafts by local artists are in each room. Complimentary breakfast. No room phones, TV in common area. Laundry facilities. No kids. No smoking. | 8 Seventh Ave. W | 218/387-2847 or 800/823-3174 | info@snuggleinnbb.com | www.snuggleinnbb.com | 4 rooms | $85–$95 | AE, D, DC, MC, V.

Super 8. This is the first hotel you come to as you approach Grand Marais from the south, and there are no lake views. It's a two-story establishment in two buildings. Complimentary Continental breakfast. In-room data ports, refrigerators. Cable TV. Hot tub, sauna. Laundry services. Business services. Some pets allowed. | 1711 Rte. 61 W | 218/387-2448 or 800/247-6020 | fax 218/387-9859 | gmhotel@worldnet.att.com | 35 rooms | $45–$99 | AE, D, DC, MC, V.

GRAND PORTAGE

MAP 3, I3

(Nearby town also listed: Grand Marais)

This is the last town you'll hit before crossing into Canada. Dakota people used this area as a launching point for travels on interior waterways. In the late 1700s, it became a major rendezvous point and supply depot for fur traders. Today it's probably best known for its Grand Portage Casino.

Information: Grand Portage Tourist Association | Box 233, 1 Casino Dr., Grand Portage, 55605 | 218/475–2401 or 800/232–1384.

Attractions
Grand Portage Casino. Here you'll find video slots, including poker and progressive machines, Keno, live blackjack tables, and a huge high-stakes bingo hall. | U.S. 61 at Marina Rd. | 800/543–1384 | Daily.

Grand Portage National Monument. *See* Grand Marais.

Dining
Howl'n Wolf Saloon & Grill. American. Antique sleds and fishing gear set the scene for pork fillet, walleye, trout, and Lake Superior bluefin. | 2066 W. Hwy. 61 | 218/387–1236 | $8–$20 | D, MC, V.

Lodging
Grand Portage Lodge and Casino. Not only do you have a great view of Lake Superior or the surrounding woods, you are just steps away from the 15,000-square-ft Grand Portage

Casino. There's also a marina and RV park for those arriving in style. Restaurant, bar (with entertainment), room service. Cable TV. Indoor pool, lake. Sauna. Hiking, dock, boating. Business services. | Rte. 61 | 218/475–2401 or 800/543–1384 | fax 218/475–2309 | www.grand-portagemn.com | 100 rooms | $56–$120 | AE, D, DC, MC, V.

GRAND RAPIDS

MAP 3, E4

(Nearby towns also listed: Deer River, Hibbing)

Best known as the birthplace of Judy Garland, this town celebrates its most famous daughter as widely as possible, with a museum and other sites dedicated to the star. Early in its history, Grand Rapids was primarily a logging town. Paper production is still big business here, but tourism has become just as important, as visitors come, not only for Judy Garland memories, but also for the area's more than 1,000 lakes, dozen golf courses, and, in winter, 1,000 mi of snowmobile trails.

Information: **Grand Rapids Area Chamber of Commerce** | 1 N.W. 3rd St., Grand Rapids, 55744 | 218/326–6619 or 800/GRANDMN | www.grandmn.com.

Attractions

Central School. Built in 1895 and listed on the National Register of Historic Places, this school houses the Itasca County Historical Society. | 10 5th St. NW | 218/327–1843 | Free | Daily. Also part of Central School, the **Judy Garland Museum** has no yellow brick road to follow, but you can view one of Garland's dresses from *The Wizard of Oz*, as well as a horse-drawn carriage featured in the movie and other mementos of the star's life. | 2727 U.S. 169S | 218/327–9276 or 800/664–5839 | www.judygarland.com | $2 | Mon.–Sat. 10–5, Sun. noon–5.

Forest History Center. This reproduction of a turn-of-the-20th-century logging camp has a camp blacksmith, a saw filer, a clerk, a cook, and lumberjacks. While visiting, you can board the moored river "wanigan," a floating cook shack used when the logs—and men—headed downstream to the mills. | 2609 County Rd. | 218/327–4482 | www.mnhs.org/places/sites/fhc/index.html | Free | June–Oct., daily 10–5; Oct.–June, Mon.–Fri. 9–4:30, closed Sat.–Sun.

Hill Annex Mine State Park. Tour guides explain how the mine operates and give a sense of northern Minnesota's rich mining history. The entrance to the 635-acre park is on the north edge of Calumet, along Highway 169. | | 218/247–7215 | www.dnr.state.mn.us/parks_and_recreation/state_parks/hill_annex_mine/index.html | $6 | Daily.

The Myles Reif Performing Arts Center. More than 10,000 exhibits, shows, and performances have been held here since the center opened in 1979. | 720 Conifer Dr. | 218/327–5780 | fax 218/327–5798 | www.reifcenter.org | Ticket prices vary | Year-round.

Pokegama Dam. The Pokegama Recreation Area backs up behind this dam, and there are RV camping sites if you want to hang around and get in some fishing. | 34385 US 2 | 218/326–6128 | $15 | Daily.

Scenic State Park. This 3,000-acre park has seven lakes with camping, boating, fishing, and hiking in summer and cross-country skiing and snowmobiling in winter. There are 102 RV and tent campsites with seasonal rate variations. | County Rd. 7 | 218/743–3362 | www.dnr.state.mn.us/parks_and_recreation/state_parks/scenic | $4 | Daily.

White Oak Society. The Learning Center provides educational programs for youth and adults who want to experience a "living history" interpretation of the fur trade era. | 33155 State Rte. 6 | 218/246–9393 | www.whiteoak.org | $6.

JUNE: *Judy Garland Festival.* The Judy Garland Museum hosts a celebration of the entertainer's life, with a musical program, films, and the appearance of some Munchkins. | 218/327–9276.

JULY: *Mississippi Melodie Showboat.* An old-time riverboat pulls up to the banks of the Mississippi as actors sing and dance, spilling onto a stage on shore to continue the revelry. | 800/722–7814.

JULY: *North Star Stampede.* Three days of rodeo fun are to be had 45 mi north of Grand Rapids, in Effie. | 218/743–3893.

AUG.: *Tall Timber Days and U.S. Chainsaw Carving Championships.* Break up summer with lumberjack competitions, chainsaw carving demonstrations, and a host of other fun events around downtown Grand Rapids. | 800/472–6366.

AUG.: *Itasca County Fair.* Arts and crafts, livestock shows, rides, and live entertainment are all on the schedule. | 218/326–6619.

Dining

Bridgeside Restaurant & Sports Bar. American. With four televisions always on, you can watch your favorite team here while eating one of the hand-tossed pizzas, crab manicotti, chicken Parmesan, or lasagna. | 29 Crystal Springs Rd. | 218/326–0235 | $9–$14 | MC, V.

Eagles' Nest Dining. Continental. Eating 70 ft above the water on an 80-ft, wraparound screened porch is a favorite summer treat for local residents. From this "million dollar view," they—or you—can choose among chicken fettuccine, duck, prime rib, trout, and walleye entrées. | 52001 County Rd., Bigfork | 218/832–3852 or 888/832–3852 | $12–$21 | MC, V.

Hong Kong Garden Restaurant. Eclectic. The menu here spans the globe. In addition to Szechuan- and Hunan-style Chinese dishes, you can order enchiladas, tacos, burritos, sizzling fajitas, and other Mexican fare—or go for American entrées such as sirloin steaks and catfish. | 118 SW 12th St. | 218/327–1131 | $10–$15 | D, MC, V.

La Rosa Mexican Restaurant. Mexican. An elegant fireplace, a fountain, and Mexican artifacts create a south-of-the-border flavor in the northland. Chicken chimichangas, seafood enchiladas, and the La Rosa sampler platter are popular. | 1300 E. Rte. 169 | 218/327–4000 | $7–$18 | AE, MC, V.

Lodging

AmericInn. Convenience is key at this two-story motel, surrounded by a movie theater, a Dairy Queen, a Wal-Mart, and a Target. Complimentary Continental breakfast. Some kitchenettes, some microwaves, some refrigerators, some in-room hot tubs. Cable TV. Indoor pool. Hot tub, sauna. Business services. | 1812 Pokegama Ave. S | 218/326–8999 | fax 218/326–9190 | www.AmericInn.com/minnesota/grandrapids.html | 35 rooms, 8 suites | $68–$78 | AE, D, DC, MC, V.

Best Western Rainbow Inn. Standing on the north edge of town, this motel is directly on the highway. Restaurant, bar (with entertainment), room service. Cable TV. Indoor pool. Hot tub, sauna. Business services, airport shuttle. | 1300 U.S. 169E | 218/326–9655 | fax 218/326–9651 | 80 rooms, 4 suites | $45–$70 rooms, $75–$90 suites | AE, D, DC, MC, V.

Budget Host. The downtown area is two blocks west of this motel. Picnic area. Cable TV. Playground. Business services, airport shuttle. Pets allowed. | 311 U.S. 2E | 218/326–3457 | fax 218/326–3795 | 34 rooms | $50–$69 | AE, D, DC, MC, V.

Country Inn. Opened in 1994, this inn is on the south edge of town next to the Judy Garland house. The handful of two-room suites are in a wing built in 2000. Complimentary Continental breakfast. Some refrigerators, some microwaves. Cable TV. Indoor pool. Hot tub. Exercise room. Some pets allowed. | 2601 U.S. 169S | 218/327–4960 | fax 218/327–4964 | www.countryinns.com | 46 rooms, 5 suites | $55–$73 | AE, D, DC, MC, V.

Judge Thwing House. You can experience living in "arts and crafts style" in this B&B, which was built during the movement's heyday. It's in a quiet valley surrounded by lakes and forested areas 1½ mi from town. Complimentary breakfast. Pets allowed. | 1604 County Rd. A | 218/326–5618 | fax 218/326–2019 | 4 rooms | $50–$60 | AE, D, MC, V.

Rainbow Inn. Built in the 1970s, this two-story hotel has direct access to a hiking trail. Restaurant, bar, in-room hot tubs. Cable TV. Pool. Hot tub, sauna. Pets allowed. | 1300 E. Rte. 169 | 218/326–9655 | fax 218/326–9851 | 85 rooms, 6 suites | $39–$69, $75 suites | AE, D, DC, MC, V.

Sawmill Inn. This two-story, locally-owned inn is one block from the Judy Garland house. Restaurant, bar, room service. Cable TV. Indoor pool. Hot tub, sauna. Laundry facilities. Business services, airport shuttle. Pets allowed. | 2301 S. Pokegama Ave. | 218/326–8501 or 800/235–6455 | fax 218/326–1039 | 124 rooms, 10 suites | $75–$80, $108–$120 suites | AE, D, DC, MC, V.

Segren's Pokegama Lodge. You can choose B&B or separate cabin accommodations at this lakefront lodge. Complimentary breakfast. In-room data ports. Cable TV. Beach, boating. | 931 Crystal Springs Rd. | 218/326–9040 | www.seagrens.com | 5 rooms, 2 cabins | $50–$70, $90–$325 cabins | AE, D, DC, MC, V.

Super 8. This 2-story, 1983 facility is on the south end of town, 4 blocks from the Judy Garland House. Complimentary Continental breakfast. In-room data ports. Cable TV. Laundry service. Business services. | 1902 S. Pokegama Ave. | 218/327–1108 | 58 rooms | $51–$57 | AE, D, DC, MC, V.

Williams Narrows Resort. Generations of families have been coming here since the resort was established in 1920. The abundant lake structure of Big Cutfoot Sioux, which leads into Lake Winnibigoshish, provides some of northern Minnesota's best fishing. Kitchenettes, refrigerators. | 43465 William Narrow Rd. | 218/246–8703 or 800/325–2475 | fax 218/246–8847 | 22 cottages | $110–$240 | Closed April–Nov. | MC, V.

GRANITE FALLS

MAP 3, C8

(Nearby towns also listed: Marshall, Redwood Falls, Tracy, Willmar)

Granite Falls sits on the Minnesota River's west bank, over massive granite bedrock. This is where most of the famous incidents and battles of the 1862 Dakota Conflict took place. The history of that conflict, which pitted white settlers against Native Americans, is recorded at monuments throughout the area and at the Upper Sioux Agency, now a Minnesota Historical Society site.

Information: **Granite Falls Area Chamber of Commerce** | Box 220, 155 7th Ave., Granite Falls, 56241 | 320/564–4039 | www.granitefalls.com.

Attractions

Camden State Park. The Redwood River flows through this 1,747-acre park, allowing for good fishing; there's also a spring-fed pond for swimming, and rustic trails for hiking. The entrance is 40 mi from Granite Falls. | Rte. 23 | 507/865–4530 | www.dnr.state.mn.us/parks_and_recreation/state_parks/camden/index.html | Free | Daily 8-5.

Lac qui Parle State Park. Sandwiched between the Lac qui Parle and Minnesota rivers, about 25 mi west of Granite Falls, this 27,000-acre park hosts activities including camping, swimming, boating, fishing, and cross-country skiing. | Cty Rd. 13 | 320/752–4736 | www.dnr.state.mn.us/parks_and_recreation/state_parks/lac_qui_parle | $4 | Daily.

Olof Swensson Farm Museum. This Norwegian immigrant was the stuff of Minnesota legend. A many-skilled Renaissance man, he built a grist mill and a 22-room brick mansion, proposed amendments to the U.S. constitution, ran for state governor, crafted his own casket and tombstone, and was a self-proclaimed minister. His 39'x39' chapel is in the mansion. | Rte. 15 | 320/269-7636 | www.montechamber.com/cchs/swensson.htm | $5 | Memorial Day–Labor Day, Sun. 1–5.

Upper Sioux Agency State Park. Nearly thirteen hundred acres of open-prairie, knolls, bluffs, and wooded slopes contain the remains of the Upper Sioux (or Yellow Medicine) Agency, which was established in 1862 to administer the terms of the *Traverse des Sioux* treaty. Trails here are ideal for horseback riding, hiking, skiing, and snowmobiling. | RR 2 | 320/564-4777 | www.dnr.state.mn.us/parks_and_recreation/state_parks/upper_sioux_agency | $4 | Daily.

Yellow Medicine County Museum. Exhibits here include two log cabins from the 1800s. You can also stand on an exposed rock outcropping that's been around for about 3.8 billion years. | 98 Rte. 67E | 320/564-4479 | $1 | May–Oct., Tues.–Fri. 11–3, Sat.–Sun. noon–4.

ON THE CALENDAR
SEPT.: *Pursuit of Excellence.* This marching band competition, a day-long event with a parade in the morning and competitions in the evening, attracts a statewide audience. | 507/532-2157.

Dining
Ninety-Fifth Club. Contemporary. Walleye, trout, fettucine Alfredo, and steak are favorites on the menu here. | Rte. 212 W at Rte. 67 | 320/564-4003 | No lunch | $8–$15 | AE, D, DC, MC, V.

Lodging
Super 8 Motel. The combination of great amenities at good prices attracts people to this two-story hotel on Rte. 212, 3 blocks west of the junction of Routes 23/67 and 212. Restaurant. Microwaves, in-room hot tubs. Cable TV. 2 pools. Hot tub. Health club. Business services. | 844 W. Rte. 212 | 320/564-4075 or | fax 320/564-4038 | www.super8.com. rooms | 63 | $40–$56 | AE, D, DC, MC.

Viking Motel. A locally owned, L-shape motel about 1 mi south of downtown, this is a 1-story drive-up, so it's good for folks who don't want to climb stairs. All beds are doubles. Cable TV. Some pets allowed. | 1250 U.S. 212W | 320/564-2411 | 20 rooms | $28–$42 | AE, D, MC, V.

HASTINGS

MAP 3, F8

(Nearby towns also listed: Minneapolis, Northfield, Red Wing, St. Paul)

Founded in 1855, this old steamboat stop is a beautiful vantage point from which to see the Mississippi River. Victorian residences, tree-lined neighborhoods, a classic Main Street downtown, and the 1871 County Courthouse give Hastings its small town character.

Information: **Hastings Area Chamber and Tourism Bureau** | 111 E. 3rd St. Hastings, 55033 | 651/437-6775 or 888/612-6122 | www.hastingsmn.org.

Attractions
Afton Alps. In winter, you can ski on 40 trails served by 18 lifts, with a 300-ft vertical drop. In summer there's golfing and mountain biking. | 6600 Peller Ave. | 651/436-5245 or 800/328-1328 | www.aftonalps.com | Nov.–Mar., daily.

Alexis Bailly Vineyard. Though the tag line at Minnesota's oldest winery is "Where the grapes can suffer," your tastebuds surely won't. This thriving vineyard was started in the 1970s and has garnered the attention of wine growers everywhere. | 18200 Kirby Ave. | 651/437–1413 | www.abvwines.com | Free | June–Nov., Fri.–Sun. 11–5.

Carpenter St. Croix Valley Nature Center. Right on the St. Croix River, this environmental education center 15 mi of hiking trails, plus an interpretive center with informative displays. | 12805 St. Croix Tr | 651/437–4359 | Free | Daily.

Hastings Family Aquatic Center. Water activities include a 200-ft-tall water slide and a step slide that drops into the water. Lifeguards are on duty, and there is also a dry-land playground. | Rte. 55 and Maple St. | 651/480–2392 | $5 | Memorial Day–Labor Day.

Historic Walking Tour. Stop by the Chamber of Commerce and pick up the booklets and maps you'll need for a self-guided tour of town. | 11 E. 3rd St. | 651/437–6775 | Daily.

Lock-n-dam Number 2. Pleasure boats and working barges pass through on route to the Mississippi River. From an observation platform, you can watch the process of raising and lowering boats 12 ft as six-million gallons of water are emptied and then fill locks, using an all-gravity system that allows the water to move through the gates. | 1350 Dam Rd. | 651/437–3150 | Free | Apr.–Oct.

Ramsey Mill. The state's first governor, Alexander Ramsey, also built the state's first flour mill. Though it's now mainly in ruins, it's still interesting to history buffs. Historical plaques give some background. It's on the National Register of Historic Places, in Vermillion Falls Park. | 21st St. | 888/612–6122 | Free | Daily.

Treasure Island Casino and Bingo. You might not really feel like you're in the Caribbean, but the kitschy theme of this hotel and casino is fun to look at, considering it's in Minnesota. Besides the casino, there are a marina, a cruise ship, and an RV park. | 5734 Sturgeon Lake Rd. | 800/222–7077 | www.treasureislandcasino.com | Daily.

ON THE CALENDAR

JULY: *Rivertown Days.* Celebrate Hastings's river heritage with boat and street parades, waterski shows, a music festival, and an arts and crafts fair. | 651/437–6775.

Dining

Levee Cafe. Contemporary. Sandwiches, grilled Cajun chicken Caesar salad, and pasta primavera are on the varied menu here, along with filet mignon, steaks, and chops. | 100 Sibley St. | 651/437–7577 | $8–$17 | MC, V.

Mississippi Belle Italian Restaurant. American. Fancy chandeliers and steel engravings bring to mind a 19th-century riverboat. Though it's not on the river, there are still some great water views. On the menu are fresh seafood, pasta, and steak. Kids' menu. | 101 2nd St. E | 651/437–4814 | Closed Mon. No lunch Tues.–Thurs., Sat. | $12–$22 | AE, D, DC, MC, V.

Steamboat Inn & River Charters. Seafood. When casual, yet gourmet dining is desired, the chef's breast of chicken in raspberry sauce, crab cakes, jumbo frog legs, salmon, walleye pike, or Wisconsin roasted duckling are good choices. | Rte. 10 at Bridge, Prescott | 651/480–8222 | $12–$28 | AE, D, MC, V.

Lodging

AmericInn. Directly off the main highway, this two-story hotel is on the town's main street, about 10 blocks south of West View Mall area shops and restaurants. Complimentary Continental breakfast. Cable TV. Pool. Hot tub. Business services. | 2400 Vermillion St. | 651/437–8877 or 800/634–3444 | fax 651/437–8184 | 27 rooms | $43–$86 | AE, D, DC, MC, V.

Hastings Country Inn & Suites. This European-style, three-story hotel serves breakfast on an indoor balcony overlooking the lobby and fireplace below. Complimentary Continental breakfast. In-room data ports. Cable TV, some in-room hot tubs. Pool. Hot tub. No pets. | 300 33 St. W | 651/437–8870 | fax 651/437–8178 | www.countryinns.com | 61 rooms, 11 suites | $65–$130 | AE, D, DC, MC, V.

Hastings Inn. This sprawling, single-story motel is 15 blocks south of town. An indoor pool makes it a nice draw for wintertime. In-room data ports. Cable TV. Indoor pool. Sauna. Game room. | 1520 Vermillion St. | 651/437–3155 | fax 651/437–3530 | 43 rooms | $28–$60 | AE, D, DC, MC, V.

Hearthwood Bed & Breakfast. A New England experience, Minnesota-style, awaits you at this Cape Cod–style B&B, where every room has antiques and a fireplace. It has an 11-acre walking trail, and is 7 mi from the casino. Complimentary breakfast. In-room hot tubs. Cable TV. | 17650 200th St. E | 651/437–1133 | www.hearthwood.com | 5 rooms | $125–$145 | AE, D, MC, V.

Super 8. This 2-story inn was built in the 1990s and has plenty of room for kids to run around on the big front lawn. It's right off Rte. 61. Complimentary Continental breakfast. Cable TV. Hot tub. No pets. | 2450 Vermillion St. | 651/438–8888 | fax 651/438–8888 | 48 rooms, 2 suites | $44–$57 | AE, D, DC, MC, V.

Thorwood Inn. Listed on the National Register of Historic Places, this 1880 Victorian is well preserved, and, what with all the quilts and fireplaces and a "bottomless cookie jar," you'll feel right at home. Complimentary breakfast. In-room data ports, some in-room hot tubs. Business services. | 315 Pine St. | 651/437–3297 or 800/992–4667 | fax 651/437–4129 | www.thorwoodinn.com | 15 rooms | $97–$257 | AE, D, MC, V.

HIBBING

MAP 3, E4

(Nearby towns also listed: Chisholm, Cook, Deer River, Eveleth, Grand Rapids, Virginia)

Hibbing calls itself the "iron ore capital of the world," and that's not an empty boast— it's home to the world's largest open-pit iron mine. In 1918, the big Hull-Rust pit had encroached on the heart of town, and Hibbing had to be transplanted 2 miles south. Other claims to fame: Hibbing is the birthplace of the Greyhound Bus system and the boyhood home of singer Bob Dylan.

Information: **Hibbing Area Chamber of Commerce** | 211 E. Howard St., Hibbing, 55746 | 218/262–3895 or 800/4–HIBBING | www.hibbing.org.

Attractions

Hill Annex Mine State Park. Eighteen miles southwest of Hibbing lies this old mining area now transformed into a state park, with 633 acres of woods and open areas, including the impressive abandoned-mine pit. You can take a guided tour of the old mining facilities, which follows an 8-mi road, and visit the mining museum. Large groups may schedule tours during the off-season. | 880 Gary St. | 218/247–7215 | Free, tour $6 | Memorial Day–Labor DayMemorial Day–Labor Day 9:30-6, Labor Day-Memorial Day 8-5. Note, during the winter hours tend to be irregular, so call in advance.

Hull-Rust Mahoning Mine. The folks at the largest iron mine in the world call it the "Grand Canyon of the North," and it's an apt title. The mine is three mi long, two mi wide, and 500 ft deep. Climb to the top of the observation building for the best view. | 3rd Ave. E | 218/262–4900 | Free | May–Sept., daily.

McCarthy Beach State Park. Dig your toes into this sandy beach along Sturgeon Lake, or launch a boat and explore Side Lake, along with another four lakes connected to the Sturgeon chain. You can also hike, ski, or snowmobile through stands of virgin pine, or camp in this 2,311-acre park. | 7622 McCarthy Beach Rd. | 218/254–7979 | www.dnr.state.mn.us/parks_and_recreation/state_parks/mccarthy_beach | Park permit required | Daily.

Paulucci Space Theatre. This multimedia theater presents programs on astronomy and other topics. Showtimes vary. | 1502 E 23rd St. | 218/262–6720 | $4.50 | Daily 9–5.

ON THE CALENDAR

FEB.: *Winter Frollick.* A queen reigns over this event, which takes place during the second week of the month; there's also an ice-fishing contest and a treasure hunt, with clues given over the radio and in the local newspaper. | 218/262–3895 or 800/4–HIB-BING.

APR.: *Last Chance Curling Bonspiel.* The world's best curlers gather to compete in this four-day event at the Hibbing Memorial Building ice rink. The sport involves playing ice hockey with brooms, while wearing shoes. | 218/262–3895.

Dining

Amelia's Family Cuisine. Italian. This centrally located restaurant uses family recipes to make its traditional Italian dinners. Old pictures of town and of Italy line the walls, and the lighting is soft. There is also a full line of specialty imported beers and wines you won't find anywhere else nearby. | 2601 First Ave. | 218/263–7141 | No lunch Sat. Closed Sun. | $7.95–$11.95 | MC, V.

Sammy's. Italian. The interior of this family-owned restaurant has been painted with mock storefronts that might make you think you're sitting in a sidewalk café. Though the menu has steaks and pasta, Sammy's is best known for combo pizzas. Kids' menu. | 106 E. Howard St. | 218/263–7574 | No lunch Sat. | $8–$12 | AE, D, DC, MC, V.

Lodging

Super 8. Built in the early 1990s, this 2-story facility has a convenient highway location about 2 mi east of downtown, at the junction of Routes 169 and 37. Cable TV. Business services. Some pets allowed. | 1411 E. 40th St. | 218/263–8982 | www.super8.com | 49 rooms | $37–$53 | AE, D, DC, MC, V.

HINCKLEY

MAP 3, E6

(Nearby town also listed: Mora)

Midway between the Twin Cities and Duluth, Hinkley is also the midpoint for travels between Duluth and St. Cloud. The city serves as a good base for those seeking outdoor recreation, gambling, and history. Since the Great Hinckley Fire of 1894, the city has rebuilt itself around those historic attractions which escaped destruction.

Information: Hinckley Visitors and Tourism Bureau | 109 Tobies Mill Pl., Hinckley, 55037 | 320/384–0126 or 800/996–4566 | www.hinckleymn.com.

Attractions

Hinckley Fire Museum. Hear the story of the great Hinckley fire, which destroyed six nearby towns and killed 400 people in just four hours. A miniature replica shows how the town looked before the fire, and a 20-minute video shows what it would have been like to live through the disaster. | 106 U.S. 61 | 612/384–7338 | www.ci.hinckley.mn.us/firemuseum/index.html | $3 | May–Oct., daily.

Hinckley Grand Casino. Enjoy round-the-clock gaming such as bingo, blackjack, slots, and video poker. | 777 Lady Luck Dr. | 800/472–6321 | www.grandcasinosmn.com | Daily.

Northwest Company Fur Post. Among the attractions at this trading post is an authentic Ojibway wigwam. Costumed guides lead you through an oral history. | 612/629–6356 | www.state.mn.us/ebranch/mhs/places/sites/nwcfp | May–Labor Day, Tues.–Sat. 10–5, Sun. noon–5.

St. Croix State Park. Two rivers run through this 34,000-acre park: the St. Croix and the Kettle. Intrepid travelers can explore them by canoe, and more placid folk can ply the waters with fishing poles. You can also swim at 34,037-acre Lake Clayton, or climb a fire tower. | Rte. 22 | 612/384–6591 | www.dnr.state.mn.us/parks_and_recreation/state_parks/st_croix | $4 | Daily.

ON THE CALENDAR
JULY: *Corn and Clover Carnival.* On the first weekend after the Fourth the town celebrates its farming roots, with a parade, a talent show, antiques appraisals, a pedal-tractor pull, and plenty of native corn-on-the-cob. | 800/996–4566.

Dining
Cassidy's. Continental. This beam-and-rock structure is as rugged looking as the menu is hearty. Steaks and chili are popular, and the salad bar, with its 80 hot and cold dishes, is a big draw. Also known for its homemade breads, soups, and a big breakfast menu, the restaurant is at the junction of I–35 and Hwy 48. Kids' menu. Beer and wine only. | 384 Fire Monument Rd. | 320/384–6129 | $7–$12 | D, MC, V.

Grand Grill Americana. American. This restaurant in the Grand Casino, 1 mi east of town, is open most hours and serves steak, prime rib, and a new dessert every month, like bread pudding with caramel sauce. | 777 Lady Luck Dr. | 320/384–7101 or 800/468–3517 | Breakfast also served | $10–$16 | AE, D, MC, V.

Tobie's. Continental. Open in one location or another since the 1950s, Tobie's has earned a good reputation for steaks, seafood, and cinnamon rolls from the on-site bakery. Lots of people stop here just to grab some pastries for the road. | 404 Fire Monument Rd. | 320/384–6174 | Open 24 hours | $6–$14 | AE, DC, MC, V.

Tommy G's Pizza. American. This popular spot serves pizzas with many toppings, as well as some sandwiches. | Hwy 48 E | 320/384–7348 | Closed Tues. No lunch | $4–$12 | No credit cards.

Lodging
Dakota Lodge Bed and Breakfast. Here you can stay in a contemporary house nestled in the woods or in your own two-bedroom cabin with a kitchen, porch, and fireplace on six wooded acres. The main house has a library and a cozy, comfortable living room with a fireplace and a scattering of antiques. It's about 10 mi east of town. Complimentary breakfast. In-room hot tubs. Laundry facilities. | Rte. 3, Box 178 | 320/384–6052 | www.dakotalodge.com | 5 rooms, 1 cabin | $58–$110, $135 cabin | D, MC, V.

Days Inn. This 2-story member of the chain was built in 1991, and is about 1½ mi from the Hinckley Grand Casino, off exit 183 on I–35. The apartment suite can sleep five. Complimentary Continental breakfast. Some refrigerators. Cable TV. Indoor pool. Hot tub, sauna. Laundry facilities. Business services. Some pets allowed. | 104 Grindstone Ct | 320/384–7751 | 69 rooms, 5 suites | $44–$85 rooms, $90–$135 suites | AE, D, DC, MC, V.

Down Home Bed and Breakfast. Seated among 40 acres of woods and open fields, this contemporary home has a three-season porch, a common room with a wood-burning fireplace, and a quiet room for reading or listening to music. One bedroom has either a twin or a king-size bed, the others have double beds. It's 5 mi southeast of town and just under 2 mi from the casino. Complimentary breakfast. TV in common area. No pets. | R.R. 2, Box 177a | 320/384–0396 or 800/965–8919 | fax 320/384–0397 | 3 rooms | $60–$100 | D, MC, V.

Hinckley Gold Pine Inn. Across the street from Hinckley Grand Casino, this two-building hostelry has some deluxe ways to blow your winnings. Check out the hot tub, Jacuzzi, and queen suites. Other rooms have two double beds. Complimentary Continental breakfast. In-room data ports, some microwaves, some refrigerators, some in-room hot tubs. Cable TV. Indoor pool. Hot tub. Exercise equipment. Video games. Laundry facilities. Business services. | 111 Lady Luck Dr. | 320/384–6112 or 800/468–3517 | fax 320/384–7610 | 154 rooms, 16 suites | $95–$105 rooms, $109–$164 suites | AE, D, DC, MC, V.

Holiday Inn Express. Built in 1994, this 2-story property is 1 mi from the casino, off I–35, exit 183, behind Tobie's restaurant. Complimentary Continental breakfast. Cable TV. Indoor pool. Hot tub, sauna. Some pets allowed ($10). | 604 Weber Ave. | 320/384–7171 | fax 320/384–7735 | 101 rooms | $69–$129 | AE, D, DC, MC, V.

Super 8. This 2-story motel is 12 mi north of Hinckley, in Finlayson, off I–35, exit 195. Complimentary Continental breakfast. Some in-room hot tubs. Cable TV. Hot tub. Game room. Laundry facilities. Business services. Some pets allowed. | 2811 Rte. 23, Finlayson | 320/245–5284 | fax 320/245–2233 | 30 rooms | $45–$57 | AE, D, DC, MC, V.

Waldheim Resort. Lodgings here are cedar cabins surrounded by pine trees, right on Big Pine Lake, 20 mi northwest of town. Each cabin has its own theme based on such northwoods animals as moose and wild boars, and is filled with wildlife pictures; floors are hardwood and furniture is made of logs. Tent and RV sites are also available. Kitchenettes. Lake. Beach, boating. Playground. Pets allowed (fee). | 906 Waldheim La. | 320/233–7405. no fax | www.waldheimresort.com | 12 cabins | $110–$145 | No credit cards.

HUTCHINSON

MAP 3, D8

(Nearby towns also listed: Litchfield, New Ulm, Willmar)

The Dakota roamed the area around Hutchinson for centuries before the first pioneers arrived in the 1850s. Since then, Hutchinson has grown to a city of more than 12,000 people. Reminders of the Dakota still remain, though: the Crow River, which flows through town, is named after Dakota Chief Little Crow and the statue near the Main Street dam was created in his honor.

Information: **Hutchinson Area Chamber of Commerce** | 206 Main St. N, Hutchinson, 55350 | 800/572–6689 | www.hutchtel.net/~hchamber.

Attractions

Crow River Art Center. Exhibits change monthly, showcasing local artworks of various media and styles. | 44 Washington Ave. | 320/587–0899 | Free | Mon.–Thurs. 9–5.

ON THE CALENDAR
SEPT.: *Arts and Crafts Fair/Taste of Hutchinson.* Over 200 crafters gather here to show quilts, clothing, knitted goods, Christmas ornaments, woodwork, and many other unique items. Also some 20 area food vendors bring delicious eatables to the fair, at Library Square Park in town, on a Friday and Saturday in mid-September. | 320/587–5252 or 800/572–6689.

Dining
McCormick's Family Restaurant. American. Great homemade soups and baked goods are the thing here, along with hearty burgers, ribs, and steak dinners. There are booths in the smoking section and tables elsewhere, and images of Ireland and novelty items from the country embellish the walls. | 1102 Rte. 15 | 320/587–4417 | Breakfast also available | $6–$11 | AE, D, MC, V.

Lodging
Best Western Victorian Inn. This 2-story Victorian-style hotel downtown, built in the 1990s, has an entrance to a state recreational trail right in its backyard. Restaurant, bar, complimentary Continental breakfast. No-smoking rooms, in-room hot tubs. Cable TV. Indoor pool. Playground. Business services. | 1000 Rte. 7W | 320/587–6030 or 800/369–0145 | fax 320/587–6030 | 52 rooms | $56–$92 | AE, D, DC, MC, V.

Glencoe Castle Bed and Breakfast. This Queen Anne fieldstone home, 14 mi southeast of town, was built to woo a young woman into marriage (it worked). The three-story house, today a B&B, has unique parquet floors and stained-glass windows, as well as a fireplace, a parlor, and many interesting rooms. Complimentary breakfast. Some in-room hot tubs. TV in common area. Some pets allowed. | 831 13th St. E | 320/864–3043 or 800/517–3334. no fax | www.glencoecastle.com | 3 rooms (2 with shared bath) | $70–$175 | AE, D, MC, V.

INTERNATIONAL FALLS

MAP 3, E2

(Nearby towns also listed: Baudette, Crane Lake, Voyageurs National Park)

Residents with a sense of humor like to call their city, which is right on the Canadian border, the "icebox of the nation." But International Falls, a city of 10,000, has turned its frigid weather into a winter wonderland. At Voyageurs National Park, Rainy Lake, and other sites, you can fish, boat, ski, hike, snowmobile, or gaze at the spectacular scenery. Fishing and hiking remain a draw through the warm weather.

Information: International Falls Convention and Visitors Bureau | 301 2nd Ave., International Falls, 56449 | 218/283–9400 or 800/325–5766 | www.rainylake.org.

INTERNATIONAL
FALLS

INTRO
ATTRACTIONS
DINING
LODGING

Attractions

Boise Cascade Paper Mill. Here, you can take a look at what the company calls the largest, fastest papermaking machine in the world. | 400 2nd St. | 218/285–5511 | Free | June–Aug., Mon.–Fri. 9–5.

Grand Mound Interpretive Center. This unexcavated site is the largest prehistoric burial mound in Minnesota. It's attributed to the Laurel Indians, who lived in the area from 200 BC to AD 800. A visitors' center tells their story. The mound is 17 mi west of International Falls, on the Rainy River. | Rte. 11 | 218/285–3332 | $2 | May–Aug., Mon.–Fri. 10–5, Sun. noon–5; Sept.–Oct., Sat. 10–5, Sun. noon–5; Nov.–Apr., by appointment.

International Falls City Beach. The sandy beach makes this a convenient city feature if you like to swim. It's actually in the village of Rainier, 2 mi from International Falls. | Old Hwy. 11 in Rainier | Free | Memorial Day–Labor Day, daily 9–9.

Rainy Lake. This scenic lake, along the U.S.–Canada border, includes 985 mi of shoreline and hundreds of mostly uninhabited islands. | Off Rte. 11E | 800/325–5766 | Free | Daily.

Smokey Bear Park. A giant statue of the famous firefighting bear and a 22-ft-tall thermometer dominate this downtown civic park, across from the town square. The landscaped area includes a band shell from 1940, two museums, and public picnic tables. | 214 6th Ave. | 800/325–5766 | Free | Daily.
The Smokey Bear Park's **Koochiching County Historical Museum** features exhibits of Indian, gold-rush, logging, homesteading, and farming artifacts. | 214 6th Ave. | 218/283–4316 | $2 for this and Bronco Nagurski Museum | May–Sept., daily 10–4.
Learn almost everything there is to know about the National Football League legend who came from International Falls at the **Bronko Nagurski Museum** in the Smokey Bear Park. | 214 6th Ave. | 218/283–4316 | $2 for this and Koochiching County Historical Museum | May–Sept., daily 10–4.

ON THE CALENDAR

JAN.: *Annual Icebox Days.* The "Freeze Yer Gizzard" Blizzard Run, a 6²/₁₀-mi foot race, and turkey bowling, in which people go bowling in the streets with frozen turkeys, are two of the many weekend events held throughout International Falls. | 218/283–9400 or 800/325–5766.

Dining

Falls Country Club. American. There are an 18-hole golf course, putting and chipping greens, and a driving range here, as well as a pro shop and a grill serving light fare. It's a mile west of town, off Hwy 71. | Golf Course Rd. | 218/283–4491 | www.fallscc.com.

Giovanni's Pizza. American. The seven or eight specialty pizzas here include taco, cheeseburger, and vegetarian pizzas, as well as a slim jim pizza with canadian bacon, ham, extra cheese, and fresh tomatoes on top. You can also get burgers, chicken, pastas, and Italian ices. An arcade game room is on the premises. | 1225 3rd St. | 218/283–2600 | $6–$15 | MC, V.

International Skillet. Eclectic. Sit in traditional diner-style booths or at the counter in this casual eatery. The taco-potato skillet comes to the table right in the pan. You might also try the oriental chicken stir-fry, or the locomotive, a whopping 1-lb burger. | 2515 22nd St. | 218/283–9494 | Open 24 hours | $5–$8 | AE, MC, V.

Panorama Dining Room. American. Part of the the Thunderbird Lodge, about 10 mi east of town on Rainy Lake, this restaurant serves steaks, burgers, pastas, and salads. | 2170 County Rd. 139 | 218/286–3151 | Breakfast also available in summer | $12.95–$18.95 | AE, D, MC, V.

Riverfront Dining Room. American. This restaurant in the Holiday Inn, about 1½ mi west of town, has views of the Rainy River and of the hotel's gardens. Specials include local walleye, breaded and deep-fried, or broiled with wine and herbs, as well as shrimp, chicken, New York strip steak, and pork chops. In summer you can also sit outside. | 1500 Rte. 71 | 218/283–8000 | fax 218/283– 3774 | Closed Sun. | $8.95–$17.95 | AE, D, MC, V.

© Corbis

THE ICEBOX

Chances are you've seen at least a few television weather reports in which the meteorologist points to a place high on the map and informs you that the lowest temperature recorded in the continental U.S. that day was in International Falls, Minnesota. Chuckle, chuckle. Twenty-two degrees below zero. Can you believe that? Bet you're glad you don't live there, eh?

You might think the people of International Falls would cringe at all that bad publicity.

No way.

International Falls revels in its reputation as a cold spot. The people there happily call their city "the nation's icebox." The annual Icebox Days festival in January features such popular events as frozen turkey bowling and the Freeze Yer Gizzard Blizzard Run. The town's 22-ft-tall thermometer is no longer the world's largest (the one in Baker, California, now holds bragging rights), but it remains a staple of morning TV talk shows and weathercasts. International Falls was also the inspiration for Frostbite Falls, the fictional hometown of the cartoon characters Rocky and Bullwinkle. Fans of the cartoon will remember that Bullwinkle was governor of Moosylvania, a small island in Lake of the Woods. At one point, Rocky and Bullwinkle's creator, Jay Ward, actually bought a real island on the lake and dubbed it Moosylvania. His campaign to gain statehood for his island failed miserably.

Rose Garden Restaurant. Chinese. On the menu here are several soups, sweet or savory pork, beef, or chicken served with rice, bean curd, and mixed vegetables, and a few noodle dishes. The dining area is light and cheerful. | 311 Fourth Ave. | 218/283–4551 | $4–$8 | D, MC, V.

Spot Firehouse. American. Almost everything related to firefighting, including fire trucks and horse carts, is on display at this 65-year-old, family-owned restaurant. Menu favorites are prime ribs, steak, lobster, and the "Grandpa Chinks" barbecued ribs, made with the secret-ingredient sauce invented by the original owner. Kids' menu. | 1801 2nd Ave. W | 218/283–2440 | Closed Sun. No lunch | $8–$20 | AE, D, DC, MC, V.

Thunderbird. American. Specialties at this formal spot in the Thunderbird Resort, 10 mi east of International Falls, include prime rib and filet mignon, accompanied by an extensive wine list. | 2170 County Rd. 139, International Falls | 800/351–5133 or 218/286–3151 | No lunch | $11–$16 | AE, D, MC, V.

Lodging

Budget Host Inn. Wood-paneled rooms have twin, double, queen-, and king-size beds. You can park at your door at this motel, which is in town, next door to restaurants and a movie theater. Picnic area. Cable TV. Playground. Pets allowed. | 10 Riverview Blvd. | 218/283–2577 | fax 218/285–3688 or 800/880–2577 | www.budgethost.com | 31 rooms | $41–$69 | AE, D, MC, V.

Days Inn. The gateway to Voyageurs National Park adjoins this two-story wood-and-cinderblock building 15 mi from the Canadian border. Complimentary Continental breakfast. Cable TV. Hot tub. Exercise equipment. Business services. Some pets allowed. | 2331 U.S. 53S | 218/283–9441 | fax 218/283–9441 | 58 rooms | $46–$70 | AE, D, DC, MC, V.

Holiday Inn. This log-sided hotel is next to the Rainy River. Restaurant, bar, room service. Some refrigerators, in-room data ports. Cable TV. Indoor pool, wading pool. Hot tub, sauna. Laundry facilities. Business services, airport shuttle. Some pets allowed. | 1500 U.S. 71 | 218/283–4451 | fax 218/283–3774 | 126 rooms, 12 suites | $74–$114, $85–$149 suites | AE, D, DC, MC, V.

Island View Lodge and Motel. Established in 1908, this two-story cedar lodge and cabins have a private beach on Rainy Lake. It's 12 mi east of International Falls, on Rte. 11. Restaurant, bar, picnic area. No air-conditioning in cottages, some kitchenettes. No TV in cottages. Beach, dock, boating. Snowmobiling on the lake. Airport shuttle. Some pets allowed. | 1817 Rte. 11E | 218/286–3511 or 800/777–7856 | iview@rainy-lake.com | www.rainy-lake.com | 9 rooms, 12 cabins | $85–$149 cottages, $65–$70 rooms in lodge | D, MC, V.

Islandview Bed and Breakfast. Directly on Rainy Lake, about 10 mi east of town, this home has guest rooms with lake views; each has a private entrance and a deck. Two common sitting rooms have fireplaces. Dining room, complimentary breakfast. Lake. Dock, boating. No pets. | 2160 County Rd. 139 | 218/286–3085 | davisele@northwinds.net | www.bedand-breakfast.com | 3 rooms (1 with shared bath) | $85 | No credit cards.

Kettle Falls Hotel. Accessible only by air or water, the hotel was built in 1910 by lumber baron Ed Rose, and rumored to have been financed by Madame Nellie Bly. Now on the National Register of Historic Places, the hotel has a main lodge building with three bathrooms serving 12 guest rooms, and a separate "villa" with 3 self-contained suites. The site is inside Voyageur National Park, on Kabetogama Lake, with a shuttle from the boat docks. Restaurant, bar. Fishing. | 10502 Gamma Rd., Lake Kabetogama | 218/374–4404 or 888/534–6835 (mid–May–Sept.); 218/875–2070 (Oct.–mid–May) | kfh@uslink.net | www.kettlefallshotel.com | 12 rooms, 3 suites | $65 rooms, $140–250 suites | Closed Oct. 1–mid-May | D, MC, V.

Northernaire Floating Lodges. Captain your own houseboat on Voyageur National Park's Rainy Lake. All "boatel houseboat" rentals include sunroofs, walkaround decks, and interiors with linens on the dining table and beds. Each boatel comes with a fishing boat. No air-conditioning. Kitchenettes. Water sports. Some pets allowed. | 2690 Rte. 94 | 218/286–

INTERNATIONAL
FALLS

INTRO
ATTRACTIONS
DINING
LODGING

5221, 800/854–7958 | nhb@northernairehouseboats.com | www.northernairehouse-boats.com | 15 power-driven floating lodges on pontoon boats | $795–$2,100 (7–day stay) | Closed mid-Oct.–mid-May | MC, V.

Super 8. This motel is five mi from town, one mi north of the airport. In-room data ports. Some microwaves, refrigerators. Cable TV. Hot tub. Laundry facilities. Business services. | 2326 U.S. 53S | 218/283–8811 | fax 218/283–8880 | 53 rooms, 7 suites | $42–$50, $49–$69 suites | AE, D, DC, MC, V.

Thunderbird Lodge. On the western edge of Voyageurs National Park, 10 mi east of International Falls, this resort has views of Rainy Lake and its many islands. A large marina is surrounded by evergreens, and cabins have private decks and two or three bedrooms with twin, double, or queen-size beds. Restaurant, bar. Cable TV. Boating. | 2170 County Rd. 139 | 800/351–5133 or 218/286–3151 | fax 218/286–3004 | tbird@northwinds.net | www.voyageurs-park.com/ | 15 rooms, 10 cabins | $59–$94, $125–$185 cabins | AE, D, MC, V.

JACKSON

MAP 3, C10

(Nearby town also listed: Fairmont)

Jackson lies in the Des Moines River valley, near the Iowa border. You can get a glimpse of history in its downtown business district, which includes many buildings listed on the National Register of Historic Places. Today, Jackson is an agricultural community and a manufacturing site for food products and industrial farm equipment.

Information: **Jackson County Tourism** | 405 4th St., Jackson, 56143 | 507/847–3867 | www.jacksonmn.com.

Attractions

Fort Belmont. Built in 1864, Belmont was one of the first forts in Minnesota. On-site are a log chapel, sod house, and flour mill, as well as a collection of antique cars. Off I–90; re-opening summer 2001. | 507/847–5840 | Free | Memorial Day–Labor Day, daily.

Jackson County Historical Society and Museum. Displays of local history, from the pioneer days to the 1950s, rotate periodically, and include items of interest from homes and families, businesses, and the army. You can do genealogical research here and pick up a free driving-tour guide of the area. | 307 Rte. 86N | 507/662–5505 | Free | May–Aug., weekdays 10–12 and 1–4, closed weekends; Sept.–Apr., Tues., Thurs. 10–12 and 1–4, closed Weds., Fri.–Mon.

Kilen Woods State Park. You can hike the woodland trail meandering along the Des Moines River, or enjoy the view from Dinosaur Ridge Overlook. The park is 9 mi southwest of Lakefield. | Rte. 24 | 507/662–6258 | www.dnr.state.mn.us/parks_and_recreation/state_parks/kilenwoods | Park permit required | Daily.

Monument to Slain Settlers. Commemorating the 1857 attack by Sioux Indians on the area's pioneer settlers, this monument is in Kilen Woods State Park. | Rte. 24 | 507/847–4235 | Free | Daily.

ON THE CALENDAR

JULY: *Jackson County Fair.* The regular attractions here include livestock exhibitions, rides, and live entertainment. | 507/847–3867.

DEC.: *Holiday Fest.* On the first Saturday of the month, the town turns out for cookies and cider, a movie, horse and wagon rides, and kids' bingo; it all winds up with a spectacular lighted parade. | 507/847–3867.

Dining

Long Horn Cafe. American. Three blocks south of Main Street, this popular breakfast spot has a morning menu of homemade biscuits and gravy, sausage, pancakes, and other favorites. Dinners include burgers as well as soup-and-sandwich specials. The horns on the walls carry out the Western motif. | 415 Rte. 71S | 507/847–5188 | Breakfast also available | $5 | No credit cards.

Lodging

Best Western Country Manor Inn. Off I–90, exit 73, this facility is about 1 mi north of downtown. Restaurant, bar. In-room data ports. Cable TV. Indoor pool, wading pool. Hot tub, sauna. Business services. | 2007 U.S. 71N | 507/847–3110 | fax 507/847–3110 | www.network1000.com/bwjackson | 42 rooms | $40–$62 | AE, D, DC, MC, V.

Budget Host Prairie Winds. This single-story brick building, constructed in 1949, is about ½ mile from I–90, exit 73. In-room data ports. Cable TV. | 950 U.S. 71N | 507/847–2020 | fax 507/847–2022 | 24 rooms | $31–$54 | AE, D, DC, MC, V.

Park-Vu Motel. Rooms have twin, double, and queen-size beds in this in-town motel. A picnic area and park are next door. Cable TV. Pets allowed. | 101 Third St. | 507/847–3440 | 18 rooms | $24–$47 | MC, V.

Super 8 Motel. Rooms have twin, double, and queen-size beds at this motel, which is 1½ mi north of town, off I–90, exit 73. Some refrigerators, some in-room hot tubs. | 2025 Rte. 71N | 507/847–3498 | fax 507/847–5881 | www.super8.com | 42 rooms, 7 suites | $59–$64 | AE, D, DC, MC, V.

LAKE CITY

MAP 3, F9

(Nearby towns also listed: Lakeville, Minneapolis, Northfield, Red Wing, St. Paul, Wabasha)

Situated on 22-mi-long Lake Pepin (actually the widest spot on the Mississippi River, and not a lake at all), Lake City is the birthplace of water skiing; the sport was invented here in 1922 when 18-year-old Ralph Samuelson experimented with two pine boards, replicas of which are displayed in the Chamber of Commerce offices. Outdoor recreation remains a large part of the city's culture: the marina has 600 boat slips; area parks totalling more than 250 acres provide warm-weather fishing, boating, or swimming, and cold-weather ice-skating or ice fishing; and 500 mi of groomed snowmobile trails, as well as 40 mi of cross-country ski trails, attract enthusiasts from all over southeastern Minnesota.

Information: Lake City Tourism Bureau | 220 S. Washington St., Lake City, 55041 | 877/525–3249 | www.lakecity.org | tourism@lakecity.org.

Attractions

Hok-Si-La Municipal Park. Part of a major migratory flyway, these 160 acres (by far the city's largest park grounds) are among southeastern Minnesota's best bird-watching spots, particularly in early spring and late fall. You can spot bald eagles, tundra swans, Canada geese, and Iceland gulls. Besides nature trails and a playground, the park has campsites, picnic areas, and a swimming beach. Most of the city's 500 mi of snowmobile trails, and all 40 mi of its ski trails, are part of this park. It's ½ mi northeast of downtown. | Rte. 61 | 877/525–3249 | www.lakecity.org | Free | Year-round.

McCahill Park. Standing alongside the boat harbor, the park has playground equipment where the kids can play while the adults fish from the pier. | Rte. 61, 3 blocks south of Rte. 63 | 877/525–3249 | www.lakecity.org | Free | Year-round.

Ohuta Park. Playground facilities, picnic areas, and a swimming beach are all directly on the lakefront. | Lyon Ave., 3 blocks east of Rte. 61 | 877/525–3249 | www.lakecity.org | Free | Year-round.

Patton Park. One square block in size, the park has a central fountain, a quaint gazebo, and paved walking paths. | Rte. 61, 1 block south of Rte. 63 | 877/525–3249 | www.lakecity.org | Free | Year-round.

Roshen Park. Besides picnic areas for large and small groups, this park at the south end of town has tennis courts, playground equipment, and fine lake views. | Rte. 61, south end of town | 877/525–3249 | www.lakecity.org | Free | Year-round.

ON THE CALENDAR

OCT.: *Johnny Appleseed Days.* During the first full weekend in October, Pepin Heights Orchards (the Midwest's largest apple grower) sponsors events including an arts and crafts fair, an apple pie sale and social, a farmers' market, and more. | 877/525–3249.

JUNE: *Water Ski Days.* To celebrate the locally invented sport, Lake City devotes the first weekend of the month to partying. Ralph Samuelson's original 2-ft by 12-ft pine board water skis are on display, and there's an arts and crafts fair, antique auto show, carnival, and beer tent, as well as nightly entertainment, an evening Venetian boat parade, and a Sunday parade with local floats, all at the Marina. | 800/369–4123 or 651/345–4123.

Dining

The Galley. American. Burgers and sandwiches are the mainstays at this family-style restaurant, which also serves breakfast. | 110 Lyon Ave. | 651/345–9991 | $5–$10 | AE, D, MC, V.

Rouletti's. American. The pizza here has won several regional awards. Other favorites are ribs and chicken. | 214 S. Lakeshore Dr. | 651/345–5333 | $7–$15 | AE, D, MC, V.

Waterman's. American. The menu here emphasizes the freshest possible ingredients, from meat to produce; locals favor the filet mignon and Porterhouse steak. Dining room windows face Lake Pepin and the surrounding bluffs. | 1702 N. Lakeshore Dr. | 651/345–5353 | Reservations suggested | $7–$20 | AE, D, DC, MC, V.

Lodging

AmericInn Motel. Many rooms here overlook Lake Pepin. A few hot-tub suites and mini-suites have private decks. Continental breakfast. Some in-room hot tubs. Indoor pool. Sauna. | 1615 N. Lakeshore Dr. | 800/634–3444 or 651/345–5611 | www.AmericInn.com | 48 rooms | $47–$132 | AE, D, MC, V.

Lake City Country Inn. Some rooms here have kitchenettes, fireplaces, or hot tubs, and all have views of Lake Pepin. Some kitchenettes. Some in-room hot tubs. Cable TV. Outdoor pool. Hot tub, sauna. | 1401 N. Lakeshore Dr. | 651/345–5351 | 21 rooms | $50–$129 | AE, D, MC, V.

The Willows. You can rent one- and two-bedroom units, fully furnished and equipped, at this resort complex. Weekly and monthly rates are available, as are golf packages. Restaurant, room service. Indoor pool. Exercise room. Dock, boating. | 100 Central Point Rd. | 651/345–9900 | www.watermansresort.com | 33 units | $159–$259 | AE, D, MC, V.

LAKEVILLE

MAP 3, E8

(Nearby towns also listed: Bloomington, Hastings, Lake City, Minneapolis, Northfield, Red Wing, St. Paul, Shakopee)

Linking the corn belt and the Twin Cities, Lakeville stands on the southern fringes of the Minneapolis metro area. Incorporated in 1967, the town has grown from a small community to a busy suburb of 36,000 residents.

Information: Lakeville Area Convention and Visitors Bureau | 20730 Holyoke Ave., Lakeville, 55044 | 612/469–2020 or 888/525–3845 | www.lakevillechambercvb.org.

Attractions

Antlers Park. This 12-acre park, 2 mi east of town, has a swimming beach on Lake Marion, a picnic area, a playground, and baseball diamonds. | 9740 201st St. W | 952/985–4600 | www.cilakeville.mn.us | Free.

ON THE CALENDAR

JULY: *Pan-O-Prog.* The Panorama of Progress involves more than a week of activities and special events, including races, picnics, pet shows, dances, a scholarship pageant, a cruise night, fireworks, and a parade. | 888/525–3845.

Dining

Chart House Restaurant. Contemporary. With its peculiar shiplike shape, this local landmark, 4 mi west of town, is unmistakeable. Inside, portholes punctuate weathered-looking blue walls, looking into fish tanks; tables are piled high with broiled and deep-fried walleye, halibut, swordfish, prime rib, steak, and chicken. Kids' menu. | 11287 Klamath Tr. | 612/435–7156 | $14–$25 | AE, D, DC, MC, V.

Lodging

Comfort Inn Lakeville. Some rooms at this hotel, 5 mi west of town, overlook a pond. Complimentary Continental breakfast. In-room dataports, microwaves, refrigerators. Cable TV. Indoor pool. Hot tub. Some pets allowed. | 10935 176th St. W | 952/898–3700 | fax 952/898–3827 | 56 rooms, 3 suites | $69.90–$89.90 | AE, D, DC, MC, V.

Friendly Host Lakeville. Some rooms at this two-story hostelry have balconies. The motel is 2 mi south of town, on the interstate frontage road near exit 85, off of I–35. Cable TV. Indoor pool. Hot tub. Game room. | 17296 I–35 | 612/435–7191 800/341–8000 | fax 612/435–6220 | imalodging.com/Lodges/W059.htm | 48 rooms | $35–$70 | AE, D, DC, MC, V.

Motel 6. Fast food places are next door to this two-story brick building 4 mi from town. | 11274 210th St. | 612/469–1900 | fax 612/469–5359 | 84 rooms | $30–$42 | AE, D, DC, MC, V.

LANESBORO

MAP 3, G10

(Nearby town also listed: Preston)

Lying in the deep Root River valley, in an area settled by Norwegian and Irish immigrants (and later by German pioneers), Lanesboro was established in 1868. The downtown area is listed on the National Register of Historic Places, and you can still detect immigrant influences in local food and conversation. The Root River State Trail winds through the center of town.

Information: Lanesboro Area Chamber of Commerce | Box 348, Lanesboro, 55949 | 800/944–2670 or 507/467–2696 | www.lanesboro.com.

Attractions

The Commonweal Theatre Company. Theater productions rotate February through December, and a live radio show broadcasts Sunday evenings from May through September. | 206 Parkway Ave. N | 507/467–2525 or 800/657–7025 | www.commonwealtheatre.org | Feb.–Dec.

The Cornucopia Art Center. Dedicated to arts education in southeastern Minnesota, this not-for-profit organization sponsors workshops, in-school programs, and six new gallery exhibits per year, highlighting the work of local artists. | 103 Parkway Ave. S | 507/467–2446 | Free | Year-round.

Root River State Trail. Around 1860, the Southern Minnesota Railway Company cut a right-of-way through the bluffs of southeastern Minnesota, and it is now one of the most popular recreational trails in America. The Root River State Trail System has more than 60 mi of paved surface bounded on the west by the city of Fountain, on the south by Harmony, and on the east by Houston, with Lanesboro forming the hub. Each year, thousands of cyclists, roller-bladers, and hikers experience the Root River valley via these meandering byways. The Minnesota Department of Natural Resources owns and maintains the trail, charging no use fees except for wintertime cross-country skiing. | Central Lanesboro | 800/944–2670 or 507/467–2696 | Free | Year-round.

ON THE CALENDAR
AUG.: *Buffalo Bill Days.* Volleyball, softball, a flea market, a parade, and nightly dances are all part of this annual festival, held in the city park. | 800/944–2670.
JUNE: *Art in Park.* Local and regional artists display their creations in the city park every Father's Day. | 800/944–2670.
OCT.: *Oktoberfest.* Polka music and ethnic food are part of this German heritage celebration. | 800/944–2670.

Dining
Das Wurst House. German. Live polka music, plus handmade German-style sauerkraut, sausages, mustards, and breads make for a real Old World dining experience. | 117 Parkway Ave. N | 507/467–2902 | $12–$18 | MC, V.

Mrs. B's Historic Lanesboro Inn. American. Creative five-course meals are served in an 1872 limestone building downtown. No preservatives are used, and the innkeepers grow their own produce. There's one dinner seating nightly with a single fixed menu. | 101 Parkway Ave. | 507/467–2154 or 800/657–4710 | Wed.–Sun. 7 PM | $26.

Old Village Hall. American. In nice weather, you can dine outside on a deck overlooking the Root River Trail. On the menu of this restaurant and pub are steak, lamb, veal, seafood, and pastas, as well as vegetarian dishes. | 111 Coffee St. | 507/467–2962 | $19–$23 | D, MC, V.

Lodging
Berwood Hill Inn. Overlooking the river valley, this 200-acre Victorian country estate has extensive gardens and, inside, period-furnished rooms, claw-foot tubs, and fireplaces. Four mi south of Lanesboro off Highway 16, the inn is adjacent to paved bike trails. Banquet facilities are available. Complimentary breakfast. Spa. No pets. No kids under 12. | off MN-16 | 800/803–6748 | www.berwood.com | 5 rooms | $155–$200 | MC, V.

Green Gables Inn. On the west end of town, the inn's facilities include four connecting suites which are ideal for large family groups. All rooms have queen-size beds and private baths. Cable TV. No smoking. No pets. | 303 Sheridan Ave. W | 507/467–2936 or 800/818–4225 | 13 rooms | $49–$79 | D, MC, V.

Historic Scanlan House B&B. Six blocks from the Root River Trail, this 1889 Queen Anne has all its original woodwork and stained glass. Each room has a private bath; some have fireplaces and whirlpools. Complimentary breakfast. Some hot tubs. | 708 Parkway Ave. S | 507/467–2158 or 800/944–2158 | www.scanlonhouse.com | 5 rooms | $70–$135 | AE, D, MC, V.

LE SUEUR

MAP 3, D9

(Nearby towns also listed: Faribault, Mankato, New Prague, St. Peter)

This Minnesota River town, one of the state's oldest, began life as a stopping place for riverboats. Later, it achieved fame of a sort when Le Sueur brand vegetables launched an advertising campaign featuring the Jolly Green Giant. Founded in 1903 as the Minnesota Valley Canning Company, Le Sueur still maintains an agricultural research center here.

Information: **Le Sueur Area Chamber of Commerce** | 213 Main St., Suite 106, Le Sueur, 56058 | 507/665–2501 | fax 507/665–4322 | chamber@prairie.lakes.com | home.le-sueur.mn.us.

Attractions

Mayo Park Arboretum. There are flowers, shrubs, and rose gardens at this site on the north edge of town, as well as a playground and picnic shelters. | Rte. 169 and Rte. 112 | 507/665–2501 | Free | Daily.

W. W. Mayo House. Costumed guides here take you on a tour of the 1859 home in which its builder, Dr. William Warrall Mayo, who founded Rochester's world-famous Mayo Clinic, first practiced frontier medicine. | 118 N. Main St. | 507/665–3250 | www.state.mn.us/ebranch/mhs/places/sites/wwmh | Memorial Day–Labor Day, Tues.–Sun. 1–4:30; Sept.–Oct., Sat.–Sun. 1–4:30.

ON THE CALENDAR
AUG.: *Giant Celebration.* The land of the Jolly Green Giant celebrates agriculture with a parade, a queen's coronation, a corn feed, food, games, and live entertainment in Legion Park, downtown. | 507/665–2501.

Dining

Welcome Inn Restaurant. American. A down-home place in the center of town, this eatery has a menu full of burgers, pizza, steaks, chicken, and fish. Don't pass up the homemade pies, made fresh daily, or the turnovers and cookies. | 205 S. Main St. | 507/665–6929 | $7–$10 | No credit cards.

Lodging

Beaver Dam Resort. These cabins stand 40 ft from the waters of Jefferson and German Lakes, 9 mi of town. Each has between one and four bedrooms, with double beds. Lake. Beach, boating, fishing. Some pets allowed. | County Rd. 13 | 507/931–5650 | 12 cabins | $70–$132 | Closed Oct.–Apr. | D, MC, V.

Downtown Motel. The only motel downtown, this facility is part of a complex that also includes offices, a deli, a hospital clinic, and a bowling alley. Restaurant, bar. Kitchenettes, no-smoking rooms. Cable TV. Some pets allowed. | 510 N. Main St. | 507/665–6246 | fax 507/665–6246 | 39 rooms | $32–$41 | AE, D, DC, MC, V.

LITCHFIELD

MAP 3, D7

(Nearby towns also listed: Hutchinson, Willmar)

Corn fields, as well as Meeker County's 200 mi of winter snowmobile trails, surround Litchfield, a rural community 65 mi west of Minneapolis. On the southwest side of town, Lake Ripley provides both summer and winter entertainment, with swimming beaches and picnic areas, a public arboretum on the northeastern shore, and a good supply of northern pike for warm- and cold-weather anglers. One of Minnesota's most popular health spas is also here.

Information: **Litchfield Chamber of Commerce** | Box 820, Litchfield, 55355 | 320/693–8184 | litch@litch.com | www.litch.com.

Attractions

Ball of Twine. A glassed-in gazebo in Darwin, 6 mi east of Litchfield, holds the *Guinness Book of World Records'* top honors as the "The Largest Ball of Twine Created by One Individual." | Free | Daily.

Meeker County Historical Society Museum and GAR Museum. Photo displays and memorabilia document the history of Meeker County. | 308 N. Marshall Ave. | 320/693–8911 | www.litch.com/attract.htm | $2 | Tues.–Sun. 12–4, or by appointment.

Built by Union soldiers for use as a garrison, the 1885 **Grand Army of the Republic Hall** is the state's only Civil War museum. The towering, fortress-like building contains period artifacts including an original Civil War cannon. | 308 N. Marshall Ave. | 320/693–8911 | www.litch.com/attract.htm | Free with historical society admission | Tues.–Sun. 12–4.

ON THE CALENDAR
JULY: *Litchfield Watercade*. Starting on the first weekend after the Fourth and continuing for a week, the town enjoys fireworks, a flea market, a waterski show on Lake Ripley, a parade, a queen coronation, and art in the park. | 320/693–8184.

Dining

Swan's Cafe. American. This is a diner-style place, ½ mi east of town, with booths, tables, and pictures of swans on the walls. For breakfast go for hash browns, pancakes, and egg dishes; burgers and chicken sandwich platters are served the rest of the day. Fresh homemade pies are a bonus. | 1015 E. Frontage Rd. | 320/693–3279 | Breakfast also available | $5.50–$6.95 | D, MC, V.

Lodging

Birdwing Spa. Rejuvenation is the goal of this 300-acre spa 8 mi southwest of town. Star Lake is on the premises, with 2½ mi of shoreline, and there are 15 mi of hiking trails. A one-night stay includes three healthful meals; spa services such as massages, facials, and makeovers; guided fitness walks; and outdoor activities. Rooms are romantic, with fireplaces, Georgia pine furniture, gingham bedding, and tile and wood floors. Dining room, complimentary breakfast. Some in-room hot tubs. Lake. Beauty salon, hot tub, massage, sauna, spa. Exercise equipment, hiking. Boating, bicycles. Cross-country skiing. No pets. | 21398 575th Ave. | 320/693–6064 | birdwing@hutchtel.net | www.birdwingspa.com | 14 rooms | $250–$374 | MC, V.

Lake Ripley Resort. Lake Ripley is directly across the street from this 1-story motel. Cable TV. | 1205 S. Sibley Ave. | 320/693–3227 | 17 rooms | $23–$37 | AE, D, MC, V.

Scotwood. This 1-story motel is on the east edge of town near a mall. Complimentary Continental breakfast. Indoor pool. Cable TV. Some pets allowed. | 1017 E. Frontage Rd. | 320/693–2496 or 800/225–5489 | 35 rooms | $45–$100 | AE, D, DC, MC, V.

LITTLE FALLS

MAP 3, D6

(Nearby towns also listed: Brainerd, Onamia, St. Cloud)

Situated in the geographic middle of Minnesota, Little Falls was named after a tempestuous Mississippi River waterfall which for centuries was a gathering place for Native Americans. Fur traders and explorers made note of the falls in their journals, and in the 1840s white settlers began to arrive. After an electricity-generating dam was built over the falls in 1887, the area experienced an economic boom, with lumber operations springing up all over. Although the falls no longer exist in their natural state, the water does continue to rush down from chutes in the dam, creating a spectacle worth seeing. A promenade alongside the dam makes a good vantage point.

Information: **Little Falls Area Chamber of Commerce** | 200 1st St. NW Little Falls, 56345 | 320/632–5642 or 800/325–5916 | lfcvb@fallsnet.com | www.littlefallsmn.com.

Attractions

Charles A. Lindbergh State Park. Situated along the Mississippi River, this 340-acre park contains a Work Projects Administration (WPA) picnic shelter and a stone water tower. A visitor center near the Lindbergh homesite has maps of the area, as well as information on three generations of the Lindbergh family. | 1200 Lindbergh Dr. S | 320/632–9050 | www.dnr.state.mn.us/parks_and_recreation/state_parks/charles_a_lindberg | Park permit required | Daily.

The famous aviator spent boyhood summers in what is now the **Charles A. Lindbergh House,** a 1906 farmhouse that still contains many of his original furnishings and family possessions. Also on the property are the original ice house and tenant farmer's house. | 1200 Lindbergh Dr. S | 320/632–3154 | www.state.mn.us/ebranch/mhs/places/sites/lh | Free | May–Labor Day, Mon.–Sat. 10–5, Sun., noon–5; Labor Day–Oct., Sat. 10–4, Sun. noon–4.

Charles A. Weyerhaeuser Memorial Museum. This building, 2 mi south of downtown, houses the county historical society. Displays contain artifacts and clothing from the 1800s. | 2151 South Lindbergh Dr. S | 320/632–4007 | Free | Mid-Oct.–Memorial Day, Tues.–Sat. 10–5; May–Oct., Sun. 1–5.

Minnesota Military Museum. At this former regimental headquarters, you can learn about Minnesota's military contributions from frontier days to the present. | 15000 Rte. 115 | 320/632–7374 | Free | June–Aug., Wed.–Sun. 10–5; Sept.–June, Thurs.–Fri. 9–4.

Primeval Pine Grove Municipal Park. Named for a stand of virgin pines on the grounds, the park has picnic and playground areas, and a small zoo with native animals. | 1200 W Broadway | 320/632–2341 | Free | May–Sept., daily.

ON THE CALENDAR

SEPT.: *Arts and Crafts Fair.* Nine hundred exhibitors from eight states come to town the weekend after Labor Day. This is one of the largest arts and crafts fairs in the Midwest. | 612/632–5155.

Lodging

AmericInn. Suites contain queen-size beds and sleep sofas at this motel ½ mi east of town. Standard rooms are also available. Complimentary Continental breakfast. Some microwaves, some refrigerators, some in-room hot tubs. Cable TV. Indoor pool. Hot tub. No pets. | 306 Lemieur St. | 320/632–1964 | fax 320/632–0810 | www.americinn.com | 30 rooms, 5 suites | $72–$112, $67–$79 suites | AE, D, DC, MC, V.

Pine Edge Inn. A veranda faces the Mississippi at this downtown redbrick hotel. The high-ceilinged rooms have Victorian-style wallpaper and furniture. Restaurant, bar, room service. Cable TV. Pool. Playground. Business services. Some pets allowed. | 308 1st St. SE | 320/632–6681 or 800/344–6681 | fax 320/632–4332 | janders@upstel.net | www.pineedgeinn.com | 56 rooms | $35–$95 | AE, D, DC, MC, V.

Super 8. One mi east of downtown, this 2-story highway motel is at the intersection of Highways 10 and 27. Cable TV. | 300 12th St. NE | 320/632–2351 | 51 rooms | $49–$61 | AE, D, DC, MC, V.

LUTSEN

(Nearby town also listed: Grand Marais)

Tourism is the main industry in Lutsen (pop. 185), a vacation destination on the north shore of Lake Superior. In summer outdoor enthusiasts flock to the Superior Hiking

Trail. In winter, Lutsen is the focal point for local skiers, who enjoy its many miles of cross-country trails.

Information: **Lutsen Tofte Tourism Association** | Box 2248, Tofte, 55615 | 218/663–7804 or 888/61–NORTH | www.61north.com.

Attractions

Lutsen Mountains Ski Area. You can gaze out at the wide expanse of Lake Superior as you ski down any one of 62 runs on four peaks, with vertical drops of 350–800 ft. There's plenty of lodging here, too, including ski-in, ski-out options. | Rte. 61 | 218/663–7281 | www.lutsen.com | Daily.
In summer at the Lutsen Mountains Ski Area, you can ride the chairlift to the top and streak down the **Alpine Slide,** a ½-mi track on a rider-controlled sled. | 218/663–7281 | $4.50 for single ride, $18 for all-day pass | June–mid-Oct., daily 10–5.
The **Gondola Skyride** lets you enjoy the view from the highest point on the north shore. It's a 2-mi trip from top to bottom. | 218/663–7281 | $8.75 | June–mid-Oct., daily 10–5.

Sawtooth Mountain Bike Park. Known as the mountain bike capital of the Midwest, this 1,000-acre park place has 50 mi of mapped, maintained trails, ranging from easy to difficult. You can use the lift to get to the top, then bike down the winding forest trails, or go straight down the fall line over roots, rocks, and mud, if you dare. | 465 Ski Hill Rd. | 218/663–7281 | $20–$23 lift and trail day pass, $14 trail-only day pass | June–Oct., daily 10–5; Oct., Nov., May 10–5, weekends.

ON THE CALENDAR

JUNE: *John Schroeder Days.* On the first full weekend of the month, the neighboring town of Schroeder has historic tours, kids' races, entertainment, arts and crafts vendors, and a spaghetti dinner. | 888/61–NORTH.

Dining

Cascade Lodge Restaurant. American. Enjoy views of Lake Superior in this elegantly rustic North Shore dining room, which has wagon-wheel chandeliers, a large stone fireplace, and walls hung with fish and animal trophies. Go for the blue cheese–crusted rib-eye steak, the salmon, or the pork tenderloin. It's 5 mi east of town. | 3719 W. Rte. 61 | 218/387–2911 or 800/322–9543 | Breakfast also available | $9.95–$15.95 | AE, D, DC, MC, V.

Lutsen Resort Dining Room. Contemporary. Halibut, walleye, duck breast, and pork tenderloin are on the menu of this lakeside restaurant with natural woodwork and a large stone fireplace, and the kitchen uses traditional Scandinavian recipes for some of its breads and desserts. | 5700 W. Rte. 61 | 218/663–7212 or 800/258–8736 | Breakfast also available | $16–$24 | AE, D, MC, V.

Mountaintop Deli. American. Take the Lutsen Mountain Tram to the very top and you can enjoy a hundred-mile-view at this lunch stop, at the top of Moose Mountain. Snacks and light lunches are available. | 465 Ski Hill Rd. | 218/663–7281 | No dinner | $3–$6 | No credit cards.

Naniboujou Restaurant. Contemporary. The ceiling of this restaurant in the Naniboujou Lodge is painted in Native American style, with bright colors and an intricate design, and the fireplace is enormous, one of the largest made of native stone in the state. The food here has such a reputation that the kitchen has generated its own cookbook. Go for the steaks at dinner; breakfast is also a delight. | 20 Naniboujou Tr. | 218/387–2688 | Breakfast also available | $8–$20 | D, MC, V.

Papa Charlie's Saloon and Grill. Contemporary. You can see the Moose and Mystery Mountains, the Poplar River, and Lake Superior from floor-to-ceiling windows at this restaurant 3 mi south of town. Lanterns illuminate the room in the evening. Try the sweet potato walleye dish, a light baked-fish meal, or the wild mushroom tamale. There's also steak, pasta, pizza, soups, and sandwiches. In summer you can sit on any of the three decks outdoors. | 467 Ski Hill Rd. | 218/663–7800 | $14–$19 | AE, D, MC, V.

Tracks Restaurant and Bar. Contemporary. The bear rug and trophy moose head on the walls are focal points in this northwoods-style dining room, in the Caribou Highlands Lodge. Specials include twin tenderloin filet with wild rice, and the seafood trio, a seafood dish containing bay shrimp, scallops, and crab over fettucine with cream, roasted red peppers, and pesto sauce. | 371 Ski Hill Rd. | 218/663–7316 | Breakfast also available | $10.95–$17.95 | AE, D, DC, MC, V.

Lodging

AmericInn. This 2-story cedar and stone building with a stone portico and columns was built in 1994. It's two blocks from the shore of Lake Superior; some rooms have limited lake views. Snowmobile trail access is available from parking lot. Temperance State Park is 2 mi west, Cascade River State Park is 20 mi east, and Lutsen Mountains Ski Area is 9 mi east. Picnic area, complimentary Continental breakfast. Microwaves, some refrigerators, some in-room hot tubs. Cable TV. Indoor pool. Hot tub, sauna. Business services. Some pets allowed. | 7261 W. Hwy. 61, Tofte | 218/663–7899 | fax 218/663–7387 | www.AmericInn.com/minnesota/tofte-MN.html | 52 rooms | $59–$139 | AE, D, DC, MC, V.

Best Western Cliff Dweller. The unique feature of this 2-story wood building is that every room has a balcony overlooking Lake Superior. It is 5 mi south of Lutsen Mountains Ski Area between Tofte and Lutsen; restaurants are 5 mi north and south. Restaurant. In-room data ports. Cable TV. Business services. Some pets allowed. | 6452 Rte. 61 | 218/663–7273 | gmhotel@worldnet.att.com | 22 rooms | $60–$99 | AE, D, DC, MC, V.

Bluefin Bay. These 2- and 3-story lakeside vacation homes along on ½ mi of lake shore have vaulted ceilings and panoramic views. Although privately owned, they're often for rent. Lutsen Mountains Ski Area is 5 mi north. Restaurant, bar. No air-conditioning, many kitchenettes, many in-room hot tubs. Cable TV. 2 pools (1 indoor). Hot tub, massage. Exercise equipment. Game room. Kids' programs. Laundry facilities. Business services. Some pets allowed. | 7198 W. Hwy. 61, Tofte | 218/663–7296 or 800/258–3346 | fax 218/663–7130 | bluefin@boreal.org | www.bluefinbay.com | 16 rooms, 56 suites | $99–$189 rooms, $175–$420 suites | D, MC, V.

Caribou Highlands Lodge. Standing among 28 wooded acres in the Sawtooth Mountains, this ski-in, ski-out lodge and outbuildings overlook Lake Superior and are 2 mi from the Lutsen Mountain ski area. The lobby has a 26-ft ceiling, a stone fireplace, a moosehead on the wall, and a bearskin rug. Restaurant, bar, picnic area, room service. Some microwaves, Some refrigerators. Cable TV. 2 pools (1 indoor). Spa. Driving range, putting green, tennis. Exercise equipment, hiking. Bicycles. Snowmobiling, sleigh rides. Game room. Kids' programs. Playground. Business services. | 371 Ski Hill Rd. | 218/663–7241 or 800/642–6036 | fax 218/663–7920 | info@caribouhighlandslodge.com | www.caribouhighlands.com | 27 inn rooms, 43 condo/apartments, 52 town homes | $49–$125 inn rooms, $80–$300 condo/apartments, $80–$685 town homes | MC, V.

Cascade Lodge. Built in 1937 and renovated several times since, the lodge is in the middle of Cascade River State Park. Lake Superior is across the street, Lutsen Mountains Ski Area is 8 mi north, and Thunder Bay, Ontario, is 90 miles north. Recreational options include hiking, canoeing, and skiing; the kitchen will pack you a box lunch if you plan to be out all day. Dining room, picnic area. No air-conditioning, Some kitchenettes, refrigerators, some in-room hot tubs. Cable TV. Hiking. Bicycles. Playground. Business services. | 3719 Rte. 61E | 218/387–1112 or 800/322–9543 (outside MN) | fax 218/387–1113 | cascade@cascadelodgemn.com | www.cascadelodgemn.com | 16 rooms (12 in lodge), 11 cabins, 4-unit motel, 16-person house | $66–$110, $106–$185 cabins, $205 house | AE, D, MC, V.

Chateau le Veaux. On a cliff over Lake Superior, this 2-story building has lake views from every room. Outdoors, a wooden deck built directly on boulders overlooks the Lake Superior shoreline. Lutsen Mountains Ski Area is 4 mi north. Kitchenettes Cable TV. Indoor pool. Lake. Hot tub. Sauna. Hiking. Snowmobiling. Playground. Some pets allowed. | 6626

W. Rte. 61, Tofte | 218/663–7223 or 800/445–5773 | fax 218/663–7124 | www.boreal.org/chateau | 34 rooms | $69–$159 | AE, D, DC, MC, V.

Dreamcatcher Bed and Breakfast. Local artwork and lots of windows and woodwork make for a welcoming glow at this contemporary house, on 26 wooded acres 14 mi northeast of town. Lake Superior is visible in the distance. Complimentary breakfast. No pets. No kids under 12. | 2614 County Rd. 7 | 218/387–2876 or 800/682–3119 | www.dreamcatcher.com | 3 rooms | $93–$102 | AE, D, MC, V.

Kah-Nee-Tah. The three cottages on this 4-acre property all have cobblestone fireplaces, spacious decks, and views of Lake Superior. They are in the middle of Cascade River State Park. Kitchenettes. Lake. | 4210 Rte. 61W | 218/387–2585 | hoffman@boreal.org | www.boreal.org/kahneetah/cabins.htm | 3 cabins | $90–$130 cabins | AE, D, DC, MC, V.

Lutsen Resorts and Sea Villas. Started in 1885, added to in 1952, and rebuilt several times, this year-round resort is on Lake Superior, at the mouth of the Poplar River. The main lodge has pine paneling, handcarved beams of native timber, massive stone hearths, and a dining room. Lutsen Mountains Ski Area is across the street, and accommodations have ski-in, ski-out access. Bar, dining room. No air-conditioning. Cable TV. Indoor pool. Hot tub, sauna. 9-hole golf course, tennis. Playground. Some pets allowed. | 5700 Hwy. 61W | 218/663–7212 or 800/258–8736 | lutsen@lutsenresort.com | www.lutsenresort.com | 32 rooms in 1 lodge, 9 cabins, 47 sea villas, 12 condominium units | $33–$135 rooms in lodge, $125–$249 cabins, $80–$219 apartments | AE, D, DC, MC, V.

Mountain Inn. This 2-story wooden ski lodge, built in 1993, is in the woods 1½ mi from Lake Superior and 2 blocks from Lutsen Mountains Ski Area. Picnic area, complimentary Continental breakfast. Cable TV. Hot tub, sauna. Driving range, putting green. Business services. Some pets allowed. | 360 Ski Hill Rd. | 218/663–7244 or 800/686–4669 (reservations) | fax 218/387–2446 | 30 rooms | $99–$119 | AE, D, DC, MC, V.

Solbakken Resort. Accommodations here include rustic, knotty pine cabins (with decks and lake views), motel rooms, lodge suites, and luxurious lake houses which sleep eight to ten people. The main lodge is a 1930s log structure, and has a fireplace parlor with board games. The resort, 2 mi east of town, is open year-round. Some kitchenettes. Lake. Hot tub, sauna. Some pets allowed (fee). | 4874 Rte. 61W | 218/663–7566 | fax 218/663–7816 | www.solbakkenresort.com | 3 lodge suites, 6 rooms 6 cabins, 3 houses | $74–$93 rooms, $77–$114 cabins, $180–$227 houses | AE, MC, V.

Spruce Falls Cabins. These are cozy, simple cabins with fireplaces, on the shore where Spruce Creek runs out into Lake Superior, 6 mi east of town. Some cabins have two bedrooms. Lake. Beach. No pets. | 4140 Rte. 61W | 218/387–2558 | 5 cabins | $84–$125 | Closed mid-Oct.– Memorial Day | No credit cards.

Superior Overlook Bed and Breakfast. This contemporary house 20 mi northeast of town has a view of the lake and 200 ft of frontage, a covered deck, modern furnishings, and a cozy common area with a woodstove. Complimentary breakfast. In-room hot tub. TV in common area. Lake. No pets. | 1620 Rte. 61E | 218/387–1571 | fax 218/387–1899 | www.boreal.org/a-superior-overlook | 2 rooms | $95–$130 | D, MC, V.

LUVERNE

MAP 3, B10

(Nearby town also listed: Pipestone)

If you want to see what open prairie might have looked like a century ago, check out Luverne. The Great Plains begin in this agricultural region, which is tucked into the extreme southwest corner of the state, about a half-hour's drive from Sioux Falls, South Dakota.

Information: **Luverne Area Chamber of Commerce** | 102 E. Main St., Luverne, 56156 | 507/283–4061 | www.ci.luverne.mn.us.

Attractions

Blue Mounds State Park. Sioux quartzite cliffs rise 100 ft from the plains here; watch a bison herd grazing on the prairie in this 1500-acre park. Bird-watchers come to see nesting blue grosbeaks, among other birds. The park is on Rte. 75, just off I–90. | 507/283–1307 | www.dnr.state.mn.us/parks_and_recreation/state_parks/blue_mounds | Park permit required | Daily.

ON THE CALENDAR

DEC.: *Winterfest.* This three-day event includes a Christmas Light Parade, hockey tournaments, a craft show, a snow sculpture contest, a radar run, a parade of homes, and a live Nativity musical. | 507/283–4061.

Dining

Magnolia Steak House and Lounge. American. Now in its third generation of business, this locally famous place, 1½ mi south of town, has its own meat market. Steaks are served grilled or broiled, and there are also walleye, shrimp, and other seafood. Scattered throughout the building are antiques from the community's farming, fishing, and hunting days, as well as train sets and a rare bottle collection. | 1202 S. Kniss Ave. | 507/283–9161 | Closed Sun. No lunch | $10–$13 | MC, V.

Lodging

Comfort Inn. Directly off the highway, this two-story motel is 5 mi south of Blue Mounds State Park. Complimentary Continental breakfast. Cable TV. Indoor Pool. Hot tub. | 801 S. Kniss (U.S. 75S) | 507/283–9488 | fax 507/283–9488 | 44 rooms | $63–$75 | AE, D, DC, MC, V.

Hillcrest Motel. This simple, no-frills place is 1 mi from the center of town, off Rte. 71N. Twin and double beds are available. Cable TV. Some pets allowed (fee). | 210 W. Virginia St. | 507/283–2363 | 16 rooms | $28–$50 | AE, D, MC, V.

Super 8. This 2-story motel highway hotel is one of the last stops before the Iowa and South Dakota borders. Cable TV. Some pets allowed. | RR 2, Box 82C, Rte. 90 | 507/283–9541 | 36 rooms | $41–$65 | AE, D, DC, MC, V.

MANKATO

(Nearby towns also listed: Faribault, Le Sueur, Mantorville, New Ulm, Owatonna, St. Peter)

The town of Mankato sprang up in the wooded valley along the banks of the Minnesota and the Blue Earth rivers, settled by pioneers from the east coast, and by immigrants from Scandinavia and Germany. "Mankato" is Native American for "blue earth," which refers to the bluish clay found along the banks of its two rivers. The city's economy is based on farming, retailing, manufacturing, and distributing.

Information: **Mankato Area Convention and Visitors Bureau** | Box 999, Mankato, 56001 | 800/657–4733 | visitors.mankato.mn.us.

Attractions

Blue Earth County Heritage Center. The gallery has local history exhibits and instructive dioramas. | 415 E. Cherry St. | 507/345–5566 | www.ic.mankato.mn.us/reg9/bechs | $2 | Tues.–Sat. 10–4.

Hubbard House. Surrounded by formal gardens, this 1871 mansard-roofed Victorian has 15 rooms filled with antiques and artifacts from 19th-century rural Minnesota. | 606 S. Broad St. | 507/345–4154 or 507/345–5566 | www.ic.mankato.mn.us/reg9/bechs/hhouse.html | $4 | Sat.–Sun. 1–4.

Land of Memories. This is a municipal campground with picnicking, fishing, boating, and nature trails. | Holly St., off Rte. 169S | 800/657–4733 | Free | Daily.

Minneopa State Park. In this 2,700-acre park, you can walk a trail encircling two water-falls, descend a limestone stairway to the valley below, and then climb the other side for a panoramic view. Seppmann Mill, a German-style stone-and-wood grist mill, is in the north-west corner of the park. And there's camping and fishing. The area is 5 mi west of Mankato. | Rte. 68 and U.S. 169 | 507/389–5464 | www.dnr.state.mn.us/parks_and_recreation/ state_parks/minneopa | Park permit required | Daily.
Learn about nature and Native American life at the **Minneopa-Williams Outdoor Learning Center** in Minneopa State Park. | Rte. 68 and U.S. 169 | 507/625–3281 | Free | Daily.

Mt. Kato Ski Area. With nearly 8 mi of trails and a 2800-ft vertical drop, this hill 4 mi south of Mankato has snowboarding and snow-tubing as well as skiing in winter and moun-tain biking in summer. | Rte. 66 | 507/625–3363 | www.mountkato.com | $20–$24 | Nov.–Apr., daily.

Sakatah Singing Hills State Trail. This 39-mi abandoned railroad bed is a good place to hike, mountain bike, or snowmobile. Mostly covered with crushed rock, it leads east to Farib-ault, passing through Sakatah Hills State Park, along Upper Sakatah Lake. You can pick up the trail north of town. | Lime Valley Rd. | 507/389–5464 | www.dnr.state.mn.us | Free | 8 AM–10 PM daily.

Sibley Park. Originally the site of Camp Lincoln, where more than 300 Dakota people were imprisoned (and 38 executed) after their revolt in 1862, this meticulously-landscaped riverside park now includes picnic areas, a playground, a zoo, and 17 ½ acres of natural ther-mal springs. | West Mankato | 800/657–4733 | Free | Daily.

Tourtelotte Park. A swimming pool, a wading pool, picnic areas, and a playground are all on the grounds here. | East Mable St. | 800/657–4733 | Free | Swimming warm months only. Park open daily.

ON THE CALENDAR
JULY: *Minnesota Vikings Training Camp.* The NFL's Vikings train and swelter on the Mankato State University campus, two times a day, six days a week all month. | Blakeslee Field | 612/828–6500.

Dining
Hunan Garden Restaurant. Chinese. This in-town spot serves traditional fare such as bar-becued sesame ribs, sweet and sour pork and chicken, and vegetarian dishes. There are pictures of goldfish on the walls. | 1400 E. Madison Ave., #104 | 507/345–8812 | $6.95–$11 | D, MC, V.

Neighbors Restaurant. American. Soup and sandwich specials are the most popular lunchtime fare at this family-oriented place, and for dinner you can order steaks, pastas, fish, and shrimp. Kids' menu. | 1812 S. Riverfront Dr. | 507/625–6776 | $10–$16 | AE, D, MC, V.

Lodging
Best Western Garden Inn. This 2-story brick North Mankato hotel occupies 10,000 square ft and has an atrium pool area. The lobby has a fireplace and lounge, and there's a walk-ing trail right outside. Restaurant, bar, room service. Cable TV. Indoor pool. Hot tub, sauna. Laundry facilities. Business services, airport shuttle. | 1111 Range St., N. Mankato | 507/625–9333 | 147 rooms | $45–$80 | AE, D, DC, MC, V.

KODAK'S TIPS FOR TAKING GREAT PICTURES

Get Closer
- Fill the frame tightly for maximum impact
- Move closer physically or use a long lens
- Continually check the viewfinder for wasted space

Choosing a Format
- Add variety by mixing horizontal and vertical shots
- Choose the format that gives the subject greatest drama

The Rule of Thirds
- Mentally divide the frame into vertical and horizontal thirds
- Place important subjects at thirds' intersections
- Use thirds' divisions to place the horizon

Lines
- Take time to notice lines
- Let lines lead the eye to a main subject
- Use the shape of lines to establish mood

Taking Pictures Through Frames
- Use foreground frames to draw attention to a subject
- Look for frames that complement the subject
- Expose for the subject, and let the frame go dark

Patterns
- Find patterns in repeated shapes, colors, and lines
- Try close-ups or overviews
- Isolate patterns for maximum impact (use a telephoto lens)

Textures that Touch the Eyes
- Exploit the tangible qualities of subjects
- Use oblique lighting to heighten surface textures
- Compare a variety of textures within a shot

Dramatic Angles
- Try dramatic angles to make ordinary subjects exciting
- Use high angles to help organize chaos and uncover patterns, and low angles to exaggerate height

Silhouettes
- Silhouette bold shapes against bright backgrounds
- Meter and expose for the background illumination
- Don't let conflicting shapes converge

Abstract Composition
- Don't restrict yourself to realistic renderings
- Look for ideas in reflections, shapes, and colors
- Keep designs simple

Establishing Size
- Include objects of known size
- Use people for scale, where possible
- Experiment with false or misleading scale

Color
- Accentuate mood through color
- Highlight subjects or create designs through color contrasts
- Study the effects of weather and lighting

From *Kodak Guide to Shooting Great Travel Pictures* © 2000 by Fodor's Travel Publications

Days Inn. This 2-story brick building has a walking path along the Minnesota River. Shopping is 3 mi east; Mankato State University is 5 mi south. Complimentary Continental breakfast. In-room data ports. Cable TV. Indoor pool. Hot tub. Business services. Some pets allowed. | 1285 Range St. | 507/387–3332 | 50 rooms | $40–$85 | AE, D, DC, MC, V.

Econo Lodge. Mankato State University is 2 mi of this motel on the north edge of town. It's also 2 mi north of the River Hill shopping mall and the Civic Center. Complimentary Continental breakfast. Cable TV. Hot tub, sauna. Business services. Free parking. Some pets allowed. | 111 W. Lind Ct. | 507/345–8800 | fax 507/345–8921 | 66 rooms | $36–$50 | AE, D, DC, MC, V.

Holiday Inn–Downtown. Built in 1980, this hotel is across the street from the Minnesota River biking and walking trail, and one block of the Civic Center. Restaurant, bar, room service. In-room data ports. Cable TV. Indoor pool, hot tub and sauna in holidome. Putting green. Exercise equipment. Laundry facilities. Business services, free parking. | 101 Main St. | 507/345–1234 | fax 507/345–1248 | www.basshotels.com/holiday-inn | 151 rooms | $59–$79 | AE, D, DC, MC, V.

Riverfront Inn. Some rooms at this 1-story motel have fireplaces. The property is ¾ mi north of downtown. In-room data ports, refrigerators. Cable TV. Business services. Some pets allowed. | 1727 N. Riverfront Dr. | 507/388–1638 | fax 507/388–6111 | 19 rooms | $30–$79 | AE, D, DC, MC, V.

Super 8. A few blocks from the River Hill shopping center, this motel is 3 mi north of downtown, on Rte. 169. In-room data ports. Cable TV. Hot tub. Business services. | RR1, Box 390 | 507/387–4041 | fax 507/387–4107 | 61 rooms | $40–$52 | AE, D, DC, MC, V.

MANTORVILLE

MAP 3, F9

(Nearby towns also listed: Austin, Faribault, Mankato, Northfield, Rochester)

Named after the Mantor brothers, who arrived in 1853 and began erecting the city, Mantorville lies in a valley alongside the Zumbro River. Nineteenth-century architectural gems earn the 12-block downtown district a listing on the National Register of Historic Places. A local limestone quarry provided building materials for many of the structures, including the Dodge County Courthouse (1871) and the Hubbell House (1856); both buildings are still in use and open to the public, as is the historic Opera House.

Information: Mantorville Chamber of Commerce | Box 358, Mantorville, 55955 | 507/635–5464 | www.kasson-mn.com.

Attractions

Dodge County Courthouse and Annex. Minnesota's oldest working courthouse was constructed between 1865 and 1871. The building's limestone walls are 40 inches thick. | Main and 6th Sts. | 507/635–6239 | Free | Year-round.

Dodge County Historical Society Museum and School. Housed in the former St. John's Episcopal Church (built in 1869), the museum has many bits of Dodge County historical memorabilia. The one-room school house is on the same site. | Box 433 | 507/635–5508 | Free | May–Oct., Tues.–Sun.

Mantorville Theatre Company. You can see a real old-fashioned melodrama in the Opera House. The audience participates by hissing and booing the villains and applauding the heroes and heroines. | Off 5th St. between Clay and Main St. | 507/635–5420 | June–Aug., weekends.

JUNE: *Old Tyme Days.* Minnesota's largest antique tractor pull, farm toy show, and craft show is held the third Sunday in June. | 507/635–5464.

SEPT.: *Marigold Days.* What began as a promotion to encourage the creative displays of marigolds throughout the city has blossomed into a weekend festival with arts and crafts, a flea market, flower show, kids' fishing contest, fiddler's jamboree, dancing, singing, and queen contests, and a Sunday parade. | 507/635–5464.

DEC.: *Old-Fashioned Christmas.* Caroling, live nativity, sleigh rides, and, of course, Santa Claus are part of this pre-Christmas festival. | 507/635–5464.

Dining
Hubbell House. American. Established in 1854, this restaurant and saloon was an important stop on the 19th-century mail route. The dining room serves large steaks and fresh fish, including a tasty walleye pike almondine. Kids' menu. | Main and 5th Sts. | www.hubbell-house.com | 507/635–2331 | Closed Mon. | $12–$36 | AE, MC, V.

Lodging
Grand Old Mansion B&B. Built in 1899, the inn is filled with Victorian antiques and collectibles. Some rooms have shared baths. The property also has two stand-alone accommodations: an 1850 log cabin with period antiques, and a 19th-century schoolhouse, which sleeps 10, improbably done up in 1970s style, with gold carpeting and avocado-colored couches. Complimentary breakfast. | Box 185 | 507/635–3231 | 4 rooms, 2 cabins | $35–$64 for two people, plus $8 per additional person in cabins.

MARSHALL

MAP 3, B9

(Nearby towns also listed: Granite Falls, Redwood Falls, Tracy)

The city's strong industrial base and the presence of Southwest State University lend a metropolitan edge to the otherwise small-town atmosphere. The town's name dates back to 1869, when the first postmaster named the post office after Gov. William Marshall.

Information: Marshall Convention and Visitors Bureau | 1210 E. College Dr., Marshall, 56258 | 507/537–1865 | www.marshall-mn.org.

Attractions
Camden State Park. Fishing enthusiasts can angle for brown trout in the Redwood River or bass and bluegills in Brawner Lake. Other activities in this 1,647-acre park include hiking the trails, cooling off in the spring-fed pool, or walking along the Dakota Valley Trail. The area is 10 mi south of Marshall. | Rte. 23 | 507/865–4530 | www.dnr.state.mn.us/parks_and_recreation/state_parks/camden | Park permit required | Daily 8–10.

Garvin Park. The 600 acres at this county park 14 mi south of town encompass trails for hiking, horseback riding, and snowmobiling, and a hill for snow-tubing and tobogganing. Camping is permitted and there is a picnic shelter. | Rte. 59 | 507/537–6767 | Free.

Southwest State University. Founded in 1967, Southwest State University has both liberal arts and professional programs, and a 215-acre campus. Its planetarium, museum, and greenhouse are open to the public. | 1501 State St. | 507/537–7021 | www.southwest.msus.edu | Daily, hours upon request.

AUG.: *International Rolle Bolle Tournament.* One hundred fifty teams gather to compete in the game of Rolle Bolle, which was originally developed in Belgium. The game is played on bare ground with stakes set 30 ft apart. Players roll their balls (bolles) down the court and try to get closest to the stake. | 507/537–1865.

AUG.: *County Fair.* This week-long agricultural fair has livestock, craft, and food competitions; a demolition derby; a rodeo; carnival rides; and a teen dance. | 507/537–1865.

Dining

Mike's Cafe. American. This cafe serves home-cooked meals all day long. Soups and sandwiches, burgers and chicken are popular. | 203 E. College Dr. | 507/532–5477 | Breakfast also available | $4–$6 | D, MC, V.

Shays Restaurant. American. In the Best Western, this restaurant is a place with linens and candles on the tables, and a large fireplace. Walleye, shrimp, crab, steak, prime rib, and pasta are on the menu. Kids' menu. | 1500 E. College Dr. | 507/532–3221 | Breakfast also available. No lunch Sat. No dinner Sun. | $7–$17 | AE, D, DC, MC, V.

Toni's Depot. American. This is basically a submarine shop on one side of a convenience store in the heart of town; the hearty pork chops, chicken, and burgers are a nice surprise. | 814 W. Main St. | 507/532–3288 | Closed Sun. | $3–$5 | No credit cards.

Lodging

AmericInn. All rooms at this hostelry, directly in town, have queen-size beds, and some have fireplaces. Complimentary breakfast. Some microwaves, some refrigerators, some in-room hot tubs. Cable TV. Indoor pool. Laundry facilities. Some pets allowed. | 1406 E. Lyon St. | 507/537–9424 | www.gomarshall.net | 36 rooms | $69–$129 | AE, D, MC, V.

Best Western Marshall Inn. A 2-story brick building built in 1973, this property is on the edge of town, at the corner of Routes 19 and 23, across the street from Southwest State University. Restaurant, bar, room service. In-room data ports. Cable TV. Indoor pool. Hot tub, sauna. Business services, airport shuttle. Some pets allowed. | 1500 E. College Dr. | 507/532–3221 | fax 507/532–4089 | 100 rooms | $44–$61 | AE, D, DC, MC, V.

Comfort Inn. This 2-story motel is next to the university and next door to a restaurant. A downstairs lounge is available for group rentals. Complimentary Continental breakfast. In-room data ports. Cable TV. Indoor pool. Hot tub. Business services. Some pets allowed. | 1511 E. College Dr. | 507/532–3070 | fax 507/537–9641 | 49 rooms | $52–$95 | AE, D, DC, MC, V.

Super 8. This two-story building, built in the 1980s, is surrounded by shops and restaurants, and within blocks of a 24-hour service station. Cable TV. Laundry facilities. Business services. Some pets allowed. | 1106 E. Main St. | 507/537–1461 | 50 rooms | $43–$51 | AE, D, DC, MC, V.

Traveler's Lodge. Marshall Square and Southwest State University are both across the street from this motel. Complimentary Continental breakfast. Cable TV. Business services, airport shuttle. Some pets allowed. | 1425 E. College Dr. | 507/532–5721 or 800/532–5721 | fax 507/532–4911 | 90 rooms | $34–$42 | AE, D, DC, MC, V.

Valentine Inn. This 3-story Victorian has a wraparound porch for sitting in warm weather. Inside is filled with antiques and collectibles. Rooms vary in size, with double or queen-size beds. About 20 mi south of town. Complimentary breakfast. No pets. No kids under 12. No smoking. | 385 Emory St. | 507/629–3827 | 4 rooms | $75–$105 | No credit cards.

MINNEAPOLIS

MAP 3, E8

(Suburbs also listed: Anoka, Bloomington, Elk River, Hastings, Lake City, Lakeville, Shakopee)

The name Minneapolis combines the Dakota word for water (*minne*) with the Greek word for city (*polis*). Put them together and you get a very accurate description of this

Midwestern metropolis. Eighteen lakes lie within the city, and the Mississippi River runs through it.

The Dakota people lived in this area for centuries before the arrival of white explorers. In 1680, a Catholic missionary named Father Louis Hennepin passed a waterfall during an expedition up the Mississippi River and named it St. Anthony Falls. White settlement did not begin in earnest for another 140 years, when Fort Snelling was constructed near the confluence of the Mississippi and Minnesota rivers. Soon soldiers from the fort built a sawmill and flour mill at Father Hennepin's waterfall. The village of St. Anthony grew up on the river's east bank. Minneapolis emerged on the west side. In 1872, the two towns united to form one city.

St. Anthony Falls proved to be the perfect place to process Minnesota grain. Large mills were built along the river, spawning several companies that still exist, including Pillsbury, General Mills, and Cargill. Today, Minneapolis remains an agricultural powerhouse, but its economy is well diversified. Manufacturing, transportation, computer technology, and banking are among the major industries here.

The revitalized downtown area is home to many fine stores, more than 30 theaters, two world-class art museums, and three professional sports teams. Much of downtown is connected by a second-story skyway system that helps keep the city running even on the coldest days. With an average temperature of 18°F in December, 12°F in January, and 18°F again in February, the opportunity to stay indoors can be a definite plus.

Information: Greater Minneapolis Convention and Visitors Association | 4000 Multifoods Tower, 33 S. 6th St., Minneapolis, 55402 | 612/348–7000 or 800/445–7412 | www.minneapolis.org.

NEIGHBORHOODS

Downtown Minneapolis. Vibrant with commercial and residential life, downtown is bordered by the Mississippi River on the north, I–35W on the east, I–94 on the south, and I–394 on the west. The heart of the area is Nicollet Mall, a 12-block pedestrian-only thoroughfare where Mary Tyler Moore tossed her hat in the opening credits of her 1970s television sitcom. It continues to serve as the city's main shopping district. Several blocks to the northwest is the **Warehouse District,** the center of the city's dining and entertainment scene. Here you'll find renovated warehouses that have been turned into apartments, condominiums, coffee houses, art galleries, bars, and restaurants. It's the place where the musician once known as Prince got his start. **Loring Park,** tucked in the southwest corner of the Downtown area, is a trendy neighborhood with turn-of-the-20th-century brick and brownstone apartments. It offers a Bohemian mixture of new condos, cultural centers, and restaurants. The eastern part of Downtown features fewer attractions. It's where you'll find remnants of the city's flour-milling past and the puffy monument to its pro-sports present: the Hubert H. Humphrey Metrodome.

Uptown. Southwest of downtown Minneapolis lies the hip Uptown area. Bordered by I–394 on the north, I–35W on the east, and Route 21 on the south, it includes the picturesque Chain of Lakes for which Minneapolis is well known. The neighborhoods surrounding Cedar Lake, Lake of the Isles, Lake Calhoun, and Lake Harriet boast some of the oldest and most impressive homes in the Twin Cities. They're magnets for thousands of walkers, runners, bikers, skaters, and boaters. Hennepin Avenue is Uptown's main street. It's lined with unique shops, and a wide assortment of restaurants, bars, coffee houses, and alternative movie theaters.

U of M District. Encompassing what are known as the **East Bank** and **West Bank** areas, the University of Minnesota district is the slice of Minneapolis that's bordered by Route 280 on the east, I–94 on the south, and I–35W on the northwest. The main campus is on the East Bank, and includes the shopping, dining, and entertainment neighborhood called **Dinkytown.** The West Bank area has a smaller collection of university buildings and a separate commercial center with restaurants, bars, and theaters.

Northeast. The mill town of St. Anthony merged with Minneapolis in 1872, becoming the city's northeastern district. Parts of the area retain the industrial flavor of their flour and lumber milling days, and in fact almost all today's residents have been there only since the mid-1980s. Today, high-rises in the area known as St. Anthony–Main offer spectacular views of the river. Farther north are residential neighborhoods with pockets of ethnic restaurants and retail establishments.

TRANSPORTATION

Airports: The blizzard scenes in the movie *Airport* were shot at the **Minneapolis/St. Paul International Airport.** It has a reputation for staying open in all but the very worst winter weather. | 612/726–5555.
Rail: National rail passenger service is via **Amtrak.** | 800/872–7245.
Bus Lines: The regional bus system is **Metro Transit.** | 612/373–3333.
Intra-city Transit: Contact the **Metropolitan Transit Commission** | 3118 Nicollet Ave. | 612/349–7000.

Attractions

ART AND ARCHITECTURE

American Swedish Institute. The turreted mansion which houses the institute is on the National Register of Historic Places. It showcases the Institute's collection of Swedish glass, decorative and fine arts, and textiles. | 2600 Park Ave. S | 612/871–4907 | www.americanswedishinst.org | $4 | Tues., Thurs.–Sat. noon–4, Wed. 12–8, Sun. 1–5.

Minneapolis City Hall. The marble statue *Father of Waters* is among the landmarks here. Self-guided tours are available. | 350 South 5th St. | 612/673–2491 or 612/673–5301 | Free | Mon.–Fri. 9–5 | www.ci.minneapolis.mn.us.

CULTURE, EDUCATION, AND HISTORY

Guthrie Theater. The resident acting company of this celebrated theater performs classic plays in rotating repertory. A typical season includes five to seven productions. | 725 Vineland Pl. | 612/377–2224 | www.guthrietheater.org.

Minneapolis College of Art and Design. The MCAD galleries exhibit works by students and by nationally known artists. | 2501 Stevens Ave. S | 612/874–3700 | www.mcad.edu | Daily.

University of Minnesota–Twin Cities. The campus of this Big 10 school sprawls over both cities, and sponsors art exhibitions, live performances, and sports competitions year-round. | 612/626–8687 | www1.umn.edu/twincities | Daily.

The **Bell Museum of Natural History** is on the University of Minnesota–Twin Cities campus at the southwest corner of 17th Ave. (Church St.) and University Avenue SE. Among the regular features is the Touch-and-See Room, where you can handle natural objects. | 10 Church St. | 612/624–7083 | www1.umn.edu/bellmuse | $3 | Tues.–Fri. 9–5, Sat. 10–5, Sun. noon–5. Free on Sunday.

MUSEUMS

Frederick R. Weisman Art Museum. With its shiny, angular exterior overlooking the Mississippi, this museum is one of the Twin Cities' most recognizable buildings. The collection numbers some 13,000 objects; the strength is in early 20th-century American art. | 333 E. River Rd. | 612/625–9494 or 612/625–9656 | hudson.acad.umn.edu/WAMinfo.html | Free | Tues., Wed., Fri. 10–5, Thurs. 10–8, Sat.–Sun. 11–5.

Hennepin History Museum. The Hennepin History Museum has some of the Twin Cities' most unique social history offerings, exhibiting historical artifacts such as toys and dolls, household implements, and Native American objects in a historic mansion setting. Its archives hold an estimated 100,000 other items of interest to researchers. | 2303 3rd Ave. S | 612/870–1329 | fax 612/870–1320 | www.hhmuseum.org | $1 | Tues. 10–2, Wed.–Sat. 1–5.

Minneapolis Institute of Arts. On display here are 85,000 objects from diverse cultures spanning 4,000 years. Check the schedule for lectures, classes, and films. | 2400 3rd Ave. S | 612/870–3131 | www.artsmia.org | Free | Tues., Wed., Fri., and Sat. 10–5, Thur. 10–9, Sun. noon–5.

Minnesota Transportation Museum. Actually a far-flung group of separate attractions, the MTM is dedicated to preserving historic modes of transportation, including trains, streetcars, and steam boats. In addition to its Minnesota holdings, the MTM owns and operates the Wisconsin-based Osceola & St. Croix Valley Railway, one hour east of the Twin Cities, where you can take a 50- or 90-minute river valley tour aboard vintage railroad equipment. The MTM's main offices and some exhibits are in the Jackson Street Roundhouse Museum. | 193 Pennsylvania Ave. E, St. Paul | 651/228–0263 | www.mtmuseum.org.

The Minnesota Transportation Museum's **Como-Harriet Streetcar Line** runs vintage trams at 15-minute intervals on restored tracks between Lake Harriet and Lake Calhoun in southwest Minneapolis. The Linden Hills Station, which houses displays of trolley technology, is at Queen Ave S and W. 42nd St., while the Lake Calhoun platform is on Richfield Road, south of W. 36th St. | www.mtmuseum.org/traction/schedule.html | $1.50 | Memorial Day–Labor Day, Mon.–Fri. 6:30 AM–dusk, Sat.–Sun. 12:30–dusk; Sept., Sat., Sun. 12:30–dusk; Oct., Sat.–Sun. 12:20–5.

Built by the Great Northern Railroad in 1907 as a maintenance shop for its steam locomotives, the **Jackson Street Roundhouse Museum** was the first such facility in the state. Now a "working museum" where the Minnesota Transportation Museum maintains and restores its railroad equipment, the roundhouse was opened to the public in 1999. | 193 Pennsylvania Ave. E, St. Paul | 651/228–0263 | Free with MTM admission | May–Oct., Sat. 10–5, Sun. 1–5.

The Minnesota Transportation Museum's only non-functioning site is the **Minnehaha Depot** in Minneapolis's Minnehaha Park. Built in 1875 as a stop on the Great Northern Rail-

SIBLING RIVALRY

The Twin Cities of Minneapolis and St. Paul usually get along just fine, but occasionally sibling rivalry takes over. Such was the case in 1890.

St. Paul had always considered itself superior to its twin. It was the capital. It was older. It had established itself as an economic power. But its self-confidence was beginning to waver. The census of 1880 had shown for the first time that more people lived in Minneapolis than in St. Paul. Luckily for St. Paul, the numbers were close enough to prevent either city from claiming outright superiority. So it was that the 1890 census would determine the official pecking order.

And it wasn't a pretty sight.

The problems started in June with the arrests of seven Minneapolis census counters who were subsequently charged with vote fraud. Then the U.S. Secretary of the Interior ordered a recount in both cities, citing voting irregularities in St. Paul as well as Minneapolis. The St. Paul count, for example, included 91 people who supposedly were living in the offices of the city's biggest newspaper.

When it was all over, Minneapolis was the winner with a census tally of 164,738. St. Paul had just 133,301. The capital city has remained runner-up in the population race ever since.

© Corbis

way, the depot now houses historical displays. | Hiawatha Ave. and Godfrey Pkwy./Nawadaha Blvd. | Donation | Memorial Day–mid-Sept., Sun. and holidays 12:30–4:30.

One of Lake Minnetonka's original 1905 "streetcar boats"—so dubbed because they shared some visual characteristics with streetcars, and ran just as dependably—the **Steamboat Minnehaha** shuttled early 20th-century commuters on a 27-stop route along the sprawling lake's 110-mi shoreline. The whole fleet was scuttled in 1926 after the passenger service closed down. Raised from the lake waters in 1980 and finally restored by the Minnesota Transportation Museum in 1996, the *Minnehaha* operates once again out of Excelsior, 20 mi southwest of Minneapolis. There are 1½-hour cruises twice daily around the lake's Big Island and 2½-hour roundtrips to Wayzata, 13 mi west. In the ticket office exhibits document trolley and steamboat transportation of days gone by. | 328 Lake St., Excelsior | 612/474–4801 or 800/711–2591 | Short cruise: adults $7, children $5; Long cruise: adults $10, children $6 | mid-May–mid-October, Sat. and Sun.

Museum of Questionable Medical Devices. The world's largest display of what the human mind has devised to cure the body without the benefit of either scientific method or common sense. See for yourself the soap that lathers off pounds, and the weight-reduction eyeglasses. | 201 Main St. SE | 612/379–4046 | www.mtn.org/~quack | Free | Tues.–Thurs. 5–9, Fri.–Sat. noon–9, Sun. noon–5.

★ **Walker Art Center.** This institution is nationally renowned for its vigorous multidisciplinary involvement in contemporary art, which you can experience in galleries, in performance spaces, and via educational programs of cutting-edge artistic work in theater, dance, video, music, film, and fine art. Exhibitions of 20th-century visual arts are often staged, and artists in residence create works for the Walker and host activities. In addition, actors stage theatrical works year-round, including an annual production of Dickens's *A Christmas Carol*. The permanent collection ranges from Edward Hopper's *Office at Night* to works by Chuck Close, Marcel Duchamp, Jasper Johns, Lorna Simpson, and others. | Lyndale Ave. and Vineland Pl | 612/375–7577 or 612/375–7622 | www.walkerart.org | $4 for gallery; performance events vary | Tues., Wed., Fri., Sat., 10–5; Thurs. 10–9; Sun. 11–5.

Across the street from the Walker Art Center, the 11-acre **Minneapolis Sculpture Garden** is a collaborative project with the Minneapolis Park and Recreation Board. Claes Oldenburg's massive *Spoonbridge and Cherry* is by far the most identifiable sculpture in the 11-acre garden. | 612/375–7622 | Free | Daily.

PARKS, NATURAL AREAS, AND OUTDOOR RECREATION

Buck Hill. Twelve slopes and nine lifts cater to skiers and snow tubers 30 mi south of Minneapolis. The hill has a 325-ft vertical drop. | 15400 Buck Hill Rd., Burnsville | 612/435–7174 | www.skibuck.com | Mon.–Fri., 10 AM–10 PM; Sat.–Sun., 9 AM–10 PM.

Chain of Lakes. Stretching between Lyndale Avenue S and the suburb of St. Louis Park, this 13³⁄₁₀-mi chain includes Lakes Calhoun and Harriet, Cedar Lake, and Lake of the Isles. Surrounded by some of the city's most impressive homes, the waters are circled by public walkways, parks, and swimming beaches. | www.minneapolisparks.org.

Eloise Butler Wildflower Garden and Bird Sanctuary. Woodland, wetland, upland, and savanna-prairie habitats fill this 14-acre native-plant garden. | 1 Theodore Wirth Pkwy., south of Glenwood Ave. | 612/348–5702 | Free | Apr.–Oct., daily.

Lyndale Gardens. Also known as the Municipal Rose Garden, this well-tended landscape, next to Lake Harriet, is one of many attractions along the Chain of Lakes. | 612/661–4806 | Free | Daily | www.minneapolisparks.org.

Majestic Oaks Golf Course. Fifteen mi north of Minneapolis, Majestic is actually three golf courses in one: Platinum (the oldest and longest), Gold (shorter, opened in 1991), and Executive (9-hole). You'll find flat to rolling terrain with mature trees. Greens undulate and are well trapped, ranging from medium to large. Some tees and greens are elevated. | 701 Bunker Lake Blvd., Ham Lake | 612/755–2142 | $23–$31 | Apr.–Oct., sunrise–sunset.

Minnehaha District. At 171-acre Minnehaha Park you can picnic, bird-watch, explore Minnehaha Falls, or walk through Longfellow House, a ⅔-scale replica of the poet's Massachusetts home, which contains the park's information center. Wind along Minnehaha Creek and watch the spring flowers as they emerge and bloom. Minnehaha District is along the 50-mi National Scenic Byway called the Grand Rounds, which also passes the Chain of Lakes. | Rte. 55 and E. Minnehaha Pkwy. | 612/661–4806 or 612/661–8942 | Free | Daily | www.minneapolisparks.org.

St. Anthony Falls. In full view of downtown Minneapolis, the St. Anthony Falls are on Nicollet Island on the Mississippi River, in the Downtown Riverfront area of the Grand Rounds. Locks and dams have taken away much of their thunder, but the falls are still fun to watch from several public viewing areas. The best view by far is from the Stone Arch Bridge, south of the falls. | 612/661–4806 | Free | Daily | www.minneapolisparks.org.

RELIGION AND SPIRITUALITY

Basilica of St. Mary. With its copper dome extending 250 ft above grade, and its white Hardwick granite exterior, the Basilica of Saint Mary is a striking landmark in western Minneapolis. Designed in 1906 by Emmanual Masqueray (1861–1917), America's first basilica has served the area since the first mass was celebrated here on May 31, 1914. St. Mary's is affiliated with the basilica of St. John Lateran, in Rome, and contains exact half-scale replicas of St. John Lateran's twelve apostle sculptures. A 9-ft statue of Our Lady of Grace overlooks the high altar, standing on a 40-ft baldachin with four marble pillars and a stone canopy. The Lady Chapel, in the southeast corner of the church, contains an icon of Mary from the congregation's original parish church, Immaculate Conception. The crucifixion tableau, carved in situ by John Garratti, was modeled after a miraculous crucifix of Lympias in Spain, and is on the east pier of the sanctuary. Two 133-ft towers flank the facade's carving of the Assumption. | Hennepin Ave. at 16th St. | www.mary.org | Free | Daily.

SHOPPING

Nicollet Mall. Perhaps best known for its background cameo at the beginning of the *Mary Tyler Moore Show*, this promenade is a vibrant shopping and dining area, extending for 12 blocks between 13th St. S and Washington Ave. S, between LaSalle Ave. to the west and Marquette Ave. to the east. Only buses and taxis are allowed. | www.nicolletmall.com.

At 57 stories, the **IDS Tower** is one of the tallest buildings between Chicago and the West Coast. The ground-floor Crystal Court has dining and shopping. | 80 S. 8th St. | Daily.

SIGHTSEEING TOURS

MetroConnections. Two excursions per day highlight the Twin Cities' most notable sites, including the Nicollet Mall, the Metrodome, Minnehaha Falls, and the Kenwood-area TV home of Mary Tyler Moore, all in Minneapolis; historic Fort Snelling, the World Trade Center, the State Capitol, and F. Scott Fitzgerald's home and haunts, in St. Paul; and the Mall of America in Bloomington. The morning tour lasts 3¼ hours, the afternoon tour 2¾ hours. Tours depart from the various downtown hotels in the morning and early afternoon. | 612/333–8687 or 800/747–8687 | www.metroconnections.com | $20 | June–Aug., daily; Sept.–Oct., Fri.–Sun.; no tours Nov.–May.

River City Trolley. Following 2-hr-long routes around the Downtown Riverfront Area and the Chain of Lakes, the trolley makes 20 stops, including the Minneapolis Convention Center, Walker Art Center, and St. Anthony Main. The two most popular embarkation points are the Convention Center and the Walker Arts Center. | 612/204–0000 | 2-hr tour $8, 1-day pass $10, 3-day pass $15 | May–Oct., Mon.–Fri. 10–4, Sat.–Sun. 10–5.

SPECTATOR SPORTS

Hubert H. Humphrey Metrodome. This domed stadium opened in 1982 and is the home of Major League Baseball's Minnesota Twins, the National Football League's Minnesota Vikings, and the University of Minnesota Golden Gophers football team. | 900 S. Fifth St. | 612/332–0386.

Minnesota Twins. The 1987 and 1991 World Series champs play major league baseball in the Hubert H. Humphrey Metrodome. Opening hours vary, so call to confirm. | 900 S. Fifth St. | 612/375–1366; tickets 800/33–TWINS | www.twinsbaseball.com | $5–$25 | Apr.–Sept.

Minnesota Timberwolves. Based at the Target Center, the team is one of the NBA's newest franchises. | 600 1st Ave. N | 612/673–1600 | www.nba.com/timberwolves | $10–$255 | Nov.–May.

Minnesota Vikings. There are no more "blizzard bowls" for the Vikings now that the NFL team plays indoors in the Metrodome. | 900 S. Fifth St. | 612/828–6500 | www.nfl.com/vikings | Aug.–Dec.

OTHER POINTS OF INTEREST

Minneapolis Grain Exchange. You can see for yourself how a grain and futures market really works. Call ahead to schedule a tour. | 400 S. 4th St. | 612/338–6212 | Free.

Minneapolis Planetarium. Stargazers study the heavens under a 40-ft domed ceiling. | 300 Nicollet Mall | www.mplanetarium.org | 612/372–6644 | $4.50.

ON THE CALENDAR

JULY: *Minneapolis Aquatennial.* A 10-day, citywide carnival includes milk-carton boat races, sand castle competitions, and Minnesota's largest parade. | 612/331–8371.
SEPT.–JUNE: *Minnesota Orchestra.* Ninety-five musicians make world-class music in a concert hall that's known for the acoustic cubes sticking out of its ceiling and stage wall. | Sept.–May | 612/371–5656.
OCT.–MAY: *University Theatre.* Student and professional actors put on musicals, comedies, and dramas in this four-theater entertainment complex at the University of Minnesota. | Rarig Center–West Bank Campus, 330 21st Ave. S | 612/624–2345.

Dining

INEXPENSIVE

August Moon. Pan-Asian. This small, cozy suburban eatery 5 mi west of Minneapolis is well-known to regulars for its food, but also for its decor which includes works from area artists (artwork changes every six weeks) as well as lava lamp lighting. Favorites includes *murgh aloo matar anand* (a marinated chicken breast stuffed with goat cheese), and the tuna with soba noodles. | 5340 Wayzata Blvd., Golden Valley | 612/544–7017 | No lunch Sat., Sun. | $8–$15 | AE, DC, MC, V.

Cafe Havana. Cuban. An arched ceiling, velvet drapes, and large leather booths bring to mind pre-Castro Havana in this small, energetic restaurant. Try the paella. | 119 Washington Ave. N | 612/338–8484 | Closed Sun., Mon. No lunch | $8–$16 | AE, D, DC, MC, V.

Emily's Lebanese Deli. Lebanese. Photographs of Lebanon serve as a reminder that this is not a standard New York–style deli. Situated in the Northeast district, the deli serves kababs, spinach pies, and anything with hummus and tabbouleh. | 641 University Ave. NE | 612/379–4069 | Closed Tues. | $5–$10 | No credit cards.

Gardens of Salonica. Greek. A narrow, turn-of-the-20th-century storefront houses this family-owned Greek café and deli, five blocks north of downtown on the other side of the Mississippi. The decor is sparse and tasteful with stone and wire artwork from local artists and walls painted to resemble the old crumbling walls of Greece. Moussaka is on the menu along with orzo and lamb in a light tomato sauce. | 19 5th St. NE | 612/378–0611 | Closed Sun. | $5–$12 | AE, D, DC, MC, V.

Mud Pie. Vegetarian. At this uptown bohemian joint you can dine indoors surrounded by abstract art, huge mirrors, and potted plants or, in warm weather, sit outside on the enclosed patio. The menu has a large selection with lots of sandwiches, salads, dips, and the like. The house specialty is the veggie burger. Beer and wine only. | 2549 Lyndale Ave. S | 612/872–9435 | $7–$16 | AE, D, DC, MC, V.

Santorini. Greek, Mediterranean. Festive Greek music and vivid murals create a Mediterranean garden setting; the Village Room, a re-created Mediterranean courtyard, is complete with clotheslines and grapevines. On the menu are saganaki, gyros, and phyllo specialties. | 9920 Wayzata Blvd., St. Louis Park | 612/546–6722 | $5–$15 | AE, D, DC, MC, V.

Shuang Cheng. Chinese. A few scattered streamers are the only visual frills at this popular stop on the University of Minnesota campus. The kitchen serves lobster, crab, and various fish preparations, as well as common Chinese fare. | 1320 S.E. 4th St. | 612/378–0208 | $5–$12 | AE, D, DC, MC, V.

Sidney's Pizza Cafe. Italian. Part of the happening Uptown area of Minneapolis. The wood-burning oven and rotisserie are in full view of diners, as cooks prepare innovative pies such as the Asian spicy chicken pizza; pasta dishes, such as fiesta chicken linguine, are equally varied, and fresh salads are an art form. Beer and wine only. | 2120 Hennepin Ave. | 612/870–7000 | $6–$12 | AE, D, DC, MC, V.

Table of Contents. Contemporary. This sophisticated eatery, the sister restaurant to the St. Paul location of the same name, has a dramatic black, gold, and mauve color scheme, an innovative martini list, and a menu full of creativity. Sun. brunch. | 1310 Hennepin Ave. | 612/339–1133 | $6–$12 | AE, D, DC, MC, V.

MODERATE

Backstage at Bravo. Contemporary. During this cheery musical revue the black-clad servers belt out songs as they pass the fried calamari and Caesar salad. The dining area looks like a theater's backstage. Top billing goes to the stuffed wontons—a different filling every day. There's open-air dining on the roof. | 900 Hennepin Ave. | 612/338–0062 | Closed Sun., Mon. No lunch | $8–$22 | AE, D, DC, MC, V.

Black Forest Inn. German. Directly south of downtown, the restaurant serves hearty German fare—including Wiener schnitzel and sauerbraten—and draft beer under a stenciled ceiling, amid displays of beer steins and German visual art. There are 18 beers on tap, including local, German, and other European brews. | 1 E. 26th St. | 612/872–0812 | $9–$17 | AE, D, DC, MC, V.

Buca di Beppo. Italian. The visual appeal here is zany and fun, with red-checkered tablecloths, Christmas lights, and walls crammed as full as library shelves with pasta boxes, clay wine jugs, and photos of soccer teams and famous Italians. Dining groups pass around family-style platters groaning with ravioli, tortellini, pizza, and eggplant Parmigiana. The garlic mashed potatoes and the fork-tender chicken marsala with enormous, wine-soaked mushrooms are favorites, as is the 15-ingredient 1893 salad. | 11 S. 12th St. | 612/341–9178 | No lunch Mon.–Sat. | $9–$25 | AE, D, DC, MC, V.

Cafe Brenda. Vegetarian, Seafood. High ceilings, terra-cotta walls, and plenty of windows distinguish this renovated warehouse, where the menu includes macrobiotic sozai of brown rice with ginger-and-maple-seasoned red beans, sautéed tofu and pickled cabbage, and a rosy salmon fillet glazed with ginger and paired with a crisp croquette. | 300 1st Ave. N | 612/342–9230 | Closed Sun. No lunch Sat. | $10–$16 | AE, DC, MC, V.

Campiello. Italian. Tuscan-style mosaics adorn the walls of this Uptown restaurant, where the thin-crusted pizzas, the pastas, and the rotisserie meats make for lots of return customers. Open-air dining. Sun. brunch. | 1320 W. Lake St. | 612/825–2222 | No lunch | $10–$15 | AE, D, DC, MC, V.

Chutneys Indian Bistro. Indian. Part of a suburban strip mall 3 mi north of Minneapolis, this large restaurant is comfortable and elegant with white linen tablecloths and soft lighting. The ambitious menu includes many dishes seldom seen in the Midwest. A good intro-

duction to the cuisine here are the appetizer platters (with spinach balls, potato cakes, stuffed samosas, and onion crisps) and the thali, a huge tray featuring two entrées, salad, lentils, naan, rice, and a syrup-soaked pastry. Cricket bats and international pennants decorate the restaurant's sports bar. | 2321 Palmer Dr., New Brighton | 651/633–6224 | $10– $20 | AE, D, DC, MC, V.

Figlio. Italian. Locals know this loud and bustling urban hangout as a place to see and be seen. The fire-roasted pepperoni pizza, with huge hand-cut slices of charred meat, marinated tomatoes, and thick mozzarella, is locally praised. | 3001 Hennepin Ave. S | 612/822– 1688 | $9–$20 | AE, D, DC, MC, V.

510. French. Chandeliers hang from 18-ft ceilings in this elegant space. Menu favorites include grilled pork tenderloin with figs and bacon in port sauce; rack of lamb encrusted with mustard and hazelnuts; smoked duck breast; and citrus-glazed salmon. | 510 Groveland Ave. at Hennepin Ave. | 612/874–6440 | Closed Sun. No lunch | $12–$25 | AE, D, DC, MC, V.

Gluek's. German. Dine in German beer hall surroundings, with wood, brick, stained glass, and photos reminiscent of the days when the building housed a brewery. Despite the decor, the food is mostly American with some German influence. Favorites include the Berliner sandwich, with roast beef, sour cream, mushrooms, and melted cheese, as well as New York steak and walleye pike. | 16 N. Sixth St. | 612/338–6621 | Closed Sun. | $8–$14 | AE, D, DC, MC, V.

It's Greek to Me. Greek. Pressed-tin ceilings, wall murals, and tile floors help create the proper Greek mood at this southside restaurant, as do the traditional Greek dishes such as kababs, moussaka, spinach pies, and lamb preparations. | 626 W. Lake St. | 612/825–9922 | Closed Mon. | $8–$15 | AE, D, MC, V.

J. D. Hoyt's. American. Diners settle into roomy booths that recall a 1950s roadhouse at this downtown hot spot known for Cajun pork chops. The prime steaks, seafood and the signature double pork chop, grilled over charcoal and served, if you wish, with herb butter and Cajun or jerk spices, are top picks. Sun. brunch. | 301 Washington Ave. N | 612/338– 1560 | $10–$38 | AE, D, DC, MC, V.

Jerusalem's. Middle Eastern. With the walls covered in colorful tapestries and billowing red cloth drooping from the ceiling, Jerusalem's evokes a desert tent in the Middle East. Indeed, the crunchy falafel, thick hummus, and shish kebabs encourage you to forget you're really in a concrete building in Minneapolis. Belly dancers perform Saturday and Sunday evenings. | 1518 Nicollet Ave. | 612/871–8883 | $10–$18 | D, DC, MC, V.

Kikugawa. Japanese. The serious approach to food and the Minneapolis skyline view make this restaurant popular among Japanese visitors. The enormous prix-fixe dinner, includes *otoshi* (little hors d'oeuvres), sashimi or yakitori, beef teriyaki, *yakisakana* (broiled marinated salmon), shrimp and vegetable tempura, *sunomono* (a crab-meat salad), miso soup, and the vegetable pickles known as oshinko—all presented in pretty dishes. | 43 S.E. Main St. | 612/378–3006 | $11–$22 | AE, D, DC, MC, V.

King and I Thai. Thai. Steps away from the Minneapolis Convention Center, this spacious restaurant contains carved elephant statues, ceremonial Buddhist figures, and museum-quality Thai crafts and antiques. The chef prepares a special curry to be served fresh every day. You might try the *pad bai ga-prow* (basil stir-fried with Thai chile and garlic seasoning). Beer and wine only. | 1346 LaSalle Ave. | kingandithai.citysearch.com | 612/332–6928 | Closed Sun. No lunch Sat. | $10–$24 | AE, D, DC, MC, V.

Linguini and Bob. Italian. Bleached wood, wicker chairs, and sponge-painted walls create a subdued setting for grilled chicken breast, lemony mashed potatoes, or chewy-crust pizzas. | 100 N. 6th St., at 1st Ave. N | 612/332–1600 | No lunch | $10–$20 | AE, D, DC, MC, V.

Lord Fletcher's of the Lake. English. High-rollers arrive by boat, wearing swimsuits; land-lubbers and dreamers travel more conventionally to this busy lakeside complex, which has sunset viewing, fireplaces, and a scattering of wine kegs presided over by a portrait of Winston Churchill. Except in the formal, reservation-only Harbor Room, the vibe is summery and casual and the menu offers up seafood, including local favorites like walleye. Sun. brunch. | 3746 Sunset Dr., Spring Lake Park | 952/471–8513 | $10–$25 | AE, D, DC, MC, V.

Lucia's. American. A separate wine bar adjoins this sunny, Uptown storefront dining spot. You might try a spicy seafood gumbo or smoky lentils with duck, or order a risotto of leeks, asparagus, fresh peas, and Parmesan. Open-air dining. Sun. brunch. | 1432 W. 31st St. | 612/ 825–1572 | $10–$18 | MC, V.

Market Bar-B-Que. Barbecue. Framed newspapers, autographed photos, and an oldies-stocked jukebox create a retro café style. Market's pork and beef ribs are decidedly on the chewy side, but to many Twin Citians they are sentimental favorites. For the indecisive, there are several combo plates, plus barbecue sandwiches and burgers for smaller appetites. | 1414 Nicollet Ave., at 14th St. | 612/872–1111 | $9–$20 | AE, D, DC, MC, V.

The Marsh. Contemporary. Low-fat eating is a watchword of this restaurant in a health and wellness resort 20 mi southwest of Minneapolis, and you can eat cafeteria-style or in a formal dining room. Paintings and sculptures with eastern themes decorate the dining room, and the menu revolves around chicken, fish, and stir-fry. In spring you can order a portobello mushroom melt and eat outside on the deck, enjoying views of the marsh that inspired the establishment's name. Kids' menu. Sun. brunch. | 15000 Minnetonka Blvd., Minnetonka | 612/935–2202 | $12–$18 | AE, MC, V.

Nye's Polonnaise. Polish. Gold-speckled booths and a sing-along piano bar are among the big draws at this retro hangout, which serves various Polish favorites including *pieroszki* (a meat- or potato-filled dumpling) and kielbasa. There's polka Thursday to Saturday nights. | 112 E. Hennepin Ave. | 612/379–2021 | No lunch Sun. | $12–$20 | AE, D, DC, MC, V.

Palomino. Mediterranean. Quiet colors and music set a perfect background for the wood-fired Roma-style pizza and the spit-roasted garlic chicken. | 825 Hennepin Ave. | 612/339– 3800 | No lunch | $8–$26 | AE, D, DC, MC, V.

Pickled Parrot. Southern. Pink flamingos and a red pontoon plane add extra whimsy to the beach-shack presentation of this Warehouse-district eatery. The championship barbecue ribs are perennial favorites. Sun. brunch. | 26 N. 5th St. | 612/332–0673 | $12–$25 | AE, D, DC, MC, V.

Ping's Szechuan Bar and Grill. Chinese. Box kites hang from the ceiling at this popular sit-down or take-out restaurant, one block from the convention center. Buffet lunch. Free valet parking. | 1401 Nicollet Ave. S | 612/874–9404 | $10–$15 | AE, D, DC, MC, V.

Pracna on Main. American. One of the Twin Cities' best outdoor dining spots, this Northeast neighborhood restaurant is on the trolley stop and has a dreamy view of St. Anthony Falls. It is known for its sandwiches, burgers, and baby corn dogs. Open-air dining. | 117 Main St. | 612/379–3200 | $12–$20 | AE, D, DC, MC, V.

Rosewood Room. Continental. Rose-patterned carpeting, rosewood paneling, and soft lighting create a romantic setting. Couples might enjoy the roast rack of lamb for two, or individual plates of cumin-crusted pork tenderloin. | 618 2nd Ave. S | 612/338–2288 | $12– $25 | AE, D, DC, MC, V.

Sawatdee. Thai. The restaurant's big windows look out on Minneapolis's rebounding riverfront district. Known for pad Thai, and a Bangkok seafood special, the kitchen also serves a buffet lunch. | 607 Washington Ave. S | 612/338–6451 | $10–$16 | AE, D, DC, MC, V.

1313 Nicollet. Contemporary. Wine racks line one of the stucco walls of this restaurant in the Regal Hotel. The kitchen turns out corn-crusted shrimp, pork poppers, chicken grills, and other interesting fare. Buffet breakfast. Kids' menu. | 1313 Nicollet Ave. | 612/332–6000 | $9–$18 | AE, D, DC, MC, V.

EXPENSIVE

Auriga. Contemporary. Modern art and concrete floors underscore the modern aesthetic here. The cuisine is subtle and delicious; you might find homemade pasta dressed with

roast rabbit, parsley root, and porcini mushrooms; or brown rice-and-walnut croquettes nestled on a bed of wilted greens, portobello mushrooms, and thin parsnip crisps. | 1930 Hennepin Ave. S | 612/871–0777 | $16–$18 | AE, D, DC, MC, V.

Bobino Cafe and Wine Bar. Contemporary. Hanging lights made from old wine bottles illuminate this dining room where the menu changes biweekly. It's a good bet for both everyday meals and for special occasions. Entrées might include grilled salmon fillet with risotto, or any number of ostrich- and rabbit-based dishes. There is also a selection of tapas. The garden-flanked patio is pleasant when the weather is accommodating. | 222 E. Hennepin Ave. | 612/623–3301 | $16–$23 | No lunch Sat., Sun. | AE, D, DC, MC, V.

Cafe Un Deux Trois. French. The banquette seating, terrazzo floor, rosy faux-marble walls, and high, painted ceiling of this French bistro recall the worlds of Colette and Edith Piaf. Roast Long Island duck and grilled salmon with lobster-infused risotto are among the more popular dishes. | 114 S. 9th St. | 612/673–0686 | Closed Sun. No dinner Sat. | $16–$28 | AE, DC, MC, V.

Giorgio. Italian. Yuppies and hipsters flock to this northern Italian eatery for romantic nights out, but just as many people regard it as their friendly neighborhood trattoria. The daily ravioli special (with a different filling each day) is by far the favorite option; also popular is the *cinghiale* (a penne pasta with wild boar sausage, oven-dried tomatoes, and caramelized onions). There's a sunny dining area for nonsmokers and dark bar for smokers. Beer and wine only. | 2451 Hennepin Ave. | 612/374–5131 | $14–$20 | DC, MC, V.

Ichiban Japanese Steak House. Japanese. You sit around huge griddles as your food is cooked, and kimono-clad waitresses take your order. All dinners include a chicken liver and mushroom appetizer sautéed in sake and butter, soup, marinated cucumber salad, vegetables, rice, and green tea. There's a small moat around the sushi bar and you can select your sushi from little boats that float by. | 1333 Nicollet Ave. | 612/339–0540 | No lunch | $17–$33 | AE, D, DC, MC, V.

Jax Café. American. Steaks top the list here. Thick as a weightlifter's neck, they're hands-down the most satisfying choices. In winter, you can sit by a fireplace in the dark Round-table Room; in summer, there's patio dining. Pianist Thurs.–Sun. Sun. brunch. | 1928 University Ave. NE | 612/789–7297 | $15–$35 | AE, D, DC, MC, V.

Loring Cafe. Contemporary. Brick arches, towering trees, and exposed ductwork add to this restaurant's cultivated counterculture atmosphere. Try shrimp with pears, or manicotti with lamb and cheese. Open-air patio. Entertainment. | 1624 Harmon Place | 612/332–1617 | $18–$36 | MC, V.

New French Café and Bar. French. This bistro is in a converted turn-of-the-20th-century warehouse in the Warehouse district. The menu reveals an Asian influence—witness the chicken paste with truffle bits, brie and watercress stuffed into spring-roll wrappers and stacked in a pyramid with Dijon mayonnaise anchoring the corners, and grilled pork tenderloin arranged over a cold horseradish-and-sweet-corn sauce and onion slaw. Open-air dining. Sun. brunch. | 128 N. 4th St., at 2nd Ave. N | 612/338–3790 | $16–$24 | AE, DC, MC, V.

Oceanaire. Seafood. Leatherette booths lend a clubby air to this restaurant, which has an oyster bar and individual relish trays. Crab cakes and cioppino are popular. | 1300 Nicollet Mall | 612/333–2277 | No lunch | $18–$30 | AE, D, DC, MC, V.

Origami. Japanese. This Warehouse-district destination is known for its sushi. The interior shimmers with lilac lights and flickering candles, and a sidewalk patio is open in summer. | 30 N. 1st St. | www.origamirestaurant.com | 612/333–8430 | Closed Sun. No lunch Sat. | $15–$21 | AE, D, DC, MC, V.

VERY EXPENSIVE

Aquavit. Scandinavian. Transplanted from New York, the restaurant sits in the atrium of a Midwestern skyscraper. Shrimp, herring, salmon, venison, lingonberries, and juniper are a starting point for complex but subtle preparations, often with an Asian twist. Locals favor the venison loin, the miso-grilled bass, and the herring tacos. | IDS Center at S. 7th St and Nicollet Mall | 612/343–3333 | No lunch Sun. | $24–$30 | AE, DC, MC, V.

D'Amico Cucina. Italian. White-linen tablecloths and exposed wood-beam ceilings distinguish this renovated space. The restaurant is known for its modern renditions of Italian classics. | 100 N. 6th St. | 612/338–2401 | No lunch | $22–$30 | AE, D, DC, MC, V.

Goodfellow's. Contemporary. Many of the restored light fixtures, mirrors, and other decorative pieces you'll see came from the popular Art Deco cafeteria that once stood here. The menu emphasizes regional products and foods made from scratch—the Wisconsin star prairie brook trout exemplifies the approach. | 40 S. 7th St. | 612/332–4800 | Closed Sun. | $20–$30 | AE, D, DC, MC, V.

Manny's Steakhouse. Steak. Waiters in white aprons squeeze between packed tables on hardwood floors in this meat-lover's landmark, which is known state-wide for its perfectly cooked dry-aged steaks. | 1300 Nicollet Mall | 612/339–9900 | No lunch | $20–$40 | AE, D, DC, MC, V.

Meadows. Continental. This restaurant is in the Radisson-Metrodome Hotel, but the dark wood, comfortable chairs, and classical music in the air feel more like an old-fashioned country club. On the menu are seafood, steak, and native game. Pianist Fri., Sat. | 615 Washington Ave. SE | 612/379–8888 | Closed Sun. No lunch | $20–$40 | AE, D, DC, MC, V.

Morton's of Chicago. Continental. The songs of Frank Sinatra are always in the background at this popular steakhouse below Nicollet Avenue. You can order a huge steak or prime rib, a Maine lobster, or a 1-lb baked potato. | 555 Nicollet Mall | 612/673–9700 | $30–$60 | AE, DC, MC, V.

Murray's. Steak. This third-generation steak house, with its pink linen–covered tables, has been in business since 1946. Steaks are well prepared, and there are garlic toast, hickory-smoked shrimp, and selections from its on-site bakery. Entertainment Thurs.–Sat. | 26 S. 6th St. | 612/339–0909 | No lunch Sat., Sun. | $20–$35 | AE, D, DC, MC, V.

Whitney Grille. American. This slice of a former Mississippi River flour mill is now a long, narrow dining room with dark woodwork and booths. By far the favorite menu item is Minnesota walleye. Open-air dining. Entertainment on Fri.–Sat. Sun. brunch. No smoking. | 150 Portland Ave. | 612/372–6405 | No dinner | $20–$30 | AE, D, DC, MC, V.

Lodging

INEXPENSIVE

Aqua City Motel. The first half of this brick motel was built in the 1950s, the second half in the 1960s, and it was bought by the present owner in 1997. It is between the city and the southern suburbs, 5 mi from both downtown and the Mall of America. Some kitchenettes. Cable TV. Outdoor pool. Free parking. | 5739 Lyndale Ave. S | 612/861–6061 or 800/861–6061 | 38 rooms | $49–$69 | AE, D, DC, MC, V.

Metro Inn. Centrally placed between downtown and the southern suburbs, this motel is about 10 mi west of the Mall of America. Cable TV. Some pets allowed (fee). | 5637 Lyndale Ave. S | 612/861–6011 | fax 612/869–1041 | 35 rooms | $35–$52 | AE, D, DC, MC, V.

MODERATE

Baymont Inn. Downtown Minneapolis is 4 mi southeast of this three-story hotel next to Earle Brown's Bowling and within a few blocks of movie theaters and the Brookdale Shopping Center. You're 22 mi from the Minneapolis/St. Paul airport. Complimentary Continental breakfast. In-room data ports. Cable TV. Business services. Free parking. | 6415 James Cir., Brooklyn Center | 763/561–8400 | fax 763/560–3189 | www.baymontinn.com | 99 rooms | $65–$84 | AE, D, DC, MC, V.

Best Western Kelly Inn. A theater in this two-story motel west of Minneapolis hosts off-Broadway productions and musicals. Restaurant, bar, room service. Cable TV. Indoor pool. Hot tub. Exercise equipment. Video games. Laundry facilities, laundry service. Business services, free parking. | 2705 Annapolis, Plymouth | 763/553–1600 | fax 763/553–9108 | www.bestwestern.com | 150 rooms | $69–$185 | AE, D, DC, MC, V.

Chanhassen Inn. Fifteen miles west of Minneapolis, this two-story brick motel caters to business travelers. The lobby has a vaulted ceiling and a large fireplace. Complimentary Continental breakfast. In-room data ports, microwaves, refrigerators. Cable TV. Laundry facilities. Business services. | 531 W. 79th St., Chanhassen | 952/934–7373 or 800/242–6466 | 74 rooms | $59 | AE, D, DC, MC, V.

Econolodge University. Two mi from the MetroDome and 1 mi from downtown. Complimentary Continental breakfast. In-room data ports. Some kitchenettes, some microwaves, some refrigerators. Cable TV. Pool. Business services. | 2500 University Ave. SE | 612/331–6000 | fax 612/331–6821 | 80 rooms | $75–$99 | AE, D, DC, MC, V.

Super 8. This two-story brick building is 1 mi north of the Brookdale Mall off I–694, exit 34, and 5 mi northwest of downtown. Complimentary Continental breakfast. Cable TV. Business services. | 6445 James Cir., Brooklyn Center | 763/566–9810 | fax 763/566–8680 | www.super8.com | 102 rooms | $73 | AE, D, DC, MC, V.

EXPENSIVE

Best Western Downtown. In the heart of downtown, this two-building, four-story hotel is the first stop for many airport limousines. Bar, complimentary Continental breakfast. In-room data ports. Cable TV. Indoor pool. Hot tub. Exercise equipment. Business services, parking (fee). | 405 S. 8th St. | 612/370–1400 | fax 612/370–0351 | www.bestwestern.com | 159 rooms | $94 | AE, D, DC, MC, V.

Comfort Inn. Built in 1996, this three-story hotel with beige stucco walls and white trim is off I–694, exit 34, 5 mi from downtown Minneapolis. Complimentary Continental breakfast. In-room data ports, some microwaves, some refrigerators. Cable TV. Hot tub, spa. Video games. Business services. Pets allowed. | 1600 James Cir. N, Brooklyn Center | 612/560–7464 | 60 rooms | $90 | AE, D, DC, MC, V.

Days Inn University. Six stories of white stucco stand on the east edge of the University of Minnesota campus. Complimentary Continental breakfast. In-room data ports, some refrigerators. Cable TV. Laundry facilities. Business services. | 2407 University Ave. SE | 612/623–3999 | fax 612/331–2152 | www.daysinn.com | 131 rooms | $99–$160 | AE, D, DC, MC, V.

Doubletree Park Place. This 16-story brick hotel is 3 mi outside of downtown, in St. Louis Park. Because the suburb charges no local hotel tax, room taxes at the facility are only 6½% (Minnesota state charges), instead of the 13% (state plus city charges) collected by downtown establishments. Restaurant, bar, room service. In-room data ports. Cable TV. Indoor pool. Hot tub. Exercise equipment. Video games. Business services. | 1500 Park Place Blvd. | 612/542–8600 | fax 612/542–8068 | www.doubletree.com | 297 rooms | $79–$154 | AE, D, DC, MC, V.

Hampton Inn. Six mi southeast of Minneapolis surrounded by shopping malls and restaurants, this hotel occupies a redbrick four-story building. Complimentary Continental breakfast. In-room data ports. Cable TV. Exercise equipment. Laundry Business services. | 10420 Wayzata Blvd. | 952/541–1094 | fax 952/541–1905 | www.hamptoninn.com | 127 rooms | $79–$109 | AE, D, DC, MC, V.

Holiday Inn–Metrodome. Four blocks from the Metrodome and 1 mi east of the business district. Restaurant, bar (with entertainment). In-room data ports. Cable TV. Indoor pool. Exercise equipment. Business services, airport shuttle. | 1500 Washington Ave. S | 612/333–4646 | fax 612/333–7910 | www.metrodome.com | 265 rooms | $99–$139 | AE, D, DC, MC, V.

Mounds View Inn. Spanish contemporary fixtures characterize this two-story hotel at the intersection of Route 35W North and Ramsey County Rd. 10, 11 mi north of downtown Minneapolis. Bar, complimentary Continental breakfast. Cable TV, in-room VCRs (and movies). Laundry facilities. Business services. | 2149 Program Ave., Mounds View | 612/786–9151 or 800/777–7863 | fax 612/786–2845 | 70 rooms | $79 | AE, D, DC, MC, V.

VERY EXPENSIVE

Crowne Plaza Northstar. Part of the business district, this luxury hotel has direct access to the city's skyway system. Restaurants, bar. In-room data ports. Cable TV. Beauty salon. Exercise equipment. Business services. | 618 2nd Ave. S | 612/338–2288, ext. 318 | fax 612/338–2288 | www.basshotels.com/crowneplaza | 226 rooms, 6 suites | $160–$175, $250–$500 suites | AE, D, DC, MC, V.

Doubletree. This all-suites hotel is one block off Nicollet Mall. Restaurant, bar. In-room data ports, microwaves, refrigerators. Cable TV. Exercise equipment. Business services. | 1101 LaSalle Ave. | 612/332–6800 | fax 612/332–8246 | www.doubletree.com | 230 suites | $144–$199 suites | AE, D, DC, MC, V.

Embassy Suites–Downtown. A six-story atrium filled with tropical plants dominates this all-suites hotel, which occupies the top seven floors of an executive office building, 4 blocks west of Nicollet Mall. Restaurant, bar, complimentary breakfast. In-room data ports, microwaves, refrigerators. Cable TV. Indoor pool. Hot tub. Exercise equipment. Business services. | 425 S. 7th St. | 612/333–3111 | fax 612/333–7984 | www.embassy-suites.com | 217 suites | $155–$189 | AE, D, DC, MC, V.

Hilton Towers. One of the most luxurious of the downtown hotels, this 25-story Victorian-style edifice is connected by skyway to the financial district. Orchestra Hall is next door. Restaurant, bar. In-room data ports. Cable TV. Pool. Hot tub. Exercise equipment. Business services. | 1001 Marquette Ave. S | 612/376–1000 | fax 612/397–4875 | www.hilton.com/hotels/MSPMHHH | 814 rooms, 30 suites | $150–$245, $700–$1,000 suites | AE, D, DC, MC, V.

Hyatt Regency. In the center of the financial district, this is accessible to the Convention Center via skywalk. Restaurants, bar. In-room data ports. Cable TV. Indoor pool. Beauty salon. Business services, airport shuttle. | 1300 Nicollet Mall | 612/370–1234 | fax 612/370–1463 | www.hyatt.com/pages/m/msprma.html | 533 rooms, 21 suites | $199–$224, $290–$800 suites | AE, D, DC, MC, V.

★ **Hyatt Whitney.** This 8-story former flour mill, a hotel since 1982, overlooks the Mississippi River and St. Anthony Falls. Restaurant, bar (with entertainment). In-room data ports, refrigerators, room service. Cable TV. Business services, airport shuttle. | 150 Portland Ave. | 612/339–9300 or 800/248–1879 | fax 612/339–1333 | www.hyatt.com/pages/m/msp-wha.html | 97 rooms, 40 suites | $160–$170, $195–$1,600 suites | AE, D, DC, MC, V.

Inn on the Farm. Housed in four renovated buildings in the Earle Brown Heritage Center, the Inn on the Farm is 5 mi north of downtown Minneapolis. All-weather-glass-enclosed walkways connect the various parts of the complex. Complimentary breakfast and afternoon snacks. Business services. Free Parking. | 6130 Summit Dr. N | 612/569–6330 or 800/428–8382 | www.innonthefarm.com | 9 rooms, 1 suite | $110–$130, $130–$150 suite | AE, D, DC, MC, V.

The Marquette. This boutique hotel in downtown Minneapolis is part of the IDS Center complex. Restaurant, bar. In-room data ports. Cable TV. Exercise equipment. Business services. | 710 Marquette Ave. | 612/333–4545 or 800/328–4782 | fax 612/376–7419 | www.hilton.com/hotels/MSPVIVI | 278 rooms, 40 suites | $229–$389, $389–$810 suites | AE, D, DC, MC, V.

Marriott–City Center. Four blocks southeast of the Target Center, this 31-story glass high-rise downtown has direct access to the city's skyway system. Restaurants, bar. In-room data

MINNEAPOLIS

INTRO
ATTRACTIONS
DINING
LODGING

ports. Cable TV. Hot tub, massage. Gym. Laundry services. Business services, parking (fee). | 30 S. 7th St. | 612/349–4000 | fax 612/332–7165 | www.marriotthotels.com/mspcc | 583 rooms, 83 suites | $188–$229, $299–$850 suites | AE, D, DC, MC, V.

Nicollet Island Inn. Nestled on Nicollet Island, across the Mississippi River from downtown Minneapolis, this former factory and men's shelter has a great view of the Minneapolis skyline. An inn since the 1970s, it's on the National Register of Historic Places. Restaurant, complimentary Continental breakfast, room service, in-room data ports. Cable TV. Business services, free parking. | 95 Merriam St. | 612/331–1800 | fax 612/331–6528 | www.nicolletislandinn.com | 24 rooms | $135–$170 | AE, D, DC, MC, V.

Northland Inn. This high-tech conference center is in an eight-story modern brick structure. All accommodations are two-room suites with whirlpools. Restaurant, bar. In-room data ports. Cable TV. Indoor pool. Hot tub. Exercise equipment. Video games. Business services. | 7025 Northland Dr., Brooklyn Park | 612/536–8300 or 800/441–6422 | fax 612/533–6607 | www.northlandinn.com | 231 suites | $129–$219 | AE, D, DC, MC, V.

Quality Inn. The closest hotel to the Target Center, this 1937 stucco hotel is downtown, a block from the Hennepin Avenue theater district. Restaurant, bar (with entertainment), room service. In-room data ports. Cable TV. Indoor pool. Hot tub. Laundry facilities. Business services. | 41 N. 10th St. | 612/339–9311 | fax 612/339–4765 | www.choicehotels.com | 192 rooms | $109 | AE, D, DC, MC, V.

Radisson Hotel and Conference Center. On 25 acres of marshland, this six-story hotel is part of the Northwest Business Center, 10 mi north of downtown Minneapolis. Restaurant, bar. Minibars. In-room data ports, refrigerators. Cable TV. Indoor pool. Hot tub. Tennis. Gym, racquetball. Business services. | 3131 Campus Dr., Plymouth | 612/559–6600 | fax 612/559–1053 | www.radisson.com/minneapolismn_plymouth | 243 rooms, 6 suites | $119–$154, $199–$325 suites | AE, D, DC, MC, V.

Radisson–Metrodome. This hotel is 1 mi east of downtown on the University of Minnesota campus, in easy reach of the Northrop Auditorium, the Weisman Art Museum, the Williams Arena, the Aquatic Center, and other university landmarks. Restaurants, bar. In-room data ports. Exercise equipment. Business services. Some pets allowed. | 615 Washington Ave. SE | 612/379–8888 | fax 612/379–8436 | www.radisson.com | 304 rooms, 34 suites | $105–$120, $145–$350 suites | AE, D, DC, MC, V.

Radisson Plaza. Connected by skyways to upscale shopping, this glass-walled skyscraper is 1½ blocks west of the Target Center and the edge of the trendy Warehouse district. Restaurant, bar (with entertainment), room service. In-room data ports. Cable TV. Hot tub. Gym. Business services. | 35 S. 7th St. | 612/339–4900 | fax 612/337–9766 | www.radisson.com/minneapolismn_plaza | 357 rooms, 42 suites | $178–$258, $310–$410 suites | AE, D, DC, MC, V.

Ramada Plaza Hotel. A double atrium dominates this hotel, 8 mi west of Minneapolis. Restaurant, bar, room service. In-room data ports. Cable TV. Indoor pool. Exercise equipment. Business services. | 12201 Ridgedale Dr., Minnetonka | 612/593–0000 | fax 612/544–2090 | www.theramadahotelminneapolis.com | 222 rooms | $119–$129 | AE, D, DC, MC, V.

Regal Minneapolis. Nicollet Mall is the site of this hostelry, the closest hotel to the Minneapolis Convention Center. Restaurant, bars. In-room data ports. Cable TV. Indoor pool. Exercise equipment. Laundry facilities. Business services, airport shuttle. Some pets allowed. | 1313 Nicollet Mall | 612/332–6000 or 800/522–8856 | fax 612/359–2160 | www.regal/hotels.com | 325 rooms, 43 suites | $189–$205, $199–$365 suites | AE, D, DC, MC, V.

Sheraton Four Points Hotel. Three mi east of downtown, the hotel has regular shuttle service to the Metrodome. Restaurant, bar (with entertainment). In-room data ports. Cable TV. Indoor pool. Hot tub. Exercise equipment. Business services, airport shuttle. | 1330 Industrial Blvd. | 612/331–1900 | fax 612/331–6827 | www.fourpoints.com | 252 rooms | $114–$205 | AE, D, DC, MC, V.

MOORHEAD

(Nearby towns also listed: Detroit Lakes, Fergus Falls)

Moorhead and its neighbor across the river, Fargo, North Dakota, dominate agricultural commerce in the region. One of the biggest businesses here is sugar refining. Moorhead refineries produce millions of pounds of sugar each year from beets raised in and around Clay County. It's also a cultural center with three colleges, a symphony orchestra, and a civic opera.

Information: Moorhead/Fargo Convention and Visitors Bureau | 2001 44th St. SW, Moorhead, 58103 | 701/282–3653 or 800/235–7654.

Attractions

Comstock Historic House. This 1882 home was built by Solomon Comstock, who established the First National Bank and Moorhead State University and helped James J. Hill build a railroad system in the Red River Valley. Ada Comstock, one of three children reared in this home, became the first dean of women at the University of Minnesota and later president of Radcliffe College. Guided tours interpret the restored house and original furnishings. Varnished oak and butternut trim and Queen Anne Eastlake furniture and tapestries brighten the rooms. | 506 8th St. S | 218/291–4211 | www.mnhs.org/places/sites/ch/index.html | Free | Late May–Sept., Sat., Sun. 1–4:15.

Heritage–Hjemkomst Interpretive Center. Interpretive exhibits chronicle the construction and voyage of the *Hjemkomst,* a Viking ship that sailed across the Atlantic in 1982. A replica of the ship is the largest display. Also on site is the Clay County Museum. | 202 1st Ave. N | 218/299–5511 | $3.50 | Mon.–Wed., Fri.–Sat. 9–5, Thurs. 9–9, Sun. noon–5.

Regional Science Center–Planetarium. Part of Minnesota State University, the planetarium runs five different shows each year. | 11th St. and 8th Ave. S | 218/236–3982 | www.mnstate.edu/regsci/planetarium.html | $3 | Call for showtimes.

ON THE CALENDAR

JUNE: *Scandinavian Hjemkomst Festival.* For four days, locals and visitors celebrate Scandinavia with Nordic arts and crafts, folk costume fashion shows, dancing, singing, and foods from Denmark, Finland, Iceland, Norway, and Sweden. The festival is held at the Heritage–Hjemkomst Interpretive Center, with additional "mini-fests" throughout Moorhead and Fargo, North Dakota, Moorhead's twin city. | 218/233–8484.

Lodging

Red River Inn. Two stories of solid brick, the hotel is 2½ mi south of the University and College. All attractions in Moorhead and Fargo, North Dakota, are within a 15-minute drive. Restaurant, bar. Cable TV. Indoor pool. Sauna. Exercise equipment. Some pets allowed. | 600 30th Ave. S | 218/233–6171 or 800/328–6173 | fax 218/233–0945 | 173 rooms | $71–$78 | AE, D, DC, MC, V.

Super 8. Concordia College and Moorhead State University are both 1 mi from this two-story stucco motel. Complimentary Continental breakfast. Cable TV. Video games. Laundry facilities. Business services. | 3621 8th St. S | 218/233–8880 | 61 rooms | $40–$43 | AE, D, DC, MC, V.

MORA

(Nearby town also listed: Hinckley)

Swedish immigrant farmers founded this town in 1882, and today's residents take pride in their Swedish heritage—they have a sister city in Sweden, also named Mora, and colorful and traditional Swedish dala horses are displayed around town. The city's biggest employers include a leading plastics manufacturer, a nationally known direct-mail marketer, and a yacht builder.

Information: **Mora Area Chamber of Commerce** | 20 N. Union St., 55051 | 320/679–5792 or 800/291–5792 | www.moramn-chamber.com.

Attractions

Ann Lake. With a maximum depth of 17 ft, this 653-acre lake is popular with walleye anglers. It's between Routes 26 and 6. | Rte. 47 | 800/291–5792 | Free | Daily.

Dala Horse. Brightly painted wooden horse sculptures are a Swedish tradition and a symbol of Mora's roots. This colorful, 22-ft-high, 18-ft-long replica of the Dala Horse of Dalacarlia, Sweden, at the Kanabec County Fairgrounds, is the largest dala horse in North America. | 701 S. Union St.

Fish Lake. Known for its resident walleye and northern pike, this reservoir southwest of town spans 407 acres. | West of Rte. 65 | 800/291–5792 | Free | Daily.

Kanabec County History Center. Craft demonstrations, hands-on activities, music, and special holiday events are held regularly here. | 805 West Forrest Ave. | www.kanabechistory.com | 320/679–1665 | $3 | Mon.–Sat. 10–4:30, Sun. 12:30–4:30.

Knife Lake. Walleye anglers like to wet their lines in this 1,266-acre lake north of town. | Between Rtes. 19 and 3 | 800/291–5792 | Free | Daily.

Snake River. Fishing and canoeing are available in this river, which winds along Mora's western border. | 800/291–5792.

ON THE CALENDAR

FEB.: *Vasaloppet–Cross-Country Ski Race.* Minnesota's largest cross-country competition, the race is run the second Sunday of the month on two woodland courses, ending at a downtown finish line. | 800/368–6672.

MAY: *Mora Snake River Canoe Race.* This two-hour race begins at the Hinckley Road Bridge on the first Saturday of the month. | 800/291–5792.

Lodging

Ann River Swedish Motel. Quiet and seclusion are the key words at this single-story motel, even though it's right in town, about a mile from Mora's only stoplight. Complimentary Continental breakfast. No-smoking rooms, in-room hot tubs. Cable TV. Some pets allowed. | 1819 Rte. 65S | 320/679–2972 | fax 320/679–2973 | 23 rooms | $35–$95 | AE, D, MC, V.

Motel Mora. Built in 1965, this one-story brick motel includes a sun deck, and is on the south side of town. Picnic area. In-room data ports, some microwaves, some refrigerators. Cable TV. Business services. Some pets allowed (fee). | 301 Rte. 65S | 320/679–3262 or 800/657–0167 | fax 320/679–5135 | 23 rooms | $40–$52 | AE, D, DC, MC, V.

MORRIS

(Nearby town also listed: Glenwood)

Founded in 1871 and named after the St. Paul and Pacific Railroad's chief engineer, Charles F. Morris, this is a railroad town. It is also a hub for agricultural research, information services, and agribusinesses, with a population of 5,600. The town has many natural areas open to hiking, bird-watching, and photography.

Information: Morris Area Chamber of Commerce | 507 Atlantic Ave., 56267 | 320/589–1242.

Attractions
Stevens County Historical Society. You can learn about the history of Stevens County through the exhibits in this former Carnegie Library, built in 1905. Among the displays are antique clothing, musical instruments, and farm implements. | 116 W. 6th St. | 320/589–1719 | Donation | Monday–Friday 9–5.

Pomme de Terre City Park. There are swimming, fishing, canoeing, picnicking, and camping in this 363-acre park next to the Pomme de Terre River on the east edge of town. | Rte. 10 | 320/589–1242 | Free | Apr.–Oct., daily.

University of Minnesota–Morris. The small campus (student enrollment is 1,980), north of downtown, has a fine arts gallery with contemporary exhibits. | 600 E. 4th St. | 320/589–6050 | www.mrs.umn.edu | Daily.

ON THE CALENDAR
JULY: *Prairie Pioneer Days.* This midsummer event includes a parade, a craft show, a bike race, food vendors, musicians, and sporting events. | 320/589–1242.
SEPT.: *Harvest Holiday Festival.* Pumpkin carvers compete at the county fairgrounds on Labor Day, and local farmers and artisans sell woodwork, stained glass, quilts, homemade candy, and local apples and pumpkins the second weekend after the holiday. | 320/795–2412.

Dining
Diamond Club. American. Candles and red tablecloths set the scene in this basement dining room, where the menu runs to prime rib, steaks, lobster, shrimp, and surf 'n' turf combinations. Many weddings take place in the two adjacent banquet halls. | 26 E 6th St. | 320/589–4611 | $8–$17 | No credit cards.

Lodging
American House Bed & Breakfast. Each bedroom of this 1900 Victorian is named after one of the owner's grandparents or great-grandparents, and has original wall stencils and heirlooms. The university campus is 1 block away. Complimentary breakfast. TV in common area. No room phones. No pets. | 410 3rd St. | 320/589–4054 | 3 rooms | $40–$60 | MC, V.

Best Western Prairie Inn. A wide expanse of lawn surrounds this two-story brick motel, which is four blocks from University of Minnesota–Morris, and 11 blocks from the Stevens County Museum. Restaurant, bar. Complimentary Continental breakfast Sun.–Thurs. Cable TV. Indoor pool, wading pool. Hot tub, sauna. Video games. Business services. Some pets allowed. | 200 Rte. 28E | 320/589–3030 or 800/535–3035 | fax 320/589–3030 | 90 rooms | $64 | AE, D, DC, MC, V.

Morris Motel. This single-story motel is on the south side of town, 5 blocks from the business district. Cable TV. | 207 Rte. 9S | 320/589–1212 | 14 rooms | $29–$35 | D, MC, V.

MORRIS

INTRO
ATTRACTIONS
DINING
LODGING

NEW PRAGUE

MAP 3, E8

(Nearby towns also listed: Bloomington, Faribault, Le Sueur, Northfield, Shakopee)

The residents of New Prague (pronounced with a long "a") have blended their town's Czech and German heritages with modern culture to produce a contemporary community with old world undertones. Forty mi southwest of Minneapolis, it has a vibrant Main Street, a growing commercial and industrial base, and a population of 4,100. The Bohemians who founded the town in the 1850s called it Orel, Bohemian for eagle. By the time the railroad arrived in 1877, they had changed the name to New Prague.

Information: New Prague Chamber of Commerce | 101 E. Main, New Prague, 56071 | 952/758–4360 | www.newprague.com.

Attractions

Yackley's Cabin. If you want to understand how early settlers really lived, stop by this tiny shack, which settlers Frederick and Katherine Yackley called home in the mid–1800's. | Corner of 2nd St. and Rte. 21, off Rte. 169 | 612/758–4360 | Free | Daily.

St. Wenceslaus Church. Built in 1906 with stained-glass windows imported from Europe, this church is on the National Register of Historic Places. The Cemetery Chapel next door, built in 1899, has solid marble walls 2 ft thick and a copper dome. | 215 E. Main St. | 952/758–3225 | Free | Daily.

Wallseum. Murals on the walls of downtown buildings depict the history of the city. A walking-tour map available from the Chamber of Commerce guides you from one to the next. | Downtown streets | 952/758–4360 | Free | Daily.

ON THE CALENDAR

SEPT.: *Dozinsky.* The ethnic food stands, multiple live bands, Czech dancers, and 400-strong antique car parade draw more than 15,000 people to this Czechoslovakian harvest festival, held mid-month along Main St. | 952/758–4360.

Dining

Fish Tail Grill. Czech. Cases of fishing lures and trophy fish fill the walls of this log restaurant; the newspaper-cum-menu bills itself as the "Fish Tail Spinner." Roasted pork with sauerkraut and dumplings is on the menu every Monday, and walleye pike and burgers top diners' choices the rest of the week. | 200 E. Rte. 37 | 952/758–8000 | Breakfast also served | $8–$15 | AE, MC, V.

Schumacher's. German. The woodwork and fireplaces in this hotel dining room bring to mind a central European inn. The food is mostly wild game, and German and Czech ethnic dishes: grilled red elk loin, Czech roasted duck, and six-sided pork tenderloin steak. All entrees include two sides and a dinner salad. There's an herb and edible flower garden outside. Sun. brunch. Kid's menu. | 212 W. Main St. | 612/758–2133 800/283–2049 | www.schumachershotel.com | $26–$36 | AE, D, DC, MC, V.

Lodging

Heritage Inn Motel. This no-frills mom-and-pop motel, built in the 1980s, is downtown, one block from the flashing-red-light intersection of Rtes. 13, 19, and 21. Air-conditioning. Some microwaves. Room phones. | 410 Main St. W | 952/758–4100 | 9 rooms | $35–$40 | D, MC, V.

Schumacher's New Prague Hotel. Designed by architect Cass Gilbert (who also designed the capitol building in St. Paul and New York City's Woolworth Building, among other prominent U.S. structures), this 2-story structure, dating from 1898, is on the National Register of Historic Places. Restaurant, bar. Business services. Free parking. | 212 W. Main St. | 952/758–2133 or 800/283–2049 | www.schumachershotel.com | 16 rooms | $140–$275 | AE, D, DC, MC, V.

NEW ULM

(Nearby towns also listed: Hutchinson, Mankato, Redwood Falls, St. Peter)

After a careful search for a new home, German immigrant farmers chose this piece of Dakota Indian country as the perfect spot, settling here in 1854. They named the town after their mother city across the Atlantic. It was built as a planned community, and still emanates a built-in orderliness. Modern-day New Ulm (pop. 14,000) is known for its German music festivals and specialty shops.

Information: New Ulm Convention and Visitors Bureau | 1 N. Minnesota St., New Ulm, 56073 | 507/354–4217 | www.ic.new-ulm.mn.us.

Attractions

Brown County Historical Museum. Three floors of displays explore Brown County and American Indian history in this former post office building. There are also extensive files for genealogical research. | 2 N. Broadway | 507/354–2016 | $2 | May–Sept., Mon.–Fri. 10–5, Sat. 1–5; Oct.–April, Mon.–Fri. noon–5, Sat. 1–5.

Flandrau State Park. The slow-moving Big Cottonwood River meanders through this 805-acre park dotted by old stone structures built in the 1930s by the Works Project Administration. During the 1940s, the park was used as a camp for German prisoners of war. It has a sand-bottom swimming pond, a picnic area, campgrounds, and a group center. | 1300 Summit Ave. | 507/233–9800 | www.dnr.state.mn.us/parks_and_recreation/state_parks/flandrau | Park permit required | Daily.

Fort Ridgely State Park. Once a thriving outpost, this 584-acre park was a battle site in the U.S.–Dakota Conflict of 1862. Today, it has a nine-hole golf course, camping facilities, hiking, cross-country skiing, and horseback-riding trails. It's 18 mi northeast of New Ulm, 12 mi north of Sleepy Eye, and 6 mi south of Fairfax. | Off Rte. 4 | 507/426–7840 | www.dnr.state.mn.us/parks_and_recreation/state_parks/fort_ridgely | Park permit required | Daily.

The Glockenspiel. In three daily performances, animated figures dance to the music of the 37-bell carillon in a 45-ft-tall clock tower downtown. | N. 4th St. and Minnesota St. | Daily at noon, 3, and 5.

Harkin Store. A costumed staff "sells" period wares in this recreated 1870s general store 9 mi northwest of New Ulm. | Rte. 21 | 507/354–2016 or 507/354–8666 | www.state.mn.us/ebranch/mhs/places/sites/hs | Free | May, Sat., Sun. 10–5; June–Aug., Tues.–Sun. 10–5; Sept.–Oct., Fri.–Sun. 10–5.

Hermann's Monument. This 102-ft monument in Hermann Park (more familiarly known as "Hermann the German") commemorates Hermann the Cheruscan, a 1st-century German hero. Although the park is open year-round, public access to the monument is restricted during the winter months due to weather conditions making the steps unsafe. The park is 10 blocks west of downtown. | Center and Summit Sts. | 507/359–8344 | Free | June–Labor Day, daily.

The John Lind House. Minnesota's Swedish-born 14th governor built this home in 1887. Now listed on the National Register of Historic Homes, the house contains Lind's furniture and oil portraits that once hung in the state capitol. | Center and State Sts. | 507/354–8802 | $1 | Apr., May, Sept.—Jan. Fri.–Sun. 1–4; Memorial Day–Labor Day Mon.–Sun. 1–4. Closed Jan.–Mar.

Schell Brewing Company. New Ulm's oldest industrial site, founded in 1860, is open for business and tours. Deer and peacocks roam the gardens outside. | 1860 Schell Rd. (Broadway and 18 South St.) | 507/354–5528 | www.schellsbrewery.com | $2 | Memorial Day–Labor Day, daily noon–5, Mon.–Fri. tours at 3 and 4, Sat.–Sun. tours at 1, 2, 3, and 4.

The Wanda Gag House. Named for the author of the 1946 children's book, *Millions of Cats*, this 1894 structure retains its original interior oil paint, including 18-inch hand-crafted ceiling borders. Anton Gag, the author's father, built the house. | 226 N. Washington St. | 507/359–2632 | June–Aug. Sat.–Sun. 1–5, Sept.–May by appt.

ON THE CALENDAR

FEB.: *Fasching*. This German Mardi Gras, held in Turner Hall, means continuous entertainment, arts and crafts, and German and American food. | 507/354–8850.

JULY: *Heritagefest*. New Ulm's largest festival, held at the fairgrounds, draws 50,000 people for entertainment from home and abroad, a keg opening, and a tuba concert. | 507/354–8850.

AUG.: *Brown County Fair*. Livestock exhibitions, rides, and live entertainment are part of the festivities at the fairgrounds for this event. | 507/354–4217.

OCT.: *Oktoberfest*. The traditional German fall festival has sauerkraut, landjaegers, German potato salad, apple strudel, and lots of live music. It's held downtown and at the Holiday Inn. | 507/354–4217.

DEC.: *Christmas Parade*. Lighted floats from area businesses glide down Minnesota Street the Friday evening after Thanksgiving. | 507/354–4217.

Dining

DJ's. German, American. On the menu of this downtown diner are a full roast-beef dinner and a quarter roasted chicken. | 1200 N. Broadway | 507/354–3843 | $7–$12 | No credit cards.

Lamplighter Family Sports Bar and Grill. American. Beer steins lining the walls and nine TVs in the bar area accent this family place downtown. Popular for its creative burgers— the Lamplighter Burger is loaded with cheese, fried onions and coleslaw—the menu also lists steaks and various pastas, including fettucine Alfredo. | 214 N. Minnesota St. | 507/354–2185 | $5–$9 | AE, D, MC, V.

Veigel's Kaiserhoff. American. Bavarian murals decorate the bar of this downtown restaurant, run since 1938 by the same owner. The menu is half German, half American. You can tuck into barbecued ribs or chow down on the German sampler plate, a marathon of ribs, bratwurst, red cabbage, German potato salad, and more. Kids' menu. | 221 N. Minnesota St. | 507/359–2071 | $10–$22 | AE, D, DC, MC, V.

Lodging

Budget Holiday. Sitting one block from the fairgrounds, this weathered motel has ground-floor and basement rooms. Microwaves and refrigerators available for rent. Cable TV. Business services. Some pets allowed. | 1316 N. Broadway | 507/354–4145 | fax 507/354–4146 | 44 rooms | $29–$40 | AE, D, MC, V.

Colonial Inn. This one-story motel lies on the north edge of town. Cable TV. | 1315 N. Broadway | 507/354–3128 | 24 rooms (10 with shower) | $25–$50 | AE, D, MC, V.

Deutsche Strasse Bed & Breakfast. This three-story brick and stucco 1893 home, four blocks from downtown, has the oak floors, beveled-glass French doors, a dining room full of pecan woodwork, and many furnishings left from a 1915 renovation. There's a baby grand piano, and breakfast is served on a sun porch. Complimentary breakfast. Air-conditioning. No room phones, no TV. No smoking. | 404 S. German St. | 507/354–3005 | glsonnen@newulmtel.net | www.bbonline.com/mn/deutsche/index.html | 5 rooms | $60–$80 | No credit cards.

Holiday Inn. A Holidome indoor recreation area is the highlight of this 1982 Tudor-style hotel 1 mi north of downtown. Restaurant, bar (with entertainment), room service. In-room data ports. Cable TV. Indoor pool. Hot tub, sauna. Exercise equipment. Video games. Business services, free parking. Pets allowed. | 2101 S. Broadway | 507/359–2941 and 877/359–2941 | fax 507/354–7147 | 126 rooms, 4 suites | $69–$89, $89–$129 suites | AE, D, DC, MC, V.

Innis House. Simple dark-wood bedframes in the guest rooms and breakfast served at the family table make this 1962 blue ranch-style bed and breakfast decidedly homey. The house is in St. Georges, a town of 25 houses 6 mi northwest of New Ulm. Complimentary breakfast. No room phones. | Rte. 3, Box 62, St. Georges | 507/359–9442, 800/597–3964 | fax 507/359–3768 | 2 rooms | $65–$75 | No credit cards.

NORTHFIELD

MAP 3, E9

(Nearby towns also listed: Faribault, Hastings, Lake City, Lakeville, Minneapolis, Mantorville, New Prague, Owatonna, Red Wing, St. Paul)

Known as the town that thwarted Jesse James, Northfield now describes itself as "the city of cows, colleges, and contentment." It got its start as a mill town on the banks of the Canon River in the 1850s, and agriculture remains a large part of the area's economy. Northfield, whose population is now 16,457, is flanked by two colleges, St. Olaf and Carleton.

NORTHFIELD

INTRO
ATTRACTIONS
DINING
LODGING

ROVING REMAINS

Every once in a while, a museum obtains an artifact that's too embarrassing to put on display. One such unexhibited artifact hides in the dark recesses of the Northfield Historical Society. It's a skeleton that may or may not be the remains of one Charlie Pitts.

Pitts was one of the participants in the Jesse James gang's famous Northfield bank raid in 1876. He escaped from Northfield but was tracked down and killed by a posse two weeks later. His body was transported to St. Paul and put on display at the State Capitol, presumably to show people what can happen to you if you rob a bank. Pitts's body eventually made it into the hands of a young medical student who dissected it and then sunk the bones in St. Paul's Lake Como to prepare them for display. The box holding the bones eventually resurfaced, convincing police and the public that they had a grisly murder on their hands. The confusion was soon cleared up but Pitts's bones then disappeared.

Or did they?

Years later, a gun museum near Shakopee displayed a human skeleton that it obtained in exchange for a firearm. The owner of the bones insisted they were the remains of Charlie Pitts. Eventually, the museum donated the bones to the Northfield Historical Society, but the society was skeptical about their authenticity and it arranged for an autopsy. The result: the skeleton was almost certainly not that of Charlie Pitts.

The Northfield Historical Society still has the skeleton and the people there still call it Charlie. But don't expect to see it on display. The society is hoping someday to arrange a proper burial.

© Corbis

Information: **Northfield Area Chamber of Commerce** | 500 Water St., Northfield, 55057 | 800/658–2548 | www.northfieldchamber.com.

Attractions

Carleton College. A liberal arts school with an enrollment of about 1,850, this nationally known school on the northeast edge of town has an 800-acre arboretum with trails for walking, biking, and skiing, and a natural habitat for rare prairie plants. | Rte. 19 | 507/646–4000 | www.carleton.edu | Daily.

Nerstrand Big Woods State Park. Home to a large maple-basswood forest—one of the last extensive stands of Minnesota's "Big Woods"—the park is also the only place in the world where you'll find the dwarf trout lily. Hiking, cross-country skiing, snowmobiling, and camping are all allowed. Northfield lies 14 mi to the north. | 9700 170th St. E, Nerstrand | 507/334–8848 | www.dnr.state.mn.us/parks_and_recreation/state_parks/nerstrand_big_woods | Park permit required | Daily.

Northfield Arts Guild. An old YMCA building now hosts exhibits of local and regional artworks. The Guild Theater presents plays and musicals by local talent. | 411 W. 3rd St. | 507/645–8877 | Free | Mon.–Sat. 10–4.

Northfield Historical Society. You can explore the history of Northfield and the surrounding area through ever-changing exhibits—some including the local theater guild in costume. A reenactment video of Jesse James's defeat is a perennial favorite. Tours are available weekends May–Sept. and by appointment. | 408 Division St. | 507/645–9268 | $3, $4 tour | Tues.–Sat. 10–4, Sun. 1–4.

St. Olaf College. On a hill overlooking Northfield, this college, with an enrollment of just under 3,000 students, has an internationally respected choir, band, and orchestra, and its Christmas concerts in early December draw visitors from around the country. | 1520 St. Olaf Ave. | 507/646–2222 | www.stolaf.com | Free | Daily.

ON THE CALENDAR

SEPT.: *Rice County Steam & Gas Engine Threshing Show.* This harvest-inspired Labor Day event centers around old farm implements threshing wheat, but also includes live music, food stands, and a flea market. | 800/658–2548.

SEPT.: *Defeat of Jesse James Days.* The live reenactment of the James-Younger gang's failed bank robbery in 1876 is part of a four-day festival the weekend after Labor Day. There are a rodeo, a tractor pull, a midway, and a parade. | 800/658–2548.

Dining

Byzantine Cafe. Mediterranean. A mural of Mykonos Island off the coast of Greece sets the scene for Greek and Middle Eastern fare, including chicken roti—curried vegetables with chicken, cashews, and raisins between crispy bread—and several vegetarian options such as hummus and spanakopita. Go for the homemade baklava for dessert. | 201 Water St. | 507/645–2400 | Closed Sunday | $7–$13 | D, MC, V.

Ole Store Cafe. American. You sit in booths dating from 1930, the date that this 1889 Scandinavian general store became a café, among local artists' watercolors of the St. Olaf and Carleton campuses. The "Ole Roll," a caramel cinnamon roll, and the seafood omelet are breakfast standouts. | 1011 St. Olaf Ave. | 507/645–5558 | Closed Mon. No dinner Tues., Wed., Sun. | $7–$14.

The Tavern. American. You'll probably keep company with college students and visiting parents in this low-ceilinged, stone-walled place in the basement of Archer House. Tuck into burgers, pastas, duck, fish, tacos, and burritos. | 212 Division St. S | 507/663–0342 | Breakfast also served | $7–$16 | AE, D, DC, MC, V.

Lodging

AmericInn. The log cabin–style lobby, complete with a fireplace, welcomes you to this hotel, constructed in 2000 on the southeast side of town. Complimentary Continental breakfast. Cable TV. Indoor pool, hot tub. Laundry facilities. | 1320 Bollenbacher Dr. | 507/645–7761 | 33 rooms, 8 suites | $70–$78, $116–$146 suites | AE, D, DC, MC, V.

Archer House. The front porch of this four-story redbrick 1877 colonial inn faces the town's main street. Room service. Some refrigerators, some in-room hot tubs. Cable TV. Laundry service. Free parking. Some pets. | 212 Division St. | 507/645–5661 or 800/247–2235 | fax 507/645–4295 | www.archerhouse.com | 18 rooms, 18 suites | $45–$55, $115–$140 suites | AE, D, MC, V.

College City Motel. This one-story motel is 1 mi north of town. Cable TV. Pets allowed. | 875 Rte. 3N | 507/645–4426 or 800/775–0455 | 24 rooms | $25–$55 | AE, D, MC, V.

Country Inn. This two-story wood hotel is across the river from downtown and ½ mi from the colleges. Complimentary Continental breakfast. Some refrigerators, some microwaves. Cable TV. Indoor pool. Hot tub. Laundry facilities. Free parking. | 300 Hwy. 3 S | 507/645–2286 | fax 507/645–2958 | 54 rooms | $70–$130 | AE, D, DC, MC, V.

Martin Oak Bed & Breakfast. All bed linens are starched and ironed, and rooms are antiques-filled at this 1869 home with a wraparound front porch and a Victorian parlor. Breakfast includes freshly squeezed orange juice and sweet breads, among other pleasures. The house stands on ½ acre in the village of Dundas, 2 mi north of Northfield. Complimentary breakfast. No TV. One room with phone. | 107 1st St., Dundas | 507/645–4644 | 3 rooms | $60–$85 | MC.

Super 8. The two-story stucco highway hotel is 2 mi south of downtown. Cable TV. Some microwaves, some refrigerators. Business Services. Pets allowed. | 1420 Riverview Dr. | 507/663–0371 | fax 800/789–1331 | 40 rooms | $54–$70 | AE, D, DC, MC, V.

ONAMIA

MAP 3, E6

(Nearby towns also listed: Aitkin, Brainerd, Little Falls)

Onamia–which means "dancing ground" in Ojibway–sits on the shore of Lake Onamia, immediately south of Lake Mille Lacs and the Mille Lacs Reservation. The city dates back to 1908, when the first trains arrived and lumbering was the major local industry. Today, Onamia is the area's largest town, with a population of 1,800 and more than 50 retail stores and other businesses.

Information: Mille Lacs Area Tourism Council | Box 362, Isle, 56342 | 888/350–2692 | www.millelacs.com/commun/Onamia.html.

Attractions

Grand Casino Mille Lacs. This grown-up playground on the west shore of Lake Mille Lacs has popular games, a luxury hotel, and restaurants. There are year-round outdoor activities: golfing, boating, fishing, snowmobiling, skiing, and ice fishing. | 777 Grand Ave. | 800/626–LUCK | Daily.

Mille Lacs Kathio State Park. Nineteen archaeological sites have been identified here, covering more than 4,000 years of human history. There are a visitors center, and swimming, boating, fishing, camping, hiking, cross-country skiing, and snowmobiling. | 15066 Kathio State Park Rd. | 320/532–3523 | www.dnr.state.mn.us/parks_and_recreation/state_parks/mille_lacs_kathio | Park permit required | Park 8 AM–10 PM daily, office 8–4:30 daily.

Mille Lacs Lake. With 150 mi of shoreline, this lake north of Onamia is one of the most popular fishing lakes in the state. Anglers regularly pull in good hauls of northern pike, walleye, crappie, and sunfish. | 218/829–2838 | Free | Daily.

ON THE CALENDAR
JUNE: *Onamia Days.* Cedar Street fills with live music, carnival rides, a bratwurst stand, a classic car show, youth sports tournaments, and other activities on the second weekend of the month. | 888/350–2692.

Dining
Grand Northern Grille. American. This bright dining room, inside the Grand Casino Mille Lacs, serves up an all-you-can-eat buffet, prime rib, pork roast, and cashew chicken stir-fry—around the clock. | 777 Grand Ave. | 800/626–LUCK | Open 24 hours | $7–$16 | AE, D, DC, MC, V.

Woodlands Steakhouse. Steak. A trickling fountain, crackling fireplace, and faux pine trees carry the theme of this restaurant in the Grand Casino Mille Lacs. White linens and candlelight set the stage for New Zealand lobster tail and steak; all the wine is non-alcoholic—the casino is on a reservation, and it's dry. | 777 Grand Ave. (Rte. 169) | 320/532–7777 | Closed Mon., Tues. No lunch | $20–$40 | AE, D, MC, V.

Lodging
Econolodge. A satellite dish provides nine TV channels at this two-story, 1990s motor hotel. Rooms have views of either Lake Mille Lacs or the woods. Complimentary Continental breakfast. | 40847 Rte. 169 | 320/532–3838 or 800/839–7006 | 30 rooms, 6 suites | $49–$79, $79–$99 suites | AE, D, DC, MC, V.

Eddy's Lake Mille Lacs Resort. The spacious lobby has a fireplace and walls of varnished woods and exposed brick, and some rooms have hot tubs and gas or wood-burning fireplaces. Non-smoking rooms are available, and a free shuttle runs to Grand Casino Mille Lacs. Restaurant, bar. Some in-room hot tubs. Sauna, spa. Exercise equipment. Hiking, volleyball. Beach, dock, boating, fishing, bicycles. Baby-sitting, playground. Some pets allowed. | 41334 Shakopee Lake Rd. | 320/532–3657 or 800/657–4704 | fax 320/532–4483 | www.eddys-resort.com | 80 rooms | $69–$129 | MAP | AE, D, DC, MC, V.

Izatys Golf and Yacht Club. A lodge and dozens of townhouses anchor this 650-acre property on Lake Mille Lacs. In winter you can rent ice-fishing houses and igloos. In summer, you can rent a boat or launch your own at the 120-slip marina with a sheltered harbor, and golfers can hone their skills on a driving range, two practice greens, practice bunkers, a chipping green, and a three-hole par-3 practice course. Restaurant, bar. Some microwaves. Cable TV. 2 pools (1 indoor). Hot tub, sauna. 18-hole golf, tennis. Dock, boating. Business services. | 40005 85th Ave. | 320/532–3101 or 800/533–1728 | fax 320/532–3208 | www.izatys.com | 59 apartments, 24 rooms in lodge, 4 suites in lodge | $115–$389 apartments, $80–$140 rooms, $130–$150 suites | AE, D, DC, MC, V.

OWATONNA

MAP 3, E9

(Nearby towns also listed: Albert Lea, Austin, Faribault, Mankato, Northfield, Rochester)

Legend says this was named after a frail Native American princess who was restored to health by the area's spring waters. A statue of Princess Owatonna stands in Mineral Springs Park. Now one of the economic centerpieces of southern Minnesota, with a population of 21,000, Owatonna stands in some of the region's richest farmland, with more than 750 local farms. It's also home to more than 500 retail, wholesale, and professional firms.

Information: Owatonna Area Chamber of Commerce | 320 Hoffman Dr., Owatonna, 55060 | 507/451–7970 | www.owatonna-today.com/chamber.html.

Attractions

Wells-Fargo Bank Building. The former National Farmers Bank occupies a 1908 building designed by famed architect Louis Sullivan. The elaborate gold-leaf arches, huge stained-glass windows, terra-cotta tiles, massive light fixtures, and Oskar Gross murals illustrate Sullivan's distinctive way with ornamentation. The building is on the National Register of Historic Buildings and was featured on a United States postage stamp in 1981 as one of four unique American buildings. Tours are available. | 101 N. Cedar Ave. | 507/455–7500 | Mon.–Fri. 8–5:30, Sat. 8–noon.

Owatonna Arts Center. The permanent collection here includes costumes by designer Marianne Young, and 14 stained-glass panels. Works by several of Minnesota's best-known artists punctuate the sculpture gardens. | 435 Garden View La. | 507/451–0533 | Free | Tues.–Sun. 1–5.

Rice Lake State Park. Native Americans once harvested wild rice by this 600-acre lake, whose shallow waters and marshy edges attract migratory waterfowl. | 8485 Rose St. | 507/455–5871 | www.dnr.state.mn.us/parks_and_recreation/state_parks/rice_lake | Park permit required | Daily 10–4.

Village of Yesteryear. Historic buildings from Owatonna's and Steele County's past line a fanciful village street. Among the structures are a blacksmith shop, a railroad depot, an 1876 church, a general store, and a barber shop. | 1448 Austin Rd. | 507/451–1420 | $4 | May–Oct., Tues.–Sun., 12–4.

ON THE CALENDAR

OCT.: *Bed Races.* Teams of five people—one on each corner of a standard, metal-frame twin bed, and one lying on the bed—race around Owatonna square the last Saturday of the month. Prizes are awarded for speed, bed decoration, and team costumes. | 507/455–0969.

Dining

Costa's Candies and Restaurant. Greek. You can order eggs and potatoes for breakfast, soup and Greek salad for lunch, and walleye pike or a gyro for dinner at this booths-and-counter diner–cum–candy shop. On your way out, grab a few chocolate creams or pecan-and-caramel turtles, all made in-house. | 112 N. Cedar St. | 507/451–9050 | Closed Sun. | $5–$11 | No credit cards.

Jerry's Supper Club. Steak. Three hundred Jim Beam decanters dominate this restaurant established in 1960. A mural depicts downtown at the turn of the 20th century, and freshly cut steaks, chops, and seafood fill the menu. Especially popular are the tournedos of beef—medallions sautéed in garlic butter and red wine with portobello mushrooms and asparagus. | 203 N. Cedar Ave. | 507/451–6894 | Closed Sun. | $12–$25 | AE, MC, V.

Timberland Steakhouse. Steak. Deer, moose, pheasant, duck, and elk mounts punctuate the log walls of this franchise steakhouse, 3 mi north of town off I–35 Exit 45 (Clinton Falls). Almost any cut of steak you can imagine is on the menu, along with token seafood. | 4455 W. Frontage Rd. | 507/444–0303 | No lunch | $15–$20 | AE, D, DC, MC, V.

Lodging

Budget Host Inn. A 2-story brick motel 1 block from I–35, exit 42A, this facility is ½ mi from Owatonna and 6 mi from the Medford Outlet Center. Complimentary Continental breakfast. Cable TV. Laundry services. Small pets allowed (fee and with permission). | 745 State Ave. | 507/451–8712 | fax 507/451–4456 | 27 rooms | $65–$95 | AE, D, MC, V.

Comfort Inn. Deer and buffalo mounts in the lobby of this three-story, log cabin–style hotel play off the theme of the neighboring sporting-goods store, Cabela's. Some rooms have whirlpool tubs. Complimentary Continental breakfast. Cable TV. Indoor pool. Hot tub. | 2345 43rd St. NW | 507/444–0818 | 63 rooms | $85–$135 | AE, D, DC, MC, V.

Northrop–Oftendahl House. Original stained glass and woodwork embellish this family-owned hostelry, an 1898 home in a residential neighborhood. Among the dozens of antiques are beds brought from Norway in the 1870s; other pieces are turn-of-the-20th-century Victorian. Complimentary breakfast. Some rooms with cable TV. No room phones. | 385 E. Main St. | 507/451–4040 | 5 rooms | $70–$95 | No credit cards.

Ramada Inn. Work by local artists decorates the lobby of this two-story brick hotel at I–35N, exit 42 (Hwy 14W). Restaurant, bar, room service. Cable TV. Indoor pool. Hot tub, sauna. Laundry facilities. Video games. Business services, airport shuttle. | 1212 I–35N | 507/455–0606 | fax 507/455–3731 | 117 rooms | $49–$80 | AE, D, DC, MC, V.

Super 8. This 2-story brick-and-stucco hostelry is 2 mi west of downtown, at I–35, exit 35 (Hwy 14W, Waseca). Complimentary Continental breakfast. Cable TV, in-room VCRs (and movies). Business services, free parking. | 1818 Rte. 14W | 507/451–0380 | fax 507/451–0380 | 60 rooms | $45–$60 | AE, D, DC, MC, V.

PARK RAPIDS

MAP 3, C5

(Nearby towns also listed: Detroit Lakes, Walker)

Park Rapids is the gateway to Itasca State Park, where the Mississippi River begins. The town is surrounded by hundreds of lakes, and more than 200 resorts are scattered throughout the park's 20-mi radius.

Information: **Park Rapids Area Chamber of Commerce** | Box 249, U.S. 71S, Park Rapids, 56470 | 218/732–4111 or 800/247–0054 | www.parkrapids.com.

Attractions

Heartland Park and Trail. Twenty-seven of the 50 miles of this trail, which runs northeast from Heartland Park to Walker, are paved. You can bike, walk, run, or roller-blade through farmlands and forest, and over scenic bridges. Within the park itself are a beach, a tennis court, a playground, and a picnic area. | Mill Rd. | 800/247–0054 | Year-round.

Itasca State Park. Minnesota's oldest state park, home of the Mississippi River headwaters, encompasses more than 32,000 acres and has more than 100 lakes. The entrance is 21 mi north of Park Rapids or 30 mi south of Bemidji on U.S. 71. | HCO5, Box 4, Lake Itasca | 218/266–2114 | www.dnr.state.mn.us/parks_and_recreation/state_parks/itasca | Park permit required | Daily; office open Mon.–Fri. 8–4:30, Sat.–Sun. 8–4.

Rapid River Logging Camp. The camp staff gives logging demonstrations and serves a lumberjack meal on tin plates. It's a short walk from the camp's log cabin to the river to see the sluiceway. | CSAH 18 East | 218/732–3444 | Free | Memorial Day–Labor Day, daily 10–6.

Smoky Hills Artisan Community. Local artists display their work at this miniature village. | Rte. 34W, Osage | 218/573–3300 | Free | Daily 9–4.

ON THE CALENDAR
AUG.: *Antique Tractor Show.* Demonstrations of threshing, plowing, and lathe-making with old farm implements complement the tractor display and parade on a weekend late in the month. | 800/247–0054.

Dining
Brother's Restaurant at Blueberry Pines. American. Locals flock to this log-cabin dining room for special-occasion dinners. Friday and Saturday prime rib is the special; you can also

order shrimp or chicken. The windows overlook the golf course, 8 mi south of town. | 39161 Rte. 71 | 218/564–4657 | Closed Nov.–Apr. no lunch, no dinner Tues. | $11–$16 | AE, D, MC, V.

Dorset Cafe. American. The 3-ft-tall white chicken in the yard leaves no doubt as to what this restaurant is about. The house specialty—broasted chicken—is chicken and potatoes pressure-cooked in oil. If fowl doesn't appeal, you can order walleye fish, pork chops, or the Dorset sizzler, seared steak served in the frying pan. The café is one of the ten buildings in Dorset, a village 5 mi east of Park Rapids. | Main St., Dorset | 218/732–4072 | No lunch Mon.–Sat. | $7–$14 | D, V.

Great Northern Cafe. American. Antique calendars and train photos adorn the walls of this greasy spoon, next to a bank downtown. Grilled sandwiches, burgers, soups, and deep-fried fish are on the lunch and dinner menus. For breakfast there is a choice of twenty different omelets, all served with hashbrowns. | 218 E. 1st St. | 218/732–9565 | $5–$10.

Rapid River Logging Camp. American. Every meal is a fixed-price, all-you-can-eat, family-style affair in this log building on the Potato River, 1 mi northeast of town. You'll sit at long, wooden communal tables next to a working steam-powered saw mill, eat from metal cups and plates, and get to know the folks next to you. Breakfast includes pancakes, eggs, ham, hashbrowns, and prunes. At dinner you choose between ham, pork, barbecued ribs, roast beef, and chicken. | Rte. 71 N of town 3 mi, right on County 18 3 mi | 218/732–3444 | Closed Labor Day–Memorial Day | $9.25 | No credit cards.

Lodging

Brookside Resort. Guest cabins line the lakeshore and river, each with a picnic table and grill. You have the choice of bringing your own sheets, pillowcases, and towels, or renting theirs (call in advance to rent bed linens). There's a seven-day minimum stay requirement. The resort is 12 mi north of town. Picnic area. Kitchenettes. No TV in rooms, TV in common area. Indoor-outdoor pool. Sauna. 9-hole golf course, miniature golf, putting green, tennis. Beach, dock, water sports, boating. Library. Kids' programs (ages 3–18). Laundry facilities. Business services, airport shuttle. | Two Inlets Lake Rd. | 218/732–4093 or 800/247–1615 | www.brookside-resort.com | 28 cottages | $1,100–$1,700 (includes a boat) | Closed Oct.–late May | MC, V.

Dickson Viking Huss Bed & Breakfast. A fireplace, oak accents, and a vaulted ceiling in the living room complement the rustic wood siding on this ranch-style house downtown. One room has a private bath, and across the street is a public park. Complimentary breakfast. Room phones. | 202 E. Fourth St. | 218/732–8089, 888/899–7292 | 3 rooms | $50–$75 | MC, V.

Douglas Lodge. Constructed in 1903–1905, the lodge was the first building serving tourists in Itasca, and stands in the center of the Itasca State Park. A park sticker is required for lodging. Dining room. No air-conditioning in some rooms. Some kitchenettes. Hiking. Bicycles. Playground. Business services. | Park Rd., Lake Itasca | 218/266–2100 or 800/246–2267 | www.dnr.state.mn.us/parks_and_recreation/state_parks/itasca | 22 cabins (all central shower area only), 28 rooms in lodge (1 with shower only) | $77–$138 cabins, $50–$77 rooms in lodge | Closed Oct.–Apr. | AE, D, MC, V.

Evergreen Lodge. Individual cottages are the accommodations at this 1918 resort, which has boating and a private beach. The hostelry is 7 mi northeast of town, on Route 4. Picnic area. Kitchenettes, microwaves. Sauna. Golf, tennis. Beach, boating. Kids' programs (ages 3–10), playground. Airport shuttle. | Big Sand Lake Rd. | 218/732–4766 | fax 218/732–0762 | 18 cabins | $660, 1–4; $575–$735 cabins for 1–4 (7-day minimum stay); $720–$875 for 1–6; $690–$965 for 1–8 | Closed Labor Day–mid-May | No credit cards.

Gateway Guest House. The papa-bear room in this 2-story gray-sided 1920s B&B is painted bright yellow and has a bed frame made from thick tree trunks. A wide front porch and parlor with a fireplace provide quiet places to relax. Complimentary breakfast. No TV. No room phones. | 203 Park Ave. N | 218/732–1933, 877/558–8614 | www.gatewayguesthouse.com | 4 rooms | $55 | No credit cards.

Loon Song Bed & Breakfast. Built in 1999, this split-log-sided home has a great-room with a fireplace and picture windows overlooking the lake and gardens. All guest rooms have private baths, and the beds are decked with quilts handmade by the innkeeper. The building is in the woods on Heart Lake, 6 mi from Itasca State Park and 35 mi north of Park Rapids. Complimentary breakfast. No TV. No room phones. Beach. Fishing. No smoking, no pets, no kids under 8. | Lake Itasca 27 | 218/266–3333, 888/825–8135 | fax 218/266–3383 | 4 rooms, one cottage | $70–$90 | MC, V.

Sunset Lodge. The largest resort in the area, on Potato Lake, 14 mi northeast of Park Rapids. Accommodations are individual cabins, and a one-week stay is required. Picnic area. Kitchenettes. Cable TV. Tennis. Beach, boating. Playground. Laundry facilities. Airport shuttle. | Potato Lake Rd. | 218/732–4671 | 11 cottages (with boat) | $540 cottages for 1–4, $720 for 2–bedroom cottage | Closed Mid-Nov.–mid-May | No credit cards.

Super 8. Hundreds of miles of snowmobiling, biking, and cross-country skiing trails surround this two-story motel 1 mi east of downtown. Complimentary Continental breakfast. In-room data ports. Cable TV. Hot tub, sauna. Laundry services. Business services. | 1020 E. 1st St., Rte. 34E | 218/732–9704 | fax 218/732–9704 | 62 rooms | $45–$75 | AE, D, DC, MC, V.

Vacationaire. The lodge and cottages are spread out over expansive grounds at the south end of Island Lake, making for an uncrowded experience. Right off Route 71, it's 9 mi north of town. Dining room, bar. Some kitchenettes. Cable TV. Indoor pool. Sauna. Tennis. Beach, dock, boating. Ice-skating. Cross-country skiing. Playground. Laundry facilities. Business services. | Island Lake Dr. | 218/732–5270 | 16 cottages, 16 rooms in lodge | $80–$250 cottages, $55–$100 rooms in lodge | AE, D, MC, V.

PINE RIVER

MAP 3, D5

(Nearby towns also listed: Brainerd, Cross Lake, Walker)

Dakota Indians were common in the Pine River area until the Ojibway began pushing them out in the early 1700s. White fur traders arrived at about the same time and established a trading post, and in the late 1800s, Pine River emerged as a hub for north-central Minnesota's logging industry. Five highways merge at the city, making it a regional center for tourism, logging, and service industries.

Information: Pine River Area Chamber of Commerce | Box 131, Rte. 371S, Pine River, 56474 | 218/587–4000 | www.pineriver.org.

Attractions

Minnesota Resort Museum. This gallery displays artifacts of early resort life in Minnesota, including cabins, boats, woodshops, a kitchen, and a dining room; a Victorian dollhouse and a display of science fiction movie miniature replicas are also here. It's at the Driftwood 9 mi east of Pine River. | Rte. 1, Box 404 | 218/568–4221 | $2 | May–Oct., daily 10–5.

ON THE CALENDAR

JUNE: *Summerfest.* The last weekend of the month, a craft show, street dance, a parade down Main St., and other activities fill downtown. There is also a "fly-in" breakfast at the airport. | 218/587–4000.

Dining

Red Pine Supper Club. American. You can order a burger, fried walleye pike, garlic-buttered rib-eye steak, or pasta at this log cabin 1½ mi south of town. A central fireplace warms the air. Sun. brunch includes omelets made to order, waffles, and pancakes. | 2793 Rte. 371 | 218/587–3818 | No dinner Sunday. No lunch | $6–$16 | D, MC, V.

Lodging

Driftwood. Established in 1900, this Scandinavian resort 5 mi east of Jenkins, off Route 371, has both lodge rooms and cabins, plus a private beach, pony rides, and sternwheel paddleboat cruises. The kitchen serves a popular smorgasbord. Dining room. Refrigerators. Pool, wading pool. 9-hole golf course, putting greens, tennis. Beach, boating, bicycles. Kids' programs (ages 3–18). Laundry facilities. Business services. | Rte. 1, Box 404 | 218/568–4221 | fax 218/568–4222 | www.driftwoodresort.com | 24 cottages | $729 per person (with 2 meals), $797 per person (3 meals) cottages (7–day stay) | Closed late Sept.–mid-May | AP, MAP | AE, D, DC, MC, V.

Piney Ridge. The 1911 Northwoods resort on Upper Whitefish Lake is a rustic family getaway with a choice of cabins or apartments. A pay phone near the entrance of the resort is the establishment's only phone. Dining room, picnic area. No in-room phones, no TV. Refrigerators. Pool, sauna. Miniature golf, 18-hole golf course, tennis. Beach, dock, boating. Kids' programs. Laundry facilities. Business services, airport shuttle. | 6023 Wildemere Dr. | 218/587–2296 | fax 218/587–4323 | piney@uslink.net | www.pineyridge.com/location.html | 14 apartments, 12 cottages | $110–$125, 2 people, 1 cabin; $1,200–$1,600 apartments; $700–$1,100 cottages for 2–6 (7–day minimum stay) | Closed late Sept.–Apr. | MAP | D, MC, V.

Travelodge. All the rooms in this two-story roadside motor lodge are no-frills rooms except for one: The Sleepy Bear room is decorated with a bear motif and equipped with a children's easy chair and free family videos. Room access is via outside corridors, and the location is ½ mi south of town between a meat market and a car dealership. Complimentary Continental breakfast. Cable TV. Hot tub, sauna. Laundry facilities. Pets allowed. | 2684 Rte. 371 SW | 218/587–4499 | 30 rooms, 1 suite | $55–$73, $95–$105 suite | AE, D, DC, MC, V.

PIPESTONE

MAP 3, B9

(Nearby towns also listed: Luverne, Tracy)

For thousands of years, Native Americans lived on the tall grass prairies of the Pipestone area, fashioning the soft stone quarried here into ceremonial pipes. Henry Wadsworth Longfellow was inspired to write of it in his poem, "Song of Hiawatha." Today, agribusiness, fiberglass manufacturing, meat processing, and tourism form Pipestone's economic backbone.

Information: Pipestone Area Chamber of Commerce | 117 8th Ave. SE, Pipestone, 56164 | 507/825–3316 | www.pipestone.mn.us.

Attractions

Family Aquatic Center. This pool complex has a zero-depth, beach-like entry, a 126-ft tube slide, a 22.5-ft drop slide, a diving board, spray geysers, lap lanes, and sun-bathing areas. | 510 6th St. SE | 507/825–5834 | $4.36, children $3.20 | Daily 1–8.

Pipestone County Museum. Local exhibits and a research library occupy the old City Hall building. | 113 Hiawatha Ave. | 507/825–5464 | www.pipestone.mn.us/museum/homepa~1.htm | $2 | Daily 8–5.

Pipestone National Monument. The federal government established this monument in 1937 to protect the unique red stone (Catlinite) from which Native Americans fashioned ceremonial pipes. The monument includes the pipestone quarries, native tallgrass prairie, quartzite bluffs, and a creek with a waterfall. | 36 Reservation Ave. | 507/825–5464 | www.nps.gov/pipe | Free | Daily.

Split Rock Creek State Park. Split Rock Lake, the largest in Pipestone County, has swimming, fishing, boating, hiking, cross-country skiing, and camping. It's 7 mi southwest of Pipestone, off Route 23. | Rte. 20, Jasper | 507/348–7908 or 800/766–6000 | www.dnr.state.mn.us/parks_and_recreation/state_parks/split_rock_creek | Park permit required | Daily.

ON THE CALENDAR

JUNE: *Watertower Festival.* The festivities include a street dance, an arts and crafts show, retail sidewalk sales, and a softball tournament. | 507/825–3316.

JULY–AUG.: *Song of Hiawatha Pageant.* Townspeople perform Longfellow's poem, "The Song of Hiawatha," at the amphitheater north of town the last two weekends in July and first weekend in Aug. | 507/825–3316.

DEC.: *Festival of Trees.* Every Holiday season, as a charitable benefit, area businesses sponsor decorated trees, which are displayed in the Calumet Inn through New Year's Day. | 507/825–3316.

Dining

Historic Calumet Restaurant. American. Cally's Lounge, in this former bank, has an 11'-by-20' antique oak bar. The dining room has antique furnishings and pottery from Red Wing. Roasted chicken and steak share the menu with specials such as a turkey and bacon croissant. Continental breakfast served daily. Sun. brunch. | 104 W. Main St. | 507/825–5871, 800/535–7610 | No dinner Sunday | $5–$10 | AE, D, MC, V.

Lange's Cafe. American. The casual, family-style restaurant has white-tiled tables, arrowback wood chairs, and Native American art. Specialties are the homemade bread, the southern breakfast served here everyday, and the roast chicken with potato salad. | 110 8th Ave. SE | 507/825–4488 | Open 24 hours | $6–$15 | MC, V.

Lodging

Arrow. Sitting on three quiet acres, this one-story motel is less than 1 mi north of Pipestone National Monument. Complimentary Continental breakfast. Cable TV. Pool. Playground. | 620 8th Ave. NE | 507/825–3331 | 17 rooms | $39 | AE, D, MC, V.

Calumet Inn. Erected in 1888 using Sioux quartzite from local pipestone quarries, this four-story hotel has an atrium and an oak staircase. Antique furniture, glassware, and Red Wing pottery decorate the lobby and dining room. Restaurant, bar, complimentary Continental breakfast. In-room data ports. Cable TV. Business services. | 104 W. Main St. | 507/825–5871 or 800/535–7610 | fax 507/825–4578 | 41 rooms | $80 | AE, D, DC, MC, V.

Pipestone RV Park and Campground. You can pitch a tent, park your RV, or sleep in a platform-mounted tepee at this prairie campground. The tepees sleep 6 adults comfortably. Picnic area. Outdoor pool. Laundry facilities. | 919 Hiawatha Ave. | 507/825–2455 | 50 sites, 2 tepees | $15–$21, $27 tepee | Open Apr. 15–Nov. 1 | MC, V.

Super 8. This two-story motel dating from 1983 is in ½ mi from the center of town. Complimentary Continental breakfast, in-room data ports. Cable TV. Some in-room hot tubs. Laundry services. Business services. | 605 8th Ave. | 507/825–4217 | fax 507/825–4219 | 39 rooms | $42–$73 | AE, D, DC, MC, V.

Wooden Diamond Bed & Breakfast. The two-bed suite in this rustic, gambrel-roofed cabin has a view of the sunset over the lake. The home was built bit by bit over the years by the innkeeper, a painter, and her husband for their family of five children. The house stands on a full acre on Lake Benton, 20 mi north of town. Complimentary breakfast. No room phone. | 504 Shady Shore Dr. | 507/368–4305 | 1 suite | $60–$85 | No credit cards.

PRESTON

MAP 3, G10

(Nearby towns also listed: Austin, Lanesboro, Spring Valley, Rochester, Winona)

Preston grew up around a bend in the Root River. It's a farming community that serves as a commercial, industrial, and recreational hub for southeast Minnesota's bluff country. Preston is the seat of Fillmore County.

Information: **Preston Area Tourism** | Box 657, Preston, 55965 | www.prestonmn.org | 507/765–2100 or 888/845–2100.

Attractions

Root River State Recreation Trail. You can rollerblade, bike, or cross-country ski on this DNR-maintained, paved trail, a former railroad line following the Root River for 24 mi. A parking lot and rest rooms are at the trailhead. | Fillmore St., off Rte. 52 | 507/467–2552 or 888/646–6367 | Free | Year-round.

ON THE CALENDAR

SEPT.: *September Fest.* You can browse a city-wide garage sale, or attend a pumpkin-carving contest and a craft fair. | 888/845–2100 | Last Sat. in Sept.

Dining

Chic's Pizza. Pizza. Hand-tossed pizzas topped with fresh vegetables and meats are the specialty at this downtown booth-filled dining room with Root River Trail maps on the walls and an always-on TV. The alley next to the building allows for a drive-through window. Hearty breakfasts of omelets and pancakes, as well as daily specials such as burgers and chicken à la king are also served. | 216 St. Paul St. | 507/765–3333 | $2–$5.

Lodging

Jail House Historic Inn. The 1869 Fillmore County jail, an Italianate building, is now an inn. The cell block retains some of its original features, such as bathroom fixtures and steel bars, though most interior accents are Victorian and Amish. Some rooms have fireplaces. Dining room, complimentary Continental breakfast. Some in-room hot tubs. Limited stay for children. No smoking. | 109 Houston St. NW | 507/765–2181 | fax 507/765–2558 | 12 rooms | $49–$149 | AE, MC, V.

Old Barn Resort. Directly on the Root River State Trail, this 44-bed hostel and 130-site campground share the site with an 1885 barn. Forty of the campsites are suitable for tents. Restaurant, bar. Kitchenettes. Cable TV. Indoor pool. Hiking. Boating. Cross-country skiing. Playground. Laundry facilities. | Rte. 3, Box 57 | 507/467–2512 or 800/552–2512 | fax 507/467–2382 | 5 rooms | $11–$35 | Closed Dec.–Mar. | AE, D, DC, MC, V.

RED WING

MAP 3, F8

(Nearby towns also listed: Hastings, Lake City, Lakeville, Northfield, St. Paul)

The earliest settlers in this region were members of the Mdewakanton Dakota tribe. The city's name recalls a succession of Mdewakanton chiefs who used dyed swan wings as their symbols. In the 1850s, Mississippi River steamboats began docking regularly in Red Wing, turning the town into a major trading center. These days, Red Wing is a favorite tourist destination and is recognized internationally as the home of Red Wing Pottery, highly collectible ceramics.

Information: **Red Wing Visitors and Convention Bureau** | 418 Levee St., Red Wing, 55066 | 800/498–3444 | www.redwing.org.

Attractions

Bay Point Park. On the Mississippi River, ¼ mi north of downtown, the park has a marina with a boat launch, picnic grounds, walking trails, and a playground. | 800/498–3444 | Free | Daily.

Cannon Valley Trail. Bikers and hikers fill this 21-mi trail along the old Chicago Great Western railroad line, connecting Cannon Falls, Welch, and Red Wing. The main trail head is about ½ mi east of Red Wing, off Route 52S on Route 19. | City Hall, 306 W. Mill Street, Cannon Falls | 507/263–0508 | www.cannonvalley.com | Apr.–Oct., $3 day pass, $12 season pass; no fee Nov.–Mar. | Year-round.

Colvill Park. Beside the Mississippi on the south side of town this is one of several river parks in Red Wing. An outdoor pool is open summers only. | Between 7th St. and Rte. 61 | 800/498–3444 | Free | Daily.

Goodhue County Historical Museum. Among the permanent exhibits are displays on local and regional history, Red Wing ceramics, and Prairie Island Native American artifacts. An extensive library, with more than 15,000 photos and 5,000 books, is used for histori-cal and genealogical research. | 1166 Oak St. | 651/388–6024 | $2 | Tues.–Fri. 10–5, Sat., Sun. 1–5. Closed weekends.

Mt. Frontenac Ski and Golf. Seven mi south of Red Wing and 6 mi north of Lake City, the ski area has variable-difficulty slopes and trails on 420 vertical feet, as well as a golf course in warm months. | 31099 Ski Rd., off U.S. 61 | 651/345–3504 or 800/488–5826 | www.ski-fron-tenac.com | Daily.

Red Wing Pottery. The showroom of the original Red Wing Pottery factory, which opened in the late 1800s and closed in 1967, continues to sell what's left of the famous salt-glazed brown dinnerware, crocks, and jugs, as well as modern stoneware and gifts. Since 1988, the shop has also hosted local potters who work onsite, throwing and decorating ceram-ics in the Red Wing style while visitors look on. | 1995 W. Main St. | 651/388–3562 or 800/228–0174 | Mon.–Sat. 8–6, Sun. 11–5.

Soldiers Memorial Park/East End Recreation Area. The park has hiking trails, picnic areas, caves to explore, and a spectacular view. | E. 7th St., 1 mi south of downtown | 800/498–3444 | Free | Daily.

Welch Village. This ski area has 36 trails and nine lifts serving 350 vertical ft. | On Rte. 7 south of Rte. 63 | 651/258–4567 | Nov.–Mar., daily.

ON THE CALENDAR
AUG.: *River City Days.* The citywide shindig, the first weekend of the month, includes a food festival, country music, dragon boat races, a car show, a parade, and fireworks. | 800/498–3444.

OCT.: *Fall Festival of the Arts.* The second week of the month, a few blocks of Bush St. and Third St. are designated to local potters, painters, woodworkers, and craftspeople who show and sell their wares. | 800/498–3444.

Dining
Liberty's. Continental. Over the years, this 1872 corner building has served as a saloon, a shoe store, a clothing store, a pool hall, and (legend has it) a speakeasy and house of ill repute. Today, the kitchen serves 3 meals a day, and lists slow-cooked prime rib *au jus* with horseradish sauce on its dinner menu. Sunday brunch. | 303 W. 3rd St. | 651/388–8877 | $6–$18 | AE, D, DC, MC, V.

Marie's Casual Dining & Lounge. American. Housed in a 1901 armory building, this restau-rant serves everything from grilled cheese sandwiches to boiled lobster. Fridays bring a fish fry and buffet, Saturdays an all-you-can-eat prime rib buffet. | 217 Plum St. | 651/388–1896 | $9–$18 | AE, D, MC, V.

Randy's Restaurant. American. After you order your fried chicken and mashed potatoes (or your sandwich and salad) at the counter, you'll seat yourself and wait to be served among the nostalgic advertisements in the dining space of this 1969 brick building downtown. Breakfast also served. | 709 Main St. | 651/388–1551 | $3–$6 | No credit cards.

Staghead. Contemporary. Exposed brick walls, oak tables, and a pressed-tin ceiling com-plement the historic maps and paintings of Red Wing on the walls of this dining room.

Serving beef tenderloin, free-range chicken, and fish, the kitchen is praised locally for a grilled pork tenderloin with applewood smoked bacon and sun-dried cherries in a sage demi-glaze. Thursday is all-Italian night. | 219 Bush St. | 651/388–6581 | No dinner Mon., closed Sun. | $8–$26 | MC, V.

Port of Red Wing. Contemporary. The dining room of downtown St. James Hotel has forest green table cloths, exposed brick, and dark-stained furniture. The menu changes seasonally, but summer dishes might include roasted rack of lamb with garlic whipped potatoes and bourbon-rhubarb glaze, or creole-style chicken with onions, peppers, and mushrooms in a spiced, red-wine tomato sauce. | 406 Main St. | 651/388–2846 or 800/252–1875 | No lunch | $18–$30 | AE, D, DC, MC, V.

Lodging

AmericInn. About 1 mi from downtown, this hotel is across the street from an outlet shopping center and a bike trail access point. Complimentary Continental breakfast. Cable TV. Indoor pool. Hot tub, sauna. Free parking. | 1819 Old West Main St. | 651/385–9060, 800/634–3444 | 43 rooms | $75–$86 | AE, D, MC, V.

Best Western Quiet House Suites. The Red Wing Pottery showroom is across the street from this white colonial-style hostelry, and the Mississippi River is 6 blocks east. In-room data ports, some refrigerators. Cable TV. Some in-room hot tubs. Indoor-outdoor pool. Hot tub. Exercise equipment. Some pets allowed. | 752 Withers Harbor Dr. | 651/388–1577 | fax 651/388–1150 | 51 rooms, 15 suites | $86–$169 | AE, D, DC, MC, V.

Candlelight Inn. Listed on the National Register of Historic Places, this 1877 Victorian B&B is three blocks west of downtown. Five of the building's eight fireplaces are in the guest rooms. Complimentary breakfast. No TV. No room phones. | 818 W. 3rd St. | 651/388–8034 | 5 rooms | $99–$169 | MC, V.

Days Inn. Colvill Park is across the street from this single-story motel. Cable TV. Indoor pool. Hot tub. Business services. Some pets allowed. | 955 E. 7th St. | 651/388–3568 | fax 651/385–1901 | 48 rooms | $58–$85 | AE, D, DC, MC, V.

Golden Lantern. This 1932 Tudor revival house served as home to three presidents of the Red Wing Shoe Company. Walnut, birch, oak, and maple are used throughout. Standing among some of Red Wing's oldest buildings, the house is 3½ blocks from downtown. Complimentary breakfast. No room phones. No smoking. Children by arrangement. | 721 East Ave. | 651/388–3315 | 5 rooms | $109–$199 | D, MC, V | www.goldenlantern.com.

Parkway Motel. Eight of the rooms here are extra large, and sleep up to six people. Standing across the highway from convenience stores, the motel is about 1½ mi from downtown. Cable TV. | 3425 Rte. 61N | 651/388–8231 or 800/762–0934 | 27 rooms | $35–$70 | AE, DC, MC, V.

Pratt Taber Inn. This 1870s Italianate mansion has original antiques, a porch, and a fireplace. Complimentary Continental breakfast. No room phones, no TV in rooms, TV in common area. No smoking. No kids under 10. | 706 W. 4th St. | 612/388–5945 | 5 rooms | $89–$110 | No credit cards.

Rodeway Inn. Next to Pottery Place Mall, this two-story motel is 1 mi southeast of downtown. Cable TV. Indoor pool. Hot tub. Business services. | 235 Withers Harbor Dr. | 612/388–1502 | fax 612/388–1501 | 39 rooms | $39–$67 | AE, D, DC, MC, V.

St. James. Listed on the National Register on Historic Places, this 1875 Victorian hotel in the heart of town has views of Hiawatha Valley and the Mississippi. Handmade quilts cover the beds. Restaurant, bars (with entertainment). In-room data ports, some hot tubs. Cable TV. Beauty salon. Business services, airport shuttle. | 406 Main St. | 612/388–2846 or 800/252–1875 | fax 612/388–5226 | www.st-james-hotel.com | 60 rooms | $120–$170 | AE, D, DC, MC, V.

Super 8. The motel is next to the Pottery Place Mall and 1 block from Cannon Valley Trail. Complimentary Continental breakfast. Cable TV. Indoor pool. Business services. | 232 Withers Harbor Dr. | 612/388–0491 | fax 612/388–1066 | 60 rooms | $43–$65 | AE, D, DC, MC, V.

REDWOOD FALLS

MAP 3, C8

(Nearby towns also listed: Granite Falls, Marshall, New Ulm, Tracy)

Boasting a huge municipal park, Redwood Falls is near the confluence of the Minnesota and Redwood rivers. It is an economic centerpiece of the Minnesota River Valley, and lies 6 mi south of the Jackpot Casino in Morton.

Information: Redwood Area Chamber and Tourism | 610 E. Bridge St., Redwood Falls, 56283 | 507/637–2828 or 800/657–7070 | www.redwoodfalls.org.

Attractions
Gilfillan Estate. You can take a guided tour of this farm house and its outbuildings 9 mi east of town. You'll see the summer kitchen, original furnishings, farm equipment, and gardens. | Rte. 67 | 507/249–2210 | $3 | Memorial Day–Labor Day Saturday, Sunday 1–4:30.

Lower Sioux Agency and History Center. The grounds were the scene of the first organized Dakota attack in the 1862 U.S.–Dakota Conflict. Trail markers provide a self-guided interpretive history of the conflict, and an indoor exhibit relates Dakota cultural history. | Rte. 2 off of Rte. 19 | 507/697–6321 | May–Labor Day, Mon.–Sat. 10–5, Sun. 1–5; Sept.–Oct., Daily 1–5; Dec.–Feb., Sat.–Sun. 1–5.

Ramsey Park. At 217 acres, this heavily wooded property is the largest municipal park in Minnesota. In northwest Redwood Falls, the park has picnicking, horseback riding, cross-country skiing, hiking, golf, and camping, as well as a small zoo. | 507/637–2828 and 800/657–7070 | Free | Daily.

ON THE CALENDAR
JUNE: *Minnesota Inventors Congress.* It's the world's oldest invention convention. | 507/637–2828 and 800/657–7070.
OCT.: *Jack O'Lantern Jamboree.* You can ride in a wagon to the pumpkin patch, pick out your own pumpkin, build a scarecrow, and have a piece of apple pie the first weekend of the month at this 20-acre orchard of over 6,000 trees. About 25 mi west of town. | 507/762–3131.

Dining
Falls Cafe. American. Burgers and homemade soups share the menu with daily specials such as pork roast and chicken à la king in this 1886 downtown favorite of lunching business people. A collection of Beanie Babies and nostalgic cookie and cracker tins is displayed above the wooden booths and tables. Breakfast also served. | 230 S. Washington St. | 507/640–3032 | Closed Sun. No dinner Mon.–Wed., Fri. | $4–$6 | D, MC, V.

Lodging
Comfort Inn. One mi north of downtown, this three-story, brick-and-stucco hotel runs a free shuttle to the Jackpot Casino 5 mi farther north. Complimentary Continental breakfast. Some in-room hot tubs. Hot tub, sauna. Some pets allowed (fee). | 1382 E. Bridge St. | 507/644–5700 or 800/569–1010 | fax 507/644–5722 | 105 rooms, 1 suite | $40–80 rooms, $120–$150 suite | AE, D, DC, MC, V.

Dakota Inn. A gaming package at this two-story hotel includes complimentary shuttle transportation to the Jackpot Casino. The hostelry is across the street from the race track and armory 1½ mi east of downtown. Complimentary Continental breakfast. Cable TV. In-door pool. Hot tub. | 410 West Park Rd. | 507/637–5444, 800/287–5443 | 118 rooms, 2 suites | $44–$54 | AE, D, MC, V.

ROCHESTER

(Nearby towns also listed: Mantorville, Owatonna, Preston, Spring Valley, Wabasha, Winona)

During the mid-1800s, this spot in the Zumbro River Valley was a wagon train cross-roads. Today, Rochester is best known for one thing: health care. Each year, thousands of people from around the world come to the Mayo Clinic seeking world-class medical treatment. The city is also developing a reputation as one of Minnesota's top technology centers; IBM has a strong corporate presence here.

Information: Rochester Convention and Visitors Bureau | 150 S. Broadway, Suite A Rochester, 55904-6500 | 507/288–4331 or 800/634–8277 | www.rochestercvb.org.

Attractions

Mayo Clinic. Jointly, the Mayo Clinic, Saint Mary's Hospital, and Rochester Methodist Hospital form an integrated, 36-structure medical center. The complex, established in 1914, now employs 1,100 staff physicians and scientists and nearly as many residents, and has 1,800 patient beds and 3 libraries. | 200 1st St. SW | 507/284–9258 | www.mayo.edu | Daily. The **Rochester Carillon**—a set of 23 or more huge tower bells played with a keyboard—is a rare instrument, and the 56-bell Rochester Carillon is a fine specimen. Three times weekly the bells (in the tower of the Plummer Building) fill the city with music. | 200 1st St. SW | Free | Mon. 7 PM, Wed. and Fri. noon.

Mayowood. Three generations of the Mayo family collected the artwork and other objects in this 50-room stone mansion, which was designed by Dr. Mayo himself. | 1195 W. Circle Dr. SW | 507/282–9447 or 507/287–8691 | http://homepage2.rconnect.com/ochs/index.htm | $10 | May.–Oct. Sat.–Sun. 10–5, July–Aug. Sun., Tue., Thurs., and Sat 10–5.

Olmsted County History Center and Museum. Antique furniture, clothing, and farm equipment are among the displays chronicling the history of Olmsted County. | 1195 W. Circle Dr. NW | 507/282–9447 | $4 | Tues.–Sat. 9–5.

WHAT TO PACK IN THE TOY TOTE FOR KIDS

- ☐ Audiotapes
- ☐ Books
- ☐ Clipboard
- ☐ Coloring/activity books
- ☐ Doll with outfits
- ☐ Hand-held games
- ☐ Magnet games
- ☐ Notepad
- ☐ One-piece toys
- ☐ Pencils, colored pencils
- ☐ Portable stereo with earphones
- ☐ Sliding puzzles
- ☐ Travel toys

*Excerpted from *Fodor's: How to Pack: Experts Share Their Secrets*
© 1997, by Fodor's Travel Publications

Whitewater State Park. The limestone bluffs and deep ravines draw crowds to this 2,700-acre park, 30 mi east of Rochester. You can swim, hike, and camp, and fish for brown, brook, and rainbow trout in the Whitewater River and Trout Run Creek. | Rte. 1, Box 256, Altura | 507/932–3007 | www.dnr.state.mn.us/parks_and_recreation/state_parks/whitewater | $4 | Daily.

Zumbrota Covered Bridge. Minnesota's only remaining original covered bridge has been restored and is now listed on the National Register of Historic Places. The bridge spans the Zumbro River and is surrounded by the 10-acre Covered Bridge Park. | 175 West Ave. | 507/288–4331 or 800/634–8277 | Free | Daily.

ON THE CALENDAR

JUNE: *Rochester Fest.* Toward the end of the month, live music and food vendors fill three streets in front of the Mayo Civic Center. | 507/285–8769.

Dining

Aviary. American. Trees, plants, and pictures of exotic birds set the stage in this tropical-theme dining room, but the menu is all-American. Everything is made from scratch, including the house specialties: blackened steak and garlic shrimp fettucine. | 4320 U.S. 52N | 507/281–5141 | $8–$12 | AE, D, DC, MC, V.

Brass Lantern. American. Sharing the building with a bowling alley, this split-level dining room has nostalgic baseball photos on the walls and aluminum-rimmed Formica booths. The signature burger comes with bacon, mushrooms, and your choice of cheese, and there is a prime rib special on weekends. The chicken fajita salad is extra large. | 1828 14th St. | 507/289–9399 | $9–$17 | D, V.

Broadstreet Cafe. American. Framed antique rugs hang around this airy dining room in an old warehouse. Ostrich tops the menu. | 300 1st Ave. NW | 507/281–2451 | No lunch weekends | $20–$28 | AE, DC, MC, V.

Canadian Honker. American/Causal. This 8,000-square-ft place across from St. Mary's Hospital is filled with pictures of the city's goose population. It serves fresh stir-fried vegetables in teriyaki sauce and several pasta dishes, as well as steaks, burgers, and—on Friday and Saturday—fresh fish flown in from both coasts. | 1203 2nd St. SW | 507/282–6572 | $6–$16 | D, MC, V.

Chardonnay. French. The tone of this turn-of-the-20th-century Victorian home provides an intimate environment for a special meal. The menu changes four times each year, and in the past has listed macadamia nut–crusted salmon and Stilton cheese–and–pear-stuffed chicken breast. | 723 2nd St. SW | 507/252–1310 | Reservations recommended | Closed Sun. No lunch Sat. | $18–$29 | AE, D, DC, MC, V.

China Dynasty. Chinese. Embroidered Chinese wall-hangings and a large fish tank are focal points at this Szechuan/Hunan restaurant, four blocks from the Mayo Clinic. Try the Happy Family—shrimp, chicken, and scallops sautéed with vegetables over rice—or General Tso's chicken. | 701 S. Broadway | 507/289–2333 | $7–$9 | AE. D, MC, V.

Daube's German and Alsatian Bistro. German. A bright and lively bakery and lunch café by day, a cozy, candlelit bistro by night, this downtown place serves authentic specialties like rouladen—sliced steak rolled around bacon, onion, and mushrooms with sour cream gravy—shoe-string potato galettes, and red cabbage. | 14 Third St. SW | 507/280–6446 | Closed Sun. | $14–$20 | DC, MC, V.

Don Pasqual's. Southwestern. Dried chili peppers, a faux-adobe hostess station, and New Mexican art on the walls prepare you for southwestern specialties with a twist—a beef-and-potato–filled burrito with your choice of red or green sauce, green chili stew, and enchiladas with blue corn tortillas. The restaurant is about 10 blocks northwest of downtown. | 530 11th Ave. NW | 507/292–8986 | No lunch Sun., Mon. | $7–$11 | MC, V.

Grandma's Kitchen. American. You can tuck into homemade meatloaf, turkey with dressing and gravy, or roast chicken in this strip-mall eatery, while sitting among antique washboards, lanterns, Singer sewing machines, and a stove from the 1800s. Pie crusts are hand rolled, and hashbrowns are made from freshly grated potatoes. Hearty breakfasts of pancakes, French toast, and eggs are also served. | 1514 N. Broadway | 507/289–0331 | Closed Sun., no dinner Mon. | $4–$7.

Henry Wellington. Continental. If you're interested in any of the antiques hanging from the walls and ceilings of the ceramic-tiled dining room, ask. They're for sale. Everything from the kitchen is made from scratch. The specialties of the house are filet or chicken Wellington, and dessert menu lists Key lime pie and German chocolate cheesecake. There is open-air dining on a side patio. | 216 1st Ave. SW | 507/289–1949 | No lunch weekends | $10–$19 | AE, DC, MC, V.

John Barleycorn. American. Photographs of farm and farming tools surround you in this barn-like structure as you munch on crusty sandwiches or the house special, prime rib. | 2780 S. Broadway | 507/285–0178 | No lunch weekends | $8–$25 | AE, D, DC, MC, V.

Michael's. American. Locally acclaimed for its steaks, this restaurant has a substantial Greek influence as well, as evidenced by its Greek salad and Greek soup. You can choose from a variety of fresh fish that can be fried, pan-fried, or broiled. Works of local artists accent the dining room. | 15 S. Broadway | 507/288–2020 | Closed Sun. | $8–$22 | AE, D, DC, MC, V.

Pannekoeken Restaurant. Dutch. Dutch art prints, lace curtains, and blue-and-white porcelain in the gift shop set the stage for this restaurant's signature dish: *pannekoeken* (a souffléed pancake, baked to puffed perfection in a frying pan). Roast beef and turkey dinners with skin-on mashed potatoes (made with sour cream and chives) are also menu favorites. The building is across the street from the fairgrounds. | 1201 S. Broadway | 507/287–0717 | $7–$9 | AE, D, MC, V.

Sandy Point. American. The old wood accents lend a slightly rustic tone to this dining room, which overlooks Lake Zambro. On the menu are prime rib, filet mignon, and shrimp dishes. | 18 Sandy Point Court NE | 507/367–4983 | No lunch weekdays | $10–$22 | AE, D, DC, MC, V.

Zorba's Greek Restaurant. Greek. Photos and postcards of Greece surround you in this small downtown restaurant, which serves such specialties as shish-kabobs, grilled chicken, and a special gyro—grilled lamb, fresh onions, and tomato, wrapped in pita bread with garlic-yogurt sauce. | 924 7th St. NW | 507/281–1540 | $9–$13 | D, MC, V.

Lodging

Alpine Inn. This three-story 1940s guest house–cum–hotel, with red awnings, flower-filled window boxes, and air-conditioning, has a combination of rooms: some with dark woods and upholstery, others with light and airy designs. Directly across from St. Mary's Hospital, the house is four blocks south of Kutzsky Park. Cable TV. Room phones. Complimentary Continental breakfast. | 1231 2nd St. SW | 507/288–2055, 800/448–7583 | 37 rooms | $41–$45 | D, DC, MC, V.

AmericInn of Stewartville. This two-story hotel stands ½ mi south of I-90, exit 209A (Hwy. 63, Stewartville), 3 mi from the Rochester Airport. A large fireplace warms the lobby. Complimentary Continental breakfast. Cable TV. Business services. Some pets allowed. | 1700 2nd Ave. NW, Stewartville | 507/533–4747 | fax 507/533–4747 | www.AmericInn.com/minnesota/stewartville.html | 27 rooms | $40–$50 | AE, D, DC, MC, V.

Bell Tower Inn. Next to the Alpine Inn, and in fact its sister hotel, this air-conditioned 1987 structure has elevator access to its three stories of guest rooms, and stands across the street from St. Mary's Hospital. Restaurant. Cable TV. Room phones. | 1235 2nd St. SW | 507/289–2233, 800/448–7583 | www.rochcc.com | 40 rooms | $45–$65 | D, DC, MC, V.

Best Western. The Mayo Clinic is 3½ blocks southeast of this four-story hotel. An atrium surrounds its indoor pool–hot tub complex. Complimentary Continental breakfast. In-room

data ports, microwaves, refrigerators. Cable TV. Indoor pool. Hot tub. Laundry facilities. Business services. Some pets allowed. | 20 5th Ave. NW | 507/289–3987, ext. 130 | fax 507/289–3987 | www.bestwestern.com | 63 rooms | $65–$85 | AE, D, DC, MC, V.

Best Western–Apache. A glass-and-wood atrium accents this hostelry next to the immense Apache Mall. Restaurant, bar, complimentary Continental breakfast, room service. In-room data ports. Cable TV. Indoor pool. Hot tub. Video games. Business services, airport shuttle. Some pets allowed. | 1517 16th St. SW | 507/289–8866, ext. 312 | fax 507/289–8866 | www.bestwestern.com | 149 rooms, 2 suites | $70–$80 rooms, $120 suites | AE, D, DC, MC, V.

Best Western Soldiers Field. You can either walk the four blocks or take a shuttle bus to the Mayo Clinic from this three-building complex. Several room configurations are available, from a one-queen-bed room to a two-bedroom suite. Restaurant, bar (with entertainment), complimentary Continental breakfast. In-room data ports, some kitchenettes, some refrigerators. Cable TV. Indoor pool. Hot tub. Exercise equipment. Shops. Laundry facilities. Business services, airport shuttle. | 401 6th St. SW | 507/288–2677 | fax 507/282–2042 | www.bestwestern.com | 128 rooms, 90 suites | $60–$75, $80 suites | AE, D, DC, MC, V.

Blondell Hotel. St. Mary's Hospital is across the street from this three-story, L-shape hotel. Restaurant, bar, room service. Cable TV. Laundry facilities. Business services. Some pets allowed. | 1406 2nd St. SW | 507/282–9444 or 800/441–5209 | fax 507/282–8683 | www.blondell.com | 58 rooms | $58 | AE, MC, V.

Colonial Inn. Guests gather in the spacious lobby of this four-story, turn-of-the-20th-century brick hotel to talk and play cards. The Mayo clinic is across the street. In the rooms, ceilings are higher than those in more modern hotels. Restaurant. Complimentary Continental breakfast Sat., Sun. Cable TV. Some microwaves, refrigerators. | 114 2nd St. | 507/289–3363 | www.rochesterlodging.com/colonialinn | 50 rooms | $45–$69 | AE, D, MC, V.

Comfort Inn and Conference Center. An indoor water slide pleases youngsters at this five-story hotel, 1 mi north of the Mayo Clinic. The hotel offers a complimentary shuttle service to and from the Clinic. Restaurant, bar, complimentary Continental breakfast, room service. In-room data ports. Cable TV. Indoor pool. Hot tub, sauna. Laundry facilities. Business services, airport shuttle. | 1625 S. Broadway | 507/281–2211 | fax 507/288–8979 | Comfort_Inn@prodigy.net | www.comfortinn.com | 164 rooms | $59–$175 | AE, D, DC, MC, V.

Days Inn. Two blocks from the Mayo Clinic, this hotel has a choice of European-theme rooms or B&B rooms. Restaurant. Some refrigerators. Cable TV. Laundry facilities. Some pets allowed. | 6 1st Ave. NW | 507/282–3801 | fax 507/282–3801 | www.daysinn.com | 71 rooms | $45–$69 | AE, D, DC, MC, V.

Days Inn–South. Three miles south of downtown, this two-story hostelry is at the intersection of Routes 52 and 63. Complimentary Continental breakfast. Cable TV. Business services, airport shuttle. Some pets allowed. | 111 28th St. | 507/286–1001 | www.daysinn.com | 128 rooms | $42–$62 | AE, D, DC, MC, V.

Econo Lodge. Across the street from the athletic field and two blocks north of Soldier's Field golf course, this two-story motel is three blocks from downtown. Some kitchenettes. Cable TV. Laundry facilities. | 519 3rd Ave. SW | 507/288–1855, ext. 300 | fax 507/288–1855 | www.econolodge.com | 62 rooms | $42–$56 | AE, D, DC, MC, V.

Executive Inn. Renovated in spring 2000, this two-story hostelry is two blocks south of the Mayo Clinic, right downtown. Complimentary Continental breakfast. Some refrigerators. Cable TV. Indoor pool. Sauna. Laundry facilities. | 116 5th St. SW | 507/289–1628 or 888/233–9470 | www.rochesterlodging.com/executiveinn | 59 rooms | $33–$59 | AE, D, DC, MC, V.

Executive Suites by Kahler. Nestled between a grocery store and the Galleria Mall, this nine-story hotel is also connected to the skyway–subway system. Restaurant, bar, complimentary Continental breakfast. In-room data ports, some refrigerators. Cable TV. Indoor pool. Hot tub. Exercise equipment. Laundry facilities. Business services, free parking. Some pets allowed. | 9 N.W. 3rd Ave. | 507/289–8646 | fax 507/282–4478 | www.kahler.com/executivesuites | 128 suites | $79–$109 | AE, D, DC, MC, V.

Fiksdal Hotel and Suites. Every 11th night is free at this independently owned six-story hotel, across the street from St. Mary's Hospital. Complimentary Continental breakfast. Cable TV. Business services, airport shuttle. | 1215 2nd St. SW | 507/288–2671 | fax 507/366–3451 | www.rochesterlodging.com/fiksdal/page2.htm | 55 rooms | $41–$75 | AE, D, MC, V.

Gaslight Inn Motel. One block west of the Mayo Clinic's St. Mary's Hospital is this two-story motel. Free city bus passes are included with your stay. Restaurant. In-room data ports, refrigerators. Cable TV. Laundry facilities. Business services. | 1601 2nd St. SW | 507/289–1824 or 800/658–7016 | fax 507/289–3611 | www.rochesterlodging.com/gaslightinn | 25 rooms | $69–$99 | AE, D, DC, MC, V.

Hampton Inn. Two miles south of downtown and 1 mi from the city's main shopping mall is this three-story hotel, which has free shuttle service to the Mayo Clinic. Restaurant. Complimentary Continental breakfast. Refrigerators. Cable TV. Indoor pool. Hot tub. Exercise equipment. Laundry facilities. Business services. | 1755 S. Broadway | 507/287–9050 | fax 507/287–9139 | www.hampton-inn.com/rochester | 105 rooms | $64–$129 | AE, D, DC, MC, V.

Hilltop Bed & Breakfast. The guest rooms of this 1928 limestone home, standing on 6 wooded acres and overlooking Silver Lake, are on the second floor. Each is decorated individually, one with a four-poster bed and floral wallpaper. It's a 10-block walk to downtown. Complimentary breakfast. TV in common room. Room phones. | 1735 Third Ave. NW | 507/282–6650 | fax 507/282–1389 | www.bedandbreakfast.com | 3 rooms | $96–$144 | AE, D, MC, V.

Holiday Inn–Downtown. In the heart of the city's cultural and commercial center and connected to the skyway-subway system, this nine-story hotel has an indoor atrium to brighten cold-weather visits. Restaurant, bar. In-room data ports. Cable TV. Business services. | 220 S. Broadway | 507/288–3231 | fax 507/288–6602 | www.kahler.com/holidayinn | 170 rooms | $99–$235 | AE, D, DC, MC, V.

Holiday Inn–South. Across from the County Fairgrounds and Graham Arena, this two-story hotel is 1½ miles south of downtown. Restaurant, bar, room service. Some kitchenettes. Cable TV. Indoor pool. Laundry facilities. Business services, airport shuttle. Some pets allowed. | 1630 S. Broadway | 507/288–1844 | fax 507/288–1844 | www.kahler.com/holidayinn | 196 rooms | $62–$75 | AE, D, DC, MC, V.

Inn at Rocky Creek. All rooms have private baths, and the sitting room has a vaulted ceiling and wood-burning fireplace. Built by the owners, this air-conditioned B&B is surrounded by oak trees in a residential neighborhood on the north edge of town. Complimentary breakfast. Cable TV in some rooms. Room phones. No smoking. No pets. | 2115 Rocky Creek Dr. NE | 507/288–1019 | rochesterlodging.com/rockycreek | 3 rooms | $85–$125 | AE, DC, MC, V.

Kahler Grand Hotel. Built in 1921, in the heart of downtown, this hotel is connected to the greater Kahler complex by a skywalk. From the domed, skylit pool to crystal chandeliers, every detail is lavish in this 12-story hostelry. Restaurant, bars (with entertainment). In-room data ports, refrigerators. Cable TV. Indoor pool. Hot tub, beauty salon. Exercise equipment. Business services, airport shuttle. Some pets allowed. | 20 2nd Ave. SW | 507/282–2581 or 800/533–1655 | fax 507/285–2775 | www.kahler.com/kahlergrand/index.html | 700 rooms, 26 suites | $59–$150, $350–$1,500 suites | AE, D, DC, MC, V.

Langdon's Uptown. This two-story motel is one block from Soldier's Field park, and three blocks south of the Mayo Clinic complex. Refrigerators. Cable TV. | 526 3rd Ave. SW | 507/282–7425 | rochesterlodging.com/langdons | 38 rooms | $25–$33 | AE, MC, V.

Maxwell Guest House. In 1922, this 3-story brick building was moved from its original location a few blocks away to its present site. Since then, it has served as a nurses' dormitory for the Mayo Clinic, two blocks away. The no-frills single and double rooms and the communal kitchen give it a casual, hostel-like feel. No room phones. Cable TV. | 426 2nd Ave. SW | 507/288–4821 | 52 rooms | $22 | No credit cards.

Rochester Marriott. A seven-story courtyard atrium is the highlight of this 10-story hotel, which is directly across the street from the Mayo Clinic. The interior lobby is done in stone and glass. Restaurant, bar (with entertainment). In-room data ports, some minibars, refrigerators. Cable TV. Indoor pool. Hot tub, beauty salon. Exercise equipment. Business services. | 101 1st Ave. SW | 507/280–6000 or 800/533–1655 | fax 506/280–8531 | www.kahler.com/marriott | 184 rooms, 10 suites | $100–$229, $295–$1,800 suites | AE, D, DC, MC, V.

Roy Sands Guest House. Two turn-of-the-20th-century homes connected by a breeze-way and surrounded by trees make up this mom-and-pop hotel, which stands across from St. Mary's Hospital and ten blocks from the Mayo clinic. Cable TV. Room phones. | 1307 2nd St. | 507/285–0554 | roomrenter@aol.com | http://rochesterlodging.com/roy-sands | 20 rooms | $40–$50 | AE, D, MC, V.

Quality Inn and Suites. This 2-story hotel is part of a small cluster of similar hotels in a residential area, next to the Olmsted County Fairgrounds. Complimentary Continental breakfast. In-room data ports. Cable TV. Laundry facilities. Business services, airport shuttle. Some pets allowed. | 1620 1st Ave. SE | 507/282–8091 | fax 507/282–8091 | rochesterlodging.com/qualityinn | 41 rooms | $69–$165 | AE, D, DC, MC, V.

Radisson Plaza. The Skyway connects this 10-story hotel with the Mayo Clinic, the Galleria Mall, and the government center. Restaurant, bar. In-room data ports, some refrigerators. Cable TV. Indoor pool. Hot tub. Exercise equipment. Laundry facilities. Business services. | 150 S. Broadway | 507/281–8000 | fax 507/281–4280 | www.radisson.com | 207 rooms, 5 suites | $155 rooms, $350–$1,200 suites | AE, D, DC, MC, V.

Ramada Limited. All rooms have microwaves and coffee makers at this 3-story hotel, 3 mi north of the Mayo Clinic complex. Restaurant. Some kitchenettes, microwaves, refrigerators. Cable TV. Indoor pool. Laundry facilities. Some pets allowed. | 435 16th Ave. NW | 507/288–9090, ext. 502 | fax 507/288–9090 | www.ramada.com | 120 rooms | $62–$125 | AE, D, DC, MC, V.

Red Carpet Inn. Each room has a dad-style recliner at this motel, ¾ mi north of downtown. Complimentary Continental breakfast. Some kitchenettes. Cable TV. Indoor pool. Laundry facilities. Business services. Some pets allowed. | 2214 S. Broadway | 507/282–7448 or 800–658–7048 | rochesterlodging.com/redcarpet | 34 rooms | $43–$53 | AE, D, MC, V.

Rochester Inn. Downtown is 2 mi north of this single-story, no-frills motel in a busy commercial area. Cable TV. Some pets allowed. | 1837 S. Broadway | 507/288–2031 | 27 rooms | $32–$40 | AE, D, DC, MC, V.

Super 8 South Broadway. Downtown is 2 mi north of this two-story motel, which is part of a busy commercial district. Complimentary Continental breakfast. Some refrigerators. Cable TV. Business services. | 106 21st St. SE | 507/282–1756 | fax 507/282–1756 | rochesterlodging.com/super8s2 | 79 rooms | $40–$59 | AE, D, DC, MC, V.

Super 8 South 1. This three-story 1980s hotel is on a commercial strip 1 mi south of downtown. In-room data ports. Cable TV. Sauna. Some pets allowed. | 1230 S. Broadway | 507/288–8288, ext. 350 | fax 507/288–8288 | rochesterlodging.com/super8s1 | 89 rooms | $52–$65 | AE, D, DC, MC, V.

ROSEAU

MAP 3, B1

(Nearby town also listed: Baudette)

Roseau calls itself the North Star City, and it's an apt description for a town within a ten-minute drive of the Canadian border; you won't find many communities farther north on the Minnesota map. Despite the town's small size, its high school hockey team is a perennial state powerhouse.

Information: Roseau Civic and Commerce | 100 2nd Ave. NE, Roseau, 56751 | 218/463–1542.

Attractions

Hayes Lake State Park. Bird watchers have spotted over 200 species in or near this 3,000-acre park, 22 mi southeast of Roseau. Summer flora include orchids, gentians, and blueberries. There's swimming and canoeing in the lake, and camping in designated areas. Trails for hiking, skiing, snowmobiling, and horseback riding connect the park the Beltrami Island State Forest. | 48990 County Rd. 4 | 218/425–7504 | www.dnr.state.mn.us/parks_and_recreation/state_parks/hayes_lake | Park permit required | Daily.

Pioneer Farm and Village. The village, 2 mi west of town, includes a blacksmith shop, a post office, a log school, a church, and a parish hall. | Rte. 11W | 218/463–2187 | Free | May–Sept., call for hours.

Roseau Bog Owl Management Unit. You might see gray owls, northern hawk owls, great horned owls, and other species on these 8,960 acres of tamarack black spruce bog, part of the Lost River State Forest 6 mi north of town, across the Sprague Creek bridge. The area is included on a list, published by the Minnesota Ornithologists' Union, of the top bird-watching areas in the state. | Rte. 310N | 218/463–1557 | Free | Daily.

Roseau City Park. Bordering the Roseau River, the park has camping and RV sites, a shelter, a boat launch, a picnic area, a horse shoe pit, and a beach volley ball court. One third of the 37-acre park is naturally forested and equipped with hiking trails. | 900 11th Ave. SE | 218/463–1542 | Free | Daily.

Roseau County Historical Museum and Interpretive Center. The artifacts and displays here include information on the area's natural history, Native Americans, and non-native Pioneers. The museum shop sells books and video tapes on these subjects. | 110 2nd Ave. NE | 218/463–1918 | www.angelfire.com/mn/rchistsocmuseum | $2 | Tues.–Fri. 9–5; Sat. 9–4; Closed Sun., Mon.

Roseau River Wildlife Management Area. The 60,000 acres of natural bog and forest create a great habitat for spotting wildlife of many kinds. | 27952 400 St. | 218/463–1557 | Free | Daily.

ON THE CALENDAR

JUNE: *Range Riders Horse Extravaganza.* Events at this lasso twirling, three-day festival may include jackpot roping, barrel and riding clinics, reining demonstrations, draft-horse logging exhibitions, and hands-on learning. The festivities occur during the second weekend of the month, at the Roseau County fairgrounds. | 218/463–1810.

Dining

American Legion Restaurant. American. Wildlife paintings by local artist Terry Redlin line the walls of this downtown dinner spot, the only smoke-free restaurant in town. The menu includes everything from pork chops and burgers to lobster and steak, and all entrées include soup and a salad bar. Friday night there is a chicken and ribs special. | 321 N. Main Ave. | 218/463–3691 | No lunch. Closed Sun., Mon. | $8–$16 | D, MC, V.

Lodging

AmericInn. A fireplace brightens the lobby of this 1988 hotel on the west side of town. A playground, picnic area, and horseshoes game outside face farmland. Complimentary Continental breakfast. Cable TV. Indoor pool. Hot tub, sauna. | 1090 3rd St. NW (Rte. 11) | 218/463–1045 | www.americinn.com | 37 rooms | $60–$94 | AE, D, DC, MC, V.

Evergreen Motel. Three single-story buildings make up the Evergreen, which is in the southwest corner of town. The original wood structure dates back to 1940. Kitchenettes. Cable TV. Some pets allowed. | 304 5th Ave. NW | 218/463–1642 | 34 rooms | $34–$37 | D, DC, MC, V.

ST. CLOUD

MAP 3, D7

(Nearby towns also listed: Elk River, Little Falls)

One of the fastest-growing metropolitan areas in the state, this thriving Mississippi River town has quite a number of cultural, social, and recreational venues, including historic theaters, internationally renowned gardens, and a sprawling university. Its central-Minnesotan location has made it a popular convention site. The city is named after the suburb of Paris where Napoleon Bonaparte had a summer residence.

Information: **St. Cloud Convention and Visitors Bureau** | 525 Rte. 10S, Ste. 1, St. Cloud, 56304 | 800/264–2940 | www.stcloudcvb.com.

Attractions

City recreation areas. St. Cloud has an extensive recreation system that ensures that its residents and visitors have plenty of outdoor activities to choose from. | 320/255–7256.

The facilities at **Riverside Park** include a picnic shelter, gardens, wading pool, tennis courts, and lighted cross-country skiing. You'll also find a monument to Zebulon Pike, the explorer who discovered the nearby Beaver Islands on the Mississippi. | 1725 Killian Blvd. | 320/255–7256 | Free | Daily.

You can launch your boat on the river or sit down with a picnic lunch at **Wilson Park.** Facilities include play equipment, picnic tables, rest rooms, horseshoe pits, a softball field and tennis courts, a boat launch, a shelter and kitchen, and a sand volleyball court. | 625 Riverside Dr. NE | 320/255–7256 | Free | Daily.

Facilities and recreation options at **Lake George Eastman Park** include a warming house, paddle boating, fishing, and picnicking. An Olympic-size outdoor pool is in the southwest corner of the park. | 425 E. Lake Blvd. | 320/255–7262 | Free | Daily.

© Corbis

FANTASY TOWN

You may have noticed that Minnesota's best-known small town is nowhere to be found in this guide. That's because it doesn't exist. If you've ever listened to public radio's "A Prairie Home Companion," you're probably aware that Lake Wobegon, Minnesota, is the product of host Garrison Keillor's imagination. Still, Keillor's descriptions of his mythical hometown are so vivid that some people remain confused about its fictional nature. After all, Keillor has provided a perfectly good explanation for why Lake Wobegon does not appear on any state maps: a surveyor simply overlooked it.

If you're intent on finding the "real" Lake Wobegon, head toward central Minnesota, in the direction of St. Cloud (which is mentioned frequently in Keillor's books). Many of the small towns there share characteristics with Keillor's invention, even if the children are not all "above average." If you're into hiking or biking, you might want to plan an excursion to the Lake Wobegon Trail. It opened in 1998 and runs 28 mi from Avon to Sauk Centre on an abandoned rail corridor.

The **Municipal Athletic Center** is the place to go in St. Cloud for indoor ice skating. | 1000 8th St. N | 320/255–7223 | $3 | Open session Fri. 9–10:30, Sun. 11–1.

The softball diamonds, soccer fields, and walking trails at 140-acre **Whitney Memorial Park** attract big crowds. | 1529 Northway Dr. | 320/255–7256 | Free | Daily.

Heritage Park, a 93-acre natural habitat, has woodland, prairie, and aquatic areas for nature study. Canoe and snowshoe rentals are available. | 225 33rd. Ave. S | Free | Daily.

College of St. Benedict. Founded in 1913 by the Sisters of the Order of Saint Benedict, this was one of the first women's colleges in the Midwest. It now has a partnership arrangement with nearby St. John's University to offer coeducational programs in a variety of fields. Among the campus facilities is the Benedicta Arts Center, featuring a 1,000-seat auditorium and a 300-seat theater. | 37 S. College Ave. | 320/363–5011 | www.csbsju.edu | Free | Daily.

St. Benedict's Monastery. Nearly 400 Benedictine women call the monastery their home. Tours of the 1912 Sacred Heart Chapel and the monastery archives are available by appointment. | 104 Chapel La., St. Joseph | 320/363–7100 | Free | By appointment.

Munsinger Gardens. Several distinct garden areas include the White Garden, which was inspired by the world-renowned White Garden at Sissinghurst Castle in Kent, England, and the Perennial Garden, which displays flowers and plants that can survive harsh Minnesota winters. | Riverside Dr. S and Michigan Ave. | 320/255–7238 | Free | Daily.

Powder Ridge Ski Area. A 310-ft vertical drop, 15 trails, and seven lifts draw snow bunnies from around central Minnesota. The ski area is 16 mi south of St. Cloud. | 15015 93rd Ave., Kimball | 320/398–7200 or 800/348–7734 | Nov.–Apr., daily.

St. Cloud State University. Founded in 1969 as a training school for elementary teachers, St. Cloud State is now a full-fledged liberal arts university with 14,000 students, the second largest university in the state. | 320/255–3151 | www.stcloudstate.edu | Daily.

Saint John's University. Founded in 1856, St. John's is now a partner in liberal arts education with the nearby College of St. Benedict. It has an enrollment of 1,700 and is sponsored by the Benedictines of St. John's Abbey. | Collegeville | 320/363–2573 | www.csbsju.edu | Daily. Thousands of medieval manuscripts on microfilm make **Hill Monastic Manuscript Library** the world's largest collection of its kind. | St. John's University, Collegeville | 320/363–3514 | www.hmml.org | Free | Mon.–Fri. 8–4:30, Sat. 10–4:30, Sun. 11–4:30.

The Benedictine monastic community of **St. John's Abbey** at St. John's University follows the 1,500-year-old tradition of worship and work through daily prayer and service. The Abbey's modern church, designed by Marcel Breuer, is widely considered an architectural gem. Tours are available. | 104 Chapel La., Collegeville | 320/363–2011 | Free | Daily.

Stearns History Museum. The state's only nationally accredited museum outside the Twin Cities, Stearns has one main, two-level gallery, one kids' gallery, two rotating exhibits, a research center, and a library. There are a self-activated video presentation, an example of Indian dwellings, a mock dairy barn, and a granite quarry model, built to scale. | 235 S. 33rd Ave. | 320/253–8424 | www.stearns-museum.org | $4 | Mon.–Sat. 10–4, Sun. noon–4.

ON THE CALENDAR

APR.: *Mississippi Music Fest.* On the last Sunday of the month, a wide array of musicians with diverse styles entertain at Riverside Park, on 10th St. | 320/255–2205.

JUNE: *Wheels, Wings and Water Festival.* This end-of-the-month celebration spans the whole city, with festivities along the Mississippi River, at the St. Cloud Regional Airport, and at Whitney Park. There are a parade, fireworks, a block party, food vendors, and a free outdoor concert. | 800/264–2940.

Dining

Anton's Fish and Whiskey. American. Steaks grilled to order and stuffed shrimp with Boursin sauce are favorites at this casual spot. For dessert, go for the seven-layer chocolate cake. | 2001 Frontage Rd. N | 320/253–3611 | No lunch Sun. | $10–$24 | AE, D, DC, MC, V.

Ciatti's. Italian. Seated among faux grape vine–wrapped columns, you might order the tortellini straw and hay, which comes with snow peas, ham, mushrooms, and a Parmesan cream sauce. Leave room for desserts such as tiramisu and cheesecake. Kids' menu. | 600 W. St. Germaine | 320/251–5255 | $9–$15 | AE, D, DC, MC, V.

D.B. Searle's. American. Antiques warm the skylighted dining rooms in this four-story brick building, built in 1886 between the Wells Fargo Building and the Radisson Hotel. Prime rib and walleye pike top the menu. | 18 S. 5th Ave. | 320/253–0655 | No lunch Sun. | $10–$20 | AE, MC, V.

McGee's Bar and Grill. American. Serving up steaks, fried chicken, and ribs, this casual eatery is in the southwest corner of town. All three dining rooms have rural decorations, such as a real tractor, an old rifle, and a mural depicting a country lodge scene. | 137 Second Ave. S, Waite Park | 320/255–1207 | $9–$16 | AE, D, MC, V.

Mexican Village. Mexican. Handpainted murals and Mexicans artifacts make this a festive place for chicken fajitas and other south-of-the-border favorites. | 509 West Germaine St., | 320/252–7134 | $7–$10 | AE, D, MC, V.

Park Diner. American. A black-and-white checkered floor and a juke box blaring '50s rock and roll help set the mood at this diner. The Stingray, one of its specialty burgers, comes with bacon, American cheese, and fries. | 1531 Division St., Waite Park | 320/252–0080 | Daily 6 AM–10 PM | $6–$9 | AE, D, DC, MC, V.

Waldo's. American. Model airplanes are scattered around this restaurant, where thick-crusted, Chicago-style pizza tops the menu. Try the Barnstormer, with Canadian bacon, sausage, and mushrooms. | 3360 W. Division St. | 320/253–7170 | $6–$23 | AE, D, MC, V.

Lodging

American Motel. On the southwest edge of St. Cloud, this 2-story motel is next door to a fast food restaurant. Complimentary Continental breakfast. In-room data ports, some kitchenettes, some in-room hot tubs. Cable TV. Indoor pool. Hot tub. Free parking. Pets allowed. | 4361 Clearwater Rd. | 320/253–6337 or 800/634–3444 | fax 320/253–6127 | 40 rooms, 5 suites | $61, $71 suites | AE, D, DC, MC, V.

Best Western Americana Inn and Conference Center. The Munsinger Gardens are three blocks from this 2-story hotel 1½ mi east of downtown. Restaurant, bar (with entertainment), room service. In-room data ports. Cable TV. Indoor pool. Hot tub, sauna. Business services. Some pets allowed. | 520 S. Rte. 10 | 320/252–8700 | fax 320/252–8700 | www.bestwestern.com | 63 rooms | $49–$104 | AE, D, DC, MC, V.

Best Western Kelly Inn. The Civic Center is right next door to this 6-story glass-and-brick hotel. Some rooms are poolside and others have views of the mighty Mississippi. Fireplace and Jacuzzi suites are available. Restaurant, bar. In-room data ports. Cable TV. Indoor pool, wading pool. Hot tub, sauna. Laundry facilities. Business services. Some pets allowed. | Rte. 23 at 4th Ave. S | 320/253–0606 | fax 320/202–0505 | www.bestwestern.com | 229 rooms | $59–$105 | AE, D, DC, MC, V.

Comfort Inn. This is a 2-story motel amid shiny strip malls 2 mi west of downtown. Complimentary Continental breakfast. Cable TV. Exercise equipment. Laundry facilities. Business services. | 4040 S. 2nd St. | 320/251–1500 | fax 320/251–1500, ext. 301 | www.comfortinn.com | 63 rooms | $46–$70 | AE, D, DC, MC; V.

Days Inn. A mile southeast of downtown, this two-story motel is 3 mi down Route 23 from the Crossroads Mall. Complimentary Continental breakfast. Cable TV. Indoor pool. Hot tub. Business services. Some pets allowed. | 420 S.E. U.S. 10 | 320/253–0500 | www.daysinn.com/ctg/cgi-bin/DaysInn | 78 rooms | $41–$125 | AE, D, DC, MC, V.

Edelbrock House. A shaded front patio welcomes you to this 1880s yellow brick farmhouse. Complimentary breakfast. No air conditioning. No room phones, TV in common area. | 216

14th Ave. N | 320/259–0071 | http://itn.bbchannel.com/bbc/p216807.asp | 4 rooms | $50–$65.

Fairfield Inn by Marriott. I–94, exit 167B, brings you to this three-story stucco building, 4 mi west of St. Cloud State University. Rooms are designed for business travelers and some have executive-size desks. Complimentary Continental breakfast. In-room data ports, some refrigerators. Cable TV. Indoor pool. Hot tub. Laundry facilities. Business services. | 4120 S. 2nd St. | 320/654–1881 | www.fairfieldinn.com/STCFI | 57 rooms | $49–$104 | AE, D, DC, MC, V.

Holiday Inn & Suites. A Holidome atrium surrounds the exercise equipment at this west side hotel, three blocks east of the Crossroads shopping mall. Restaurant, bar. Some kitchenettes. Cable TV. 2 indoor pools, wading pool. Hot tub. Exercise equipment. Business services. | 75 37th Ave. S | 320/253–9000 | fax 320/253–5998 | www.basshotels.com/holiday-inn/ | 257 rooms | $67–$90 | AE, D, DC, MC, V.

Motel 6 St. Cloud. Waite Park is a residential suburb of St. Cloud and this chain is in the middle of it, four blocks from the Crossroads Mall. In-room data ports. Cable TV. Business services. | 815 S. 1st St., Waite Park | www.motel6.com | 320/253–7070 | fax 320/253–0436 | 93 rooms | $36–$46 | AE, D, DC, MC, V.

Quality Inn Pool and Water Park. A 2½-story water slide and kiddie pool with fountain are right inside the hotel. All this fun is 3 mi from both St. Cloud State University and the Civic Center. Cable TV. Hot tub, sauna. Some pets allowed. | 70 37th Ave. S | 320/253–4444 | fax 320/259–7809 | www.qualityinn.com | 89 rooms | $50–$130 | AE, D, DC, MC, V.

Radisson Suite Hotel. The Civic Center is attached to the hotel by a skyway. Plenty of coffee shops, stores, bars, restaurants lie within a three-block radius. Restaurant, room service. In-room data ports, some in-room hot tubs. Cable TV. Indoor pool. Hot tub, sauna. Exercise room. Laundry service. Business service, free parking. | 404 St. Germaine | 320/654–0779 | fax 320/654–0779 | www.radisson.com | 103 suites | $104–$249 | AE, D, DC, MC, V.

Ramada Limited. Standing at the intersection of Route 22 and Route 15, this hotel caters to business travelers, and has a large desk in every room. Complimentary Continental breakfast, room service. In-room data ports, some kitchenettes. Cable TV. Indoor pool. Hot tub, spa. Exercise room. Video games. Laundry facilities, laundry services. Business services, free parking. | 121 Park Ave. | 320/253–3200 or 800/272–6232 | fax 320/253–7082 | www.ramada.com | 52 rooms, 13 suites | $65–$80, $150 suites | AE, D, DC, MC, V.

Super 8. The Crossroads Mall is across the street from this two-story brick motel. Complimentary Continental breakfast. Cable TV. Business services. Some pets allowed. | 50 Park Ave. S | 320/253–5530 | fax 320/253–5292 | www.super8.com | 68 rooms | $36–$43 | AE, D, DC, V.

Travelodge. This two-story, east-side motel sits among auto-repair shops and tire stores, and is a half mile off of I–94 Exit 171 (St. Augusta), 4 mi south of downtown. Bar, complimentary Continental breakfast. Cable TV. | 3820 Roosevelt Rd. | 320/253–3338 | www.travelodge.com | 28 rooms | $40–$60 | AE, D, DC, MC, V.

ST. PAUL

MAP 3, E8

(Suburbs also listed: Anoka, Bloomington, Elk River, Hastings, Lake City, Lakeville, Le Sueur, Northfield, Red Wing, Shakopee, Stillwater, Taylor Falls)

You wouldn't guess it, looking at St. Paul today, but Minnesota's capital city began as a squatter's camp. Its first resident was a one-eyed moonshiner named Pierre "Pig's Eye" Parrant, who had twice run afoul of the authorities at nearby Fort Snelling. In the late 1830s, Parrant set up a saloon and shack in a muddy swamp down-river from the fort, and within no time his little settlement had become a popular stopping point for rivermen and settlers. People called the area Pig's Eye Landing until some civic-minded settlers decided to name their town after a little log church that a missionary had built. They called it St. Paul.

In 1847, St. Paul became the capital of the new Minnesota territory. The effect on the village was profound: within three weeks, it doubled in size. Settlers began streaming in, carried to the new capital on steamboats.

At first, fur trading was the big local business. Then it was lumber. Eventually, the railroads arrived and Minnesota's capital became a center of rail commerce. St. Paul prospered and grew. Grand mansions, a majestic Roman Catholic cathedral, river-spanning bridges, and other architectural marvels arose within a short distance of the place where Pig's Eye Parrant had once set up shop. Today you'll find that many of those architectural landmarks have survived in remarkably good condition. They and other

KODAK'S TIPS FOR PHOTOGRAPHING THE CITY

Streets
- Take a bus or walking tour to get acclimated
- Explore markets, streets, and parks
- Travel light so you can shoot quickly

City Vistas
- Find high vantage points to reveal city views
- Shoot early or late in the day, for best light
- At twilight, use fast films and bracket exposures

Formal Gardens
- Exploit high angles to show garden design
- Use wide-angle lenses to exaggerate depth and distance
- Arrive early to beat crowds

Landmarks and Monuments
- Review postcard racks for traditional views
- Seek out distant or unusual views
- Look for interesting vignettes or details

Museums
- Call in advance regarding photo restrictions
- Match film to light source when color is critical
- Bring several lenses or a zoom

Houses of Worship
- Shoot exteriors from nearby with a wide-angle lens
- Move away and include surroundings
- Switch to a very fast film indoors

Stained-Glass Windows
- Bright indirect sunlight yields saturated colors
- Expose for the glass not the surroundings
- Switch off flash to avoid glare

Architectural Details
- Move close to isolate details
- For distant vignettes, use a telephoto lens
- Use side light to accent form and texture

In the Marketplace
- Get up early to catch peak activity
- Search out colorful displays and colorful characters
- Don't scrimp on film

Stage Shows and Events
- Never use flash
- Shoot with fast (ISO 400 to 1000) film
- Use telephoto lenses
- Focus manually if necessary

From *Kodak Guide to Shooting Great Travel Pictures* © 2000 by Fodor's Travel Publications

attractions such as the Native American burial grounds overlooking the Mississippi River make St. Paul a fascinating place to visit.

Information: St. Paul's Convention and Visitors Bureau | 175 W. Kellogg Blvd., St. Paul, 55102 | 651/265–4900 or 800/627–6101 | www.stpaulcvb.org.

NEIGHBORHOODS

Central. Central St. Paul sits in a basket created by Kellogg Blvd. on the south and by University Ave. and the State Capitol complex on the north. The **downtown business district** dominates this area. Western downtown is the cultural corridor, and contains such attractions as the Minnesota Historical Society History Center, Landmark Center, and the Science Museum of Minnesota. **Lowertown,** on the eastern edge of downtown, has established itself as a thriving arts community. Near the State Capitol is the neighborhood known as **Frogtown.** It developed at the turn of the 20th century around three Catholic parishes composed of Irish, German, and Polish immigrants.

★ **Summit-Grand.** The Summit-Grand area, also called Summit Hill, is a mixture of the traditional and the trendy. Standing west of downtown, it fills the slice of St. Paul that's created by I–94 to the north and I–35E to the southeast. The neighborhood overlooks downtown and consists mostly of Victorian mansions, many of which are listed as state and national historic structures. The writer F. Scott Fitzgerald lived in or frequented several of them. Grand Avenue runs parallel to Summit Avenue, and as it stretches west it turns into an urban shopping and dining haven. The street features everything from college campuses to cozy cafés and restaurants.

Midway–Como–St. Anthony Park. The northwest corner of St. Paul is an amalgam of neighborhoods known as Midway–Como–St. Anthony Park. A large chunk of Midway is devoted to the Minnesota State Fairgrounds. Lake Como is the centerpiece of the Como neighborhood, which contains a large public park and charming homes built in the early to mid-20th century, but has few commercial or retail establishments. St. Anthony Park is a vibrant community known for stable residential neighborhoods and businesses, well-tended gardens, and convenient shopping areas.

West Side. The bump of St. Paul that lies south of the Mississippi River is confusingly called West Side. Perhaps more than any other community, this one reflects the city's ethnic, economic, and cultural diversity. Its vast collection of Mexican, Lebanese, Central American, Filipino, and Asian-American grocery stores and restaurants makes it a great destination for anyone interested in ethnic foods. The lower West Side is prone to flooding when the Mississippi rises, and is primarily a commercial and industrial area.

TRANSPORTATION INFORMATION

Airports: The **Minneapolis/St. Paul International Airport** has a reputation for staying open in all but the very worst winter weather. The blizzard scenes in the movie *Airport* were shot here (612/726–5555).
Amtrak offers national rail passenger service (800/872–7245).
Bus Lines: Metro Transit is a regional bus system (612/373–3333).
Intra-city Transit: Contact the **Metropolitan Transit Commission** (3118 Nicollet | 612/349–7000).

Attractions

ART AND ARCHITECTURE

Alexander Ramsey House. Guides dressed as Anna Ramsey's servants take you on a tour of the home that once belonged to her and her husband, Alexander, the first territorial governor of Minnesota. Their Victorian home is one of the best preserved in the country, remarkable for its carved walnut woodwork, marble fireplaces, crystal chandeliers, and many

ST. PAUL

INTRO
ATTRACTIONS
DINING
LODGING

original furnishings. Tours begin hourly. | 265 S. Exchange St. | 651/296–8760 | www.mnhs.org/places/sites/arh | $5 | May–Dec., Tues.–Sat. 10–3.

City Hall and Court House. Construction for this Art Deco building lasted from 1928 to 1931. Its centerpiece is a three-story Italian marble statue, "Vision of Peace" by Carl Milles, that depicts a Native American surrounded by his disciples. | 15 W. Kellogg Blvd. | 651/266–8023 | Free | Weekdays 8–4:30.

James J. Hill House. The builder of the Great Northern Railway moved into his rugged, red sandstone residence in 1891. The home has 43 rooms (including 13 bathrooms) and exquisite details such as carved woodwork, stained glass, and a skylit art gallery. | 240 Summit Ave. | 651/297–2555 | www.mnhs.org/places/sites/jjhh | $6 | Wed.–Sat. 10–3:30.

Sibley Historic Site. The 1836 home of Henry Hastings Sibley, the state's first governor, is the focal point of the site. Adjacent to his home is Faribault House, a museum that focuses on Native American and fur trade history. | 1357 Sibley Memorial Rte., Mendota | 651/452–1596 | www.mnhs.org/places/sites/shs | $4 | May–Oct., Tues.–Sat. 10–5, Sun. noon–5.

State Capitol. St. Paul native Cass Gilbert designed this Italian Renaissance building, made of Georgian marble and St. Cloud granite, which was constructed between 1896–1905. If weather permits, the tours pass the Quadriga, a sculpture of golden horses that graces the Capitol's exterior; from here you'll have a panoramic city view. Tours last 45 minutes. | 75 Constitution Ave. | 651/296–2881 | Free | Weekdays 10–4, weekends 1–4.

CULTURE, EDUCATION, AND HISTORY

Luther Theological Seminary. This is the largest of the eight seminaries of the Evangelical Lutheran Church in America (ELCA), with an attendance of 790 students. The campus, on the west side of town, between St. Paul and Minneapolis, includes the Old Muskego Church, the first American church built by Norwegian immigrants. | 2481 Como Ave. | 651/641–3456 | www.luthersem.edu | Daily.

Minnesota Vietnam Veterans' Memorial. The names of over a thousand Minnesotan soldiers, either killed in the war or missing in action, cover a large granite wall on the State Capitol grounds. | 75 Constitution Ave. | 651/536–1792 | Free | Daily.

Saint Paul Public Library. This Italianate structure's two-story arched windows overlook the riverfront. It houses an extensive collection of books and articles. | 90 W. Fourth St. | 651/266–7000 | Free | Mon. 11:30–8, Tues., Wed., Fri. 9–5:30, Thurs. 9–8, Sat. 11–4.

University of Minnesota, St. Paul Campus. This branch of the U of M's Twin Cities is often referred to as the "agricultural campus." It consists of five colleges concentrating on agriculture, veterinary sciences, environmental sciences, natural resources, and similar areas of study. Campus tours and barn tours are available. | Cleveland Ave. and Larpenteur Ave., Falcon Heights | 651/625–5000 | www1.umn.edu/twincities/ | Daily.

MUSEUMS

Gibbs Farm Museum. Costumed interpreters tell the story of the Gibbs family, who established this farm in 1840. As a child, Jane Gibbs had lived in New York, and was kidnapped by missionaries traveling to Minnesota to work with the Dakota people. Later, as a married woman, Jane renewed her ties to the Dakota, who would pass through on their way to harvest wild rice, pitching their tepee on the farm for week-long visits. The tour takes in a Dakota-style garden planted with corn of a type grown in AD 1100, as well as the Gibbs farmhouse, a one-room schoolhouse, the gardens, the original barn, and various farm animals. Gibbs Farm Museum is northwest of the state fairgrounds. | 2097 W. Larpenteur Ave., Falcon Heights | 651/646–8629 | www.rchs.com/gbbsfm2.htm | $5 | May–Oct., weekdays 10–4, weekends 12–4.

Landmark Center. This former federal courthouse and post office was built in 1902. Now a cultural center and home to 13 arts organizations, it houses the Minnesota Museum of American Art and the Stepping Stone Theatre for Childhood Development. Tours highlight

St. Paul's gangster-era history. The center hosts many special events, for which there is a fee. | 75 W. 5th St. | 651/292–3233 or 651/929–3230 (tours) | www.landmarkcenter.org | Free | Mon.–Wed., Fri. 8–5, Thurs. 8–8, Sat. 10–5, Sun. 1–5.

Minnesota Children's Museum. It's fun to learn in these hands-on galleries of adventure and knowledge. You can crawl through a giant ant hill, model prairies or bluff caves, and create in the inventors' workshop. | 10 W. 7th St. | 651/225–6000 | www.mcm.org | $6 | Tues., Wed., Fri.–Sun. 9–5, Thurs. 9–8. Closed Mon.

Minnesota Historical Society History Center. The building's distinctive exterior is made of Rockville granite and Winona limestone. Inside, you'll find interactive exhibits, a grain elevator you can climb aboard, and a library with extensive genealogical holdings. | 345 Kellogg Blvd. W | 651/296–6126 or 800/657–3773 | www.mnhs.org/places/historycenter | Free | Tues. 10–8, Wed.–Sat. 10–5, Sun. noon–5. Closed Mon. Call for library hours.

Minnesota Museum of American Art–Landmark Center. As St. Paul's only visual arts museum, the MMAA has explored a wide variety of topics including American Indian fine arts, the historical forces in photography, contemporary crafts, and American Impressionist painting. | 5th and Market Sts. | 651/292–4355 | www.mtn.org/MMAA | Free | Tues., Wed., Fri., Sat. 11–4, Thurs. 11–7:30, Sun. 1–5.

Minnesota Transportation Museum. *See* Minneapolis.

The Science Museum of Minnesota. One of the most-visited museums in the Upper Midwest, this downtown St. Paul riverfront institution is known for its world-class collection of dinosaurs, Omnimax theater, 3-D laser show, hands-on exhibits, and priceless collections. You can see the Mississippi River from all parts of the museum. | 120 W. Kellogg Blvd. | 651/221–9444 | www.smm.org | $9 | Tues., Wed. 9:30–5:30, Thurs.–Sat. 9:30–9, Sun. 10:30–5:30.

Housed in an annex of the Science Museum is the **Great American History Theatre.** Shows are typically adaptations of historical literature and biographies. | 30 E. 10th St. | 651/292–4323 | $19–$25.

Ordway Center for the Performing Arts. A major performing arts center serving more than a half million patrons a year, the Ordway is the only Minnesotan facility of its kind. The center produces spectacles in theater, music, dance, and multidisciplinary performing arts, hosts educational programs, and serves as home to The Minnesota Opera, the St. Paul Chamber Orchestra, the Schubert Club, and the Minnesota Orchestra. Within it are two theaters, a 1,900-seat main hall, and the 322-seat McKnight Theatre. | 345 Washington St. | Ticket information: 651/224–4222; Tours: 651/282–3000 | www.ordway.org | Year-round.

PARKS, NATURAL AREAS, AND OUTDOOR RECREATION

Como Park. Between 70-acre Como Lake (which has paddleboat rental and fishing for bass and walleye pike), the 18-hole golf course, the small zoo (one of only four free-of-charge zoos in the United States), the amusement park, and over a mile of walking paths, there's a lot of fun to be had in this 450-acre city park, which is 2 mi north of I–94's Lexington Pkwy exit. | 1360 Lexington Pkwy. N | 651/266–6400 | www.2havefun.com/Places/Metro/como-park.shtml | Free | Sunrise to sunset.

The towering Victorian aluminum-and-glass **Como Conservatory** houses several exquisitely designed garden areas with plants, streamlets, and bright natural light. You enter via the Palm Room, full of upswept trees and lush ferns; small birds flit overhead. There's also a sunken garden, a fern room, and a bonsai display. | 1325 Aida Pl. | 651/487–8200 | www1.stpaul.gov/depts/parks/?loc=/depts/parks/garden/index.html | $1 | Oct.–Mar., daily 10–4; Apr.–Sept., daily 10–6.

Carefully placed glacial rock accents a pond and waterfall landscaped in the Sansui mountain-and-water style at the **Como Ordway Memorial Japanese Garden.** You enter through the Como Conservatory. | 1325 Aida Pl. | 651/487–8200 or 651/487–8240 |

www1.stpaul.gov/depts/parks/?loc=/depts/parks/garden/index.html | $1 | Mother's Day–Labor Day, daily 10–6.

Fort Snelling State Park. Rising in the heart of the Twin Cities, the park has extensive biking, hiking, and skiing trails, which link to Minnehaha Park and the Minnesota Valley National Wildlife Refuge. | 1 Post Rd., St. Paul | 612/725–2390 or 612/725–2389 | www.dnr.state.mn.us/parks_and_recreation/state_parks/fort_snelling | Park permit required | Daily.

At **Historic Fort Snelling** you'll encounter costumed guides, crafts demonstrations, historical skits, and military drills. One mile east of the airport, the restored 1820s stone fortress overlooks the confluence of the Mississippi and Minnesota rivers. | Junction of Minnesota Hwys. 5 and 55 | 651/725–2413 | www.mnhs.org/places/sites/hfs | $5 | June.–Sept., Wed.–Sat. 10–5, Sun. 12–5; May, Sept.–Oct. Sat. 10–5, Sun. 12–5.

Harriet Island. A Y2K re-opening celebration, complete with fireworks and fanfare, ended the massive, multi-year renovation of this park, on the Mississippi River across from downtown. The project added a riverwalk, performance stages, playgrounds, rock gardens, scenic overlooks, a 12-acre Great Lawn, and an expansion of the Grand Pavilion, originally built in 1941. Today, you may board a paddlewheeler from the 600-ft pier, take a self-guided bicycle trek from the park to Lilydale, or stay the night aboard a refurbished tugboat. | Plato Blvd. | 651/266–6409 | Free | Daily.

Keller Golf Course. Built in 1929, this par-71 course has rolling terrain, tree-lined fairways, and only a few water obstacles. In the '50s, '60s, and '70s it hosted several PGA and LPGA golf tournaments, and was a regular stop on both professional tours. | 2166 Maplewood Dr. | 651/484–3011 | $26 | Apr.–Oct., sunrise to sunset.

Lake Phalen. St. Paul's largest recreational lake is the headquarters for many civic festivals. The surrounding park allows for picnicking, golfing, and cross-country skiing. | Wheelock Pkwy. and Arcade St. | 651/266–6400 | Free | Sunrise to sunset.

Mounds Park. Prehistoric Native American burial mounds occupy part of this 25-acre park, above the Mississippi River. From both picnic sites and ball fields you have stunning views of the river, downtown St. Paul and, in the distance, downtown Minneapolis. | Earl and Mound Sts. | 651/266–6400 | Free | Sunrise to sunset.

Town Square Park. This indoor tropical garden, the site of many a wedding, contains waterfalls, pools, and thousands of tropical plants. | 445 Minnesota St. | 651/266–6400 | Free | Daily.

RELIGION AND SPIRITUALITY

Cathedral of St. Paul. The design of this massive cathedral, with its 175-ft-tall dome, is based on St. Peter's in Rome. It houses six chapels which serve as the "shrine of nations." | 239 Selby Ave. | 651/228–1766 | Free | Daily 8–6.

SHOPPING

Farmer's Market. All kinds of Minnesota foods and produce are on sale here, including fruits and vegetables, wild rice, maple syrup, honey, eggs, cheeses, and meats. | 290 E. 5th St. and 7th Place Mall | 651/227–8101 | www.stpaulfarmersmarket.com | Free | May–Nov., Sat. 6 AM–1 PM; late June–Oct. Tues. at 290 E. 5th St., Thur. 10–2 at 7th Place Mall.

Norwest Center Skyway. Shopping and dining in what used to be a five-story parking garage. | 55 E. 5th St. | 612/344–1200 | Daily.

SIGHTSEEING TOURS

Gray Line. The standard Twin Cities tour lasts 3½ hours, plus an additional 2-hour boat ride. Five others are available. | 835 Decatur Ave. N | 651/591–0999 | May–Oct. | $15–$32.

Capital City Trolley. The regular trolley route loops between the Minnesota History Center, the downtown area, and the State Capitol. Hour-long narrated tours and historical tours are available by reservation. | 807 E. 7th St. | www1.stpaul.gov/welcome/transportation/trolley | 651/223–5600 | $7 | May–Oct.

Metro Connections. *See* Minneapolis.

Minnesota Brewing Company. You can take a 1-hr tour at the home of Pig's Eye Pilsner, Grain Belt Premium, and Yellow Belly Bear. A video detailing the history of the brewery is also shown. | 882 W. 7th St. | 651/290–0209 | Free | Mon.–Fri. 10–1, gift shop Mon.–Fri. 8–4.

Sightseeing cruises. Tour the Mississippi River on a paddlewheeler from Harriet Island Regional Park. The *Harriet Bishop, Anson Northrup, Betsey Northrup,* and *Jonathan Padelford* make 1½-hour round-trips to Fort Snelling. The *Anson Northrup* travels through the lock at St. Anthony Falls in Minneapolis. Boats dock across the Wabasha Street Bridge from downtown. | Plato Blvd. | 651/227–1100 | www.padelfordboats.com | $10 | Memorial Day–Labor Day, daily noon and 2.

ON THE CALENDAR

JAN.–FEB.: *St. Paul Winter Carnival.* In 1885, a *New York Times* reporter wrote that St. Paul was the "Siberia of America," and questioned whether it was fit for human habitation. Offended by this attack on its city, the local chamber of commerce decided to prove not only that St. Paul was habitable, but also that its citizens were very much alive during winter, the dominant season. Thus was born the St. Paul Winter Carnival. More than 115 years later, it's still going strong with parades, elaborate ice castles, and entertainment, including a giant snow slide. | 651/223–4700 or 800/488–4023.

AUG.–SEPT.: *Minnesota State Fair.* One and a half million people attend the fair each year, making it one of the biggest and best-attended state fairs in the country. It may take you all 12 days to see everything there is to see on the 300-acre fairgrounds. | Minnesota State Fairgrounds, 1265 Snelling Ave. N | 651/642–2200.

SEPT.–JUNE: *St. Paul Chamber Orchestra.* Established in 1959, SPCO has the distinction of being the only full-time professional chamber orchestra in the United States. | Ordway Music Theater, 345 Washington St. | 651/291–1144.

Dining

INEXPENSIVE

Babani's. Middle Eastern. Brightly colored walls and photographs may transport you to Kurdish territory, in northern Iraq. *Dowjic,* a tangy, lemony, chicken soup, is a local favorite. | 544 St. Peter St. | 651/602–9964 | No lunch Sat., Sun. | $8–$14 | AE, D, MC, V.

Cecil's Delicatessen, Bakery and Restaurant. Delicatessen. One hundred eighty-five items constitute the menu at this deli, which has been serving St. Paul for nearly a half century. Try one of the oversized Reuben varieties—Chicago, Russian, spicy, and veggie. | 651 S. Cleveland | 651/698–0334 | $5–$8 | MC, V.

Dixie's. Southern. Cajun music and jambalaya may place you south of the Mason–Dixon. The dining room is covered with framed flags from southern states. House specialties include the Shak sandwich—pulled pork with spicy barbecue sauce—and coconut fried shrimp. A rotating specials menu highlights other southern delicacies. | 695 Grand Ave. | 651/222–7345 | Sun. brunch | $6–$16 | AE, D, DC, MC, V.

India Palace. Indian. Specializing in curry, vindaloo, korma, masala, and saag, this restaurant also has a lunch buffet where you can sample a little of everything. | 2570 Cleveland Ave. N, Roseville | 651/631–1222 | $8–$14 | AE, D, DC, MC, V.

Sawatdee. Thai. Here you can look out at the St. Paul skyline while dining on chicken satay and pad Thai. | 289 E. 5th St. | 651/222–5859 | No lunch Sun. | $8–$12 | AE, D, DC, MC, V.

MODERATE

Caravan Serai. Afghan. Live music accompanies Egyptian dancers Friday and Saturday nights, and you'll order from a menu steeped in the culinary traditions of the Middle East, North India, Greece, and Afghanistan. Lamb, chicken, and vegetarian entrées are served on brass tables in the pillow room. The tandoori chicken is prepared in traditional clay ovens. | 2175 Ford Pkwy. | 651/690–1935 | $9–$18 | AE, DC, MC, V.

Ciatti's. Italian. Design your own personal pan pizza or order from a variety of house-made concoctions including the prosciutto and wild mushroom pizza with sliced tomatoes, artichoke hearts and Parmesan. This downtown spot, on the corner of Victoria and Grand, also specializes in interesting pasta dishes. Kids' menu. Sun. brunch. | 850 Grand Ave. | 651/292–9942 | $12–$16 | AE, D, MC, V.

Lexington. Continental. The stately black marble entryway of this west side turn-of-the-20th-century building leads you into a chandelier-lit dining room, a real find hung with oil paintings. The simple menu includes steaks, a renowned prime rib, and pasta specials. | 1096 Grand Ave. | 651/222–5878 | $12–$20 | Reservations essential | AE, D, DC, MC, V.

Mancini's Char House. Steak. Tunes by Sinatra and Tony Bennett play over the speakers in this Chicago-theme restaurant whose walls are covered in brick and bright red paint. From your booth you have a clear view of the open pit broiler, on which the juicy steaks are seared. Live entertainment Wed.–Sat. | 531 W. 7th St. | 651/224–7345 | No lunch | $12–$30 | AE, MC, V.

Muffuletta in the Park. Contemporary. The fresh fish and daily specials keep locals coming to this neighborhood bistro done in earthy colors. Dining is intimate and the menu is varied, so it's fun to order several entrées and split them among friends. Try the harvest farfalle with roast chicken, cranberries, and pecans, served in a squash cream sauce. The patio is open in fine weather. | 2260 Como Ave. | 651/644–9116 | Sun. brunch, no lunch Sat. | $9–$20 | AE, D, DC, MC, V.

No Wake Cafe. American. From the wraparound windows of this tugboat-turned-restaurant, still afloat, you'll have stunning views of the sun setting over the Mississippi. The menu changes yearly, but usually includes seafood, beef, and sandwiches. Breakfast also served. | 100 Yacht Club Rd., Pier 1, Harriet Island | 651/292–1411 | Reservations recommended for dinner | Closed Oct.–Apr. and Mon. | $12–$18 | AE, MC, V.

Ristorante Luci. Italian. Homemade pasta, cheese, and bread make this small, family-owned restaurant a real delight. | 470 Cleveland Ave. S | 651/699–8258 | No lunch | Reservations essential | $11–$29 | AE, MC, V.

Sakura. Japanese. The spacious sushi bar occupies much of the space in this converted loft, between 4th and 5th. Hot entrées are on the menu as well. | 338 St. Peter St. | 651/224–0185 | $12–$18 | AE, D, DC, MC, V.

Table of Contents. Contemporary. Works by local artists, varying in medium from paintings to metal work, cover the sea-green walls at this intimate, 55-seat restaurant. The menu changes every four weeks and draws on cuisines from around the world. Entrées always include a pasta, a vegetarian selection, and free-range chicken, fresh ocean fish, and whole roasted fish dishes. Sun. brunch. | 1648 Grand Ave. | 651/699–6595 | $12–$25 | AE, D, DC, MC, V.

Toby's on the Lake. Continental. Overlooking Tanner's Lake, this pub-like restaurant may be the perfect, low-key place to unwind. Try the steak or the chicken piccata, and save room for the homemade desserts—the variety of cheesecakes is as decadent as the crème brûlée. | 249 Geneva Ave. N | 651/739–1600 | No dinner Sun. | $10–$25 | AE, D, DC, MC, V.

Venetian Inn. American. After a hearty pizza or bowl of pasta in the theatrically themed dining room—it's decked out with playbills and theater memorabilia—you can move into the bar area for entertainment by female impersonators. Little Canada is 6 mi north of St. Paul. Kids' menu. | 2814 Rice St., Little Canada | 651/484–7215 | Closed Sun. | $9–$20 | AE, D, DC, MC, V.

Zander Cafe. Contemporary. No detail was spared in this stylish neighborhood bistro, which has a wine bar, geometric furniture, and wood floors. After your grilled meat or crab cake dinner, plus a good night's sleep, you might try Zander's sister café, Z's, across the street, for breakfast or lunch. | 525 Selby Ave. | 651/222–5224 | Closed Mon. | $10–$25 | D, DC, MC, V.

EXPENSIVE

Buca Di Beppo. Italian. Arrive hungry for the heaping plates of pasta served family style in this huge dining room, splattered with hanging Christmas lights and photographs of Sophia Loren. Open-air dining, weather permitting. | 2728 Gannon Rd. | 651/772–4388 | No lunch | $13–$18 | AE, DC, MC, V.

Chet's Taverna. Contemporary. This storefront restaurant has checked linoleum floors, European posters, and a loyal neighborhood clientele. The kitchen prepares predominately organic and locally farmed produce and meats. Daily pasta specials, potato gnocchi, and risotto are house favorites, along with braised lamb chops and bone-in pork chops. | 791 Raymond Ave. | 651/646–2655 | Closed Mon. No lunch weekends | $15–$20 | AE, D, DC, MC, V.

Forepaugh's. French. Built in 1870, this three-story Victorian mansion–turned–restaurant serves upscale, inventive dishes including seafood, veal, and poultry. Be sure to try the stuffed breast of pheasant, beef Wellington, or tornedos of beef, which is two petit tenderloin fillets with bearnaise and bordelaise sauces. | 276 S. Exchange St. | 651/224–5606 | No lunch Sat. Sun. brunch | $13–$21 | AE, DC, MC, V.

Gallivan's. Steak. With its soft lighting and mahogany paneling, this is a comfortable destination for business meals and a classy after-work and weekend party spot, with entertainment Friday and Saturday nights. Steaks are the favorite, but you can mix turf with some surf or choose from a generous list of pasta entrées. | 354 Wabasha St. | 651/227–6688 | No lunch Sun. | $15–$25 | AE, D, DC, MC, V.

Green Mill Brewing Company. American. From six taps flow golden home-brewed beer, two seasonal beers and four in-house staples such as Swamp Buck Stout. Stained-glass windows cast colorful light across the tavern wooden tables and booths. On the menu are Caribbean sirloin steak and pasta Pavarotti (a decadent blend of penne, chicken, sun-dried tomatoes and Alfredo sauce). | 57 S. Hamline Ave. | 651/698–0353 | $13–$18 | AE, DC, MC, V.

Kozlak's Royal Oak. Continental. Eleven miles north of St. Paul, in Shoreview, linen table cloths and fancy roast duck dishes fill the menu. All entrées come with homemade clam chowder or a trip to the salad bar, plus fresh bread. Garden dining in summer. | 4785 Hodgson Rd., Shoreview | 651/484–8484 | $16–$22 | AE, D, DC, MC, V.

Lake Elmo Inn. Continental. This 1880 stagecoach stop and inn, 15 mi northeast of St. Paul, specializes in chops, lamb, pork, and other meaty fare. Sunday and Tuesday there is a champagne brunch buffet, and in fair weather you may dine outside under an umbrella. Kids' menu. | 3442 Lake Elmo Ave., Lake Elmo | 651/777–8495 | Sun. brunch | Reservations essential | $15–$24 | AE, D, DC, MC, V.

Leeann Chin Chinese Cuisine. Chinese. With five entrées, four appetizers, dumplings, and sides, this all-you-can-eat buffet is not for the faint of heart. Some table service is available. | 214 E. 4th St. | 651/224–8814 | $15 | AE, D, DC, MC, V.

Lindey's. Steak. The centerpiece of this steak-lover's paradise, 11 mi north of St. Paul, is a grand stone fireplace topped with a ship in a bottle. Each of the three top sirloin varieties here come in 1-lb slabs, and are served with salad, hash browns and watermelon pickles. | 3600 Snelling Ave. N, Arden Hills | 651/633–9813 | Closed Sun. No lunch | $15–$24 | No credit cards.

Pazzaluna Urban Trattoria and Bar. Italian. At the corner of 5th and St. Peter, across the street from the St. Paul Hotel, you'll find hand-made gnocchi prepared with your choice of sauces: four-cheese, butter and sage, four-meat, or tomato and basil. Or try a risotto, either chicken with asparagus and saffron, or duck with dried cherries. | 360 St. Peter St. | 651/223–7000 | Closed Sun., Mon. No lunch | $15–$30 | AE, D, DC, MC, V.

ST. PAUL

INTRO
ATTRACTIONS
DINING
LODGING

Saint Paul Grill. American. From the windows of the hardwood-floored dining room you can see Rice Park. Try the chicken Vesuvio, a midwestern specialty, or any of the steak selections. | 350 Market St. | 651/224–7455 | $17–$30 | Sun. brunch | AE, D, DC, MC, V.

Tulips. French. In the Cathedral Hill area of St. Paul is this gem with rose-colored walls, dried flowers, and strings of tiny lights. A typical meal might begin with a wild mushroom strudel appetizer, followed by escargots, and finally boneless duck breast with Bordeaux sauce. If you still have room for dessert, try the crème brûlée. | 452 Selby Ave. | 651/221–1061 | No lunch Sat. | $13–$23 | AE, DC, MC, V.

W.A. Frost and Company. Continental. In this romantic Victorian house dating from the 1880s, each dining room is carpeted with oriental rugs and has a fireplace and marble-topped tables. Country French and Mediterranean flavors predominate in the cuisine. The roast venison in juniper sage reduction, served with leek-flavored mashed potatoes and wild forest mushrooms, is not to be missed. Kids' menu. Sun. brunch. No smoking. | 374 Selby Ave. | 651/224–5715 | www.wafrost.com | Sun. brunch | $15–$30 | AE, D, DC, MC, V.

VERY EXPENSIVE

Dakota Bar and Grill. Contemporary. Live jazz music plays nightly and the lighting is soft in this dining room with a menu of roast game, including pheasant and venison. You can also get grilled fish and lamb shank; specials change frequently. Sun. brunch. | 1021 E. Bandana | 651/642–1442 | No lunch | $17–$25 | AE, D, DC, MC, V.

Kincaid's. American. With several locations in Minneapolis, this winner finally crossed the river. Romantic lighting, rich wood trim, and high ceilings set the scene for steaks and seafood. Sun. brunch. | 380 St. Peter St. | 651/602–9000 | fax 651/602–9158 | Reservations recommended | No lunch weekends | $18–$25 | AE, D, DC, MC, V.

Lodging

INEXPENSIVE

Exel Inn. Five mi north of St. Paul, this 3-story motel is off of the White Bear Ave. exit of I-94. Complimentary Continental breakfast. In-room data ports, refrigerators. Cable TV. Laundry facilities. Business services. Some pets allowed. | 1739 Old Hudson Rd. | 651/771–5566 | fax 651/771–1262 | www.exelinns.com | 100 rooms | $44–$64 | AE, D, DC, MC, V.

Maplewood Super 8. Two blocks from the 3M world headquarters overlooking Tanner's Lake, this four-story chain hotel, built in 1986, is also 6 mi east of St. Paul. Take I-94, exit 51 (Century Avenue). Picnic area, complimentary Continental breakfast. In-room data ports. Cable TV. Laundry facilities. Business services, airport shuttle. Some pets allowed (fee). | 285 N. Century Ave., Maplewood | 651/738–1600 | fax 651/738–9405 | www.super8.com | 107 rooms, 3 suites | $47–$80, $127–$159 suites | AE, D, DC, MC, V.

Red Roof Inn St. Paul/Woodbury. Ten miles east of St. Paul, at I-494, exit 59 (Valley Creek Road), you'll find this two-story, two-building motel. In-room data ports. Cable TV. Business services. Some pets allowed. | 1806 Wooddale Dr., Woodbury | 651/738–7160 | fax 651/738–1869 | www.redroof.com | 108 rooms | $40–$70 | AE, D, DC, MC, V.

MODERATE

Best Western Maplewood Inn. St. Paul is 6 mi east of this two-story motel, which lies across the street from the Maplewood Mall. An in-house comedy club and poolside video games provide entertainment. Some rooms have Mississippi River views. Restaurant, bar (with entertainment), room service. In-room data ports. Cable TV. Indoor pool. Hot tub, sauna. Video games. Laundry facilities. Business services. Some pets allowed (fee). | 1780 E. County Rd. D, Maplewood | 651/770–2811 | www.bestwestern.com | 118 rooms | $74–$129 | AE, D, DC, MC, V.

ONE LAST TRAVEL TIP:

Pack an easy way to reach the world.

Wherever you travel, the MCI WorldCom Card℠ is the easiest way to stay in touch. You can use it to call to and from more than 125 countries worldwide. And you can earn bonus miles every time you use your card. So go ahead, travel the world. MCI WorldCom℠ makes it even more rewarding. For additional access codes, visit **www.wcom.com/worldphone**.

EASY TO CALL WORLDWIDE

1. Just dial the WorldPhone® access number of the country you're calling from.
2. Dial or give the operator your MCI WorldCom Card number.
3. Dial or give the number you're calling.

Canada	1-800-888-8000
Mexico	01-800-021-8000
United States	1-800-888-8000

EARN FREQUENT FLIER MILES

6 "I'm thirsty"s, 9 "Are we there yet"s, 3 "I don't feel good"s,
1 car class upgrade.
At least something's going your way.

Hertz rents Fords and other fine cars. ® REG. U.S. PAT. OFF. © HERTZ SYSTEM INC., 2000/005-00

Make your next road trip more comfortable with a free one-class upgrade from Hertz.

Let's face it, a long road trip isn't always sunshine and roses. But with Hertz, you get a free one car class upgrade to make things a little more bearable. You'll also choose from a variety of vehicles with child seats, Optional Protection Plans, 24-Hour Emergency Roadside Assistance, and the convenience of NeverLost, the in-car navigation system that provides visual and audio prompts to give you turn-by-turn guidance to your destination. In a word: it's everything you need for your next road trip. Call your travel agent or Hertz at **1-800-654-2210** and mention PC# **906404** or check us out at **hertz.com** or AOL Keyword: **hertz**. Peace of mind. Another reason nobody does it exactly like Hertz.

Hertz
exactly.®

Como Villa Bed and Breakfast. Period antiques can be found all throughout this 1875 Victorian home, which is 4 mi northeast of downtown and 2 mi from I–94. Some rooms have private balconies that overlook huge oak trees. Complimentary Continental breakfast. No room phones, TV in common area. | 1371 W. Nebraska Ave. | 651/647–0471 | 3 rooms (2 with shared bath) | $69–$89 | AE, MC, V.

Garden Gate Bed and Breakfast. Built in 1907, this Victorian home is two blocks from several restaurants and boutiques. Complimentary Continental breakfast. No room phones, no TV. | 925 Goodrich Ave. | 651/227–8430 | fax 651/225–9791 | www.gardengatebandb.com | 3 rooms | $70 | AE, D, MC, V.

Hampton Inn–Shoreview. The I–69, Lexington Ave. exit takes you to this motel, 12 mi north of downtown St. Paul. Restaurant, bar, complimentary Continental breakfast, room service. In-room data ports. Cable TV. Indoor pool. Hot tub. Exercise equipment. Laundry facilities. Business services. | 1000 Gramsie Rd., Shoreview | 651/482–0402 | fax 651/482–8917 | www.hamptoninn.com | 120 rooms | $69–$89 | AE, D, DC, MC, V.

Travel Inn. Standing next to the State Capitol, this three-story motel is ½ mi from a handful of fast food eateries. Free parking. | 149 University Ave. E | 651/227–8801 | 50 rooms | $50–$100 | AE, D, DC, MC, V.

EXPENSIVE

Best Western Drover's Inn. Equidistant from both downtown St. Paul (which is 10 mi north) and the Mall of America (10 mi west), this four-story brick hotel has complimentary shuttle service to both destinations. Restaurant, bar, complimentary Continental breakfast, room service. Cable TV. Indoor pool. Hot tub. Business services, airport shuttle. | 701 S. Concord St., South St. Paul | 651/455–3600 | fax 651/455–0282 | www.bestwestern.com | 85 rooms | $79–$99 | AE, D, DC, MC, V.

Best Western Kelly Inn. All six poolside video games thrill kids at this 10-story hotel across the street from the Minnesota Histories Center, between St. Paul Cathedral and the Capitol. Restaurant, bar, room service. In-room data ports, some microwaves. Cable TV. Indoor pool, wading pool. Hot tub, sauna. Video games. Business services. Some pets allowed. | 161 St. Anthony Blvd. | 651/227–8711 | fax 651/227–1698 | www.bestwestern.com | 126 rooms | $80–$195 | AE, D, DC, MC, V.

Chatsworth Bed and Breakfast. Rooms in this 1902 Victorian home are individually themed and decorated, ranging from Victorian to Oriental. Some rooms have private decks overlooking the garden. Complimentary breakfast. Business services, free parking. No kids under 13. | 984 Ashland Ave. | 651/227–4288 | www.stpaulcvb/welcome2.htm | 5 rooms (2 with shared bath) | $80–$135 | AE, D, MC, V.

Country Inn by Carlson. Some rooms have fireplaces in this four-story hostelry 5 mi south of St. Paul. Restaurant, bar, complimentary Continental breakfast, room service. In-room data ports. Cable TV. Indoor pool. Hot tub. Exercise equipment. Video games. Laundry facilities. Business services. | 6003 Hudson Rd., Woodbury | 651/739–7300 or 800/456–4000 | fax 651/731–4007 | www.countryinns-suites.com | 158 rooms | $85–$105 | AE, D, DC, MC, V.

Holiday Inn–St. Paul North. Lush trees surround the building here, 10 mi north of downtown. Take I–694, exit 43A (Lexington Avenue). Restaurant, bar, complimentary breakfast. Some refrigerators. Cable TV. Indoor pool. Hot tub. Exercise equipment. Laundry facilities. Business services. | 1201 Rte. 2nd E, Arden Hills | 651/636–4123 | fax 651/636–2526 | www2.basshotels.com/holiday-inn | 156 rooms, 18 suites | $79–$149 | AE, D, DC, MC, V.

Holiday Inn–East. This eight-story tower is one block from the 3M world headquarters, 5 mi from downtown. Take I–94, exit 246 (McKnight Rd.). Restaurant, bar, room service. In-room data ports. Cable TV. Indoor pool. Hot tub. Exercise equipment. Laundry facilities. Business services. | 2201 Burns Ave. | 651/731–2220 | fax 651/731–0243 | www.basshotels.com/holiday-inn/ | 192 rooms | $86–$96 | AE, D, DC, MC, V.

Holiday Inn Express. A railroad track runs right through the lobby of this former round-house, where train cars were once painted and repaired. It's 2 mi west of downtown. Complimentary Continental breakfast. In-room data ports, some refrigerators. Cable TV. Indoor pool, wading pool. Hot tub, sauna. Business services. | 1010 Bandana Blvd. W | 651/647–1637 | fax 651/647–0244 | www.basshotels.com/holiday-inn | 109 rooms, 12 suites | $81–$131 | AE, D, DC, MC, V.

Holiday Inn Select–Minneapolis Airport/Eagan. This motel is 12 mi southwest of downtown and 5 mi east of the airport and the Mall of America; shuttles take you to either. Restaurant, bar. In-room data ports. Cable TV. Indoor pool. Hot tub. Exercise equipment. Laundry facilities. Business services, airport shuttle. | 2700 Pilot Knob Rd., Eagan | 651/454–3434 | fax 651/454–4904 | www.basshotels.com/holiday-inn | 187 rooms, 21 suites | $79–$159 | AE, D, DC, MC, V.

Sheraton–Midway. Three miles east of St. Paul, this upscale hotel runs shuttles to the Mall of America and the airport on request. An airport ticket counter is on site. Restaurant, bar, room service. In-room data ports. Cable TV. Indoor pool. Hot tub. Exercise equipment. Business services. | 400 Hamline Ave. N | 651/642–1234 | fax 651/642–1126 | www.sheraton.com | 198 rooms, 15 suites | $95–$125 | AE, D, DC, MC, V.

VERY EXPENSIVE

Covington Inn. A 1946 towboat was converted to a B&B, one of the few such establishments in North America. The rooms in the three-story boat resemble the cabins they used to be, finished in wood and brass, with built-in storage. Each has a working fireplace and a private bathroom. Complimentary breakfast. No TV. | 100 Yacht Club Rd., Pier 1, Harriet Island | 651/292–1411 | towboat@mninter.net | www.covingtoninn.com | 5 rooms | $135–$235 | AE, MC, V.

Embassy Suites. Built in 1986, this 10-story all-suites hotel is surrounded by gardens and centered around an atrium. It's right downtown. Restaurant, bar, complimentary breakfast. In-room data ports, microwaves, refrigerators. Cable TV. Indoor pool. Hot tub. Exercise equipment. Laundry facilities. Business services, airport shuttle. | 175 E. 10th St. | 651/224–5400 | fax 651/224–0957 | www.embassy-suites.com | 210 suites | $109–$169 | AE, D, DC, MC, V.

Radisson Riverfront. From the 22nd-floor revolving restaurant atop this riverside hotel on the south edge of town, you can enjoy some of St. Paul's best views of the Mississippi. Also on site are a working carousel and poolside cabanas. Restaurant, bar. Some microwaves, in-room data ports, some refrigerators. Cable TV. Indoor pool. Exercise equipment. Business service. Some pets allowed. | 11 E. Kellogg Blvd. | 651/292–1900 | fax 651/224–8999 | www.radisson.com | 475 rooms | $120–$155 | AE, D, DC, MC, V.

Saint Paul Hotel. One of several landmark buildings encircling Rice Park, this 12-story, marble-pillared 1910 landmark has been a stopover for presidents, heads of state, and celebrities. It's within 7 blocks of the Ordway Theatre, the Civic Center, and the Children's Museum. Restaurant, bar. In-room data ports. Cable TV. Exercise equipment. Business services. | 350 Market St. | 651/292–9292 or 800/292–9292 | fax 651/228–9506 | info@stpaulhotel.com | www.stpaulhotel.com | 254 rooms, 32 suites | $150–$675 | AE, D, DC, MC, V.

Wingate Inn–Oakdale. Five miles east of downtown St. Paul, this three-story hostelry is in the suburb of Oakdale, one mi from I–94. Restaurant, bar. Complimentary breakfast. In-room data ports. Cable TV. Hot tub. Exercise equipment. Video games. Laundry facility. Business services. Free parking. Pets allowed. | 970 Helena Ave. N | 651/578–8466 | fax 651/578–0763 | www.wingateinns.com | 83 rooms, 3 suites | $115–$125, $155 suites | AE, D, DC, MC, V.

ST. PETER

(Nearby towns also listed: Faribault, Le Sueur, Mankato, New Ulm)

Founded in 1853, St. Peter is one of the state's oldest cities and home to 12 sites listed on the National Register of Historic Places. Two miles north of town is the *Traverse des Sioux*, a Minnesota River fording place used for hundreds of years by Dakota tribespeople traveling from the woodlands in the west toward the bison prairies in the east. In 1851, these people signed a treaty ceding 24 million acres to the U.S. government, in return for payments of goods and money on which they were to live, to be paid annually at the *Traverse des Sioux*; over the next decade, skipped annuity payments and theft by corrupt traders and government agents led to widespread famine and sickness among the Dakota. Finally, in 1862, a Native American uprising led to the U.S.–Dakota conflict, the only documented war ever fought on Minnesota lands. Today, farming is an economic mainstay in St. Peter, and the town is an agribusiness center for the region.

Information: St. Peter Tourism and Visitors Bureau | 101 S. Front St., St. Peter, 56082 | 507/931–3400 | www.tourism.st-peter.mn.us.

Attractions

Eugene Saint Julien Cox House. Cox was the first mayor of St. Peter, and generations of his family lived in this Victorian house from 1871, when it was built, to 1969, when his grandson gave it to the local historical society for restoration. Now costumed guides give you tours of the home with its many artifacts. | 500 N. Washington Ave. | 507/625–1768 | www.tourism.st-peter.mn.us/nicollet.php3 | $3 | May, Sat., Sun. 1–4; June–Aug., daily 1–4; Sept., Sat., Sun. 1–4; Closed Oct.–Apr.

Gustavus Adolphus College. The campus of this liberal arts college is on 340 acres in the Minnesota River Valley, one hour southwest of Minneapolis/St. Paul. Founded in 1862 by Swedish Lutheran immigrant and pastor Eric Norelius, it now has an enrollment of about 2,500 students. | 800 W. College Ave. | 507/933–8000 | www.gac.edu | Daily.
Linnaeus Arboretum showcases the state's three natural ecosystems: A hardwood deciduous forest sandwiched between a prairie and a conifer woodland. Cultivated rose and perennial gardens and trees from around the world surround the interpretive center. Also on the grounds are an 1866 settler's cabin, moved here and restored in the 1980s, and a winding trail punctuated by bluebird houses. | 800 W. College Ave. | 507/933–8000 | jgilbert@gustavus.edu | www.gac.edu/oncampus/academics/Arboretum/index.html | Daily.

St. Peter Regional Treatment Center. The state's first residential psychiatric treatment facility, established in 1866, covers 580 wooded acres. A small museum in the "Old Center" building houses medical artifacts used at the hospital in the late 1800s. Photographs and furniture tableaux depict hospital life at the turn of the 20th century. | 100 Freeman Dr. | 507/931–7250 | Free | Museum open by appointment only.

Treaty Site History Center. Exhibits cover the 1851 Treaty of Traverse des Sioux, as well as the history of the Dakota people and the explorers, traders, and settlers they encountered. | 1851 N. Minnesota Ave. | 507/934–2160 | www.tourism.st-peter.mn.us/treaty.php3 | $2.50 | Mon.–Sat. 10–4, Sun. 1–4.

Dining

Whisky River. American. Everyone from college students to families comes to this casual spot for burgers and pasta. Kids' menu. | Rte. 99E | 507/934–5600 | Breakfast also available | $8–$13 | AE, MC, V.

Lodging

AmericInn. The Gustavus Adolphus campus is 2 mi from this two-story hostelry on the north side of downtown. Complimentary Continental breakfast. Some in-room hot tubs. Pool. Hot tub, sauna. | 700 N. Minnesota Ave. | 507/931–6554 or 800/634–3444 | fax 507/931–2396 | www.AmericInn.com/minnesota/stpeter.html | 50 rooms | $66–$130 | AE, MC, V.

Engesser House. Rooms are oversized and contain period antiques in this 1880 Victorian with a full wraparound porch. The original carved fireplace on the first floor is the centerpiece of the home, which lies on the south side of St. Peter. Complimentary breakfast, dining room. No room phones. | 1202 S. Minnesota Ave. | 507/931–4121 | 4 rooms | $75–$120.

SAUK CENTRE

MAP 3, C7

(Nearby towns also listed: Alexandria, Glenwood)

If you've read *Main Street* by Sinclair Lewis, you are already familiar with Sauk Centre. Lewis grew up here and used his home town, disguised as Gopher Prairie, as the setting for this novel. Since Lewis's day, agriculture has fuelled the city's economic engine. The town is near the center of the state on the southern tip of Big Sauk Lake, off I–94/Hwy 71.

Information: **Sauk Centre Area Chamber of Commerce** | 1220 S. Main St., Sauk Centre, 56378 | 320/352–5201 | www.saukcentre.com.

Attractions

Sinclair Lewis Boyhood Home. You can see original furnishings and family memorabilia in the restored home of America's first Nobel Prize–winning novelist. | 812 Sinclair Lewis Ave. | 320/352–5201 | www.saukherald.com/lewis/home.html | $3 | Memorial Day–Labor Day, daily 8–5.

Sinclair Lewis Interpretive Center. Exhibits include original manuscripts, photographs, and letters. The center is at the junction of Route 71 and I–94, exit 127 (Sauk Centre). | 1220 S. Main St. | 320/352–5201 | www.saukherald.com/lewis/center.html | Free | Memorial Day–Labor Day, Mon.–Fri. 8:30–5, Sat.–Sun. 9–5.

ON THE CALENDAR

JULY: *Sinclair Lewis Days.* The third weekend of the month brings auto races, parades, craft shows, live music, and milk carton boat races to town. | 320/352–5201.

Dining

Main St. Cafe. American. A few antiques dress up this small café. Try the taco salad or a hearty cheeseburger. Kids' menu. | 303 Main St. | 320/351–3512 | $4–$6 | No credit cards.

Lodging

Hillcrest. First-floor rooms in this two-story downtown motel have parking spaces right outside their doors. Cable TV. | 965 S. Main St. | 320/352–2215 or 800/858–6333 | 21 rooms | $25–$35 | AE, D, MC, V.

Palmer House Hotel. There's an antiques shop in the lobby of this three-story 1901 brick house. A beautifully restored grand piano stands in the living room. Restaurant, bar, complimentary Continental breakfast. Cable TV. Library. No smoking. | 228 Original Main St. | 320/352–5602 or 888/222–3431 | www.palmerhouse@saukherald.com | 10 rooms, 6 suites | $69–$99, $85–$99 suites | AE, D, DC, MC, V.

Super 8. This 2-story motor hotel is in a rural area 2 mi south of Sinclair Lewis's Boyhood Home, and 1 mi north of I–94, exit 127 (Sauk Centre). Cable TV. Pool. Business services. Some pets allowed. | 322 12th St. S | 320/352–6581 | fax 320/352–6584 | www.super8.com | 38 rooms | $43–$62 | AE, D, DC, MC, V.

SHAKOPEE

(Nearby towns also listed: Bloomington, Lakeville, Minneapolis, New Prague, St. Paul)

This residential suburb southwest of Minneapolis is a popular destination, both for Twin Cities residents and for visitors.

Information: **Shakopee Convention and Visitors Bureau** | 1801 E. County Rd. 101, Shakopee, 55379-0716 | 612/445–1660 | www.shakopee.org.

Attractions

Canterbury Park. There are horse racing in summer, snowmobile racing in winter, and the Midwest's largest arts and crafts show in April and November. | 1100 Canterbury Rd. | 612/445–7223 | www.canterburypark.com | Free | Daily.

Historic Murphy's Landing. At this 88-acre "living history village," costumed interpreters spin tales and explain the daily lives of the 19th-century men, women, and children who inhabited the Minnesota River Valley. More than 40 period buildings have been moved to the site for preservation and restoration. | 2187 E. County Rd. 101 | 612/445–6901 | www.murphyslanding.com | $8.50 | Sat., Sun. 10–5, and selected holidays.

Minnesota Landscape Arboretum. The arboretum has 905 acres of rolling hills, native woods, a restored prairie, formal display gardens, and a wide variety of plant collections in a pristine landscape. | 3675 Arboretum Dr., Chanhassen | 612/443–2460 | www.arboretum.umn.edu | $5 | May–Sept., daily 8–dusk; Oct.–Apr., daily 8–5:30.

Minnesota Zoo. Five trails meander through replications of natural wildlife habitats, and more than 2,300 animals, including 15 species on the endangered list, live among them. If you'd rather ride than walk, you can tour the 500 acres via monorail, while an on-board naturalist explains the sights; you're likely to see hardy, Northern Hemisphere animals such as Siberian tigers, Bactrian camels, Asian wild horses, and moose. An IMAX theater presents educational and entertaining films. | 13000 Zoo Blvd., Apple Valley | 952/431–9200 or 800/366–7811 | www.mnzoo.com | $10 | Memorial Day–Labor Day, daily 9–6; Labor Day–Memorial Day, daily 9–4.

Scott County Historical Society/Stans Museum. Several hundred years of fur and other commodity trading along the Minnesota River are the subjects of most exhibits here. The Stans House, a Dutch Colonial home dating from 1908, is across the street. | 235 Fuller St. | 888/325–2575 | fax 952/445–4154 | www.co.scott.mn.us/historic | Free | Tues., Wed, Fri. 9–4, Thur. 9–8, Sat. 11–3.

Valleyfair. This 68-acre amusement park has more than 50 rides, including four roller coasters, three water rides, and an old-fashioned carousel. Food and souvenirs abound. | 1 Valleyfair Dr. | 612/445–6500 or 612/445–7600 | www.valleyfair.com | $26.

ON THE CALENDAR

AUG.–SEPT.: *Renaissance Festival.* Costumed players entertain in this re-created 16th-century Renaissance village for 7 weekends beginning mid-month. | 612/445–7361.
SEPT.: *Great Scarecrow Festival.* Scarecrow contests and displays are highlights of this outdoor harvest festival at Emma Krumbee's Apple Orchard, off U.S. 69 in Belle Plaine. | 612/873–4334.

Dining

Brew Station Brewery. American. You can't miss the railroad theme in this brew pub filled with antique lightposts and luggage. It's known for its burgers, home-brewed beer, and sodas. Kids' menu. | 1128 Vierling Ct | 612/403–9950 | Closed major holidays | $8–$16 | AE, D, MC, V.

Dangerfield's. Eclectic. Overlooking the Minnesota River, this restaurant is decorated with wood furnishings and offers an extensive selection of international dishes. Lots of folks enjoy the broiled walleye, which is flown in three times a year from Prince Edward Island, Canada. | 1583 1st Ave. E | 952/445–2245 | $15–$20 | AE, D, DC, MC, V.

Lodging

Country Inn and Suites. This 3-story establishment is 2 mi south of downtown, in a commercial area 10 mi south of Valleyfair. Complimentary Continental breakfast. In-room data ports, some in-room hot tubs. Cable TV. Pool. Hot tub. Laundry facilities. Business services. | 1204 S. Ramsey St. | 612/445–0200 | fax 612/403–0680 | 63 rooms | $84–$150 | AE, D, DC, MC, V.

Holiday Inn Express. Downtown is 1 mi from this three-story hotel. There's fast food across the street, and Route 169 is 1 mi north. Complimentary Continental breakfast. In-room data ports. Cable TV. Indoor pool. Hot tub. Laundry facilities, laundry services. | 511 Marshall Rd. | 952/445–9779 | fax 952/445–9725 | www.hiexpress.com/shakopeemn | 57 rooms, 9 suites | $79–$99, $129–$149 suites | AE, D, DC, MC, V.

SPRING VALLEY

MAP 3, F10

(Nearby towns also listed: Austin, Preston, Rochester)

A group of land-seeking farmers from Pennsylvania founded Spring Valley in 1855, and the Laura Ingalls Wilder family was later on the local church membership. Standing between a tallgrass prairie and a hardwood forest, the town has hiking and fishing areas, as well as underground caves in the area state park. Historically an agricultural center, Spring Valley has begun establishing an industrial and commercial base that includes manufacturing and food processing.

Information: Spring Valley Tourist Information Center | 112 W. Courtland St., Spring Valley, 55975 | 507/346–1015 | www.ci.spring-valley.mn.us. .

Attractions

Forestville/Mystery Cave State Park. Fishing, hiking, and horseback riding are among the outdoor activities available in this 3,000-acre park nestled in the Root River valley, about 6 mi south of Wykoff. It is also home to Historic Forestville, a restored 1800s village operated by the Minnesota Historical Society. | County Rd. 118 | 507/352–5111 | www.dnr.state.mn.us/parks_and_recreation/state_parks/forestville_mystery_cave | Park permit required | Daily.
Mystery Cave, the state's longest, with over 12 mi of passages, shows off stalactites, stalagmites, and underground pools. Park naturalists lead 1-hr tours. | 507/352–5111 | $7, park permit required | Memorial Day–Labor Day, weekdays 11–5, weekends 10:30–5; spring and fall weekends 11–4.

Methodist Church Museum. Attended by Laura Ingalls Wilder and her husband from 1890–91, this 1876 Victorian Gothic church is listed on the National Register of Historic Places. Two floors of exhibits cover the history of the area, and include special displays on former residents Laura Ingalls Wilder and Richard Sears, of Sears Roebuck. The site is one block west of downtown. | 221 W. Courtland St. | 507/346–7659 | $3 | Memorial Day–Labor Day, daily 10–4.

Pioneer Home Museum. Period furnishings, quilts, farm equipment, and toys fill the 10 exhibit areas in this two-story 1865 frame house operated by the Minnesota Historical Society. The sunken bedroom, costume room, and children's room are among the most interesting corners of the house. | 220 W. Courtland St. | 507/346–7659 | $4 | Memorial Day–Labor Day, daily 10–4:30.

ON THE CALENDAR
AUG.: *Wilder Fest.* Spring Valley celebrates author Laura Ingalls Wilder with street dances, a parade, car shows, and games on the third weekend of the month. | 507/346–1015.

Dining
Elaine's Cafe. American. Comfort food such as hot beef with mashed potatoes and gravy is served up at this small café. For dessert, you might try one of Elaine's homemade pies. | 125 S. Broadway | 507/346–7492 | $4–$6 | No credit cards.

Lodging
Super 8. Opened in June of 1999, rooms at this two-story motel have views of the rural countryside. Downtown Spring Valley is 1 mi south. Complimentary Continental breakfast. Some in-room hot tubs. Cable TV. Video games. Laundry facilities. Business services. Pets allowed. | 745 N. Broadway | 507/346–7788 | fax 507/346–7254 | www.super8.com | 36 rooms, 4 suites | $50–$70, $70–$85 suites | AE, D, DC, MC, V.

William Strong House. This two-story Victorian mansion downtown is complete with porch and gardens. It's on the National Register of Historic Places. Dining room. In-room hot tubs. | 508 Huron Ave. N | 507/346–2850 | 5 rooms | $95–$135 | AE, D, DC, MC, V.

STILLWATER

MAP 3, F8

(Nearby towns also listed: St. Paul, Taylors Falls)

Before white settlers began arriving in the early 1800s, Stillwater was Dakota and Ojibway Indian country. Now listed on the National Register of Historic Places, the old logging town stands among the bluffs of the St. Croix River, 25 mi east of St. Paul. Downtown, hundred-year-old brick and limestone buildings, once mercantile stores, house antiques shops, rare-book dealers, restaurants, and inns.

Information: Stillwater Convention and Visitors Bureau | Box 516, 423 S. Main St., Stillwater, 55082 | 651/439–4001 | www.ilovestillwater.com.

Attractions
Minnesota Zephyr. Aboard this restored 1940s dining train, live '40s and '50s music accompanies a five-course meal as you chug along the banks of the St. Croix River. The trip lasts 4½ hours, the meal 3½, with menu choices including prime rib, Atlantic salmon, and Cornish game hen. The depot has a railroad museum and a gift shop. | 601 N. Main St. | 651/430–3000 | Reservations essential | www.minnesotazephyr.com | $65–$75 | Sunday, noon; Nightly, 7:30.

Washington County Historical Museum. Built in 1853, and once a prison warden's house, the museum displays tools and other artifacts from the region's lumber-era past. | 602 N. Main St. | 651/439–5956 | www.wchsmn.org | $3 | May 1–Oct. 31, Tues., Thurs., Sat., Sun. 2–5.

William O'Brien State Park. Directly on the St. Croix River, this 1,500-acre park has plenty of places to swim, fish, canoe, cross-country ski, and camp. | 16821 O'Brien Tr. N | 651/433–0500 | www.dnr.state.mn.us/parks_and_recreation/state_parks/william_obrien | Park permit required | Daily.

MAY: *Rivertown Art Fair.* Local artists display and sell their work in Lowell Park the third weekend of the month. | 651/439–7700.

JUNE: *Taste of Stillwater.* Forty area restaurants converge upon Lowell Park, along the St. Croix River, the third weekend in June. You can purchase small samples rather than entire entrées so that you can have a taste of everything. | 651/439–4001.

JULY: *Lumberjack Days.* Head into town for polka in the park, a lumberjack show, a parade, a treasure hunt, races, and fireworks the last weekend of the month. | 651/430–2306.

Dining

Afton House. Continental. Part of an 1867 inn listed on the National Register of Historic Places, this dining room has some tableside cooking and is known for its Caesar salad, steak Diane, and cherries Jubilee. Kids' menu. Sun. brunch. | 3291 S. St. Croix Tr., Afton | 651/436–8883 | Closed Mon., Jan.–Mar. | $15–$25 | AE, D, MC, V.

Bayport American Cookery. Contemporary. Sitting behind an unassuming storefront and hung with the work of local artists, this restaurant serves five-course dinners, with one seating nightly. The menu changes weekly and highlights seasonal ingredients such as fresh truffles in January, morel mushrooms in spring, and garlic in fall. A pan-seared breast of duck with white bean ragoût is typical. No smoking. Beer and wine only. | 328 5th Ave., North Bayport | 651/430–1066 | www.bayportcookery.com | Reservations essential | Wed.–Sun. 7 PM. No lunch | $34 | AE, D, DC, MC, V.

Dock Cafe. American. This restaurant gives you a great view of the oldest lift bridge in the state. Specialties include a gravlax (cured salmon), grilled seafood, and chicken saltimbocca (with melted cheese, tomatoes, and sage). Kids' menu. | 425 E. Nelson | 651/430–3770 | $9–$20 | AE, D, DC, MC, V.

Esteban's. Tex-Mex. This is an anchor restaurant of a small chain serving such Tex-Mex staples as fajitas and chimichangas. Kids' menu. | 423 S. Main St. | 651/430–1543 | $8–$15 | AE, D, DC, MC, V.

Freight House. American. Housed in an old train station listed on the National Register of Historic Places, the restaurant overlooks the St. Croix River. Specialties include steak, seafood, sandwiches, and salads. Kids' menu. | 305 Water St. | 651/439–5718 | $8–$16 | AE, D, DC, MC, V.

Gasthaus Bavarian Hunter. German. There's open-air dining (summertime only) in the beer garden of this restaurant tucked into the woods near town. On the menu are German specialties such as Wiener schnitzel and sauerbraten. An accordionist performs Fri. evenings and Sun. afternoons. Buffet lunch Sun. Kids' menu. | 8390 Lofton Ave. N | 651/439–7128 | $10–$20 | AE, MC, V.

Harvest Inn. Continental. Walleye is a strong local favorite at this restaurant, which has an outdoor dining patio, used in summer. Early-bird suppers. Kids' menu. Beer and wine only. No smoking. | 114 Chestnut St. | 651/430–8111 | Closed Sun. No lunch Sat. | $17–$21 | AE, D, MC, V.

La Belle Vie. French. Big windows in this bistro look out on Stillwater's main street. You can dine à la carte, or go for a five-course meal and with dishes such as cumin-and-honey-marinated chicken breast or ravioli with turnip purée. | 312 S. Main St. | 651/430–3545 | $19–$27 | AE, D, DC, MC, V.

Lowell Inn. American. Parts of a tourist-attracting 1880 inn listed on the National Register of Historic Places, three themed dining rooms serve lobster, lamb, and prime cuts of beef in period splendor. Each table in the George Washington Room has a centerpiece of English Spode china, Colonial glassware, and sterling flatware. In the Garden Room, a spring-fed trout pool, flagstone flooring, and abundant greenery make for a calming freshness in the air. The Matterhorn Room, dedicated to Swiss woodcarving and surrounded by carved panels and ropes used to climb the Matterhorn, has a fixed-price menu of Swiss provincial foods such as rosebud salad and fondue *bourguignonne* (tenderloin beef cubes and jumbo shrimp with four accompanying sauces). Kids' menu. | 102 2nd St. N | 651/439–1100 | fax 651/439–4686 | www.lowellinn.com | $22–$60 | AE, MC, V.

Vittorio's. Italian. Weather permitting, open-air dining is a highlight of this restaurant, which specializes in pastas and pizzas. Kids' menu. | 402 S. Main St. | 612/439–3588 | $7–$20 | AE, D, DC, MC, V.

Lodging

Afton House. Some rooms have balconies overlooking the St. Croix River at this two-story National Register of Historic Places–listed hostelry dating from 1867. It's 15 mi south of Stillwater. Restaurant. Some in-room hot tubs. Cable TV. Business services, airport shuttle. | 3291 S. St. Croix Tr., Afton | 651/436–8883 | fax 651/436–6859 | info@aftonhouseinn.com | www.aftonhouseinn.com | 16 rooms | $70–$160 | AE, D, MC, V.

Ann Bean Mansion. Formerly the home of a lumber baron, this four-story downtown mansion dating from 1878 has two towers with panoramic views of the St. Croix River Valley. An ornately carved oak fireplace and grand piano adorn the double parlor. You can eat your four-course breakfast in the dining room, or have it brought to your room. Complimentary breakfast. Some in-room hot tubs. No room phones, no TV. | 319 Pine St. | 651/430–0355 | fax 651/351–2152 | kstimack@prodigy.net | www.annbeanmansion.com | 5 rooms | $109–$199 | AE, D, MC, V.

Aurora Staples Inn. Period antiques and oriental rugs characterize this 1890s Queen Anne home overlooking the St. Croix River. It is three blocks from the downtown area, I–36, and I–95. Complimentary breakfast. Some in-room hot tubs. No room phones, no TV. Library. No kids under 12. | 303 N. Fourth St. | 651/351–1187 | fax 651/430–9755 | info@aurorastaplesinn.com | www.aurorastaplesinn.com | 5 rooms | $115–$180 | MC, V.

Best Western Stillwater Inn. Standing in a commercial and recreational area 1½ mi south of downtown, this motel has a rustic, Scandinavian-style lobby with a fireplace. Complimentary Continental breakfast. In-room data ports, some in-room hot tubs. Cable TV. Hot tub. Exercise equipment. Business services. Some pets allowed. | 1750 Frontage Rd. W | 651/430–1300 | fax 651/430–0596 | www.bestwestern.com | 60 rooms | $55–$75 | AE, D, DC, MC, V.

Country Cove Bed and Breakfast. With a fireplace and grand piano inside, and a large lawn and gazebo outside, this B&B's quiet setting is right for relaxation. It is 3 mi west of downtown Stillwater, within waving distance of the Minnesota Zephyr's train route. Complimentary breakfast. No room phones. No kids. | 11591 North McKusick Rd. | 651/430–3434 | www.countrycove.com | 3 rooms | $99–$149 | MC, V.

Country Inn and Suites. This country-style hotel is in a suburban shopping area 2 mi west of downtown, on the St. Croix River. Complimentary Continental breakfast. In-room data ports, some microwaves, refrigerators, some in-room hot tubs. Cable TV. Pool. Hot tub. Exercise equipment. Laundry facilities. Business services. | 2200 Frontage Rd. W | 651/430–2699 | fax 651/430–1233 | 52 rooms, 20 suites | $69–$85, $85–$129 suites | AE, D, DC, MC, V.

James A. Mulvey Inn. A porch, a parlor, a formal dining room, carved staircases, and lots of antiques characterize this two-story 1870 inn, on the north end of town. The black walnut trees around the house were planted by the home's original owner. Complimentary breakfast. Some in-room hot tubs. No room phones. No kids under 12. No smoking. | 622 W. Churchill St. | 651/430–8008 or 800/820–8008 | www.jamesmulveyinn.com | 4 rooms, 3 suites | $99–$169, $149–$199 suites | D, MC, V.

Lowell Inn. Built in 1924 as a private home, this white-columned mansion has been a inn since 1927. The dining rooms are striking and the accommodations comfortable. One room has a shower in the round; another has a double Jacuzzi. Restaurant, bar. Some in-room hot tubs. Business services. | 102 N. 2nd St. | 651/439–1100 | fax 651/439–4686 | www.lowellinn.com | 21 rooms (12 with shower only) | $59–$269 | MC, V.

Lumber Baron's. Built by lumberjacks in 1890, this two-story Victorian hotel, beside the St. Croix River in downtown Stillwater, has a patio and a saloon where you can meet some interesting locals. Restaurant, bar, complimentary breakfast. In-room hot tubs. Cable TV. Business services. | 101 Water St. S | 651/439–6000 | fax 651/430–9393 | www.lumber-barons.com | 36 rooms | $139–$199 | AE, D, DC, MC, V.

Rivertown Inn. Nineteenth-century poets and writers inspired guest-room themes in this mansion built in 1882; there's a Christina Rosetti bedchamber with pre-Raphaelite-style cherub statuary and wallcoverings and a Byron suite with red draperies, tiled fireplace, and whirlpooth bath with a waterfall faucet. The inn is 3 blocks southwest of downtown. Complimentary breakfast. In-room hot tubs. No room phones. No smoking. | 306 W. Olive St. | 651/430–2955 | fax 651/430–0034 | rivertn@aol.com | www.rivertowninn.com | 4 rooms, 4 suites | $79–$169 | AE, D, DC, MC, V.

Super 8. This two-story motel is 2 mi west of downtown. Complimentary Continental breakfast. Cable TV. Laundry facilities. Business services. | 2190 Frontage Rd. W | 651/430–3990 | fax 651/430–3990 | 49 rooms | $43–$70 | AE, D, DC, MC, V.

TAYLORS FALLS

MAP 3, F7

(Nearby towns also listed: St. Paul, Stillwater)

Sitting directly over the St. Croix River, atop a rocky canyon known as the St. Croix Dalles, Taylors Falls is the last Minnesotan town on Route 95, before you cross into Wisconsin. Originally the site of a French fur-trading settlement, the town itself was established in 1838 as a steamboat navigation hub for the riverway, supplying nearby communities and logging camps with goods shipped from afar. Today, tourism is the major industry, thanks to a host of river activities, two nearby state parks, and a historic district with specialty and antique shops.

Information: Taylors Falls Chamber of Commerce | Box 171, Taylors Falls, 55084 | 651/465–6700 | www.taylorsfalls.com.

Attractions

Angel Hill Historic District. White clapboard buildings in this New England–style neighborhood date from the town's earliest days in the mid-1800s, and include the state's oldest schoolhouse (built in 1852) and the 1861 Methodist church, which was originally served by itinerant preachers. | Basil St. | 651/465–6700 | Free | Daily.

The **W.H.C. Folsom House,** part of the historical district, was built in 1851 by lumber baron William Henry Carman Folsom, who ran a grist mill, a store, and other enterprises in town, and served as a state senator. The five-bedroom mansion is maintained and operated by the Minnesota Historical Society, which opens it to visitors in summer and the first two weekends after Thanksgiving for the Taylors Falls Lighting Festival. | 272 W. Government St. | 651/465–3125 | folsomhouse@mnhs.org | www.state.mn.us/ebranch/mhs/places/sites/fh | $3 | Late May–mid-Oct., daily 1–4:30.

Boat Excursions. During your 30- or 80-minute trip through the St. Croix Dalles, aboard either the *St. Croix Princess* or the *St. Croix Queen,* guides point out the interesting rock formations left behind as glaciers retreated thousands of years ago. A highlight of the trip is the natural rock face called the Old Man of the Dalles. | Landing near the Minnesota–Wisconsin bridge | 651/465–6501 or 800/996–4448 | www.wildmountain.com/scenicboat.html | $6.25–$8.50 | May–Oct., daily.

Interstate State Park. The nation's first interstate park, owned jointly by Minnesota and Wisconsin, was established in 1895 (the Minnesota part) and 1900 (the Wisconsin part) to preserve the St. Croix River Dalles from a growing threat of area mining. Today, the 293-

acre park gives you chances at canoeing the flat water, kayaking the rapids, climbing the Dalles themselves, or hiking on either side of the river. | Rte. 8, at Rte. 95 | 651/465–5711 | www.dnr.state.mn.us/parks_and_recreation/state_parks/interstate | Park permit required | Daily.

St. Croix National Scenic Riverway. The 252-mi riverway, which includes both the St. Croix and the Namekagon rivers, was one of the first designated under the Wild and Scenic River Act of 1968. The corridor forms part of the Minnesota–Wisconsin border. The Riverway provides canoeing and other boating activities, and is a diverse wildlife habitat. | 651/483–3284 | www.nps.gov/sacn.

Wild Mountain Ski Area. This 100-acre ski area has 23 runs, four quad chairlifts, and a vertical drop of 300 ft. | 37200 Wild Mountain Rd. | 651/465–6315 | www.wildmountain.com/winterhome.html | Nov.–Mar., daily.

In summer, Wild Mountain becomes a **Water Park,** with water slides, alpine slides, and go-carts. | 612/465–6315 or 612/257–3550 | $11–$20 | May–Aug., daily.

Wild River State Park. Camping, hiking, horseback riding, canoeing, interpretive programs, self-guided trails, and cross-country skiing are available at this 6,800-acre park along the St. Croix River. | 39797 Park Tr., Center City | 651/583–2125 | www.dnr.state.mn.us/parks_and_recreation/state_parks/wild_river | Park permit required | Daily.

ON THE CALENDAR
NOV.: *Lighthouse Festival.* Local businesses, homes, and landmarks throughout Taylor Falls are covered with Christmas lights and ornaments, beginning the weekend after Thanksgiving. | 651/456–6700.

Dining
Border Bar and Grill. American. In downtown Taylors Falls, this lively bar and restaurant is known for its ¾-lb "Border burger." | 367 Bench St. | 651/465–1011 | $4–$20 | MC, V.

Chisago House Restaurant. American. A large fireplace dominates this dining room, which serves breakfast all day, including apple-cinnamon dumplings served with vanilla ice cream. The prime rib buffet on weekends is also very popular. Kids' menu. | 361 Bench St. | 651/465–5245 | Breakfast also available | $9–$14 | AE, D, MC, V.

Drive-In Restaurant. American. On Thursdays, customers arriving in classic cars get 10% off any menu item at this '50s-style drive-in. Carhops in poodle skirts serve you burgers, root beer, and fries. | 572 Bench St. | 651/465–7831 | taylorsfalls.com/drivein.html | mid-Apr.–mid-Oct., daily noon–7 | $7–$11 | AE, D, MC, V.

Lodging
The Cottage. Designed to resemble an 18th-century English country house, this two-story cottage stands 1 mi south of downtown, on a secluded bluff overlooking the St. Croix River. The suite has a private entrance and dining area. Dining room. | 30495 Herberg Rd. | 651/465–3595 | www.the-cottage.com | 1 suite | $95–$115 suite | AE, MC, V.

McClaine House Bed and Breakfast. This two-story 1863 yellow country home is five blocks north of downtown. Rooms contain handmade quilts and American antiques. Complimentary Continental breakfast. No room phones. TV in common area. | 519 Bench St. | 651/465–4832 | fax 651/465–6403 | csm@quixnet.net | 3 rooms | $85–$95 | No credit cards.

Old Jail Co. Bed and Breakfast Built in 1851 as a stable, the main building of this B&B complex has housed a newspaper office, a general store, and a saloon; it's now on the National Register of Historic Places. You can also lodge in an original 1885 jail, which has a fireplace, loft bedroom, and private balcony. The cottage and suites are stocked with popcorn, coffee, tea, and hot cocoa, and some have views of the wooded hillside. The B&B is on the southwest side of town. Complimentary breakfast. No room phones, TV in common area. | 102 Government St. | 651/465–3112 | www.oldjail.com | 3 suites | $110–$125 | MC, V.

Springs Country Inn. The St. Croix River is visible from the upper floors of this inn, which is on the southwestern side of town. Restaurant, bar, complimentary Continental breakfast. In-room hot tubs. Cable TV. Business services. Some pets allowed (fee). | 361 Government St. | 651/465–6565 or 800/851–4243 | fax 651/822–4258 | 29 rooms | $45–$95 | AE, D, DC, MC, V.

THIEF RIVER FALLS

MAP 3, B3

(Nearby town also listed: Crookston)

Named "Thief River" by the Dakota and Ojibway people, this area was the site of a 40-family Ojibway village until 1904, several years after white people established a lumber-mill town, adding "Falls" to the name in 1896, when a dam turned the river rapids into a waterfall. Later, the city became a major agricultural area, due partly to the rich soil left by the ancient glacial Lake Agassiz. Today, Thief River Falls is northwest Minnesota's regional center for commerce, education, health, government, and transportation, and the seat of Pennington County.

Information: **Thief River Falls Area Chamber of Commerce and Convention and Visitors Bureau** | 2017 Rte. 59 SE, Thief River Falls, 56701 | www.ci.thief-river-falls.mn.us | 218/681–3720 or 800/827–1629.

Attractions

Agassiz National Wildlife Refuge. This 61,500-acre refuge is one of two in the continental U.S. known to have resident packs of eastern gray wolves. The forests, water, and marshland here protect 280 bird species and 41 mammal species. It's 12 mi north of Thief River Falls, on Route 32. | 218/449–4115 | www.fws.gov/r3pao/agassiz | Free | Daily.

Peder Engelstad Pioneer Village. A replica of a northern Minnesota town as it might have appeared 100 years ago, the village has 19 artifact-filled buildings, including two railroad depots, a one-room school house, a church, a blacksmith shop and seven log cabins. | Oakland Park Rd. | 218/681–5767 | $3 | Memorial Day–Labor Day, daily 1–5.

ON THE CALENDAR

JULY: *All Nations Cultural Festival.* This two-day cultural celebration in St. Hilaire, 7 mi south of Thief River Falls, draws ethnic performers from around the world. There are model fur-trading and Native-American encampments, and a kids' carnival. | 218/681–7363.

Dining

Dee's Kitchen. American. With an in-house bakery and a menu filled with comfort food, this restaurant is a real country delight. Especially popular are the hot beef and pork sandwiches topped with mashed potatoes and gravy, and Dee's homemade pies and pastries make for fine desserts. | 811 Atlantic Ave. N | 218/681–9907 | $5–$8 | No credit cards.

Lodging

Best Western Inn. One mile south of downtown in a commercial area, this two-story hotel caters to families. Restaurant, bar (with entertainment). In-room data ports, refrigerators. Cable TV. Pool. Hot tub. Exercise equipment. Business services, airport shuttle. | 1060 Rte. 32S | 218/681–7555 | fax 218/681–7721 | www.bestwestern.com | 78 rooms | $59–$70 | AE, D, DC, MC, V.

C'mon Inn. A residential area off Route 59, on the south end of town, is the setting for this small, two-story motel. Complimentary Continental breakfast. In-room data ports. Cable

TV. Pool. Some in-room hot tubs. Business services. Some pets allowed. | 1586 U.S. 59S | 218/681–3000 or 800/950–8111 | fax 218/681–3060 | 44 rooms | $60–$99 | AE, D, MC, V.

Hartwood Motel. Seven blocks north of downtown, this single-story motel has been in business since the early 1950s. There is a café across the street. Cable TV. Pets allowed. | 1010 N. Main Ave. | 218/681–2640 | 34 rooms | $31–$38 | AE, D, MC, V.

Super 8. This highway motel is in a commercial area 1½ mi southeast of town. Complimentary Continental breakfast. Some in-room hot tubs. Cable TV. Business services. | U.S. 59SE | 218/681–6205 | fax 218/681–7519 | www.super8.com | 46 rooms | $40–$60 | AE, D, DC, MC, V.

TOWER

MAP 3, F3

(Nearby towns also listed: Babbitt, Cook, Crane Lake, Ely, Eveleth, Virginia)

Founded in 1883, shortly after the discovery of iron ore at the site of the present Soudan Mine, Tower is the oldest mining town in northern Minnesota. It now serves as a major retail shopping hub for residents and visitors in the Lake Vermilion area and the Superior National Forest.

Information: Tower-Soudan Chamber | Box 776, Tower, 55790 | 218/753–2301 or 800/648–5897 | www.towermn.com.

Attractions

Lake Vermilion. At 40 mi long, with 1,200 mi of shoreline and more than 350 islands, this lake is a water lover's dream. Most of Vermilion falls within the borders of Superior National Forest. It's an all-around recreational lake with fishing, boating, and snowmobiling. | Rte. 169 and Rte. 77N | 218/753–2301 | Free | Daily.

Soudan Underground Mine State Park. This park encompasses the state's first underground iron mine, which is on the southeastern shore of Lake Vermilion. As a guest, you'll put on a hard hat and go down 2,400 ft in a "cage," then ride the rails back into the mine and listen to stories of the mining days. | 1379 Stuntsbay Rd. | 218/753–2245 | www.dnr.state.mn.us/parks_and_recreation/state_parks/soudan_underground_mine | Park permit required | Daily.

Steam Locomotive and Coach. The locomotive once belonged to the Duluth and Iron Range Railroad, and pulled cars loaded with Iron Range ore to ships on Lake Superior. The coach is now a museum specializing in mining history. | 404 Pine St. | 218/753–2301 | $1 | Memorial Day–Labor Day, daily 10–4.

Vince Shute Wildlife Bear Sanctuary. Fifty miles northwest of Tower, this 360-acre sanctuary is home to black bears, bald eagles, whitetail deer, and many other species. An elevated observation deck gives safe, up-close views of the bears. | County Rd. 514, Orr | 218/757–0172 | www.americanbear.org | Free | Memorial Day–Labor Day, Tues.–Sun. 5 PM–dusk.

ON THE CALENDAR

JULY: *Tower Fourth of July Celebration.* Highlights of this day-long party include a parade down Main St. and a fireworks display. | 218/753–6100.

Dining

Black Bear Cafe. American. Philly cheesesteak sandwiches are among the more popular items at this café, 10 mi south of downtown. A separate bar area is adorned with Minnesota Viking memorabilia. | 6699 Rte. 169 | 218/749–2460 | $6–$16 | MC, V.

Wayside Cafe. American. This small café has been in business since the early 1950s. Burgers and cold cut sandwiches dominate the menu. | 3114 Coney Rd. 77 | 218/753–4828 | Breakfast also available | $3–$10 | MC, V.

Lodging

Daisy Bay Resort. Each rustic lakeside cabin here has its own private dock. The resort is off Route 77, on Lake Vermilion. Kitchenettes. Cable TV. Lake. Hiking. Beach, dock, boating, fishing. Baby-sitting, playground. Some pets allowed. | 4070 Rte. 77 | 218/753–4958 or 800/449–8306 | www.lakevermilionresorts.com/daisy.html | 9 cabins | $65–$140 | AE, MC, V.

End of Trail Lodge. Trees and year-round recreational activities abound at this secluded resort, which has five log cabins on Lake Vermilion. Kitchenettes. Lake. Sauna. Beach, dock, boating, fishing. Some pets allowed. | 4284 End of Trail La. | 218/753–6971 or 800/353–0123 | www.endoftrail.com | 5 cabins | $130–$156 | AE, MC, V.

Fortune Bay Resort and Casino. Overlooking Lake Vermilion in the heart of Superior National Forest, this four-story resort is connected to the casino. Many rooms have private balconies and fireplaces. Trails on the grounds are clearly marked for hiking. Restaurant, 3 bars. In-room data ports, kitchenettes, microwaves, some in-room hot tubs. Cable TV. Indoor pool. Hot tub, sauna. Exercise equipment. Shops, video games. Laundry facilities, laundry services, airport shuttle. | 1430 Bois Forte Rd. | 218/753–2710 | fax 218/753–3600 | www.fortunebay.com | 84 rooms, 30 suites | $69–$99, $99–$149 suites | AE, D, MC, V.

Glenwood Lodge. The only resort on the northeast section of Lake Vermilion, and one of the most isolated in the region, Glenwood has a lodge and cabins, as well as an on-site grocery and bait shop. Kitchenettes. Lake. Sauna. Hiking. Beach, dock, boating, fishing. Cross-country skiing, snowmobiling. Playground. Some pets allowed. | Rte. 408 | 218/753–5306 | www.GlenwoodLodge.com | 5 cabins | $290–$635 weekly | AE, D, DC, MC, V.

Marjo Motel. Built in 1957, this motel is ¼ mi west of the town center. West Two River, which leads to Lake Vermilion, flows next to the motel. No room phones. Cable TV. Pets allowed. | 712 Rte. 169 | 218/753–4851 | 8 rooms | $40–$55.

TRACY

MAP 3, B9

(Nearby towns also listed: Granite Falls, Marshall, Pipestone, Redwood Falls)

First and foremost a railroad town, Tracy started life as Shetek Bend in 1875. A few years later, it was renamed Tracy in honor of a former railroad president. Today it remains a regular stop on the Dakota, Minnesota, and Eastern Railroad, part of a rich agricultural region.

Information: **Tracy Area Chamber of Commerce** | 372 Morgan St., Tracy, 56175 | 507/629–4021 | www.tracymn.com.

Attractions

Lake Shetek State Park. The Des Moines River begins here, with its headwaters in Lake Shetek. You can walk to Loon Island, a 45-acre bird sanctuary, or visit the Koch Cabin and Monument, which memorialize pioneer settlers. | 163 State Park Rd., at Rtes. 11 and 38 | 507/763–3256 | www.dnr.state.mn.us/parks_and_recreation/state_parks/lake_shetek | Park permit required | Daily.

Laura Ingalls Wilder Museum and Tourist Center. Fans of Wilder's *Little House on the Prairie* books enjoy the history and memorabilia in these buildings, which include an 1898 railroad depot and an 1880s school chapel. A quilt hand-made by Laura herself is of special interest. | 330 8th St. | 507/859–2358 | www.walnutgrove.org/page3.html | $3 | Apr. and Oct.:

Wed.–Sat. 10–4, Sun. noon–4; May and Sept.: Wed.–Sat. 10–5, Sun. noon–5; June–Aug.: daily 10–6; Jan.–Mar.: by appointment, Nov.–Dec. 10–4, Sun. noon–4, weather permitting.

ON THE CALENDAR
JULY: *Laura Ingalls Wilder Pageant.* The Ingalls family history is acted out at an outdoor theater on the banks of Plum Creek. | 507/859–2174.

Dining
Red Rooster. American. Seven blocks from downtown Tracy, this casual spot serves up hearty American fare. The burgers and the specialty biscuits with gravy are quite popular. Kids' menu. | 1333 330th Ave. | 507/629–9959 | Breakfast also available | $4–$7 | No credit cards.

Lodging
Cozy Grove Motel. This single-story motel has been in business since 1950. Rooms overlook Route 14 and there are three restaurants within 5 blocks. Cable TV, some microwaves, some refrigerators. | 1000 Craig Ave. | 507/629–3350 | 22 rooms | $38 | No credit cards.

Valentine Inn. This B&B, two blocks from Highway 14 west of town, has Victorian-theme room motifs. Non-smoking rooms are available. Dining room. Cable TV. | 385 Emory St. | 507/629–3827 | 5 rooms | $65–$95 | AE, D, DC, MC, V.

TWO HARBORS

MAP 3, G4

(Nearby towns also listed: Cloquet, Duluth)

Two Harbors lies in a scenic area of deep forests and rugged Lake Superior shorelines in northeastern Minnesota, 15 mi northwest of Duluth. It owes its existence to the railroad and to the local presence of iron ore, which has been shipped from here to destinations around the country since the 1880s. Today, at the docks in Agate Bay, boats still take on iron ore and taconite pellets destined for eastern steel mills. In addition to the area's mineral resources, timber, game animals, and trophy fish fill the area's waters and woodlands. Burlington Bay is preserved for recreational activities.

Information: **Two Harbors Chamber of Commerce** | 603 7th Ave., Box 39, Two Harbors, 55616 | 218/834–2600 or 800/777–7384 | www.twoharbors.com/chamber.

Attractions
Depot Museum. Formerly a depot of the Duluth and Iron Range Railroad, the structure is now a museum specializing in geological and iron mining history. Displays include a 1941 locomotive and steam engine. | 520 South Ave. | 218/834–4898 | $2 | Sat. 10–4.

Gooseberry Falls State Park. Upper, middle, and lower falls on the Gooseberry River thunder into Lake Superior from a deep river gorge. Abundant wildlife, Civilian Conservation Corps log and stone buildings, and more than 18 mi of hiking trails are among the big attractions at this 1,662-acre park on the shores of Lake Superior. There are also extensive biking and cross-country skiing trails. A visitors center, constructed entirely of recycled materials, has displays, a park video, a nature store, and more. | 3206 Rte. 61 | 218/834–3855 | www.dnr.state.mn.us/parks_and_recreation/state_parks/gooseberry_falls/index.html | Free | Daily, dawn to dusk.

Lighthouse Point and Harbor Museum. The lighthouse still works, and the museum explores the history of mining and shipping in the area. | 520 South Ave. | 218/834–4898 | $2 | May–Oct., daily 10–4.

Split Rock Lighthouse State Park. Best known for its lighthouse, which guided ships to safe waters from the early to mid-1900s, the 2,075-acre park also has year-round hiking, camping, and fishing, and Lake Superior splashes at the beach. | 3713 Split Rock Lighthouse Rd. | 218/226–6377 or 218/226–6372 | www.dnr.state.mn.us/parks_and_recreation/state_parks/split_rock_lighthouse | Park permit required | Daily, park; noon–4, lighthouse and visitors center.

ON THE CALENDAR

JULY: *Heritage Days.* This Scandinavian festival goes from Thursday to Sunday the second full week of the month. Highlights include the lutefisk-throwing contest between Norwegian and Swedish Americans, and the parade on Saturday. | 800/777–7384.

Dining

Judy's Cafe. American. Two blocks from downtown, this café is popular for its hearty steak and eggs and all-day breakfast. Pictures and a wooden sculpture of the famous *Edna G.* tugboat adorn the walls. Kids' menu. | 623 7th Ave. | 218/834–4802 | Breakfast also available | $5–$9 | No credit cards.

Lodging

Breezy Point Resort. Four miles south of downtown Two Harbors, this resort is in a serene setting on Lake Superior. All cabins have lake views, and several have fireplaces and private decks. Kitchenettes. Cable TV. Water sports. Playground. | 540 Old North Rd. | 218/834–4490 | www.breezyonsuperior.com | 12 cabins | $94–$200 cabins | MC, V.

Country Inn by Carlson. This cozy 2-story motel is off Route 61, right in town, 1 mi west of Lake Superior. Restaurant, complimentary Continental breakfast. Some microwaves, some refrigerators. Cable TV. Pool. Hot tub, sauna. Laundry facilities. Business services. Some pets allowed (fee). | 1204 7th Ave. | 218/834–5557 or 800/456–4000 | fax 218/834–3777 | www.countryinns.com | 46 rooms | $70–$130 | AE, D, DC, MC, V.

Superior Shores. Standing in a woodsy area 1 mi north of town, this resort has full access to all Lake Superior recreational activities. Restaurant, bar. Some kitchenettes, microwaves, refrigerators. Cable TV, in-room VCRs (and movies). 3 pools. Hot tub, sauna. Tennis. Hiking. Business services. Some pets allowed. | 1521 Superior Shores Dr. | 218/834–5671 or 800/242–1988 | fax 218/834–5677 | supshores@norshor.dst.mn.us | www.superiorshores.com | 57 rooms, 47 suites, 42 apartments | $99–$169 rooms, $179–$329 suites, $179–$429 apartments | AE, D, MC, V.

VIRGINIA

MAP 3, F4

(Nearby towns also listed: Babbitt, Chisholm, Cook, Crane Lake, Eveleth, Hibbing, Tower)

Situated in the heart of Minnesota's Iron Range, Virginia calls itself the Queen City of the North. The first settlers came here in 1890, lured by prospects of streets paved with gold and, later, by the uncovering of iron deposits. The town now serves as the region's retail centerpiece, with sales from its main mall and historic district exceeding those of many larger communities.

Information: **Virginia Area Chamber of Commerce** | 403 1st St. N, Virginia, 55792 | 218/741–2717 | www.virginiamn.com.

Attractions

Mine View in the Sky. This overlook, off Highway 53 1 mi south of town, sits atop a 20-story pile of rock, giving you a bird's-eye view of the area's deepest open-pit mine, 650 ft below. A visitor center has exhibits on the history of iron mining in Virginia. | 218/741–2717 | www.irontrail.org/rouchleau.htm | Free | May–Sept., daily 9–6.

Floating Loon. Listed in the *Guinness Book of Records* as the World's Largest Floating Loon, this 20-ft-long, 10-ft-high fiberglass bird spends it summers bobbing on Silver Lake. It migrates to storage in winter. | Chestnut St. and 6th Ave. | www.infomagic.net/~martince/wlflloon.htm.

Olcott Park. With more than 40 landscaped acres, plus a greenhouse and playground, the park is a popular spot for picnics. The Virginia Historical Society's Heritage Museum is also here, displaying artifacts of the area's mining history. | N. 9th St. at 9th Ave. | 218/741–1136 | Daily.

ON THE CALENDAR

JUNE: *Land of the Loon Ethnic Arts and Crafts Festival.* This celebration, held annually the third weekend of the month, includes a parade as well as ethnic food and dance. | 218/749–5555 or 800/777–8497.

Dining

Four Seasons Restaurant and Lounge. Eclectic. Popular items at this upscale spot include the breaded or broiled walleye pike, the chicken and wild rice salad, and the popovers with honey butter. Lemon meringue pie and cheesecake are after-dinner favorites. | Rte. 169 and Rte. 53 | 218/741–4200 | $11–$15 | MC, V.

Lodging

Lakeshore Motor Inn. This small motel, right in town, has a lake in its backyard. Some in-room hot tubs. Cable TV. Some pets allowed. | 404 N. 6th Ave. | 218/741–3360 or 800/569–8131 | 18 rooms | $32–$89 | AE, D, DC, MC, V.

Park Inn International. A handful of fast food restaurants stand within a four-block radius of this four-story hotel, and Olcott Park is 1 mi northwest. Restaurant. In-room data ports. Cable TV. Indoor pool, hot tub. Laundry facilities. Business services. No pets. | 502 Chestnut St. | 218/749–1000 | fax 218/749–6934 | mail@parkinnvirginia.com | www.parkinnvirginia.com | 46 rooms, 4 suites | $79, $99–$175 suites | AE, D, DC, MC, V.

Ski View Motel. A golf course is next door to this motel on the north side of town. Complimentary Continental breakfast. Cable TV. Sauna. Some pets allowed. | 903 N. 17th St. | 218/741–8918 | 59 rooms | $30–$70 | AE, D, DC, MC, V.

VOYAGEURS
NATIONAL PARK

INTRO
ATTRACTIONS
DINING
LODGING

VOYAGEURS NATIONAL PARK

MAP 3, F2

(Nearby towns listed: Crane Lake, Grand Marais, International Falls)

Named after French-Canadian *voyageurs*, 19th-century fur traders who traveled these waterways in 20-ft birch-bark canoes, this 219,000-acre park has some of the world's oldest exposed rock formations. Fifteen mi east of International Falls, and on the border of Ontario, the area consists of hills, boreal forest, bogs, swamps, beaver ponds, and lakes, with the land forms accessible mostly by watercraft. The bedrock, part of the Canadian Shield, has been carved and gouged by at least four glacial periods, leaving a rugged, though beautiful, terrain. A system of Coast Guard buoys marks some of the rocks, reefs, and sand bars which appear and disappear with water fluctuations, and several visitors centers have maps of the area, as well as books, tapes, videotapes, and other merchandise. You can fish, boat, camp, hike, snowmobile, cross-country ski, snowshoe. Or simply drive around the area marveling at its splendor. | 301 2nd Ave. | 800/325–5766 | www.nps.gov/voya | Free | Daily.

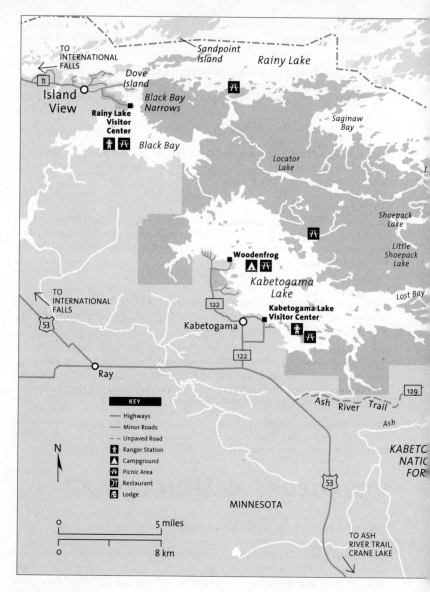

Attractions

Kabetogama Lake. More than 200 remote islands are scattered throughout this 25,000-acre lake 24 mi south of International Falls. Anglers flock to Lake Kabetogama to fish for walleye, bass, and jumbo perch. | Rte. 53 | 218/875-2111 | Free | Daily.

WABASHA

MAP 3, F9

(Nearby towns also listed: Lake City, Rochester, Winona)

Minnesota's earliest settled community, Wabasha provided the small-town backdrop for the Walter Matthau/Jack Lemmon film, *Grumpy Old Men*, and its sequel. Several

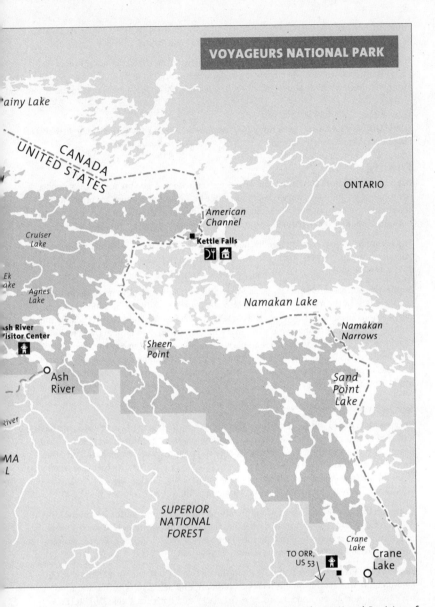

VOYAGEURS NATIONAL PARK

Rainy Lake

CANADA
UNITED STATES

ONTARIO

American Channel

Cruiser Lake

Kettle Falls

Ek ake

Agnes Lake

Namakan Lake

Ash River Visitor Center

Namakan Narrows

Sheen Point

Ash River

River

Sand Point Lake

MA L

SUPERIOR NATIONAL FOREST

Crane Lake

TO ORR, US 53

Crane Lake

buildings and the central business district are listed on the National Register of Historic Places, and the town has worked to resist franchise architecture and billboards. It is the seat of Wabasha County, 90 mi southeast of Minneapolis and St. Paul.

Information: **Wabasha Area Chamber of Commerce** | 154 Pembroke Ave., Wabasha, 55981 | 651/565–4158 or 800/565–4158 | www.wabashamn.org.

Attractions

Eagle Watch. Wabasha's eagle population soars during fall and spring migrations, and this Audubon group is dedicated to fostering environmental stewardship and celebrating eagles. You can visit the eagle observation deck on the Mississippi River in downtown Wabasha, where volunteers explain eagle activity. The National Eagle Center plans to complete new facilities in Wabasha in 2003, including an aviary with 60 eagles. | 152 Main St. | www.eaglewatch.org | Free; donations accepted | Year-round.

Historic Commercial District. Downtown Wabasha is listed on the National Register of Historic Places. You can visit the city library to get information on walking tours and other subjects and view a slide show. | 168 Alleghany Ave. | 651/565-3927 | Free | Year-round.

ON THE CALENDAR

JUNE: *Slippery's Annual "Let's Have Fun" Memorial Fishing Contest.* Held on Father's Day, this fishing contest is a family affair. | 651/565-4158 or 800/565-4158.

Dining

Grandma Anderson's Dutch Kitchen. American. Fresh homemade breads, chicken noodle soup, baked raisin beans, stuffed beef rolls, apple brandy pie, and more are served family style in a relaxed atmosphere. The Sunday breakfast buffet has a nice variety of fruits, meats, eggs, and breads. | 333 W. Main St. | 651/565-4524 or 800/535-5467 | $10–$20 | MC, V.

Papa Tronnio's. American. Housed in the local bowling alley, this eatery serves generous portions of pizza, chicken, spaghetti, shrimp, and burgers. | 218 2nd St. W | 651/565-3911 | $5–$10 | MC, V.

Slippery's. American. Originally just a shack for beer, bait, and burgers, Slippery's was made famous by the movies *Grumpy Old Men* and *Grumpier Old Men*. The land where Slippery's stands used to be the site of the old Wabasha Boat Yard and Marina. The existing building dates back to 1979 when the shack burned down, and Slippery and his wife, Gladys, rebuilt it as a resort, with boat rentals and a gas dock. Next to the Mississippi River, the place attracts boaters, snowmobilers, and eagle watchers. The menu is extensive and includes items such as "morons chicken" and the "putz burger." | 10 Church Ave. | 651/565-4748 | $12–$25 | AE, D, MC, V.

Lodging

Bridgewaters B & B. One block off the Mississippi River, directly in town, this 1903 inn has a wraparound porch with wicker seating. The rooms, named for bridges over the river, are designed in turn-of-the-20th-century style, with spoon-carved headboards and other touches. Some rooms have hot tubs or fireplaces. Three rooms have private baths, two rooms share. Complimentary breakfast. No smoking. No pets. | 136 Bridge Ave. | 651/565-4208 | www.bridgewatersbandb.com | 5 rooms | $79–$145 | MC, V.

Eagles on the River B&B. Overlooking the Mississippi River ³/₄ mi southeast of town, this B&B has CDs and CD players in all rooms, and fireplaces and whirlpools in some. Complimentary breakfast. Some in-room hot tubs. | 1000 E. Marina Dr. | 800/684-6813 or 651/565-3417 | www.eaglesontheriver.com | 4 rooms | $119–$159 | AE, D, MC, V.

Eagles on the River InnTel & Suites. Standing on on two secluded acres at the base of Coffee Mill Bluff, this establishment has both standard and deluxe rooms. Standard rooms have two double beds. Some rooms have fireplaces and hot tubs. Cable TV. | Rte. 60 W | 800/482-8188 | www.eaglesontheriver.com | 21 rooms | $49–$159 | MC, V.

WALKER

MAP 3, D4

(Nearby towns also listed: Bemidji, Park Rapids, Pine River)

You can't talk about Walker without mentioning Leech Lake, the state's third largest fishing lake, and one of its most popular. Walker, in north central Minnesota, has fewer than 1,000 residents, but it welcomes thousands of visitors each year, in large part because of the forest and lake. The town is named for a pioneer lumberman and landowner.

Information: Leech Lake Area Chamber of Commerce | Box 1089, Walker, 56484 | 218/547–1313 or 800/833–1118 | www.leech-lake.com.

Attractions

Heartland Trail. You can bike, walk, or run along this 29-mi trail, which starts on the upper west side of town and runs between Walker and Park Rapids. | Off Rte. 371 | 800/833–1118 | Free | Daily.

Leech Lake. Situated in the southwestern part of 660,000-acre Chippewa National Forest, and lying at the junction of Highways 200 and 371, this 110,000-acre lake is popular among walleye and muskie anglers. | Free | Daily.

ON THE CALENDAR
JULY: *Moondance Jam.* This outdoor rock and country music festival attracts about 50,000 people each year to Moondance Ranch, 7 mi east of Walker. | 877/MOO–NJAM.

Dining

Jimmy's. American. Usually filled with families, this casual spot serves breakfast all day, and prime rib, chicken teriyaki sandwiches, and other lunch and dinner dishes. Kids' menu. | Rte. 371 N | 218/547–3334 | Breakfast also available | $6–$15 | AE, D, DC, MC, V.

Lodging

AmericInn. Some rooms have fireplaces at this two-story motel downtown. Conference rooms are available, and a restaurant is next door. Complimentary Continental breakfast. Some refrigerators. Some in-room hot tubs. Cable TV. Pool. Hot tub, sauna. | 907 Minnesota St. | 218/547–2200 or 800/634–3444 | fax 218/547–2200 | www.americinn.com | 37 rooms | $61–$106 | AE, D, DC, MC, V.

Big Rock. All the cottages at this year-round resort, which is 10 mi east of Walker, overlook a protected harbor on Leech Lake. Kitchenettes. Cable TV. Pool. Hot tub. Tennis. Beach, docks, boating. Playground. Airport shuttle. | Rte. 84, Leech Lake | 218/547–1066 or 800/827–7106 | fax 218/547–1402 | www.bigrockresort.com | 8 cottages | $450–$690 1–3 bedroom cottages (7–day stay) | D, MC, V.

ForestView Lodge. Serving Leech Lake visitors since 1924, the ForestView has log-and-stone cottages, each with a view of the lake, and each with a log-mantle fireplace. A private marina is on the grounds. Restaurant, bar. No room phones. No TV. Some in-room hot tubs. | 7127 Forestview Rd. NW | 218/836–2441 or 800/223–6922 | fax 218/836–6078 | www.fishandgame.com/forest | 21 cottages | $65–$210 | Closed mid-Oct.–mid-May | AE, D, MC, V.

WILLMAR

MAP 3, C7

(Nearby towns also listed: Granite Falls, Hutchinson, Litchfield)

Ninety-eight mi west of Minneapolis, Willmar is in west-central Minnesota's Little Crow Lake region, on rolling farmlands which were once the disputed hunting grounds of the Dakota and Ojibway. The town was named after an English bondsman who handled investments in the railroad that came through town in 1869. Today, Willmar's economy relies on a mix of industry, health care, education, and government, as well as retail and wholesale trade.

Information: Willmar Convention and Visitors Bureau | 2104 E. U.S. 12, Willmar, 56201 | 320/235–3552 or 800/845–TRIP | www.willmarcvb.com.

Attractions

Kandiyohi County Historical Society Museum. The lobby looks like a train depot, and the main attraction is a real Great Northern steam locomotive. Other exhibits focus on the railroad, Dakota Indians, and pioneer life. | 610 Rte. 71NE | 320/235–1881 | Free | Mon.–Fri. 9–5.

Mr. B Chocolatier. More than 50 kinds of Belgian chocolates and Swiss truffles are churned out at this small chocolate factory. Tours are given to groups upon request. | 540 W. Benson St. | 320/235–1313 | Free | Mon.–Fri. 9–5, Sat. 9–3.

Sibley State Park. A patchwork of forest, farmland, prairie knolls, and lakes is visible below the hike-up overlook in this 3,000-acre park, which was named after Minnesota's first governor. In summer, you can swim, boat, and fish on 800-acre Lake Andrew. The park also has campgrounds, a picnic area, a modern group center, horseback camps, and interpretive programs. It is 15 mi north of Willmar, on Highway 7. | 320/354–2055 | www.dnr.state.mn.us/parks_and_recreation/state_parks/sibley | Park permit required | Daily.

ON THE CALENDAR

SEPT.: *Willmar Fall Festival.* Willmar says goodbye to summer on the third Thursday of the month. Festival highlights include hands-on arts and crafts demonstrations, food vendors, and a petting zoo. | 320/231–0403.

Dining

Edinbary's Restaurant and Lounge. American. Casual by day and candlelit by night, this specializes in healthy dishes such as broccoli Benedict and vegetarian Alfredo. Kids' menu. | 701 Rte. 71N | 320/235–7862 | $9–$15 | AE, MC, V.

Frieda's Cafe. American. In business for more than six decades, this downtown diner is Willmar's oldest eatery. Open for breakfast and lunch only, it is known for huge buttermilk pancakes. | 511 W. Benson Ave. | 320/235–2865 | Breakfast also available. No dinner. Closed Sun. | $4–$5 | No credit cards.

McMillan's. American. Hanging lamps and nature photographs surround you as you order your grilled chicken sandwich or chicken Alfredo. The all-day breakfast is very popular, especially the Belgian waffles. Kids' menu. | 2620 S. First St. | 320/235–7213 | Breakfast also available | $6–$9 | AE, D, MC, V.

Lodging

AmericInn. Next to the Willmar Convention Center, this motel is one block west of the intersection of routes 12 and 17. Complimentary Continental breakfast. Cable TV. Pool. Hot tub. Business services. | 2404 U.S. 12E | 320/231–1962 or 800/634–3444 | fax 320/231–1962 | www.AmericInn.com/minnesota/willmar.html | 30 rooms | $75–$90 | AE, D, DC, MC, V.

Buchanan House Bed and Breakfast. Wicker furniture and pastel colors decorate the rooms in this two-story home. There is an gazebo surrounded by a deck in the backyard. Complimentary breakfast, dining room. No room phones, some in-room hot tubs. Hot tub. No TV. Library. No kids under 12. | 725 5th St. | 320/235–7308 | davidjea@willmar.com | www.thebuchananhousebandb.com | 3 rooms | $89–$99 | MC, V.

Colonial Inn. Across the street from several restaurants, this motel is on a lively thoroughfare two blocks south of downtown. In-room data ports, microwaves, refrigerators, some in-room hot tubs. Cable TV. Pets allowed. | 1102 S. 1st St. | 320/235–3567 or 800/396–4444 | 19 rooms, 3 suites | $42, $69–$89 suites | AE, D, MC, V.

Days Inn. The Civic Center is ¼ mi north of this stucco motel at the junction of routes 71 and 12 and the Route 23 bypass. Complimentary Continental breakfast. Some in-room hot tubs. Cable TV. Hot tub. Exercise equipment. Some pets allowed. | 225 28th St. SE | 320/231–1275 | www.torgersonproperties.com/daysinnwillmar/index.html | 59 rooms | $43–$54 | AE, D, DC, MC, V.

Holiday Inn. Visible from Highway 71, this 4–story hotel is 1 mi east of downtown. Restaurant, bar, room service. In-room data ports. Cable TV. Pool, wading pool. Hot tub. Business services. Some pets allowed. | 2100 U.S. 12E | 320/235–6060 | fax 320/235–4731 | www.TorgersonProperties.com | 98 rooms | $85–$95 | AE, D, DC, MC, V.

Super 8. This hotel is 1 mi from the Willmar lakes area, on the south edge of town. Cable TV. Business services. Some pets allowed. | 2655 1st St. S | 320/235–7260 | fax 320/235–5580 | www.super8.com | 60 rooms | $37–$55 | AE, D, MC, V.

WINONA

MAP 3, G9

(Nearby towns also listed: Preston, Rochester, Wabasha)

Established by a steamboat captain in 1851, on an island in the Mississippi River which, in time, became connected to the shore, Winona is in southeast Minnesota. Its name is taken from the Dakota Sioux word for "firstborn daughter." Within two years of its founding, Winona was a full-fledged river town, the last dockage for immigrants— many of them German or Polish—traveling upstream and then heading west to make homes. The steamboat era is still reflected in the city's buildings, and in its ongoing relationship with the river.

Information: Winona Convention and Visitors Bureau | 67 Main St., Winona, 55987 | 507/452–2272 or 800/657–4972 | www.visitwinona.com.

Attractions

Julius C. Wilkie Steamboat Center. This full-size steamboat replica houses a museum and a collection of miniature steamboats. It's at Levee Park, between Walnut and Johnson Sts. on the Mississippi River. | 507/454–1254 | www.winonanet.com/visitors/welcome.html | Free | June–Oct., Tues.–Sun. 10–4.

Prairie Island Park and Nature Trail. Half of this municipal park is maintained in near-pristine condition, and has a 1-mi interpretive nature trail which stops by an enclosed deer park, a flood-plain forest, and an observation deck overlooking a Mississippi River backwater slough. Also in the park are a visitors center, boat launches, picnic and camping areas, and playgrounds. | 1120 Curry Island Rd. | 507/452–8550 | Free | Daily.

Upper Mississippi River National Wildlife and Fish Refuge. Extending 261 mi along the Mississippi River, from the Chippewa River in Wisconsin almost to Rock Island, Illinois, this is the longest wildlife refuge in the continental U.S., providing habitat for huge numbers of plants, fish, migratory birds, and other animals. | 51 E. 4th St. | 507/452–4232 | www.emtc.nbs.gov/umr_refuge.html | Free | Daily.

Winona County Historical Society Museum. Housed in a former armory, the museum has extensive historical archives, plus exhibits on Native Americans, logging and lumbering, steamboats, transportation, and pioneer life. | 160 Johnson St. | 507/454–2723 | www.winona.msus.edu/historicalsociety | $3 | Daily.

Maintained by the Historical Society, **Bunnell House** is an example of rural Gothic architecture. It's built of northern white pine and contains furniture and objects from the mid- to late 1800s. Guides walk you through three floors of pioneer life, describing the era when Native American canoes gave way to steamboats and game-trails became roads and highways for Euro-Americans. Bunnell House is 5 mi downriver from Winona, off Highway 61, in Homer. | 507/452–7575 | www.winona.msus.edu/historicalsociety/sites/bunnell.asp | Free | Memorial Day–Labor Day, Wed.–Sat. 10–5, Sun. 1–5.

ON THE CALENDAR

MAR.: *Eagle Watch Weekend.* Naturalists' lectures, at the Quality Inn on Makato Ave., precede a bus ride along the Mississippi River, during which you can see bald eagles in the midst of their migration. | 800/657–4972.

JULY: *Winona Steamboat Days.* The July 4 week brings fireworks, a carnival, a parade, and a food fair. | 800/657–4972.

SEPT.: *Victorian Fair.* Craftspeople ply their trades in an old-time setting with music, food, and festivities. | 507/454–2723.

Dining

Beier's Family Food and Cocktails. American. On the west end of town, this casual spot serves breakfast until 3 PM and has a daily soup and salad bar, plus a popular prime rib sandwich. | 405 Cottonwood Rd. | 507/452–3390 | Breakfast also available | $7–$10 | AE, D, DC, MC, V.

Lodging

Best Western Riverport Inn. This full-service facility is right in town, at the junction of Highways 61 and 43. Restaurant, bar, complimentary Continental breakfast, room service. Some refrigerators. Cable TV. Pool. Hot tub. Some pets allowed (fee). | 900 Bruski Dr. | 507/452–0606 | fax 507/457–6489 | www.bestwestern.com | 106 rooms | $56–$99 | AE, D, DC, MC, V.

Days Inn. Downtown is ¼ mi east of this two-story hotel off Route 14, one block south of the intersection of routes 14 and 61. Complimentary Continental breakfast. Cable TV. | 420 Cottonwood Dr. | 507/454–6930 | fax 507/454–7917 | www.daysinn.com | 58 rooms | $40–$70 | AE, D, DC, MC, V.

Quality Inn. A half mile south of downtown, this 35-year old motel is among the area's oldest structures. Restaurant, bar, room service. Cable TV. Pool. Hot tub. | 956 Mankato Ave. | 507/454–4390 | fax 507/452–2187 | winquin@luminet.net | www.choicehotels.com | 112 rooms | $60–$95 | AE, D, DC, MC, V.

Sterling. This is a drive-up-to-your-room motel on the west side of town. Cable TV. | 1450 Gilmore | 507/454–1120 or 800/452–1235 | 32 rooms | $36–$49 | AE, D, DC, MC, V.

Sugar Loaf Motel. Surrounded by trees at the foot of one of the area's taller peaks, this single-story motel is 3 mi south of downtown. A snowmobiling/hiking trail starts on the property. Some microwaves, some refrigerators. Cable TV. Pets allowed (fee). | 1066 Homer Rd. | 507/452–1491 | fax 507/452–5334 | 20 rooms | $35–$75 | AE, D, DC, MC, V.

Super 8. Three mi south of town, this hotel is 2 mi southeast of the Mississippi River. Complimentary Continental breakfast. Cable TV. | 1025 Sugarloaf Rd. | 507/454–6066 | fax 507/454–6066 | www.super8.com | 61 rooms | $43–$63 | AE, D, DC, MC, V.

TOP TIPS FOR TRAVELERS

Smart Sightseeings

Don't plan your visit in your hotel room. Don't wait until you pull into town to decide how to spend your days. It's inevitable that there will be much more to see and do than you'll have time for: choose sights in advance.

Organize your touring. Note the places that most interest you on a map, and visit places that are near each other during the same morning or afternoon.

Start the day well equipped. Leave your hotel in the morning with everything you need for the day—maps, medicines, extra film, your guidebook, rain gear, and another layer of clothing in case the weather turns cooler.

Tour museums early. If you're there when the doors open you'll have an intimate experience of the collection.

Easy does it. See museums in the mornings, when you're fresh, and visit sit-down attractions later on. Take breaks before you need them.

Strike up a conversation. Only curmudgeons don't respond to a smile and a polite request for information. Most people appreciate your interest in their home town. And your conversations may end up being your most vivid memories.

Get lost. When you do, you never know what you'll find—but you can count on it being memorable. Use your guidebook to help you get back on track. Build wandering-around time into every day.

Quit before you're tired. There's no point in seeing that one extra sight if you're too exhausted to enjoy it.

Take your mother's advice. Go to the bathroom when you have the chance. You never know what lies ahead.

Hotel How-Tos

How to get a deal. After you've chosen a likely candidate or two, phone them directly and price a room for your travel dates. Then call the hotel's toll-free number and ask the same questions. Also try consolidators and hotel-room discounters. You won't hear the same rates twice. On the spot, make a reservation as soon as you are quoted a price you want to pay.

Promises, promises. If you have special requests, make them when you reserve. Get written confirmation of any promises.

Settle in. Upon arriving, make sure everything works—lights and lamps, TV and radio, sink, tub, shower, and anything else that matters. Report any problems immediately. And don't wait until you need extra pillows or blankets or an ironing board to call housekeeping. Also check out the fire emergency instructions. Know where to find the fire exits, and make sure your companions do, too.

If you need to complain. Be polite but firm. Explain the problem to the person in charge. Suggest a course of action. If you aren't satisfied, repeat your requests to the manager. Document everything: Take pictures and keep a written record of who you've spoken with, when, and what was said. Contact your travel agent, if he made the reservations.

Know the score. When you go out, take your hotel's business cards (one for everyone in your party). If you have extras, you can give them out to new acquaintances who want to call you.

Tip up front. For special services, a tip or partial tip in advance can work wonders.

Use all the hotel resources A concierge can make difficult things easy. But a desk clerk, bellhop, or other hotel employee who's friendly, smart, and ambitious can often steer you straight as well. A gratuity is in order if the advice is helpful.

Nebraska

Nebraska has everything from city sophistication to country charm. There are places so rugged and wild they still conjure images of the Old West frontier, and there are cosmopolitan cities that offer almost any choice in the way of culture and the arts. The terrain varies from the rolling hill country along the Missouri River, where foliage is lush and varied, to the grasslands of the Sandhills, to the Panhandle's rough breaks with their bluffs and buttes. The Platte River flows east to west, and climatic changes occur in the vicinity of the 100th meridian, which runs north to south approximately midway through the state. At the 100th meridian, the humid climate of the Midwest or East gives way to the arid conditions of the West.

Traveling across Nebraska on I–80, the land seems rather flat and the scenery monotonous, but if you divert yourself from the fast interstate highway and take U.S. 30—the first transcontinental highway and known as the Lincoln Highway—you'll begin to discover the charm that exists in Nebraska. On the Lincoln Highway are small towns like Gothenburg, Sidney, and Kimball, and cities like Fremont, Columbus, Grand Island, and Kearney. Of course you'll pass by most of those same places when driving I–80—but the key phrase is "pass by." In most cases, you'd have to make a conscious decision to stop at any of those towns if you are traveling the interstate; on U.S. 30, you'll naturally drive right through them and learn for yourself the friendliness of Nebraskans whenever you stop. Other routes across the state provide equal opportunity to experience the variety that is Nebraska, as well as to meet some of the people who live here.

There is great ethnic diversity here, created in part by the homesteading emigrants of the latter portion of the 1800s and early 1900s. Thus, Nebraska has an "Irish Capital" (O'Neill), a "Czech Capital" (Wilber), and a "Danish Capital" (Dannebrog). This is a state where you can still find a hamburger for a couple of bucks, and where a fried

CAPITAL: LINCOLN	POPULATION: 1,578,385	AREA: 77,355 SQUARE MI
BORDERS: KS, CO, WY, SD, IA, MO	TIME ZONES: CENTRAL AND MOUNTAIN	POSTAL ABBREVIATION: NE
WEB SITE: WWW.VISITNEBRASKA.ORG		

chicken dinner is likely to be served family-style: with a platter of chicken, a bowl of potatoes, and pitcher of gravy.

The wealth of wildlife—particularly waterfowl—will astound you at times, especially during the great spring migrations of sandhill cranes as they travel through the Central Flyway. A state declared part of the "Great American Desert" by government explorer Stephen Long in 1820 today actually has 23,000 mi of rivers and streams and 246 public lakes and reservoirs that also attract an estimated 10 million ducks and 2 million snow geese—and water recreation enthusiasts who like to fish or float.

This is the only state in the nation with a unicameral legislature (with a single legislative chamber), and it is a place where some great literary talents received their early inspiration, including Willa Cather, Mari Sandoz, and John Neihardt, who brought to the world the vision of Oglala (Sioux) holy man Black Elk in his classic *Black Elk Speaks*.

The only completely man-made National Forest in the country is in Nebraska, created by people who wanted to bring trees to the treeless plains, an outgrowth, no doubt, of the efforts of Nebraskan J. Sterling Morton, who is recognized as the "father" of Arbor Day, the national tree-planting holiday that started here as a state celebration in 1872.

Driving almost any road except I–80, you will undoubtedly experience what is known as the "Nebraska Wave." It varies and can be the "V" of two fingers held up, a head nod, thumb waggle, or a one-finger (index, not middle) salute. Any one of those signs is simply Nebraskans' way of saying "howdy." It doesn't matter that the driver waving doesn't know you and may never even see you again; the wave is just a friendly acknowledgment that you're sharing a road in a big state, where sometimes there won't be another car for miles.

History

Nebraska was initially populated by the Pawnee nation, Native Americans whose origins date back to the 1200s. Early in the 19th century, there were more than 10,000 Pawnees along the North Platte River. They unwillingly began to cede their lands to the U.S. Government in 1833 and were completely relocated to what is now known as Pawnee County by 1875.

French explorers and later traders made early claims to the region encompassing Nebraska. The earliest documented explorations in Nebraska took place in 1714 and 1720, when Spanish explorer Don Pedro de Villasur made his way across the area, ultimately confronting the Pawnee (and perhaps a few French traders) in the vicinity of present-day Columbus. The mighty river that bisects the region was at one point named the Shell River by the Lakota and the Nebraskier River by the French explorer Étienne de Bourgmont. It was renamed the Platte River (as in *plate*) by the Canadian brothers Pierre and Paul Mallet, who in 1836 led a French expedition from Canada to establish a trade route to Santa Fe.

In 1804 Meriwether Lewis and William Clark, along with their Corps of Discovery, made their epic exploratory journey of the Louisiana Purchase territory, which included

NE Timeline	8000 BC	1675	1720	1730
	Paleo-Indians cross the Bering Strait and migrate to the Great Plains.	French traders first encounter Pawnee villages along the Republican River.	French traders and Pawnee allies attack the Spanish explorer Pedro de Villasur and his troops near Columbus.	The Kiowa migrate into northwestern Nebraska, eventually becoming the Kiowa Apaches.

parts of Nebraska. Lewis and Clark had campsites at various spots along the Missouri River, and they participated in the first "council" between the western Native American tribes and the United States at a bluff area in the vicinity of today's Omaha.

By the early 1800s, fur traders—variously representing Spain, France, and the United States—moved into the region near where the Platte and Missouri rivers converge. In 1806, American Lieutenant Zebulon Pike, searching for a route to Santa Fe from St. Louis, made his way up the Republican River across the southern portion of the present-day state. Pike met with the Pawnee and convinced them to remove the French flag flying in their village and replace it with an American flag. When Stephen Long led an American military expedition across the region in 1820, he called it "The Great American Desert," a misnomer to be certain, but one that stuck for decades.

The first great movements of European Americans into the region occurred with Oregon Trail migration that began in earnest in 1843. By 1870, when the continent was linked from east to west by the Union Pacific Railroad, more than 400,000 emigrants had traveled across Nebraska en route not only to Oregon, but also to California and Utah. Travel by Mormons to Utah started in 1847, while the California Gold Rush began in 1849.

Until 1854, when the Nebraska Territory was created, travelers were moving through Native American country claimed by a number of tribes, including the Omaha, Osage, Ponca, Otoe, Missouria, Pawnee, Sauk, Fox, and Kansas in the eastern portion of today's state, and the Arapaho, Cheyenne, Comanche, Kiowa, and Lakota (Sioux) in the western areas. Today, there are several small reservations in Nebraska.

With the passing of the Kansas-Nebraska Act of 1854 and the granting of territorial status in the emotionally charged climate prior to the Civil War, Nebraska entered the United States as a "free" state, which made it an important location during the years leading up to and during the Civil War. Slaves attempting to escape bondage needed only to cross the Missouri River from Missouri, or the border from Kansas, which entered the United States as a "slave" state under the same act, to find freedom. As a result, several areas in eastern Nebraska became important stops along the Underground Railroad.

Two extremely significant pieces of national legislation forever changed Nebraska Territory in 1862: The Homestead Act and the Pacific Railway Act. The first led to settlement of the plains regions, including the land in present-day Nebraska, and the second led to construction of the Union Pacific Railroad and telegraph line, extending from the Missouri River to the Pacific Ocean.

In 1867, Nebraska Territory became the present-day state, and a battle for the location of the state capital raged between people living north of the Platte, "the North Platters," and those living south of the river, "the South Platters." Although the early, short-lived capitals were in Bellevue and later in Florence, the permanent capital was established at Lancaster, a town developing south of the Platte in a salt-producing region. Its name was quickly changed to Lincoln. Though the region along the Missouri River

1795	1803		1803	1804
James Mackay opens the first fur-trading post in Nebraska near Bellevue.	The Sioux move into northwestern Nebraska, forcing the Kiowa Apaches, the Crow, and the Cheyenne out of the region. The Cheyenne form alliances with the Sioux, however, and	remain in the Black Hills and farther west, eventually living near the Sioux.	On April 30, the United States acquires Nebraska Territory through the Louisiana Purchase.	Meriwether Lewis and William Clark explore the Louisiana Territory; they return in 1806 on their way back to St. Louis from the Oregon coast.

and in the vicinity of Bellevue, Florence, and Omaha has always had a larger population base, Lincoln has maintained its status as the state's capital, and it is now also the home of the University of Nebraska.

While the Homestead and Pacific Railway acts spurred settlement and development, irrigation from the state's many rivers quickly established it as a major crop-production area and agriculture center. The rivers also served as major routes and shipment points for cattle herded in from Texas in the 1870s. Some of the major industries in the state even today relate to livestock production and processing, or to agricultural practices—ranging from companies that feed and slaughter beef to those that build pivot sprinkler systems.

World War I (1914–18) proved very lucrative for Nebraska's farmers, but their luck ran out during the Great Depression. The downturn in the national economy, along with local droughts and dust storms, substantially reduced crop prices and yields. The federal government assisted by building reservoirs and dams and expanding irrigation. Over the subsequent 50 years, the amount of irrigated land in the state increased nearly ninefold. Then, in the 1980s Nebraska suffered yet another economic collapse. Even federal farm subsidies failed to prevent land values and crop prices from plummeting. Many farmers were forced into bankruptcy, and it wasn't until the end of the decade that other industries, such as tourism, health care, insurance, and telecommunications, began to stabilize the economy.

Today, there are almost 100 state parks and recreation areas in Nebraska, including Fort Kearny, Fort Robinson, and the ranch of William F. Cody (the impresario also known as Buffalo Bill). There is an abundance of natural attractions, historic sites, and monuments. Cultural oases include Omaha's Joslyn Art Museum, Omaha Magic Theatre, the Oregon Trail Museum at Scotts Bluff National Monument, which displays a collection of 63 paintings by the artist William Henry Jackson, and the Nebraska Museum of History and the Sheldon Memorial Art Gallery in Lincoln.

Regions

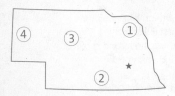

1. NORTHEASTERN NEBRASKA

Northeastern Nebraska is bordered on the north and east by the Missouri River and on the south by the Platte River and stretches west to just beyond Highway 281. The southeastern quarter of this region is the state's most densely populated area and includes the Omaha metropolitan area, as well as such other communities as Fremont, Columbus, Blair, Wayne, Grand Island, and Norfolk. The closer you are to the Missouri River, the more hills and vegetation you will encounter and the more humid the climate will be. This is a region tied to agricultural production along the Elkhorn River.

1806	1812	1815	1819	1819–20
Zebulon Pike crosses through southeast Nebraska en route to Santa Fe, meeting with the Pawnee near Guide Rock.	Manuel Lisa opens a fur-trading post at Bellevue, later known as Fort Lisa.	Omaha Native Americans negotiate their first treaty with the U.S. government at Portage des Sioux.	The U.S. military establishes Cantonment Missouri (later Fort Atkinson) as their first western outpost.	Major Stephen Long launches his exploration of the western country and reaches Nebraska in the steamboat *Western Engineer*. He calls the area "The Great American Desert."

INTRODUCTION
HISTORY
REGIONS
WHEN TO VISIT
STATE'S GREATS
RULES OF THE ROAD
DRIVING TOURS

Towns listed: Ashland, Bancroft, Bellevue, Blair, Columbus, Crofton, Dannebrog, Fremont, Grand Island, Neligh, Norfolk, Omaha, Royal, St. Paul, South Sioux City, Wayne, West Point, York.

2. SOUTHERN NEBRASKA

Southern Nebraska constitutes the region south of the Platte River and really consists of two halves—east and west. The section from the Missouri River west to the Little Blue River has rolling countryside, lush vegetation, and a humid climate. River towns, including Plattsmouth, Nebraska City, Brownville, and the state capital of Lincoln, as well as the communities of Beatrice and Wilber, are in this part of the region. From the Little Blue extending west to the Colorado border, the climate becomes increasingly drier and the land flatter. This is the land crossed by the Oregon and California trails, and you can still see wagon ruts from Rock Creek Station near Fairbury to Fort Kearny and then along the Platte River to Ogallala. Some of the interesting and important communities in this area are Fairbury, Wilber, Hastings, Minden, McCook, and Red Cloud.

Towns listed: Auburn, Beatrice, Brownville, Eustis, Fairbury, Hastings, Lincoln, McCook, Minden, Nebraska City, Plattsmouth, Red Cloud, Wilber.

3. THE SANDHILLS

The vast diamond-shape area of Nebraska known as the Sandhills is a geological wonder. It is a place of rolling hills made almost entirely of sand held in place by a carpet of tough prairie grasses. As such, it is an important cattle- and bison-ranch region. Bordered roughly by U.S. 281 in the east, the Platte River in the south, Route 61 in the west, and South Dakota in the north, the Sandhills have fewer residents, roads, and communities than any other portion of Nebraska, even though this is the largest region of the state. It is a place to experience the quiet of the prairie and to appreciate the wonders of nature—ranging from the hand-planted Nebraska National Forest to the many natural lakes and the abundant wildlife. The primary roads crossing the Sandhills from east to west are Route 2 and U.S. 20, while the major north-south roads are U.S. 281, 183, and 83, and Routes 97 and 61.

Towns listed: Broken Bow, Burwell, Cozad, Gothenburg, Kearney, Lexington, North Platte, Ogallala, O'Neill, Thedford, Valentine.

4. THE PANHANDLE

Bordered by Colorado in the south, Wyoming to the west, South Dakota in the north, and Route 61 in the east, the Nebraska Panhandle more closely resembles its neighboring states than it does the rest of Nebraska. The country here shifts from prairie in the south to high plains in the north as buttes, bluffs, and the rough breaks of the Black Hills appear in the northwestern corner. In addition to grass, you'll find sagebrush and prickly pear cactus. There are dozens of tiny natural lakes in the eastern portion

1828	**1833**	**1837**	**1841**	**1843**
Hiram Scott dies near the bluff that now bears his name.	The Pawnee enter their first treaty with the U.S. government.	Alfred Jacob Miller sketches Chimney Rock, probably the first artist to do so.	The Bidwell–Bartleson wagon train crosses the plains, carrying the first emigrants on the Oregon Trail.	Oregon migration begins; during the next 30 years, more than 400,000 emigrants cross Nebraska en route to Oregon and California.

of the region. The Oregon, California, and Mormon Trails followed the North Platte River through here from 1843 to 1869, while the Sidney–Deadwood Trail made its way from Sidney to the Black Hills during the gold rush there in the mid-1870s.

Towns listed: Alliance, Bayard, Bridgeport, Chadron, Crawford, Gering, Harrison, Kimball, Scottsbluff, Sidney.

When to Visit

The best time to visit Nebraska is in the spring and fall, when temperatures and humidity levels—particularly in the eastern half of the state—are more moderate than at other times of the year. Be aware, however, that Nebraska lies in "tornado alley," a region in the central part of the United States where significant numbers of tornadoes occur each year from late April through early June. Pay attention to warning sirens (and rapidly building dark clouds) and take cover when dire weather threatens. Even when tornadoes don't develop, major thunderstorms can pound the area, dumping several inches of rain in the span of a few hours and causing lowland flooding.

Many museums and attractions are open only during the high season from Memorial Day to Labor Day, but many do have extended hours during the summer, and you will seldom have difficulty finding a place to stay or eat.

Though you likely won't encounter snow and ice in the late spring or early fall, you almost certainly will at times in the winter, and the fringe seasons of early spring and late fall. Driving across Nebraska during a plains blizzard is extremely dangerous, so watch the weather forecast and spend an extra day wherever you are rather than venturing out into such weather.

If you must drive in the winter, be sure to have winter survival gear in your vehicle, including (at a minimum) a sleeping bag or blankets, water, food, and a flashlight. A cell phone is a good idea, especially in the Sandhills, where it can be many miles between towns and there will be little traffic under the best of conditions. Most important, if at all possible, tell somebody when you're leaving, when you should arrive at your destination, and your route.

CLIMATE CHART
Average Temperatures (°F) and Monthly Precipitation (in inches)

	JAN.	FEB.	MAR.	APR.	MAY	JUNE
NORTHEAST	20.9	26	34.7	47.4	58.2	65.7
	.43	.55	1.39	2.15	3.37	3.53

	JULY	AUG.	SEPT.	OCT.	NOV.	DEC.
	74.2	71.8	61.6	50.1	35.1	23.8
	3.20	2.57	2.05	1.24	.87	.57

1846	1847	1849	1854	
Brigham Young and the first of the Mormons cross the Missouri River and establish winter quarters at Florence.	Mormon migration from winter quarters to Utah begins.	Thousands of gold seekers follow the California Trail.	On March 15–16, in exchange for two reservations, the Otoe, Missouria, and Omaha Native Americans cede lands west of the Missouri River, opening most of eastern Nebraska	to white settlement.

	JAN.	FEB.	MAR.	APR.	MAY	JUNE
SOUTHEAST	23	28.3	39.4	52.1	62.8	72.4
	.61	.78	2.21	2.71	4.16	4.10

	JULY	AUG.	SEPT.	OCT.	NOV.	DEC.
	77.4	74.7	65.7	54.3	39.9	27
	3.54	3.69	3.70	2.25	1.34	.94

	JAN.	FEB.	MAR.	APR.	MAY	JUNE
CENTRAL	21.6	27	36.5	49.2	59.8	69.7
	.41	.67	1.81	2.42	3.80	4.07

	JULY	AUG.	SEPT.	OCT.	NOV.	DEC.
	75.1	72.4	62.7	51.1	36.3	24.7
	3.18	2.83	2.52	1.61	1.02	.71

	JAN.	FEB.	MAR.	APR.	MAY	JUNE
PANHANDLE	23.3	28.2	35.1	45.5	55.5	65.7
	.37	.38	.99	1.75	3.12	2.90

	JULY	AUG.	SEPT.	OCT.	NOV.	DEC.
	72.6	70.2	60	48.5	34.9	25.2
	2.50	1.62	1.34	.85	.52	.41

FESTIVALS AND SEASONAL EVENTS
WINTER

Nov.–Dec. **Holidays in the Haymarket.** On the Fridays between Thanksgiving and Christmas, you'll find music and dancing, along with visits from Santa Claus, in Lincoln's historic district. | 402/435–7496.

The Light of the World Christmas Pageant. Minden's annual pageant is 60 years old now, but still a favorite way for many Nebraskans to begin their holiday season. The performances are held at 7 PM November 24th and December 2nd and 9th outdoors in the town square and end with the lighting of 10,000 Christmas lights. | 308/832–1811.

Feb. **ABATE Lincoln Motorcycle Show.** Hundreds of motorcycle enthusiasts journey to Lincoln for this annual event at the State Fairgrounds. | 402/434–5348.

Feb.–Apr. **Sandhill Crane Migration.** More than 400,000 sandhill cranes migrate up the Central Flyway from Mexico to Canada, stopping along the Platte River in central Nebraska for several weeks to feed and rest. You'll find many sites for watching

1854	1854	1857	1860	1860–61
On May 30, Congress approves the Kansas-Nebraska Act, establishing Nebraska Territory. The Kansas-Nebraska Act repeals the 1820 Missouri Compromise.	Richard Brown crosses the Missouri and starts the town of Brownville; Bellevue and Omaha are already founded.	On September 24, Pawnees sign away the last of their land in Nebraska in the Table Rock Treaty in Nebraska City; they move to a reservation at Genoa.	Congress approves a subsidy for development of a telegraph line from western Missouri to San Francisco.	William Russell, Alexander Majors, and William Waddell of Nebraska City start the Pony Express.

them eat during the day, then fly into their nighttime retreats, and tours and viewing bunkers are available. If you really get into crane-viewing or are a photo bug, you can spend the night with the big birds in the photography blinds right at the roosting sites at the Audubon Society's Rowe Bird Sanctuary—but you cannot leave between 5 PM and 8 AM the next morning. For general information, call: Kearney Visitors Bureau, 308/237–3101 or 800/652–9435; Grand Island Visitors Bureau, 308/382–4400 or 800/658–3178; Crane Meadows Nature Center, 308/382–1820; Rowe Bird Sanctuary, 308/468–5282.

SPRING

Mar.   **St. Patrick's Day Celebration.** In O'Neill, the Irish Capital of Nebraska, events include a fun run, parade, Irish dancing, food, kids' games, and an art show. | 402/336–2355.

May   **Willa Cather Festival.** You can view films made from the books and stories of Willa Cather, then tour the region where those same stories are set, as well as attend discussions of the works of this Nebraska author. Events take place in Red Cloud at the Willa Cather Pioneer Memorial. | 406/746–2653.

Spring Fling Antique Flea Market. Many people—and many antiques dealers—begin their summer by coming to Lexington for the Memorial Day weekend antiques flea market at the Dawson County Fair Grounds off Highway 283. | 308/987–2633 or 308/324–5504.

Lady Vestey Victorian Festival. In the town of Superior, about 25 mi from Red Cloud, Lady Vestey time means a look at earlier times with tours of Victorian homes and an old-fashioned teas—or you can take your pleasure the more modern way, with driving tours, a carnival, and entertainment. | 402/879–3419.

May and Sept.   **Annual Spring and Fall Flea Markets.** You may find treasures; you may find only what you'd call trash, but the hunt is the thing at the Brownville Historical Society's flea markets that now have been going on for more than 40 years. Most of the action is on Brownville's Main Street. | 402/825–4131.

SUMMER

June   **Annual Homestead Days.** This historical celebration in Beatrice includes a kids' parade, tractor pull, crafts show, music,

1862	1862	1867	1868	
President Abraham Lincoln signs the Pacific Railway Act, leading to construction of the Union Pacific Railroad across Nebraska.	Congress approves the Homestead Act; the first homestead in the nation claimed under the act is that of Daniel Freeman, which is now part of Homestead National Monument near Beatrice.	On March 1, Nebraska becomes a state; Lincoln becomes its permanent capital.	The Sioux agree to a treaty at Fort Laramie that stipulates they will receive annuities distributed to them along the North Platte River; later they receive goods along the White	River in northeastern Nebraska. Agencies are set up to collect the annuities.

INTRODUCTION
HISTORY
REGIONS
WHEN TO VISIT
STATE'S GREATS
RULES OF THE ROAD
DRIVING TOURS

and demonstrations of native crafts, plus a land-records symposium for those trying to build their own family tree. | 402/223–3514.

Grundlovsfest. The annual Danish Days festival in Dannebrog recognizes the area's heritage with ethnic dancers, Danish foods, melodrama, art show, antiques show, and parade. | 308/226–2237.

Nebraskaland Days. This four-day extravaganza has options for almost any taste, from cowboy poetry and country and western music to concerts, art shows, and ethnic foods, the state rodeo in the Wild West Arena opposite Buffalo Bill Cody's old ranch, the Miss Nebraska pageant, and other events all over North Platte. | 308/532–7939.

Rock Creek Trail Days. The buffalo stew the westward-heading settlers made was probably a great break from the dry fare of most of their meals. You can sample a modern version at the annual buffalo stew cookout during this festival, when Fairbury sets up a crafts show, living-history demos, and an entertainment site on the path of the Oregon Trail. | 402/729–3000.

South Central Nebraska Czech Festival. One of several areas settled by Czech immigrants, Hastings remembers its past with a rollicking festival of ethnic foods, entertainment, and lots of dancing, at the VFW Post. | 402/462–6775 or 800/967–2189.

Sugar Valley Rally. This antique car rally in Scottsbluff features races of pre-1952 automobiles utilizing a computerized course. Drivers travel more than 300 mi in the Nebraska panhandle. | 308/632–2133.

Summer Arts Festival. More than 175 visual artists participate in this Omaha festival that also includes live entertainment and an assortment of ethnic foods from Italian to Chinese. | 402/963–9020.

Wurst Tag. The polka music makes a lively background beat to this celebration of Eustis's German heritage with a volksmarch, road race, displays, ethnic foods, pretzel and sausage contests, and a street dance, all outdoors on Main Street the second Saturday of June. | 308/486–5615 or 308/486–3611.

1869	1869	1872	1877	1878
The first Texas cattle ship to market on the Union Pacific Railroad from Schuyler, Nebraska.	The University of Nebraska gets its charter. It opens in Lincoln in 1871.	The Nebraska State Department of Agriculture approves Arbor Day as a holiday.	On September 5, a sentry at Fort Robinson stabs and kills Lakota Chief Crazy Horse.	On November 27, homesteaders Ami Ketchum and Luther Mitchell shoot and kill cattleman Bob Olive in the first deadly encounter between homesteaders and cattlemen in

July   **Nebraska's Big Rodeo.** Phones in towns miles away start ring-
        ing in March as people seek rooms for this professionally
        sanctioned rodeo in Burwell the last weekend in July. Now 80
        years old, it draws about 15,000–20,000 to the traditional
        slate of contests from calf roping to bulldogging and bronc
        riding, chuck wagon races, and much, much more. | 888/328–
        7935 or 308/346–5121.

        Oregon Trail Days. You can revisit the past at a historical play,
        but this four-day festival in Gering also has a range of other
        activities, including a Western art show, international food
        fair, quilt show, lots of music and dance events, a 5-mi run,
        and the state championship chili cookoff. | 308/436–4457.

        Old West Trail PRCA Rodeo. Before the professional rodeo
        cowboys do their thing in two nights of sanctioned tradi-
        tional riding and roping competitions, the kids get a turn in
        the spotlight with their own gymkana on Thursday night. The
        annual 4th of July weekend event in Crawford also includes
        fireworks and a dance. | 308/665–1400 or 308/665–2800.

Aug.   **Kool-Aid Days.** The drink mix nearly every kid loves was cre-
        ated in the town of Hastings, and the city celebrates with the
        "world's largest Kool-Aid stand," exhibits, and games. | 800/
        967–2189.

        Neihardt Day. This tribute to the famed Nebraska poet com-
        bines serious workshops with lighter musical and artistic pre-
        sentations celebrating his literary works on Native Americans.
        It's all outdoors at Bancroft's Neihardt Center. | 888/777–4667
        or 402/648–3388.

        Wilber Czech Festival. You can attend serious presentations
        about the Czech culture, or you can just go and share all the
        fun of the clogging, costumes, parade, food, and many other
        activities in Wilber, the "Czech Capital of Nebraska" and of the
        USA. | 888/494–5237.

        Greater Siouxland Fair and Rodeo. This week-long annual
        event is both a sporting event for rodeo fans and a fair where
        everyone can enjoy a parade, musical entertainment, a carni-
        val, or just eating lots of food. | 402/494–5522.

Aug.–Sept. **Nebraska State Fair.**The state's big fair runs for 11 days and
        has exhibits of crafts and livestock, a kids' zone and a midway,
        and NASCAR auto racing, as well as some top-name enter-
        tainment, at Lincoln's State Fair Park. | 402/473–4109.

		1880s	1872	1881
Nebraska. Olive's brother Print leads a vigilante group that hangs Mitchell and Ketchum. Even-tually someone burns the home-steaders' bodies, and Nebraska becomes known as	the "Man Burner State."	Omaha becomes a center of livestock shipping and pro-duction processing centers.	April 22 becomes Arbor Day as the holiday spreads nationwide.	William F. Cody organizes his first Wild West Show in Columbus, Nebraska.

Sept.

Heritage Days Celebration. This hometown celebration in the downtown area of McCook, which produced three Nebraska governors and Senator George W. Norris, includes a parade, crafts and food booths, games, and entertainment. | 308/345–3200.

Annual Harvest Festival Celebration. Begun in 1941, this Gothenburg festival still recognizes the need to play after the work of the harvest. You'll find a parade, a carnival, entertainment, an art show, and food and crafts booths. | 308/537–3505.

Husker Harvest Days. More than 100,000 people from all over the world attend this agricultural show in Grand Island, the largest of its kind in the country, for live field demonstrations of irrigation machinery and other presentations on new farming technology. It's the third week of September, at the Cornhusker Army Ammunition Plant, on Husker Highway off Highway 30. | 308/382–4400.

River City Roundup. A western-heritage festival comes to the big town, Omaha, with all the fun of a pancake feed, PRCA rodeo, trail rides, western and wildlife art show, concerts, dances, food, and other activities, at Aksarben Coliseum. | 402/554–9611.

Sept.–Oct.

Living History at Arbor Lodge. What did artisans do before they had access to electricity? For a month of Sundays, you can watch re-creations of the way everyone used to live, plus Civil War programs, on the grounds of Arbor Lodge in Nebraska City. You might even want to stock up on apple cider from an 1876 Keystone cider press. | 402/873–7222.

Oct.

Oktoberfest. It's a Nebraska version of the traditional German festival, in Sidney, and you'll find lots of free entertainment, dances, food, exhibits, and a 10K run. | 308/254–5851.

Old West Days and Poetry Gathering. The town of Valentine's cowboy poetry gathering also has a bit-and-spur show, mountain man rendezvous, and powwow, plus a melodrama, quilt show, trail ride, and parade. | 800/658–4024.

World Famous Ugly Pickup Parade and Contest. The main event at this competition and parade in Chadron is to determine who has the ugliest farm pickup, in several categories, but there's also the crowning of "Miss Ugly PU" and a chili cook-off. | 308/432–4401.

1881	1896	1902	1917	1931
On May 11, a wayward soldier kills Second Lieutenant Samuel A. Cherry, whose name is now associated with Cherry County, the largest of Nebraska's counties.	William Jennings Bryan of Lincoln, "The Great Commoner," is the Democratic candidate for U.S. President.	President Theodore Roosevelt creates the Nebraska National Forest, a completely manmade preserve.	Father Edward Flanagan starts Boys Town near Omaha.	Sioux holy man Black Elk shares his vision with John Neihardt, who writes the classic *Black Elk Speaks*.

State's Greats

Forests and Parks

Limestone bluffs, open ranges, and hand-planted cedar and pine trees interweave into a dramatic landscape for hiking in the 90,000 acres of the **Nebraska National Forest,** which officially also includes the Oglala Grasslands, Pine Ridge National Recreation Area, and other lands in both Nebraska and South Dakota in its jurisdiction. The **Eugene T. Mahoney State Park** is jam-packed with recreational opportunities, ranging from swimming in a complex complete with water slides and a theater to miniature golf, camping, and an RV park. **Lake McConaughy State Recreation Area,** nicknamed (of course) Big Mac, has 100 mi or shoreline and recreational facilities around nearly 36,000 acres of water where fishermen have caught the kind of record-size fish they dream of. **Indian Cave State Park,** set in the bluffs overlooking the Missouri River, is a popular place for hiking and camping, as well as cross-country skiing and sledding. **Ponca State Park** offers a variety of hiking and camping opportunities.

Culture, History, and the Arts

The overland trails diverged widely as immigrants from the East headed for California and Santa Fe as well as Oregon. The trails began to bear the signs of hardship as travelers chose survival over continuing to carry the pianos and mirrors and rocking chairs they'd hoped to have in their new life. But their wagons were still heavy when they came through Nebraska—and nearly all the various routes lumped under the name **Oregon Trail** did come through Nebraska. **Scotts Bluff National Monument** near Gering was a major guidepost to the wagonmasters; **Chimney Rock National Historic Site,** a tall, rocky spire just south of Bayard, was another and is supposed to have been mentioned more than any other landmark in the journals of those 19th-century travelers. At both those sites and at many others, you will find good historical displays on the Trail and the people who followed it. In several areas—most notably at the Scotts Bluff monument, at **Rock Creek Station State Historical Park,** at **Ash Hollow State Park,** and in Carter Canyon near Scottsbluff—you can still see the signs of those full wagons in the deep ruts they marked in the earth, wagon following wagon.

Around the same time, the Mormons were headed west to seek religious freedom. The **Mormon Trail Visitors Center** outside Omaha tells their particular story, next to a cemetery marking the final resting spots for some 700 of them who died before reaching Utah.

Nebraska also has three other outstanding historical parks representing the frontier military era. **Fort Robinson State Historical Park and Museum,** a state park since 1956, was an active military post for more than 70 years. Among other things, this is the place where the Oglala Sioux Chief Crazy Horse was killed and where many German prisoners of war were detained during World War II. You can rent bicycles to pedal around the grounds, enjoy the crafts center, ride the stagecoach, take a jeep tour

1934	1950	1970	1986	1993
Nebraska adopts a unicameral, nonpartisan legislature.	Swanson Foods of Omaha develops chicken pot pie and three years later begins production of TV Dinners™.	The construction of I–80 across Nebraska is complete.	Kay Orr becomes Nebraska's first female governor.	Hundreds of people follow Nebraska's Oregon Trail in wagons and on horseback in a commemoration of the trail's sesquicentennial.

INTRODUCTION
HISTORY
REGIONS
WHEN TO VISIT
STATE'S GREATS
RULES OF THE ROAD
DRIVING TOURS

to see a buffalo herd in Smiley Canyon, fish for trout, have a cookout, ride horses, swim in an indoor pool, and take in performances at the summer stock theater. At **Fort Hartsuff State Historical Park,** you can see restored stables, officers quarters, and barracks. The originals were built by infantry soldiers between 1874 and 1881. Until it was abandoned in 1827, Fort Atkinson, which at one time housed 1,000 men, was the first and only military presence west of the Missouri. A re-created fort with barracks and log walls now occupies the site at **Fort Atkinson State Historical Park.**

The **Neligh Mill State Historic Site** in Neligh offers a superb example of a 19th-century flour mill, with original equipment in the original building, first put into use in 1873. The Railroad Town section of the **Stuhr Museum of the Prairie Pioneer** in Grand Island is a noteworthy re-creation of a prairie community using actual barns, stables, houses, and other old buildings. The town appears so authentic it has been the background for several films.

Outstanding cultural attractions in the state include the **Joslyn Art Museum** in Omaha, an Art Deco structure with a modern addition that houses one of the best collections of art of the American West, and the **Sheldon Memorial Art Gallery and Sculpture Garden** with a showcase white marble building designed by Phillip Johnson on the University of Nebraska campus in Lincoln.

Sports

River rafting is popular on the **Niobrara River,** and fishing and boating opportunities abound on **Lake McConaughy** and the **Missouri River,** as well as in many other state recreation areas. Nebraskans' favorite sport is **Husker Football,** played at Husker Stadium at the University of Nebraska in Lincoln. Games have been sold out for decades, and as long as the teams continue to win national championships, that's unlikely to change.

Rules of the Road

License Requirements: General driver's licenses are available at age 16, though some special permits for resident youth are allowed at younger ages.

Right Turn on Red: Unless otherwise posted, right turns on red are permitted *after* a full stop. Left turns on red are allowed where such a turn would not cross an oncoming traffic lane.

Seat Belt and Helmet Laws: Seat belts are required of the driver and all front-seat passengers. Children under age five, or weighing less than 40 pounds, must be secured in a car seat that meets federal guidelines. All motorcycle operators and passengers must wear approved motorcycle helmets.

Speed Limits: Interstate: 75 mph except in metropolitan areas around Lincoln and Omaha. State highways: generally 60 mph; some stretches are 55 mph. City and town streets:

1995	1995	1996
On New Year's Day, the Nebraska Huskers become National College Football Champions.	South Sioux City advertises for people to "Return to Sioux Land" in order to have adequate workers for an expanding labor market.	The Nebraska Huskers repeat their New Year's Day victory as National College Football Champions.

25 mph in residential districts, 20 mph in business districts unless otherwise posted. County roads: 55 mph; 50 mph on unpaved county roads, unless otherwise posted.

For More Information: Nebraska State Patrol | 402/471–4545. Emergency Highway Help Line | 800/525–5555. Department of Motor Vehicles | 402/471–2281.

Lewis and Clark's Journey: Missouri River Driving Tour
FROM BROWNVILLE TO CROFTON

Distance: 404 mi   Time: Minimum 5 days
Breaks: Overnight stops in Nebraska City, Omaha, Crofton

This tour takes you along the Missouri River, following essentially the same route that Lewis and Clark took in 1804. You will visit river towns such as Brownville and Nebraska City, plus and the state's major metropolitan area, Omaha, and begin to experience the agricultural prosperity of the Midwest as you head north to South Sioux City and Crofton.

❶ Begin in **Brownville,** a town that is proud of its heritage as a riverboat community, one of the first established when Congress created the Nebraska Territory. The **Brownville Historic District** includes many buildings dating back to the 1860s and 1870s, such as the Captain Bailey House, which houses the **Brownville Museum,** the **Carson House,** and the **Governor Furnas Home.** Once you've explored the historic district, stroll down to the waterfront for a visit to the *Meriwether Lewis,* a former Missouri River dredge that's now operated as a riverboat museum. Several local companies offer cruises on the river.

❷ From Brownville, go to Route 64E, then head south on Route 64E for approximately 9 mi until you get to **Indian Cave State Park.** The park, which sprawls over 3,000 acres along the Missouri River, takes its name from a sandstone overhang with Native American rock carvings. Stop for a quick hike—you'll probably see (and hear) many species of birds, ranging from wild turkeys to bright red cardinals.

❸ When you're ready to leave the park, head north on U.S. 75 to **Nebraska City,** which is known as the City of Seven Hills. National Arbor Day holiday was born here, and the best place to learn to appreciate the importance of trees is at **Arbor Lodge State Historical Park and Arboretum** and the **Arbor Day Farm.** Historical attractions include **John Brown's Cave,** where fleeing slaves were hidden during the Civil War era, and the **Old Freighter's Museum.**

❹ When you're finished exploring Nebraska City, continue north on Highway 75 to **Bellevue,** the site of a fur-trading post established in the early 1800s, making this one of the oldest European American communities in the state of Nebraska. **The Sarpy County Historical Museum** provides information about early settlement, as well as about Native Americans who knew this as their homeland for generations prior to arrival of the white people.

❺ Leaving Bellevue, head north on U.S. 75 to enter **Omaha,** the state's major metropolitan area. You can plan to spend one or several days in the Omaha region. Whatever you decide, you will leave the area with things you'd still like to do. The opportunities

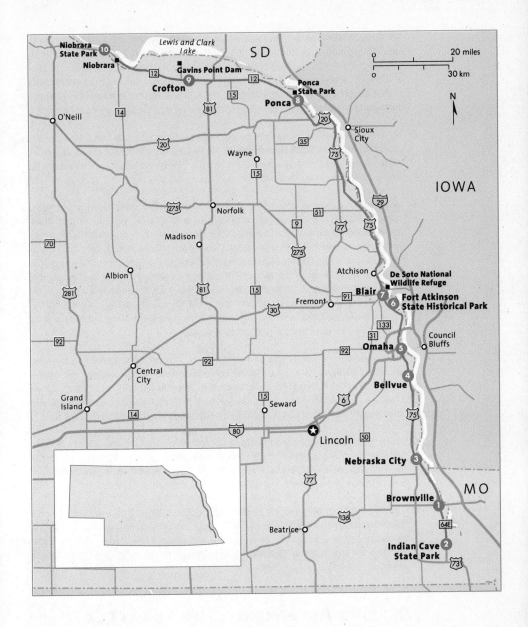

range from shopping and museums to parks, nature centers, and recreation areas. Some of the top attractions include the **Durham Western Heritage Museum** in the historic Union Station and the **Joslyn Art Museum.** In the **Old Market,** 12 blocks of 19th-century buildings, you'll find shopping opportunities galore—from antiques and books to Persian rugs. Horse-drawn carriages or tandem bicycles can provide transportation. **Father Flanagan's Boys Town** is a national historic landmark. At the **Mormon Trail Visitors Center,** you can see the cemetery that is the final resting place for some 700 Mormons who died during the winter of 1846–47, when the group had stopped while en route to Utah.

For the kids, take time to spend a day at the **Henry Doorly Zoo** with its Lied Jungle, the world's largest indoor rain forest, the Scott Aquarium, and, of course, a variety of animals, from puffins and penguins to North America's largest "Cat Complex." Within the city, you'll discover many sites for appreciating nature, such as the **Neale Woods Nature Center** and the **Botanical Gardens,** or you can tour former President **Gerald Ford's birthplace** or a World War II minesweeper that's now berthed in **Freedom Park.**

❻ When you've finished exploring Omaha, head north on U.S. 75 to Fort Calhoun, near Blair. **Fort Atkinson State Historical Park** is a re-creation of the first U.S. military fort built west of the Missouri River and is close to the site where Lewis and Clark met with local Native Americans in 1804.

❼ When you exit the park, go onto U.S. 75 and head north. After approximately 9 mi, you'll come to **Blair** at the intersection of U.S. 75, Route 133, Route 131, and Route 91. **Black Elk/Neihardt Park** is a special place dedicated to the Sioux holy man and the Nebraska poet laureate who helped spread Black Elk's vision to the world. Three miles east of the park, you'll find **DeSoto National Wildlife Refuge,** the site where the steamboat *Bertrand* went down in the Missouri River in 1865 while en route to Fort Benton, Montana. The refuge straddles the Nebraska–Iowa state line and has a visitor center where relics of the *Bertrand* are on permanent display. The refuge attracts half-a-million geese, mallards, and bald eagles as they migrate south in the fall and is a year-round home for deer, birds, beaver, and muskrats.

❽ Continue north on U.S. 75 and turn west onto U.S. 20, then north on Route 12 to the community of **Ponca,** where you can visit **Ponca State Park.** The 892-acre park has impressive views of the Missouri River and attracts people who like to hike or ride horses on trails. As a part of the Lewis and Clark National Historic Trail, this is one place where the river still looks much as it might have when the Corps of Discovery first saw it.

❾ From Ponca, continue west on Route 12 to **Crofton,** which is a good place to stop for the night and take time to enjoy the recreational activities in the northeastern corner of Nebraska. **Lewis and Clark Lake** was formed by **Gavins Point Dam,** which has a hatchery, aquarium, power plant, and a visitor center of historical exhibits.

❿ Leaving Crofton, head west on Route 12 for approximately 28 mi until you come to **Niobrara State Park,** a 1,640-acre preserve about a mile from the town of Neeligh. The Niobrara and Missouri rivers converge here, and you can hike along a stretch of the Lewis and Clark National Historical Trail and explore Basile Creek Wildlife Area, a wetlands used by migratory birds.

Native Americans, the Fur Trade, Emigrants, and Cowboys Driving Tour

OGALLALA TO SCOTTSBLUFF AND CHADRON

Distance: 350 mi   Time: Minimum 3 days
Breaks: Overnight stops in Scottsbluff/Gering and Chadron

This is a loop tour that lets you explore the Nebraska Panhandle, a region marked by Native American conflict, fur-trading posts, and the route of the Oregon, California, and Mormon trails. The land is rugged, with outcrops that are the beginning of the

Pine Ridge country. You'll see sagebrush and prickly pear, along with small natural lakes and pine forests. Begin your trip in Ogallala and drive west on U.S. 26 to Scottsbluff, then head north on Route 71 to Crawford before turning east on U.S. 20 to Chadron. At Chadron, you can either continue the circle, returning south on Highway 385 through the Panhandle to Alliance and Sidney, or head east into the cowboy country of the Nebraska Sandhills.

INTRODUCTION
HISTORY
REGIONS
WHEN TO VISIT
STATE'S GREATS
RULES OF THE ROAD
DRIVING TOURS

❶ Start in **Ogallala.** To cowboys who drove cattle herds here in the late 1800s, this was the promised land of roaring saloons and friendly ladies. **Boot Hill Cemetery** is the resting place of some of those cowboys, while the **Front Street/Cowboy Museum** gives a glimpse into what life was like here during the days this part of Nebraska was the Old West and the **Mansion on the Hill** shows how the wealthy folk lived during the cowboy period.

❷ As you leave Ogallala, take U.S. 26 west for approximately 27 mi to **Ash Hollow State Park.** Bones of ancient rhinos and mammoths found here may date back 6,000 years, and you can see the ruts where Oregon Trail immigrants skidded their wagons down a steep hill. The interpretive center also has information about the 1855 Battle of Blue Water (also called the Harney Massacre), in which Army troops commanded by General William S. Harney attacked the Lakota in retaliation for a fight the previous year near Fort Laramie that left 28 soldiers dead.

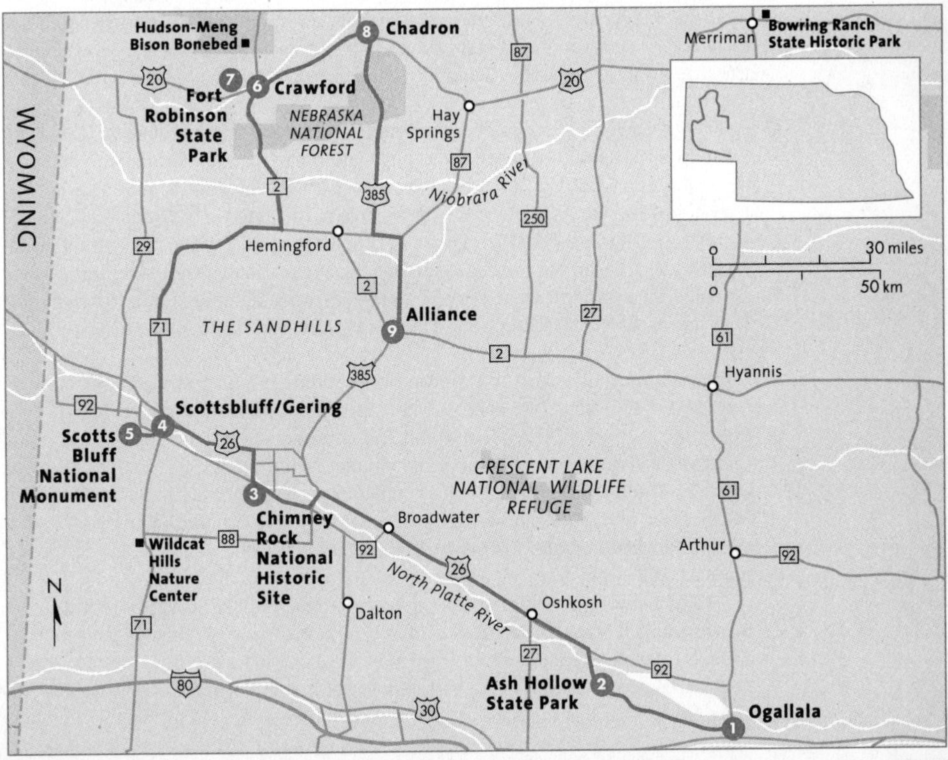

❸ When you've finished exploring Ash Hollow, head west on Highway 26 for approximately 100 mi to **Chimney Rock National Historic Site.** Chimney Rock was one of the most recognized landmarks on the Oregon Trail. You aren't allowed to get right up to the rock any more, but you can visit a little cemetery just east of it. Or you can ride actual trail ruts with Bayard's **Oregon Trail Wagon Train,** headquartered on a ranch on Oregon Trail Road off Highway 26, which takes you near the rock in a covered wagon. (Allow about three hours for the tour.)

❹ Leaving Chimney Rock, follow Highway 26 west for about 15 mi to **Scottsbluff/Gering.** Settle in one of these towns—they're separated only by the North Platte River—for a day or so to explore not only the Oregon Trail sites, but also some nice recreational opportunities. At the **Wildcat Hills Nature Center,** you can see herds of elk, buffalo, and sometimes longhorn cattle, as well as displays related to the flora and fauna of western Nebraska, while the **Wildcat Hills State Recreation Area** provides an area for hiking and camping. The **Farm and Ranch Museum** has some authentic pioneer homes and cabins and lots of old horse-drawn and steam-powered farm equipment, and **Robidoux Pass** has a reconstructed trading post in Carter Canyon.

❺ As the wagon trains headed west, they guided themselves by natural landmarks—and the fortresslike rock we now know as **Scotts Bluff National Monument,** 2 mi west of the junction of Routes 71 and 92, was one of their major guideposts. You can hike or drive to the top of the monument for a view of the North Platte River Valley—and see it from afar at places such as Scottsbluff's Riverside Zoo.

❻ When you leave Scottsbluff, head north on Route 71 and then take Route 2 for about 74 mi to **Crawford.** Crawford is in the center of an area that was inhabited by Native Americans as far back as 10,000 years ago. About 4 mi north of Crawford on Route 2, turn west into Toadstool Road, then go 15 mi north to reach the **Hudson-Meng Bison Bonebed,** an archaeological site within the Oglala National Grasslands where excavations have uncovered more than 600 bison skeletons dating to prehistoric times. From mid-May through September, you can see scientists at work at the fossil dig. Before or after that visit, you might want to see some interesting rock formations that look like toadstools at **Toadstool Geological Park,** on Toadstool Road just west of Route 2.

❼ Heading 3 mi west of Crawford on Highway 20, you'll come to **Fort Robinson State Park.** Established as a military post during the Plains Indian Wars, Fort Robinson remained in use through World War II, when it was a K-9 training center and the site of a German prisoner-of-war camp. Many of the troops who participated in the major battles (and appalling incidents) of the Plains wars were in companies stationed at Fort Robinson. Nearby, you also can see the Red Cloud Agency, where Lakota received annuities after agreeing to land-rights treaties and before eventually being settled on reservations. The state park includes lodging and a restaurant, interpretive programs, and a museum.

❽ Going east from Crawford on Highway 20, **Chadron** is about 20 mi away. Chadron is the home of Chadron State College, where the **Mari Sandoz Heritage Room** pays tribute to the author of *Cheyenne Autumn* and other books on the history of Nebraska. Chadron's early existence came about in part due to fur-trading posts, and the **Museum of the Fur Trade,** on the site of the 1837 Bordeaux Trading Post, has many artifacts from that era and way of life. Recreational activities abound in **Chadron State Park** and at the **Pine Ridge National Recreation Area,** where motorized vehicles aren't allowed, though mountain bikes are.

From Chadron, continue east on Highway 20 for about 80 mi to Merriman and the **Bowring Ranch State Historic Park.** About 1½ mi north and 2 mi east of Merriman on a gravel road off Route 61, this has been preserved as a working cattle ranch that also houses the extensive glassware and china collections of Nebraska's only female U.S. Senator.

○ If you prefer, from Chadron, you can loop south on Highway 385 to **Alliance** to visit **Carhenge,** a unique reproduction of England's Stonehenge made with 26 cars instead of large blocks of stone. Other sculptures made of automobiles are nearby. If you're interested in Native American and pioneer history, make a stop at the **Knight Museum.** Then continue on south to **Sidney,** home of the headquarters and showroom of **Cabela's,** the nation's largest sports outfitter, and the **Fort Sidney Museum and Post Commanders Home,** one of the few buildings left of an army garrison built here in the 1880s to protect railroad crews. Once you've reached Sidney, head east on I–80 for about 47 mi to return to Ogallala.

ALLIANCE

MAP 11, B2

(Nearby towns also listed: Bridgeport, Chadron, Crawford)

Alliance, initially known as Broncho Lake, was established in 1888, when the Burlington Railroad arrived, and the town, now the county seat, remains a railroad town through and through. It is an important rail-switching location and the center of a large agricultural area. Carhenge, James Reinders's strange display of old cars tipped up and arranged to replicate Stonehenge, is just north of town off U.S. 385.

Information: **Alliance Chamber of Commerce** | Box 571, Alliance 69301 | 308/762–1520 | chamber@ricochet.net | www.premaonline.com.

ALLIANCE

INTRO
ATTRACTIONS
DINING
LODGING

Attractions

Carhenge. This reproduction of England's Stonehenge, in a big field on Highway 87 3½ mi north of Alliance, is one of the stranger sights in western Nebraska—instead of large blocks of stone, it has 26 cars pointing to the heavens. Nearby, the "car art reserve," as locals call it, has other sculptures made of automobiles. | 308/762–1520 | Free | Daily.

In June, Carhenge observes **Summer Solstice** with a special celebration on the longest day of the year, much as many Britons do at the real Stonehenge and other sites in England. | 308/762–1520 | Free.

Knight Museum. The emphasis here is on early Nebraska, using artifacts and other exhibits to trace the history of the Native Americans who lived here and the pioneers who came here to live. | 908 Yellowstone Ave. | 308/762–2384 | Free | May–Labor Day, Mon.–Sat. 10–6, Sun. 1–5; Labor Day–Apr. by appointment.

Dining

Elms Restaurant and Lounge. American. Popular with Alliance locals, this restaurant has two main dining areas; one has mirrored walls, red tablecloths, candles, and linen napkins, and the other is more family-oriented, with exposed-brick walls and ceiling fans. Dress is casual in both spaces. Favorite menu items include the 14-oz rib eye and chicken-fried steaks. | 1015 E. 3rd St. | 308/762–3425 | www.mallofalliance.com/elms.htm | $10–20 | AE, D, MC, V.

Lodging

Holiday Inn Express. At the edge of town on Highway 385, which is also 3rd Street, this motel has country views all around, and an indoor pool for relaxing after sightseeing. Truck parking is available. Complimentary Continental breakfast. Some in-room hot tubs. Cable TV. Indoor pool. Hot tub. No pets. | 1420 W. 3rd St. | 308/762–7600 or 800/465–4329 | fax 308/762–6468 | 56 rooms, 4 suites | $67–$105 | AE, D, DC, MC, V.

ASHLAND

MAP 11, H4

(Nearby towns also listed: Bellevue, Lincoln, Omaha)

Just beyond the Omaha metropolitan area, this small town founded in 1866 has always been an agricultural community, but for the past few years it has also been home to the Strategic Air Command Museum, where you can see aircraft ranging from the B-17 Flying Fortress of World War II to the SR-71 Blackbird of jet-plane times.

Information: **Ashland Chamber of Commerce** | Box 5, Ashland 68003 | 402/944–2050.

Attractions

Eugene T. Mahoney State Park. You'll find many of the expected outdoor activities in this 700-acre park about halfway between Lincoln and Omaha on I–80. But besides the swimming, hiking, and picnicking areas, it also has water slides, a theatrical playhouse, miniature golf, a greenhouse, an observation tower, crafts sites, and a lodge (*see* Peter Kiewit Lodge) and restaurant. Or you can opt for overnight stays in the tent-camping areas, an RV park, or cabins. | 28500 W. Park Hwy. | 402/944–2523 | etmsp@ngpc.state.ne.us | ngp.ngpc.state.ne.us/parks/etm/etm1.html | Neb. Parks Permit required; camping, $7; RV sites, $13 | Daily.

Strategic Air Command Museum. The 33 planes, six missiles, and countless smaller items exhibited here can give real shape to the development of our country's air power for the last four decades of the 20th century. Along with seeing World War II's B-29, the supersonic B-58 Hustler, and the U-2 spyplane, you can pause in a glass-walled hangar and watch more planes being restored. | 2819 W. Park Hwy. | 402/944–3100 or 800/358–5029 | $6 | Daily 9–5.

The Lee G. Simmons Wildlife Safari Park. Around the next bend, you might see a buffalo whose ancestors once thundered across this same ground, for this drive-through wildlife park, at exit 426 off I–80, an extension of Omaha's Henry Doorly Zoo, concentrates on the bison, elks, pronghorn antelopes, and wolves that once roamed free across early Nebraska. | 16406 N. 292nd St. | 402/944–9453 | $5 per car | Apr.–Oct., weekdays 9:30–5, weekends 9:30–6; after Labor Day, weekends 9:30–5.

Willow Point Gallery/ Archie Hightshoe Big Game Collection. A native of Nebraska, Gene Roncka is a well-known local artist whose career includes designing for the prestigious ad agency Young & Rubicam, *Time* magazine, and General Motors. Many of his oils depict Nebraska subjects. Roncka also painted the backdrop for the Archie Hightshoe Big Game Collection, an exhibit that features stuffed wildlife, including huge polar bears. | 1431 Silver St. | 402/944–3613 | www.generoncka.com | Free | Mon.–Sat. 10–6, Sun. 12–4.

ON THE CALENDAR

JULY: *Ashland Stir-up Days.* This three-day annual event takes place in the heart of Ashland and comes complete with a carnival, parade, rodeo, bull-riding show, movies in the park, and a big country street dance. You can enjoy BBQ beef sandwiches, hot dogs, and hamburgers and quaff a cold brew or two in the beer garden. | 402/344–2050.

Dining

Cheri O's. American. This multi-theme luncheon and snack stop has something for everybody. The basement Cigar Cellar has a shuffleboard and a big-screen TV. On the main floor, you'll find a room dedicated to the 1950s and '60s, with old records on the walls, a Ladies Tea Room filled with antique valentines and teatime trappings, and a dining area done in old-fashioned soda-fountain style, with spindly legged wire café tables. There's even a deck at the back with large, umbrella-covered tables. You might try an old-fashioned cherry soda to wash down a chicken sandwich or char-grilled burger. | 1404 Silver St. | 402/944–9499 | Breakfast also available, no dinner | $4–$6 | No credit cards.

Lodging

Peter Kiewit Lodge. Staying within Mahoney State Park will let you be near all the activities but still have your own private space. Some rooms in the two-story lodge have sleeping lofts and fireplaces; most have decks overlooking the Platte River. The light-housekeeping cabins range from two bedrooms to four bedrooms and include some treetop cabins where your deck and grill are at bird's-eye level. Restaurant. Room phones. Kitchenettes in cabins. | 28500 W. Park Hwy. | 402/944–2523 | fax 402/944–7604 | ngp.ngpc.state.ne.us/parks/etm/etm1.html | 40 rooms, 51 cabins | $55–$75 lodge rooms, $80–$210 cabins; 2–night minimum | MC, V.

AUBURN

(Nearby towns also listed: Beatrice, Brownville, Nebraska City)

When the towns of Sheridan and Calvert merged in 1882, they became Auburn, named for a city in New York. Today, Auburn is known for its antiques shops, with several stores catering to folks who like old china. If you visit Indian Cave State Park just outside Brownville, you will also pass through a tract of land between the Nemaha and Little Nemaha rivers that was set aside as a Native American reservation following the 1830 Treaty of Prairie Du Chien.

Information: Auburn Chamber of Commerce | 1211 J St., Auburn 68305 | 402/274–3521 | fax 402/274–4020 | cc60618@navix.net | www.ci.auburn.ne.us/.

Attractions

Auburn Legion Park. A smallish municipal park, the Auburn Legion Park has lighted tennis courts, a basketball court, sand volleyball courts, four baseball/softball fields, and two small fishing lakes. | J St. | 402/274–3521 | Free | Daily.

ON THE CALENDAR

OCT.: *Fall Festival*. This annual two-day event turns the streets of downtown Auburn into sites for a flea market, car show, food booths, beer garden, and street dance. | 402/274–3521.

Dining

Camp Rulo. American. Along the Missouri River on the west edge of town on Highway 159, this casual eatery serves what comes naturally—carp and catfish caught in the river before being battered and fried. The walleye fillets and the battered chicken livers and gizzards are also local favorites. | 402/245–4096 | 11–8:30 | Closed Mon. | $7–$15 | MC, V.

Wheeler Inn. American. The atmosphere is rustic and casual in this country dining room and its lounge and keno lounge on Highway 75. You can go light with a meal from the salad bar offerings or try the specialty lobster. | 1905 J St. | 402/274–4931 | 5–9 | $10–$17 | AE, DC, MC, V.

Lodging

Auburn Inn. This remodeled two-story, red brick motel, built in the late '70s, has kitchenettes for your snacking after a visit to Indian Cave State Park, about 10 mi away. Complimentary Continental breakfast. Microwaves, refrigerators. Cable TV. Pets allowed (fee). | 517 J St. | 402/274–3143 or 800/272–3143 | fax 402/274–4404 | 36 rooms | $30–$50 | AE, D, DC, MC, V.

Palmer House. Though this 1940s brick one-story motel has an old-fashioned feeling to the exterior, guest rooms are outfitted with modern furnishings. Cold-weather hookups are available. Refrigerators. Cable TV. | 1918 J St. | 402/274–3193 or 800/272–3193 | fax 402/274–4165 | 22 rooms, 8 suites | $30–$53 | AE, D, DC, MC, V.

BANCROFT

MAP 11, H2

(Nearby towns also listed: Blair, Norfolk, South Sioux City, Wayne, West Point)

The lore and history of Native Americans have greatly impacted the area around this small town in the Missouri River country. It is near the reservations of the Omaha and Winnebago tribes and was the home of Susette LaFlesche Tibbles, an Omaha, and her husband, Thomas Tibbles, who were influential in activities that led to laws granting rights to Native Americans. The community is known for the John G. Neihardt Center, which has memorabilia related to the esteemed poet whose *The Cycle of the West* drew on legends learned while he lived among the Omaha in the early years of the 20th century.

Information: **Bancroft Village Office** | 502 Main St., Bancroft 68004 | 402/648–3332.

Attractions

John G. Neihardt Center. Exhibits here relate to both the life and the literature of Nebraska's famous poet laureate, whose best-known individual work was *Black Elk Speaks*. You'll also see a small library for researchers, a prayer garden, and the little cabin Neihardt used as his study. | Washington at Elm St. | 888/777–4667 or 402/648–3388 | Neihardt.com | Free | Mon.–Sat. 9–5, Sun. 1:30–5.

ON THE CALENDAR

AUG.: *Neihardt Day.* For more than 30 years, noted authors, poets, musicians, and artists have come to tiny Bancroft the first Sunday of August to pay tribute to John Neihardt with many forms of their own creative expressions. All the entertainment takes place outdoors at Neihardt Center. | 888/777–4667.

Dining

Country Pub Steak House. Steak. Wooden tables and the rustic baskets and candles on the walls make for a low-key, country-style feeling in the dining area here. There's a BBQ rib-and-fried chicken buffet on Thursday, and Friday night brings an expansive fish buffet with cod, walleye, and catfish. | 409 Main St. | 402/648–7458 | Closed Sun. nights | $8–14 | D, MC, V.

Lodging

Hotel Palace. A turn-of-the-20th-century monument in Pender, this three-story brick building has acres of hardwood, an ornate main staircase, and a spot on the National Registry of Historic Places. Residential apartments and some office spaces co-exist with guest rooms here. No air-conditioning. No room phones, no TV. No pets. | 404 Main St., Pender | 402/385–3036 | fax 402/385–2154 | 43 rooms | $25 | AE, D, DC, MC, V.

BAYARD

MAP 11, B3

(Nearby towns also listed: Alliance, Bridgeport, Gering, Scottsbluff)

This tiny farming community, which dates to 1888, is known as the closest community to Chimney Rock National Historic Site, one of the best-known of the rocky landmarks in Nebraska's "Monument Valley" along U.S. 26.

Information: **Bayard City Office** | 445 Main St., Bayard 69334 | 308/586–1121 | fax 308/586–1834 | bayard@navix.net.

Also: **Scottsbluff–Gehring United Chamber of Commerce** | 1517 Broadway, No. 104, Scottsbluff 69361 | 308/632–2133 or 800/788–9475 | fax 308/632–7128 | tourism@visitscottsbluff.com | www.visitscottsbluff.com.

Attractions

Chimney Rock National Historic Site. This tall, rocky spire 4½ mi south of Bayard was mentioned more than any other landmark in the journals kept by those who traveled the Oregon Trail in the mid-19th century. No one is allowed right up at the rock, but you can go into an old cemetery to the east of it. Displays in the Chimney Rock Center, on Highway 26 a mile south of the junction with Highway 92, explore many views of the rock and other historical bits about the Oregon Trail—and include an exhibit teaching children what they might have packed for a wagon train headed west. | Chimney Rock Rd. | 308/586–2581 | www.nps.gov/chro/ or www.nebraskahistory.org | $2 | Apr.–Sept., daily 9–6; Oct.–Mar., daily 9–5.

Oregon Trail Wagon Train. You can travel part of the route of the Oregon Trail and the Pony Express in an old-fashioned wagon train in these excursions that go fairly close to Chimney Rock. The trips last from three hours to four days and include chuck wagon cookouts with homemade ice cream and sourdough bread. The home ranch, off Highway 26, also has an RV park, log cabins, canoeing, and spaces for tent camping. | Oregon Trail Rd. | 308/586–1850 | www.prairieweb.com/oregonwagon | Reservations required | $50—$525 | May–Aug.

ON THE CALENDAR

SEPT.: *Chimney Rock Pioneer Days.* You could get kidnapped by outlaws—that's one of the Old West touches to this lively festival in Bayard's Library Park the first weekend after Labor Day. You'll also find food booths, street dances, a saloon, crafts fairs, a car show, a horseshoe competition, and a parade Saturday morning. | 308/586–2830.

Lodging

Landmark Inn. Built in the 1962, this single-story, blue-and-white building is right off the highway and next to a barn emblazoned with the Landmark Inn logo. The motel is just 1 mi from Chimney Rock. Cable TV. | 246 Main St. | 308/586–1375 | 9 rooms | $44 | MC, V.

BEATRICE

MAP 11, H5

(Nearby towns also listed: Auburn, Fairbury, Lincoln, Wilber)

You could say that both homesteading and culture in the West had their start in Beatrice. The 1862 Homestead Act was put into effect on January 1, 1863, when Daniel Freeman, home on leave from his Civil War regiment, obtained the title to land just west of Beatrice. His homestead is believed to be the first recorded in the West and is now part of Homestead National Monument, as is the school he built for his children.

Culture arrived in 1889, in the form of the Beatrice Chautauqua, named and patterned after the legendary educational/artistic movement of upstate New York. Residents constructed an assembly hall for the programs and later added cottages for housing. The Chautauqua presentations attracted some 10,000 people in 1905, due in part to special rates offered by the railroads, but participation began to wither, and the community held its last Chautauqua in 1916.

Information: **Beatrice Chamber of Commerce** | 226 S. 6th St., Beatrice 68310 | 402/223–2338 or 800/755–7745 | fax 402/223–2339 | info@beatrice-ne.com | www.beatrice-ne.com.

Attractions

Gage County Historical Museum. Housed in the 1906 Neoclassical Revival-style Burlington Depot on Highway 136, the museum focuses on the history of area towns. | 101 N. 2nd St. | 402/228–1679 | Free | Memorial Day–Labor Day, Tue.–Fri. 9–noon, Sat. 9–noon, Sun. 1–5.

Homestead National Monument of America. The museum has various displays related to the way the Homestead Act opened the plains to settlers after Daniel Freeman filed his claim in 1862. More displays are in the 1867 log cabin on the grounds and in the Freeman schoolhouse a short drive away. You also can take a short walk to see a 100-acre tall-grass prairie abloom with wildflowers. | 8523 Hwy. 4W | 402/223–3514 | www.nps.gov/home | Free | Daily.

ON THE CALENDAR

MAY: *Heartland Storytelling Festival.* Regionally and nationally known artists gather at the Homestead National Monument each year to tell tales of the Midwest and its pioneers that span time and distance. | 402/223–3514 or 402/223–2338.

JUNE: *Annual Homestead Days.* If you're trying to put together a history of your family in this area, you can attend a land-records symposium. If not, you can still take part in such activities as a kids' parade, craft show, duck derby, demonstrations of native crafts, historical musicals, horseshoes, and an old-time baseball game. | 402/223–3514.

Dining

Hallie's. American. Started by three sisters, this restaurant in a restored Victorian home in a village 25 mi from Beatrice offers good food made from scratch. Locals think the homemade whole wheat buns for sandwiches, freshly made rhubarb pie, private-recipe poppyseed dressing on the romaine salad, and special sauce topping the "Gold Award" chicken are worth the drive. Take Highway 136 to Route 4, then south on Route 50, which becomes Route 604, to Pawnee City, a very small town. It's inside the second Victorian house south of KC's store. | 604 9th St., Pawnee City | 402/852–2445 | Closed Sun., Mon. | $8–$15 | No credit cards.

HOMESTEAD—OREGON TRAIL COUNTRY

Nebraska has a unique place in the development of the West. The first major cross-country trail—the Oregon Trail—cut across the state. Nebraska is also the region of the first homestead, claimed by resident Daniel Freeman under the 1862 Homestead Act. In southern Nebraska, you can visit the Freeman homestead, now part of the Homestead National Monument on the Blue River just west of Beatrice.

From Beatrice, head west on U.S. 136 to Fairbury, where you'll cross the Oregon Trail. Just south of town is Rock Creek Station, an important traveler's stop on the overland routes to Oregon and California, a station on the Pony Express circuit, and the place where Wild Bill Hickok first became known as an Old West gunfighter. The site is now a state historical park with living historical interpretations, a campground, and picnic area.

West of Fairbury, roads that keep you close to the Little Blue River also take you near the Oregon Trail route. In the region between Hastings and Fort Kearny, the trail parallels the Platte River. Here you'll find re-created fort buildings as well as monuments to the pioneers at Fort Kearny, which has living history presentations throughout the summer.

© Corbis

Lodging

Beatrice Inn. This brick structure with shake-shingle roof on Highway 77 across from the airport is within 10 mi of Homestead National Monument and Rock Creek Station State Historical Park. Truck parking and cold-weather hookups are available. Restaurant, bar. Cable TV. Pool. Laundry facilities. Pets allowed. | 3500 N. 6th St. | 402/223–4074 or 800/232–8742 | fax 402/223–4074 | 65 rooms | $29–$42 | AE, D, DC, MC, V.

Holiday Villa. You can can choose from the main three-story brick building or the 25 one-story stucco cabins at this complex on the north edge of town, about 5 mi northeast of Homestead National Monument and Rock Creek Station State Historical Park. Truck parking and cold-weather hookups are available. Some kitchenettes. Cable TV. Playground. Pets allowed. | 1820 N. 6th St. | 402/223–4036 | fax 402/228–3875 | 25 rooms, 25 cabins | $29–$41 | AE, D, DC, MC, V.

Victorian Inn. Right along Route 77, the exterior of this motor inn has a faintly Victorian look, but the interiors were planned for 20th-century road-travelers. Truck parking is available. Complimentary Continental breakfast. Cable TV. Pets allowed. | 1903 N. 6th St. | 402/228–5955 | fax 402/228–2020 | 44 rooms | $35–$55 | AE, D, DC, MC, V.

BELLEVUE

MAP 11, I3

(Nearby towns also listed: Ashland, Omaha, Plattsmouth)

When Meriwether Lewis and William Clark hoisted an American flag in the vicinity of present-day Bellevue on July 23, 1804, it likely was the first time the United States banner had ever flown over Nebraska. Bellevue's strategic position near the juncture of the Platte and Missouri rivers made it an important site for early French, Spanish, and eventually American traders and explorers. In 1795, James Mackay, working as a trader for Spain, established a fur trading post in the area, followed later by a post put up by Manuel Lisa. By 1846, a ferry across the Missouri had further opened the region to both settlers and travelers.

In 1881, the United States Army put up Fort Omaha there as well, the first stage in what eventually would be the area's significant role in our military history. Later renamed Fort Crook, the post became Offutt Field during World War II, when it was a construction center for bombers built by the Glenn L. Martin Company. Two of the most famous planes to come from that facility were the *Enola Gay*, which dropped the atomic bomb on Hiroshima, and the *Bocks Car*, which unleashed "the Fat Man," the second bomb, on Nagasaki three days later.

After the war, the Strategic Air Command (SAC) headquartered its long-range bombers at Offutt and—as many Cold War-era schoolchildren were well aware—planted the crucial War Room beneath the Nebraska soil. The Air Force eventually used the site to manage its intercontinental ballistic missiles. Today, the 4,000-acre base still employs more than 10,000 civilian and military personnel, mostly in reconnaissance and control operations.

Information: Bellevue Chamber of Commerce | 204 W. Mission Ave., Bellevue 68005 | 402/291–5216 | fax 402/291–8729 | bellevue@bellevuenebraska.com | www.bellevuenebraska.com.

Attractions

Bellevue Little Theater. This small community theater has been around since 1968 and produces about five plays a year, drawing cast and production crews from the Bellevue area. Theater group volunteers also run a thrift shop next door to help fund productions. | 203 Mission St. | 402/291–1554 | Call for prices.

Fontenelle Forest Nature Center. More than 1,300 acres of hilly woodlands, wetlands, and land fronting the Missouri River on the northern edge of town are laced with more than 25 mi of trails, including about a mile of boardwalk accessible to travelers using wheelchairs. The Nature Center has nature and historical displays and a variety of programs, including guided hikes. | 1111 Bellevue Blvd. N | 402/731–3140 | $7.50 | Daily 8–5, weekends 8–6.

Historic Bellevue. Guides lead visitors on 90-minute tours through the state's oldest train depot, church, bank, and cemetery, plus an original log cabin. | 112 W. Mission Ave. | 402/293–3080, 800/467–2779 | Free | Daily.

The Sarpy County Historical Museum. Displays cover the early history of Sarpy County, home to some of the state's first settlements, with items related to the early explorers, fur traders, and trappers as well as Native American artifacts, then move forward in time to period rooms re-creating the home styles of the turn of the 20th century. | 2402 Clay St. | 402/292–1880 | $2 | Mon.–Fri. 9–5.

ON THE CALENDAR

AUG.: *Offutt Air Force Base Open House.* Vintage and contemporary military aircraft take to the skies at Nebraska's largest airshow, which also has live music, exhibits, and food booths, as well as displays of still more planes on the ground. Best entry point for the two-day event, always held the last weekend of August, is the SAC gate on Capehard Road. | 402/294–3663.

Dining

Amarillo Barbecue. Barbecue. The quiet dining room has a mix of antiques and "Texas-like" touches, such as metal signs. You can opt for booths or tables, but the country music is standard with either choice. Known for the stuffed baked potatoes, smoked meat sandwiches, and dinners of good portions with such side orders as corn bread with jalapeño peppers, plus the cobblers for dessert. | 303 Fort Crook Rd. N | 402/291–7495 | $4–$15 | AE, MC, V.

Nettie's Fine Mexican Food. Mexican. The name says it all—Mexican food, in an easy-going setting with a range of beef, chicken, and other specialties, all served south-of-the-border style. There's a separate lounge for socializing. | 7110 Railroad Ave. | 402/733–3359 | Closed Sun., Mon. | $7–$8 | No credit cards.

Stella's. American. This neighborhood bar and lounge known for its burgers, burgers, burgers is almost a lunchtime institution for personnel from nearby Offutt Air Force Base. Pictures of the owner's relatives and friends are on the walls. The TV's always on, but the volume's rarely up—except during Nebraska football games. Sandwiches and burgers are served on napkins, the fries in a bowl. No forks and knives needed here. | 106 Galvin Rd. S | 402/291–6088 | Closed Sun. | $2–$8 | No credit cards.

Lodging

Quality Inn Crown Court. This large two-story brick structure with an atrium, near Fontenelle Forest and downtown Bellevue, has a heated indoor pool for your morning laps, followed by a complimentary "power breakfast" hot buffet. Restaurant, bar, complimentary breakfast, room service. Some refrigerators, some minibars, some microwaves. Cable TV. Hot tub. Game room. Laundry facilities. Business services. No pets. | 1811 Hillcrest Dr. | 402/292–3800 or 800/228–5151 | fax 402/292–6373 | QualityInnOmaha@Prodigy.net | 126 rooms | $53–$110 | AE, D, DC, MC, V.

Super 8 Motel. There is an eating area in the lobby, although you may wish to prepare your own snacks using the in-room microwaves and refrigerators. Cold-weather hookups are available. Complimentary Continental breakfast. In-room data ports, hot tubs. Cable TV. Business services. | 303 Fort Crook Rd. | 402/291–1518 | fax 402/292–1726 | 40 rooms | $42–$70 | AE, D, DC, MC, V.

BLAIR

(Nearby towns also listed: Bancroft, Fremont, Omaha, West Point)

Sometimes considered a suburb of Omaha, Blair is a small, vital community with a rich heritage tied both to Dana College, started in 1884 as a seminary by the Danish Evangelical Lutheran Church, and to Oglala Sioux holy man Black Elk, immortalized by the poet John Neihardt. Blair was settled by Danes but named for railroad magnate John I. Blair. Today, it is an industrial center that is home to several nationally known companies. Nearby attractions include Fort Atkinson, a stopover for Lewis and Clark that later became the first American military fort in present-day Nebraska, and the DeSoto National Wildlife Refuge, home to artifacts from the *Bertrand*, a supply boat that went down in the Missouri River on April 1, 1865, while en route from St. Louis to Fort Benton, Montana Territory.

Information: Blair Area Chamber of Commerce | 1526 Washington St., Blair 68008 | 402/533–4455 | fax 402/533–4456 | blairchamber@huntel.net | www.blairchamber.org.

Attractions

Black Elk/Neihardt Park. The 80-acre park includes a pavilion and picnic shelters as well as a monument depicting the visions of the Oglala seer Black Elk. | 31st St. and College St. | 402/426–5025 | Free | Daily.

Boyer Chute National Wildlife Refuge. A new preserve 10 mi southeast of Blair on County Road 34 alongside the Missouri River, the Boyer Chute is a restored river channel surrounded by 2,000 acres of grassland, woodland, and wetlands, with two short nature trails and a 4-mi hiking loop. | 712/642–4121 | Free | Daily dawn to dusk.

DeSoto National Wildlife Refuge. Up to half-a-million snow geese pause here for a few weeks during their southbound migration each fall. You can view them from an outdoor area or from within the glass-walled galleries of the visitor center, 3 mi east of Blair. Besides displays about the flora and fauna of the refuge, which is partially in Iowa, the center has more than 200,000 well-preserved articles recovered from the steamboat *Bertrand*, which sank in the region in 1865. No-wake boating and fishing are permitted on the lake, and you'll find plenty of hiking trails on the grounds. | 1434 316th Lane, Missouri Valley, IA | 712/642–4121 | $3 per car | Daily except winter holidays.

Fort Atkinson State Historical Park. The original fort, for some years the only military presence west of the Missouri, was built in 1820 close to the site where Lewis and Clark met with local Native Americans in 1804. A re-created fort with barracks and log walls now occupies the grounds, which are 10 mi south of Blair, with living-history programs the first weekend of each month from May through October to give you a deeper feeling for the life of the 1,000 men billeted there. | 7th and Madison, Fort Calhoun | 402/468–5611 | ngp.ngpc.state.ne.us/parks/ftatkin.html | Neb. Parks Permit required | Grounds: daily 8–7. Visitor Center: Memorial Day–Labor Day, daily 9–5 PM.

ON THE CALENDAR

DEC.: *Sights and Sounds of Christmas*. To keep alive the Scandinavian customs brought from the Old World, this annual observance at Dana College on the first Sunday in December includes storytelling, making tree ornaments, concerts by Dana College students, and a groaning board of traditional foods. The big smorgasbord begins at 10:30 in the morning and turns over seating every 45 minutes until 6:15 PM. | 2848 College Dr. | 402/426–7216.

BLAIR

INTRO
ATTRACTIONS
DINING
LODGING

Dining

Jake's Bar and Grill. American. There's been a restaurant of one kind or another here since 1972, but Jake's took over the space in 1999. Now it's a sports bar, with several strategically placed televisions throughout the dining area, plus a big-screen TV. The crowd at Jake's is largely made up of locals who come for the ground-steak burgers and loaded nachos—and their favorite sports events. | 218 S. 8th St. | 402/426–9928 | $4–$9 | No breakfast | AE, D, MC, V.

Lodging

Landmark Inn. Erected in 1891 as the Keeley Rehabilitation Institute, this two-story frame building is downtown, right across from the old train depot. The lobby and main staircase are from the original structure and display photos of the Institute's opening. Throughout, you'll see original antique furniture and fixtures. Some dorm-style rooms share baths; others are like small apartments. Microwaves, refrigerators. Cable TV. Some room phones. | 1465 Front St. | 402/426–2650 | 20 rooms | $30–40 | No credit cards.

Rath Inn. After a day at Fort Atkinson State Historical Park, 7 mi away, you can return to this inn for a relaxing evening in the deck furniture on the covered front porch. This red-brick two-story building on the southern edge of town has a gently traditional look inside, and there is parking for trucks. Complimentary Continental breakfast. Refrigerators in suites. Pool. Pets allowed (fee). | 1355 Hwy. 30S | 402/426–2340 | fax 402/426–8703 | 32 rooms | $39–$60 | AE, D, DC, MC, V.

Super 8 Motel. If you'd like a real roof over your head after a day exploring the log walls of Fort Atkinson, this motel is only 5 mi from the park, on Highway 75 on the southern edge of Blair. Truck parking and cold-weather hookups are available. Complimentary Continental breakfast. Cable TV. | 558 S. 13th St. | 402/426–8888 | fax 402/426–8889 | 48 rooms | $48–$84 | AE, D, DC, MC, V.

BRIDGEPORT

MAP 11, B3

(Nearby towns also listed: Alliance, Bayard, Gering, Scottsbluff, Sidney)

After gold was discovered in the Black Hills of South Dakota in 1874, many dreamers and prospectors railroaded to Sidney, then crossed the Platte River on the Camp Clarke Bridge. When entrepreneurs saw that those travelers would need supplies, the town of Bridgeport grew up around the bridge. Though the span no longer exists, the town is still a supply center for the agricultural region.

Information: **Bridgeport Chamber of Commerce** | Prairie Winds Community Center, 428 Mack St., Bridgeport 69336 | 308/262–1825 | fax 308/262–0229 | pwcc98@hamilton.net | www.bridgeport-ne.com.

Attractions

Bridgeport State Recreation Area. Located in the valley of the North Platte River, this region offers hiking, primitive camping, picnicking, boating, and swimming. Follow Highway 26 east just until you cross the railroad tracks, then take the next left, and you should run right into the park. | 800/826–7275 or 308/262–1825 | Neb. Parks Permit required; camping, $6 with electricity | Daily.

Courthouse and Jail Rocks. For the pioneers who took the Oregon Trail to build new lives in the West, these two large rocky outcroppings were some of the first they saw after they'd crossed the long, dusty miles of the plains. The rocks are 5 mi south of Bridgeport on Route 88, with hiking trails leading around them. | 308/262–1825 | Free | Daily.

AUG.: *Greek Festival.* Sponsored by the Greek Orthodox Church, this celebration of the Aegean heritage in this community is always on the weekend closet to August 15. The Saturday night dinner is followed by entertainment and dancing to that rousing music familiar from so many films. | 308/586–1926 or 308/262–1825.

Dining
Bell Motor Inn Restaurant. American. If you find yourself stricken with a mid-afternoon craving for a home-cooked breakfast, consider heading to this casual, family-run restaurant, in the Bell Motor Inn on Highway 385N, for cheesy scrambled eggs and hand-grated hash browns. Large windows in the dining area illuminate the green-and-burgundy interior. For dinner, there are chicken-fried steak and several shrimp preparations. | Hwy. 385N | 308/262–0557 | Closed Sun. after 4 | $5–$15 | AE, MC, V.

Lodging
Bell Motor Inn. Handily next to a gas station and convenience store, this blond brick motel on Highway 385N is about 5 mi from the Courthouse and Jail Rocks and near the Platte River. Restaurant, bar. Cable TV. Pets allowed. | Hwy. 385N | 308/262–0557 | fax 308/262–0923 | 22 rooms | $35–$44 | AE, D, MC, V.

Bridgeport Inn. This single-story, family-run motel was built in 1930, but remodeled in 1997. It has a quiet, almost rural demeanor—you'll find lawn chairs for lounging on the front lawn and recliners and rocking chairs in the lobby. In-room data ports. Cable TV. Business services. Pets allowed (fee). | 517 Main St. | 308/262–0290 | sandmaur@hamilton.net | 12 rooms | $46.50 | AE, MC, V.

BROKEN BOW
MAP 11, E3

(Nearby towns also listed: Burwell, Dannebrog, Lexington)

The town that got its name when an early settler found a broken Native American bow here is in the heart of Nebraska's prime ranching country. Sandhills grasslands still cover the rolling hills all around, providing a good habitat for various types of wildlife—especially the pheasants that have drawn such notables as Neil Armstrong and Norman Schwarzkopf to the annual One Box Pheasant Hunt.

Information: Broken Bow Chamber of Commerce | 444 S. 8th Ave., Broken Bow 68822 | 308/872–5691 | fax 308/872–6137 | bbchamber@alltel.net | www.custercounty.com.

Attractions
Custer County Historical Museum. The museum is right on the town square with its century-old bandstand. Its collection of memorabilia from 1880s pioneer life to the present includes photographs by Solomon Butcher documenting the Plains lifestyle of homesteaders in the late 19th century. | 445 S. 9th Ave. | 308/872–2203 | Free | June–Aug., 10–5; Sept.–May, 1–5.

Victoria Springs State Recreation Area. Originally known for its mineral waters, Victoria Springs is a wooded oasis amid Nebraska's Sandhills, 6 mi east of the town of Anselmo. Besides areas for tent camping and RVs, it has two modern housekeeping cabins overlooking the lake where visitors can fish or ride on paddleboats. There's also a one-room schoolhouse that can be opened by appointment. From Broken Bow, drive 20 mi west on Route 2 to Anselmo, then east on Route 21A. | 308/749–2235 | ngp.ngpc.state.ne.us/parks/vspring.html | Neb. Parks Permit required; camping, $7–$10; cabins, $50 | Grounds, daily; cabins, Memorial Day–late Nov.

ON THE CALENDAR

SEPT.: *Kite Fly.* Anyone can enter the annual stunt kite competition Labor Day weekend, but you must register. If you just want to watch the soaring fliers, bring your own lawn chair or blanket—it all takes place in the open space of Callaway Golf Course 6 mi southeast of Callaway on Route 40. | 308/836–2245.

Dining

Lobby Restaurant. American. On the first floor of the Arrow Hotel, the Lobby Restaurant has plenty of good food, including a lunch buffet, in an old-fashioned country setting. The menu is mostly American, with some twists now and then, like the gyros and Greek salad on the dinner list along with steaks and prime rib. | 509 S 9th St. | 308/872–3363 | $6–16 | Mon.–Fri., Sun. 7–2, 5–10 | AE, D, MC, V.

Uncle Buck's. Steak. The Old West is still alive, though ever so well-mannered, at this steakhouse/inn/saloon along the North Loup River on Route 7 in Brewster, about 50 mi from Broken Bow. The building, on a working ranch, is 100-plus years old, with pressed tin ceilings, hardwood furnishings, and a long polished oak bar, an adjacent dance hall, and—just like in the old days—guest rooms upstairs (*see* Uncle Buck's Lodge). You'll find steaks and sandwiches, and there are always a salad bar and homemade pies (the apple pie is especially popular). | 308/547–2210 | $2–$22 | D, MC, V.

Lodging

Arrow Hotel. When this downtown hotel in an historic 1928 building by the town square was modernized in the 1980s, its flapper-era rooms were made into minisuites with their own kitchenettes. Restaurant, bar. Cable TV. | 509 S. 9th St. | 308/872–6662 | 22 suites | $40–$85 | AE, D, MC, V.

Gateway Motel. This motel in a commercial area on Route 2 on the east end of town, has simple accommodations, but it is near Sylvester's Lounge, a local hang-out for the music on weekends. Cable TV. Sauna. Pets allowed. | 628 E. South E St. | 308/872–2478 | 23 rooms | $25–$40 | AE, D, DC, MC, V.

Super 8 Motel. You can spend your quiet times as you wish at this motel on the east end of town. Built in 1990, it has a fitness center if you want to work out, and many rooms have a high-backed easy chair and floor lamp if you'd rather sit and read. Complimentary Continental breakfast. In-room data ports. Cable TV. Exercise equipment. Laundry facilities. | 215 E. South E St. | 308/872–6428 | fax 308/872–5031 | 32 rooms | $43–$62 | AE, D, DC, MC, V.

Uncle Buck's Lodge. In the Old West tradition, this B&B on a 10,000-acre ranch has eight sleeping rooms and one suite above a restaurant and saloon, with hunting trophies and classic quilts displayed in the great room. Accommodations in the 100-year-old structure are generally modernized, although amenities vary by room. These spaces and campground spaces are available as part of the ranch's vacation or "Sandhills Adventures" hunting packages; call for rates and other information. Restaurant, bar with entertainment. No air conditioning in some rooms. | Hwy. 7, Brewster | 308/547–2210 | www.unclebuckslodge.com | 8 rooms, 1 suite | D, MC, V.

Wagon Wheel. This modest motel on Route 2, which is E Street, has been in town since the 1940s, but all the rooms have since been remodeled, and a sauna and heated pool have been added. Truck parking and RV hookups are available. The Broken Bow Municipal Airport is 5 mi away. Cable TV. Heated pool. Sauna. Hot tub. Playground. Some pets allowed. | 1545 South E St. | 308/872–2433 or 800/770–2433 | 15 rooms | $23–$37 | AE, D, DC, MC, V.

William Penn Lodge. Rooms in this traditional, white clapboard motor inn on Route 2 have refrigerators for your cold snacks, and some have microwaves, too. You are near the Sandhills here, and the parking area has spaces for trucks, with cold-weather hookups. Refrigerators, some microwaves. Cable TV. Pets allowed. | 853 E. South E St. | 308/872–2412 | fax 308/872–6376 | 28 rooms | $35–$55 | AE, D, MC, V.

BROWNVILLE

(Nearby towns also listed: Auburn, Nebraska City)

In 1854, Richard Brown crossed the Missouri River and built a cabin in the newly formed Nebraska Territory. Two years later, Brownville was incorporated, and it soon became an important riverfront town and a jumping-off point for travelers headed farther west. It continued to grow, especially after the *Nebraska Advertiser* promoted opportunities in Brownville, and developed a thriving cultural life with band performances and dances at the Brownville House.

After plans for a railroad link to Fort Kearny failed in the late 1860s, population declined, and Brownville withered. But it didn't die. A century later, the town experienced a revival with the forming of the Brownville Historical Society and the Brownville Fine Arts Association. These groups began sponsoring cultural events and undertook restoration of historic homes and buildings. The Brownville Village Theater, Nebraska's oldest summer rep theater, has now been active for more than 30 years, the Brownville Concert Series attracts national and international artists, and several companies operate riverboats for sightseeing jaunts or dinner cruises on the river.

Information: Brownville Chamber of Commerce | 116 Main St., Brownville 68321 | 402/825–4131 or 800/305–7990 | jm62006@navix.net.

Attractions

Brownville Historic District. Although the description *antebellum* fits the buildings and homes in the district in time terms, it is antebellum with a Midwestern sensibility. Many of the structures are in red brick, with a spare, squared-off shape, yet the ornately carved accents and the size of the lots around them bear testimony to this prosperity of their owners and this riverside community in the mid-1800s. The area, which covers most of downtown, is today a popular tourist attraction and the site of a number of town events. | 116 Main St. | 402/825–6001 or 402/825–4131 | Free; fee at some homes | June–Labor Day, daily 10–5; Labor Day–June, weekends 10–5.

In a gabled brick building in the historic area, the **Brownville Museum** has many objects that were in daily use when Brownville was a bustling port on the Missouri. | 4th and Main Sts. | 402/825–6178 | $1 | June–Aug., daily 1–5; Sept.–mid-Oct., weekends and by appointment.

Another popular attraction in the Brownville Historic District is the **Carson House.** Built in 1860 by Brownville's founder, Richard Brown, who then sold it to John Carson, southeast Nebraska's leading banker, this home is filled with original furnishings left by the Carson family. | 3rd St. at Main St. | 402/825–6001 | $1 | Memorial Day–Labor Day, daily 1–5.

In Brownville's heyday of almost a century and a half ago, many people knew about the house in Brownville Historic District that is now known as the **Governor Furnas Home** because the 2½-story structure, which shows both Italianate and Gothic Revival influences, was the home of Robert Furnas, Nebraska's second elected governor. | 6th St. at Water St. | 402/825–6001 or 402/825–4131 | Donations accepted | Weekends 1–5.

Brownville Mills. Long ago, Brownville produced many *firsts* in the new state of Nebraska—including the first hotel, first lawyer and first woman lawyer, first marriage, and first postmaster. This downtown enterprise dates only to the 1950s, but is the state's oldest health-food store, selling its stone-ground flours and other products from a building that housed the Lone Tree Saloon in the 1860s. | 116 Main St. | 800/305–7990 | Mon.–Sat. 9–5, Sun. 1–5.

Brownville State Recreation Area. On the eastern edge of town, just before the Missouri bridge, this park has primitive camping, picnicking, and fishing areas, as well as access to the Steamboat Trace, a 21-mi hiking and biking trail. | 402/883–2575 | ngp.ngpc.state.ne.us/parks/brownvil.html | Neb. Parks Permit required; camping $5 | Daily.

Brownville Village Theater. In a one-time church just off Main Street, this repertory theater presents a variety of stage productions from June through the Labor Day weekend. | 222 Water St. | 402/825–4121 | Fri. 7:30, Sat. and Sun. 2 and 7:30.

Indian Cave State Park. Named after an overhanging sandstone bluff that carries Nebraska's only known examples of the Native American rock carvings called petroglyphs, the park also includes the ruins and some reconstructed buildings of the old river community of St. Deroin. You'll find areas for hiking, camping, cross-country skiing, and sledding, as well as a modern RV campground. It's about 9 mi south of Brownville on Route 64E. | 402/883–2575 | icavesp@ngpc.state.ne.us | ngp.ngpc.state.ne.us/parks/icave.html | Neb. Parks Permit required, camping $8–$12 | Daily; camping Mar.–Nov.

Meriwether Lewis Dredge and Missouri River History Museum. Brownville's past as a riverboat town is memorialized in the museum on the *Captain Meriwether Lewis*, a retired steam-powered, sidewheel vessel used to dredge the Missouri River for more than 30 years. | 402/825–3341 | $2 | May–mid-Oct., daily 10–6.

River Cruises. Several companies have river tours, for daytime outings or dinners on the water. The best known is the two-deck paddlewheeler *Spirit of Brownville*, which plies the the Missouri from Memorial Day to Labor Day on weekend sightseeing sojourns to Indian Cave State Park south of town, with moonlight dinner cruises Thursday through Sunday. For information, call 402/825–6441. For names of other cruise companies, contact the Brownville Chamber of Commerce at 402/825–4131 or 800/305–7990.

Verdon Lake State Recreation Area. Like many other state recreation areas, this is a small, quiet place, 1 mi west of the town of Verdon on Highway 73, where you can kick back, relax, and drop a fishing line, or perhaps just come for the picnicking or primitive camping. | 402/883–2575 | ngp.ngpc.state.ne.us/parks/verdon.html | Neb. Parks Permit required; camping $3 | Daily.

ON THE CALENDAR

MAY: *Nemaha County Great Missouri River Boat Race.* To herald the summer season, the *Spirit of Brownville* and a guest contender re-enact the great steamboat races of yesteryear in a Memorial Day weekend competition. The race, which takes about two hours, begins at Brownville State Recreation Area, and guests are allowed to ride the boats. | 402/825–6441.

MAY AND SEPT.: *Annual Spring and Fall Flea Markets.* You may find a prize or a trifle, but you know what they say about one man's junk being another man's treasure. For more than 40 years, the Brownville Historical Society's flea markets have been drawing people to the Brownville historic area. | 402/825–6001.

Lodging

Rock Port Inn Motel. Although it sits just off I–29 across the border in Missouri, about 7 mi from Brownville, this two-story, Colonial-style building is in a quiet rural area with a large lawn and trees out back. Inside, the lobby carries out the country feeling with lots of bird feeders and flowers. Some refrigerators, some microwaves. Cable TV. Pool. Laundry facilities. Pets allowed. | 1200 Hwy. 136W, Rock Port, MO | 660/744–6282 | 36 rooms | $43–$50 | AE, D, DC, MC, V.

BURWELL

MAP 11, F3

(Nearby towns also listed: Broken Bow, Dannebrog, St. Paul)

Settled in the 1870s by homesteaders who started farms near Fort Hartsuff, Burwell is still a productive farming and ranching region that draws about 15,000 to 20,000 people to the 80-year-old event known as Nebraska's Big Rodeo.

Information: **Burwell Chamber of Commerce** | 147 S. 8th St., Burwell 68823 | 308/346–5121.

Attractions

Calamus Reservoir State Recreation Area. You'll find fishing, boating, picnicking, swimming, and camping sites all around the Calamus Reservoir 7 mi northwest of Burwell on Highway 96. | 308/346–5666 | ngp.ngpc.state.ne.us/parks.calamus.html | Neb. Parks Permit required; camping $3–$12 | Camping May–late Sept. only.

Fort Hartsuff State Historical Park. Infantry soldiers arrived here in the Loup River Valley in 1874. Their fort with nine lime-concrete buildings was the main defense for the area until 1881. The restored buildings, 4 mi north of the town of Elyria, include stables, officers' quarters, and barracks around a square parade ground. | 308/346–4715 | npg.ngpc.state.ne.us/parks/hartsuff.html | Neb. Parks Permit required | Daily.

ON THE CALENDAR

JULY: *Nebraska's Big Rodeo.* The riding and roping and other contests are in a classic Western-style arena, with wooden chutes and pens, that is listed on the National Register of Historic Places. Besides the professionally sanctioned competitions, the program includes chuck wagon and wild horse races and junior steer wrestling. Elsewhere on the 40-acre rodeo grounds, on Highway 11 on the southeast edge of town, you can visit a carnival or quilt, livestock, and classic car shows. | 888/328–7935 or 308/346–5121.

Dining

Maverick Cafe. American. Catering to long-haul truckers and road-weary travelers, this rough-and-tumble local fixture has metal siding on the outside and classic early '70s wood paneling within. The Maverick double cheeseburger (a pair of massive beef patties with lettuce, tomato, and mayo, with a mountain of hash browns or fries on the side) is a local favorite. Sunday brunch buffet. | Hwy. 11 at Hwy. 91 | 308/346–5699 | $3–$5 | No credit cards.

CHADRON

MAP 11, B1

(Nearby towns also listed: Alliance, Crawford, Harrison)

Around Chadron, the rolling Sandhills give way to the breaks of Pine Ridge to the west. It is a ranching and farming region but also a college town, home of Chadron State College, and one of the largest cities in the Nebraska Panhandle.

The area was traditionally used by the Lakota, Cheyenne, and Kiowa tribes, and it was the site of one of the first fur-trading posts in this part of North America. At the Museum of the Fur Trade, you'll see many everyday items from the 30 years Frenchman James Bordeaux ran that trading center, along with other frontier-life necessities dating back to the early 1800s.

Information: **Chadron Chamber of Commerce** | 706 W. 3rd St., Chadron 69337 | 308/432–4401 or 800/603–2937 | fax 308/432–4757 | chamber@chadron.com | www.chadron.com/. Also: **Dawes County Travel Board** | Box 746, Chadron 69337 | 800/603–2937 or 308/432–4401.

Attractions

Chadron State College/Mari Sandoz Heritage Room. This memorial space in the college's administration building honors area native Mari Sandoz, who wrote *Cheyenne Autumn* (later made into a gripping epic film), *Old Jules, Crazy Horse,* and other books about the history and people of western Nebraska. | 1000 Main St. | 308/432–6276 | Free | By appointment only.

Chadron State Park. It's easy to see why this spot in the beautiful rugged Pine Ridge 8 mi south of Chadron became Nebraska's first state park. Many trails lead through the back country, where you may meet wild deer or shy, retreating porcupines. In the evening, you're likely to hear coyotes yipping in the distance. You can tour by Jeep, horseback, or just take the hiking and biking trails on your own. There are a crafts center, picnic areas, a lagoon for fishing and paddleboating, camping sites, and 22 cabins for rent. | 15951 Hwy. 385 | 308/432–6167 | ngp.ngpc.state.ne.us/parks/chadron.html | Neb. Parks Permit required; camping, $7–$14; cabins, $50–$60 | Daily; camp sites, May–Nov.; cabins, Apr.–Nov.

Museum of the Fur Trade. On the land where James Bordeaux ran his trading post, the museum has constructed a replica of his original outpost behind the main building. Exhibits show trade goods, weapons, furs, and other items that kept life going in the early 19th century. | 6321 E. Hwy. 20 | 308/432–3843 | $2.50 | Memorial Day–Labor Day, daily 8–5; Sept.–May, by appointment only.

Pine Ridge National Recreation Area. Part of the Nebraska National Forest, this area along the Pine Ridge is one of rugged beauty, with limestone bluffs, buttes, and open ranges. Hiking trails wind through the site, or you can bring your horse and ride. Mountain bikes are permitted, but motorized vehicles are not. Camp sites are available. It's about 14 mi southwest of Chadron, and one of the best entry points is the Roberts Trailhead off Bethel Road. The Nebraska National Forest also includes the Oglala National Grasslands and other federally managed reserves in both Nebraska and South Dakota. (*See* listings under Crawford, Harrison, and Thedford.) Call 308/432–0300 or 308/432–4401 for specific directions to other areas of interest. | 16524 Hwy. 385 | 308/432–4475 | Free; camping, $5 | Mon.–Fri., 7:30–4:30.

ON THE CALENDAR

JULY: *Fur Trade Days.* This festival the second weekend of July includes arts and crafts shows, a parade, music, fireworks, a fun run, a flea market, and—straight from the days when traders and settlers had to create their own amusements—a buffalo chip-throwing contest. | 800/603–2937.

OCT.: *World Famous Ugly Pickup Parade and Contest.* The judges will make their decisions, but you may want to decide for yourself which is the ugliest pickup, the prettiest entrant in the "Miss Ugly Pickup" contest, and the best recipe in the chili cookoff. The international event honoring the rural farm truck is always on the Friday closest to Halloween, downtown at Flag Plaza. | 308/432–4401.

Dining

Garden Level. American. In the Elks Building downtown, this spot is below street-level and adjacent to a comfortable bar and lounge. One of the few places in town with a wine list, Garden Level also features menu items such as New York strip steak, prime rib, and filet mignon. Locals are fond of the Thursday night all-you-can-eat ribs special. | 247 Bordeaux St. | 308/432–5084 | Sun. | $8–$16 | MC, V.

Lodging

Best Western West Hills Inn. The light and airy pale brick motel sits on a hill near the scenic Pine Ridge, 3 mi from the Fur Trade Museum. The rooms, in soft beiges and browns, have hot tubs, and many include two easy-curling chairs with a reading lamp. Complimentary Continental breakfast. Some microwaves, some refrigerators. Cable TV. Indoor pool. Hot tub. Exercise equipment. Laundry facilities. Pets allowed. | 1100 W. 10th St. | 308/432–3305 | fax 308/432–5990 | 66 rooms | $55–$115 | AE, D, DC, MC, V.

Economy 9. This modest one-story brick motel is at the junction of Highway 20 and Highway 385 in the north part of town, with a hot tub for easing sore muscles after a hike along the ridge. Cable TV. Hot tub. Pets allowed. | 1201 W. Highway U.S. 20 | 308/432–3119 | fax 308/432–3119 | 21 rooms | $30–$50 | AE, D, DC, MC, V.

Olde Main Street Inn. A three-generation female operation, this B&B, two blocks north of the town's single stoplight, dates to 1890. Built like a fort, the three-story brick structure was once headquarters for General Nelson Miles, who commanded U.S. Army troops at Wounded Knee in nearby South Dakota in 1891. Now a rustic country inn of suites and mini-suites, it has a real well, a running fountain, a fireplace in the dining room, and preserved remnants of the original wallpaper. Truck parking and cold-weather hookups are available. Restaurant, bar, complimentary breakfast. Some rooms with shower only. Cable TV. Pets allowed. | 115 Main St. | 308/432–3380 | www.chadron.com/oldemain | 9 rooms | $30–$72 | AE, D, MC, V.

Our Heritage Bed and Breakfast. A working, family-run ranch since 1887, this B&B is on a clover-dotted prairie, nestled between pine-topped hills, 100-year-old cedar trees, and the fossils-filled Badlands. You'll be put up for the night in a private two-room guest house with a full kitchen and, if you wish, you can participate in a "working ranch experience," including fixing fences and feeding livestock. Complimentary Continental breakfast. No air-conditioning. Pond. Fishing. | 1041 Toadstool Rd. | 308/665–2810 or 308/665–1613 | jnkolling@bbc.net | www.bbc.net/ohbedandbreakfast/ | 2 rooms | $150 | No credit cards.

Super 8 Motel. If you've come from the east, you may want to reset watches. At this beige-and-stucco motel ½ mi east of the junction of Highways 20 and 385, you are definitely in the Mountain Time Zone. Renovated in 1996, it has some suites with recliners and coffeemakers. Truck parking and cold-weather hookups are available. Complimentary Continental breakfast. Cable TV. Indoor pool. Hot tub. Laundry facilities. Pets allowed. | 840 U.S. 20W | 308/432–4471 | fax 308/432–3991 | Super8chadron@aol.com | 45 rooms | $44–$64 | AE, D, DC, MC, V.

COLUMBUS

MAP 11, G3

(Nearby towns also listed: Fremont, Grand Island, York)

When the Spaniard Don Pedro de Villasur reached the area near the confluence of the Loup and the Platte rivers in 1720, he drove off the Spanish traders who were already there and attacked the Pawnee tribe. That conflict is believed to be the first involving European explorers in Nebraska.

More than a century later, as the Plains Indian Wars heated up, Frank and Luther North recruited Pawnees to be scouts for the American Frontier Army. Those Pawnee scouts were probably the first Native Americans to ally themselves officially with the frontier troops against other western Native American tribes.

The North brothers also became acquainted with scout William F. "Buffalo Bill" Cody and helped him develop his Buffalo Bill Wild West Show. Long before the show won international acclaim touring Europe with Annie Oakley, Buffalo Bill's troupe presented its first performance in Columbus in 1881.

Old and new are interwoven throughout Columbus. Downtown, more than 100 buildings in the National Historic District date to the 1870s. The 1857 cabin of Fredrick Gottschalk, one of the town's original 13 settlers, remains intact within one of the four 1912 buildings that make up the Platte County Museum, and in Pawnee Park, you'll hear the peals from the Quincentenary Belltower, constructed in 1992 as a monument to the 500th anniversary of Columbus's arrival in America using bells from the churches of our own era.

Information: Columbus Chamber of Commerce | 764 33rd Ave., Columbus 68602-0515 | 402/564-2769 | fax 402/564-2026 | chamber@megavision.com | www.ci.columbus.ne.us.

Attractions

Genoa Indian School. Young Native Americans once were housed and schooled here, 20 mi west of Columbus off Highway 22, in an attempt to assimilate them into European-based cultures. At the site, you also can see the Genoa Museum, with exhibits on the Pawnees and on the Mormon Trail. | 209 E. Webster Ave., Genoa | 402/993–2349 | $2.50 | Fri.–Sun. 2–4:30, or by appointment.

Lake North. Around Lake North, you'll find 2 mi of sandy beaches for good swimming and picnicking, along with boating and camping, and the starting point for a beautiful 7 mi trail. Lake Babcock, a wetlands preserve and reservoir area, sits across the roadway. The lakes are about 4 mi north of Columbus. | Monastery Rd. | 402/564–3171 | Free | Daily until the water freezes in winter.

Pawnee Park. To bring a new view of the surrounding territory, there's a living tree museum, a grove of trees representing all the native species of the area. At this 40-acre park on the southern edge of town, you'll also find a 1904 steam locomotive, playgrounds, a pool, a rose garden, tennis and basketball courts, and fishing and ice skating areas. | 7th St. and Hwy. 81 | 402/564–0914 | Free | Daily.

Platte County Museum. An 1857 cottonwood cabin that housed a former Platte County settler has been preserved inside the museum's main building, one of four 1911 schools in the complex. Other displays tell of local town and farm life in the early 20th century, with antique farm equipment around the grounds. | 2916 16th St. | 402/564–1856 | $2 | May–Labor Day, Fri.–Sun. 1–4; Sept.–May, by appointment.

ON THE CALENDAR

MAY: *Gold Rush Days.* You can really kick up your heels at the Saturday night hoedown during this four-day event, which also includes a wagon train camp, craft exhibits, and lots of kids' activities, at the Agricultural Society site the locals call Ag Park. | 402/564–2769.

AUG.: *Columbus Days.* There's always a Sunday parade, but other activities, at various sites around the city the third weekend of the month, show a range of interests old and new in such events as a baby show, lip sync contest, horseshoe-tossing, turtle races, and a tractor pull. | 402/564–2769.

JULY–SEPT.: *Horse Racing.* Through the modern technology of simulcasts and satellite uplinks to other racing facilities, you can participate in pari-mutuel thoroughbred racing in this three-month "race meet" at Ag Park. Food and beverages are available. | 402/564–0133.

Dining

Dusters/Gottberg Brew Pub. American. The building was once an automobile factory; now it houses two distinctive approaches to dining. At Dusters, which is open daily, you'll find exotic items such as alligator along with traditional veal, lamb, seafood, and steaks. The brew pub, which is closed on Sunday, has a more casual menu but with such unusual items as buffalo burgers—plus its six types of brews, including beer, root beer, and cream soda. | 2804 13th St. | 402/564–8338 | $7–$25 | AE, D, MC, V.

Lodging

Berkey Motel. This modest, two-story brick motel built on the scenic "old Lincoln" highway in the late 1940s is just a block from the city park and pool. It's been remodeled several times in the years since its birth, and now both and Highways 80 and 81 pass right in front. Cable TV. | 3220 8th St. | 402/564–2729 or 800/288–3658 | 21 rooms | $34–$38 | MC, V.

Eco-Lux Inn. This in-town motel is popular with long-distance truckers because it's just a short haul from the interstate, and cold-weather hook-ups are available. A number of chain restaurants are within a block. Complimentary Continental breakfast. Cable TV. Laundry facilities. Business services. No pets. | 3803 23rd St. | 402/564–9955 | fax 402/564–9436 | 39 rooms, 1 suite | $35–$50 | AE, D, DC, MC, V.

Johnnie's. Within walking distance of several restaurants and stores, this white brick motor inn has one section built in the 1950s and another added in the 1960s. It is 16 mi from Columbus and one block from Highway 15, with truck parking and cold-weather hookups. Cable TV. Some pets allowed. | 222 W. 16th St., Schuyler | 402/352–5454 | 30 rooms | $37–$45 | AE, D, DC, MC, V.

New World Inn. Well-tended plants add interest to the interior courtyard of this mid-range motel that has several rooms overlooking the Loup River. It's about eight blocks from shopping areas and the city park, but has volleyball and picnic areas right on site. Restaurant, bar, picnic area, room service. Cable TV. Indoor pool. Volleyball. Laundry facilities. Business services, airport shuttle. | 265 33rd Ave. | 402/564–1492 or 800/433–1492 | fax 402/563–3989 | 154 rooms | $65–$75 | AE, D, DC, MC, V.

St. Benedict Religious Retreat and Conference Facility. The St. Benedict Center on Highway 15 in Schuyler is an ecumenical spiritual retreat that offers rooms, meals, and quiet walks. Spiritual direction is provided if requested, and guests can participate in daily religious ceremonies and prayer with the monks if they choose. Both individual and group retreats may be arranged, with or without meals. No room phones, no TV. | 1126 Rd. I, Schuyler | 402/352–8819 | fax 402/352–8884 | 44 rooms | $20–$30 | MC, V.

Super 8 Motel. This in-town motel still offers personalized wake-up calls, along with a "modified superstart breakfast" and round-the-clock coffee in the lobby. King and Queen rooms have recliners. Cable TV. Business services. | 3324 20th St. | 402/563–3456 | fax 402/563–3679 | 64 rooms | $47–$56 | AE, D, DC, MC, V.

COZAD

MAP 11, E4

(Nearby towns also listed: Eustis, Gothenburg, Lexington)

Cozad is where the East meets West—literally. It is on the 100th meridian, the demarcation line between the "wet" east and the "dry" plains. Just east of Cozad, more than 20 inches of rain falls annually; just west of town, less than half that amount reaches the ground each year.

The town, in the center of a farming region, was named for John Cozad, the man who arrived wearing a tailcoat and diamond stickpin. One of the town's best-known residents was his son, Robert Henry, who changed his name to Robert Henri and became an accomplished artist who helped start the Ashcan school of painting. His work hangs in New York's Museum of Modern Art and at the Robert Henri Museum and Historical Walkway in Cozad.

Information: Cozad Chamber of Commerce | 211 W. 8th St., Cozad 69130 | 308/784–3930 | fax 308/784–3509.

Attractions

100th Meridian Museum. Named, of course, for Cozad's special geographical position, this museum of local memorabilia also has a Yellowstone stagecoach, like so many that once were a primary means of transportation across the meridian. | 206 E. 8th St. | 308/784–1100 or 308/784–3930 | $1 | Memorial Day–Labor Day, weekdays 10–5, Sat. 1–5; Sept.–May, by appointment only.

Robert Henri Museum and Historical Walkway. Artist Robert Henri, a founder of the Ashcan school of painting, came from this town, a fact recalled at the museum in the Hotel Hendee. Along the Historical Walkway, you also can visit a Pony Express station and old church and school buildings. | 218 E. 8th St. | 308/784–4154 | $2 | June–Sept., Mon.–Sat. 10–5; Sun. and Oct.–May, by appointment only.

SEPT.: *Hay Days.* You can cheer at the Saturday parade, go to the carnival, play silent critic—or fervent admirer—at the art show and crafts exhibits, and observe the kids at their own special activities. This downtown program has something for almost every interest. | 308/784–3770 or 308/784–3930.

Dining
PJ's Restaurant. American. Flowery wallpaper, cozy booths, and soft lighting make for a friendly setting. The regulars think highly of the prime rib, followed by a slice (or two) of PJ's made-from-scratch pies—everything from butterscotch to sour cream–and–raisin to good old-fashioned apple. | 103 E. Monroe St. | 308/784–4777 | $4–$20 | AE, D, MC, V.

Plainsman. American. You'll get home-style cooking, including homemade pies and rolls, served country-style in this large dining area with big windows and both booths and tables. It's known for broasted chicken, but the town secret is the coconut cream pie. | 128 E. 8th St. | 308/784–2080 | Closed Mon. | $2–$6 | No credit cards.

Lodging
Budget Host Circle S Motel. This motel option and its outdoor pool are just a just ¼ mi from exit 222 on I–80, and you'll find three restaurants within a quarter of a mile in the surrounding commercial area. It's also ¼ mi from the Robert Henri Museum and Pony Express station. Restaurant. Cable TV. Pool. Pets allowed. | 440 S. Meridian | 308/784–2290 or 800/237–5852 | fax 308/784–3917 | 49 rooms | $34–$48 | AE, D, MC, V.

CRAWFORD

MAP 11, B1

(Nearby towns also listed: Alliance, Chadron, Harrison)

For many years, the Lakota considered the area around present-day Crawford their territory. White settlers came after Fort Robinson was established on the White River in 1874, and hostilities between the native peoples and the frontier army became the pattern. Crazy Horse, one of the greatest of all Lakota warriors, died when he was stabbed while troops were trying to arrest him at Fort Robinson.

After the fighting with the Northern Plains tribes had been largely settled, Crawford was officially formed in 1885—and went from being a tent city to a community of 200 in a matter of days. The area is still mostly agricultural, but extremely popular with tourists who come to explore several unusual geological sites and Fort Robinson State Park.

Information: **Crawford Area Chamber of Commerce** | 308/665–1817 or 800/647–3213.

Attractions
Fort Robinson State Historical Park. An active military post for more than 70 years, Fort Robinson has been a state park since 1956 and has long been regarded as Nebraska's premiere state park. Among the well-known incidents of its early days, the fort was the scene of the Cheyenne Outbreak, recounted in Mari Sandoz's book *Cheyenne Autumn* and the film made from her work. Later the fort became a training center for military dogs, and it finally ended its military service as a camp for German prisoners of war during World War II. Today, you can ride bicycles, horses, or take a stagecoach ride; camp out or stay in the lodge created from the former officers' quarters and the cavalry barracks (*see* Fort Robinson Lodge); fish for trout or swim in an indoor pool; visit a crafts center or take in performances at the summer stock theater; or take a Jeep tour to Smiley Canyon to see a buffalo herd. Soldier Creek Wilderness, a 7,794-acre national forest within the park, has 10 mi of trails open year-round. It all starts about 3 mi west of Crawford on Highway 20. | 308/665–

2660 | fprobst@bbc.net | ngp.ngpc.state.ne.us/parks/frob.html and www.fs.fed.us/r2/
nebraska/soldier.html | Neb. Parks Permit required; camping, $7–$10 | Daily; amenities, Memorial Day–Labor Day.

The telling is, indeed, in the details at the **Fort Robinson Museum,** which traces the history of the fort's military life through the everyday belongings of early cavalry troopers, the Native Americans they fought, and the German POWs detained there during World War II. The museum is right on Highway 20, in the two-story Post Headquarters built in 1905. | 3200 Highway 20 | 308/665–2919 | Memorial Day–Labor Day, Mon.–Sat. 8–5, Sun. 9–5; Apr., May, Sept., weekends only; Oct.–Mar., Mon.–Fri., 8–5.

The former post theater at Fort Robinson is now occupied by the **Trailside Museum,** a branch of the University of Nebraska State Museum devoted to the natural history of the region. Its collection of fossils—some of which are 30 million years old—and geological displays are dominated by the 14-ft-high skeleton of a mammoth found north of the fort. You can arrange tours of northwest Nebraska from here, including guided trips to Toadstool Geological Park. | 308/665–2929 | Free with park pass | Memorial Day–Labor Day, Mon.–Sat. 8–5, Sun. 9–5.

Hudson–Meng Bison Bonebed. You can watch researchers at work digging for clues to the reason that hundreds of bison died here en masse about 10,000 years ago. Theories range from ancient Native Americans driving them to their deaths to a massive lightning strike and other natural phenomenon, such as prairie fires or hail storms. The visitor center has scientific information on the bison. You can arrange to participate in the digs by calling ahead. The site, within the Oglala National Grassland, is about 4 mi north of Crawford, off Toadstool Road. | 1811 Meng Dr. | 308/432–0300 or 308/665–3900 | $3 | Mid-May–Sept., daily 9-5.

Toadstool Geological Park. The terrain looks more like an arid moonscape than part of Nebraska. Trails lead to unusual rock formations throughout the park, on Toadstool Road just west of Route 2. As you hike, you can see tracks left by animals 30 million years ago as they wandered across what was then a wetland. Picnic tables and a campsite are available. | 308/432–4475 | Memorial Day–Labor Day, $3 per vehicle; Sept.–May, free | Daily dawn to dusk.

ON THE CALENDAR

JUNE: *Hike the Ridge.* An annual guided hike explores the Pine Ridge on National Trails Day, the first Saturday in June. The starting point differs each year. | 308/432–4475.

JULY: *Old West Trail PRCA Rodeo.* Big-name cowboys from throughout the West come to Crawford City Park for this annual three-day event over the July 4th weekend. Besides the traditional competitions, there's a gymkana for the kids on Thursday night, a Rodeo Queen contest, and a huge fireworks display. | 308/665–2800 or 308/665–1400.

Dining

Frontier Restaurant. American. Booths line the walls and tables run through the center of this classic American spot with a bar and lounge just beyond big wooden double doors. Beef is a specialty, and the wine list features bottlings from Nebraska vineyards. | 342 2nd St. | 308/665–1872 | $7–$16 | AE, D, MC, V.

Lodging

Fort Robinson Lodge. You can choose from a variety of overnight accommodations at the historic fort. The onetime barracks units have been converted into single guest rooms, and the old officers' quarters are now duplex apartments, ranging from two to nine bedrooms, all with full kitchens. The rentals list also includes a number of cabins and "Brick Houses," from two to four bedrooms each, and the Peterson Ranch House, where you can rent stalls for your own horses. For group events, Comanche Hall accommodates 60 people. You can rough-it at primitive campsites year-round or park your RV at modernized sites mid-April to mid-November. Besides ordering full meals at the Inn, you can buy snacks at Sutter's Store in the Activity Center. Rentals require a two-night minimum and a Nebraska Parks Permit and include access to park facilities; reservations are taken up to a year in advance. Restaurant. No room phones. Indoor pool. Tennis. Playground. | 3200 Hwy. 20 | 308/665–2900 | fax 308/665–2906 | ftrobsp@bbc.net | www.ngpc.state.ne.us/parks/frob.html | 22 rooms, 34 cabins | $34–$160; camping, $7–$10 | Closed mid-Nov.–mid-Apr. | MC, V.

Hilltop Motel. This small single-story motel on the south end of town is about 5 mi from the Fort Robinson State Park. Cable TV. Some pets allowed. | 304 McPherson St. | 308/665–1144 or 800/504–1444 | fax 308/665–1602 | 13 rooms | $35–$60 | D, MC, V.

CROFTON

MAP 11, G1

(Nearby town also listed: South Sioux City)

Although Lewis and Clark spent a week in 1804 crossing the Missouri just north of where Crofton now sits, the area remained unsettled until railroad workers pitched their tents on a hill in 1892 as they constructed a route linking Norfolk, Nebraska, and Yankton, South Dakota. Railroad promoter J. T. M. Pearce liked the spot and started a town, named for Crofton Courts, his home in England. By 1906, Crofton had evolved from the tents to dugouts to being a real town with a substantial business district. Some of the area was flooded when the Gavins Point Dam was constructed on the Missouri River in the 1950s, but many Midwestern cities, industries, and farmers now know of Crofton as the place where their electricity is generated.

Information: **Crofton Chamber of Commerce** | Box 81, Crofton 68730 | 402/388–4385 | fax 402/388–4161 | aii@bloomnet.com | www.crofton-ne.com.

Attractions

Lewis and Clark State Recreation Area. If there were trails all the way around Lewis and Clark Lake, you'd be off on a 90-mi hike. Six recreation areas on the Nebraska side of this dammed portion of the Missouri, Nebraska's second largest reservoir, have picnicking, camping, fishing, swimming, and boating facilities, plus rental cabins and a marina that has gas available for boats 24/7. Ice-fishing, snowmobiling, and other winter sports continue through the cold months; February and March are said to be good for bass fishing. The park entrance is 21 mi from Crofton, off Highway 54C. | 402/388–4169 | lcsra@ngpc.state.ne.us | ngp.ngpc.state.ne.us/parks/lewclark.html | Neb. Parks Permit required; camping, $3–$11; cabins, $70 | Year-round; camping, May–mid-Sept.; cabins, Apr.–Dec.

The **Lewis and Clark Lake Visitor Center,** maintained by the U.S. Army Corps of Engineers 10 mi north of Crofton on Route 121, sits on a bluff overlooking river, lake, and dam. Inside, you can see exhibits about the upper Missouri from the days of Lewis and Clark to the advent of hydroelectric dams. Outside, the Dorian Prairie Garden is lush with nature's exhibits of grasses and wildflowers.

ON THE CALENDAR

AUG.: *Lewis and Clark Festival.* The fourth weekend of August, the Visitor Center hosts the annual Lewis and Clark Festival, commemorating the famous expedition with re-enactments, speakers, and demonstrations. | 402/667–7873 | Free | Memorial Day–Labor Day, weekdays 8–6, weekends 10–6; Sept.–Nov. and Feb.–May, Mon.–Fri. 8–4:30, weekends 10–6.

Dining

Argo Hotel. American. Stepping into the dining and lounge areas of the Historic Argo Hotel B&B is like stepping back into the elegance of the past, when all fine rooms were aglow with chandeliers, an oak staircase, a tin ceiling, and fireplaces. The menu in the candle-lit restaurant includes seafood and steaks, as well as a "chocolate temptation" with home-made cream sauce and a cheesecake that's the best for miles. The two cocktail lounges continue the romantic pattern with music played on a baby grand, a cigar room, a 100-year-old oak bar with bullet holes, and space for dancing. | 211 W. Kansas St. | 800/607–2746 or 402/388–2400 | $8–$25 | AE, D, MC, V | Daily 5–10.

Lodging

Historic Argo Hotel Bed and Breakfast. Transformed anew into a semblance of *Titanic*-era luxury, this small brick 1912 building is filled with early 20th-century decorative details and such furnishings as brass beds in the guest rooms. Restaurant, bar (with entertainment), complimentary breakfast. Cable TV. Free parking. No kids under 12. No smoking. | 211 W. Kansas St. | 402/388–2400 or 800/607–2746 | fax 402/388–2525 | 17 rooms, 1 suite | $50–$110 | AE, D, MC, V.

DANNEBROG

MAP 11, F4

(Nearby towns also listed: Broken Bow, Burwell, Grand Island, St. Paul)

Dannebrog is likely the best-known Danish community in the state, in part because Nebraska's best-known folklorist, Roger Welsch, author of *It's Not the End of the Earth, But You Can See It from Here* and other books, settled here when he retired from the University of Nebraska. After he became the anchor of CBS's "Sunday Morning" program, he often broadcast from Dannebrog—and he was responsible for the popular "Postcard from Nebraska" program that airs in Denmark.

The community works to live up to its nickname "Danish Capital of Nebraska" with Danish products in many stores, the Grundlovsfest festival each June and an annual Danish Christmas festival, complete with Danish costumes, stories, food, and a visit from Denmark's Old Father Christmas. But you don't have to be Danish to join in another local tradition, the story-telling contests periodically held at Eric's Bar, which bills itself as "The National Liars Hall of Fame."

Information: Dannebrog Area Booster Club | 522 E. Roger Welsch Ave., Dannebrog 68831 | 308/226–2237 | fax 308/266–2237.

Attractions

Liars Hall of Fame. This tongue-in-cheek "museum" in a corner of Eric's Tavern houses extensive exhibits celebrating the art of telling whoppers and spinning yarns. There are biographies of "professionals" in the field, live demonstrations, and living-history presentations, pageants, and parades. | 106 S. Mill St. | 308/226–2222 | Free | Wed.–Sun. 9–5.

ON THE CALENDAR

JUNE: *Grundlovsfest*. Everything's Danish at this annual festival the first weekend in June. The program's packed with ethnic dancers, Danish foods, an art show, an antiques show, and a parade, but all activities are within easy walking distance in the small downtown area. | 308/226–2237.

EUSTIS

MAP 11, E4

(Nearby towns also listed: Cozad, Gothenburg, Kearney, Lexington, McCook)

A small town in the heart of rolling hill country of farms and cattle ranches, Eustis was founded by German immigrants. Their traditions are remembered in several events

EUSTIS

INTRO
ATTRACTIONS
DINING
LODGING

through the year—and in the town's billing of itself as the "Sausage Capital of Nebraska."

Information: **Eustis Chamber of Commerce** | Box 173, Eustis 69028 | 308/486–5615 | fst-bnk@swnebr.net | www.eustis.ne.us.

Attractions
Gallagher Lake. You'll find sites for primitive camping here, as well as boating and fishing. The lake and surrounding wooded recreation acreage are about 7 mi from Eustis. To get there, take Route 21N to Johnson Lake Road. | 308/486–5615 | Neb. Parks Permit required | Daily.

ON THE CALENDAR
JUNE: *Wurst Tag*. The polka music makes a lively background beat to this celebration of Eustis's German heritage with a volksmarch, road race, displays, ethnic foods, pretzel and sausage contests, and a street dance, all outdoors on Main Street the second Saturday of June. | 308/486–5615.

Dining
Eustis Pool Hall. Mexican. Built in the early 20th century, the downtown building did house a classic pool hall—and the restaurant still has tin ceilings, wood floors, and pool tables as a backdrop. You can expect south-of-the-border favorites such as burritos, enchiladas, and chile rellenos, plus great nachos and a few surprises, such as freshwater shrimp platters. | 112 E. Railroad St. | 308/486–3801 | Closed Sun. | $3–$12 | AE, D, MC, V.

Lodging
Hotel Eustis Bed and Breakfast. Like its neighbor, the old pool hall, this B&B was built around the turn of the 20th century, but remodeling and modern decorating have given it a rustic yet contemporary look inside, without much clutter or frilly antiques. Rooms do not have private baths. No room phones, no TV. Steam room. No smoking. | 114 E. Railroad St. | 308/486–5345 | fax 308/486–5346 | 5 rooms | $36–$42 | AE, D, MC, V.

FAIRBURY

MAP 11, H5

(Nearby towns also listed: Beatrice, Wilber)

James Butler "Wild Bill" Hickok launched his career as an Old West gunfighter when he shot and killed David McCanles and two hired men on July 12, 1861, at Rock Creek Station, now a state historical park, just south of present-day Fairbury. In the early 1900s, Fairbury was the home of the Campbell Brothers Circus, the second largest circus in the world at that time, and displays at the Fairbury City Museum include many items from the circus. Fairbury has been restoring its historic district, and more reminders of its past—and especially its ties to the history of the Oregon Train and the days of the Pony Express—are bound to appear as this work progresses.

Information: **Fairbury Chamber of Commerce** | 518 E St., Fairbury 68352 | 402/729–3076 | fax 402/729–3185 | jp03415@navix.net | www.oregontrail.org.

Attractions
Alexandria Lakes State Recreation Area. This spring-water lake is as clear a bell, and it is frequently restocked for fishing. Campsites are primitive, but the park, on Daykon Road off Highway 136, also has areas for day-trip hiking, hunting, picnicking, and low-power boating, as well as a parking area for trailers. | 402/729–3000 | ngp.ngpc.state.ne.us/parks/alexan.html | Neb. Parks Permit required; camping, $3–$6 | Daily.

Rock Creek Station State Historical Park. Although the station's buildings and covered wagons are re-creations, the ruts are real, just as they were cut into the soil by the thousands who traveled the Oregon Trail. The visitor center, 6 mi from town, covers the history of the trail and the station's connection with Wild Bill Hickok, who was a young ranch hand when he killed three men in a dispute over rent money and began his path to becoming part of the lore of the West. If you ride, you and your horse will be welcome at Rock Creek's horse camp. Campgrounds are about 5½ mi east of Fairbury, off Route 15. | 402/729–5777 | ngp.ngpc.state.ne.us/parks/rcstat.html | Neb. Parks Permit required; camping, $7–$11 | Visitor center: Memorial Day–Labor Day, daily 9–5; primitive camping, year-round; modern camping facilities, May–mid-Sept.

Rock Island Depot. Once upon a time the Rock Island Railroad was big news in these parts, and this museum in the one-time depot downtown is home to a collection of rail-related artifacts and other exhibits interweaving the story of the rails with the local history of the area. | 910 2nd St. | 402/729–5131 | $2 | Wed.–Fri. 1–5.

ON THE CALENDAR
JUNE: *Rock Creek Trail Days.* The buffalo stew the westward-heading settlers made was probably a great break from the dry fare of most of their meals. You can sample a modern version at the annual buffalo stew cookout during this festival, when Fairbury sets up a crafts show, living-history demos, and an entertainment site on the path of the Oregon Trail. | 402/729–3000.
SEPT.: *Germanfest.* A German king and queen, prince and princess are chosen to reign over this merry celebration in downtown Fairbury with lots of live music, polka-dancing, and German foods. | 402/729–5777 or 402/729–3000.

Dining
TrailBlazers. Steak. Once a department store, this space was made into a restaurant in 1990. Now, it has oak furnishings, soft lighting, and high ceilings and looks out onto a tiled courtyard. There's a light brunch on Sundays, but the regular menu has such favorites as chicken quesadillas and chicken-fried steak, doused in rich, homemade gravy. | 500 4th St. | 402/729–5205 | Sun., Mon. nights | $10–$18 | AE, D, MC, V.

Lodging
Capri. This motel on Highway 136 on the east end of town was built in 1973, but now has a Victorian-esque interior with such turn-of-the-20th-century touches as lace curtains and dried flower arrangements. Truck parking is available. Cable TV. | 1100 14th St. | 402/729–3317 or 800/932–0589 | 45 rooms | $39–$57 | AE, D, MC, V.

FREMONT

MAP 11, H3

(Nearby towns also listed: Blair, Columbus, Omaha)

Fremont was named for John C. Fremont, the controversial explorer, soldier, and one-time Republican candidate for President whose writings did much to influence many Americans to head west to seek a new life. A cottonwood tree near Fremont was also one of the many places where Clerk William Clayton left messages for later travelers on the Mormon Trail—in this instance, his white flag was the signal for a note with directions to a riverside camp. Many travelers of our own time come to Fremont specifically to shop at the hundreds of antiques outlets, or to take another trip, the entertaining ride aboard the Fremont–Elkhorn Dinner Train.

Information: **Fremont Area Chamber of Commerce** | 605 N. Broadway, Fremont 68025 | 402/721–2641 or 800/727–8323 | fax 402/721–9359 | www.visitdodgecountyne.org.

Attractions

Fremont and Elkhorn Valley Railroad. The cars date to the 1920s and 1940s; the rail line they take on the 17-mi round trip to Nickerson or the 30-mi excursion to historic Hooper was laid out in 1869. Along the way, you'll cross the path of an old Native American trail, as well as the Mormon Trail. In the evenings, the railroad runs the popular Fremont Dinner Train (*see* Dining). | 1835 N. Somers Ave. | 402/727–0615 | fdt@fremont-online.com | www.fremont-online.com/fdt | Sat. $7, Sun. $11 | Reservations suggested | Apr.–Oct., weekends only, 1:30.

Fremont Lakes State Recreation Area. On U.S. 30 just 3 mi west of Fremont, campsites around 20 small lakes near the Platte River provide for swimming, boating, tent or RV camping, and picnicking. | 402/727–3290 | ngp.ngpc.state.ne.us/parks/fremont.html | Neb. Parks Permit required; camping, $8–$11 | Daily; modern camping facilities, May–mid-Sept. only.

Louis E. May Historical Museum. Living-history programs bring the past to life at this Dodge County Historical Society complex that includes a large brick Victorian mansion, a Victorian garden, and an 1868 log home. | 1643 N. Nye Ave. | 800/727–8323 or 402/721–4515 | www.connectfremont.org | $2 | Apr.–Dec., Wed.–Sun. 1:30–4:30, closed Sun.
On warm August evenings, you can get a fresh breeze at the **Concerts on the Lawn** around the mansion at the Louis E. May Historical Museum. You'll need to bring your own blankets or chairs for sitting on the grass. | 1643 N. Nye Ave. | 402/721–4515.

The Old Poor Farm. Once, many of Nebraska's people lived on farms like the one at this four-acre 1800s farmstead on Route 1 in Nickerson. You can tour the original buildings and watch a variety of demonstrations—and see more than 200 birds and animals in the adjacent mini-zoo. Call for information and directions. | 402/721–8087 | www.visitdodge-countyne.org | By reservation only.

ON THE CALENDAR

JULY: *John C. Fremont Days.* You can mix history with pure fun during this weekend tribute to the man known as "The Pathfinder." Activities, held throughout the city on the the second full weekend of July, range from living-history encampments to arts and crafts shows, antiques displays, and magic and car shows to a carnival, a rodeo, and other sporting events. | 402/727–9428.

Dining

Bank-Quit. American. You can go into the vault, now displaying antiques and crafts, in this former bank building that stood empty for six decades. In the town of Dodge 26 mi northwest of Fremont, the restaurant has roast beef lunch specials, homemade coconut cream pie, tea in the afternoon, and cappuccino. As another touch from the building's former life, you pay at a teller's cage on the way out. | 331 2nd St., Dodge | 402/693–4165 | Closed Sun. | $4–$5 | No credit cards.

Carey Cottage. American. You can come for lunch or wait a while and come just for the English-style afternoon tea with scones. In a small downtown house with a courtyard, the restaurant, which caters to shoppers at nearby antiques stores, has a gentle tea room atmosphere. Lunches include salads, soups, sandwiches, and excellent desserts, such as coconut cream pie and bread pudding. | 732 Park Ave. | 402/721–7640 | Closed Sun., Mon. | $7–$10 | No credit cards.

Franky and Oly's. American. This downtown eatery is what it is: a sportsbar that does beef and brew. You'll see the expected sports pictures on the walls, a bar in the center of the room, and 21 working televisions, placed even in the rest rooms. The burgers are half-pounders, and you might want to try the "Irish beef nachos," made with fried potato skins instead of nachos. | 353 W. 23rd St. | 402/727–4119 | Mon.–Fri. 11–1 AM, Sun. 12–8 | $4–$9 | AE, D, MC, V.

Fremont Dinner Train. American. It is a throwback to that time when reporters met cross-country trains to photograph the day's arriving movie stars—usually with a coat draped over their shoulders. The cars on the Fremont train actually date back to the 1940s and serve a five-course feast in a traditionally elegant setting, along with murder mysteries and other dinner theater. Try the Cornish hen, prime rib, salmon, quail, or orange roughy. Each trip lasts about 3½ hours. | 1835 N. Somers Ave. | 402/727–8321 or 800/942–7245 | fdt@fremont-online.com | www.fremont-online.com/fdt | May–Oct., Fri. and Sat. 7:30; Sun. 1:30; Nov.–April, Fri. and Sat. 6:30; Sun. 1:30 | Reservations essential | $38–$61.95 | AE, D, MC, V.

KC's. American. In a downtown that has slews of antiques shops, this restaurant is, appropriately, decorated with its own collection of antique and collectible signs. It's known for the broccoli salad and "Rose's pepper steak," named for the owner's mother. Kids' menu. | 631 N. Park St. | Closed Sun., Mon. | $7–$15 | AE, MC, V.

Office Bar and Grill. American. In a historic building in Hooper's historic district, about 18 mi north of Fremont, this outpost of old-time Americana has its original tin ceiling and wood floors. Specialties include broasted chicken and homemade desserts, such as the banana cream pie served only on Tuesday, often sold out before noon. | 121 Main St., Hooper | 402/654–3373 | Closed Mon. No lunch Sun. | $4–$10 | No credit cards.

Lodging

Budget Host Relax Inn. This one-story motel, 1 mi east of the junction of Highways 77 and 30, has recliners and queen beds, usually covered in quiet, dark-toned fabrics. Truck parking and cold-weather hookups are available. Complementary coffee. Cable TV. No pets. | 1435 E. 23rd St. | 402/721–5656 or 800/616–9966 | fax 402/727–8029 | 35 rooms | $39–$57 | AE, D, MC, V.

Comfort Inn. This pale-toned two-story motel, 3 mi from Fremont Municipal Airport, takes a different tack inside, using lots of burgundy-colored fabrics. Suites also have sofabeds. Complimentary Continental breakfast. Some in-room data ports, microwaves, refrigerators. Cable TV. Indoor pool. Hot tub. Business services. Pets allowed. | 1649 E. 23rd St. | 402/721–1109 | fax 402/721–1109 | 48 rooms | $50–$69 | AE, D, DC, MC, V.

Holiday Lodge. This brick motel has indoor and outdoor entrances to the rooms and a pleasant atrium and indoor pool for relaxing moments. Truck parking and cold-weather hookups are available. Restaurant, bar. Cable TV. Hot tub. Exercise equipment. Business services. Pets allowed. | 1220 E. 23rd St. | 402/727–1110 or 800/743–7666 | 100 rooms | $49–$70 | AE, D, DC, MC, V.

Prairie Garden Bed and Breakfast. In this part of the world, this B&B's crisply contemporary exterior may remind you of Frank Lloyd Wright's Prairie School architecture, now almost a century old. Furnishings are modern; you'll find a sunroom, a large screened porch, and a shared bath. It's in the town of Howells, right on Route 91, which is also 3rd Street. Complimentary breakfast. | 216 S 3rd St., Howells | 402/986–1251 | 2 rooms | $40–$50 | No credit cards.

Super 8 Motel. Right beside the Platte River and a mall, this in-town motel helps you start the day with complimentary toast and coffee in the lobby. The free parking includes spaces for trucks and RVs. Bar. Cable TV. Pets allowed. | 1250 E. 23rd St./Hwy. 30 | 402/727–4445 or 800/800–8000 | fax 402/727–4445 | 43 rooms | $38–$66 | AE, D, DC, MC, V.

GERING

MAP 11, A3

(Nearby towns also listed: Bayard, Bridgeport, Kimball, Scottsbluff)

Gering was organized in 1887 as a central stop on the Union Pacific Railroad. The Scottsbluff–Gering metropolitan area is on the Oregon, California, and Mormon trails in the vicinity of the Scotts Bluff National Monument, a natural sandstone outcrop that was a major trail marker for overland travelers.

Information: **Gering and Scottsbluff Chamber of Commerce** | 1517 Broadway, Ste. 104, Scotsbluff 69361 | 308/632–2133 | fax 308/632–7128 | www.scotsbluff.net/chamber.

Attractions

Farm and Ranch Museum. In this agricultural area, farm and ranch equipment has always been important, and the displays here include items that go back to the days when most farm machinery was horse- or human-drawn, as well as steam-powered machines. | 9230 M St. | 308/436–1989 | $2 suggested | May–Sept., Mon.–Sat. 10–5, Sun. 1–5; Oct.–Apr., by appointment.

North Platte Valley Museum. This regional history museum examines the impact of the Oregon, Mormon, and California trails on the development of the valley, but it also looks at the lives of those who were most influential—the pioneers who stopped here and stayed—with a fur trapper's boat, a log cabin, an 1889 homestead dwelling, and a later ranch house, as well as smaller artifacts like tools and weapons. | 11th and J Sts. | 308/436–5411 | www.wyobraskagoldpages.com/npvmuseum | $3 | May–Sept., Mon.–Sat. 8:30–5, Sun. 1–5; Oct.–Apr., Mon.–Fri., 8:30–5.

Robidoux Pass. As you drive through Carter Canyon, 12 mi from Gering, the ruts you'll see intersecting the gravel road are the visible depressions made by the thousands of wagons that came this way as they headed west. Though the Oregon Trail originally ran south of here, through the Robidoux Pass, which looks much the same today as it did 150 years ago, the route quickly shifted north to the more forgiving landscape by Scots Bluff National Monument. | Carter Canyon Rd. | 800/788–9475 | Free | Daily.

Scotts Bluff National Monument. Originally called Me-a-pa-te, for "the hill that is hard to go around," this fortresslike rock formation must certainly have seemed just that to pioneers on the Oregon Trail. But they found their way around it, leaving wagonwheel ruts that can be seen today near the visitor center, on Highway 92W, 2 mi west of the junction with Route 71. You also can drive to the summit, which overlooks the oldest concrete road in the state, or hike there on the $1^6/_{10}$-mi Saddle Rock Trail. | 308/436–4340 | www.nps.gov/scbl | $5 per car | Memorial Day–Labor Day, daily 8–8; Sept.–May, daily 8–5.

Wildcat Hills Nature Center. The nature center is in the rugged Wildcat Hills, where elk, buffalo, and sometimes longhorn cattle live in a refuge. You can hike, bike, or camp along the various trails, but parking at the nature center, 10 mi south of Gering off Highway 71, is limited to 20 minutes. | 308/436–3777 | ngp.ngpc.state.ne.us/parks/wildcat.html | Neb. Parks Permit required; camping, $3 | Grounds and camping, daily; nature center: Memorial Day–Labor Day, daily 8–4:30; Sept.–May, weekdays 8–4:30.
Within the boundaries of the Wildcat Hills Nature Center lies the land that is officially the **Wildcat Hills State Recreation Area,** with sites for various types of outdoor recreation as well as camping. | 308/436–3777 | ngp.ngpc.state.ne.us/parks/wildcat.html | Neb. Parks Permit required; camping, $3 | Grounds and camping, daily. Nature center, Memorial Day–Labor Day, daily 8–4:30; Sept.–May, weekdays 8–4:30.

Wildlife World at the Wyo-Braska Natural History Museum. More than 250 mounted animals from six continents are exhibited in this museum in a renovated train station, including Baluchithere, a 30-ft-long dinosaur. | 950 U St. | 308/436–7104 | $3.50 | May–Sept., weekdays 9–5, Sat. 9–noon, Sun. 1–4; Oct.–Apr., Tues.–Fri. 10–4, Sat. 9–noon.

ON THE CALENDAR

JULY: _Hoop-La._ You'll see players from 12 to 60—and sometimes older—trying to slam-dunk their way to the $1,000 grand prize. Athletes from all over the country come to Gering for the Hoop-La basketball tournament, which has been going strong since 1989, when town streets are closed off as teams play pick-up-style at Garner Park. All games are "make your own calls" except for the World Class division, in which certified refs call the games. | 308/436–6886.

JULY: *Oregon Trail Days.* You can revisit the past at a historical play, but this four-day festival in Gering also has a range of other activities, including a Western art show, international food fair, quilt show, lots of music and dance events, a 5-mi run, and the state championship chili cookoff. | 308/436–4457.

Dining
Gaslight Restaurant and Lounge. American. Chandeliers throw soft, goldish light onto the wooden tabletops and etched-glass panels engraved with scenes and symbols of the area's vibrant past. Locals often come here especially for the "Family Meal," which has chunks of chicken, shrimp, and/or beef, salad, and a side all served in one big bowl. The Gaslight also makes its own coleslaw from scratch. | 3318 10th St. | 308/632–7315 | $10–$37 | D, MC, V.

Lodging
Circle S Lodge. Along the routes of the Oregon trail and the Pony Express, this 1950s brick motel on Route 92 offers ground-level rooms in a mostly commercial area about 8 mi from the Wildcat Hills Nature Center and Scotts Bluff National Monument. Truck parking is available. Cable TV. Pets allowed. | 400 M St. | 308/436–2157 | fax 308/436–3249 | 30 rooms | $34–$44 | AE, D, MC, V.

GOTHENBURG

MAP 11, E4

(Nearby towns also listed: Cozad, Eustis, Lexington, North Platte)

Although many historians speak of the Oregon Trail as if the pioneers followed some precise little path, there actually were several routes—and Gothenburg is right on one of the most popular ones. It is also at the center of 15,000 acres of land that yield about 60 million pounds of popcorn annually.

Information: Gothenburg Area Chamber of Commerce | 1021 Lake Ave. 69138 | 308/537–3505 or 800/482–5520 | fax 308/537–2541 | gothenburg@alltel.net | www.ci.gothenburg.ne.us.

Attractions
Pony Express Station. Originally a fur-trading post and ranch house, this log structure later was a stop for riders of the Pony Express. Some years ago, it was moved intact to Gothenburg's Ehmen Park, on Route 47 about 1 mi north of exit 211 on I–80. In the summer, you can take carriage rides around the park. | 308/537–2143 | Free | Daily.

Sod House Museum. Homesteaders in the prairie regions often started their new lives in sod houses built from the dirt they'd claimed, like this example now resting near a typical windmill and a barn, in town, off Route 47. Exhibits include unusual barbed wire sculptures of a man atop a horse and a buffalo. | 308/537–2076 | Free | May, Sept., daily 9–6; June–Aug., daily 8–8.

ON THE CALENDAR
JULY: *Annual South Loup River Blues and BBQ.* BBQ is very much the traditional fare at this summer program that's been drawing blues fans since 1993 to the town of Arnold, about 35 mi due north of Gothenburg up Route 47 to Route 40. The gates of Old Mill Park open at 11 for performances that run from noon to 11:30. Camping is permitted. | 308/872–5881 or 800/228–4307.
JULY: *Pony Express Rodeo.* After two days of cheering their favorite riders—or maybe the bulls and broncs—fans of this annual event at the rodeo grounds on the northwest side of Gothenburg can ooh and aah at the traditional Independence Day fireworks before they head home. | 308/537–3505.

SEPT.: *Annual Harvest Festival.* Attractions at this celebration the third week in September, which has been a town event since 1941, include food and crafts booths, a parade, a carnival, an art show, and entertainment—and sometimes tractor-pulling competitions. | 308/537–3505.

Lodging

Western Motor Inn. This two-story brick motor hotel off I–80 is surrounded by popular chain restaurants and about a mile from the Pony Express Station. If you're traveling with a child, you can arrange for a crib or roll-away bed. Some truck parking is available. Cable TV. Pets allowed. | 207 Lake Ave. | 308/537–3622 | fax 308/537–3650 | 26 rooms | $27–$49 | AE, D, MC, V.

© Corbis

CRANE WATCH

One of the most incredible displays of waterfowl occurs from mid-February to mid-April along the Platte River—especially between Grand Island and Kearney—as hundreds of thousands of sandhill cranes and other waterfowl migrate from southern to northern habitats. The Central Flyway narrows like an hourglass in this region of the Platte River. Between 450,000 and 500,000 cranes are concentrated in a 40-mile stretch along the river, interrupting their long journey to rest and eat for two months, then heading northward again.

Since 1970, thousands of people have also migrated to the region during the "Crane Watch" period. The birds, which stand nearly three feet tall, roost at night on the river, mostly around the Audubon Society's Rowe Bird Sanctuary. As sundown nears, they start gathering, often near the bridge at Fort Kearny, swirling through the air and landing in great masses, all the while crying and calling for family members.

Crane families generally include three animals, the male and female, who mate for life, and one young crane. So if you watch the birds swirl, you will almost always be able to pick out families; and individual birds also have different "voices" so "mom" and "dad" can recognize "junior."

The cranes need the river habitat for nighttime roosting because it protects them from predators. They also benefit from the farmers' fields in the region both north and south of the river, where they can eat remnants of the corn crops. In the daytime, you can drive along U.S. 30 or county roads both north and south of the Platte River and chance upon cranes eating in the fields. If you use your car as a blind, you can often sit and watch or photograph the big birds—sometimes even seeing them dancing through one of their mating rituals. In the evening or early morning hours, your best viewing sites will be near the river around Kearney and Grand Island. There are several places where you can pay a small fee to sit in a blind and watch as the cranes arrive or depart.

But there are so many birds that you may be able to see them in many parts of the region between Lexington and Grand Island. When you are crane-watching, be sure not to disturb the birds—and be careful not to block roads or bridges.

GRAND ISLAND

(Nearby towns also listed: Columbus, Dannebrog, Hastings, Kearney, St. Paul, York)

Grand Island is at the eastern edge of the land where the magnificent sandhill cranes always stop during their northward spring migration. German immigrant William Stolley led the settlement of Grand Island in 1857, and soon he had planted more than 50 varieties of trees in the area that is now a part of the Stolley Recreation Area.

When the Union Pacific Railroad passed through, it divided the community along economic lines, with the well-to-do citizens living south of the tracks and the less prosperous citizens north of the rail line. But Grand Island isn't nearly so divided these days, and it proudly displays reminders of all of its history at the Stuhr Museum of the Prairie Pioneer, which has been used as a location for such films as *My Antonia*, *Home at Last*, and *Sarah Plain and Tall*.

Information: Grand Island/Hall County Convention and Visitor's Bureau | 309 W. 2nd, Grand Island 68801 | 308/382–4400 or 800/658–3178 | fax 308/382–1154 | info@visitgrandisland.com | www.visitgrandisland.com or www.gionline.com.

Attractions

Stuhr Museum of the Prairie Pioneer. This fine complex of 70 buildings has one of the nation's best living-history programs. The modern white Stuhr Building, on an island surrounded by a moat, contains pioneer artifacts and historical displays. Nearby, the Fonner Rotunda has a rich assortment of Native American and Old West items. A short walk from there and you'll be in Railroad Town, a re-created prairie community of actual historic buildings, including the childhood home of famed actor and Nebraska native son Henry Fonda. You also can visit a general store and hotel, shops, barns, stables, and homes, creating an Old West town that appears so authentic it has been used by movie production crews. | 3133 Hwy. 34W | 308/385–5316 | www.stuhrmuseum.com | $7.25 | Daily 9–5.

Traditional lanterns create magic in the winter night as they light the way for you to see the holiday decorations of Railroad Town, the Stuhr's Museum's turn-of-the-20th-century village, and a log cabin settlement during the **Old-Fashioned Christmas** program the first two weekends of December. Many residents join in the spirit of the celebration by decorating their own homes in similar holiday dress and going carolling downtown during those weekends. | 3133 Hwy. 34W | 308/385–5316 or 308/387–9210.

Crane Meadows Nature Center. This interpretive center about 6 mi west of Grand Island, south of I–80 exit 305, describes the role of the Platte River in the annual spring migration of the sandhill cranes and of the whooping cranes who start coming, two or three at a time, in April. Along the 7½ mi of hiking trails, you also may see migrating hummingbirds and such resident wildlife as turtles and wood ducks. There is a pedestrian footbridge across the Platte River with an observation tower, plus van tours during the crane season. Reservations for space in a crane-viewing bunker are taken from January 1. | 9325 S. Alda Rd., Wood River | 308/382–1820 | info@cranemeadows.org | www.cranemeadows.org | $2; crane tours, $10; crane blinds, $15 | Mon.–Sat. 9–5, Sun. 1–5.

Edgerton Explorit Center. One of Nebraska's newest science centers, this institution explores the world of physics with interactive exhibits for all ages. The center, in Aurora, 3 mi north of I–80 on Route 14, is named for Dr. Harold Edgerton, an Aurora native who invented electronic strobes for photographic use. | 208 16th St., Aurora | 402/694–4032 | www.hamilton.net/aurora/city/edgerton.htm | $4 | Mon.–Sat. 9–5, Sun. 1–5.

Great Platte River Road Archway. If you've only whizzed under it, you may not know the details. This eight-story-high archway, the length of a football-field, that spans I–80 between Grand Island and Kearney is the only historical educational monument granted air rights over an interstate highway. Inside the big red structure, you'll find 79,000 square ft of historical exhibits, many of them detailing the place of the Platte River Valley in the westward migration of the 19th century. Follow the signs from exit 272. | $7.50 | May 1–Sept. 30, daily 8 AM–10 PM; Oct. 1–Apr. 30, weekdays 11–6, Sat.–Sun. 8 AM–10 PM.

Mormon Island State Recreation Area. After founder Joseph Smith was murdered, the Mormons sought their own religious haven in the west in the middle of the 19th century— and stopped here during their journey. Now, it is a prime recreational spot where you can sun on the beach, swim in the lake, picnic at the shelters, or boat, fish, or camp. | 7425 Highway 281S, Doniphan | 308/385–6211 or 800/658–3178 | ngp.ngpc.state.ne.us/parks/mormon/html | Neb. Parks Permit required; camping, $7–$12 | Daily; modern camping facilities, May–mid-Sept.

Plainsman Museum. A whole series of 19th-century buildings have been gathered at this site 3 mi north of the town of Aurora on Route 14. In the Agricultural Museum, for example, you can see a homestead house, farm equipment, a farm scene replica, a barn, and a blacksmith shop. Other structures include the General Deleven Bates historic home, which dates to 1876, and a one-room school where classes met from 1848 to 1950. | 210 16th St., Aurora | 402/694–6531 | smpolak@hamilton.net | www.plainsmanmuseum.org | $6 | Apr.– Oct., Mon.–Sat. 9–5, Sun. 1–5; Nov.–Mar., daily 1–5.

Fonner Park. From mid-February to mid-May, you can sit in the glass-enclosed, heated grandstand and watch the thoroughbreds race; the rest of the year, you can come for simulcast racing and keno—and such special events as the Hall County Fair. | 700 E. Stolley Park Rd. | 308/382–4515 | www.fonnerpark.com | $1.50 | Daily.

Island Oasis Water Park. This swimming complex is designed for the entire family, from young waders to those who want to spin round and round on the slides before splashing into the water. The 750-ft "lazy rider" is a big attraction. | 321 Fonner Park Rd. | 308/385– 5381 or 800/658–3178 | $4.75 | Memorial Day–Labor Day, daily noon–10.

ON THE CALENDAR

FEB.–APR.: *Sandhill Crane Migration.* More than 400,000 sandhill cranes migrate up the Central Flyway from Mexico to Canada, stopping along the Platte River in Central Nebraska for several weeks to feed and rest. For general information on the cranes' arrival and viewing sites around Grand Island, call 308/382–4400 or 800/658–3178; for specifics on programs, viewing tours, and bunkers at Crane Meadows Nature Center, call 308/382–1820.

JULY: *Central Nebraska Ethnic Festival.* The traditions of many cultures, European and Native American, come together at this downtown festival the last week of July with crafts booths, continuous live entertainment on two stages, street dances, food, and an education pavilion. | 308/385–4400.

SEPT.: *Husker Harvest Days.* More than 100,000 people from all over the world attend this agricultural show, the largest of its kind in the country, for live field demonstrations of irrigated-agriculture machinery and other presentations on new farming technology. It's the third week of September, at the Cornhusker Army Ammunition Plant, on Husker Highway off Highway 30. | 308/382–9210.

OCT.: *Harvest of Harmony Parade.* Downtown Grand Island resounds with music during this annual parade and competition among high school bands from Nebraska and several neighboring states. The floats are judged, too, and a queen is chosen. | 308/382– 9210.

Dining

Coney Island Lunch Room. American. All-beef hot dogs have been the mainstay of this downtown eatery with 13 stools and one booth since 1933. You can add homemade chili and onions, if you wish, as well as large milkshakes and fries, but the coney sauce "uses real meat not gravy," so it's pretty rich all by itself. | 104 E. 3rd St. | 308/382–7155 | Breakfast also available, no dinner Sat., closed Sun. | $2–$9 | No credit cards.

Dreisbach's. American. There are booths and large tables for groups at this family-friendly restaurant a block from Fonner Park that has real baking powder biscuits and five types of homemade salad dressing. Try the "chunk sirloin," their own special cut. Buffet brunch Sunday. Kids' menu. Earlybird suppers for seniors. | 1137 S. Locust St. | 308/382–5450 | Mon.–Thurs. 5–9, Fri. and Sat. 5–10, Sun. 5–9 | $6–$25 | AE, D, DC, MC, V.

El Tapatio. Mexican. Among brightly colored serapes and warm, adobe-colored walls, large portions of good Mexican food are the norm here. Try the cactus chicken or the *mojarra frita* (fried fish). For dessert, treat yourself to the *sopapilla* delight (a pastry sprinkled with cinnamon and served with honey). | 2610 S. Locust St. | 308/381–4511 | $8–$17 | AE, D, MC, V.

Nonna's Palazzo. Italian. The many antiques add a classic note throughout the dining and living rooms of this turn-of-the-20th-century mansion at the edge of the downtown area. The chef/owner/dishwasher has made everything from scratch since 1983, including the ice cream. Try the lemon parsley chicken with fettuccine or the hearty marinated T-bone steak—and the mouth-watering desserts such as chantilly (a meringue shell with chocolate and strawberries), and double-crust sour cream-raisin pie with caramel. | 820 W. 2nd St. | 308/384–3029 | Thur.—Sat. 5–9 | $9–$12 | D, MC, V.

Ski's Bar & Grill. American. The feeling is casual, but the Mexican tiles and a fountain in the dining room are nicely dressy touches. Known for char burgers, chicken mushroom and Swiss sandwiches, and chicken strips. | 3311 W. Stolley Rd. | 308/381–6426 | Mon.–Thur. 5–9, Fri.–Sat. 10–10, Sun. 10–9 | $6–$10 | AE, MC, V.

Lodging

Best Western Riverside Inn. With 10 meeting rooms, this two-story buff-colored brick motor hotel draws many group events. Off Highway 34E, it's about 2 mi from the interstate and a mile from the horse-racing at Fonner Park. In other leisure hours, you can cool off in the indoor pool or shape up at the fitness center. Most rooms have sofas, and guests receive a complimentary cocktail. Restaurant, bar, complimentary breakfast, room service. Cable TV. Hot tub. Laundry facilities. Business services, airport shuttle. Pets allowed. | 3333 Ramada Rd. | 308/384–5150 or 800/422–3485 | fax 308/384–6551 | 183 rooms | $52–$62 | AE, D, DC, MC, V.

Days Inn. Off Highway 281 on a side road, this northside motel is in a generally quite location, with a sauna and hot tub to help you refresh yourself after a long drive. The parking area includes spaces for trucks and cold-weather hookups. Complimentary Continental breakfast. Cable TV. Laundry facilities. Business services. Pets allowed. | 2620 N. Diers Ave. | 308/384–8624 | fax 308/384–1626 | 62 rooms | $40–$85 | AE, D, DC, MC, V.

Holiday Inn–Midtown. On the south side of town about 5 mi from I-80, this hotel has about a dozen restaurants within eight blocks. If you're really chilled from sitting in an unheated bunker to watch the cranes, the "Holidome" has both an indoor pool and a hot tub to help you recuperate. Truck parking and cold-weather hookups are available. Restaurant, bar, room service. Cable TV. Indoor pool, wading pool. Hot tub. Exercise room. Laundry facilities. Business services. | 2503 S. Locust St. | 308/384–1330 | fax 308/382–4615 | 200 rooms | $64–$74 | AE, D, DC, MC, V.

Super 8 Motel. If you like to start the day with brisk exercise, you can trot along the lake behind this buff-colored motel in the south end of town—or do a few laps in the indoor pool. Truck/RV parking is available. Complimentary Continental breakfast. Cable TV. Hot tub. Pets allowed. | 2603 S. Locust St. | 308/384–4380 or 800/800–8000 | fax 308/384–5015 | 80 rooms | $43–$55 | AE, D, DC, MC, V.

HARRISON

MAP 11, A1

(Nearby towns also listed: Chadron, Crawford)

This small town is considered an access point for the Agate Fossil Beds National Monument and is not far from several other natural attractions, including the Oglala National Grasslands and Toadstool Geological Park. It's also known for the Warbonnet skirmish, where Buffalo Bill Cody killed Cheyenne warrior Yellow Hair (sometimes called Yellow Hand) not long after the 1876 Battle of the Little Bighorn, which claimed the lives of George Armstrong Custer and all the men under his immediate command. Cody is reputed to have said he "took the first scalp for Custer."

Information: **Community Club Inc.** | Box 156, Harrison 69346 | 308/668–2466 | fax 308/668–2467.

Attractions

Agate Fossil Beds National Monument. Tipped off by the discovery of fossilized burrows left by ancient beaverlike animals, paleontologists eventually realized that these grounds were rich with the fossils of animals that lived here up to 22 million years ago. They've since recovered the fossils of bear-dogs, gazelle-camels, ancient horses, and rodents the size of sheep. You can see examples in the visitor center, about 25 mi from Harrison, which also has a display of Native American artifacts, and you can walk the trails leading to some of the original dig sites. | 301 River Rd. | 308/668–2211 | www.nps.gov/agfo | $5 per car or $2 per person | Memorial Day–Labor Day, daily 8–6; Sept.–May, daily 8–5 except holidays.

Oglala National Grassland. When you're standing within this 94,400-acre grassland, the high plains appear to stretch on forever. Toadstool Geological Park and the Hudson–Meng Bonebed are in its boundaries, as are three reservoirs where you can fish. If you're there at the right times, you can expect to see antelopes, turkeys, mule and white tail deer, grouse, swift foxes, prairie dogs, and various songbirds. Locals note that the grasslands are open year-round—if you can get through the snow. The grasslands officially are about 15 mi north of Harrison, but you will find other access points near Crawford and Chadron. Call for directions to specific areas of interest. | 308/432–4475 | www.fs.fed.us/r2/nebraska/toadstooltemp. and www.fs.fed.us/r2/nebraska/hudsonmeng | Free | Daily dawn to dusk.

ON THE CALENDAR
AUG.: *Sioux County Fair and Rodeo.* This three-day event at the Sioux County Fair Grounds has scores of food booths, a beer garden, a parade, as well as a rodeo. Follow Monroe Canyon Drive 2 mi north from Harrison. | 308/668–2466.

Dining
Sioux Sundries. American. The northwesternmost community in Nebraska is also home to the Coffee Burger. Named after a rancher, this hamburger is not made with coffee, but it does pack a lot of beef—about 28 well-seasoned ounces. If you're not a beef person, you'll find choices such as chicken or shrimp in a basket, but do try the malts and cyclones, especially the peanut butter flavor. The restaurant is in an old-fashioned general store in the heart of town, so you can wander the aisles before or after your meal. | 201 Main St. | 308/668–2577 | Mon.–Fri. 6:30–5:30; Sat. 6:30–7 | Breakfast available, no dinner. Closed Sun. | $5–$8 | MC, V.

Lodging
Sowbelly Bed and Breakfast Hideaway. This small B&B is an earth-sheltered structure with three sides backed into Sowbelly Canyon, so they seem to be totally underground, but it has 60 ft of glass facing south. Built in 1984, the house is about 5 mi outside Harrison, on a winding dirt road off Route 29 and near Fort Robinson State Park and Agate Fossil Beds

National Monument. You're likely to see all kinds of wildlife, from wild turkey to elk. Lodging includes a full ranch-style breakfast. No pets. No smoking. | 407 Sowbelly Rd. | 308/668–2537 | 2 rooms | $40 | No credit cards.

HASTINGS

(Nearby towns also listed: Grand Island, Kearney, Minden, Red Cloud, York)

Outside the region, Hastings is perhaps best known for its connections to big-time military weapons production and to the familiar little packages of fruit-drink concentrate known as Kool-Aid. Hastings resident Edwin Perkins had been bottling and selling a drink called Fruit-Smack. In 1927, he developed a powdered concentrate of his formula—and kids ever since have been tearing open the packages at kitchen tables or setting up Kool-Aid stands on their street corners.

During World War II, when the Navy opened opened a naval ammunition depot east of the city, thousands of employees worked 60-hour weeks—at 74 cents an hour—to manufacture the bombs, mines, rockets, and needed to fight the war. At peak operation in World War II and during the Korean War, the 49,000-acre Harrison NAD facility was the Navy's largest inland munitions plant. The buildings are still there, but no longer affiliated with the Navy.

To local residents, however, Tom Osborne is the town's claim to fame. Though some might not recognize the name, sports fans, and particularly Nebraska Husker fans, know that Tom Osborne is the coach with the most wins in college football history who led the University of Nebraska to multiple national titles.

Hastings is close enough to the Platte River that you may see some of the thousands of sandhill cranes who congregate around Kearney from February to April. If you are going to be in the area, the Adams County Convention and Visitors Bureau may be able to alert you to crane-sightings and viewing spots.

Information: Adams County Convention and Visitors Bureau | Box 941, 100 Northshore Dr., Hastings 68902 | 402/461–2370 or 800/967–2189 | fax 402/461–7273 | hastingsnevisit@tcgcs.com | www.hastingsnet.com/visitors/.

Attractions

Crystal Lake State Recreation Area. You can hike, swim, and play tennis here, but only low-power boating is permitted on the lake. Campsites at this park, on Highway 281 about 1½ mi from Ayr, are primitive, but there's a covered shelter for some cooking. | 800/826–7275 or 800/967–2189 | ngp.ngpc.state.ne.us/parks/crylkmp.html | Neb. Parks Permit required; camping, $3–$6 | Daily.

Hastings Museum and Lied IMAX Theater. You can explore several worlds of thought at this northside complex that includes an IMAX theater, the Discovery Center, and the McDonald Planetarium. The various museum galleries are devoted to such subjects as early life on the Great Plains, birds of the world, insects, seashells and corals, rocks and minerals, fossils, North American mammals, and antique vehicles, plus an exhibit on the development of Kool-Aid. | 1330 N. Burlington Ave. | 402/461–2399 | www.hastingsnet.com/museum | $5; IMAX Theater, $7 | Mon. 9–5, Tues.–Sat. 9–8, Sun. 10–8.

Landmark Center's Hastings Hall of History & Aspen Art Gallery. Here, you can see an antique shoe-shine chair and photos from the old days in Hastings. A huge world map hangs next to clocks set for Tokyo, San Francisco, Hastings, New York, and Moscow time. In the Aspen Art Gallery, you can view sculpture, prints, paintings, and the work of regional artists. | 2727 W. 2nd | 402/463–0546 | www.hastingsnet.com/visitors/ | $3–$5 | Mon. 9–5, Tues.–Sat. 9–8, Sun. 10–8.

ON THE CALENDAR

JUNE: *Cottonwood Prairie Festival.* This outdoor festival, in Brickyard Park on the southwest edge of town, is planned as a family event, with arts and crafts exhibits, entertainment, unusual foods, and children's activities. | 402/461–2368 or 800/967–2189.

JUNE: *South Central Nebraska Czech Festival.* No matter where your ancestors were born, you can join in the polka dancing and enjoy the ethnic foods, entertainment, and other activities at this lively annual gathering at the Hastings VFW Post. | 402/462–6775 or 800/967–2189.

JULY: *Friends of the Library Book Sale.* This sale of used books, which runs from Friday evening through Sunday in the City Auditorium, is one of the state's largest. You can choose from approximately 100,000 books of all types, including about 13,000 romance novels, plus pounds of magazines, sold just that way—by the pound. | 402/461–2346.

AUG.: *Kool-Aid Days.* The city bills this family festival at the Hastings Museum as the "world's largest Kool-Aid stand." You'll find special exhibits, games, and other family activities. | 800/967–2189.

Dining

Bernardo's Steak House. Steak. A fixture on the west side of Hastings for many years, Bernardo's offers family-style dining in a setting with lots of polished wood and paintings on the walls. There's a lounge for additional socializing. Locals praise the tournedos (a fillet of beef with a mushroom sauce) and peanut butter pie. The nut crunch ice cream isn't bad, either. Kids' menu. | 1109 S. Baltimore St. | 402/463–4666 | Mon.–Fri. 5–10, weekends 5–11, Sun. 5–9 | $9–$17 | AE, D, MC, V.

Taylor's Steakhouse. Steak. There's a fireplace to dine by and a lounge with darts—and specialty drinks—that closes "whenever." This downtown restaurant is known for the filet mignon, of course, but also for its spicy chicken wings, crab legs, lobster, and carrot cake. Kids' menu. | 1609 N. Kansas St. | 402/462–8000 | Mon.–Sat, 4:30–10 | $10–$25 | AE, MC, V.

Lodging

Holiday Inn. This modern two-story cream-colored brick building on the north edge of town has an enclosed courtyard and such room niceties as irons, ironing boards, and hair dryers. Truck parking with cold-weather hookups is available. Restaurant, bar, complimentary Continental breakfast, room service. In-room data ports. Cable TV. Indoor pool. Hot tub, sauna, exercise equipment. Business services. | 2205 Osborne Dr. E | 402/463–6721 | fax 402/463–6874 | 101 rooms | $69–$72 | AE, D, DC, MC, V.

Super 8 Motel. Rooms in this buff-and-brown two-story motel have a quiet mix of pale walls and dark fabrics and include some "whirlpool suites." Just 26 mi from the Grand Island Airport and not far from the Hastings Convention Center, it is right off Highway 281, behind a Dairy Queen. Complimentary Continental breakfast. Cable TV. Pets allowed. | 2200 N. Kansas St. | 402/463–8888 or 800/800–8000 | fax 402/463–8899 | 50 rooms | $44–$54 | AE, D, DC, MC.

U.S.A. Inns. This motel option just off Highway 281 on the north side of town, built in the 1980s, is near the college and local attractions. Truck parking and cold-weather hookups are available. Some refrigerators. Cable TV. Pets allowed. | 2424 Osborne Dr. E | 402/463–1422 or 800/348–0426 | fax 402/463–2956 | 63 rooms | $41–$44 | AE, D, DC, MC, V.

X-L. A one-level brick-block motel built in the 1960s, this lodging option on the combined Highway 6/34 is adjacent to the fairgrounds. The pool is heated but open only during the summer season. Truck parking and cold-weather hookups are available. Complimentary Continental breakfast. Kitchenettes, refrigerators, some microwaves. Cable TV. Pool. Hot tub. Laundry facilities. | 1400 W. J St. | 402/463–3148 or 800/341–8000 | fax 402/463–3148 | 43 rooms | $38–$43 | AE, D, DC, MC, V.

KEARNEY

(Nearby towns also listed: Eustis, Grand Island, Hastings, Lexington, Minden)

Hundreds of thousands of sandhill cranes, headed up the central flyway from Mexico to Canada, settle in Kearney for about two months from about mid-February of each year. From the bridge near Fort Kearny, you usually can see lots of them as the birds return from their daytime haunts along the Platte River to spend the night around Rowe Bird Sanctuary, but because crowds of crane-watchers on the bridge can be a safety hazard, the city has had to establish several public viewing sites with off-road parking.

Kearney gets its name from nearby Fort Kearny, but due to a mid-1800s postal spelling error, the town's name gained an extra "e" that somehow was never removed. Today, Fort Kearny is a re-creation of the important military post established in 1847 to protect emigrants headed west on the Oregon Trail.

Information: Kearney Chamber of Commerce and Visitors Bureau | Box 607, 1007 2nd Ave., Kearney 68848 | 308/237–3101 or 800/652–9435 | fax 308/236–8785 | www.ci.kearney.ne.us.

Attractions

George W. Frank House. Built in 1889 for one of the community's early leaders, this three-story sandstone mansion, on Highway 30W on the campus of the University of Nebraska at Kearney, has hand-carved oak woodwork, tile fireplaces, and Tiffany glass. | 308/865–8284 | $3 | Memorial Day–Labor Day, Tues.–Sun. 1–5.

Museum of Nebraska Art. The Museum of Nebraska Art houses the official visual art collection for the state of Nebraska. The neo-classical building, a former post office, is on the National Register of Historic Places. In addition to the Cliff Hillegass Sculpture Garden, MONA includes works of art about Nebraska and by such present and former Nebraskans as John James Audubon, Thomas Hart Benton, George Catlin, and Robert Henri. | 2401 Central Ave. | 308/865–8559 | monet.unk.edu/mona | Free | Tues.–Sat. 11–5, Sun. 1–5.

SCULPTURE GARDEN

They call it the "Museum without Walls," a collection of modern art sculptures at nine rest areas along I-80's 500-mi stretch across Nebraska. Rest areas on the westbound lanes include the York, Kearney, Brady, Ogallala, and Sidney stops; if you're headed eastbound, you can see some of the works at the Platte River, Blue River, and Grand Island rest areas. Travelers headed in either direction can see another example at the Nebraska/Omaha Travel Information Center in Omaha.

The sculpture project commemorates the United States Bicentennial in 1976. It was first proposed in 1973 amid a storm of controversy—many felt the sculptures were too "abstract." Though none of the works that eventually found homes in the 500-mi-long "Sculpture Garden" were created by Nebraska artists, they do represent the state's history. The sculpture *Roadway Confluence* at the Sidney westbound rest area, for example, is a 35-ft-tall shiny aluminum piece that commemorates the state's role in the development of transcontinental transportation.

The major difference between these sculptures and those you'll find inside a museum is the fact that this roadside art is designed to be touched and even climbed upon by youngsters as families take a break from driving.

© Artville

Fort Kearny Museum. Historical and multicultural exhibits representing the events of many centuries are in this in-town museum at a channel of the Platte River. Glass-bottom boats on a nearby lake allow visitors to see fish native to Nebraska waterways and lakes, including catfish, bluegill, bass, carp, and gar. | 131 S. Central Ave. | 308/234–5200 or 308/237–3101 | $2. Boat rides: $2.50 | Memorial Day–Labor Day, Thurs.–Sat. 10:30–5, Sun. 1–5.

Fort Kearny State Historical Park. From 1848 to 1871, a military outpost stood here, where the Oregon Trail met the Platte River and then followed it for hundreds of miles to the west. Now, you can see a re-created sod blacksmith shop, stockade, and powder magazine, along with the outlines of other buildings used by the troops trying to keep peace in the wide-open territory. Displays in the visitor center detailing the fort's role, and there are special programs held here during the crane season. | 1020 V Rd. | 308/865–5305 | ngp.ngpc.state.ne.us/parks/ftkearny.html | Neb. Parks Permit required | Grounds, year-round; visitor center, Memorial Day–Labor Day, daily 9–5; Sept.–Mar., by appointment; sandhill crane tours, mid-Mar.–mid-Apr., please call for times.

The state acquired the 150-acre **Fort Kearny State Recreation Area** specifically to be a recreational addition around the historical park. Here, you will find eight sand-pit lakes, with one beach for unsupervised swimming, fishing, hiking trails, and 110 fee campsites. The Hike-Bike Bridge, about ⅓ mi from the parking lot, is especially recommended for watching the sandhill cranes for about an hour before sunrise and an hour before sunset. You also may see many examples of the 10 million ducks and 2 million snow geese who also pause in the area during the migration seasons. To reach the parks from Kearney, go 4 mi south on Route 14, then 4 mi east on L50A. | 1020 V Rd. | 308/865–5305 | ngp.ngpc.state.ne.us/parks/ftkearny.html | ftkrny@ngpc.state.ne.us | Neb. Parks Permit required | Daily; modern camping facilities, May 1–Oct. 1.

Kearney Area Children's Museum. Interactive exhibits are designed to involve and amuse kids as they learn. The train depot and dress-up displays seem to be especially popular. | 2013 Ave. A | 308/236–5437 | $2 | Thurs.–Sat. 1–6, Sun. 1–5.

Trails and Rails Museum. This collection both tells about railroads and their role in making the West a real part of the United States and about the life that grew up as the tracks headed toward the Pacific. In an old Union Pacific depot, you can see lots of memorabilia and historical exhibits. Outside are a steam engine and caboose, an 1880s hotel, and an 1871 school. | 710 W. 11th St. | 308/234–3041 or 308/237–3101 | Free | Memorial Day–Labor Day, Tues.–Sat. 11–5, Sun. 1–5.

Rowe Bird Sanctuary. The National Audubon Society established the 1,150-acre Lillian Annette Rowe Sanctuary just outside Kearney in Gibbon especially to be a refuge for migratory birds—and the birds have been happy campers ever since. This is where the sandhill cranes spend the night when they're pausing along the Platte. For the best views of the cranes, you can arrange to watch from one of the three large wooden blinds, carpeted but unheated, open 5–8 AM and 5–8 PM. Or you can join the "photographer's tour" and spend the night there; you are not allowed to leave between 8 PM and 5 AM. Call for dates, details, photography rules, and recommended items to bring to stay warm. | 44450 Elm Island Rd., Gibbon | 308/468–5282 | rowe@nctc.net | www.rowesanctuary.org | Crane blinds, $15; photographer's nights, $100.

ON THE CALENDAR

FEB.–APR.: *Crane Watch.* You may suddenly see some of the big white sandhill cranes anywhere along the waterways and in the fields of the area around Kearney. To plan a crane-watching expedition, see the programs listed at Fort Kearny State Recreation Area and the Rowe Sanctuary in Kearney and at Crane Meadows Nature Center near Grand Island. The visitor bureaus in the various towns may also be able to direct you to other tours. The town of Kearney also has established several sites for safe crane-viewing, all with free off-road parking. These include the Richard Plantz platform site, 1½ mi south of I-80 exit 285; the Alda site, 2 mi south of I-80 exit 305; and roadside turnouts west of the Rowe Bird Sanctuary on Elm Island Road, and one on the south side and one on the east side of Platte River Drive off I–80 exit 305. If you see some larger cranes in April, you may be seeing the rare whooping cranes, still on the endangered species list. In all the world, there are now about 400 whooping cranes, up from 21 in the early 1940s, and the 200 in the U.S. flock all visit the Platte River Valley in April and October—but are harder to spot than the sandhills because the whooping cranes come two or three at a time and generally stay only for a night or two.

MAY: *Living History Days.* Fort Kearny State Historical Park celebrates the time when Fort Kearny was an active military post on the Oregon Trail. The various demonstrations include the firing of cannon. | 1020 V Rd. | 308/865–5305 | Neb. Parks Permit required.

JUNE: *Pony Express Reride.* Another Old West legend is commemorated at Fort Kearny State Historical Park. This event recalls the days when riders of the Pony Express used to pass through the region. Riders re-trace the route of the fabled mail service, and and food and music are on hand for spectators. | 1020 V Rd. | 308/865–5305 | Neb. Parks Permit required.

Dining

Alley Rose. American. Plush rooms shine softly with dark woods, brass accents, and a fireplace. The salad bar has homemade dressings and breads that are baked fresh daily. Check out the shrimp marsala, the chicken cordon bleu, or the magnificent seven (a cake made of seven different chocolates). Piano player weekends. Kids' menu. | 2013 Central Ave. | 308/234–1261 | No dinner Mon–Thurs. Closed Sun. | $6–$18 | AE, D, MC, V.

French Café. French. Small sidewalk tables bring a touch of Europe to the plains at this café inside the Kaufman Center mall downtown. You can choose from croissants and quiches, American deli-style sandwiches—with five kinds of homemade bread—soups, salads, pasta, and pastries and espresso. | 2202 Central Ave. | 308/234–6808 | Mon.–Fri. 8–4, Sat. 7–3 | $2–$8 | No credit cards.

Grandpa's Steak House. Steak. This spacious dining room with an inviting fireplace is known for specialty menus and thick-sliced cuts of meat, but you may also want to try the fried calamari, escargot, and cheese cakes. Buffet lunch Sunday. Kids' menu. | 13 Central Ave. | 308/237–2882 | $10–$35 | AE, D, MC, V | Mon.–Sat. 5–11, Sun. 11–3.

Lodging

Best Western. About 7 mi from the Kearney Municipal Airport, this two-story white motel with crisp dark trim has a sauna and a heated outdoor pool—and hairdryers in the rooms if you need one after your swim or steam session. Truck and RV parking is available, with cold-weather hook-ups. Restaurant, complimentary breakfast. Cable TV. Indoor pool, wading pool. Hot tub, sauna. Exercise equipment. Business services, airport shuttle. Pets allowed. | 1010 3rd Ave. | 308/237–5185 or 800/359–1894 | fax 308/234–1002 | 62 rooms | $72–$79 | AE, D, DC, MC, V.

Budget Host Western Inn. If you came from the east, you zipped under the Great Platte River Road Archway just before you exited the interstate, so you know where that is. The quiet in-town motel, about 1½ mi north of I–80, is also within a mile of the glass-bottom boats at Fort Kearny Museum. Truck parking is available. Restaurant, bar. Cable TV. Pool. | 1401 2nd Ave. | 308/237–3153 or 800/333–1401 | fax 308/234–6073 | 34 rooms | $36–$57 | AE, D, MC, V.

Budget Motel South. This motel option is only about four blocks from I–80 exit 272. Within the surrounding 5 mi, you'll find many of the town's attractions as well as shopping. Truck parking is available. Cable TV. Indoor pool. Sauna. Laundry facilities. Pets allowed. | 411 S. 2nd Ave. | 308/237–5991 | fax 308/237–5991 | 69 rooms | $40–$70 | AE, D, DC, MC, V.

Holiday Inn. With 20,000 square ft of meeting space, this two-story motel caters to a lot of groups—but doesn't forget the families. In the indoor water recreation area, you'll find two 30-ft water slides into the pool, plus slides and a water cannon at the kids' pool (and hairdryers in the rooms). There is a complimentary shuttle to tourist attractions within 10 mi of the hotel, which covers most of the in-town sites. Truck parking with cold-weather hookups is available. Restaurant, bar, room service. In-room data ports. Cable TV. Hot tub. Exercise equipment, volleyball. Video games. Laundry facilities. Business services. Pets allowed. | 110 S. 2nd Ave. | 308/237–5971 | fax 308/236–7549 | 163 rooms | $69–$89 | AE, D, DC, MC, V.

Quality Inn. This modern stucco motel less than a block from I–80 is about 6 mi from the Fort Kearny State Historical Park, with the crane-viewing at the Hike/Bike Bridge in the State Recreation Area just a couple of miles beyond that, or a short 17-mi drive from all the collectibles at the Harold Warp Pioneer Village in Minden. Truck parking and cold-weather hookups are available. Restaurant, bar, complimentary Continental breakfast. Cable TV. Pool. Exercise room. Laundry facilities. Some pets allowed (fee). | 800 2nd Ave. | 308/234–2541 or 800/652–7245 | fax 308/237–4512 | 103 rooms | $45–$53 | AE, D, MC, V.

Ramada Inn. Remodeled in 2000, this casually modern motor hotel now has refrigerators and irons in the rooms. Just ½ mi from I–80, it is 2 mi from the Great Platte River Archway and a mile from the Trails and Rails Museum. Truck parking and cold-weather hookups are available. Restaurant, bar, complimentary Continental breakfast, room service. Refrigerators. Cable TV. Indoor pool, wading pool. Hot tub, sauna. Video games. Laundry facilities. Business services. Pets allowed. | 301 S. 2nd Ave. | 308/237–3141 or 800/652–1909 | fax 308/234–4675 | 209 rooms | $55–$85 | AE, D, DC, MC, V.

Western Inn South. Playing to its name both indoors and out, there is a wagon in front of this motel, and wood paneling and art with Old West themes in the lobby. Some rooms have kitchenettes, but the hotel provides a full hot breakfast from Oct. 15 to May 15. Truck parking with cold-weather hookups is available. Complimentary Continental breakfast. Some kitchenettes. Cable TV. Indoor pool. Hot tub, sauna. Pets allowed. | 510 S. 3rd Ave. | 308/234–1876 or 800/437–8457 | fax 308/237–2169 | 44 rooms | $39–$60 | AE, D, DC, MC, V.

KIMBALL

MAP 11, A3

(Nearby towns also listed: Bayard, Gering, Scottsbluff, Sidney)

In extreme western Nebraska, Kimball is just 17 mi from the highest point in the state—and in the center of the largest collection of ICBMs (intercontinental ballistic missiles) in the world. In fact, the town capitalized on this by securing an obsolete giant Titan I missile to display in Kimball's small Gotte Park. Around this agricultural area, an estimated 200 Minuteman III ICBMs stand ready in underground silos in the immediate tri-state area, but when you look at the wheatfields all around, you'll see few signs of the powerful missiles.

Information: **Kimball/Banner County Chamber of Commerce** | 119 E. 2nd St., Kimball 69145 | 308/235–3782 | fax 308/235–3825 | kbccc@megavision.com | www.ci.kimball.ne.us.

Attractions

Oliver Reservoir State Recreation Area. This popular recreation area, 8 mi west of Kimball on Highway 30, hums with outdoors activities year-round, from boating, water-skiing, fishing, and swimming in mild weather to ice-fishing and ice-skating when the lakes freeze over. Primitive campsites are available. | 308/235–4040 or 308/235–3782 | ngp.ngpc.state.ne.us/parks/oliver.html | Neb. Parks Permit required; camping, $3 | Daily.

Panorama Point and Three-State Marker. Panorama Point is Nebraska's highest point, 5,424 ft above sea level. To the southwest, the Three-State Marker denotes the juncture of Nebraska, Colorado, and Wyoming. The Kimball/Banner County Chamber of Commerce has a map and directions for finding Panorama Point, about 27 mi southeast of Kimball and described as being "in the middle of nowhere." | 308/235–3782 | Free | Daily.

Lodging

Days Inn. This compact sand-colored stucco motor hotel was remodeled, with all-new room furnishings, in 2000. A mile north of I–80 and next door to Kimball Event Center, it's also about 40 mi from the buffalo and elk herds at the Wildcat Hills Nature Center near Gering. Complimentary Continental breakfast. In-room data ports. Cable TV. Indoor pool. Pets allowed (fee). | 611 E. 3rd St. | 308/235–4671 or 800/329–7466 | fax 308/235–3557 | www.daysinn.com | 30 rooms | $46–$85 | AE, D, MC, V.

Super 8 Motel. This modest two-story motel built in 1990 at the I–80 junction with Route 71 helps you start the day with a free newspaper. It's about 8 mi from the Oliver Reservoir State Recreation Area—and only about 30 mi from Cabela's sporting goods store if you need to jaunt over to Sidney to stock up on new equipment. Truck and RV spaces are available. | 104 E. River Rd. In-room data ports. Cable TV. Some pets allowed (fee). | 308/235–4888 or 800/800–8000 | fax 308/235–2838 | 58 rooms | $52–$72 | AE, D, DC, MC, V.

LEXINGTON

MAP 11, E4

(Nearby towns also listed: Broken Bow, Cozad, Eustis, Gothenburg, Kearney, Minden)

Lexington started as a frontier trading post called Plum Creek because it was near the spot Plum Creek poured into the Platte River. The Plum Creek Station became widely talked about when the Cheyenne attacked a train of freight wagons there on August 8, 1864, and left several men dead. The old post relocated after the coming of the Union Pacific Railroad caused a decline in wagon travel, and the community became Lexington in 1889. Today, it is a prosperous farming and stock-raising area.

Information: Lexington Area Chamber of Commerce | 709 E. Pacific St., Lexington 68850 | 308/324–5504 or 888/966–0564 | fax 308/324–5505 | lexcoc@krvn.com | www.lexington-ets.com.

Attractions

Dawson County Historical Museum. The story of Dawson County is told through displays of farm machinery, rooms of period furnishings, quilts, glassware, and other relics of everyday life in pioneer times. The grounds also have a schoolhouse, a train depot, and a log cabin. | 805 N. Taft St. | 308/324–5340 | Free | Mon.–Sat., 9–5.

Heartland Museum of Military Vehicles. This collection of military vehicles, polished and shiny like new, includes Jeeps, trucks, and ambulances from World War II, helicopters from Vietnam, and Soviet-manufactured tanks and American Bradley fighting vehicles from Desert Storm. | 606 Heartland Rd. | 308/324–6329 | Free | Daily 10–5.

Johnson Lake State Recreation Area. About 7 mi south of Lexington off Highway 283, the lake has areas for fishing, boating, and swimming, as well as state and private fee campgrounds. If you go in the winter and think you're seeing a bald eagle, you're probably right—our national bird flocks to the region during its northward migration and might be seen diving for fish on any of the lakes around here. | 308/785–2685 | ngp.ngpc.state.ne.us/parks/johnson.html | Neb. Parks Permit required; camping, $7–$11 | Daily; modern camping facilities, May–mid-Sept.

ON THE CALENDAR
MAY: *Spring Fling Antique Flea Market.* Many people—and many antiques dealers— begin their summer by coming to Lexington for the Memorial Day weekend antiques

flea market at the Dawson County Fair Grounds off Highway 283. | 308/987–2633 or 308/324–5504.

JAN.–FEB.: J-2 Eagle Viewing Center. The bald eagles—our country's national symbol—also visit along the Platte during their migration, gathering especially to fish around the Johnson No. 2 hydroplant in Holdrege, at the junction of Highways 6 and 183 southeast of Lexington. You can drive to the observation facility or arrange to join professional and hobbyist photographers in special viewing blinds. For other viewing tours, call 308/995–8601. | 308/284–2332.

Lodging

Budget Host—Minute Man. On Highway 283, this one-story red brick-and-wood motel is only about 2 mi north of I–80, in an area where you'll find many dining options. Truck parking with cold-weather hookups is available. Cable TV. Pets allowed (fee). | 801 Plum Creek Pkwy. | 308/324–5544 or 800/973–5544 | 36 rooms | $34–$40 | AE, D, DC, MC, V.

1st Interstate Inn. Off exit 237 of I–80, this modest motel is only about 30–35 mi from several good crane-viewing sites near Kearney. If you follow 283 south of the interstate, you are also within minutes of the J-2 Eagle Viewing Facility. Truck parking is available. Complimentary Continental breakfast. Cable TV. Pool. Pets allowed. | 2503 S. Plum Creek Rd. | 308/324–5601 | fax 308/324–4284 | 52 rooms | $43–$58 | AE, D, DC, MC, V.

Gable View Inn. The building is modern, but the eight peaks of the roofline give it a slightly Victorian look. The small motel is only about a quarter of a mi from I–80 and within 10 mi of the Johnson Lake State Recreation Area. Truck parking is available. Cable TV. Pool. Pets allowed. | 2701 Plum Creek Pkwy. | 308/324–5595 or 800/341–8000 | fax 308/324–2267 | 24 rooms | $32–$40 | AE, D, MC, V.

Super 8 Motel. To reach this motel option, follow Highway 283 south from I–80 until you see a truck stop with Kirk's restaurant. Turn into the driveway and take the access road to the motel, only about 7 mi from Johnson Lake. Truck parking with cold-weather hookups is available. Complimentary breakfast. Cable TV. Hot tub. | 104 E. River.Rd. | 308/324–7434 or 800/800–8000 | fax 308/324–4433 | 48 rooms | $45–$52 | AE, D, DC, MC, V.

LINCOLN

MAP 11, H4

(Nearby towns also listed: Ashland, Beatrice, Nebraska City, Wilber, York)

Lincoln rises to meet you as you drive along I–80, its skyline dominated by the 400-ft spire of the Nebraska State Capitol Building—topped by the sculpture *The Sower* towering over the surrounding plains.

Omaha is much larger than Lincoln, and when Nebraska became a state in 1867, a fierce battle broke out about which town would be the location of the state's capitol. Lincoln didn't exist at the time, but its predecessor community, Lancaster—with a population of about 30—did. The citizens of Lancaster fought a political battle with the residents of Omaha for the honor of being named permanent state capitol, and they were victorious. Legislation was passed to move the capitol from its temporary home in Bellevue to Lancaster, which was at the same time renamed Lincoln.

After winning its new status, Lincoln began building a city suitable for state government. The first state capitol building stood until 1881, when it was replaced; the present capitol building was constructed between 1922 and 1932, and it remains the most prominent structure in the downtown area.

As Lincoln grew, it annexed neighboring towns, including the villages of Havelock, Yankee Hill, and Bethany. Besides the University of Nebraska, Lincoln has three other colleges—Southeast Community College, Nebraska Wesleyan University, and Union

College. In the fall, Husker football at the University of Nebraska becomes a way of life for nearly all Nebraskans. Since November 3, 1962, every Husker Game in the 73,650-seat Memorial Stadium has been sold out.

With more than 6,000 acres of parks, nine municipal swimming pools, an aquatic center with a water slide, seven recreation centers, 11 public golf courses, and more than 60 mi of hiking and biking trails, Lincoln has much to offer if you enjoy outdoor recreation. If you prefer the indoors, there are also ample choices, including the Lied Center for Performing Arts, the Sheldon Memorial Art Gallery, the National Museum of Roller Skating, the Museum of Nebraska History, the State Museum of Natural History, and the Nebraska State Historical Society, arguably one of the nation's best archives of Western history.

Information: Lincoln Chamber of Commerce | Box 83006, 1135 M St., Lincoln 68501 | 402/436–2350 | fax 402/436–2360 | pmmccue@lcoc.com | www.lcoc.com. **Lincoln Convention and Visitors Bureau** | Box 83737, 1135 M St., 3rd Fl, Lincoln 68501 | 402/434–5335 or 800/423–8212 | fax 402/436–2360 | info@lincoln.org | www.lincoln.org.

NEIGHBORHOODS

Historic Haymarket. You can shop for antiques or the newest fad fashions here, dine or drink, or relax with a sandwich and expresso at an outdoor café. By night or day, the Historic Haymarket district is one of Lincoln's hot spots. Within the six-block area of restored 19th-century commercial buildings, shops sell antiques, books, and clothing, and there are galleries to visit and a wide choice of bars, restaurants, and other evening hang-outs. On Saturday mornings between May and October, it's the site of a farmer's market where you can stock up on fresh fruits and vegetables, flowers, handicrafts, and homemade pastries—and you may really want to wipe the word *calorie* from your mind for Haymarket's annual **Chocolate Lover's Fantasy** in February. It's a fund-raiser to benefit work on the district, tempting your eyes and tastebuds with all manner of chocolate creations by professional and celebrity chefs, as well as art and other items. (For information: 402/434–6900.)

University Place. Once in decline, this ethnically diverse neighborhood has been revitalized. Today, coffee shops, live entertainment venues, and art galleries line 48th Street, and at almost any time, you'll see students from nearby Nebraska-Wesleyan University who've made it their "patch." A mainstay among the younger businesses is the University Place Art Center at 2601 N. 48th St. For more than two decades, this multi-faceted complex in the former City Hall building has built a diverse program that now includes displays of works by more than 125 artists and artisans. One wing houses the Gladys Lux Historical Gallery and its collection of more than 1,600 dolls, from a 1775 Nyphenburg pottery example to the cloth and wood dolls hugged by frontier children to a few Barbies from the 1950s. In addition to special exhibitions throughout the year, the center has a benefit auction every spring to fund future expansion. (For information: 402/466–8692.)

TRANSPORTATION

Airports: Lincoln Municipal Airport (402/475–7243) is served by United, TWA, U.S. Airways Express, Air Midwest, and Northwest AirLink/Mesaba. Taxis to downtown cost about $10. **Eppley Express** runs an airport van from Lincoln Municipal Airport to Eppley Airfield in Omaha. | 308/234–6066 or 800/888–9793.

Rail: Twice a day, **Amtrak** trains stop at Lincoln Station, departing for the west at 1:45 AM and for the east at 4:52 AM. | Seventh and P Sts. | 402/476–1295 or 800/872–7245; baggage information: 402/476–9335.

Bus Lines: Like the spokes of a wheel radiating outward, **Greyhound** routes connect Lincoln by bus to points all across the nation (940 P St. | 402/474–1071 or 800/231–2222), and several other carriers run from Lincoln to various other parts of the state: **Good**

Life Transportation (402/467–2900); **Eppley Express** (800/888–9793); **Arrow Stage Lines** (402/488–6622); **Big Red Bus** (402/473–3800).

Intra-city Transit: Within the city, local bus service is provided by **StarTran** (402/476–1234).

Driving around Town: A local wag once dubbed Lincoln the "one-way street and island capital of the world." Be warned: If you find yourself on the wrong side of the street, you may have to drive some distance before you can get around and back to the other side of the island that divides many streets. The good news is that rush hours are normally light and parking is readily available and inexpensive. Meters cost 50 cents per hour (8–6 Mon.–Sat.). The color of a meter signals the maximum time available in that spot: 10 minutes at white meters; 30 minutes at red ones; an hour at the yellows; 90 minutes for orange; 2 hours at greens; 5 hours at browns; and 10 hours at blue meters. These limits are strictly enforced; tickets for expired meters cost $7. Garages are plentiful and usually cost less than a parking ticket. Numbered streets run east and west; lettered streets run north and south. In general, because the city is small, walking is a good idea. For more information, call 402/441–6472.

Attractions

ART AND ARCHITECTURE

State Capitol. Nebraska's capitol building, its 400-ft tower topped by a 19-ft bronze sculpture that can be seen for miles, is one of the more unusual ones in our nation. Designed by Bertram Goodhue, it also displays many art treasures, including mosaics, paintings, and busts of such famous Nebraskans as Willa Cather, General John Pershing, Buffalo Bill Cody, and the poet John Neihardt. The last murals in the original 1930s plan were installed on the 14th floor near the observation platform only in recent years. | 1445 K St. | 402/471–0448 | Free | Weekdays 8–5, Sat. 10–5, Sun. 1–5; architectural tours by appointment.

Although the governor's private quarters are not open to the public, you can visit the public spaces of the white-columned **Executive Mansion,** next door to the Capitol grounds, and see such items as a collection of dolls in copies of inaugural gowns worn by Nebraska's First Ladies and a silver tea service from the early battleship USS *Nebraska.* | 1425 H St. | 402/471–3466 | Free | Thurs. 1–4.

University of Nebraska—Lincoln. The state's major university is home to several colleges, a large student body, and the Cornhusker football team, which has earned several conference championships as well as four national titles. Q Street near 16th Street is a good

PACKING IDEAS FOR HOT WEATHER

- ☐ Antifungal foot powder
- ☐ Bandanna
- ☐ Cooler
- ☐ Cotton clothing
- ☐ Day pack
- ☐ Film
- ☐ Hiking boots
- ☐ Insect repellent
- ☐ Rain jacket
- ☐ Sport sandals
- ☐ Sun hat
- ☐ Sunblock
- ☐ Synthetic ice
- ☐ Umbrella
- ☐ Water bottle

*Excerpted from *Fodor's: How to Pack: Experts Share Their Secrets*
© 1997, by Fodor's Travel Publications

point of entry for strolling around the city campus; group tours of Memorial Stadium may be arranged. | Daily.

The university looks to its own roots in the **Great Plains Art Collection,** which includes bronzes by Frederick Remington and Charles Russell as well as paintings. Its library houses more than 4,000 volumes of works related to the Great Plains and Americana. | 1155 Q St. | 402/472–6220 | www.unl.edu/plains/artcol.html | Free | Tues.–Sat. 10–5, Sun. 1:30–5; closed between academic sessions.

The **Lied Center for Performing Arts** has become a major cultural resource for the city, bringing to Lincoln the likes of the Joffrey Ballet, the Broadway musical "Les Miserables," and choirs under the direction of such conductors as the late Robert Shaw, to name only a few examples. | 12th and R Sts. | 402/472–4747 or 800/432–3231 | www.liedcenter.org | Box office, weekdays 11–5.

Architect Phillip Johnson became known the world over for his "Glass House" in Connecticut. For this art showcase in the American heartland, he chose white travertine marble, which was quarried near Rome and installed here under the supervision of an Italian foreman who spoke no English. Inside the **Sheldon Memorial Art Gallery and Sculpture Garden,** intimate gallery spaces display the important collection of 20th-century art, especially from the Cubism, Realism, and Abstract Expressionism movements. Outside, 32 sculptures grace a 20-acre sculpture garden. | 12th and R Sts. | 402/472–2461 | www.sheldon.unl.edu | Tues.–Wed. 10–5, Thurs.–Sat. 10–5 and 7–9, Sun. 2–9.

Nicknamed Elephant Hall—and easily recognized by the mammoth elephant sculpture in front of the building—the **State Museum of Natural History,** on the UNL campus, has extensive displays on the prehistoric elephants whose remains have been found in Nebraska, as well as on geology and human biology and a walk-in wildlife diorama. Another section is devoted to the Lenz Center for Asian Culture, with exhibits of art and objects reflecting Asian philosophies. | 14th and U Sts. | 402/472–2642 | Free | Mon.–Sat. 9:30–4:30, Sun., holidays 1:30–4:30.

Sharing the State Museum of Natural History site, the **Ralph Mueller Planetarium** has popular laser shows on astronomical subjects on Friday and Saturday afternoons. You also can view the heavens through the telescope—"when weather permits." | 14th and U Sts. | 402/472–2641 | www.spacelaser.com | Free | Mon.–Sat. 9:30–4:30, Sun., holidays 1:30–4:30; laser shows, Fri., Sat. at 2.

CULTURE, EDUCATION, AND HISTORY

American Historical Society of Germans from Russia. Preserving the heritage of Germans who settled in Russia before immigrating to the U.S. beginning in the 1870s, this center has extensive well-catalogued archives, such as "surnames by ship lists," to aid in family research about the people once called "The Czar's Germans." | 631 D St. | 402/474–3363 | www.ahsgr.org | Free | Weekdays 9–4 plus Tues. 7–9 PM, Sat. 9–1.

Bess Streeter Aldrich House and Museum. This was the home of the author of *Miss Bishop* and eight other novels, plus more than 100 short stories, now a small museum in Elmwood where you can see how she lived and worked during a writing career that spanned the years from 1909 to 1945. | 204 E. F St., Elmwood | 402/994–3855 | $3 | Wed., Thurs., Sat., Sun. 2–5, or by appointment.

Museum of Nebraska History. The state's premier historical museum, on the Centennial Mall in downtown Lincoln, covers the presence of man in the central plains from prehistoric times to the present, including exhibits that focus on Native Americans and the early settlers, as well as period rooms from many other eras. | 131 Centennial Mall North | 402/471–3270 | www.nebraskahistory.org | Free | Daily.

Thomas P. Kennard House. The home of Nebraska's first secretary of state, Thomas Kennard, this trim, two-story yellow Italianate home, built in 1869, is thought to be the oldest structure in Lincoln. The furnishings reflect those of an upper-middle-class family of the 1870s. | 1627 H St. | 402/471–4764 | www.nebraskahistory.org | $2 | Tues.–Fri. 9–noon, 1–4:30; Memorial Day–Labor Day, also weekends 1–5.

MUSEUMS

Lincoln Children's Museum. Many of the interactive exhibits in this downtown museum are designed to teach children what really happens at real-world places they might see every day, including a kid-scaled bank, radio station, and supermarket, along with a lunar lander, a face-painting area, giant bubble makers, and a special toddler area. | 1420 P St. | 402/477–0128 | www.lincolnchildrensmuseum.org | $4 | Sun., Mon. 1–5, Tues.–Sat. 10–5.

National Museum of Roller Skating. The only museum in the world dedicated to the fun of skating on wheels displays skates, costumes, and related films and artwork from the first leisure wheels in 1819 to the present. | 4730 South St. | 402/483–7551 | www.roller-skatingmuseum.com | Free | Weekdays 9–5.

PARKS, NATURAL AREAS, AND OUTDOOR RECREATION

Antelope Park and Sunken Gardens. Winding along Antelope Creek, this downtown city park seems to be many sites rather than one. You'll find the quiet and beautiful gathering places, such as the rose garden or the terraced Sunken Gardens, as well as many sculptures and fountains, plus the activity-oriented golf course, trails, tennis courts, swimming pool, and playgrounds. In Veterans Memorial Garden, you can view a half-scale replica of the Vietnam Wall naming all Nebraskans who were killed, became POWs, or are listed as MIAs from that conflict, plus memorials to those who served in World War II, Korean, and Desert Storm. | 3140 Sumner St. | Free | Daily.

Bluestem Lake State Recreation Area. This area south of the city, on Route 33 about 2 mi west of Sprague, is noted for the variety of fish in the 325-acre lake, from bass and bluegill to pike and walleye. You'll also find picnicking, swimming, and primitive camping sites and an archery range here. | 402/471–5566 | ngpc.state.ne.us | Neb. Parks Permit required; camping, $3–$5 | Daily.

Branched Oak Lake State Recreation Area. When you feel a tug on your line in Branched Oak Lake, it could be from any of three different kinds of catfish. The largest of the Salt Valley Lakes, 3½ mi north of Malcom on Route 55M, covers some 1,800 acres. In addition to camping, boating, swimming, and picnicking sites, the park also is home to an arboretum with more than 100 species of trees and shrubs and an 800-acre dog trail where championship sledding events are held in the winter. | 402/783–3400 | ngpc.state.ne.us | Neb. Parks Permit required; camping, $3–$12 | Daily; modern camping facilities, May–mid-Sept.

Conestoga Lake State Recreation Area. In these parts, Conestoga, 2 mi north of Denton on Route 55A, is almost a baby lake—it only covers 250 acres. But the 486 acres of land around it have many sites for picnicking, primitive camping, and just relaxing in the outdoors. | 402/471–5566 | ngpc.state.ne.us | Neb. Parks Permit required; camping, $3–$8 | Daily.

Holmes Lake Park. Surrounding a manmade lake, this city park has a marina with rental boats; fishing, picnicking, playgrounds, golf, ballfields, and ice-skating. You also can visit Hyde Memorial Observatory, which is within the park grounds, for various exhibits or special shows on astronomy. | 70th and Bandorn St. | Observatory: 402/441–7847 | Observatory: www.blackstarpress.com/arin/hyde | Free | Daily.

Pawnee Lake State Recreation Area. Pawnee, 2 mi north and 1½ mi west of Emerald on Route 6, is the second-largest of the Salt Valley Lakes parks, with a 750-acre lake for boating or fishing. Other recreational sites in the 1,800 land acres around it include a clay-target shooting area and a hunting preserve open in the fall. | 402/471–5566 | ngpc.state.ne.us | Neb. Parks Permit required; camping, $3–$12 | Daily; modern camping facilities, May–mid-Sept.

Pioneers Park. This 900-acre city park blends heavily wooded areas with open fields linked by bridle paths and hiking and biking trails. It also has an amphitheater for outdoor entertainment events, plus a golf course, at 3403 W. Van Dorn. The Nature Center in the southwest part of the park has its own set of trails through prairie, woodlands, and wetlands near natural habitats where buffalo and elk roam. | 3201 S. Coddington | 402/441–7895 | Grounds, daily; Nature Center, June–Aug., Mon.–Sat. 8:30–8:30, Sun. 12–8:30; Sept.–May, Mon.–Sat. 8:30–5, Sun. 12–5.

OTHER POINTS OF INTEREST

Folsom Children's Zoo and Botanical Gardens. More than 300 animals—representing 95 species from African dwarf crocodile to zebra mice—live here amid gardens with more than 7,000 annuals and 30 types of trees. The animal displays include an aviary and a forest area. In the Critter Encounter Area, kids can meet some animals up close and can ride ponies or a miniature train. | 1222 S. 27 St. | 402/475–6741 | www.lincolnzoo.org | $5 | Apr. 15–Oct. 15, daily 10–5; Nov. 24–25 and Dec. 1–2, noon–4.

James Arthur Vineyard. Some of James Arthur Jeffers's French-American hybrid grapes like the Nebraska soil so much that they grow 20–25 ft a year. You can tour the winery, then sample a glass or two from gazebos overlooking the vineyard, perhaps with the Edelweiss, which won the winery a double-gold at the prestigious Orange County Fair in 1999. | 2001 W. Raymond Rd. | 402/783–5255 | Free | Apr.–Oct., Mon.–Thurs. 10–6, Fri., Sat. noon–9, Sun. noon–6; Nov.–Mar., weekdays 10–5, Sat. noon–9, Sun. noon–6.

ON THE CALENDAR

FEB.: *ABATE Lincoln Motorcycle Show.* Hundreds of motorcycle enthusiasts journey to Lincoln for this annual event at the State Fairgrounds. | 402/434–5348.

MAR.: *Sesostris Annual Shrine Circus.* The circus comes to town, filling Pershing Auditorium with the time-old daredevil acts, clowns, and animal performances. | 402/441–8744.

JUNE: *Horse racing.* From mid-May through mid-July, the thoroughbreds take over State Fair Park. Post times for the races are 4 PM Thursday and Friday and 1 PM on Saturday. The rest of the year, you can go to the races via simulcasting in the State Fair Park Grandstands. | 402/473–4205.

JULY: *Camp Creek Thrashers Show.* The antique thrashers displayed here were once the backbone of Nebraska farm and village life. Along with demonstrations of threshers and steam-powered engines, this 25-year-old annual program, 2 mi east of Middle School on Bluff Road in Waverly, has a train, old-fashioned schoolhouse, a blacksmith shop and a broom-maker, and a parade each day. | 402/786–3003.

JULY: *Fourth of July Celebration.* Nebraska's official Fourth of July city hosts a grand, family-oriented event. The program includes more than 100 activities, most of them downtown, including exhibits and a splendid parade. The day ends with fireworks over the lake in Holmes Park, 70th at Normal St. | 402/643–4189.

JULY: *July Jamm.* Downtown jumps to many happy beats during this weekend festival of art, music, and fine food. | 402/434–6900.

AUG.–SEPT.: *Nebraska State Fair.* The biggest fair in the state runs for 11 days at State Fair Park includes a midway and carnival rides, traditional agriculture shows and competitions, and live music programs that feature some top-ranked entertainers. | 1800 State Fair Park Dr. | 402/473–4109.

OCT.: *Boo at the Zoo.* Folsom Children's Zoo opens again at Halloween (Oct. 26–30) for this event designed to provide a place for safe trick or treating. The Train of Terror rides the rails, and kids can freely shriek—or laugh—at all manner of spook booths. | 1222 S. 27 St. | 402/475–6741.

NOV.–DEC.: *Holidays in the Haymarket.* You can celebrate the holidays in the Historic Haymarket district with music and dancing and a visit with Santa. | 402/435–7496.

WALKING TOUR

(approximately 2 hours to all day)
The Haymarket Historic District in downtown Lincoln is a great place to begin a walk. The route features antiques stores, art galleries, bookstores, and a variety of food

options—in restaurants or, during the summer, at the open farmers' market. When you venture just beyond the Haymarket, you can spend anywhere from a couple of hours to all day exploring museums and state historic sites.

Begin your walk at the **Star City Visitors Center,** at 7th and P streets, then wind your way through and around the six-block **Haymarket District,** bordered by 7th Street to the west, 9th Street to the east, O Street to the south, and R Street to the north. Within this area, you'll find eight art galleries, dozens of specialty shops, several antiques stores, and a variety of places providing food and libations. Public rest rooms are in the Lincoln Station, at 201 N. 7th Street.

From the Haymarket, head east on R Street, where you'll be crossing the southern edge of the University of Nebraska campus. At 1500 North R Street, visit the **Nebraska State Historic Society,** to view displays on the past in this region and see the extensive files available to aid researchers delving into Western history. Upon exiting the Nebraska State Historic Society, turn south down the wide Centennial Mall and head toward the Nebraska State Capitol. Before reaching the capitol, however, take the time to stop at the **Museum of Nebraska History,** at 15th and P streets. There, you will be able to explore many exhibits related to Central Plains history, from the influence of Native Americans to pioneer life, as well as special displays on such topics as Nebraskans in the U.S. military and wedding finery and traditions.

Then continue south on 15th Street to the **Nebraska State Capitol,** with its elegant sculpture of "The Sower" on top of the rotunda, relief carvings around the exterior, and murals on the interior walls. If the legislature happens to be in session, you can enter the visitor's gallery and watch the lawmakers at work in the only state in the nation with a unicameral legislature (one legislative chamber). After leaving the capitol, you can continue south on 16th Street to H Street and the site of the **Thomas P. Kennard House,** which is the Nebraska Statehood Memorial and home of Nebraska's first secretary of state. Constructed in 1869, the spacious yellow house is furnished throughout in the style of the 1870s. After touring the Kennard House, walk west on H Street for two blocks to the corner of 14th Street to visit the **Governor's Mansion** and its collection of dolls depicting Nebraska first ladies in their inaugural gowns. From there, walk north on 13th Street, then turn west on O Street, where you will find the **Nebraska Children's Museum,** with hands-on exhibits related to science, technology, history, fine arts, and culture. To come full circle, just keep on walking west and you will again be at the Historic Haymarket District, where you can conclude your walking tour with a meal or refreshments.

Dining

INEXPENSIVE

El Mercadito Mexican Market. Mexican. In downtown Lincoln, this take-out restaurant and Mexican grocery also puts tables outside during pleasant weather. Some of the staff is not very fluent in English, but portions, such as one-pound burritos, are generous. Tortillas are made to order, as are chicken and steak tacos. | 1028 O St. | 402/435–6774 | $4–$7 | No credit cards.

Rock 'N Roll Runza. German. Runzas, which are German-Russian baked sandwiches of spicy ground beef and cabbage, are made and sold in Runza Huts across Nebraska. This outpost in downtown Lincoln plays up its rock 'n roll name with lots of 1950s memorabilia, including some of Marilyn Monroe's original possessions. Try the runza with home-made hand-dipped onion rings. | 210 N. 14th St. | 402/474–2030 | $2–$8 | No credit cards.

Wigwam Cafe. American. This typical small-town café has been in business for more than six decades. Its high ceilings, brick walls, and black tabletops and counters are set off by original artifacts from the 1930s. Roast beef and chicken-fried steak are local favorites. | 146 E. 5th St., Wahoo | 402/443–5575 | Closed Tues. | $4–$7 | No credit cards.

MODERATE

★ **Billy's.** Continental. Billy's is near the state capitol in a historic mansion decorated with political mementos, especially photos and artifacts recalling the famed William Jennings Bryan, the Nebraska-born orator and three-time Presidential nominee who also figured prominently in the infamous Scopes trial of 1925. On the menu: the filet mignon, crab, lobster, veal, lamb, and rib-eye. | 1301 13th St. | 402/474–0084 | Closed Sun. | $8–$20 | AE, D, DC, MC, V.

Jabrisco. American. This eclectic place in the downtown historic district takes a low-key approach to decorating, but there's an open kitchen with a wood-fired oven and a variety of pizzas, pastas, salads, breads, and soups. | 700 P St. | 402/434–5644 | $6–$18 | AE, D, DC, MC, V.

The Oven. Indian. Huge murals and dim lights set the tone in this upscale Indian restaurant in the historic Haymarket district. If you'd rather have your foods from the land of the Taj Mahal in a slightly different setting, there's a generous outdoor dining space. No smoking is allowed. Try the chicken *tikka* (boneless chicken marinated and cooked tender) or the mixed grill (a combination of chicken, shrimp, and lamb). | 201 N 8th St. | 402/475–6118 | Closed Sun. | $10–$18 | AE, D, DC, MC, V.

Shogun. Japanese. You can watch the chefs in this teppenyaki restaurant prepare your food on the skillet table—the portions are huge. Try the sampler with scallops, shrimp, and lobster. | 56th and Hwy. 2 | 402/421–7100 | $10–$26 | MC, V.

Terrace Grill. American. On the first floor of the Cornhusker Hotel, this downtown restaurant has garden-scene murals and a wide-ranging menu, serving up sandwiches, salads, and pasta for a lighter lunch or dinner, but offering New York strip, rib-eye steak, chicken cannelloni, smoked pork chops, or crab-stuffed shrimp Provençal for diners with time for a more leisurely meal by a faux marble column. | 333 S. 13th St. | 402/474–7474 | $10–$21 | AE, D, DC, MC, V.

★ **Valentino's Restaurant.** Italian. Besides pizza with original or home-style crust, this restaurant also serves specials and "dessert pizzas" with such toppings as cherries and cream cheese. | 3457 Holdrege St. | 402/467–3611 | $5–$20 | AE, D, MC, V.

EXPENSIVE

Misty's. Steak. There's no question that you are in Big Red country here, as you can see from the restaurant's football-shape bar and the University of Nebraska team memorabilia. Husker fans and others have made this a hang-out since the 1970s for prime ribs and steak specialties. | 6235 Havelock Ave. | 402/466–8424 | $5–$40 | AE, D, DC, MC, V.

Renaissance. Continental. On the second floor of the Cornhusker Hotel, the Renaissance is a traditional white-tablecloth restaurant where dining is by candlelight and some dishes are prepared right at the table. Try the smoked or grilled salmon, veal bergino, or grilled New York steak—or the bobwhite quail that could have come from Nebraska. | 333 S. 13th St. | 402/479–8200 | Closed Sun. | $19–$26 | AE, D, DC, MC, V.

Lodging

INEXPENSIVE

Best Western Villager Courtyard and Garden. Renovated in 1999, these five two-story wooden buildings are set in landscaped grounds with a wildflower garden, a heated pool, and walking paths. Downtown is 3 mi away. Restaurant, bar. Hot tub. Laundry facilities. Free parking. Pets allowed (fee). | 5200 O St. | 402/464–9111 or 800/356–4321 | fax 402/467–0505 | 193 rooms | $69–$84 | AE, D, DC, MC, V.

Budget Host Great Plains. It's almost in the shadow of the spire, this two-story motel on Highway 6 only 16 blocks from the State Capitol, and it's only a mile from all the action at the University of Nebraska. Complimentary Continental breakfast. Cable TV. | 2732 O St. |

402/476–3253 or 800/288–8499 | fax 402/476–7540 | crocker@inetnebr.com | 42 rooms | $40–$46 | AE, D, DC, MC, V.

Fairfield Inn. This three-story hotel is 4 mi from Lincoln Municipal Airport and 2 mi from the State Fairgrounds and Nebraska's biggest fair. Rooms include workdesks, and complimentary weekday newspapers are available in the lobby. Cable TV. Indoor pool. Hot tub. Laundry services. Free parking. No pets. | 4221 Industrial Ave. | 402/476–6000 or 800/228–2800 | fax 402/476–6000 | 55 rooms, 8 suites | $84–$90 | AE, DC, MC, V.

Hampton Inn—Airport. Just ½ mi from the airport and 5 mi from both the State Fair Park and Lied Center downtown, this motor inn has in-room hairdryers and irons to help you get ready for functions. King Study suites also have sleeper sofas and desk/work areas. Complimentary Continental breakfast. In-room data ports, some refrigerators. Cable TV. Pool. Hot tub. Business services, airport shuttle. No pets. | 1301 W. Bond Cir. | 402/474–2080 or 800/426–7866 | fax 402/474–3401 | 111 rooms | $65–$85 | AE, D, DC, MC, V.

Ramada Limited South. Remodeled in 1998, this two-story brick structure is 3 mi north of downtown and 8 mi from Lincoln Municipal Airport. All rooms have two-line phones, and executive suites come with refrigerators and sleeper sofas. More than half the rooms are non-smoking. Truck parking with cold-weather hookups is available. Complimentary Continental breakfast. In-room data ports. Cable TV. Pool. Exercise equipment. Airport shuttle, free parking. | 1511 Center Park Rd. | 402/423–3131 or 888–298–2054 | fax 402/423–3155 | 80 rooms | $62–$76 | AE, D, DC, MC, V.

Red Roof Inn. This hostelry, around the corner from the 27th Street exit off I–80, is 5 mi from the airport and 3 mi northwest of downtown Lincoln. Complimentary Continental breakfast. In-room data ports. Cable TV. Indoor pool. Hot tub. Pets allowed. | 64 rooms | 6501 North 28th St. | 402/438–4700 | fax 402/438–9007 | $50–$60 | AE, D, DC, MC, V.

Sleep Inn. The Lincoln Municipal Airport is 1 mi from this hotel at Exit 399 on I–80. Some rooms have microwaves and refrigerators for late-night snacking. | 80 rooms. Complimentary Continental breakfast. In-room data ports, some refrigerators, some microwaves. Cable TV. Pool. Laundry facilities. Airport shuttle. | 3400 N.W. 12th St. | 402/475–1550 | fax 402/475–1557 | $54 | AE, D, DC, MC.

MODERATE

Comfort Inn—Airport. The best way to reach this small two-story hotel a mile from the airport is through the parking lot of Perkins Restaurant. Rooms are basic but include hairdryers and irons and refreshing massage showerheads. Complimentary Continental breakfast. In-room data ports, microwaves, refrigerators. Cable TV. Indoor pool. Hot tub. Video games. Business services. Pets allowed. | 2940 N.W. 12th St. | 402/475–2200 or 800/228–5150 | fax 402/475–2200 | 67 rooms | $85 | AE, D, DC, MC, V.

Cornhusker. Downtown Lincoln's most famous hotel uses lots of glossy dark woods and wingback chairs throughout its 10 stories, with many other lush touches. The tables and lounge chairs make the indoor pool a most inviting gathering space. 2 restaurants, bar, room service. Cable TV. Indoor pool. Exercise equipment. Business services. Airport shuttle. | 333 S. 13th St. | 402/474–7474 or 800/793–7474 | fax 402/474–6006 | www.thecornhusker.com | 290 rooms | $115–$160 | AE, D, DC, MC, V.

Days Inn Airport. Hugging the ground like a sleek prairie ranch in the sunset, this earth-toned motel a mile from the airport, and only 2½ mi from the Historic Haymarket District, was renovated in 1997. Morning niceties include free newspapers and a coffee-maker in each room. The parking area includes truck spaces and cold-weather hookups. Complimentary Continental breakfast. In-room data ports, microwaves, refrigerators. Cable TV. Airport shuttle. | 2920 N.W. 12th St. | 402/475–3616 or 800/329–7466 | fax 402/475–4356 | 84 rooms | $85 | AE, D, DC, MC, V.

Holiday Inn Lincoln Downtown. This 16-story full-service hotel is right in the downtown area, 2 mi from the children's museum and 5 mi from the airport—or 20 mi from Mahoney State Park if you'd like to get outdoors and hike. Restaurant, bar, room service. In-room data ports. Cable TV. Indoor pool. Hot tub. Exercise equipment. Video games. Business services. No pets. | 141 N 9th St. | 402/475–4011 | fax 402/475–9011 | inkdt.sale@alltel.com | 230 rooms, 4 suites | $109 | AE, D, DC, MC, V.

Rogers House Inn B&B. A long flight of steps across a wide green lawn takes you up to this family-owned B&B in the historic district, a three-story gabled house in Queen Anne style—but with prairie-toned shingles. All rooms have antique furnishings, and some have sunrooms or fireplaces. The Garret Suite, which takes up the entire third floor, has a canopy bed and whirlpool for two. Complimentary breakfast. Some room phones. No kids under 10. No smoking. | 2145 B St. | 402/476–6961 | fax 402/476–6473 | www.rogershouse-inn.com | 12 rooms | $63–$135 | AE, D, MC, V.

EXPENSIVE

Chase Suites. The lobby of this complex on the east side of town has cathedral ceilings and a soaring stacked-stone fireplace where evening hospitality hour is held. Accommodations range from studio layouts to two-bedroom suites with fireplaces or lofts; all have separate breakfast areas. Picnic area, complimentary breakfast. Kitchens, microwaves. Cable TV. Pool. Hot tub. Tennis. Exercise equipment. Laundry facilities. Business services. Pets allowed (fee). | 200 S. 68th Pl. | 402/483–4900 or 800/331-3131 | fax 402/483–4464 | 120 suites | $102–$141 | AE, D, DC, MC, V.

Embassy Suites. You can view the indoor waterfalls from a glass elevator that shoots through the center of this hotel's nine-story atrium, then dine in at the hotel's Athletic Bar and Grill or find a slew of choices in the surrounding Haymarket District. Restaurant, complimentary Continental breakfast. In-room data ports. Cable TV. Indoor pool. Hot tub, sauna. Exercise equipment. Laundry service. No pets. | 252 rooms | 1040 P St. | 402/474–1111 | fax 402/474–1144 | $129–$149 | AE, D, DC, MC, V.

MCCOOK

MAP 11, D5

(Nearby towns also listed: Eustis, North Platte)

The coming of the Burlington Railroad in the 1880s led to McCook's first wave of growth. The Army was responsible for its second era of development, when more than 15,000 servicemen and 500 civilian employees were at the World War II air base that trained young Americans for duty with heavy bombers. Later in the war, it was also the site of a prisoner-of-war camp. The captured Germans decorated the plasterboard walls of their barracks with their own paintings, and McCook's High Plains Museum has preserved some of those efforts in a poignant display among more familiar artifacts of heartland America.

McCook, the home of three Nebraska governors, has several classic buildings from the past along its original bricked streets, including the Carnegie Library, the 1915 U.S. Post Office, and the former federal courthouse. There, too, you will find the home of George W. Norris, who, first as a U.S. Representative, then as a senator, represented Nebraska in Congress for 40 years. He authored the 20th Amendment to the U.S. Constitution, which moved the beginning of the President's term to January, and is considered the father of the bills that led to the Tennessee Valley Authority and the 1935 Rural Electrification Act—which brought electricity to rural people throughout the country.

Today, the area around McCook is known for its plentiful sites for fishing and upland game-bird hunting, especially those on the four Southwest Reservoirs created from 1949 to 1962 in a massive federal flood control and irrigation project.

Information: Southwest Nebraska Convention and Visitors Bureau/McCook Chamber of Commerce | 107 Nooif Ave., Box 337, McCook 69001 | 308/345–3200 or 800/657–2179 | fax 308/345–3201 | mccookchamber@navix.net | www.ci.mccook.ne.us.

Attractions

Frank Lloyd Wright House. Renowned architect Frank Lloyd Wright was noted in his early career for his earth-hugging designs he called "prairie-style." This private residence, built in 1906, is one of the few Wright houses west of the Mississippi. It is not open to the public, but you can walk or drive by it at 602 Norris Avenue in the McCook historic area.

George W. Norris House State Historic Site. The home of one of Nebraska's most influential politicians ever, who was also responsible for the structure of the state's one-house legislature, is both a state and a national historic site. The simple house hosts quilt and needlework shows in March, June, and September. | 706 Norris Ave. | 308/345–8484 | www.nebraskahistory.org | $2 | Tues.–Sat. 9:30–12, 1–5.

Museum of the High Plains. The museum's eclectic mix of exhibits explore various facets of earlier life in Red Willow County and southwest Nebraska. Among them are Native American artifacts and the farm implements used by the Germans from Russia and other early settlers; the story of the former McCook Air Base and the B-24 crews who trained there during World War II; a room of railroad mementos; period rooms, including an old drug store; and the DAR Museum. | 413 Norris Ave. | 308/345–3661 | Free | Tues.–Sat. 1–5, Sun. 2–4.

Medicine Creek Reservoir State Recreation Area. At the head of a 5,665-ft-long earth-filled dam, the 1,850-acre lake is known for its king-size crappie and walleyes that usually start biting in June. It's about 2 mi west and 7 mi north of Cambridge, and the 29 mi of shoreline have many sites for camping, swimming, and picnicking, plus hunting areas for pheasant, quail and deer. | 800/826–PARK | www.ngpc.state.ne.us/parks/swreser.html#medicine | Neb. Parks Permit required; camping, $3–$12 | Daily; modern camping facilities, May–mid-Sept.

Red Willow Reservoir State Recreation Area. Red Willow recognizes that its 6,000 acres, 11 mi north of McCook on Highway 83, serve many interests. Hunters may put up blinds during waterfowl season, as well as hunt for pheasants, rabbits, and deer, but the native prairie dog village has been carefully protected so man will not harm the small creatures whose antics are such a delight for children. There are also a display herd of longhorn cattle, plus swimming, picnicking, and camping areas around the 1,628-acre lake. | 308/345–

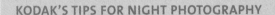

KODAK'S TIPS FOR NIGHT PHOTOGRAPHY

Lights at Night
· Move in close on neon signs
· Capture lights from unusual vantage points

Fireworks
· Shoot individual bursts using a handheld camera
· Capture several explosions with a time exposure
· Include an interesting foreground

Fill-In Flash
· Set the fill-in light a stop darker than the ambient light

Around the Campfire
· Keep flames out of the frame when reading the meter
· For portraits, take spot readings of faces
· Use a tripod, or rest your camera on something solid

Using Flash
· Stay within the recommended distance range
· Buy a flash with the red-eye reduction mode

From *Kodak Guide to Shooting Great Travel Pictures* © 2000 by Fodor's Travel Publications

6507 | ngp.ngpc.state.ne.us/parks/swres.html#redwillow | Neb. Parks Permit required; camping, $3–$12 | Daily; modern camping facilities, May–mid-Sept.

Swanson Reservoir State Recreation Area. Swanson is the largest of the Southwest Reservoirs, with 4,794 acres of water at the 8,620-ft-long dam 2 mi west of Trenton on Highway 34. It's popular for camping, boating, and picnicking, and especially with fishermen who go after the white bass from July to September. For the lucky ones, the Spring Canyon Campground has a cleaning station—and short-order food and groceries available to those who didn't catch a fish to fry. | Neb. Parks Permit required; camping, $3–$12 | Daily; modern camping facilities, May–mid-Sept.

ON THE CALENDAR
JUNE: *Buffalo Commons Storytelling Festival.* This annual gathering of the storytellers includes workshops as well as performances of stories in song, cowboy poetry, and ghost tales—at Norris Park, the Fox Theater, and the High Plains Museum. | 308/345–6223.
JULY: *Red Willow County Fair and Rodeo.* Along with the bull-riding and other tests of man against animal, the rodeo at the county fairgrounds includes a tractor pull and concerts, all in conjunction with the county fair. | 308/345–3200.
SEPT.: *Heritage Days.* The family-oriented event in the downtown area has a wealth of entertaining activities, including a parade, a face-painting areas for the children, crafts and food booths, bingo and other games, entertainment, and an ice cream social. | 308/345–3200.

Dining
Country Kitchen. American. Baskets and kitchenware decorate this homey restaurant. Try the sirloin steak, the country-fried steak, or big country burger with grilled onions, Wisconsin cheese, peppered bacon, and special secret sauce. Lunch buffet on Sundays. | 606 W. B St. | 308/345–1560. | AE, D, MC, V.

Lodging
Best Western Chief. This two-story motel is only ½ mi from the Museum of High Plains and from the Heritage Hills Golf Course, consistently rated among the top public golf courses in the country. Truck and RV parking and cold-weather hookups are available. Restaurant, complimentary Continental breakfast. Cable TV. Indoor pool. Hot tub. Exercise equipment. Business services, airport shuttle. Pets allowed. | 612 W. B St. | 308/345–3700 | fax 308/345–7182 | 111 rooms | $54–$84 | AE, D, DC, MC, V.

Holiday Inn Express McCook. Downtown McCook is 2 mi from this hotel at the junction of Highways 6 and 34 with Highway 83, which has refrigerators in case you want to stock your own juice to have the minute you get up. Complimentary Continental breakfast. In-room data ports, refrigerators. Cable TV. Indoor pool. Hot tub, sauna, spa. Exercise equipment. Laundry facilities. Business services. Pets allowed. | 50 rooms | 1 Holiday Bison Dr. | 308/345–4505 | fax 308/345–2990 | holiday@ocsmccook.com. | AE, D, DC, MC, V.

Super 8 Motel. This one-story building, constructed in 1982, is at the junction of Highways 6 and 34, and only 10 blocks from downtown. The parking area has spaces for trucks and RVs. Cable TV. Pets allowed. | 1103 E. B St. | 308/345–1141 or 800/800–8000 | fax 308/345–1141 | 40 rooms | $34–50 | AE, D, DC, MC, V.

MINDEN

MAP 11, F4

(Nearby towns also listed: Hastings, Kearney, Lexington)

Minden's annual display of holiday lights has brought it the informal nickname "Christmas City." J. W. Haws put up the first lights in 1915, stringing them from the railroad station to the town square to welcome Union veterans to a convention of the Grand Army of the Republic organization. After that, he hung up lights near the courthouse every Christmas. In 1942, the town broadened its tradition by presenting a "Light of the World" pageant that ended with the illumination of 10,000 bulbs.

Minden is also the home of Harold Warp's Pioneer Village, a collection of more than 50,000 artifacts ranging from vehicles to furniture to fountain pens and salt shakers. He started gathering objects about 50 years ago, and the items now are said to represent every era of "Man's Progress since 1838." You'll know you're there when you see the full-size Conestoga wagon atop the roof of the entrance building and an antique car perched on the Pioneer Village sign.

Information: **Minden Chamber of Commerce** | 325 N. Colorado Ave., Box 375, Minden 68959 | 308/832–1811 | fax 308/832–1949 | colloo4@navix.net.

Attractions

★ **Harold Warp Pioneer Village.** Harold Warp's monumental display of the objects people have lived with for the past 150 years is at the junction of Highways 6 and 34 with Route 10. Along with the thousands of small items, you can see such buildings as a general store, log cabin, and sod house; a steam-powered merry-go-round; 350 vehicles; a replica of the Wright Brothers' Flier; and one of the nation's earliest jet fighters. | 138 E. Hwy. 6 | 308/832–1181 or 800/445–4447 | $7 | Daily 8–sundown.

Minden Opera House. Fiberoptic lights illuminate a ceiling mural and create a stars-in-the-sky effect at this former hardware store, gutted and transformed into a performing arts facility. | 322 East Fifth St. | 308/832–0588 | Box office, Mon.–Sat. 10–5, Sun. 1–5.

ON THE CALENDAR

NOV.–DEC.: *The Light of the World Christmas Pageant.* This annual event is 60 years old now, but still a favorite way for many Nebraskans to begin their holiday season. The performances are held November 24th and December 2nd and 9th outdoors around the county courthouse on the town square. They still end with the lighting of 10,000 Christmas lights. | 308/832–1811.

AUG.: *Kearney County Classic Car and Craft Show.* You can enjoy an art show, classic car show, games and activities, street dancing, and food at this summer event in Minden's Courthouse Square. | 308/832–1811.

Dining

Shay's. American. On the stage in the large bar area, you can join in the karaoke on weekends or see bands perform at this local hang-out with a country-style dining room and large dance floor. It's also the place to come after local sports events or to watch games on the big-screen TV. Try the prime rib or the roasted chicken. | 521 North Colorado Ave. | 308/832–0201 | Closed Sun. | $4–$15 | MC, V.

Lodging

Harold Warp Pioneer Village Motel. Next door to Pioneer Village, the motel spreads through two two-story buildings built in the late 1970s. On the same site, there is a 135-space campground. The parking area includes spaces for trucks; cold-weather hookups are available. Admission to Pioneer Village is included in room rentals. Restaurant, bar. Cable TV. Pets allowed. | 224 E. Hwy. 6 | 800/445–4447 | fax 308/832–2750 | 90 rooms | $40–$47 | D, MC, V.

Home Comfort Bed and Breakfast. A mile north of Pioneer Village, this colonial-style house with a barn and outbuildings—and barnyard animals around the grounds—sits on 14 scenic acres. The house is decorated with an eclectic mixture of antique and modern furnishings. You can have dinner in the formal dining room and coffee in a smaller area that's is also used as a coffee house. Dining room, complimentary Continental breakfast. Pets allowed. No smoking. | 4 rooms | 1523 N. Brown | 308/832–0533 or 888/969–2475. | No credit cards.

NEBRASKA CITY

MAP 11, I4

(Nearby towns also listed: Auburn, Brownville, Lincoln, Plattsmouth)

Nebraska City started as a trading post, ferry crossing, and riverboat stop where boatloads of goods were unloaded to be shipped west by ox teams. Among the first freight companies to set up in Nebraska City was the firm of William Russell, Alexander Majors, and William Waddell, which gained a national reputation when it launched the Pony Express in 1861. Despite its place in the romantic lore of the West, the Express delivered mail from St. Joseph, Missouri, to California only for an 18-month period that ended when the Creighton Telegraph linked the continent with an even faster form of communication.

Today, Nebraska City is regarded as the guiding spirit of Arbor Day, the national tree-planting holiday held every April. The dream of J. Sterling Morton, an early Nebraska City resident, Arbor Day became a state holiday in 1872 and a nationally recognized holiday in 1885. His family home, Arbor Lodge, is a State Historic Site and tourist attraction noted for its beautiful gardens and huge old trees—many of them likely planted by J. Sterling himself more than 100 years ago.

Other Nebraska City attractions include the Arbor Day Farm Lied Conference Center, the multi-purpose facility built of renewable and recycled resources, and John Brown's Cave, named for abolitionist John Brown to recognize his work with the Underground Railroad. It is believed that early Nebraska City residents often provided sanctuary for fleeing slaves, hiding them in underground caverns—including the one known as John Brown's Cave—not far from the Missouri River.

Information: Nebraska City Chamber of Commerce | 806 1st Ave., Nebraska City 68410 | 402/873–6654 or 800/514–9113 | fax 402/873–6701 | city@alltel.net | www.nebraskacity.com.

Attractions

Old Freighter's Museum. The three-story house used as the headquarters for the company that founded the Pony Express has a number of items related to the way freight companies supplied the Army on the Oxbow and Cutoff trails from 1855 to 1863. | 407 N. 14th St. | 402/873–9360 or 402/837–3508 | $2 | By appointment only.

Arbor Day Farm. Originally part of the land owned by J. Sterling Morton, this apple orchard is also a National Historic Landmark. You can't pick apples on your own, but you can walk the trails and buy fresh-pressed cider made from "antique" recipes no longer used by other orchards. | 100 Arbor Ave. | 402/873–8710 | Free | Mon.–Sat. 9–5, Sun. 12–5.

★ **Arbor Lodge State Historical Park and Arboretum.** What began as a four-room frame home grew into a 52-room neo-Colonial mansion. You can see all the furnishings and a one-lane bowling alley used by the family of J. Sterling Morton, a territorial governor and U.S. Secretary of Agriculture. | 2600 Arbor Ave. | 402/873–7222 | ngp.ngpc.state.ne.us/parks/arbor.html | Neb. Parks Permit required; mansion tours $3 | April–Memorial Day and Labor Day–Nov 1st, daily 11–5; Memorial Day–Labor Day, daily 9–5; Nov. 1st–Dec., daily 1–4.

John Brown's Cave. Allen Mahew's cabin has been certified as the oldest building in Nebraska still standing. The westernmost stop on the Underground Railroad of the Civil War days, it has a trap door leading to underground chambers and a tunnel used by escaping slaves. A small village of authentic early 20th-century buildings has been assembled around the grassy commons. | 20th St. and 4th Corso | 402/873–3115 | $6 | Late Apr.–late Nov., daily 10–5, Sun. 12–5.

NEBRASKA CITY

INTRO
ATTRACTIONS
DINING
LODGING

ON THE CALENDAR

APR.: *Arbor Day Celebration*. This citywide celebration includes environmental games, presentations, tree-seedling giveaways, living-history programs, a crafts show, entertainment, and a parade. | 402/873–3000.

SEPT.: *Applejack Festival*. Recognizing the place of apple-growing in the city's history and economy, this citywide festival has a parade, air show, crafts and quilt show, and living-history demonstrations, as well as an apple bowl game, scarecrow contest, and apple jam fest. | 402/873–3000.

OCT.: *Living History at Arbor Lodge*. See demonstrations of how life was lived before electricity in a special program at Arbor Lodge State Historical Park and Arboretum. | 402/873–7222.

Lodging

Apple Inn. This motel has grown from one building in 1950 to four prairie-colored structures around a swimming pool. Almost everything in town is within a few miles, including a nine-hole public golf course ½ mi away and the Factory Stores of American outlet mall at the junction of Highway 75 and Route 2. The town trolley, which circles among various attractions, stops at the lobby. Complimentary Continental breakfast. Some refrigerators. Cable TV. Pool. Laundry facilities. Business services. | 707 1st Corso | 402/873–5959 or 800/659–4446 | fax 402/873–6640 | 65 rooms | $44–$56 | http://appleinn.net | AE, D, DC, MC, V.

Arbor Day Farm Lied Conference Center. The sprawling four-story white structure overlooks 260 acres of oak and hickory trees across the creek from the Arbor Lodge grounds. Inside, the architecture switches to very modern, angular lines—in the guest rooms, the skylighted indoor pool, and the soaring lobby with a 50-ft-tall fireplace. Meals are included in most rate plans. Restaurant, bar. In-room data ports. Cable TV. Indoor pool. Hot tub. Exercise equipment. Laundry facilities. Airport shuttle. | 2700 Sylvan Rd. | 800/546–5433 | www.adflcc.com | 144 rooms | $89–$199 | AE, D, DC, MC, V.

Days Inn. This neatly landscaped two-floor motel with a red roof takes on a relaxed country air inside, with sheer curtains and a wood-railed bannister on the staircase. Complimentary Continental breakfast. Refrigerators. Cable TV. | 29 rooms | 1715 S. 11th St. | 402/873–6656 | fax 402/873–6676. | AE, D, DC, MC.

Sparrow's Rest Bed and Breakfast. This house, built in the 1880s, has covered oak floors, woodwork, beautiful French doors, and an antique piano. The oldest Methodist church in Nebraska is directly across the street. Complimentary Continental breakfast. TV in common area. No kids. No pets. No smoking. | 3 rooms, 2 with shared bath | 1102 1st Ave. | 402/873–4166. | MC, V.

Whispering Pines Bed and Breakfast. This family-owned B&B, built in 1883, is a traditional countryside B&B. Sitting on 6½ acres of oaks and pine trees 2½ blocks east of Arbor Lodge, it has a goldfish pond, stream, and waterfall for you to explore, plus an old-time porch swing and large deck and a spa enclosed within a gazebo. Two rooms share a bath, but all the spaces are individually decorated with antiques. Picnic area, complimentary breakfast. Some room phones, no TV in some rooms. Hot tub. No smoking. | 2018 6th Ave. | 402/873–5850 | 5 rooms | $60–$75 | D, MC, V.

NELIGH

MAP 11, G2

(Nearby towns also listed: Norfolk, O'Neill, Royal)

Fertile farmland and the vision of an entrepreneurial pioneer led to the early prosperity of Neligh. In 1873, John D. Neligh (pronounced NEE-lee) built a flour mill on the bank of the Elkhorn River and made the town a vital center of the growing agricultural region around it. The structure served area farmers until 1959, when it was purchased by the

Nebraska State Historical Society. Today, agricultural production remains a mainstay of the local economy, although visitors also know it as the gateway to Niobrara State Park.

Information: Neligh Chamber of Commerce | Box 266, 202 W. 4th St., Neligh 68756 | 402/887–4195 or 888/266–4195 | lnewton@pluggers.esu8.k12.ne.us.

Attractions

Neligh Mill State Historic Site. This four-story mill is the state's only example of a 19th-century flour mill with its machinery intact. On the Elkhorn River, the mill was originally powered by water. | N St. at Wylie Dr. | 402/887–4303 | $2 | May–Sept., Mon.–Sat. 8–5, Sun. 1–5; Oct.–Apr., Mon.–Fri. 8–5, weekends by appointment.

Niobrara State Park. Set on bluffs overlooking the meeting of the Niobrara and Missouri rivers, this park about a mile from Neeligh on Route 12 has tent campgrounds, Adirondack shelters, housekeeping cabins, a swimming pool, and a wheelchair-accessible hiking and biking trail that crosses the Niobrara River on an old railroad bridge. Activities include horseback rides, fishing, picnicking, and cross-country skiing. | 89261 522 Ave. | 402/857–3373 | www.ngpc.state.ne.us/parks/niob.html | Neb. Parks Permit required; camping, $5–$11 | Grounds, year-round; lodging, mid-Apr.–Dec.

ON THE CALENDAR
JULY: *Neligh Old Mill Days.* This citywide festival includes an ice cream social, a dance, and a pancake feed, as well as water fights, nature walks, a golf shoot, fishing contests, turtle races, horseshoes, swimming, a scavenger hunt, a kids' tractor pull, a flea market, and a Fourth of July parade. | 402/887–9040.

Dining

Hungry Horse Saloon. American. Of course an authentic Old West saloon will have a bar, and this outpost in Ericson does, along with wood paneling decorated with branding irons and mounted deer antlers. You'll find prime rib and steaks on the menu every day, plus seafood on Thursdays. | 1 Main St., Ericson | 308/653–3100 | $2–$12 | No credit cards.

Lodging

Plantation House. This century-old Georgian-style mansion is now a B&B that still retains its polished woodwork, five fireplaces, two winding staircases, and many stained-glass windows. Besides the classically detailed guest rooms, it also has a separate one-bedroom cottage with a trundle daybed in the living room, about 10 mi from Neligh and 35 mi from fresh-baked bread and a glass of wine at Cuthills Vineyard in Pierce (*see* Norfolk). Complimentary breakfast. No room phones, TV in common area. One in-room hot tub. | 401 Plantation St. | 402/843–2287 or 888/446–2287 | plantation@gpcom.net | www.plantation-house.com | 5 rooms, 1 cottage | $55–$75 | No credit cards.

Rose Garden Inn Bed and Breakfast. Flowers and a white picket fence surround this small, quiet Victorian B&B in Plainview, 17 mi from Neligh. Outside are a gazebo and fountain; inside, the staircase is carved oak, and period antiques fill every room. Complimentary Continental breakfast. | 3 rooms, 2 with shared bath | $50–$65 | 305 North 3rd, Plainview | 402/582–4708 or 402/582–4808 (reservations). | MC, V.

NORFOLK

MAP 11, G2

(Nearby towns also listed: Bancroft, Columbus, Neligh, Wayne, West Point)

Norfolk is a vibrant community surrounded by farming country and is host to a large, well-known livestock auction. But the town may be best known for some of its native sons and start-up businesses. Johnny Carson of "The Tonight Show" TV fame once lived here at 306 South 13th Street, known now as Johnny Carson Boulevard. Thurl Raven-scroft, who supplied the voice of Kellogg's Tony the Tiger ("They're grrreat!"), is also a Norfolk native, and Hallmark Cards founders Joyce Hall and brothers William and Rollie made their first foray into business with their Norfolk Post Card Company.

Information: **Norfolk Chamber of Commerce** | 405 Madison Ave., Box 386, Norfolk 68702 | 402/371–4862 | fax 402/371–0182 | nacc@ncfcomm.com | www.norfolk.ne.us.

Also: **Madison County Convention and Visitors Bureau** | 405 Madison Ave., Box 386, Norfolk 68702 | 402/371–2932 or 888/371–2932 | fax 402/371–0182 | mcvb@ncfcomm.com | www.norfolk.ne.us.

Attractions

The Cowboy Trail. When this 320-mi trail from Norfolk to Chadron is finished, it will be the longest rails-to-trails project in the nation, turning old rail lines into paths for hikers, bicyclists, horseback riders, and cross-country skiers. At present, the finished segments run from Ta-HaZouka Park in Norfolk to Neligh, Inman to O'Neill, and near Valentine. You must purchase a pass from the Game and Parks Commission or at one of the boxes along the trail. | 402/370–3374 | www.ngpc.state.ne.us/parks | Daily dawn to dusk.

Cuthills Vineyards and Winery. More than a dozen varieties of wine grapes are grown in two vineyards, with a 1927 barn serving as the winery. The tasting room offers samples with the winery's home-baked breads. Cuthills has special tastings and dinners through the year, then opens the grounds in August for the annual two-day Wine and Wings Festival. | Pierce | 402/329–6774 | fax 404/329–4181 | www.cuthills.com | Grounds, free; tours, $1.50 | Jan.–Apr., Fri.–Sun. 1–5; May–Dec., Wed.–Sat. 11–6, Sun. 1–6.

ON THE CALENDAR

AUG.: *Wine and Wings Festival.* Cuthill Vineyards holds this 2-day event featuring blues and jazz bands, food vendors, wine seminars and tastings, winery tours, hay wagon rides, and huge kites taking wing overhead. | 402/329–6774 | fax 404/329–4181 | www.cuthills.com | Grounds, free; various event fees.

SEPT.: *LaVitsef Celebration.* In an area that was originally settled by 44 German families, this citywide festival includes a traditional German family meal, along with barbecue, horseshoes, a crafts show, a farmers market, and a parade and concerts. | 402/371–4862.

Dining

Brass Lantern. Steak. For almost 60 years, this family-owned steakhouse has been serving its cuts of beef—and the trimmings, of course—around a fireplace that adds its extra cheer to winter evenings. Kids' menu. | 1018 S. 9th St. | 402/371–2500 | $7–$14 | AE, D, DC, MC, V.

Granary. American. Country-style dining is the basis for this local standby, where you'll find a menu that ranges from hamburgers to fried shrimp and rib-eye steaks, with lots of good desserts. Kids' menu. | 922 S. 13th St. | 402/371–5334 | Closed Sun. | $2–$8 | No credit cards.

Marilyn's Tea Room. American. In an antiques-filled 1886 Queen Anne home, this restaurant shares space with a quilt shop that adds its colors and patterns to the friendly bustle. The menu features meatloaf, fried chicken, and pork roast, as well as sandwiches, and everything is homemade, down to the crackers. Open only for lunch. | 417 E. 3rd St., Beemer | 402/528–3282 | Tues.–Sat. 11–2 | $5–$6 | No credit cards.

Prenger's. American. With its classic oak furnishings, this looks at first glance like an ad for Ye Old Tavern, but a full-service restaurant awaits you inside, including prime ribs and steak. | 116 E. Norfolk Ave. | 402/379–1900 | $5–$15 | AE, D, MC, V.

Lodging

Days Inn. This two-floor motel is 3 mi from Norfolk's Memorial Airport and a mile from downtown Norfolk, and you'll find coffee available 24 hours a day. Complimentary Continental breakfast. In-room data ports. Cable TV. Indoor pool. Exercise equipment. Laundry facilities. | 1001 Omaha Ave. | 402/379–3035 | fax 402/371–1307 | 40 rooms | $52 | AE, D, DC, MC, V.

Holiday Inn Express. Every room has two phone lines in this motel, as well as a microwave and refrigerator in case you like to snack while you work. It's 3 mi from downtown Norfolk and the Norfolk Arts Center, about 40 mi from the zoo in Royal if you're traveling with the kids. Complimentary Continental breakfast. In-room data ports, microwaves, refrigerators. Cable TV. Indoor pool. Hot tub, spa. Exercise equipment. Laundry services. Business services. No pets. | 86 rooms | 920 S. 20th St., at U.S. 275 | 402/379–1524 | fax fax 402/379–1735 | holidayinn@conpoint.com. | AE, D, DC, MC, V.

Norfolk Country Inn. This two-story motel is only six blocks from downtown and a couple of blocks' walking distance to Sunset Plaza, the big shopping area at Highway 81 and the 275 Bypass. Truck parking and cold-weather hookups are available. Restaurant, bar, room service. Cable TV. Pool. | 1201 S. 13th St. | 402/371–4430 or 800/233–0733 | fax 402/371–6373 | 127 rooms | $54 | AE, D, DC, MC, V.

Ramada Inn. It may be steaming outside or streaming buckets, but you can find a nice oasis from any weather at the indoor tropical garden in this two-story motel at the intersection of Highways 81 and 275. Truck and RV parking is available, with cold-weather hookups. Restaurant, bar, room service. Cable TV. Indoor pool. Playground. Business services, airport shuttle. Some pets allowed. | 1227 Omaha Ave. | 402/371–7000 or 800/272–6232 | fax 402/371–7000 | 98 rooms | $65–$78 | AE, D, DC, MC, V.

Super 8. Renovated in 1999, this two-story motel on Highway 275 at Highway 81 has a breakfast area set aside from the main lobby—and keeps the coffee brewing 24 hours a day. Data-port phones are available, and the King rooms have recliners. The parking area has truck and RV spaces with cold-weather hookups. Complimentary Continental breakfast. Cable TV. | 1223 Omaha Ave. | 402/379–2220 or 800/800–8000 | fax 402/379–3817 | 66 rooms | $48–$58 | AE, D, DC, MC, V.

NORTH PLATTE

MAP 11, D4

(Nearby towns also listed: Gothenburg, Ogallala, McCook, Thedford)

When "Buffalo Bill" Cody wasn't touring with his Wild West Show or hanging out with Frank and Luther North and their Pawnee Scouts, he hung his wide-brimmed hat in North Platte. Cody had two homes in the area: a ranch in the Sandhills with his friends, the North brothers, and a ranch and home in North Platte. That North Platte mansion, filled with memorabilia, is now the focal point of the Buffalo Bill State Historical Park.

Not far across the road from Cody's Scout's Rest Ranch is the North Platte Canteen. Troop trains crossing the United States during World War II regularly made their way through North Platte. In December of 1941, a local girl, hearing that Company D of the Nebraska National Guard would be riding through town, organized friends and neighbors to hand out cookies, cakes, gum, and cigarettes at the station. Although it turned out that the train wasn't carrying members of the Nebraska National Guard, the gifts were distributed anyway, inaugurating the town's wartime effort. The North Platte Canteen officially opened on Christmas Day 1941 and remained in operation until April 1, 1946. Workers at the Canteen met every troop train passing through the city, sometimes handing out as many as 2,000 to 3,000 items. The building used for the Canteen is now the Lincoln County Historical Museum.

North Platte is still very much tied to the railroad. The Union Pacific tracks run through the city, and North Platte is known as a "hump yard," where trains congregate as cars are switched.

Information: North Platte Chamber of Commerce | 502 S. Dewey St., North Platte 69101 | 308/532–4966 | fax 308/532–4827 | chamber@northplattechamber.com | www.NorthPlatteChamber.com.

North Platte/Lincoln County Convention and Visitors Bureau | 219 S. Dewey St., Box 1207, North Platte 69103 | 308/532–4729 or 800/955–4528 | fax 308/532–5914 | lisap@nque.com | www.northplatte-tourism.com.

Attractions

Dancing Leaf Earth Lodge. This unusual structure 2 mi east of Wellfleet is a re-creation of the type of earthen, dome-shaped lodge used by Native Americans who lived on the Great Plains a thousand years ago. You may take a 90-minute tour of the structure, as well as see a medicine wheel and calendar pole, visit the nature trail, or go canoeing on the lake. Buffalo stew suppers and overnight stays can be arranged. | 6100 E. Opal Springs Rd., Wellfleet | 308/963–4233 | Tours, $7 | Reservations required for overnight stays | Memorial Day–Labor Day, daily; tours at 9 and 2.

Lincoln County Historical Museum. The North Platte Canteen, which became a sweet memory for thousands of troops who passed through here during World War II, is one of several structures from the past used now to display implements, tools, wagons, weapons, and other items from the region's frontier days. | 2403 N. Buffalo Bill Ave. | 308/534–5640 or 800/955–4528 | $1 (suggested) | Memorial Day–Labor Day, daily 9–8, Sun. 1–5; Labor Day–Sept. 30th, weekdays 9–5.

Arnold Lake State Recreation Area. The Y-shape lake in this smaller state state recreation area along the Loup River ½ mi south of Arnold on Highway 40 can afford many hours of quiet fishing. Primitive camping is allowed. | 308/749–2235 | Neb. Parks Permit required; camping, $3–$9 | Daily.

Buffalo Bill Ranch State Historical Park. Spangles and buckskins mixed glamorously in Buffalo Bill's Wild West Shows, and you can see many samples of the paraphernalia in a large barn on the site of Bill Cody's Scout's Rest Ranch. Many personal items of the legendary buffalo hunter-become-internationally known showman are in the 18-room Victorian mansion built in 1886. You also can arrange trail rides through the 25-acre park on Highway 30 off Highway 83. | N. Buffalo Bill Ave. | www.ngpc.state.ne.us/parks/cody.html | Neb. Parks Permit required | Memorial Day–Labor Day, daily 10–8; Apr., May, Sept., Oct., weekdays 9–5; trail rides, Memorial Day–Labor Day, Wed.–Sat.

Cody Park. A Wild West Memorial is in the works for this city park off North Highway 83 along the North Platte River, also the site of the Railroad Museum. There you can see an authentic old depot and the Union Pacific's *Challenger 3977*, one of the largest steam engines ever made, and the line's 6922, one of the largest diesel-electric engines, all sharing park space with a children's playground, a swimming pool, tennis courts, and wildlife displays. | 800/955–4528 | Free | Daily, dawn to dusk.

Lake Maloney State Recreation Area. Six miles south of North Platte on U.S. 83, Lake Maloney offers swimming, boating, primitive camping, and picnicking on the east shore of the 1,650-acre reservoir and a par-72 golf course on the west shore. | 308/535–8025 | ngpc.state.ne.us/parks/maloney.html | Neb. Parks Permit required; camping, $3 | Daily.

Bailey Railroad Yard. From an observation platform above the yard, on West Front Street, you can watch the day-to-day work at the world's largest reclassification railroad yards, where rail cars are separated from trains, then attached to new units headed for different destinations. The platform is open 24 hours a day, with an audio presentation explaining the operation. | 308/532–4729 | Free | Daily.

Fort McPherson National Cemetery. Once the grounds of a fort guarding the Oregon Trail, Nebraska's only National Cemetery is 13 mi east of North Platte, 2 mi south of exit 190 on I-80. Established in 1873, the cemetery includes the white marble headstones of 70 Buffalo Soldiers, the African-American cavalry troopers, two of whom won the Medal of Honor. | Free | Daily, 24 hours.

ON THE CALENDAR

JUNE: *Mexican Fiesta.* Mariachis and other happy sounds of Mexican music take over the Wild West Arena, at Buffalo Bill Avenue and County Road 21, across the road from Buffalo Bill Ranch State Historical Park, for this ethnic festival with entertainment, games, special foods, crafts displays, and dancers. | 308/532–4156.

JUNE: *Nebraskaland Days.* The four-day schedule is jam-packed with big-draw events that pull people from all over the state to North Platte for Nebraskaland Days. The state rodeo, sanctioned by the national rodeo association, brings all the traditional rodeo excitement to the Wild West Arena opposite Buffalo Bill Ranch State Historical Park. At various sites around the city, you also can choose from the Miss Nebraska pageant, performances by top-name entertainment, the governor's western and wildlife art show, readings by cowboy poets, parades, a kids' festival, a quilt show, and a carnival. | 308/532–7939.

Dining

Branding Iron BBQ. American. Deer heads, saddles, hats, and pictures of Buffalo Bill and other Western legends decorate this Western-style restaurant, and an animated puppet sings and tells stories to the kids. All meats are cooked over an all-wood smoker. Try the beef brisket sandwiches. | 202 E. Leota St. | 308/532–8584 | $8–$12 | AE, D, MC, V.

Brick Wall. Continental. Connected to a gourmet market, this downtown eatery in an early 20th-century building is decorated throughout with antique furnishings and fixtures. It's known for its salads and vegetable entrées, as well as the shrimp pasta with basil butter, chicken and broccoli crêpes with mushroom sauce, quiches, and desserts such as mousse pies. | 507 N. Dewey St. | 308/532–7545 | $5–$7 | AE, MC, V.

Butch's Bar. American. Originally a small bar that was a local secret, this rural restaurant has expanded to handle the new business brought in by word-of-mouth reputation for good meals. The pork chops and chicken-fried steaks are popular menu items. | 101 W. 1st St., Hershey | 308/368–7231 | Closed Sun. | $4–$17 | AE, D, MC, V.

Country Market. Eclectic. Antique rocking horses on the tables and antique country pictures on the walls decorate the dining room. This popular local restaurant serves a variety of foods, from Italian to American to Chinese. Try the steak or the Chinese honey sesame chicken platter. Kids' menu. | 3400 Newberry Rd. | 308/532–4999 | $8–$14 | AE, D, MC, V.

Depot Grill & Pub. American. Railroad and antique Coca-Cola memorabilia decorate this eatery in one of the oldest buildings in town. This restaurant is also popular with business people. Try the prime rib, homemade chicken-fried steak, and the blackened shrimp salad. | 520 N. Jeffers St. | 308/534–7844 | $9–$25 | AE, D, MC, V.

Golden Dragon. Chinese. If your mouth starts to water when you think of Oriental food, you'll find many favorites at this Asian outpost in North Platte. Regulars especially praise the chow chicken, beef with broccoli, and fried rice. It serves beer and wine only. | 120 W. Leota | 308/532–5588 | $7–$10 | AE, D, MC, V.

La Casita. Mexican. Around since the early 1960s, La Casita is a fixture in the area. The decorations includes tributes to the Pope, Elvis, and John F. Kennedy, but the food is authentically Mexican, with homemade tamales and such favorites as flour and corn tostadas, chili relleno, chicken mole, and chicken and beef fajita dinners. | 1911 E. 4th St. | 308/534–8077 | Closed Mon. | $5–$8 | AE, D, MC, V.

Lodging

Best Western Chalet Lodge. This two-story motel in a residential area is a mile from Buffalo Bill Ranch State Historical Park and 2 mi from the Factory Stores Outlet Mall. Many rooms have recliners, and all have in-room coffee. Cold-weather hookups are available. Complimentary Continental breakfast. Some refrigerators. Cable TV. Heated indoor pool. Pets allowed (fee). | 920 N. Jeffers St. | 308/532–2313 or 800/622–2313 | fax 308/532–8823 | 38 rooms | $50–$66 | AE, D, DC, MC, V.

Comfort Inn. Downtown North Platte is 2 mi away from this two-floor motel hotel with an indoor pool, and Buffalo Bill's ranch is about 3 mi. Complimentary Continental breakfast. In-room data ports. Cable TV. Indoor pool. Hot tub. Business services. No pets. | 94 rooms | 2901 S. Jeffers St. | 308/532–6144 | fax 308/532–6144 ext. 401. | AE, D, DC, MC, V.

Country Inn Motel. This two-story building is only a short walk from downtown, but if you've overdone on the walking—or hiking or golfing—you might try what the motel calls its therapy pool, with whirlpool, sauna, and hot tub. Truck parking is available, with cold-weather hookups. Some kitchenettes. Cable TV. Pool. Hot tub. Pets allowed. | 321 S. Dewey St. | 308/532–8130 or 800/532–8130 | fax 308/534–0588 | 40 rooms | $40–$54 | AE, D, MC, V.

Days Inn. This two-story hotel, at the intersection of I–80 and Highway 83, is ¼ mi from from Cody Park. Some family rooms and king suites are available. Complimentary Continental breakfast. Cable TV. Indoor pool. Spa. | 49 rooms | 3102 S. Jeffers St. | 308/532–9321 or 800/544–8313 | fax 308/534–9203. | AE, D, DC, MC, V.

Hampton Inn. Deep green grass handsomely sets off this four-story white building 4 mi from Lee Bird Airport and only 3 mi from Cody Park. Rooms use a lot of deep-toned fabrics and have a comfortable corner chair and floor lamp for reading, as well as irons, hairdryers and coffeemakers. Cold-weather hookups are available. Complimentary Continental breakfast. Cable TV. Indoor pool. Hot tub. Gym. Business services. No pets. | 200 Platte Oasis Pkwy. | 308/534–6000 | fax 308/534–3415 | 110 rooms | $84 | AE, D, DC, MC, V.

Knoll's Country Inn Bed & Breakfast. In a quiet setting, you can enjoy a view of the canal from the deck of this B&B while eating a homemade breakfast. Malloney Lake is 7 mi down the road, and Lake McConaughy is 50 mi east. Complimentary Continental breakfast. Hot tub. No pets. No smoking. | 4 rooms, only 1 with private bath | $60–$75 | 6132 S. Range Rd. | 308/368–5634 or 877/378–2521. | No credit cards.

Motel 6. This motel with two floors, off I–80 at exit 177, is 5 mi from the Lincoln County Historical Museum and Buffalo Bill's Ranch. Cable TV. Indoor pool. Pets allowed. | 61 rooms | $56 | 1520 S. Jeffers St. | 308/534–6200 | fax 308/532–5276. | AE, D, DC, MC, V.

Ramada Limited. At the junction of I–80 and Highway 83S, this two-story motel, renovated in 1998, is about 6 mi from Lee Bird Airport. If your morning minutes on the exercise machines leave you feeling wrung out, you can finish with a dip in the outdoor pool during summer months. The parking area includes spaces for trucks and RVs. In-room data ports. Cable TV. Pool. Hot tub. Exercise equipment. Laundry facilities. Pets allowed. | 3201 S. Jeffers St. | 308/534–3120 or 800/272–6232 | fax 308/532–3065 | 78 rooms | $64–$76 | AE, D, DC, MC, V.

Sands Motor Inn. A mile from downtown, this two-story motor inn was renovated in 1990. There's an outdoor pool for warm months, and—because the heartland can sometimes be blustery—cold-weather hookups during the winter. The parking area includes truck spaces. Restaurant. Cable TV. Pool. | 501 Halligan Dr. | 308/532–0151 | fax 308/532–6299 | 81 rooms | $50–$59 | AE, D, DC, MC, V.

Stanford Motel. A one-story building in a commercial area, this motel is just 10 blocks from downtown and about a mile from the Wild West Arena and Buffalo Bill Ranch State Historical Park. Truck parking and cold-weather hookups are available. Cable TV. Pets allowed. | 1400 E. 4th St. | 308/532–9380 or 800/743–4934 | fax 308/532–9634 | 32 rooms | $39–$44 | AE, D, MC, V.

Stockman Inn. This two-story building, renovated in 1999, is ½ mi from downtown and ½ mi north of I–80 and Hwy. 83. Room service is available, and there is a restaurant on the premises. The parking area has spaces for trucks, with cold-weather hookups. Restaurant, room service. Cable TV. Pool. Exercise equipment. Business services, airport van. Pets allowed. | 1402 S. Jeffers St. | 308/534–3630 or 800/624–4643 | fax 308/534–0110 | 140 rooms | $66 | AE, D, DC, MC, V.

Super 8. With Scout's Rest Ranch only 5 mi away, this two-story motel uses round wooden tables and frosted-glass lights in wagon-wheel fixtures to give an Old West feeling to its breakfast area off the lobby. Some whirlpool suites are available, along with truck and RV spaces with cold-weather hookups. Complimentary Continental breakfast. Cable TV. Exercise equipment. Laundry facilities. Pets allowed. | 220 Eugene Ave. | 308/532–4224 or 800/800–8000 | fax 308/532–4317 | 112 rooms | $58 | AE, D, DC, MC, V.

OGALLALA

MAP 11, C3

(Nearby towns also listed: North Platte, Sidney)

OGALLALA

INTRO
ATTRACTIONS
DINING
LODGING

Historically, Ogallala, which was named for the Native American tribe but is spelled differently, was a rough and rowdy cowtown. During the 1870s, it was the end of the trail for many herds, and sometimes there might be tens of thousands of beef cows waiting along the Platte River to be transported to eastern markets. The cowboys themselves grazed at watering holes such as the Cowboy's Rest or the Crystal Palace, and quite a few ended up in Boot Hill Cemetery instead of heading back down the Texas Trail.

The town's modern-day livestock auction and annual rodeo still make some think of it as a "cowboy capital," but the biggest attraction around Ogallala these days is "Big Mac," the 36,000-acre Lake McConaughey. And when it isn't a good day for fishing or swimming, you might detour slightly north to Arthur to see the world's smallest courthouse and a church formed from bales of hay.

Information: Ogallala/Keith County Chamber of Commerce | 204 E. A Street, Box 628, Ogallala 69153 | 308/284–4066 or 800/658–4390 | fax 308/284–3126 | ccinog@megavision.com | www.ci.ogallala.ne.us.

Attractions

Front Street/Cowboy Museum. This re-creation of the town's main street as it was in the 1880s, when Ogallala was called both the "Queen of the Cowtowns" and the "Gomorrah of the Plains," includes some saloon-like structures, but you can take your kids to the Crystal Palace Revue's musicals without worrying about the content. | 519 E. First St. | 308/284–6000 | Museum, free; Crystal Palace Dancehall Revue, $4 | Museum, daily 11–9; dance hall, Memorial Day–mid-Aug., shows daily at 7:15.

Mansion on the Hill. Harkening back to the money the cattle business could make, this three-story Victorian Italianate home, built in 1887, has been restored to its original condition and is furnished with antiques from the cattle-drive era. | 1004 W. 10th, at Spruce St. | 308/284–4066 | $2 | Memorial Day–Sept. 15, Tues.–Sun. 9–4.

Ash Hollow State Park. You can follow a walkway along Windlass Hill to look down at the deep ruts made when immigrants on the Oregon Trail locked the wheels on their wagons and skidded them down to the spring below. But archeological records show that humans were using this canyon off Highway 26, about 3½ south of Lewellen, long before that, and bones of ancient rhinos and mammoths found here may date back 6,000 years. You can find out about the history in the visitor center, as well as tour a restored schoolhouse and take a hike along a nature trail. | 308/778–5651 | www.ngpc.state.ne.us/parks/hollow.html | Neb. Parks Permit required | Grounds, daily; visitor center, Memorial Day–Labor Day, daily 8–6.

Champion Mill State Historical Park. You can see the only still-functioning water-powered flour mill in Nebraska here, as well as hear interpretive programs about the restored mill, off Route 6 near Champion, fish on the mill pond, or try one of the primitive campsites. | 308/882–5860 | www.ngpc.state.ne.us/parks.champion.html | Neb. Parks Permit required; camping, $3 | Memorial Day–Labor Day, daily 8–5; Labor Day—Memorial Day, daily by appointment.

Crescent Lake National Wildlife Refuge. Crescent Lake, about 28 mi north of Ogallala, between Highway 26 and Route 2 near Oshkosh, was established as a refuge for nesting and migratory birds, but you may also see antelope and white-tail deer on its 46,000 acres. More than 273 kinds of birds, including eagles, pelicans, and snow and Canada geese, have been spotted here. Fishing is permitted, as well as seasonal hunting in controlled areas, but camping is not. | 308/762–4893 | Free | Daily dawn to dusk.

★ **Lake McConaughy State Recreation Area.** It's big. Created when part of the North Platte River was dammed in 1941, the 36,000-acre Lake McConaughy—Nebraska's own "Big Mac," 8 mi north of Ogalla—has 100 mi of shoreline with white-sand beaches, a multitude of campsites, and facilities for water sports from scuba to snow-boating. Activities are listed according to 12 named recreation areas. The state's record walleye, a 16-pound-plus giant of a fish, was caught here, and some bass are thought to be from fish-stockings of the 1970s and '80s. Locals also say to keep your eyes open around the Lone Eagle area because a particular bald eagle dropped in from the power company's nearby eagle sanctuary, seemed to like the name, and hangs around there. You'll know you're in Big Mac country when you follow Highway 61 across the top of the 3½-mi-long Kingsley Dam. | 308/254–8800 | neparks@megavision.com. | www.ngpc.state.ne.us/parks/bigmac.html or www.lakemcconaughy.com | Neb. Parks Permit required; camping, $3–$14 | Park, daily year-round; modern camping, May–mid-Sept. only.

Lake Ogallala State Recreation Area. It's often called the "little lake," this 320-acre body of water created with fill dirt removed during the building of Kingsley Dam. It's on Highway 61, about 8 mi from Ogallala, at the eastern end of the Lake McConaughy complex. You'll find boating and fishing facilities, as well as 116 campsites and a controlled shooting area for the fall hunting season. | 308/284–8800 | ngpc.state.ne.us/parks/lakeog.html | Neb. Parks Permit required; camping, $3–$14 | Daily; modern camping facilities, May–mid-Sept.

Boot Hill Cemetery. Some of those who died with their boots on during the time that Ogallala was the golden land of saloons and dance halls at the end of the Texas Trail ended up here, their graves marked by wooden planks in the graveyard in downtown Ogallala. | 10th and Parkhill Dr. | Free | Daily.

Haybale Church. Made in 1928 from bales of hay that were then plastered over, this church is the only one of its kind in the United States. A note on the door will tell you where to find the key. Two blocks west and a block south, in the City Park on Highway 61, you also can see the world's smallest courthouse, as documented by *Ripley's Believe It or Not*. The key for that is in the modern courthouse next door. | Park, Main Street, Arthur | Donations suggested | Daily.

ON THE CALENDAR

JUNE: *Ash Hollow Pageant* To present a different look at the dramatic story of the pioneers who crossed the plains to settle the West, Ash Hollow State Park hosts this event every June. It's an outdoor presentation that includes readings from the journals of those who actually traveled the Oregon Trail. The festival has a good measure of fun with fiddle music and a chuck wagon supper. | 308/778–5548.

JUL.–AUG.: *Kites and Castles.* The action is *over* the lake and around the edges when the skies and the sands in the Martin Bay area just north of the dam are the arenas for this annual competition at Lake McConaughy State Recreation Area. You can compete in several size categories of kites—and the really big entrants make make you think more of sailboats in the sky than kites—with the sandcastle-building set up by age groups. | 308/726–7266 | lakemac@megavision.com.

SEPT.: *Governor's Cup Sailing Regatta.* The graceful, water-dancing sailboats turn Nebraska's largest body of water into a picture-postcard scene every Labor Day weekend. Most of the action takes place in the Arthur Bay section off Highway 92, about the midpoint of the shoreline road.

Dining

Hill Top Inn. American. Overlooking Lake McConaughy, this casual restaurant boasts a Southwestern look, and is known for its prime ribs and shrimp. | 197 Kingsley Dr. | 308/284–4534 | Closed Jan.–Mar. | $8–$18 | AE, D, MC, V.

Junie Mae's Roadhouse Barbecue. Barbecue. A picture of a winged pig greets you when you arrive at Junie Mae's, but after that, serious barbecue takes over. You can dine indoors in the homey redwood building or outside on a deck, just north of Kingsley Dam and overlooking Lake McConaughy. At breakfast, you'll find homemade Polish, Italian, and Cajun sausages, along with fresh cinnamon rolls from the restaurant's bakery. Later in the day, the menu includes prime rib, brisket, and barbecued chicken. There's also a beer garden, plus plenty of espressos and cappuccinos. | 1815 Hwy. 61N | 308/726–2626 | juniemaes@lakemac.net | $5–$10 | Tues.–Wed. | MC, V.

Ole's Big Game Steakhouse And Lounge. American. The buffalo steaks, buffalo burgers, and chicken-fried steak are local favorites, but you may remember more about the look of this restaurant at the Days Inn in Paxton. The late Ole Herstedt, who opened his tavern one minute after Prohibition ended in 1933, hunted on every continent—and mounted more than 200 big-game trophies on these wood-paneled walls. You might be seated under an elephant's tusks or by a glass case holding a stuffed polar bear. | 107 N Oak St., Paxton | 308/239–4500 | $7–$16 | D, MC, V.

Lodging

Best Western Stagecoach Inn. When I–80 gets as far as this two-story white-columned motel at the junction with Route 61, you are in the Mountain Time Zone. By the river, the rust-colored building is 12 mi from Lake McConaughy's outdoor facilities and 2 mi from the Mansion on the Hill if you'd rather explore the finery of the past. Some family rooms are available. The parking area includes truck and RV spaces, with cold-weather hookups. Restaurant, bar. In-room data ports. Cable TV. Heated indoor pool. Hot tub. Exercise equipment. Playground. Laundry facilities. Business services, airport shuttle. Some pets allowed (fee). | 201 Stagecoach Trail | 308/284–3656 or 800/662–2993 | fax 308/284–6734 | 100 rooms | $50–$65 | AE, D, DC, MC, V.

Comfort Inn. This two-story building, renovated in early 2000, is 9 mi from Lake McConaughy and ¼ mi from an antiques mall. Family and whirlpool suites come with a microwave and refrigerator. Complimentary Continental breakfast. Cable TV. Indoor pool. Hot tub. Exercise equipment. Laundry facilities. | 110 Pony Express Rd. | 308/284–4028 or 800/228–5150 | fax 308/284–4202 | 49 rooms | $52–$65 | AE, D, DC, MC, V.

Days Inn. This ranch-style motel has two floors and is a convenient resting place between fishing, boating, or jet skiing outings at Lake McConaughy, 9 mi away, or Lake Ogallala, 13 mi away. Complimentary Continental breakfast. In-room data ports, refrigerators. Cable TV. Pets allowed. | 31 rooms | 601 Stagecoach Trail | 800/544–8313 or 308/284–6365 | fax 308/284–2351. | AE, D, DC, MC, V.

Ramada Limited. Renovated in 1991, this two-story motor hotel and conference center near the Highway 29/61 junction helps you start the day with a free weekday newspaper and an iron, if you need to touch up your meeting clothes. The water sports at Lake McConaughy are about 10 mi away, as are several golf courses. Truck parking with cold-weather hookups is available. Restaurant, bar, complimentary Continental breakfast, room service. In-room data ports. Cable TV. Pool, wading pool. Gym. Laundry facilities. Business services. Pets allowed. | 201 Chuckwagon Rd. | 308/284–3623 or 800/573–7148 | fax 308/284–4949 | 152 rooms | $69 | AE, D, DC.

Super 8. This two-floor motel just off I–80 is 10 mi from all the goings-on at Lake McConaughy. The parking area includes spaces for trucks and RVs. Dining room. Cable TV. Laundry services. Pets allowed (fee). | 91 rooms | $55–$63 | 500 E. A South | 308/284–2076 or 800/800–8000 | fax 308/284–2590. | AE, D, DC, MC, V.

OMAHA

MAP 11, H3

(Nearby towns also listed: Ashland, Bellevue, Blair, Fremont, Plattsmouth)

Omaha was originally the homeland of the Omaha and Otoe Native Americans. The first fur traders established posts on the western bank of the Missouri River in the early 1800s, but a government decree in 1834 made the land "Indian territory," where whites could not settle, but only "pass through." In 1846, Mormons fleeing from Illinois received permission from Big Elk, the chief of the Omahas, to cross the river. They stopped at a couple of temporary camps, then built a city for 4,000 at what they called "Winter Quarters." About 700 people died that winter—from disease, malnutrition, and exposure—and their graves remain in a hillside cemetery in outlying Florence, although Brigham Young and his followers moved on toward Utah.

Omaha grew fairly quickly after the Nebraska Territory was created in 1854. It expanded further in 1863, when it became the terminus of the Union Pacific Railroad linking the east and the west. The city quickly became a blue-collar railroad town. Later, agriculture flourished, as ranchers shipped cattle, sheep, and hogs to the Omaha Livestock Market. Meat packers and producers, including industry giants Swift, Armour, and Cudahy, soon set up businesses here. Today, the meat-packing industry is dominated by ConAgra, which has its headquarters not far from the historic stockyards.

Other industries now help diversify Omaha's economic base. The city is an insurance center—with more than 30 companies, including Mutual of Omaha in its distinctive gilded, domed building. Throughout much of its history, the military has also had a presence. From 1868, when the Omaha Barracks was placed there to protect railroad workers, what became Fort Omaha was closed down and re-opened several times to serve as a support center, a school for balloonists in World War I, and an Italian prisoner-of-war work camp during World War II.

Omaha is made up of residents of many ethnic backgrounds, and it is an extremely friendly Midwestern city. The Lied Jungle at the Henry Doorly Zoo is the world's largest indoor rain forest, Union Pacific's historic Union Station has been given a new life as the Durham Western Heritage Museum, and the site of the old fort now contains the Douglas County Historical Society's archives.

Many people know of Omaha through Boys Town. An incorporated community in its own right, Boys Town was founded when Father Edward J. Flanagan raised $90 just before Christmas in 1917 and used it to rent a house in Omaha for boys who had nowhere else to go. Father Flanagan's work, emphasizing moral, religious, and vocational education, revolutionized juvenile care. Boys Town expanded several times, eventually settling at its present location just west of Omaha—where you yet can see the statue of a boy carrying his younger brother that was made so famous by the old Spencer Tracy movie.

Information: Greater Omaha Convention and Visitors Bureau | 6800 Mercy Rd., Ste. 202, Omaha 68106-2627 | 402/444–4660 or 800/332–1819 | fax 402/444–4511 | info@visitomaha.com | www.visitomaha.com.

Also: **Greater Omaha Chamber of Commerce** | 1301 Harney St., Omaha 68102 | 402/346–5000 or 800/852–2622 | fax 402/346–7050 | gocc@accessomaha.com | www.accessomaha.com.

TRANSPORTATION

Airports: Omaha's **Eppley Airfield** (402/422–6817 | www.eppleyairfield.com), on the eastern side of the city at 4501 Abbott Drive, is served by 12 major carriers and three commuter lines. **Eppley Express** (308/234–6066 or 800/888–9793) runs airport vans from Eppley Airfield to Lincoln Municipal Airport, leaving at 11:10 AM Mon.–Fri., 2:55 PM Mon.–Sat., and 6:10 PM Sun.–Fri. The fare is $21 one way; reservations are required. The vans proceed to Kearny, Grand Island, and York (additional fares required).

Rail: If you prefer rail travel, **Amtrak** (402/342–1501 or 800/872–7245) trains make two arrivals and two departures each day from a station at 9th and Pacific streets, and **Greyhound** (800/231–2222) offers long-distance bus service from 16th and Jackson streets. Several intrastate carriers run from Omaha to various other parts of the state.

Intra-city Transit: Omaha city buses are operated by **Metro Area Transit** (402/341–0800), and there are six taxi firms.

Attractions

Joslyn Art Museum. A modern addition to the original Art Deco structure has greatly expanded space for the Joslyn's respected collection of art of the American West as well as many other examples from 19th- and 20th-century Europe and America. The original building has a courtyard and concert hall, and a restaurant is in the atrium connecting the two buildings. | 2200 Dodge St. | 402/342–3300 | www.joslyn.org | $5; free Sat. 10–noon | Tues.–Sat. 10–4, Sun. 12–4.

Great Plains Black Museum. In a former telephone exchange building now listed on the National Register of Historic Places, the museum depicts the history of African-Americans on the Great Plains through photographs, documents, paintings, and rare books. | 2213 Lake St. | 402/345–2212 | Donations requested | Weekdays 10–2.

Durham Western Heritage Museum. In Omaha's restored Union Station, the museum's exhibits detail various facets of Omaha's history. There are railroad cars and a steam

KODAK'S TIPS FOR PHOTOGRAPHING WEATHER

Rainbows
· Find rainbows by facing away from the sun after a storm
· Use your auto-exposure mode
· With an SLR, use a polarizing filter to deepen colors

Fog and Mist
· Use bold shapes as focal points
· Add extra exposure manually or use exposure compensation
· Choose long lenses to heighten fog and mist effects

In the Rain
· Look for abstract designs in puddles and wet pavement
· Control rain-streaking with shutter speed
· Protect cameras with plastic bags or waterproof housings

Lightning
· Photograph from a safe location
· In daylight, expose for existing light
· At night, leave the shutter open during several flashes

From *Kodak Guide to Shooting Great Travel Pictures* © 2000 by Fodor's Travel Publications

engine, as well as the Byron Reed Coin and Document Collection. An old-time soda fountain still operates on the main level, its frothy concoctions illuminated by light streaming through salmon-colored windows. | 801 S. 10th St. | 402/444–5071 | www.dwhm.org | $5 | Tues.–Sat. 10–5, Sun. 1–5.

El Museo Latino. Works of art, films, dance, performing arts, and classes related to the Latino people of the Americas are all found here. Bilingual programs include lectures, workshops, and dance classes. | 4701 S. 25th St. | 402/731–1137 | $5 | Mon., Wed., Fri. 10–5, Tues., Thurs. 1–5, Sat. 2–5, closed Sun.

Gerald Ford Birth Site. A rose garden and colonnade similar to those at the White House commemorate the site where the childhood home of former President Ford once stood. An adjacent structure, the Gerald R. Ford Conservation Center, houses research into document preservation and also has a permanent display of exhibits on the 38th president. | 32nd St. and Woolworth Ave. | 402/444–5955 | Free | Daily 7:30–dusk.

General Crook House. Originally owned by General George Crook, who fought the region's Native Americans despite sympathizing with their cause, this two-story Victorian was the first brick house inside old Fort Omaha. Today, the house and a Victorian Heirloom Garden, part of the state arboretum system, are on the campus of Metropolitan Community College. | Building 11B, 30th and Fort Sts. | 402/455–9990 | $3.50 | Weekdays 10–4; guided tours, Sun. 1–4.

Mormon Trail Visitors Center at Winter Quarters. In a building near the cemetery established when the Mormons paused here enroute in the late 1840s, you can learn about the history of the Mormon Trail. On a less serious note, you will find up to 300 gingerbread creations displayed here each Christmas, which are given to charitable institutions after the show. | 3215 State St. | 402/453–9372 | Free | Daily 9–9.

Omaha Childrens Museum. Kids can play on a real fire truck, visit a scaled-down version of the Omaha skyline, experiment with scientific displays, deliver the news on a closed-circuit television set, and take classes at this downtown location. | 500 S. 20th St. | 402/342–6164 | $4 | Tues.–Sat. 10–5, Sun. 1–5.

Botanical Gardens. Divided into several different specialty areas, the 75-acre Gardens overlooking the Missouri River include large rose, herb, children's, and spring flowering gardens. | 5th and Cedar Sts. | 402/346–4002 | Free | Apr.–Oct., Tues.–Sun. 9–4.

Freedom Park. Paying tribute to some of the nation's wartime vessels, this park along the Missouri River is now the berth of the *USS Hazard*, a decorated World War II minesweeper; the training submarine *USS Marlin*; the landing craft LSM-45, as well as a Coast Guard helicopter and naval aircraft. | 2497 Freedom Park Rd. | 402/345–1959 | www.freedomparknavy.org | $5 | Apr.–Oct., daily 9–6.

Louisville State Recreation Area. This park near the Platte River, on Route 50 near Louisville, allows the use of power boats as well as rowboats. Day-trippers will also find many picnicking and swimming spots. | 402/234–6855 | ngpc.state.ne.us/parks/lville.html | Neb. Parks Permit required; camping, $7–$12 | Daily; modern camping facilities, May–mid-Sept.

Neale Woods Nature Center. The northern section of Fontenelle Forest in Bellevue, this 550-acre nature center has 9 mi of trails through forested hills, prairie, and wetlands near the Missouri River. | 14323 Edith Marie Ave. | 402/731–3140 | $3.50.

N. P. Dodge Park. This city park has access to the Missouri from two boat ramps and has cricket, softball, and soccer fields, as well as camping sites. | 11005 J. J. Pershing Dr. | 402/444–4673; camping reservations, 404/444–5955 | Free | Daily.

Platte River State Park. Camping is not permitted in this 418-acre park 3 mi west of Louisville, off Highway 66, but you can rent cabins with refrigerators or tepees that sleep six to eight. Activities include swimming, hiking, tennis, archery, volleyball, horseback trail rides, buffalo stew cookouts, and paddleboating. | 14421 346th St., Louisville | 402/234–

2217 | prsp@ngpc.state.ne.us | ngp.ngpc.state.ne.us/parks/prsp.html | Nebraska Parks Permit required | Lodging season, late Apr.–late Oct.; some cabins open year-round.

Schramm Park State Recreation Area. These grounds, 20 mi from Omaha along the Platte River, include the Schramm Park National Recreation Trail, the Ak-Sar-Ben Aquarium—which showcases fish native to Nebraska—and the Fish Hatchery Museum. No camping is allowed, but you'll find abundant small wildlife and unusual rock formations along the hiking trails. | 21502 Hwy. 31W, Gretna | 402/332–3887; aquarium, 402/332–3901 | www.ngpc.state.ne.us/parks/schramm.html | Neb. Parks Permit required | Grounds: daily; museum and aquarium: Memorial Day–Labor Day, daily 10–4:30; Labor Day–Nov. and Apr.–Memorial Day, Wed.–Mon. 10–4:40; Dec.–Mar., Wed.–Sun. 10–4:30.

Two Rivers State Recreation Area. You can camp at this 644-acre park off Route 92 near Venice, but the sought-after spots are the 10 old Union Pacific cabooses transformed into rental cabins–still sitting on rail tracks on a siding. The several small lakes formed from sand pits are also especially popular among trout fishermen. | 27702 F St., Waterloo | 402/359–5165 | fax 402/359–9040 | ngpc.state.ne.us/parks/2rivers/html | Neb. Parks Permit required; camping, $7–$24; call for caboose rates | Reservations required for cabooses; 2-night min | Grounds, daily; cabins, camping, Memorial Day–Labor Day.

Father Flanagan's Boys Town. The world-renowned center for boys is now officially Boys and Girls Town, but admirers everywhere will probably always think of it as Father Flanagan's Boys Town. At its large campus setting in west Omaha, you can tour Father Flanagan's House, the rose and Biblical gardens, the chapel, and other facilities. | 13628 Flanagan Blvd., Boy's Town | 402/498–1140 | Free | May–Aug., daily 8–5:30; Sept.–Apr., daily 8–4:30.

Fun Plex. Entertainment comes in many forms here, where there are get-yourself-wet water slides, a wave pool, and lazy river, as well as go-carts, bumper cars, kiddie rides, miniature golf, and batting cages. | 7003 Q St. | 402/331–8436 | unlimited ride pass, $12.95; unlimited water pass, $10.95; combined pass, $16.95 | Mon.–Fri. 11–10, weekends 11–11.

Henry Doorly Zoo. You can feel the steam of the jungle and the chill of the Arctic here. The zoo's Lied Jungle is the world's largest indoor rain forest, displaying the flora and fauna found in Africa, South America, and Asia. It has North America's largest cat complex, with rare white tigers as well as more familiar big beasts. The fish in the Scott Aquarium swim in waters that duplicate the conditions of habitats from the tropics to the Antarctic—and you can walk through a 70-ft glass tunnel with sharks swimming on both sides of and above you. There's an IMAX theater, plus a petting zoo for small fry. | 3701 S. 10th St. | 402/330–4629 or 402/733–8400 | www.omahazoo/com | $7.75 | Daily 9:30–5.

Old Market. A historic district of early 20th-century brick warehouses, the Old Market is a blend of trendy boutiques, galleries, restaurants, lounges with live music, and loft apartments running from 10th to 13th streets, Farnum to Jackson. Most of the shops along the cobblestone streets are open from 10 to 9, and you can take Old Market's horse-drawn carriages to see the waterfalls and lagoons of the 10-acre Gene Leahy Mall, a park at 14th and Farnum. | 402/341–7151 or 402/346–4445 | Free | Daily.

ON THE CALENDAR

JUNE: *NCAA College Baseball World Series.* Partisan rooting is encouraged when the leading collegiate baseball teams come to Rosenblatt Stadium to compete for the national championship. The stadium is on 13th Street South, off I-80 exit 454. | 402/444–4750.

JUNE: *Summer Arts Festival.* Live entertainment, ethnic food, and more than 175 visual artists are featured in this Omaha festival. | 402/963–9020.

JUNE–JULY: *Nebraska Shakespeare Festival.* You can view professional Shakespearean presentations performed in the outdoor setting of Elmwood Park, with seminars and Elizabethan music before the nightly performances. | 402/280–2391.

JUL.–AUG.: *Jazz on the Green.* The Joslyn Art Museum presents a series of evening concerts every summer. The players use the front steps of the museum as their stage; you must bring your own blankets or chairs for lawn-sitting. | 2200 Dodge St. | 402/342–3300.

AUG.: *Greatest Festival in Town.* This festival has food, carnival rides, live music, and game booths, most celebrating the Croatian heritage, at Saints Peter and Paul Church. | 402/731–4578.

SEPT.: *River City Roundup.* This Western-style festival at Aksarben Coliseum includes a PRCA rodeo, a pancake feed and agriculture fest, hot air balloons, train rides, western and wildlife art shows, concerts, dances, and food. | 402/554–9611.

Dining

Bohemian Café. Czech. Its red-tile roof has been an Omaha landmark since the 1920s, and regulars especially praise the roasted duck and jager schnitzel. On Fridays and Saturdays, an accordionist adds merry European sounds with his strolling serenades. | 1406 S. 13th St. | 402/342–9838 | $5–$12 | D, MC, V.

Brazen Head. Irish. Although the Brazen Head is in a strip mall, dark wood furnishings imported from Ireland recreate the feeling of a traditional Irish pub. Divided into three areas—one open and airy for a casual meal, the second quiet and cozy for a more romantic evening, and the third, the Robert Emmet Room, a cigar room and bar that feels like a private club. On the menu: fish and chips, Jameson Whiskey steak, corned beef, chicken, stew, and Irish coffee. | 319 N. 78th St. | 402/393–3731 | fax 402/393–3789 | $6–$19 | AE, MC, V.

Butsy Le Doux's. Cajun. There's open-air sidewalk dining as well as indoor tables, but all serve such Louisiana standbys as jambalaya and a combination plate with red beans and rice. In the summer, there's entertainment on Friday and Saturday nights. | 1014 Howard St. | 402/346–5100 | Closed Sun. | $5–$15 | AE, DC, MC, V.

Charlie's on the Lake. Seafood. Paintings of fish are everywhere in the dark wood interior, and just outside, you'll see a real lake. Try the fish special or the raspberry salmon, corn-fed beef, a mixed grill, and daily desserts. | 4150 S. 144th St. | 402/894–9411 | $14–$28 | AE, D, MC, V.

Chu's Chop Suey. Chinese. At Chu's, there's a lot more to choose than chop suey; the sweet-and-sour pork is particularly popular, along with the chicken chow mein, and you'll find steak and pork chops on the menu. Kids' menu. | 6455 Center St. | 402/553–6454 | Closed Tues. | $5–$10 | AE, D, DC, MC, V.

Farm House Café. American. This spacious, quiet restaurant with rich woodwork and private booths sits at the end of a small mall and has hamburgers, generous deli sandwiches, barbecued ribs, and fried chicken. There are also such farmhouse classics as homemade soups and desserts, and, if you're around at breakfast, freshly baked pastries. | 3461 S. 84th St. | 402/393–0640 | $6–$12 | AE, D, DC, MC, V.

Flatiron Cafe. Contemporary. There's a view from both sides of the dining room in this ground-floor outpost of a tall, wedge-shaped commercial building. Outstanding dishes include saffron angel hair pasta with tiger shrimp, diver scallops and muscles with saffron, tomato, and bell pepper sauce, and crispy twice-cooked duck on basmati rice with braised cabbage and star anise ginger broth. | 1722 Howard St. | 402/344–3040 | Closed Sun. | $8–$25 | AE, D, DC, MC, V.

French Café. French. An institution within the Old Market area, this restaurant kick-started the rebirth of the old warehouse district. Black-and-white photos of French scenes adorn the interior, and in good weather, the patio is open. It's known for fresh fish, including salmon piccata, pasta and pepper steak, lemon blackberry vinaigrette on a walnut-asparagus salad, and garlic potato blini with frog's legs. | 1017 Howard St. | 402/341–3547 | www.french-cafe.com | $17–$29 | AE, D, DC, MC, V.

Garden Café Downtown. American. The all-American potato, particularly in potato casseroles, is the specialty of this local chain with five locations. There also are many freshly made desserts and a full range of breakfast choices. Kids' menu. No smoking. | 1212 Harney and 3 other locations | 402/422–1574 | $5–$15 | AE, D, DC, MC, V.

Gorat's Steak House. Steak. Four generations of Gorats have run this steakhouse since 1944. There is entertainment Thursday through Saturday nights, but don't expect any frills here; it's a casual family restaurant. Try the filet mignon or Omaha strip steak. | 4917 Center St. | 402/551–3733 | Closed Sun. | $7–$20 | AE, MC, V.

Grandmother's Lounge. American. Here you'll find a variety of chicken dishes named after different cities, pasta, steak, and fish, and desserts. Kids' menu. | 8989 W. Dodge Rd., 402/391–8889 | 82nd & L Sts., 402/339–6633 | $5–$16 | AE, D, DC, MC, V.

Imperial Palace. Chinese. The building resembles something rom the Forbidden City in the days when the emperor ruled. The menu has specialty dishes like four-flavored chicken. | 11201 Davenport St. | 402/330–3888 | $6–$8 | AE, MC, V.

Indian Oven. Indian. Traditional decorations and statues lend ethnic texture to this restaurant that specializes in tandoori chicken, chicken tikke, and other dishes from the north of India. Outside, there's a patio for open-air dining at glass-topped tables with dramatic black linens. | 1010 Howard St. | 402/342–4856 | Closed Sun. | $10–$19 | AE, D, DC, MC, V.

Joe Tess'. Seafood. Joe Tess' is all about fish, from the albino catfish in its fountain to stuffed fish on the walls and posters and neon beer signs showing still more fish. The menu includes fresh carp, catfish, homemade chowder, shrimp, oysters, farm-raised coho salmon, rainbow trout, and jacket fries. | 5424 S. 24th St. | 402/731–7278 | $2–$11 | AE, MC, V.

Johnny's Cafe. American. This family-owned steakhouse is an Omaha institution. First opened in 1922, it's now run by the family's third generation, offering casual dining or more elaborate meals. Try the filet mignon or the prime ribs. Kids menu. | 4702 S. 27th St. | 402/731–4774 | Closed Sun. | $7–$18 | AE, D, DC, MC, V.

La Strada 72. Italian. You can dine indoors, among the large windows, brick-and-ceramic tile walls, and tables set with white linens, or outdoors on an enclosed patio. Either way, veal and fresh seafood are menu standouts, with homemade pastries for dessert. | 3125 S. 72nd St. | 402/397–8389 | Closed Sun. | $10–$25 | AE, D, DC, MC, V.

Le Café De Paris. French. The mood is one of understated elegance, but the Continental touches make it a popular choice for dress-up dining. Known for fresh fish, including Dover sole, as well as veal, seasonal fowl, and homemade breads. | 1228 S. 6th St. | 402/344–0227 | Reservations essential | Jacket and tie | Closed Sun. | $25–$40 | AE.

Lo Sole Mio Ristorante Italiano. Italian. If it's made in Italy, it's made here, from antipasti and *zuppa* (soup) to pizza, pasta, and dinners of chicken, veal, fish, and steak. | 3001 S. 32nd Ave. | 402/345–5656 | Closed Sun. | $6–$19 | MC, V.

Omaha Press Club. Continental. Formerly an elegant private club, this restaurant is now open to the public. It's on the top floor of the First National Bank Building in downtown Omaha, with tiered seating to give all diners panoramic views of the city from 22 stories up. The menu has cashew chicken, prime steaks, sea bass, and other seafood. | 1620 Dodge St. | 402/345–8008 | Closed Mon. night, Sun. Open Sat. noon | $6–$21 | MC, V.

Passport. Continental. On the ground floor of a former warehouse in the Old Market. Passport has a piano and cigar room for those inclined to enjoy them. Menu favorites include porterhouse steaks, Australian cold-water lobster tail, and other seafood. | 1101 Jackson St. | 402/344–3200 | No lunch | $18–$30 | AE, D, DC, MC, V.

Trini's. Mexican. On the lower level of the Passageway, a narrow brick corridor within the Old Market, Trini's offers a quiet setting for specialties like Enchilada de Jocoque. | 1020 Howard St. | 402/346–8400 | Closed Sun. | $4–$16 | AE, DC, MC, V.

Upstream Brewery. American. Upstream Brewery has turned a one-time firehouse in the Old Market into a restaurant, bar, and on-site brewery. The bar scene is friendly, the first-floor dining area and brewery are bustling, and the loft-style second floor has its own pleasures at its bar and billiards room. | 514 S. 11th St. | 402/344–0200 | $6–$20 | AE, D, DC, MC, V.

V. Mertz. Continental. Despite its out-of-the-way location in the Passageway, V. Mertz is still one of the more sought-after fine restaurants in Omaha. Soft lights illuminate the tables in the otherwise dark dining room. The menu is known for its pepper steak, tuna, and salmon, and its wine selection earned the restaurant the *Wine Spectator*'s Award of Excellence in 2000. | 1022 Howard St. | 402/345–8980 | $21–$35 | AE, D, DC, MC, V.

Vivace's. Italian. In the Old Market commercial district, Vivace's has casual sidewalk seating in pleasant weather and an elegant dining room with an antique back bar. Try the Italian dishes with homemade breads and desserts, including the osso buco (veal), or other Mediterranean standbys such as paella. | 1110 Howard St. | 402/342–2050 | $8–$24 | AE, D, DC, MC, V.

Lodging

Baymont Inns. This chain has many changes and renovations underway all around the country. This two-story outpost on the west side of town offers simple accommodations 15 mi from the SAC Museum and 3 mi from the shops of Oakview Mall. Cold-weather hookups are available. Complimentary Continental breakfast. In-room data ports. Cable TV. Business services. Pets allowed. | 10760 M St. | 402/592–5200 or 800/428–3438 | fax 402/592–1416 | 97 rooms | $56–$74 | AE, D, DC, MC, V.

Best Inn. This three-story motel, at the junction of I–80 and Highway 50, is 3 mi from the Prairie Capital Convention Center and about 11 mi from the zoo. Bar, complimentary Continental breakfast. In-room VCRs. Hot tub. Exercise equipment. Laundry facilities. Free parking. Pets allowed (fee). | 9305 S. 145th St. | 402/895–2555 | fax 402/895–1565 | 56 rooms | $42–$56 | AE, D, DC, MC, V.

Best Western—Central. Set off by a swath of green lawns, this five-story white building was renovated in 1998–99. Just off I–80, it is also just down the street from the sports events at Aksarben Coliseum and has in-room movies. Truck parking is available. Restaurant, bar, room service. In-room data ports. Cable TV. Indoor pool. Hot tub, sauna. Laundry facilities. Business services, airport shuttle. Pets allowed. | 3650 S. 72nd St. | 402/397–3700 or 800/446–6242 | fax 402/397–8362 | 212 rooms | $79 | AE, D, DC, MC, V.

Best Western Omaha Inn. Deep burnished reds play against creamy taupe colors in the spacious lobby of this downtown three-story building, renovated in 1996, about 3 mi from the charter services at Millard Airfield. Morning newspapers are complimentary, and the lounge has karaoke Friday and Saturday nights. Truck parking is available. Bar, complimentary Continental breakfast. In-room data ports, some refrigerators. Cable TV. Indoor pool. Hot tub. Exercise equipment. Business services. | 4706 S. 108th St. | 402/339–7400 or 877/819–6210 | fax 402/339–5155 | 102 rooms | $59–$79 | AE, D, DC, MC, V.

Best Western Redick Plaza. This 11-story building, renovated in 1999, has a slightly frontier look in the play of dark woods against the bright whites of the lobby. Just 4 mi from Eppley, it's about 8 mi east of downtown. Bar, complimentary breakfast, room service. In-room data ports. Cable TV. Exercise equipment. Business services. No pets. | 1504 Harney St. | 402/342–1500 | fax 402/342–2401 | 89 rooms | $109–$179 | AE, D, DC, MC, V.

Clarion Hotel Carlisle. Sparkling chandeliers and cherrywood paneling help give a refined grace to the lobby of this three-story hotel about 3 mi from the stores of Regency Fashion Court. The spacious rooms include a full-sized desk. Truck parking is available. Restaurant, complimentary Continental breakfast, room service. In-room data ports. Cable TV. Indoor pool. Hot tub. Laundry facilities. Business services, airport shuttle. Some pets allowed (fee). | 10909 M St. | 402/331–8220 or 800/526–6242 | fax 402/331–8729 | 137 rooms | $89–$125 | AE, D, DC, MC, V.

Comfort Inn. A six-story cream-and-green building 9 mi east of downtown and within 2 mi of Westroads Mall, this hotel helps you greet the new day with a complimentary newspaper and a European-style breakfast that includes a Belgian waffle. Parking for tour buses is available. Complimentary Continental breakfast. In-room data ports, some microwaves, some refrigerators, some in-room hot tubs. Cable TV. Indoor pool. Exercise equipment. Hot tub. Video games. Laundry service. Business services. | 8736 W. Dodge Rd. | 402/343–1000 | fax 402/398–1784. | 105 rooms | $85 | AE, D, DC, MC, V.

Comfort Inn. Walls of windows make the bring the sunshine in around the indoor pool at this motel next door to the Henry Doorly Zoo. It's 2 mi from downtown Omaha and the Old Market district and 2 mi from casinos. Complimentary Continental breakfast. In-room data ports, some microwaves, some refrigerators, some in-room hot tubs. Cable TV. Indoor pool. Hot tub. Business services. | 2920 S. 13th Ct. | 402/342–8000 | fax 402/342–8069 | 79 rooms. | $60 | AE, D, DC, MC, V.

Cornerstone Bed and Breakfast. You are in the heart of Omaha's historic Goldcoast district when you stay in this French Chateau–style mansion built in 1894. Dining room, complimentary Continental breakfast. Cable TV. Business services. | 40 N. 39th St. | 402/558–7600 | fax 402/551–6598 | savoy1@home.com | http://hometown.aol.com/cornerstonebandb/Cornerstone.html. | 6 rooms, 1 carriage house | $80–$110 | AE, D, MC, V.

Days Inn. This modern two-floor hotel is about 13 mi from the Joslyn Art Museum and Old Market and 15 mi from the Bluff Run Dog Track. The parking area includes spaces for trucks and RVs. Complimentary Continental breakfast. Cable TV. Indoor pool. Spa. Free parking. | 10560 Sapp Brothers Rd. | 402/896–6868 or 800/544–8313 | fax 402/896–6868. | 66 rooms | $54–$60 | AE, D, DC, MC, V.

Doubletree Guest Suites. Each suite in this six-story building has a sitting room balcony open to the hotel's five-story atrium of tropical plants around a peaceful fountain. Renovated in 1999, the hotel is 10 mi from Eppley and 7 mi from the zoo. Restaurant, complimentary breakfast. In-room data ports. Cable TV. Indoor pool. Hot tub. Exercise equipment. Laundry facilities. Business services, airport shuttle. | 7270 Cedar St. | 402/397–5141 | fax 402/397–3266 | 187 suites | $89–$114 | AE, D, DC, MC, V.

★ **Doubletree Hotel Downtown.** At 19 stories, this is the largest and tallest of downtown Omaha's hotels, and its top-floor restaurant has panoramic views of the city and the valley of the Missouri River. Renovated in 1999. It is next to office buildings and banks and the Joslyn Art Museum. Restaurant, bar (with entertainment). In-room data ports, some refrigerators. Cable TV. Indoor pool. Beauty salon, hot tub. Exercise equipment. Business services, airport shuttle. | 1616 Dodge St. | 402/346–7600 or 800/228–8733 | fax 402/346–5722 | 413 rooms | $89–$134 | AE, D, DC, MC, V.

Econo Lodge. With a gray mansard roof over the low white entry, this simple two-story motel is well placed for visits to the SAC Museum, 5 mi away, or the Henry Doorly Zoo, 4 mi east. Cable TV. | 3511 S. 84th St. | 402/391–4321 or 800/553–2666 | 79 rooms | $45–$110 | AE, D, DC, MC, V.

Econo Lodge. The two-story lodging is 2 mi from I–80, about 2 mi from Westroads Mall, and five blocks from Nebraska Crossroads Mall. Free coffee is always available, along with truck and bus parking, and extended-stay rooms have microwaves and refrigerators. Restaurant. Some in-room hot tubs. Cable TV. Pool. Laundry facilities. Pets allowed. | 7833 W. Dodge Rd. | 402/391–7100 | fax 402/391–7100 | 48 rooms | $45–$100 | AE, D, DC, MC, V.

Embassy Suites. Although this seven-story building is next to the Old Market, it has an atrium and a courtyard for quiet moments away from the busy downtown scene, plus outdoor decks where you can work on your tan. Each suite has a separate bedroom and living room. Restaurant, bar, complimentary breakfast, room service. Cable TV. Microwave, refrigerator, in-room data ports. Indoor pool. Hot tub. Fitness center. Business services, airport shuttle. Pets allowed. | 555 S. 10th St. | 402/346–9000 or 800/362–2779 | fax 402/346–4236 | 249 suites | $129–$179 | AE, D, DC, MC, V.

Four Points Hotel Omaha. With a red roof topping its classically styled six stories, this hotel in southwest Omaha has minibars and coffemakers in each room, as well as complimentary weekday newspapers. About 8 mi from Nebraska Crossroads Mall, it provides complimentary shuttles to the corporate/charter facilities at Millard Airport. Restaurant, room service. Cable TV. Heated indoor pool, wading pool. Hot tub, sauna. Gym. Laundry facilities. Business services. Pets allowed. | 4888 S. 118th St. | 402/895–1000 | fax 402/895–9247 | 163 rooms | $69–$129 | AE, D, DC, MC, V.

Hampton Inn. This four-story motel is 9 mi east of downtown, 8 mi from the Joslyn AArt Museum, and 1 mi from Westroads Mall. If you want to wear a new purchase tonight, you'll find an iron in your room for touch-ups. Complimentary Continental breakfast. In-room data ports. Cable TV. Business services, free parking. | 9720 W. Dodge Rd. | 402/391–5300 or 800/426–7866 | fax 402/391–8995 | 129 rooms | $59–$179 | AE, D, DC, MC, V.

Hampton Inn Southwest. Off I–80 in southwest Omaha, this motel is 6 mi from the Fun-Plex amusement park and 12–13 mi from Harvey's Casino or the dog races at Bluff Run. Complimentary Continental breakfast. In-room data ports. Cable TV. Pool. Business services. No pets. | 10728 L St. | 402/593–2380 or 800/426–7866 | fax 402/593–0859 | 135 rooms | $65–$115 | AE, D, DC, MC, V.

Holiday Inn Express. A six-story brick building on the west edge of downtown, this hotel renovated in the spring of 2000 is less than 1½ mi from the Great Plains Black History Museum and the Children's Museum and within 5 mi of three casinos in Council Bluffs, Iowa. Rooms have two-line phones, a sauna, and a hot tub. Complimentary Continental breakfast. In-room data ports, refrigerators. Cable TV. Hot tub. Exercise equipment. Laundry facilities. Business services, airport shuttle, free parking. | 3001 Chicago St. | 402/345–2222 or 800/465–4329 | fax 402/345–2501 | hieomaha@aol.com | 122 rooms, 10 suites | $69–$79 | AE, D, DC, MC, V.

J. C. Robinson House Bed and Breakfast. Built in 1905, this neoclassical two-story mansion surrounds you with an eclectic array of country antiques. It's 11 mi from I–80, an easy drive into Omaha. Complimentary breakfast. No smoking. | 102 E. Lincoln Ave., Waterloo | 402/779–2704 or 800/779–2705 | fax 402/779–3235 | 4 rooms, 3 with shared bath | $50–$80 | No credit cards.

La Quinta. With crisp white exterior and refurbished guest rooms with dark wood furniture, this two-story motel on the northeast side of town is about 5 mi from the Children's Museum and 15 mi from downtown. Complimentary Continental breakfast. In-room data ports. Cable TV. Pool. Laundry facilities. Pets allowed. | 3330 N. 104th Ave. | 402/493–1900 or 800/687–6667 | fax 402/496–0757 | 129 rooms | $52–$59 | AE, D, DC, MC, V.

Marriott. This L-shape six-story hotel is 10 mi from the Old Market area and just across the street from the shopping at Regency Fashion Court. Restaurants, bar, room service. In-room data ports. Cable TV. Indoor-outdoor pool. Hot tub. Exercise equipment. Business services. Pets allowed. | 10220 Regency Cir. | 402/399–9000 | fax 402/399–0223 | 301 rooms, 4 suites | $109–$149 | AE, D, DC, MC, V.

Ramada-Central. At I–80 and 72nd St., this 10-floor motel draws a lot of group events to its 10 meeting rooms, and there's a concierge desk to help with special services. It's about 7 mi from the Joslyn and the Gerald Ford Birth Site, and 5 mi from the zoo. Restaurant, bar, room service. In-room data ports, some refrigerators, some microwaves. Cable TV. Indoor pool. Hot tub, sauna. Playground. Business services, airport shuttle. Pets allowed. | 7007 Grover St. | 402/397–7030 or 800/228–5299 | fax 402/397–8449 | 215 rooms | $79–$99 | AE, D, DC, MC, V.

Sheraton Hotel. The 1920s downtown building, designed around an open-air courtyard, has a sense of the French in its architecture and decor. A concierge is on duty 24 hours. Some suites have fireplaces, and the fitness center has massages and saunas available to everyone. Restaurant, bar, room service. In-room data ports. Cable TV. Spa, hot tub. Gym. Business services, airport shuttle, free parking. | 1615 Howard St. | 402/342–2222 or 800/937–8461 | fax 402/342–2569 | 123 rooms, 22 suites | $159–$225 | AE, D, DC, MC, V.

Sleep Inn. A creamy three-story building close to Freedom Park and the Missouri River, this motel is less than 5 mi from Rosenblatt Stadium and about 8 mi from the Crossroads Mall. Most rooms have only showers, no tubs. Truck/RV parking is available. Complimentary Continental breakfast. In-room data ports. Cable TV. Airport shuttle. | 2525 Abbott Dr. | 402/342–2525 or 800/688–2525 | fax 402/342–2525 | 93 rooms, 12 suites | $62 | AE, D, DC, MC, V.

Suburban Inn. You can play "Big Red Keno" in the lobby or relax with a stroll through the inn gardens. The Joslyn Art Museum is about 13 mi away. Cable TV. Pool. Laundry facilities. | 11023 Sapp Brothers Rd. | 402/332–3911 | fax 402/332–3750 | subinn@radiks.net | www.suburbaninn.com | 72 rooms | $40–$65 | AE, MC, V.

Super 8. Renovated in 2000, this three-story motel near the SAC Museum is 10 mi from Eppley Airport. Some rooms have data ports, or you can relax with an in-room movie. Cold-weather hookups are available. Complimentary Continental breakfast. Cable TV. | 10829 M St. | 402/339–2250 or 800/800–8000 | fax 402/339–6922 | 116 rooms | $54–$68 | AE, D, DC, MC, V.

Wyndham Garden Hotel. Right at the Miracle Hills Office Park downtown, this two-floor hotel 13 mi from Eppley Airfield caters to business travelers. By night, umbrella-topped tables create a patio-like spot for relaxing beside the pool. Boys' Town is 4 blocks away. Restaurant, complimentary Continental breakfast. In-room data ports. Cable TV. Indoor pool. Hot tub. Laundry services. Business services. | 11515 Miracle Hills Dr. | 402/496–7500 | fax 402/496–0234 | www.wyndham.com/Omaha/ | 137 rooms, 15 suites | $59–$175 | AE, D, DC, MC, V.

O'NEILL

MAP 11, F2

(Nearby towns also listed: Neligh, Royal, Valentine)

In 1969, Governor Norbert Tiemann proclaimed O'Neill "the Irish capital of Nebraska." You can see evidence of the community's roots in the green shamrocks painted on streets and sidewalks and in the Irish products you can buy year-round. Here, St. Patrick's Day is the year's major event, including dancing on the world's biggest shamrock, covering the pavement where highways 281, 20, and 275 come together.

Information: O'Neill Chamber of Commerce | 315 E. Douglas St., O'Neill 68763 | 402/336–2355 | fax 402/336–4563 | oneill@inetnebr.com | www.inetnebr.com/~oneill.

Attractions

Atkinson Lake State Recreation Area. This 54-acre state park, 18 mi west of O'Neill off U.S. 20, offers primitive camping, picnicking and fishing astride the Elkhorn River. | 402/336–2355 | www.ngpc.state.ne.us/parks/atknlake.html | Neb. Parks Permit required; camping, $3–$6 | Daily.

Carney Park. This park on the south edge of O'Neill on Highway 281 South acts as a mini-sports complex, with horseshoe courts, a riding arena, a softball field, a sand volleyball court, and a fishing pond. The campground has 18 camping spaces with electricity and water and additional sites for tent camping. | 402/336–3640 | $6 parking after 7 days.

ON THE CALENDAR

MAR.: *St. Patrick's Day Celebration.* On this city's shamrock-painted streets, St. Patrick's Day is a celebration all around the town, with a fun run, parade, Irish dancers, Mulligan stew, kids' games, a fox hunt, dances, and an art show. | 402/336–2355.

Dining

Allison's Restaurant. American. In the heart of downtown O'Neill, this dining destination lets you choose the mood you want. In the café, more casual in setting and menu, you can opt for homemade chicken or ham salad or the prime rib sandwich. For dinner, the "white tablecloth" steak house has rose cloths on the tables, as well as rose draperies, for dining by candlelight on filet, rib eye, or porterhouse steak. There's also a full-service bar. | 432 E. Douglas St. | 402/336–1336 | $7–$15 | AE, D, DC, MC, V.

Karen's Kitchen. American. Among the comfort foods you can order any time of day in this country-style eatery, the hash browns and the homemade bread rate pretty highly with the regulars. | 403 E. Douglas St. | 402/336–2022 | $3–$7 | No credit cards.

Tom's Madison Street Tavern. American. You can step up to the bar and munch on nachos, the house specialty, while watching the game on the big-screen TV in this sports bar decorated with Huskers paraphernalia. | 102 S. Madison St. | 402/336–9999 | $5–$7 | No credit cards.

Lodging

Cross J Ranch Bed and Breakfast. Surrounded by the natural beauty of the prairie with its abundance of wildlife, this B&B 23 mi north of O'Neill has been a working cattle ranch since the 1800s, with the ranchhouse dating to 1916. You can use the living and dining rooms, kitchen, screened-in porch, and fireplace in the two-story guest ranch, and you can board your own horse. Tours and hunting trips are available. Dining room, complimentary Continental breakfast. No pets. | HC 85 | 402/336–2007 or 877/427–6775 | fax 402/336–2007 | rgstewart@elkhorn.net | 2 rooms, 1 suite | $65–$75 | MC, V.

Elms Best Value Inn. This small one-story motel on Highway 20 is 29 mi from Ashfall Fossil Beds State Historical Park and 50 mi from the Fort Randall casino. Truck parking and cold-weather hookups are available. Cable TV. Playground. Pets allowed. | 414 E. Douglas St. | 402/336–3800 or 800/526–9052 or 888/315–2378 | fax 402/336–1419 | 21 rooms | $40–$45 | AE, D, MC, V.

Golden Hotel. This three-story hotel has seen many travelers since it was built in 1913. Renovated in 1998, each room has a different style of decorative theme. The Ashfall Fossil Beds are 29 mi away. Complimentary Continental breakfast. Some kitchenettes. Cable TV, in-room VCRs and movies. Beauty salon. Laundry facilities. Free parking. Some pets allowed. | 406 E. Douglas St. | 402/336–4436 or 800/658–3148 | fax 402/336–3549 | 24 rooms | $29–$50 | AE, D, MC, V.

PLATTSMOUTH

MAP 11, I4

(Nearby towns also listed: Bellevue, Nebraska City, Omaha)

The region where the Platte River flows into the Missouri River was the domain of the Otoe and Pawnee Native Americans until Libias Coon built a bridge in 1846. From then on, the European Americans were in control. In 1853, a trading post opened, and by the 1870s, Plattsmouth was one of the primary livestock shipping points in eastern Nebraska, second only to Schuyler. Still a thriving commercial center, Plattsmouth also remains one of the area's most beautiful spots along the river.

Information: **Plattsmouth Chamber of Commerce** | 136 N. 5th St., Plattsmouth 68048 | 402/296–6021 | fax 402/296–3600 | www.plattsmouth-ne.com.

Attractions

Cass County Historical Society Museum. Permanent exhibits show both the golden age of steamboating on the Missouri River and the importance of the train and farm production since the county was opened for settlement in 1854. The site includes a log cabin, a caboose, and an old school, which can be seen by appointment only. | 646 Main St. | 402/296–4770 | April–Oct., Tues.–Sun. noon–4 | Free.

ON THE CALENDAR

SEPT.: *Korn Karnival.* Since the Depression days of 1932, Plattsmouth's residents have had their own spirit-lifting festival on Main Street every year. Among the many events, you'll find the crowning of a king and queen, an ugly pickup contest, firemen's water fights, parades, art, flowers and crafts shows, and a flea market and farmer's market. | 402/296–6021.

Dining

Golden Dragon. Chinese. You'll find many familiar Oriental dishes, like sweet and sour chicken and cashew chicken, as well as the lesser known crab Rangoon, all served on fine china with traditional motifs. | 828 Chicago Ave. | 402/296–5777 | Closed Sun. and Mon. | $3–$7 | No credit cards.

RED CLOUD

(Nearby town also listed: Hastings)

As you drive into Red Cloud, you can't miss the sign of a plow in silhouette, welcoming all to the prairie. Not just any prairie: Red Cloud was the long-time home of American author Willa Cather, who wrote such classics as *My Antonia, O Pioneers,* and *A Lost Lady* and often described local sites in her books. The Willa Cather Memorial Prairie south of town recalls when this part of the nation was the endless sea of grass where the Pawnee, Omaha, and Otoe lived—even though Red Cloud is named for a Lakota chief.

Information: Red Cloud Chamber of Commerce | 322 N. Webster, Box 327, Red Cloud 68970-2466 | 402/746–3238.

Attractions

Willa Cather State Historic Site. Guided tours of Catherland take you to many places connected to Pulitzer Prize–winning author Willa Cather. Or you can buy carefully prepared maps and find your own way to many of the town's 29 sites, plus another 26 on the "country map." Tours include her childhood home, which remains as she knew it, including the attic room she wallpapered as a teenage girl, and the Pavelka homestead, home of the title character in *My Antonia.* You also can make arrangements to visit Cather's later home, which is privately owned. | 326 N. Webster | 402/746–2653 | www.willacather.org | Tours $5 | House, Mar.–Nov., Mon.–Sat. 8–5, Sun. 1–5; Nov.–March, Mon.–Fri. 8–5, Sat. 9–12, Sun. 1–5; tours, March–Nov., 9:30, 11, 1:30, and 3, Nov.–March, Mon.–Fri. 10:30 and 2, Sat. by appt | 402/746–3183.

Harlan County Reservoir. This large reservoir off Route 136 south of Alma, part of the Harlan Lakes system, has long been a favorite for water sports or hiking. Five campgrounds are administered by the U.S. Army Corps of Engineers. On these waters, people know that spring has come when the white pelicans return. | 308/799–2105 | Free; camping, $6–$14 | All campgrounds, May–Oct.; Hunter Cove, also Nov.

The Theatre of the American West. On the northeast corner of the Harlan Reservoir, this dinner theater off Highway 136 in Republican City follows the old Midwestern circle rep tradition—and often presents comedies from the 1920s. | 308/799–2056 | Show, $10; dinner, $9 | Apr.–Oct., Fri–Sat. dinner 6, show 8; Nov.–Dec., Fri.–Sat. dinner 6:30, show 8; all season, Sun. show 3, dinner after.

ON THE CALENDAR

MAY: *Annual Cather Festival*. This annual conference includes tours of parts of Catherland, a panel discussion, presentation of scholarly papers, and entertainment. Registration fee. | 402/746–2653 | info@willacather.org.

MAY: *Lady Vestey Victorian Festival*. For this citywide celebration, most of the town seems to take on the airs of a century earlier, although activities range from tours of Victorian homes and old-fashioned teas to this century's crafts, driving tours, a carnival, entertainment, a flea market, and a parade. | 402/879–3419.

Dining

The Palace. American. Most regulars come early so they can play on the game room's pinball machines or six pool tables while waiting for an order of steak or prime rib in a dining room decorated with wall mirrors. | 125 W. 4th St. | 402/746–9951 | Closed Sun. | $10–$12 | D, DC, MC, V.

Lodging

Green Acres Motel. Made of brick and wood, this small one-floor motel, 1 mi from downtown Red Cloud and 1 mi from the Willa Cather girlhood home, has its own picnic area. Cable TV. Pets allowed (fee). | N. Hwy. 281 | 402/746–2201 | 17 rooms | $40 | AE, D, MC, V.

ROYAL

(Nearby towns also listed: Neligh, O'Neill)

This small community attracts many visitors because of the big dig northwest of town—the Ashfall Fossil Beds State Historical Park. Most animal remains are discovered in pieces, but at the site of what some have called the "Prairie Pompeii," paleontologists have found complete skeletons of animals who evidently were immediately killed at their waterhole when they were buried in ash from a volcanic eruption some 10 million years ago. Jointly administered by the University of Nebraska and the Nebraska Game and Parks Commission, it is an ongoing exploration that has received national attention—and you are invited to ask questions as the scientists work.

Information: For information about the town and area attractions, including the zoo, contact **Northeast Nebraska Zoo** | 402/893–2002.

Attractions

Ashfall Fossil Beds State Historical Park. You can watch as paleontologists brush away the dirt covering the fossils of animals that roamed here in prehistoric times, and you'll see the skeletons of a herd of barrel-chested rhinos, along with the bones of four-tusked elephants and three-horned deer. From Royal, the dig is about 2 mi west, then 6 mi north of Highway 20. | 402/893–2000 | www.museum.unl.edu or ngp.ngpc.state.ne.us/parks/ashfall.html | Neb. Parks Permit required; $3 | May, Tues.–Sat. 10–4; Memorial Day–Labor Day, Mon.–Sat. 9–5, Sun. 11–5; Labor Day–mid-Oct., Tues.–Sat. 10–4, Sun. 1–4.

Northeast Nebraska Zoo. This five-acre zoo two blocks south of I–20 has a chimpanzee that knows sign language, a miniature horse and donkey, bald eagles, white-tail deer, llamas, mountain lions, snow monkeys, and a Przewalski horse (an ancestor of the modern domestic horse). | 1st and Carson | 402/893–2002 | $3 | Labor Day–Memorial Day, Tues.–Sat. 10–4:30, Sun. noon–4:30; Memorial Day–Labor Day, Mon.–Sat. 9:30–5:30, Sun. noon–5:00.

DEC.: *Winter Light Display.* More than 25,000 lights, from plain colored bulbs to some in fanciful animal shapes, are displayed throughout the Northeast Nebraska Zoo during this 14-day event with music, entertainment, and food. | 402/893–2002.

Dining
Green Gables of Pleasant Valley. American. This restaurant, 4 mi east and 2 mi north of Orchard on Highway 20, about 10 mi from Royal, is in a restored barn with a distinctive burgundy color, green roof, and green gables. The dining room is decorated with antiques, family photos, and vintage memorabilia. Try the homemade pies. | Rte. 1, Orchard | 402/893–5800 | $6–$10 | Closed Nov.–Apr. | No credit cards.

Lodging
Verdigre Bed and Breakfast. Musical instruments decorate the interior, and roses surround the exterior of this two-story Victorian house built around 1900. It's in the village of Verdigres, an area settled by Czech emigrants, off Highway 20. Complimentary Continental breakfast. Some kitchenettes. Cable TV. Playground. No pets. | 305 Third Ave., Verdigres | 402/668–2277 | verdinn@juno.com | 3 rooms, 1 suite | $55 | No credit cards.

ST. PAUL

MAP 11, F3

(Nearby towns also listed: Burwell, Dannebrog, Grand Island)

Settled by Danes in the 1880s, the community was originally known as Athens. When residents discovered that another town had already registered that name, they changed their name to St. Paul. It prospered with the coming of the railroad, but even today, agriculture remains a mainstay of the local economy.

Information: St. Paul Chamber of Commerce | 524 Howard Ave., St. Paul 68873 | 308/754–5558.

Attractions
Gruber House/Baseball Museum/Historical Village. Built in 1908, this restored home especially features local baseball hero Grover Cleveland Alexander because he came from this region, but exhibits also cover four other players in the Baseball Hall of Fame who called Nebraska home. The historical village, across the street from the house, includes four pioneer buildings. | 619 Howard Ave. | 308/754–4454 | museum, $3 | Memorial Day–Labor Day, Baseball Museum, Mon.–Fri. 10–2; other areas, Sun. 1–4, or by appointment.

Happy Jack Chalk Mine. Inside this one-time chalk mine, on Route 11 about 2 mi south of Route 22 in the town of Scotia, you can tour about 6,000 ft of honeycombed caverns. The grounds have picnicking areas, hiking and walking trails, and a good overlook of the valley of the North Loup River. | 308/245–3276 | Grounds free; tours $3.50 | Grounds, daily dawn to dusk; the mine, Memorial Day–Labor Day, daily 10–6, weekends 10–8.

JULY: *Grover Cleveland Alexander Days.* A citywide celebration with a parade, street dance, and car show honors the hometown hero of St. Paul and Elba, Grover Cleveland Alexander, the great pitcher who had 90 shutouts in his 20-year career. | 308/754–5558.

Dining
Sweet Shoppe. American. This small café and bakery serves full meals, but regulars know to save room for the homemade pie. The pan-fried chicken at the Wednesday buffet lunch

is a local favorite, as is the Swiss steak, although kids may prefer the taco bar. | 605 Howard Ave. | 308/754–4900 | $5–$7 | No credit cards.

Lodging

Super 8. On the west edge of town on Highway 281, this two-floor motel built in 1996 is 3 blocks from downtown St. Paul. All rooms have electronic locks. Complimentary Continental breakfast. In-room data ports. Cable TV. Business services. Pets allowed. | 116 Howard Ave. | 308/754–4554 or 800/800–8000 | fax 308/754–5685 | 36 rooms | $37–$53 | AE, D, DC, MC, V.

SCOTTSBLUFF

MAP 11, A3

(Nearby towns also listed: Bayard, Bridgeport, Gering, Kimball)

When Stephen Long passed through Scottsbluff in 1820, he declared it "The Great American Desert." Today, thanks to modern irrigation around the North Platte River, this city 20 mi from the Wyoming border is in the heart of a rich agricultural district sometimes called "the valley of the Nile." The primary crops are potatoes, beans, and sugar beets, and the town considers its sugar beet factory, built by the Western Sugar Company in 1910, a heritage landmark.

The region has many notable attractions, variously listed with Scottsbluff or Gering addresses, since the two towns face each other across the North Platte. For example, the famed Scotts Bluff National Monument, that truly monumental hunk of granite that served as a signpost for westward-bound wagon trains, was named for the larger city although it is 3 mi west of Gering. Most city facilities spell the town's name as one word, while the county and some attractions may use two words, as does the national monument.

Information: Scottsbluff County Tourism Board | 1517 Broadway, No. 104, Scottsbluff 69361 | 308/632–2133 or 800/788–9475 | fax 308/632–7128 | tourism@prairieweb.com | www.scottsbluff.net/chamber.

Attractions

West Nebraska Arts Center. This downtown center in the former Carnegie Library has a number of artists-in-residence as well as rotating exhibits in the visual arts gallery and local and visiting performing arts programs, a children's theater, and an elderhostel program in the summer and fall. | 106 E. 18th St. | 308/632–2226 | Free | Weekdays 9–4, Sat. 1–5.

Lake Minatare State Recreation Area. A stone lighthouse is a photographer's favorite here, but this park 6 mi west and 8 mi north of Scottsbluff off Highway 26 has a full range of water activities around its 2,000-acre lake. | 291040 The Point Rd. | 308/783–2911 | www.ngpc.state.ne.us/parks/minatare.html | Neb. Parks Permit required; camping, $3–$11 | Grounds, mid-Jan.–Sept., daily; camping, May–mid-Sept.; lighthouse, April–Sept. 9, Fri.–Sun. 9–8.

Riverside Zoo. More than 175 specimens of animals, including spider monkeys, mountain lions, and prairie dogs, live here in simulated natural habitats. The Scotts Bluff National Monument is visible across the river. | 1600 S. Beltline Hwy. W | 308/630–6236 | $3.75 | May–Sept., weekdays 9:30–4:30, weekends 9:30–5:30; Oct.–Apr., daily 10:30–4:30.

ON THE CALENDAR

JUNE: *Sugar Valley Rally.* Classic pre-1953 cars follow a 300-mi computerized course around the valley and try to match the ordained perfect times from post to post. | 308/632–2133.

Dining

18th Street Bar & Grille. Casual. A large window separates the sports bar, with its big-screen TV, from the dining area. Try the chicken breast stuffed with feta cheese and spinach or the pinwheel flank steak rolled and stuffed with feta cheese. Kids' menu. | 1722 Broadway | 308/632–6977 | Closed Sun. | $7–15 | MC, V.

El Charrito Restaurant and Lounge. Mexican. The metal building may not look like much, but inside, you'll find Tex-Mex classics such as pork chili, guacamole, and sopaillas, as well as the expected enchiladas, tacos, and burritos. You order at the counter before sitting in the dining room among pictures of western Nebraska's natural landmarks. | 802 21st Ave. | 308/632–3534 | Closed Mon. | $1–$7 | MC, V.

Grampy's Pancake House. Casual. For lazy mornings on the road, you can choose from a variety of pancakes, omelettes, blintzes, and other breakfast treats. | 1802 E. 20th Pl. | 308/632–6906 | $8 | AE, D, MC, V.

Lodging

Barn Anew Bed and Breakfast. In this converted barn, built in 1907, you could be sleeping a few yards from—or even on—paths taken by Oregon Trail wagonmasters as they headed for the Scotts Bluff National Monument, visible from the guest rooms. The dining room has a four-wall mural of life around the barn in the first days of the 20th century, and a mini-museum is housed in a barracks from a 1940s prisoners-of-war camp. Complimentary breakfast. | 170549 County Rd. L | 308/632–8647 | fax 308/632–5518 | barnanew@all-tel.net | www.prairieweb.com/barnanew | 4 rooms | $65–$80 | AE, D, DC, MC, V.

Candlelight Inn. This two-story building is in the downtown area, but plays up a country theme in its interiors. Truck parking and cold-weather hookups are available. Bar, complimentary Continental breakfast. Microwaves, refrigerators. Cable TV. Pool. Exercise equipment. Airport shuttle. | 1822 E. 20th Pl. | 308/635–3751 or 800/424–2305 | fax 308/635–1105 | 56 rooms | $75–$80 | AE, D, DC, MC, V.

Comfort Inn. Renovated in January 2000, this simple two-story building is only 2 mi from Scotts Bluff County Airport and 5 mi from the zoo. The parking area has spaces for trucks and buses. Complimentary Continental breakfast. Some refrigerators. Cable TV. Indoor pool. Hot tub. Exercise equipment. Laundry facilities. | 2018 Delta Dr. | 308/632–7510 or 800/221–2222 | fax 308/632–8495 | 46 rooms, 4 suites | $65 | AE, D, DC, MC, V.

Fontenelle Inn Bed and Breakfast. Built in 1917, this country inn has a veranda on the second floor and a leisure room where you can relax after sightseeing. Lunch, dinner, and box lunches are available. Complimentary Continental breakfast. No pets. No kids. No smoking. | 1424 Fourth Ave. | 308/632–6257 | font-inn@prairieweb.com | 11 rooms, 4 with shared baths | $55–$125 | MC, V.

Holiday Inn Express Hotel and Suites. A mile from downtown, this three-story motel built in 1997 is 21 mi from Chimney Rock and 42 mi from the Agate Fossil Beds National Monument near Harrison. If business keeps you from tromping around any outdoor sites, the exercise room includes a treadmill. Complimentary breakfast bar. Some microwaves, some refrigerators, some in-room hot tubs. Indoor pool. Gym. Video games. Airport shuttle. No pets. | 1821 Frontage Rd. | 308/632–1000, 800/465–4329 | fax 308/632–8777 | checkin@prairieweb.com | 70 rooms, 15 suites | $55–$124 | AE, D, DC, MC, V.

Scottsbluff Inn. This hotel just off Highway 26 has an atrium around the indoor pool and soft rose and blue colorings in many rooms, in keeping with the theme of the hotel's Rose Garden Restaurant. Restaurant, bar. In-room data ports. Cable TV. Indoor pool. Laundry services. Airport shuttle. | 1901 21st Ave. | 308/635–3111 or 800/597–3111 | www.scottsbluffinn.com | 138 rooms | $49–$99 | AE, D, MC, V.

SIDNEY

MAP 11, B3

(Nearby towns also listed: Bridgeport, Kimball, Ogallala)

Just say the word "Sidney" anywhere within 150 mi of this small town and you'll almost always see recognition in people's eyes as they respond: "Yeah, that's where Cabela's is." Cabela's is the great sportsman's—and sportswoman's—outfitter that draws shoppers from throughout a 20-state region. Even if you're not in the market for camping gear or fishing equipment, you might want to visit the huge wood-and-glass store to see the hundreds of fish in huge tanks and the displays of animals mounted on the walls.

Sidney's own rich history is largely a product of the settlers' movement west to the plains and beyond. The Oregon, California, and Santa Fe trails passed through here, as well as the Pony Express. After the Union Pacific pushed through here in 1867, it became a major jumping-off point for the Sidney-to-Deadwood Trail during the Black Hills Gold Rush of the mid-1870s.

Information: Cheyenne County Chamber of Commerce | 740 Illinois, Sidney 69162 | 308/254–5851 or 800/421–4769 | fax 308/254–3081 | ccchamber@hamilton.net | www.sidney-nebraska.com.

Attractions

Fort Sidney Museum and Post Commander's Home. The residence of the army post commander is one of the few buildings left from the Army garrison built here in the 1880s to protect railroad crews. The museum, in the old officers' quarters, tells the stories of the fort's history on the Sidney-to-Deadwood Trail leading to the goldfields in the Black Hills. | 1153 6th Ave. | 308/254–2150 | Free | Memorial Day–Labor Day, daily 9–11, 1–3.

Cabela's. It's known as the nation's largest sporting outfitter, and, indeed, it seems to have just about everything one could want for camping, fishing, hunting, and other outdoor activities, with good buys, too, in the Bargain Cave. | 115 Cabela Dr. | 308/254–5505 | Free | Mon.–Sat. 8–8, Sun. 10–6.

Legion Park and Living Memorial Gardens. Nebraska's tallest flagpole makes a natural guidepost to this site that includes a railroad monument as well as the gardens and the War Memorial. | 10th St. and Toledo St. | 308/254–3307 | Daily, dawn to dusk | Free.

ON THE CALENDAR

JULY: *Cabela's Sidewalk Sale.* This is a bargain hunter's bonanza, with items throughout the store moved out to the parking lot for the annual event. | 115 Cabela Dr. | 308/254–7889.

JULY: *July 4th Ice Cream Social.* In the days before TV and jet planes, ice cream socials were summer events in small towns across America, and Sidney re-creates all that old feeling with this warm-hearted holiday get-together at Legion Park. | 308/254–4859 or 308/254–5851.

OCT.: *Oktoberfest.* There's continuous free entertainment at this Nebraska version of the traditional German festival, with booths, exhibits, dances, and a 10K run. | 308/254–5851.

Dining

Country Kettle. American. Homemade roast beef and chicken-fried steak are the specialties in this popular hometown restaurant, where oak wood furnishings and pictures of outdoor scenes create a low-key country feeling. Kids' menu. | 1144 Illinois St. | 308/254–2744 | $7 | MC, V.

Virgil's Mexican Food. Mexican. The familiar sombreros scattered through a red, green, and blue color scheme make this restaurant a bright and comfortable place to eat up the tostada deluxe. | 2600 11th Ave. | 308/254–2524 | Closed Sun. | $6 | No credit cards.

Lodging

Comfort Inn. When you're ready to go, this small hotel has courtesy cars to the Sidney airport, 2 mi away, and to Cabela's Outfitters—which is just an easy-striding third of a mile away. It is also about 4 mi from Fort Sidney Museum and 6 mi from the Cheyenne County Fairgrounds. Truck parking and cold-weather hookups are available. Complimentary Continental breakfast. In-room data pots. Cable TV. Hot tub. Laundry facilities. No pets. | 730 E. Jennifer La. | 308/254–5011 or 800/228–5150 | fax 308/254–5122 | 55 rooms | $65 | AE, D, DC, MC, V.

Days Inn. This two-story motel on I–80 uses its architecture to dramatic effect in full-height wall of windows at one end of the indoor pool, so the space always seems light and airy, no matter how blustery the outside world might be. The parking area includes spaces for trucks and RVs. Complimentary Continental breakfast. In-room data ports, some refrigerators. Cable TV. Indoor pool. Hot tub. Exercise equipment. Laundry facilities. Business services. | 3042 Silverberg Dr. | 308/254–2121 | 47 rooms | $64–$79 | AE, D, DC, MC, V.

Holiday Inn and Conference Center With many businesspersons here for meetings, this two-story motel built in 1996, only 4½ mi from downtown, has two phones in every room, plus irons, hair dryers, and coffeemakers—and its own putting and chipping greens. Restaurant, bar. In-room data ports, some in-room hot tubs. Cable TV. Indoor pool. Hot tub. Gym. Video games. Laundry services. Airport shuttle. | 664 Chase Blvd. | 308/254–2000, 800/ 647–4363 | fax 308/254–0970 | 85 rooms | $89–$130 | AE, D, DC, MC, V.

Super 8. Renovated in 2000, this two-story motel with the blue-gray roof has complimentary weekday newspapers for you to take to the table in the breakfast room. Truck and RV spaces are available. In-room dataports. Refrigerators. Cable TV. | 2115 Illinois St. | 308/254–2081 or 800/800–8000 | fax 308/254–2236 | 59 rooms | $48–$76 | AE, D, DC, MC, V.

SOUTH SIOUX CITY

MAP 11, H2

(Nearby towns also listed: Crofton, Bancroft, Wayne)

South Sioux City was known as the "wildest little town on the Missouri" in frontier times, and the Missouri River still frames much of the city's life. It is known now as a regional trade, convention, and recreational area, although many of the visitor attractions—from museums to casinos—lie in the larger Sioux City, Iowa, so close that the two towns can see each other's lights reflect off the water.

Information: South Sioux City Chamber of Commerce | 2700 Dakota Ave., South Sioux City 68776 | 402/494–1626 or 800/793–6327 | fax 402/494–5010. **South Sioux City Convention and Visitor's Bureau** | 2700 Dakota Ave., South Sioux City 68776 | 402/494– 1307 or 800/793–6327 | fax 402/494–5010 | cvb@sscdc.net | www.sscdc.net.

Attractions

Ponca State Park. Overlooking an untamed stretch of the Missouri, this park, 2 mi north of Ponca on S-26E off Route 12, has a lake and many recreational facilities, including a modern pool, but its 17 mi of hiking trails are especially prized for viewing birds like ruby-throated hummingbirds. There are 14 cabins as well as campgrounds, and the Highland Oaks public golf course is on its southern boundary. | 402/755–2284 | poncasp@ngpc.state.ne.us | www.ngpc.state.ne.us/parks/ponca.html | Neb. Parks Permit required; camping, $8–$11, two-night minimum | Daily dawn to dusk.

Tarbox Hollow Living Prairie. At this working buffalo ranch, 1 mi south of Highway 20 between mile markers 401 and 402, you can take a covered wagon to see bison grazing on a 15-acre tract of virgin prairie and watch demonstrations of spinning and other home arts in a general store. | 57957 871st Rd., Dixon | 402/584–2337 | $5 | May–Sept., Wed.–Sat. | reservations required.

ON THE CALENDAR

AUG.: *Greater Siouxland Fair and Rodeo.* This week-long annual event is both a sporting event for rodeo fans and a fair where everyone can enjoy a parade, musical entertainment, a carnival, and lots of food. | 402/494–5522.

Dining

Bluestem. Contemporary. On top of some of the newest waves in cooking, the chef here creates such signature dishes as molasses-grilled salmon with mashed sweet potatoes or duck spring rolls made fresh with local ingredients. It's in the Sioux City (Iowa) historic district, 100 yards from South Sioux City, and weekends feature live music and malt scotches and martinis, the house specialties. | 1012 4th St. | 712/279–8060 | Closed Sun. | $15 | AE, D, MC, V.

Kahill's. Steak. The river views are most dramatic at night, as this restaurant with mahogany wood furnishings opens up to a full panorama of rippling water and city lights across the way. Porterhouse is a specialty of this upscale dining option in the Marina Inn. Kids' menu. | 4th and B Sts. | 402/494–5025 | $10–$50 | AE, D, DC, MC, V.

USEFUL EXTRAS YOU MAY WANT TO PACK

- ❏ Adapters, converter
- ❏ Alarm clock
- ❏ Batteries
- ❏ Binoculars
- ❏ Blankets, pillows, sleeping bags
- ❏ Books and magazines
- ❏ Bottled water, soda
- ❏ Calculator
- ❏ Camera, lenses, film
- ❏ Can/bottle opener
- ❏ Cassette tapes, CDs, and players
- ❏ Cell phone
- ❏ Change purse with $10 in quarters, dimes, and nickels for tollbooths and parking meters
- ❏ Citronella candle
- ❏ Compass
- ❏ Earplugs
- ❏ Flashlight
- ❏ Folding chairs
- ❏ Guidebooks
- ❏ Luggage tags and locks
- ❏ Maps
- ❏ Matches
- ❏ Money belt
- ❏ Pens, pencils
- ❏ Plastic trash bags
- ❏ Portable TV
- ❏ Radio
- ❏ Self-seal plastic bags
- ❏ Snack foods
- ❏ Spare set of keys, not carried by driver
- ❏ Travel iron
- ❏ Travel journal
- ❏ Video recorder, blank tapes
- ❏ Water bottle
- ❏ Water-purification tablets

Karousel and the Main Event. American. Carousel horses guard the entrance of the Karousel, which serves breakfast and lunch. The Main Event is the steak house, which specializes in prime rib, with salad dressings that are considered the best in the area. | 1501 Dakota Ave. | 402/494–2048 | Closed Mon. | $14 | AE, D, MC, V.

Lodging

Best Value Inn. You'll know this single-story motel by the Victorian-style gazebo, lacy and white on a patch of green lawn at the entrance, right beside the pool. Cold-weather hookups are available. Restaurant, lounge. In-room dataports. Cable TV. Pool. Laundry facilities. No pets. No smoking. | 1201 1st Ave. | 402/494–2021 or 888/315–2378 | fax 402/494–5998 | 52 rooms | $45–$51 | AE, D, DC, MC, V.

Econo Lodge. This two-story motel is about 4 mi from Historic 4th Street across the river in Sioux City and 6 mi from Sioux City Museum. Truck parking and cold-weather hookups are available. Complimentary Continental breakfast. Cable TV. Pool. Hot tub, sauna. Laundry facilities. Business services. | 4402 Dakota Ave. | 402/494–4114 or 800/553–2666 | fax 402/494–4114 | 60 rooms | $55–$61 | AE, D, DC, MC, V.

English Mansion Bed and Breakfast. Nine original hand-painted murals of flora and cherubs decorate the ceiling of this 1894 Colonial Revival mansion, home of the Stackerl and English families for four generations. The mansion has been restored, complete with period furnishings, and is listed in the National Register. Complimentary Continental breakfast. In-room data ports, microwaves, refrigerators. Cable TV. Airport shuttle. | 1525 Douglas St. | 712/277–1386 | fax fax 712/255–1346 | www.siouxland.com/theenglishmansion/ | 4 rooms, 2 with shared bath | $90–$110 | AE.

Flamingo Inn. Like most of South Sioux City, this hotel is only a short drive from the boating facilities and events on the river. Historic 4th Street, across the bridge in Sioux City, Iowa, is less than 4 mi away. Complimentary Continental breakfast. In-room data ports. Cable TV. Pool. Hot tubs, sauna. Exercise equipment. Laundry services. Pets allowed. | 2829 Dakota Ave. | 402/494–8874 | 80 rooms | $40–$75 | AE, D, DC, MC, V.

Marina Inn. Most rooms in this two-building complex have patios or balconies, giving you a 24-hour view of river and Iowa skyline. Inside, you'll find an exercise room and indoor pool. Truck parking and cold-weather hookups are available. Restaurant, bar, room service. Cable TV. Indoor pool. Hot tub, sauna. Exercise equipment. Airport shuttle. Pets allowed. | 4th and B Sts. | 402/494–4000 or 800/798–7980 | fax 402/494–2550 | 182 rooms | $89–$104 | AE, D, DC, MC, V.

Travelodge. This two-story motel renovated in 1990 is a mile from downtown, close to the Missouri River and about two blocks from the convention center and a keno casino. There's in-room coffee, and a morning newspaper awaits in the lobby. Truck/RV parking spaces are available. Cable TV. Business services. Pets allowed. | 400 Dakota Ave. | 402/494–3046 or 800/578–7878 | fax 402/494–8299 | 61 rooms | $43–$48 | AE, D, DC, MC, V.

THEDFORD

MAP 11, D2

(Nearby towns also listed: North Platte, Valentine)

Homesteaders settled the area around Thedford, and it remains a farming and ranching town, through and through. Just east of Thedford is the 90,000-acre Nebraska National Forest, established under the conservation-promoting policies of President Theodore Roosevelt in the first years of the 20th century.

Information: Cherry County Visitors Committee | Box 201, 329 S. Main St., Valentine 69201 | 402/376–2969 or 800/658–4024.

Attractions

The Thedford Art Gallery. Many of the local artists showing their works at this regional center emphasize rustic Western themes from the area around them. If you're an artist, talk to the gallery about adding your art to its lineup. | 509 Court St. | 308/645–2586. | Free | Daily 9–5.

Nebraska National Forest–Bessey Ranger District. The state's only fire tower doubles as a 60-ft-high observation post at this preserve 17 mi east of Thedford on State Spur 86B, off Route 2 west of Halsey. In the largest hand-planted forest in the country, this region has fee camping, tennis courts, a swimming pool, and 12 mi of trails. | 308/533–2257 | Grounds, free; pool, $2 | Grounds, daily, dawn to dusk; pool, June–Aug.

ON THE CALENDAR

AUG.: *Thomas County Fair.* This four-day event on the courthouse lawn has a number of events just for kids, including a rodeo and a fashion show of clothes the kids made themselves, as well as craft and vegetable exhibits, a parade, musical entertainment, and plays. | 308/645–2586.

Dining

Stub's Fine Dining. American. A familiar downhome kind of place, this casual eatery has fried chicken, pork chops, shrimp, and fish. | East Hwy. 2 | 308/645–2642 | $8 | MC, V.

Lodging

Rodeway Inn. This modern, two-floor motel 1 mi east of Thedford uses part of its lobby to exhibit local artists' paintings, many of them depicting wildlife or local scenes. Complimentary Continental breakfast. In-room data ports, some microwaves, some refrigerators. Cable TV. Hot tubs. Laundry services. Pets allowed (fee). | Rte. 2 and Hwy. 83 | 308/645–2284 | fax 308/645–2630 | rodeway@neb/sandhills.net | 42 rooms | $46–$67 | AE, D, DC, MC, V.

VALENTINE

MAP 11, D1

(Nearby towns also listed: O'Neill, Thedford)

This city on the Niobrara River is much more than "Heart City," as inhabitants occasionally refer to their home. It is the county seat of Cherry County—the largest county in Nebraska and a region larger than several eastern states. Outdoors enthusiasts come here, to the northern edge of Nebraska's Sandhills, to canoe or raft on the Niobrara, to visit Smith Falls, the state's highest waterfall, or to hike on one of the completed sections of the Cowboy Trail. The view from an old railroad trestle bridge 150 ft above the Niobrara about 2 mi east of Valentine is consistently praised as the most beautiful on the trail.

Valentine is not far from the remains of the historic Fort Niobrara, now a wildlife refuge. Like Fort Robinson, Fort Niobrara was one of the outposts where the famed "Buffalo Soldiers," the African-American troops of the 9th and 10th Cavalry units, were assigned during the final days of the Plains Indian Wars.

Information: Valentine Chamber of Commerce/Cherry County Visitor's Committee | Box 201, 329 S. Main St., Valentine 69201 | 402/376–2969 or 800/658–4024 | fax 402/ 376–2688 | tourism@valentine-ne.com | www.valentine-ne.com.

Attractions

Cherry County Historical Museum. Along with the restored 1882 log cabin on its grounds, the museum has rooms filled with artifacts from Fort Niobrara and displays on the lives of the area's Native Americans and the early days of settlers, ranchers, and the town. | Main St. and Hwy. 20 | 402/376–2015 | $1 | Memorial Day–Labor Day, Wed.–Sun. 1–6.

Arthur Bowring Sandhills Ranch State Historical Park. When Eva Bowring, Nebraska's only female U.S. Senator, died in 1985, she left instructions that this 7,202-acre ranch be preserved as a working cattle ranch open to the public. Besides seeing the outbuildings and cattle, you also can view the extensive collection of glassware and china she amassed in her 93 years. The park is about 60 mi west of Valentine, 1½ mi north and 2 mi east of Merriman on a gravel road off Route 61. | 308/684–3428 | www.state.ne.us/parks/bowring.html | Neb. Parks Permit required | Grounds, buildings, Memorial Day–Labor Day, daily 8–5; Labor Day–Memorial Day, daily 9–5; tours by appointment.

Fort Niobrara National Wildlife Refuge. Set against a backdrop of prairie and pine-laden hills, the elk and buffalo roam and the longhorns graze as visitors drive through the 19,000-acre preserve where more than 200 species of birds have been counted. Hiking trails on the grounds of this former fort, 5 mi east of Valentine on Route 12, lead to Fort Falls, one of many waterfalls that tumble into the Niobrara. | 402/376–3789 | Free; boat launch, $2 per vessel | Memorial Day–Labor Day, daily 8–4:30; Labor Day–Memorial Day, weekdays 8–4:30.

Merritt Reservoir State Recreation Area. You'll find boating, swimming, picnicking, and primitive camping areas along the 3,000-acre reservoir, which blocks the Snake River 26 mi south of Valentine off Highway 97. A few miles north is the state's largest waterfall, Snake River Falls, which is on private land but open for viewing for a small fee. There is no electricity. | 402/376–3437 | www.state.ne.us/parks/merritt.html | Neb. Parks Permit required; camping, $3 | Daily.

Niobrara River. Consistently rated as one of the top 10 canoeing rivers in the United States, the gently flowing, shallow Niobrara passes through five ecosystems within a 30-mi stretch. Along the way, you can catch sight of meadows, towering bluffs, and several waterfalls. About a dozen outfitters provide canoes, tubes, camping equipment, and drop-off/pickup services.

Some of the outfitters are: **Graham Canoe Outfitters** (402/376–3708 or 800/322–3708), **Supertubes** (402/376–2956), **Little Outlaw Canoes/Tubes** (800/238–1867), and **Sunny Book Camp and Outfitters** (402/376–1887).

Samuel R. McKelvie National Forest. Despite its name, this 115,703-acre preserve is mostly grasslands where you may chance upon antelopes, white-tail deer, grouse, or prairie chickens. The Steer Creek Campground has 23 campsites. The best route from Valentine is to take Highway 20 west to the center of Nenzel, then go south on S-16F for 10 mi. | 402/823–1154 | www.fs.fed.us/r2/nebraska | Free | Daily dawn to dusk.

Smith Falls State Park. A pedestrian bridge leads across the Niobrara to the site where Smith Falls cascades 70 ft from a glacier-formed spring. You then can follow a boardwalk through the steep valley, 15 mi northeast of Valentine on Route 12, for other views of the scenic 200-acre park. The park has primitive camping and is an access point for canoeing and tubing on the Niobrara. | 402/376–1306 | ngpc.state.ne.us/parks/smith.html | $2.50, Neb. Parks Permit also required; camping, $3 | Daily.

The Valentine National Wildlife Refuge. Established in 1935, this 71,500-acre refuge in the middle of the Sandhills has dozens of lakes and more than 260 species of birds and other wildlife. Hunting for upland game, deer, and waterfowl is allowed, and observation blinds are provided in spring. The refuge is 25 mi south of Valentine on Highway 83 and 5 mi east on Highway 12. | Hwy. 12 | 402/376–3789 or 800/658–4024 | www.r6.fws.gov/refuges/valentin/valentin.htm | Free | Daily.

White Horse Ranch. In the 1940s, herds of beautiful white horses were trained here to perform in Thompson's White Horse Troupe. At its height of the troupe's popularity, as many as 10,000 people attended its performances near the ranch. The ranch is now a National Historic Site and Museum with barns and a general store, campsites, and fishing areas. Or you can bring your own horse for trail rides. The ranch is 5 mi south of Naper on Route 12, then 2 mi east. | 402/832–5560 | Free; camping, $5–$10 | Mon., Thurs.–Sat. 9–6; Sun. 1–6; closed Tues., Wed.

ON THE CALENDAR

JUL.: *Nebraska Star Party*. Astronomy enthusiasts from around the country gather to star gaze at Merritt Reservoir State Recreation Area. | Neb. Parks Permit required | 402/376–3437.

AUG.: *Annual National Country Music Festival*. East City Park comes alive with the sounds of eight categories of music competition for fiddlers, pickers, singers, and vocal groups, plus a Nebraska auctioneers' calling competition and entries in a songwriters' contest. The program also includes square dancing, a car show, a horseshoe tournament, and free pancakes Saturday in the park. You'll need to bring your own lawn chairs. | 402/387–2844 or 387–2724.

OCT.: *Old West Days and Poetry Gathering*. Besides cowboy poets, this frontier-oriented festival includes a bit-and-spur show, melodrama, a trail ride, a mountain man rendezvous, a powwow, a quilt show, and musical jamboree, with events in the high school auditorium and at the fairgrounds. | 800/658–4024.

Dining

Bunkhouse Restaurant and Lounge. American. The name does fit here, for the menu at this family-style eatery is as solidly American as a cowboy's Stetson. For lunch, try the Indian taco or hamburger steak sandwich; for dinner, most regulars prefer the all-American T-bone, rib-eye, or Swiss steaks. Kids' menu. | 109 W. Highway 20 | 402/376–1609 | $5–$10 | MC, V.

Jordan's. American. Jordan's has a sports bar, small family-style café, and intimate steakhouse, and diners arrive in everything from Cadillacs to pickup trucks pulling horse trailers, but you'll get home-style food, as well as prime rib and steaks, no matter where you sit. | E. Highway 20 | 402/376–1255 | Steakhouse closed Sun., Mon. | $3–$15 | AE, D, MC, V.

Mean Gene's. Casual. Every small town needs a place like this, a casual, familiar hometown spot where you can sit and have chicken or pizza in the restaurant or pick up a take-out to carry home or along on an outing. | 101 W. Hwy. 20 | 402/376–2283 | $3–$7 | No credit cards.

Peppermill. Steakhouse. Built in the 1900s, the Peppermill was formerly known as the Jordan Hotel Restaurant. It is known for aged Nebraska beef, jumbo Gulf shrimp, Cordon Bleu rice pilaf, and fried chicken. There are specials for lunch and dinner, a large dessert selection, and summer entertainment in an outdoor beer garden. | 112 N. Main St. | 402/376–1440 | $5–$10 | AE, D, MC, V.

Snake Falls Sportsman Club Restaurant. American. This rustic café with pine-paneled walls quite possibly has the most spectacular dining view anywhere in Nebraska—it looks out to the rocky, pine-flecked canyon of the Snake River. You can walk over and, for a small fee, see Nebraska's largest waterfall. The restaurant is a favorite for its breakfast lineup, as well as its hamburgers, chicken, steaks, and pizza. | 402/376–3667 | Reservations essential | Closed Tues., Wed. | $5–$17 | No credit cards.

Lodging

Comfort Inn. Take your choice (or maybe try both): At this small motel in the sandhills, you are 4 mi from the outdoor activities of the Fort Niobrara National Wildlife Refuge or 9 mi from the indoor excitement of the Rosebud Casino. Built in 1996, it has irons in every room and some in-room hot tubs, plus bus and truck parking. Complimentary Continental breakfast. In-room data ports. Cable TV. Indoor pool. Hot tub. Exercise equipment. Laundry facilities. | 101 Main St. | 402/376–3300 or 800/478–3307 | fax 402/376–2349 | 50 rooms, 5 suites | $65–$70 | AE, D, DC, MC, V.

Dunes. If you want the shelter of a motel roof at night but want to stay close to outdoor recreation, this one-story motel is near canoeing points on the Niobrara as well as the other hiking and fishing sites and wildlife refuges that so mark this region. Cable TV. | 340 U.S. 20 E | 402/376–3131 | 24 rooms | $27–$35 | AE, D, MC, V.

Heartland Elk Guest Ranch. In these 800-square-ft timbered log cabins, you awaken to the sounds of birds in the surrounding trees, only steps from paths leading to the rim of a canyon overlooking the Niobrara. Each cabin has a gas fireplace to take the edge off chilly days or nights, and RV hookups are available. The ranch, which also has some individual rooms for rent, is 17 mi east of Valentine, 2½ mi south of Route 12. Complimentary breakfast. Kitchenettes. No room phones. No smoking. | HC 13 | 402/376–1124 | fax 402/376–2553 | heartland@valentine-ne.com | 4 cabins | $99–$289 | MC, V.

Holiday Inn Express Hotel and Suites. Only a couple of years old, this pale-colored three-story hotel is on Highway 20 about a mile east of downtown. There's a fireplace in the breakfast bar area, some suites have whirlpools, and if you make arrangements in advance, the hotel will help you secure a recommended baby-sitter if you want a day at the Rosebud Casino, 10 mi away, or Smith Falls, 20 mi away. Complimentary Continental breakfast. Some kitchenettes. Cable TV. Indoor pool, hot tubs. Exercise equipment. Business services. No pets. | 802 U.S. 20E | 402/376–3000 or 877/376–3003 | fax 402/376–1133 | 41 rooms, 19 suites | $59–$105 | AE, D, DC, MC, V.

Lord Ranch Resort. From Canada geese to tiny lizards, you can see all types of wildlife at this family-owned, working Sandhills cattle ranch 1 mi east of Route 16B. The cabins are private, all decorated in a Southwestern motif. For outdoor sports, it is 15 mi east of Merritt Reservoir. Kitchenettes, microwaves, refrigerators. | HC 47, Box 41 | 402/376–2475 or 800/270–0181 | fax 402/376–2475 | lordd@inetnebr.com | www.valentine-ne.com/lord | 5 cabins | $69 | No credit cards.

Lovejoy Ranch Bed and Breakfast. You'll see panoramic views in all directions from this B&B with a geodesic dome creating the front part of the structure. Guest rooms are decorated in varying themes, one with a brass bed, and another with a sleigh-style bed, both with lots of filmy drapery. The ranch is 17 mi south of Valentine, 1 mi east of Highway 83. Complimentary breakfast. | HC 37 | 402/376–2668 or 800/672–5098 | lodging@lovejoyranch.com | 2 rooms, 1 suite | $75–$95 | MC, V.

Motel Raine. In the heart of Valentine off Highway 20, Motel Raine was built in the 1960s and renovated in the '90s. Truck parking and cold-weather hookups are available. Cable TV. Airport shuttle. Some pets allowed. | U.S. 20W | 402/376–2030 or 800/999–3066 | fax 402/376–1956 | 34 rooms | $46–$56 | AE, D, DC, MC, V.

Rosebud Casino Quality Inn. This casino hotel, decorated with woven wall hangings and furnishings in Southwestern and Native American styles, is on the Rosebud Sioux Reservation, where more than 30 wacipis, or powwows, are held every year. The hotel is in South Dakota, 9 mi north of Valentine on Highway 83, and about 15 mi from the water sports of the Niobrara. Restaurant, complimentary Continental breakfast. Cable TV. Indoor pool. Hot tubs. Exercise equipment. No pets. | Hwy. 83, Mission, SD | 605/378–3360 | fax 605/378–3367 | mktg@rosebudcasino.com | www.rosebudcasino.com/info/contact.html | 60 rooms | $80 | MC, V.

Super 8. This one-story motel with dark detailing against a pale exterior, at the junction of Highways 20 and 83, is 15 mi from Smith Falls and the tubing and rafting on the Niobrara, and 3 blocks from downtown Valentine and the fun of the country music festival. Complimentary Continental breakfast. Cable TV. Pool. Hot tubs, sauna. Laundry services. Business services. Pets allowed. | 223 E. Hwy. 20 | 402/376–1250 or 800/800–8000 | fax 402/376–1211 | 60 rooms | $70 | AE, D, MC, V.

Trade Winds Lodge. For guests who've had a successful day on lake or river, this quiet country lodge a mile southeast of Highways 20 and 83 on HC 37 has indoor fish-cleaning and freezer facilities. After the chores, there's a pool to try—and recliners and in-room movies for relaxing. Truck parking and cold-weather hookups are available. Cable TV. Pool. Airport shuttle. Pets allowed. | 402/376–1600 or 800/341–8000 or 888/315–3651 | fax 402/376–3651 | 32 rooms | $38–$61 | AE, D, DC, MC, V.

WAYNE

MAP 11, H2

(Nearby towns also listed: Bancroft, Norfolk, South Sioux City)

Wayne is home to Wayne Industries and its subsidiaries and to Wayne State Teacher's College, but it's best known for the Annual Wayne Chicken Show, which is billed as "Cheep fun for the family. Take the whole brood." The celebration started as an arts and crafts festival, but has grown and grown, especially since being featured on "The Tonight Show."

Information: **Wayne Area Chamber of Commerce** | 108 W. 3rd St., Wayne 68787 | 402/375–2240 | fax 402/375–2246 | chamber@bloomnet.com | www.waynene.net.

Attractions

Fred G. Dale Planetarium. The centerpiece of the region's only planetarium, a teaching facility for Wayne State College, is laser equipment that can project the exact position of the stars, moon, and planets on any day in history. Some shows are given for the public—call for dates and times. | 1111 Main St. | 402/375–7343 or 402/375–7329 | Free.

ON THE CALENDAR

JULY: *Chicken Show.* This is the town's big event, with an antiques, crafts, and quilt show, a parade, games, contests, variety shows, chicken-feeding, an omelet breakfast, and the National Cluck-Off, all in Bressler Park downtown. | 402/375–2240.
AUG.: *Wayne County Fair.* You'll find the carnival rides, exhibits, and displays found at many county fairs, but at this fair about a mile east of Wayne, you also can whoop at a demolition derby and tractor pulls. | 402/375–3462.

Dining

Geno's Steak House. Steak. Cherubs and baskets filled with coffee beans decorate the walls of this cheerful restaurant where you can enjoy an 8-oz hand-cut fillet or hand-breaded deep-fried shrimp. | 121 W. 1st St. | 402/375–4774 | Closed Mon. | $10–14 | AE, D, MC, V.

Lodging

Super 8. This two-floor motel with timber-look accents against a pale exterior is 1 mi from downtown Wayne. If you wear yourself out with the Chicken Show activities, you can always try the in-room movies. Complimentary Continental breakfast. Cable TV. No pets. | 610 Tomar Dr. | 402/375–4898 or 800/800–8000 | fax 402/375–4898 | 40 rooms | $42–$57 | AE, D, DC, MC, V.

WEST POINT

MAP 11, H2

(Nearby towns also listed: Bancroft, Blair, Norfolk)

In the heart of a major ranching region, West Point, the county seat of Cuming County, lies along the Elkhorn River at the intersection of Routes 272 and 32. The community was founded by John Neligh, who opened a sawmill and brickyard in 1857 and hoped to start a commercial center, but the town's economy turned to agriculture and manufacturing, which remain its staples today.

Information: **West Point Chamber of Commerce** | 500 S. Main, Box 125, West Point 68788 | 402/372–2981 | fax 402/372–5832.

Attractions

Cuming County Historical Museum. Part of the Chicago Northwestern rail depot at the Cuming County Fair Grounds on Park Street, the museum complex has a Union Pacific caboose, a country church, and a one-room schoolhouse, as well as antique agricultural equipment. | 402/372–3401 | Free | Call for hours.

ON THE CALENDAR

SEPT.: *Last Fling Til Spring.* With nearly 700 vehicles on display, this annual one-day car show in downtown West Point draws enthusiasts from all over the United States to see all types of horseless carriages, from classic automobiles to modern cars, as well as many models of motorcycles. | 402/372–3390 | free.

Dining

Chef's Corner. Casual. From the local farmer to the business person to the neighbors across the road, you can meet all types of people while eating the chef burger, roasted chicken, or one of the Mexican entrees here. | 243 S. Lincoln St. | 402/372–5717 | www.wpnews.com/brochure6.htm | $8 | No credit cards.

Lodging

Benson Bed and Breakfast. This 1905 railroad rooming house in Oakland, 14 mi east of West Point, was turned into a B&B after a 1993 renovation. For quiet relaxing, there is an enclosed sun porch, plus a whirlpool for two. Complimentary breakfast. | 402 N. Oakland Ave., Oakland | Sanderson@genesisnet.net | 3 rooms | $52–$60 | D.

Von Schweigert Haus Bed and Breakfast. You can sink into antique beds piled high with feather mattresses and relax in the claw-foot bathtub in this restored 1895 house surrounded by trees and a wraparound yard. Complimentary breakfast. | 606 N. Lincoln | 402/372–5945 | fax 402/372–5945 | 3 rooms with shared bath | $50–$65 | No credit cards.

WILBER

MAP 11, H4

(Nearby towns also listed: Beatrice, Fairbury, Lincoln)

Czech emigrants began moving to Nebraska in the late 1800s, drawn by the homestead laws' promises of land. Even today, about 65 percent of the Wilber population is of Czech descent, and they have kept their culture alive—and turned the small town 36 mi west of Lincoln into a tourist mecca—with brightly painted murals on brick walls of businesses, a Czech Museum, and especially the annual Czech Festival that often brings 30,000 people to this town of 1,600.

Information: **Wilber Chamber of Commerce** | 101 W. 3rd, Box 1164, Wilber 68465 | 402/821–2732 or 888/494–5237 | www.ci.wilber.ne.us.

Attractions

Wilber Czech Museum. In a town where Czech symbols shine from every street, the museum emphasizes the home front, with replicas of early immigrant houses and exhibits of the dishes, dresses, dolls, and laces those early settlers brought with them to help carve out a new life in the American heartland. | 201 3rd St. | 402/821–2183 or 402/821–2485 for appointments | Free | Daily 1–4.

ON THE CALENDAR

AUG.: *National Czech Festival.* Just about everyone—and every public site—in town seems to get involved in this three-day festival the first weekend in August. Events range from barrel water fights by the volunteer fire department to all manner of dances, clogging, and other entertainment to serious lectures on the Czech heritage. | 888/494–5237.

Dining

Yostie's Drive In. Casual. Pictures of apples, chickens, and farm scenes set the scene in this country-style eatery where you'll find such menu choices as tacos, chicken fajitas, or chef's salad. | 511 S. Main | 402/821–2646 | $3–$7 | No credit cards.

Lodging

Hotel Wilber. Built in 1895, the old hotel, now on the National Register of Historic Places, has retained the highly polished oak woodwork and pressed tin ceiling of its late Victorian birth and filled the lacy-curtained guest rooms with antiques of the period. Outside, old-style lamp posts glow in a shaded garden. Restaurant. Cable TV. No room phones. No smoking. | 203 S. Wilson Ave. | 402/821–2020 or 888/332–1937 | fax 402/821–2020 | 11 rooms | $45–$55 | MC, V.

YORK

MAP 11, G4

(Nearby towns also listed: Columbus, Grand Island, Hastings, Lincoln)

The South Platte Land Company brought settlers to the area in 1869, many of them German emigrants, and they named the new town York after York, England, and the Pennsylvania town where some of them had previously lived. Along the "Nebraska City cut-off" of the Oregon Trail, York quickly became a trading center with such early industry as a brick-and-tile plant, plus a public library founded by the Women's Club in 1885 and York College, established in 1890. Today, it is a bustling town with industry tied to the agricultural production of the region and a highly visible 121-ft-high water tower painted to look like a hot air balloon.

Information: **York Area Chamber of Commerce** | 116 S. Lincoln Ave., Ste. 1, York 68467 | 402/362–5531 or 888/733–9675 | fax 402/362–5953 | yco3219@navix.net | www.yorkchamber.org.

Attractions

Anna Bemis Palmer Museum. This museum of the Daughters of the American Revolution, in the York Community Center, has several period rooms as well as other historical displays. | 211 E. 7th St. | 402/363–2630 | Free | Weekdays 8–4.

Kirkpatrick North Wildlife Management Basin. Between March and May, ducks and geese migrate to this wildlife preserve in the rainwater basin 1 mi west of York, ½ mi north and 1 mi east of Exit 348 off I–80. Call for hours. | 402/362–5531 or 402/362–5953 | Free.

ON THE CALENDAR

SEPT.: *York Fest.* At its annual three-day celebration, the York community puts on a parade, a figure-8 race, a craft show, a kiddie fair and parade, a Harley Davidson show, a fishing tournament, art and photography show, and a coronation of the fair king and queen. | 402/362–5531 or 402/362–5953.

Dining

Chances R Restaurant & Lounge. American. Chances R isn't a small-town restaurant pretending to be good—it *is* good. Four dining areas, including a beer garden, offer options from casual to formal. The 60-year-old restaurant serves breakfast, lunch and dinner, brunch on Sunday, and a prime rib buffet Saturday night. The pan-fried chicken, homemade mashed potatoes, barbecued ribs, pork chops, and homemade desserts are staples worth mentioning. | 124 W. 5th St. | 402/362–7755 | $6–$18 | AE, D, MC, V.

Garden Gate. American. In a tea room where the tables and chairs are antiques and the pictures on the walls are all of leisurely bygone eras, glazed ham balls and other delicacies are offered for lunch, tea, and coffee. | 115 E. 6th St. | 402/362–5540 | Closed Sun. | $4–$7 | AE, MC, V.

Manny's. Casual. Replicas of guns and other artifacts bring a remembrance of Nebraska's Wild West days to this restaurant in a Holiday Inn between Highway 81 and I–80. Try the prime rib or the jambalaya pasta with spicy sauce. | 4619 S. Lincoln Ave. | $9–$17 | AE, D, DC, MC, V.

Lodging

Best Western Palmer Inn. In a commercial area 1 mi south of York, this rusty-toned building sits in its space like a prairie hill at sunset–if prairie rises had white columned porticos. It's about 2 mi from the Palmer Museum and the York airport. The parking area includes truck and RV spaces and cold-weather hookups. Restaurant, complimentary Continental breakfast. Cable TV. Heated pool. Playground. Laundry facilities. Airport shuttle. Some pets allowed. | 2426 S. Lincoln Ave. | 402/362–5585 or 800/452–3185 | fax 402/362–6053 | 41 rooms | $45–$65 | AE, D, DC, MC, V.

Days Inn. On Highway 81 just north of the junction with I–80, this motel built in 1992 is in a commercial area but has an indoor pool and exercise center, so you don't need to miss your daily workouts. Cold-weather hookups are available. Complimentary Continental breakfast. Cable TV. Heated pool. Hot tub. | 3710 S. Lincoln St. | 402/362–6355 | fax 402/362–2827 | 39 rooms | $38–$45 | AE, D, DC, MC, V.

Holiday Inn. Rooms in this two-story motel have hair dryers, irons, and whirlpool tubs. It's about 3 mi from York at the junction of I–60 and Highway 81 and 45 mi from the Lincoln airport. Van service is available through Eppley Express. Restaurant, bar, complimentary Continental breakfast, room service. Refrigerators. Cable TV. Indoor pool. Hot tub. Exercise equipment. Pets allowed (fee). | 4619 S. Lincoln Ave. | 402/362–6661 or 800/934–5495 | fax 402/362–3727 | 128 rooms | $44–$63 | AE, D, DC, MC, V.

Quality Inn. The Old York historic area and the Anna Palmer Museum are 3 mi from this hotel, or if you need a refuge after a game at the UNL stadium, 45 mi away, some baths have heat lamps and massage heads on the showers. Complimentary Continental breakfast. In-room data ports, some microwaves, some refrigerators. Cable TV. Indoor pool. Laundry facilities. Business services. No pets. | 3724 S. Lincoln Ave. | 402/362–1686 | fax 402/362–1726 | 50 rooms | $45–$70 | AE, D, DC, MC, V.

Super 8. A skywalk joins together two separate buildings, one with two stories and one with three, at this hotel. Complimentary Continental breakfast. Cable TV. Indoor pool. Pets allowed. | 4112 South Lincoln Ave. | 402/362–3388 or 800/800–8000 | fax 402/362–3604 | 95 rooms | $30–$65 | AE, D, DC, MC, V.

Wayfarer II. This single-story motel is in Henderson, 11 mi west of York, off I–80 Exit 342. There is a restaurant right behind the main building, and a play area for kids. Restaurant. Cable TV. Pool. Playground. | 904 Road B, Henderson | 402/723–5856 or 800/543–0577 | fax 402/723–5856 | 34 rooms | $36–$42 | AE, DC, MC, V.

Yorkshire Motel. This small, three-story motel, remodeled in April 2000, is 1 mi off I–80, about 45 mi from the UNL stadium or other Lincoln attractions, and 4 mi from Anna Bemis Palmer Museum. Truck parking and cold-weather hookups are available. Restaurant. Cable TV. Playground. | 3402 S. Lincoln Ave. | 402/362–6633 or 888/362–6633 | fax 402/362–5197 | 29 rooms | $45–$50 | AE, D, DC, MC, V.

North Dakota

North Dakota was once described by broadcaster and native son Eric Sevareid as "the blank spot on the nation's mind." The state is indeed a huge blank expanse of rolling prairies under intense blue skies, much of it unchanged since the expedition led by Lewis and Clark in 1804 and 1806. Between Minnesota and Montana, along the Canadian border, North Dakota is a large rectangle. The eastern edge, marked by the Red River, is rich soil on land so flat you can see the horizon as a straight line. The Red River is one of only two rivers in the contiguous 48 states that flows north. Normally sleepy, the river floods every spring; in 1997 a catastrophic flood devastated the town of Grand Forks. Recovery from that disaster has happened quickly through the Red River Valley. Grand Forks is in the process of rebuilding its downtown areas with many new community park and recreation areas.

Moving westward, the flat land gradually begins to show slopes and hills. Small valleys, lakes, and prairie potholes are scattered throughout, the remnants of shape-shifting glaciers that used to cover much of the state. The Missouri River juts like a giant elbow into the southwestern section of the state and defines the border between the Central and Mountain time zones. The west banks of the river also mark the end of the Rocky Mountain foothills. Continue into the southwestern corner and the Badlands will surprise you with their rugged terrain and raw beauty. North Dakota also marks the geographic center of the North American continent (technically 16 mi south, 7 mi west of Rugby).

The length of the state—360 mi—can be traveled by two excellent east–west highways, I–94 and U.S. 2. North to south—212 mi—can be traveled along I–29 and U.S. 83. Due to these routes, often parallel to railways, North Dakota has for years served as a "pass through" state. However, tourism efforts are changing North Dakota into a primary destination, especially for family and theme vacations. The remarkable

CAPITAL: BISMARCK	POPULATION: 641,000	AREA: 70,665 SQUARE MI
BORDERS: MN, SD, MT, CANADA	TIME ZONES: CENTRAL AND MOUNTAIN	POSTAL ABBREVIATION: ND
WEB SITE: WWW.NDTOURISM.COM		

Badlands are home to Theodore Roosevelt National Park, a popular tourist area that has been described both as "the Grand Canyon in miniature" and as "hell with the fires put out." Nearby is Medora, a frontier town famous for its summer cowboy musical, museums, and quaint shops.

Agriculture continues to be a major force in North Dakota's economy. Grain silos and elevators define the prairie skyline. (Even the visitor center in Fargo was built to resemble a grain elevator.) The state ranks first in production of durum wheat, spring wheat, barley, canola, flaxseed, dry edible beans, pinto beans, navy beans, oats, and sunflowers. On occasion, you can still see the old bread-style haystacks. The main live-stock raised here are beef cattle, dairy cattle, and hogs. And the cooperatives and companies that process durum into pasta and sugar beets into the refined product are giving the state an additional source of income.

The state's second largest industry is energy. Since the 1970s Arab oil embargo, North Dakota has been a leader in providing oil and gas. It ranks ninth in the nation in annual production. The state also has one of the world's largest deposits of lignite coal. Private companies operate seven large strip mines, and the nation's first coal gasifi-cation plant was built in North Dakota to convert lignite into natural gas. Seven coal-fired steam plants and Garrison Dam create electric power that is exported to several surrounding states.

The Energy Trail follows part of the Lewis and Clark Trail along the Missouri River. Two highways in North Dakota—aptly labeled 1804 and 1806—follow much of the explorers' original route through this scenic country. It was in North Dakota that Sakakawea, whose image appears on the U.S. gold dollar, joined Lewis and Clark as their guide and interpreter. (North Dakota has formally adopted this spelling of Sakakawea's name, although she is otherwise known as Sacagawea.) North Dakota also is home to four Native American reservations: Spirit Nation and Standing Rock (various Sioux bands), Turtle Mountain (Chippewa, Metis, Cree), and Fort Berthold (Mandan, Hidatsa, Arikara). About 26,000 Native Americans still live in the state. A small portion of the Sisseton-Wahpeton Sioux reservation of South Dakota is in the south-east corner of North Dakota; but it's not considered part of North Dakota's count. Others calling North Dakota home at one time or another include Sitting Bull, General George Armstrong Custer, Theodore Roosevelt, bandleader Lawrence Welk, baseball great Roger Maris, basketball coach Phil Jackson, and author Louis L'Amour.

More notable than its famous residents, however, is the state's reputation for friendly, courteous people with a strong work ethic. North Dakotans—a mix of Scan-dinavians, Germans, English, Scots, Irish, Persians, and others—realized early on that their neighbors' survival often meant their own. When an injured farmer needs help taking off the crops, neighbors pool combines, trucks, and other resources in a spec-tacular display of friendship. The word "dakota" is a Sioux word that means friendly; it's therefore fitting that North Dakota represents the nation as co-host of the Inter-national Peace Garden, the living tribute to peace and friendliness between the United States and Canada. The garden straddles the 49th parallel, the world's longest unfor-tified border.

ND Timeline

ca. 9500 BC	1682	1738	1794
Paleo-Indian peoples initially occupy the Northern Plains, hunting mammoths, giant bison, and other animals. Knife River flint was mined and exported to other tribes.	LaSalle claims the Mississippi River drainage for France, including the Missouri River in North Dakota.	The French explorer La Verendrye visits Mandan Native American villages near the Missouri River. This is the first known European American expedition in the area now North Dakota.	René Jusseaume builds a fur-trading post near present-day Washburn along the Knife River.

INTRODUCTION
HISTORY
REGIONS
WHEN TO VISIT
STATE'S GREATS
RULES OF THE ROAD
DRIVING TOURS

Despite the distinctive rural picture, in 1987 North Dakota was redefined as an urban rather than rural state when the population became more concentrated in cities and towns than on farms. That's remarkable, considering that North Dakota has only nine cities with more than 10,000 residents, and 17 cities with more than 2,500 residents. About 40 percent of the population lives on 10 percent of the land, concentrated in the Red River Valley. Two-thirds of the state's counties are classified as frontier, with fewer than six residents per square mile. There are 53 counties in all, which are represented in the state's two-house legislature that meets every other year. The governor may be elected to an unlimited number of four-year terms, and the state has three Congressional seats: two senators and one representative.

In a state this large (ranked 17th among the 50 states) with so few people (an average of 9.3 people per square mile), the long stretches of uninterrupted highway are an accurate indication of the amount of elbow room North Dakotans enjoy. North Dakota has more miles of road per capita than any other state: 106,632, or 166 mi of road for every 1,000 people. The state also has more registered vehicles than residents, and more dirt race tracks per capita than any other state.

In North Dakota, it's legal to have your hunting rifle mounted in the back window of your pickup truck. With 60 wildlife refuges—more than any other state—North Dakota has abundant waterfowl, upland birds, and big game. More ducks reproduce in North Dakota wetlands—and roadside ditches—than anywhere else in the nation. An important flyway, the state almost reverberates with honking Canada geese during the fall migration. Ring-necked pheasants and wild turkeys frequently scoot across county roads. Common game animals are white-tailed deer and mule deer; big game animals include moose, pronghorn antelope, and bighorn sheep. A license is required to hunt. On average, 72,000 fishing licenses and 90,000 deer hunting licenses are issued each year.

Bison, the once-plentiful stately sentinels of the prairie, now exist mainly in protected herds such as those at Theodore Roosevelt National Park and the National Buffalo Museum at Jamestown. These majestic beasts of the past also represent the future. Hunted nearly to extinction, they're now reviving an agriculture industry in need of diversification. Speaking of extinction, tourists have started coming to North Dakota to view the footprints and bones of another long-gone herd that once roamed these parts—dinosaurs.

These days, North Dakota is not so much a blank spot as a blank canvas, where the adventures you experience are limited only by your imagination.

History

For hundreds of millions of years, southwestern North Dakota was intermittently covered by a great sea stretching up from the Gulf of Mexico while the rest of the state was studded with glaciers. By the time the sea withdrew for good, the Badlands had been carved and layers of sediment trapped ancient marine and animal life, preserving skeletons and footprints. Ice-age glaciers scraped and molded the rest of the land,

1800		1803	1804	1806
Alexander Henry, Jr. starts a fur-trading post at Park River and moves it to Pembina in 1801. The post attracts the first white settlement in North Dakota. A trade route connects	posts between Lake Winnipeg and the Missouri River Native American villages.	The United States buys the western half of the Mississippi River basin from France with the Louisiana Purchase.	Meriwether Lewis and William Clark enter North Dakota and winter near the present town of Washburn. Their post, Fort Mandan, is visited by nearby Native Americans.	The Lewis and Clark Expedition returns on its way back to St. Louis.

leaving an assortment of debris trails as they retreated. Melting glaciers eventually formed Lake Agassiz. The lake bed—about a 40-mi-wide strip—is now the Red River Valley in the eastern part of the state, with some of the richest soil in the world.

Paleo-Indians, the first people of North Dakota, arrived more than 10,000 years ago, following herds of giant buffalo and mammoth. Gradually they formed small groups of hunters and gatherers, and some eventually became farmers taking up residence near Knife River. They also became exporters of Knife River flint. Strong and easy to shape into spear points, arrowheads and other tools, Knife River flint found its way across most of the nation by AD 100.

Several centuries later, the introduction of the horse changed the lives of Plains Native Americans, allowing greater mobility and the ability to follow migrating bison herds. North Dakota's first non–Native American visitor, the explorer La Verendrye, arrived from Canada in 1738. La Verendrye's visit began a fur-trading era that lasted more than 100 years. The intermingling of mostly French fur traders and Chippewa women created a new nation of people, the Metis, who tried unsuccessfully to establish their own nation.

After the Louisiana Purchase in 1803, President Thomas Jefferson commissioned Meriwether Lewis and William Clark to make their famous expedition up the Missouri River and to the West Coast. Commerce, in the form of fur trade, grew. By 1861, settlement of the Northern Plains began in earnest, and the Dakota Territory was organized by Congress. The Federal Homestead Law granted 160 acres of land to anyone who would live on it and farm a portion of it for five years. By 1869, the first homesteaders were staking claims in the eastern part of the state. Immigration and a settlement boom ensued. To protect routes and railroad construction, military forts were erected. Reservations for Indians were negotiated, then reduced; then portions were opened for settlement. In 1876 General George Custer and the 7th Cavalry, stationed near Bismarck, left in search of Native Americans who refused confinement on reservations. The resulting annihilation at Little Big Horn made names such as Custer, Crazy Horse, and Sitting Bull famous. Dakota Native Americans were chased relentlessly, and Sitting Bull finally surrendered at Fort Buford (near Williston) in 1881. He was killed at his home on the Standing Rock Indian Reservation in 1890.

Between 1879 and 1886, more than 100,000 people—mostly Scandinavians and Germans—entered the Dakota Territory. In 1889 North Dakota and South Dakota became states simultaneously. A second boom, between 1905 and 1920, increased the population from 191,000 to 646,000. Strong grassroots movements began to form, eventually leading to the Nonpartisan League (NPL) in 1915. The NPL united progressives, reformers, and radicals on a political platform of improving state services, full suffrage for women, and state ownership of banks, mills and elevators, and insurance companies. The NPL legacy continues today: The Bank of North Dakota, opened in 1919, and the State Mill and Elevator, completed in 1922, are the only state-owned institutions of their kind in the nation. The NPL consolidated with the Democratic Party in the 1950s.

The 1920s and 1930s were tough times for North Dakota. An economic depression started with the 1920 collapse of grain prices; the Great Depression of the 1930s saw

1818	1842	1862	1863	1868
The 49th parallel becomes the boundary between the United States and Great Britain in a treaty that gave the U.S. the upper Red River drainage.	The first Red River ox-cart caravan travels from Walhalla to St. Paul, Minnesota.	Dakota Territory is opened for homesteading. The Homestead Act gives 160 acres of land to anyone who lives and farms a portion of it for five years.	An immigrant party attacked by Sioux Native Americans circles their covered wagons and builds a sod wall around themselves for protection.	A peace treaty defines Sioux lands as those west of the Missouri River in Dakota Territory.

INTRODUCTION
HISTORY
REGIONS
WHEN TO VISIT
STATE'S GREATS
RULES OF THE ROAD
DRIVING TOURS

a crisis of farm foreclosures and bank failures. Yet the North Dakota Farmers Union continued to build elevators and organize oil cooperatives. Rural schools began consolidating, and federal relief programs improved highways, state parks, and city services.

World War II brought changes, however. Some 60,000 North Dakotans served in the armed forces; the state's population invested some $397 million in government bonds. Isolationism gave way to conservatism. Good crops and good prices brought prosperity, and farm debt dropped markedly. Land was available at low prices. Demand for irrigation and flood control led to the construction of Garrison Dam in 1946. Completed in 1953, the dam tamed the Missouri River and created Lake Sakakawea. The big lake engulfed some of the Fort Berthold Indian Reservation and created a recreational industry for the area in boating, skiing, and fishing. The dam's hydropower helped to feed the state's growing demand for electricity. In 1935, only 2.3 percent of the state's farms had electricity from central power stations; by 1954, 90 percent of North Dakota's farms had electricity. North Dakota further diversified when two air force bases were completed in the 1960s. Still active today, the bases are an economic force in Minot and Grand Forks.

With 11 public institutions of higher learning, more roads per capita than any other state, and a declining population to pay taxes, North Dakota struggles with its boom-and-bust cycles exemplified so well by the energy industry. Oil was discovered in the west portion of North Dakota in the early 1950s and since then has driven two of the state's major cities through lean and lucrative times based on the value of crude. Today, telecommunications garners serious attention, with telemarketing companies staking claims in numerous small communities. It's this ability by most North Dakotans to reinvent themselves that will continue to drive the economy and culture forward.

Regions

1. RED RIVER VALLEY

North Dakota rises like a series of steps from east to west, beginning with the Red River Valley. The northern portion of the Red River defines the North Dakota–Minnesota border, following an old glacial lake bed (Lake Agassiz) north to where the river can empty into Hudson's Bay in Canada. The flat, fertile valley extends 30-40 mi from the river. At the southern end of North Dakota, the elevation is 965 ft; at the Canadian border, the elevation is 750 ft, the lowest point in the state. Marking the western border of the valley is the Pembina Escarpment (a steep slope), prominent enough in the north that it can be seen at times while traveling I-29.

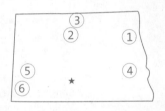

About one-fourth of the state's population lives in this region, congregated particularly in Fargo and Grand Forks. During the settlement period a century ago, valley land was quickly claimed and planted with grains. Homesteads gave way to bonanza farms that turned pioneers into wheat kings. Today, in a state where wheat is still paramount,

1869	**1872**	**1876**	**1882**	**1887**
Fort Berthold Indian Reservation is established. Treaties with the Sioux and Chippewa cede most of eastern North Dakota to the government.	The Northern Pacific Railway is built from the Red River to Jamestown; the main line doesn't reach the Montana border until 1881.	The 7th Cavalry, led by General George A. Custer, leaves Fort Abraham Lincoln near Bismarck to join the Sioux expedition. They are defeated at the Little Big Horn River in Montana.	The last great Indian buffalo hunt occurs. The Turtle Mountain Reservation is established.	The Standing Rock Indian Reservation is opened to homesteading.

early buildings are treasured monuments to the past, like Bagg Bonanza Farm near Wahpeton, Bonanzaville USA in West Fargo, Myra Museum in Grand Forks, and Pembina State Museum in the northeast corner, which reaches back millions of years to document the history of the area.

Driving the valley can be monotonous without stops in Fargo and Grand Forks. Both are university towns with courteous residents, worthy attractions, and a variety of local eateries. Both towns also are on major crossroads, with Fargo at the junction of I–29 and I–94, and Grand Forks at the junction of I–29 and U.S. 2, making them ideal beginning or ending destinations on a statewide tour.

Towns listed: Cavalier, Fargo, Grafton, Grand Forks, Pembina, Wahpeton.

2. NORTHERN DRIFT PRAIRIE

The drift prairie, also called glaciated plains, is a gently rolling landscape that rises gradually toward the west and southwest. Glaciers created pockets in the land that are now lakes and nesting grounds for hundreds of thousands of migratory waterfowl. The area stretches from the Pembina Escarpment in the east to nearly the northwest corner of the state; and from the Canadian border south to the center of the state. The elevation rises from 300 to 2,000 ft above the Red River Valley.

Devils Lake, in the heart of this region, is a fishing and hunting center for walleye, northern pike, white bass, Canada geese, duck, and white-tailed deer and mule deer, to name a few. The large natural lake is salty and has no outlet; recent years of above-average precipitation has caused the lake to swell. Nearby is Fort Totten State Historic Site, the best-preserved military fort–turned–boarding school west of the Mississippi River. Follow U.S. 2 west of Devils Lake to Rugby, a small community whose claim to fame is its proximity to the true geographic center of the continent.

Towns listed: Carrington, Devils Lake, Kenmare, Minot, New Rockford, Rugby.

3. TURTLE MOUNTAINS

Tucked along the Canadian border is a pretty woodland area known as the Turtle Mountains. Rising about 500 ft above the surrounding plains, the hills have been the home of bands of Chippewa Native Americans and the Metis, a people who grew out of the intermingling of French fur trappers and Native Americans. To the east is the Pembina Gorge, a spectacularly carved and forested valley. In the center, near the hills, is Lake Metigoshe, a popular recreation area. And to the west is the exquisite International Peace Garden, straddling the unfenced Canadian–U.S. border. Because this area is far from towns of any size, establish a nearby home base and make day trips to enjoy these great sites. *Town listed:* Bottineau.

4. SOUTHERN DRIFT PRAIRIE

The south-central section of North Dakota is similar to the northern drift prairie, dominated by rolling hills, lakes, and small valleys. The exception is that this area isn't

1889	1890	1915	1929	1942
North Dakota becomes the 39th state.	Ghost Dance activities among the Sioux cause panic among settlers. Sitting Bull is killed on Standing Rock Indian Reservation.	The socialistic Non-partisan League organizes, influencing state politics for the next 40 years. Republicans, however, dominate most elections for the better part of a century.	June is the driest month on record in North Dakota; drought conditions continue through the Great Depression, thus giving the period the name "Dirty Thirties."	The 164th Infantry becomes the first American unit to fight in the Pacific during the battle of Guadalcanal.

INTRODUCTION
HISTORY
REGIONS
WHEN TO VISIT
STATE'S GREATS
RULES OF THE ROAD
DRIVING TOURS

broken up by small mountains or large forests. From the Pembina Escarpment in the east to the Missouri River in the west, and down to the North Dakota–South Dakota border, farms and dairies fill out the countryside.

Two of the state's 10 largest cities anchor this area. Valley City, on I-94, is a popular jumping off point for travelers who enjoy scenic byways. In this case, Route 32 south of Valley City for about 30–40 mi shows off everything from prairie to valley, farms to dairies, and wildflowers to thick stands of trees. Continuing west on I-94, you'll find Jamestown, home of the world's largest (concrete) buffalo, the world's only live albino buffalo, a live herd of buffalo, and—yes—a museum dedicated to the buffalo.

Towns listed: Jamestown, Valley City.

5. GREAT PLAINS

Encompassing the northwest corner of the state, following the Missouri River east and then south to the North Dakota–South Dakota border, are the Great Plains. The Great Plains vary considerably in elevation, from 1,800 to 2,400 ft. (White Butte, in the southwest pocket of the state, reaches 3,506 ft above sea level, making it the highest point in North Dakota.)

Bismarck, Minot, Williston, and Dickinson define the perimeter of the Great Plains region. Bismarck, the state's capital, is a pretty city with a 19-story Capitol building—a skyscraper by North Dakota standards. Bismarck is home to a community that loves dining out enough to keep a disproportionate number of restaurants in business. While the zoo in Minot may be the town's best permanent attraction, the annual State Fair in July and Norsk Hostfest in October give its residents plenty to brag about. Each spanning about 10 days, these events attract nearly 100,000 visitors apiece. Near Williston is Fort Union, a national park site that is a huge, authentically recreated fur trade post complete with an impressive palisade, teepee area, and fabulous view of the Missouri River. South in Dickinson you'll find the region's treasures proudly displayed in the Dakota Dinosaur Museum, which has a dozen complete skeletons.

Towns listed: Bismarck, Fort Yates, Garrison, Linton, Mandan, New Town, Washburn, Williston.

6. BADLANDS

West of Dickinson and reaching north almost to Williston are the Badlands. This strip of rough, breathtaking land is 6–20 mi wide and about 190 mi long. Never covered by glaciers, this land of sandstone, shale, and clay has been carved into intricate shapes by wind and water for the last half million years or more. Just imagine the Grand Canyon in miniature, and you'll have the Badlands. Some of the area is preserved in Theodore Roosevelt National Park and is well worth a visit. Medora is an entertaining base for exploration. It's a restored frontier town with dozens of gift shops, a few museums, and a family-oriented musical in an amphitheater.

1946	1951	1956	1961	1969
Construction begins on Garrison Dam.	Oil is discovered near Tioga.	The Nonpartisan League and the Democratic Party merge.	Roger Maris of Fargo breaks Babe Ruth's single-season home run record.	Zip to Zap party bash by college students is ended by the Army National Guard.

Towns listed: Amidon, Bowman, Dickinson, Killdeer, Medora, Theodore Roosevelt National Park.

When to Visit

The weather varies as much as the regions in North Dakota. The eastern end of the state is notorious for the constant winds; in Fargo, winds average 14 mi per hour every day. Fargo and other Red River Valley cities also usually receive the most snowfall in the state. Combined with the winds, blizzard conditions erupt quickly and are dangerous. The interstate system is equipped with gates at exits in major cities to prevent travelers from daring nature when no travel is advised. To check road reports, call 701/328–7623.

The state's record low temperature, -60°F, was set on February 15, 1936, in Parshall. Yet, despite its reputation as a cold state, North Dakota's average winter temperature is 7° above zero; it always feels colder because of the wind-chill factor. On the brightest, coldest days in the state, you'll see the weather phenomenon called sun dogs, when sunlight refracts off ice crystals in the air and forms a bright arc on each side of the sun.

Winter can come early and stay late. The arid southwest corner of the state regularly has the warmest temperatures and least precipitation, regardless of the season. Across the state, summer temperatures average 70° and can soar into the 80s and 90s, usually in July or August. The hot temperatures are important to the wheat crops that thrive in an otherwise short growing season. The state's record high temperature, 121°F, was set on July 6, 1936, at Steele.

The average annual rainfall ranges from 13 inches in the west to 20 inches in the east, for a statewide average of around 16.5 inches. The average annual snowfall ranges from 26 to 38 inches for a statewide average of 32 inches. A record snowfall of 118 inches during the winter of 1996–97 buried Fargo.

Finally, North Dakota is a sparsely populated state, which affects the availability of some services. When planning your road trip, don't count on gas stations or dining establishments to be open late or on Sundays in small towns or rural areas. If you're planning to drive a lot of miles, end your long day at one of the state's largest cities (along I–29, I–94, and U.S. 2) to be sure the services you want are open.

CLIMATE CHART

Average High/Low Temperatures (°F) and Monthly Precipitation (in inches)

	JAN.	FEB.	MAR.	APR.	MAY	JUN.
BISMARCK	20.2/-1.7	26.4/5.1	38.5/17.8	54.9/31.0	67.8/42.2	77.1/51.6
	0.51	0.43	0.77	1.67	2.18	2.72

	JUL.	AUG.	SEPT.	OCT.	NOV.	DEC.
	84.4/56.4	82.7/53.9	70.8/43.1	58.7/32.5	39.3/17.8	24.5/3.3
	2.14	1.72	1.49	0.90	0.49	0.51

1982
The movie *Northern Lights*, about the Nonpartisan League in North Dakota, wins the Neil Simon Award for best picture.

1989
North Dakota celebrates its centennial.

1990
Farms number 33,500; in 1980, the number was 40,000; in 1933, farm numbers peaked at 86,000.

1997
Annual spring flooding sets records in April when the Red River of the North spills over its banks by more than a mile in some places. The river devastates the city of Grand Forks.

INTRODUCTION
HISTORY
REGIONS
WHEN TO VISIT
STATE'S GREATS
RULES OF THE ROAD
DRIVING TOURS

DICKINSON

	JAN.	FEB.	MAR.	APR.	MAY	JUN.
	23.0/3.7	29.0/9.4	39.8/19.0	54.4/30.7	66.6/41.6	76.1/51.0
	0.38	0.35	0.71	1.88	2.57	3.23
	JUL.	AUG.	SEPT.	OCT.	NOV.	DEC.
	84.1/56.1	82.6/54.3	70.0/43.6	58.4/33.5	40.1/19.5	26.7/7.3
	2.08	1.45	1.67	0.96	0.44	0.39

WILLISTON

	JAN.	FEB.	MAR.	APR.	MAY	JUN.
	19.6/-1.8	26.8/5.3	39.4/17.4	55.8/30.5	68.3/42.2	78.0/51.4
	0.53	0.42	0.69	1.28	1.99	2.28
	JUL.	AUG.	SEPT.	OCT.	NOV.	DEC.
	84.8/56.5	83.3/54.1	70.1/42.4	58.1/31.4	38.0/16.3	23.6/2.8
	2.10	1.25	1.33	0.77	0.45	0.58

JAMESTOWN

	JAN.	FEB.	MAR.	APR.	MAY	JUN.
	17.2/-1.9	23.5/4.2	36.1/17.2	53.7/31.0	68.2/42.7	77.5/52.9
	0.62	0.47	0.88	1.54	1.86	2.99
	JUL.	AUG.	SEPT.	OCT.	NOV.	DEC.
	84.1/58.0	82.4/55.4	69.9/44.5	57.3/33.8	37.2/18.6	21.8/3.5
	2.76	2.07	1.76	0.96	0.59	0.48

FARGO

	JAN.	FEB.	MAR.	APR.	MAY	JUN.
	15/-4	21/3	35/17	54/32	69/44	77/54
	0.67	0.45	1.06	1.82	2.45	2.82
	JUL.	AUG.	SEPT.	OCT.	NOV.	DEC.
	83/59	81/56	69/46	57/35	37/19	20/3
	2.70	2.43	1.99	1.88	0.73	0.65

FESTIVALS AND SEASONAL EVENTS

WINTER

Jan. **Fargo Farm Show.** This is one of the area's largest farm shows. More than 700 farm- and ranch-related exhibits come together at the Fargodome on the campus of North Dakota State. | 701/241–9100 or 701/298–2777 (event line) | www.fargodome.com.

Jan.–Feb. **KMOT Ag Expo.** This gigantic indoor farm show in Minot includes seminars, exhibits, and a living ag classroom. | 701/852–4101 or 800/472–2917 | www.kmot.com.

SPRING

Mar. **North Dakota Winter Show.** Ignore the cold and join the throngs who delight in this indoor version of a state fair. Thousands come to Valley City for the horse show, livestock show, rodeo, and farm and home exhibits. | 701/845–1401.

May **Dakota Cowboy Poetry Gathering.** In Medora, local and national cowboy poets read their works during a weekend that includes a Western art show and crafts display. | 701/623–4444 or 800/633–6721.

SUMMER

June **Fort Union Trading Post Rendezvous.** Near Williston, this event reenacts a rendezvous typical of the fur-trading era of the early 1800s, with mountain men and Native American encampments around Fort Union, near the Missouri River. | 701/572–9083 | www.nps.gov/fous.

July   **North Dakota State Fair.** A traditional fair in Minot shows off the best in agriculture, from 4-H projects to the latest in farm equipment. | 701/852–3247 or 701/857–7620.

Red River Downtown Street Fair. More than 300 exhibitors from 30 states and more than 50 food booths cover eight city blocks in downtown Fargo. | 701/241–1570 | www.fargomoorhead.com.

AUTUMN

Sept.   **United Tribes Technical College International Powwow.** One of the largest powwows in North America, this powwow in Bismarck draws contestants in Native American dancing and singing. | 701/255–3285 or 701/222–4308 | www.united/tribes.tech.nd.us.

Oct.   **Edge of the West Rodeo.** Many of the nation's best cowboys compete in Bismarck in this grand finale of more than 20 circuit rodeos in North Dakota and South Dakota. | 701/222–6487 or 701/222–4308.

Norsk Hostfest. In the middle of the month, Minot's All Seasons Arena turns into a sea of RVs, housing a generation that still speaks English with a bit of an accent, for the largest (and still growing) Scandinavian festival this side of the Atlantic. | 701/852–2368 | www.hostfest.com.

State's Greats

Authenticity is the key to North Dakota's experiences. No celluloid, no Web site, no hologram can replace the reverberation of powwow drums calling another dance or the starkness of a pioneer shanty whose flimsy walls barely kept its occupants from freezing. You'll find the cowboy way is lived daily in western North Dakota, where hats, boots, and shiny belt buckles are common sights. In North Dakota you can truly get away from it all, only to find that you want to get away from the endless rolling prairie underneath a sky so huge it holds every cloud formation. When the enormous expanse of space starts to feel comfortable, you'll notice the subtle beauty of the landscape in shifting shades of gold and green, broken occasionally by bursts of wildflowers. The state harbors lakes, forests, scenic gorges, and the awe-inspiring Badlands.

Hospitality and courtesy are practiced religiously in North Dakota, although differently depending on the region of the state. In the Scandinavia-influenced eastern part of the state, efficient service is prized. In the German/Slavic west, settle in for a cup of coffee and a story or two.

Forests and Parks

Although known for wide open spaces, North Dakota has four state forests. Two of these, **Turtle Mountain State Forest** and **Homen State Forest,** hug Lake Metigoshe at the Canadian border and have stands of oak, aspen, birch, green ash, and willow. **Tetrault Woods State Forest,** in the northeast corner near Walhalla, is the smallest and includes the spectacular **Pembina Gorge,** one of the most scenic areas in the state.

Competing for "spectacular" honors is **Theodore Roosevelt National Park,** with two major sections encompassing some of the state's Badlands. With hundreds of miles of intricately carved canyons, herds of bison and wild horses, prairie dog towns, and golden eagles, the rich terrain invites you to slow down, catch your breath, and savor the soul-restoring solitude. If flowers make your heart sing, travel north to the Canadian border to the **International Peace Garden.** Here you can stroll among 2,300 acres of flowers, trees, and shrubs in a garden straddling the world's longest unfortified border.

Culture, History, and the Arts

North Dakota is one of those rare states where you can truly walk in the footsteps of giants: dinosaurs. The fossil-rich beds in the southwest have yielded a dozen skeletons now displayed in the **Dakota Dinosaur Museum** in Dickinson. To explore the history of the past millennia in North Dakota, visit the **Pembina State Museum** in the northeast corner. The museum showcases stories of numerous geologic eras—including the age of reptilian dinosaurs—through settlement periods, and affords a great view from a seven-story tower. Bismarck is home to the state's largest museum, the **North Dakota Heritage Center,** which has interpretive exhibits ranging from a woolly mammoth to a tractor. Switching from history to art, make a stop at the **Plains Art Museum** in Fargo. The museum's collections, showcasing local and international artists, have earned a reputation for being the finest between Minneapolis and Seattle.

Several Native American, frontier, and military history sites are worth a tour. **Knife River Indian Villages National Historic Site,** near Washburn, documents at least 8,000 years of Plains Native American communities living on or near the site. This also is the area where Lewis and Clark met Sakakawea, who served as guide and translator for their expedition. The explorers themselves are the focal point of the **Lewis and Clark Interpretive Center** in Washburn, which includes a complete set of prints by Karl Bodmer, the artist who traveled the Missouri River after Lewis and Clark. In the northwest corner of the state, near Williston, is **Fort Union Trading Post National Historic Site,** the fur trade post used by trappers and traders in the Upper Midwest for the first half of the 19th century. Equally impressive is **Fort Totten State Historic Site,** just south of Devils Lake. With 16 original buildings, this is the largest and best preserved fort of its kind west of the Mississippi River. From 1867 to 1959, Fort Totten evolved from a military post to a Native American boarding school. **Fort Abraham Lincoln,** while less impressive structurally, may be better known because it was the departure point for General George Custer and the 7th Cavalry for a date with destiny at Little Big Horn. Adjacent to the fort is **On-A-Slant Indian Village,** a Mandan village abandoned long before Custer's appearance.

Events also celebrate North Dakota's cultural richness—powwows, the immense **Norsk Hostfest** Scandinavian celebration, the **Edge of the West Rodeo,** and the **North Dakota State Fair.**

Sports

In North Dakota, modern-day adventurers can relive frontier experiences such as camping out on a starry night under the blazing northern lights and walking in solitude through fields of wildflowers. Licensed professional guides can show you how to track elk and where the walleye are biting.

Snowmobiling, skiing, snowshoeing, sledding, skating, and ice fishing are big—winter is, after all, the state's longest season. North Dakota has 2,200 mi of snowmobile trails statewide. Downhill and cross-country skiing are available at five resorts; the most popular are Frost Fire near Walhalla, Bottineau Winter Park near Bottineau, and Huff Hills near Mandan. **Frost Fire Mountain Ski and Summer Resort** has nine runs that are modestly challenging. **Bottineau Winter Park** claims the most challenging runs and **Huff Hills** is a favorite for folks who want some practice before heading for the Rockies.

Team sports—high school, college, and semi-pro—pack in the crowds. The State Class B High School Boys Basketball Tournament, held in March, may be the best attended sports event in the state. In Grand Forks, the UND Fighting Sioux hockey team consistently ranks in the top nationally. North Dakota's pro and semi-pro teams are the Bismarck Bobcats (hockey), Bismarck Wizards (basketball), Fargo Beez (basket-ball), Fargo RedHawks (baseball), Minot Snowbears (basketball), and the Minot Mallards (baseball).

In western North Dakota, eager cyclists rarely wait for spring's arrival to begin train-ing for summer events. Bicycling is the state's number one participation sport. Paved bike trails, distance rides, and off-road mountain biking all have routes in North Dakota. The seven-day, 424-mi **Cycling Around North Dakota in Sakakawea Country (CANDISC)** brings up to 300 cyclists who pedal through Lewis and Clark historic areas along the Missouri River.

Hiking trails are marked in most of the state's parks and grasslands, including **Cross Ranch Centennial State Park, Icelandic State Park** and **Theodore Roosevelt National Park.** Cross Ranch Centennial State Park and Icelandic State Park are green even during dry years; prairie grasses, tall cottonwood trees, and a bison herd flourish in the former, while Icelandic State Park has better developed interpretive trails. Some of the most challenging horse trails are found in the **Badlands.** Canoeists enjoy the Little Missouri River (not to be confused with the Missouri River), the only designated State Scenic River. Campers have more than 400 campgrounds for the choosing. **Lake Sakakawea** itself is a major recreation area for boating and waterskiing. **Devils Lake** is well known for its jumbo perch, northern pike, and walleye fishing.

The heat of a North Dakota summer can be as intense as the cold of winter, and heat waves seem to invariably arrive during the **Prairie Rose State Games** where triathletes, archers, softball teams, and others compete for state honors in more than two dozen events.

Doves, sandhill cranes, sharp-tailed grouse, Hungarian partridges, snow geese, and ring-necked pheasants and other species make for good bird watching at refuges such as **Audubon National Wildlife Refuge** and **Sully's Hill National Game Preserve.**

Other Points of Interest

More than a century ago, settlers crossed a relentless prairie that was rarely interrupted by a tree. Today, you can still experience that sense of space in three national grass-lands in North Dakota. These wild, open lands share their bounty with cattle grazing associations, hunters, hikers, and campers. The largest and most diverse of these is the **Little Missouri National Grassland,** covering 140 mi along U.S. 85 in the southwest. You can hike, camp, follow a driving tour route, or view the wildlife in this area.

Rules of the Road

Licence Requirements: The minimum driving age in North Dakota is 16. You may not drive in North Dakota if you are under 16, even if you are licensed in another state.

Right Turn on Red: You may turn right on a red light after stopping when the inter-section is clear of both pedestrians and vehicles, unless otherwise posted.

Safety Belt and Helmet Laws: North Dakota law requires all front-seat occupants to wear safety belts. Children under age 3 must be properly secured in an approved child restraint seat, and children age 3 to 10 must be properly secured in either an approved child restraint seat or a safety belt. North Dakota does not have a motorcycle helmet law.

Speed Limits: The speed limit is 70 mi per hour on interstate highways, except when otherwise posted around major cities. On all other primary and secondary highways, the speed limit is 65 mi per hour unless otherwise posted.

For More Information: Contact the North Dakota Department of Transportation | 608 East Boulevard Ave., Bismarck. For general assistance, call | 701/328–2500. For road reports, call | 701/328–7623. For emergency assistance, call | 800/472–2121 | www.state.nd.us/dot/.

Frontier Driving Tour

FROM BISMARCK TO WILLISTON TO MEDORA

Distance: 475 mi   Time: 4 days

Breaks: Bismarck is a good starting point, or for breaks—there are many sights in or near the city. The casino in New Town makes the next good break, strategically located midway on the tour and in a scenic area. You may, however, continue to Williston, another convenient stopping place. Medora anchors the last leg of the trip.

This tour covers Native American history, frontier exploration and commerce, a famous military post, and the early cowboy way of life. Along the way, you will travel from the bluffs overlooking the Missouri River to the open prairie, wind through the majestic Badlands, and finish in the cow town of Medora. At the height of summer, ripening grain fields bow to the ever-present wind, the "big lake"—Lake Sakakawea—glistens, and the rugged terrain of the Badlands wears deep hues of sandy browns and taupes. Spring and fall seasons release sudden splashes of color in this otherwise subtle landscape. Don't forget that the Missouri River forms the dividing line between the Central and Mountain time zones. This tour is not recommended for winter; many of the sights will be closed, and the roads may be covered with snow or ice, making travel difficult.

❶ As capital city, **Bismarck** prides itself on its well-maintained residential areas, bustling downtown and shopping districts, and its many sights. Across the Missouri River, sister city **Mandan** was once called the Gateway to the West by novelist John Steinbeck. Mandan is a logical starting place for a busy day of sightseeing. Start with **Fort Abraham Lincoln State Park,** the headquarters for General Custer and the 7th Cavalry. On the fort grounds, the Custer House has been reconstructed and hosts tours. Also at the park is **On-A-Slant Indian Village,** with recreated dwellings called earthlodges from the Mandan people, who lived there from 1650 to 1750. After visiting the park and exhibits, head to Mandan and the **Five Nations Arts** for one-of-a-kind gifts—quillwork, beadwork, star quilts, sculptures, and more—made by Native American artists. Just across the street and down a block is **Mandan Drug,** where you can get a sandwich, some homemade soup, and old-fashioned hard ice cream. After lunch, head for Bismarck and the **State Capitol,** where you can enjoy a free tour of the 19-story Art Deco building. Across the street is the **North Dakota Heritage Center,** home to a museum with numerous period exhibits, from a wooly mammoth to a 1940s tractor. For an evening of entertainment, consider dinner and gaming at **Prairie Knights Casino.** The drive is scenic, the food is delicious, and the Vegas-style tone is punctuated with Native American pieces.

❷ Begin day two with a pleasant drive north to **Washburn,** where you can visit the **Lewis and Clark Interpretive Center.** Exhibits include artifacts from nearly every major tribe encountered by the 19th century explorers. From the center, turn west on Route 200A and watch for signs for **Fort Mandan,** only 1½ mi away on Rte. 17. Fort Mandan is a replica of the 1804–05 winter quarters used by Lewis and Clark and their expedition.

❸ Return to Rte. 200A and travel west, past rolling ranchlands and farm fields to **Fort Clark State Historic Site,** the spot of a former fur-trading post. While nothing remains, plaques tell the history of commerce and tragedy: During the summer of 1837, a passenger steamboat brought smallpox to the nearby Mandan Indian village, wiping out 90 percent of its people.

❹ Continue west on Rte. 200A about 8 mi to Stanton and **Knife River Indian Villages National Historic Site,** which was inhabited for thousands of years. Besides exhibits, enjoy a visit to a full-size reconstructed earthlodge.

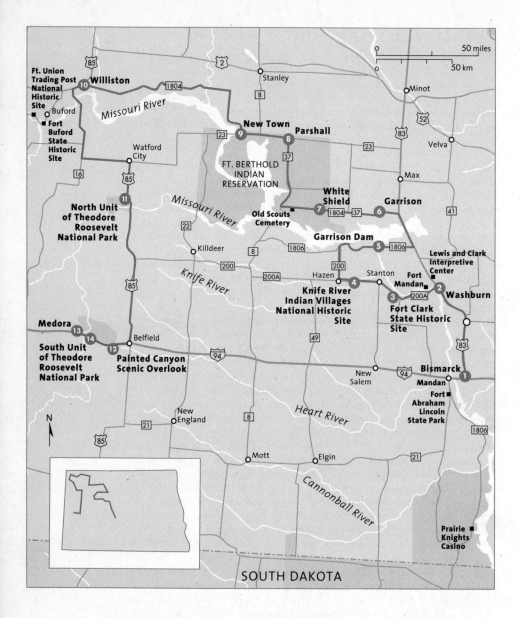

SOUTH DAKOTA

❺ Get back on Rte. 200A and travel west 3 mi to Hazen, then north 19 mi on Rte. 200 to Pick City, and then east on Rte. 1806. Enjoy the panoramic rolling farmland along the route, and then prepare to drive over the jaw-dropping **Garrison Dam** from Pick City to Riverdale. The mile-long dam, built between 1947 and 1954, created Lake Sakakawea from the Missouri River and generates hydroelectric power. Free tours are available weekdays.

❻ From Garrison Dam, continue on Rte. 1806 and connect with U.S. 83. Travel north 12 mi on U.S. 83, and turn west on to Rte. 37, which will take you to **Garrison.** At the edge of town is a service station. There's fuel for your vehicle and yourself; the place serves up German food.

❼ Traveling west from Garrison, Rte. 37 becomes Rte. 1804. Continue on 1804 as you enter the Fort Berthold Indian Reservation, home of the Three Affiliated Tribes—Mandan, Hidatsa, and Arikara. About 1 mi into the reservation is **White Shield.** Just 3 mi west of White Shield is the **Old Scouts Cemetery.** This small, serene cemetery is the final resting place for some of Custer's Arikara scouts and war veterans.

❽ Continue on Rte. 1804 as it veers north and reconnects with Rte. 37 to **Parshall,** about 25 mi. Houses and pastures dot the reservation's hills, interspersed with the occasional gorgeous gully dotted with juneberry bushes. Parshall is home to the unique **Paul Broste Rock Museum,** which has an incredible collection of specimens from around the world. After you've visited the museum, turn west on Rte. 23 and travel along the north edge of the reservation.

❾ Just 17 mi west of Parshall, **New Town** is the seat of tribal government. Here you can find the **Three Affiliated Tribes Museum.** If you're up for about another hour of travel, continue west on Rte. 1804 to **Williston,** and make this your stopping place for the evening.

❿ Begin day three of your tour with a jaunt to two forts just west of Williston on Rte. 1804. The first stop is **Fort Buford State Historic Site,** just 21 mi from Williston. A military post established in 1866, Fort Buford is noted for its famous prisoners, Sitting Bull and Chief Joseph. Drive 2 mi west, again on Rte. 1804, and you'll see **Fort Union Trading Post National Historic Site** clearly from the road. Between 1828 and 1867 this post dominated the fur trade along the upper Missouri River. If you're ready for a bite to eat, return to Williston for lunch.

⓫ From Williston, travel south on U.S. 85 about 60 mi and enjoy the unfolding prairie, dotted with ranches and an occasional tree. Then prepare for a startling change of scenery, as the dramatic buttes that make up the Badlands begin to appear. The **North Unit of Theodore Roosevelt National Park** is a primitive area where you can see buffalo and deer roam, eagles and hawks soar, and prairie dogs scamper. After touring this portion of the park, continue south on U.S. 85 about 50 mi and connect with I–94, traveling west.

⓬ **Painted Canyon Scenic Overlook** is your next breathtaking stop. The visitor center overlooks a panoramic view of the Badlands, called Mako Shika ("land bad") by the Sioux.

⓭ Just off I–94, the very walkable frontier town of **Medora** hosts the mouth-watering Pitchfork Steak Fondue on the bluffs overlooking Medora. For $19.50, you get a full dinner with rib-eye steak as the entrée. After dinner, stroll over to the **Burning Hills Amphitheater** for the foot-stomping Medora Musical.

⓮ Day four of your Frontier Tour allows you to linger and enjoy tiny Medora, founded by a French nobleman and named for his American wife. Visit the **Chateau de Mores State Historic Site,** a 26-room mansion that served as the summer home for the Marquis de Mores and his wife from 1884 to 1886. About 1 mi across from the site is the entrance to the **South Unit of Theodore Roosevelt National Park.** The visitor center has a film and exhibits, and just a short walk away is the **Maltese Cross Ranch Cabin,** from one of Theodore Roosevelt's two North Dakota ranches. The drive through the South Unit shows off more of the Badlands' incredible terrain. After having lunch in Medora, check out the many museums, including the **Medora Doll House, Museum of the Badlands, and Harold Schafer Heritage Center.** If you'd like to purchase something special, travel to Beach just 26 mi west and visit **Prairie Fire Pottery.** The owner supplies the world's zoos with animal-print tiles and handcrafts exquisite pottery with a unique, shimmery glaze.

To return to Bismarck, travel east along I–94 from Beach (about a 2½-hour trip) or Medora (about a two-hour trip).

Wide Open Spaces Driving Tour
FROM WAHPETON TO FARGO AND GRAND FORKS AND BEYOND

Distance: 270 mi   Time: 4 days

Breaks: This tour covers prairie settlement, gigantic wheat farms, tiny roadside chapels, and a look at what the future might be like in space. Both Fargo and Grand Forks are natural stopovers because of attractions, lodgings, and their convenience. Pembina has an exceptional museum and makes a nice departure point if you're considering a jaunt into Canada and up to Winnipeg, but does not have many options for an overnight stay. Better choices for lodging would be Cavalier and Walhalla.

This tour gives a glimpse of settlement and farming history, the history of frontier commerce, and a famous military post–turned–Native American boarding school. Although spring is a muddy and unglamorous time, summer and fall present a tableau of natural colors taken from the fields and trees. This tour is not recommended for winter, as many of the sights are closed and the roads may be covered with snow or ice, making travel difficult.

❶ Anchoring the southeast corner of the state is **Wahpeton,** the starting point of this tour. A fun way to start your day of sightseeing is a visit to **Chahinkapa Zoo.** Next door, you can enjoy a nostalgic ride on an exotic horse with the **Prairie Rose Carousel.** The 1926 Spillman carousel housed in a climate-controlled building, is one of only 150 operating antique carousels in the nation. From here, have an early lunch and prepare for an interesting zigzag tour to two significant historical sites. The first site is about 10 mi west of Wahpeton on Rte. 13. **Bagg Bonanza Farm** is America's only remaining bonanza farm and has 12 original buildings, many of which have been restored. (Bonanza Farms came to be when 5,000-acre parcels of land were sold by the bankrupt Northern Pacific Railroad in the 1860s.) After a leisurely stroll, return to I–29 and travel 25 mi north to Exit 37. Make your way to **Fort Abercrombie State Historic Site.** The first military post in the area that became North Dakota, the fort was established in 1858.

❷ From Fort Abercrombie State Historic Site, return to I–29 and make your way to **Fargo** and West Fargo, your first overnight stop and the state's largest community.

Day two starts out with a trip to **Bonanzaville USA.** More than 40 original and re-created buildings show life in an 1880s Dakota Territory pioneer village. If you have children with you, stop at the **Children's Museum at Yunker Farm.** Check out the live bee hive. After lunch, cross the Red River to Moorhead, Minnesota, for a visit to the **Heritage–Hjemkomst Interpretive Center,** site of a Viking ship. Just a few blocks away in Fargo is the **Plains Art Museum,** one of the largest fine arts museums between Minneapolis and Seattle, housed in a turn-of-the-20th-century warehouse. After this, call it a day and head for dinner or the West Acres Mall, where you can make a quick trip down sports memory lane and visit the **Roger Maris Baseball Museum.** This exhibit honors Fargo native Maris, whose 1961 season of 61 home runs was a record until Mark McGwire and Sammy Sosa bested it in 1998.

INTRODUCTION
HISTORY
REGIONS
WHEN TO VISIT
STATE'S GREATS
RULES OF THE ROAD
DRIVING TOURS

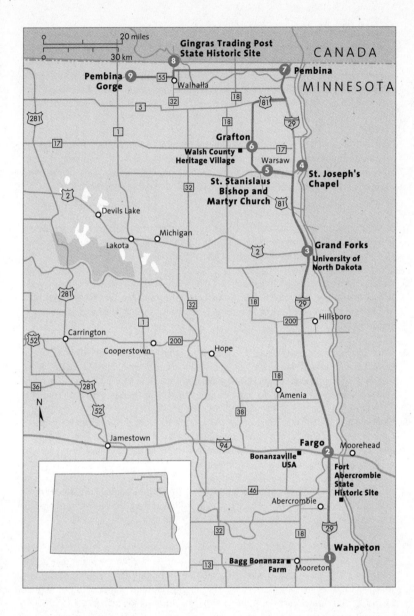

❸ Bright and early on day three, head north on I–29. Arriving in **Grand Forks,** take Exit 138 to 32nd Avenue South, turn north on Columbia Road, then turn west on University Drive to explore the prettiest campus in North Dakota. Founded in 1883—prior to statehood—the **University of North Dakota** is the state's oldest university. Follow Centennial Drive, which will take you past stately brick buildings to the **North Dakota Museum of Art.** The remodeled gym houses contemporary art exhibits.

This is a convenient time to head to downtown Grand Forks (DeMers Avenue) for a look at a scene of devastation and hope resulting from the 1997 flood. Even worse, a fire raged during the flood, destroying more than half a dozen downtown institutions.

Some buildings have been restored and again house boutiques, coffee shops, and offices. Lunch is available at three popular local establishments in the area: **Bonzer's,** known for its sandwiches; across the river in East Grand Forks, Minnesota, the **Blue Moose Bar and Grill**; and, also in East Grand Forks, **Whitey's,** with its 1930s horseshoe-shape bar. All three pubs were flooded and relocated near their original sites. For chocoholics, it's essential to visit Fargo's **Widman's,** home of the original chocolate-covered potato chip.

Conclude your visit to Grand Forks at **Odegard School of Aerospace Sciences,** a jewel in the university's crown, whose high-tech buildings house an atmospherium, tubular walkways, and cutting-edge technology. (Call ahead for a tour.) Or visit the **Myra Museum,** where you'll see an early settler's house and exhibits dedicated to pioneer women.

❹ Start the morning of day four by traveling 20 mi north of Grand Forks to see **St. Joseph's Chapel.** Just large enough for a priest and two altar servers, this quaint roadside chapel is one of the smallest in the United States.

❺ At this point, you can continue north on I–29 to Pembina. Or make the side trip west to tiny Warsaw, where you'll find **St. Stanislaus Bishop and Martyr Church.** Dedicated in 1901, this Gothic-Revival church reflects the Polish heritage of the surrounding community.

❻ From the church, continue west to U.S. 81, and turn north until you reach **Grafton,** where you can see **Elmwood House,** a Victorian mansion on 20 acres alongside the Park River. Also in Grafton is **Walsh County Heritage Village,** with more than 20 turn-of-the-20th-century buildings. After your visit, continue north on U.S. 81, then I–29 north to Pembina.

❼ **Pembina** anchors the northeast corner of the state. It's the oldest community in North Dakota and is an excellent departure point for excursions into Canada. While in Pembina, visit the **Pembina State Museum,** which exhibits everything from fossils to artifacts relating to fur trade and transportation.

❽ After lunch, head west out of Pembina about 30 mi to **Gingras Trading Post State Historic Site.** You'll find a hand-hewn oak log house and general store that served the community between 1843 and 1878.

❾ **Pembina Gorge** is your next destination. From Gingras, travel south on Rte. 32 to Walhalla, and then west on Rte. 55, where you'll find yourself in the midst of a largely undisturbed tract of 12,500 acres. The pristine and beautiful area's top asset is a forested valley created by glaciers and the winding Pembina River. In July or August, include a side trip to **Frost Fire Mountain Ski and Summer Resort,** to catch a matinee or evening performance of a Broadway musical in its amphitheater. Stay in Walhalla for the night (the bakery is a must for breakfast in the morning) or head to Cavalier to stay.

The most efficient way of returning to Wahpeton is to retrace your route to I–29, and follow it south (not quite a five-hour drive). For a pleasant change of scenery, you can choose Rte. 32 south from Walhalla to U.S. 2. It's about 75 mi of gently rolling farm country and tiny communities. When you connect to U.S. 2, travel east to Grand Forks, and then turn south on I–29 to return to Wahpeton.

AMIDON

(Nearby towns also listed: Bowman, Dickinson, Medora)

This tiny community, with a population of about 25, is the smallest county seat in the United States. The town was established in 1910 with high hopes that it would become the terminus for the Milwaukee Road Railroad. The railroad didn't come through, and the population peaked in 1930 with 162 residents. Dominated by ranches, the area is notable for its scenic drives, including the Little Missouri National Grasslands. Even more memorable is the traffic control; watch out for the patrol car permanently parked at the edge of town. The officer inside is a real dummy.

Information: Bowman Chamber of Commerce | Box 1143, Bowman, ND 58623 | 701/523–5880 or 701/523–3805 during summer | fax 701/523–3322 | www.bowmannd.com.

Attractions

Burning Coal Vein. An underground coal vein has been burning for more than a century on this National Grasslands site. A primitive campground is maintained in the area by the U.S. Forest Service. | USDA Forest Service, 1511 E Interstate Ave., Bismarck 58501 | 701/250–4443. | Free | Daily.

White Butte and Black Butte. At 3,506 ft, White Butte is North Dakota's highest point. Directly opposite is Black Butte, which is equally striking. Both are on private land. Hiking is permitted at White Butte with permission of the landowner. | 6 mi south of Amidon on Rte. 85 | 701/523–5880 | Free | Daily.

ON THE CALENDAR

AUG.: *Slope County Farmers Fair.* This old-fashioned three-day country fair has watermelon-eating contests, egg tosses, and three-legged races, with exhibits of pies and baked goods, canning, photography, vegetables, fruits, and crafts. On Saturday there's a live band, livestock show, demolition derby, horseshoe tournament, team penning contest, and stage show with local talent. Sunday has ecumenical services at the fairgrounds, a parade of champions with all 4-H trophy winners, a quilt show, rodeo, and black powder fun shoot. The fair ends with a pig roast and sweet corn supper, with a free will donation to charity. | 701/879–6270.

Lodging

Logging Camp Ranch. On a fourth-generation, 10,000-acre working cattle and buffalo ranch about 20 mi northwest of Amidon you can find three hand-built log cabins with modern facilities, trapshooting, and horseback riding. The rooms, three with bunk beds, have handmade log furnishings and photos of wildlife and cowboys at work. No air-conditioning in some rooms, some kitchenettes, some microwaves, some refrigerators, no TV in rooms, no room phones. Hiking, horseback riding, fishing. | HCR3 Box 26A, Bowman | 701/279–5501 | fax 701/279–5501 | www.loggingcampranch.com | 5 rooms, 3 cabins | $65 rooms; $50 cabins | MC, V.

BISMARCK

(Nearby towns also listed: Fort Yates, Linton, Mandan, Washburn)

Bismarck was started by railroad magnates as they laid their iron tracks across the prairie. First named Edwinton in 1872, the city was renamed in 1873 in honor of the Chancellor of Germany, Prince Otto von Bismarck, with hopes of attracting German investments

BISMARCK

INTRO
ATTRACTIONS
DINING
LODGING

in transcontinental railroads. By the time General George Custer arrived in 1874 at nearby Fort Abraham Lincoln, Bismarck was thriving as a transportation town with the Northern Pacific Railway crossing the steamboat-laden Missouri River. Custer remained here until 1876, when he left for the Battle of Little Big Horn. The *Bismarck Tribune* was the first newspaper to report Custer's demise. The story was based on notes found on the body of the *Tribune*'s reporter, Mark Kellogg, who died at the battle.

In 1889 North Dakota became a state, with Bismarck as its capital. The city thrived in the booms that followed the emergence of the railroad industry, gold rushes in the Black Hills, and, most recently, the discovery of oil and the development of synthetic fuels. Bismarck is economically and culturally dependent on its status as North Dakota's state capital. It's one of the smallest of the nation's 50 capitals and has no public transportation system. The city has thousands of acres of parks and riverfront development. Every other year, Bismarck hosts the Prairie Rose State Games, North Dakota's largest multi-sport Olympic-style festival.

Information: Bismarck-Mandan Convention and Visitors Bureau | Box 2274, 58501 | 701/222-4308 or 800/767-3555 | www.bismarck-mandancvb.org.

NEIGHBORHOODS

The most interesting section of **Downtown Bismarck** is from 6th Street in the east to Mandan Street in the west, and from Rosser Avenue in the north to Main Avenue in the south. On the corner of 6th Street and Thayer Avenue is the Belle Mehus Auditorium, the original civic auditorium built in 1914 and restored in the 1990s. The three-story 1930 Art Deco Burleigh County Courthouse straddles 6th and 5th streets. On 4th Street is the Tribune Building, former site of the state's first newspaper, now used for office space. On Main Avenue is the Patterson Hotel, built in 1910, which became the seat of state government for a couple of years when the Capitol building burned in 1930. Directly across Main Avenue is the Northern Pacific depot, a 1901 landmark notable for its Spanish mission style and now home to the restaurant Fiesta Villa.

Fifth Street Art Gallery displays the work of area artists; many other shops are nearby. Two blocks south is the Bismarck Art and Gallery Association, called BAGA, with a small gallery for the latest exhibit by area artists.

The **Historic Cathedral District** is a residential area bounded by Raymond Street to the west, 2nd Street to the east, Thayer Avenue to the south, and Boulevard Avenue to the north. The best part of the district, however, is along avenues A and B West near Washington Street. Here you can see several two-story, single-family homes in a variety of architectural styles, mostly dating from 1910 to 1920. Prairie School, Art Deco, Colonial Revival, Tudor Revival, and Bungalow are some of the architectural styles represented in this district, named for the Catholic Cathedral of the Holy Spirit.

WALKING TOUR

Historical and Arboretum Tour (minimum 2 hours)

For a compact slice of North Dakota—history, politics, art, and even gardening—try this walking tour of the Capitol grounds. From the parking lot between the State Capitol and the North Dakota Heritage Center, walk toward the front steps of the Capitol building. At the corner is the **John Burke statue,** in honor of the former North Dakota governor and later treasurer of the United States under President Woodrow Wilson from 1913 to 1921. Walk just a few steps beyond to admire the grand steps leading to Memorial Hall, the main hall of the North Dakota Capitol building. The steps are made from 1.8 billion-year-old granite. You get an impressive view of the Moderne-style **Capitol Building.** Then walk behind the Burke statue to the tunnel and ground floor entrance to the Capitol. Inside and to your right is an information booth with guides who can take you on a 30-minute tour of the building. Or try it yourself. The ground floor hosts the **North Dakota Rough Rider Hall of Fame,** with oil portraits of the state's famous sons and daughters. Go up one level to the first floor to the 40-ft-high **Memorial Hall** and admire the impressive 12-ft-long Art Deco lights. The House and Senate chambers are on the west end in **Legislative Hall,** with its rich rosewood inlaid with curly maple; to the east are the offices for the governor, attorney general and secretary of state. Travel up to the second floor for a balcony view of Memorial Hall. Then, from here, go to the 18th floor and the **observation deck.**

Exit the Capitol building at the tunnel and turn right (west). In the trees, head for the **Horse Sculpture.** Named *Cortes,* the Arabian horse was created by North Dakota artist Bennett Brien and erected in 1994. Also from here you can join an **arboretum trail.** About five minutes along this path, you can see the **Petrified Log and Stumps,** dominated by a 60-million-year-old redwood log. Opposite is **Centennial Grove,** dedicated in 1989 when President George Bush was on hand to help the state celebrate this anniversary. Continue on the southbound arboretum trail to the **Pioneer Family sculpture** at the end of the Capitol mall. Cast in bronze and dedicated in 1947, parents, son and infant symbolize the undying spirit of frontier life. Resume the arboretum trail to the **All Veterans Memorial,** dedicated in 1989. Nearby are shaded benches and a small brass sculpture, **Pioneers of the Future,** dedicated to children. The memorial is behind the North Dakota Heritage Center, and just beyond the memorial is the **Gratitude Train,** presented to North Dakota in 1949 by the people of France.

Backtrack just a bit on the path to the **North Dakota Heritage Center.** The museum has permanent and temporary exhibits, houses the state's archive collection, and sells North Dakota–related products in its gift store. Downstairs is a collection of sterling silver that graced the U.S.S. *North Dakota* and is now used for official state functions.

After you've enjoyed the museum, stroll outside and up the sidewalk. To your right will be the **Buffalo Sculpture,** erected in 1986. Continue up the sidewalk to the **statue of Sakakawea.** Dedicated in 1910, this 12-ft bronze sculpture honors the woman who guided Lewis and Clark on their 1804–1806 expedition. Given the many spellings of the Shoshone guide's name, the State of North Dakota has officially adopted this spelling of her name. From Sakakawea, walk across the parking lot to the front steps of the Capitol Building where you can find your starting point at the **John Burke statue.**

TRANSPORTATION INFORMATION

Airports: Bismarck Municipal Airport is served by Northwest and United Express. | Airport Rd. | 701/222–6502.

Bus: The town is served by **Greyhound Lines and Minot–Bismarck Bus Service.** | 3750 E. Rosser Ave. | 701/223–6576. | www.greyhound.com.

Car Travel: Bismarck is a relatively small metropolitan area, so it's easy to explore the downtown area on foot. There are only two one-way streets, 7th and 9th streets. Rush hours are short and traffic is light. Right turns are permitted on red unless signs indicate otherwise. There are no parking meters, so you can park on the street wherever you find a space; time is limited to one or two hours. Indoor parking areas cost about $5 for a day. Get more information from the Bismarck Parking Authority | 701/222–8954.

Attractions

ART AND ARCHITECTURE

State Capitol. The 19-story building is one of only two U.S. state capitols without a traditional dome. The structure, with a Moderne-style exterior and Art Deco interior, was built in the early 1930s after a Christmas fire destroyed the building from the territorial days. | 600 E. Boulevard Ave. | 701/328–2480 | fax 701/328–3710 | Free | Memorial Day–Labor Day, weekdays 8–5, Sat. 9–4, Sun. 1–4; Labor Day–Memorial Day, weekdays 8–5, closed Sat.–Sun.

Dedicated in 1989, the **All Veterans Memorial** pays tribute to North Dakotans who died in military service since statehood.

Along the **Arboretum Trail** you can see 73 varieties of trees and shrubs, including pine, oak, European larch, linden, honeysuckle, chokecherry, buffalo berry, Russian olive, and more.

Contemporary artist Bennett Brien created the **Buffalo Sculpture** out of steel-reinforcing bar. Exposure to the elements has rusted the steel since it was erected in 1986, returning the buffalo to its natural coloring.

In 1989, **Centennial Grove** was dedicated by President George Bush for the state's 100th birthday celebration. | 612 E. Boulevard Ave.

The **Gratitude Train** was presented to North Dakota in 1949 by the people of France in gratitude for our nation's efforts during World War II.

Like the Buffalo Sculpture, the **Horse Sculpture,** a graceful Arabian horse named *Cortes,* was also created by Bennet Brien out of steel-reinforcing bar. The sculpture was erected in 1994.

The **John Burke Statue** honors the former North Dakota governor and later treasurer of the United States under President Woodrow Wilson from 1913 to 1921.

Accented with rich rosewood inlaid with curly maple, **Legislative Hall** is home to the state's House and Senate chambers. Cross Memorial Hall at the east end and see the mahogany, teak, and oak-paneled offices of the governor, attorney general, and secretary of state. | 701/328–2480 | Free | Memorial Day–Labor Day, weekdays 8–5, Sat. 9–4, Sun. 1–4; Labor Day–Memorial Day, weekdays 8–5, closed Sat.–Sun.

The Rough Rider Award is the state's highest honor, and portraits of recipients hang in the **North Dakota Rough Rider Hall of Fame** in the Capitol building. On the ground floor are oil portraits of authors Era Bell Thompson and Larry Woiwode, journalist Eric Sevareid, actresses Dorothy Stickney and Angie Dickinson, band leader Lawrence Welk, and basketball coach Phil Jackson, all North Dakotans. | 612 E. Boulevard Ave. | 701/328–2480 | Free | Memorial Day–Labor Day, weekdays 8–5, Sat. 9–4, Sun. 1–4; Labor Day–Memorial Day, weekdays 8–5, closed Sat.–Sun.

The best view of the city is from the Capitol's **observation deck** on the 18th floor. | 701/328–2480 | Free | Memorial Day–Labor Day, weekdays 8–5, Sat. 9–4, Sun. 1–4; Labor Day–Memorial Day, weekdays 8–5, closed Sat.–Sun.

About 60 million years old, the **Petrified Log and Stumps** are sections of an 80-ft petrified redwood.

Created by sculptor Avard Fairbanks, *The Pioneer Family* symbolizes the era of wagon trains and the frontier spirit.

Life-size bronze figures of a girl and boy look ahead and into space, representing future generations in *Pioneers of the Future.* The sculpture was created by Jeffrey W. Barber.

In front of the North Dakota Heritage Center is a large outdoor **Statue of Sakakawea,** who is looking west into the distance and carrying her infant, Baptiste.

CULTURE, EDUCATION, AND HISTORY

Camp Hancock State Historic Site. In 1872 Camp Hancock sheltered work crews on the Northern Pacific Railroad. The site has a museum, one of Bismarck's oldest churches, and a Northern Pacific steam locomotive. | 101 W. Main Ave. | 701/328–2666 | fax 701/328–3710 | www.state.nd.us/hist | Free | Mid-May–mid-Sept., Wed.–Sun. 1–5, closed Mon.–Tues.

Double Ditch Indian Village State Historic Site. The ruins of a Mandan earthlodge village, 7½ mi north of Bismarck, on Rte. 1804, make up this site, named for its twin-ditch fortification that protected up to 150 lodges. | 701/328–2666 | fax 701/328–3710 | www.state.nd.us/hist | Free | Daily dawn to dusk.

When it Comes to Getting Cash at an ATM, Same Thing.

Whether you're in Yosemite or Yemen, using your Visa® card or ATM card with the PLUS symbol is the easiest and most convenient way to get cash. Even if your bank is in Minneapolis and you're in Miami, Visa/PLUS ATMs make getting cash so easy, you'll feel right at home. After all, Visa/PLUS ATMs are open 24 hours a day, 7 days a week, rain or shine. And if you need help finding one of Visa's 627,000 ATMs in 127 countries worldwide, visit **visa.com/pd/atm**. We'll make finding an ATM as easy as finding the Eiffel Tower, the Pyramids or even the Grand Canyon.

It's Everywhere You Want To Be®

Find America *with a Compass*

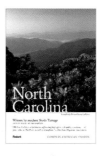
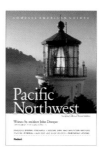
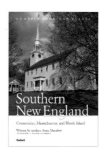

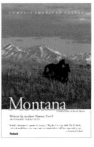

Written by local authors and illustrated throughout with images from regional photographers, Compass American Guides reveal the character and culture of America's most spectacular destinations. Covering more than 35 states and regions across the country, Compass guides are perfect for residents who want to explore their own backyards, and for visitors seeking an insider's perspective on all there is to see and do.

Fodor's Compass American Guides

At bookstores everywhere.

Former Governors' Mansion State Historic Site. This 1884 Victorian structure was home to 21 governors from 1893 to 1960. | 320 E. Ave. B | 701/328–2666 | fax 701/328–3710 | www.state.nd.us/hist | Free | Memorial Day–Labor Day, Wed.–Sun. 1–5, or by appointment.

Fort Dilts State Historic Site. In 1864 a 97-wagon party with a cavalry escort was attacked by Hunkpapa Sioux Native Americans. The caravan was corralled for 14 days behind a hastily built 6-ft-high and 2-ft-thick sod wall until troops rescued them. This may be the only documented instance that settlers actually circled their wagons for defense. Today there is little to see other than a simple marker on the site. | 612 E Boulevard Ave., Bismarck | 701/328–2666 | fax 701/328–3710 | www.state.nd.us./hist | Free | Daily.

Ward Earthlodge Indian Village Site. About 43 depressions mark where the earthlodges made up this Mandan village. Take the trail off of Burnt Boat Dr., right along Missouri River in Bismarck. | 701/328–2666 | Free. | Daily dawn–dusk.

MUSEUMS

North Dakota Heritage Center. The state's largest museum and archive, there's a permanent exhibit that covers everything from dinosaurs to tractors, and from Native Americans to immigrants. | 612 E. Boulevard Ave. | 701/328–2666 | fax 701/328–3710 | www.state.nd.us/hist | Free | Weekdays 8–5, Sat. 9–5, Sun. 11–5.

PARKS, NATURAL AREAS, AND OUTDOOR RECREATION

McDowell Dam Nature Park. An area popular with families, this park has a 65-acre fishing lake with a beach and picnic shelters. | 1951 93rd St. NE | 701/222–6455 or 701/223–7016. | www.bispark.org | Free | Daily 7 AM–10 PM.

Sertoma Riverside Park. Huge trees, picnic shelters, miniature golf, a large slide, and kiddie rides make this park along the Missouri River popular in the summer. | Bismarck Parks and Recreation Department, 420 E. Front Ave. | 701/222–6455 | fax 701/221–6838 | www.bisparks.org | Free | Daily 8 AM–11 PM.

YOUR CAR'S FIRST-AID KIT

- ❑ Bungee cords or rope to tie down trunk if necessary
- ❑ Club soda to remove stains from upholstery
- ❑ Cooler with bottled water
- ❑ Extra coolant
- ❑ Extra windshield-washer fluid
- ❑ Flares and/or reflectors
- ❑ Flashlight and extra batteries
- ❑ Hand wipes to clean hands after roadside repair
- ❑ Hose tape

- ❑ Jack and fully inflated spare
- ❑ Jumper cables
- ❑ Lug wrench
- ❑ Owner's manual
- ❑ Plastic poncho—in case you need to do roadside repairs in the rain
- ❑ Quart of oil and quart of transmission fluid
- ❑ Spare fan belts
- ❑ Spare fuses
- ❑ Tire-pressure gauge

*Excerpted from *Fodor's: How to Pack: Experts Share Their Secrets*
© 1997, by Fodor's Travel Publications

RELIGION AND SPIRITUALITY

Cathedral of the Holy Spirit. This gleaming white stucco Catholic church with a prominent spire was built in 1945 in the Art Moderne style. | 520 N. Raymond St. | 701/223–1033 | Daily.

SHOPPING

Kirkwood Mall. With more than 100 specialty shops and four major department stores, this one-level mall is several acres large. | Corner of 7th Street and Bismarck Expressway | 701/223–3500 | Weekdays 10–9, Sat. 10–6, Sun. noon–6.

SIGHTSEEING TOURS

Lewis and Clark Riverboat. This 100-ft paddlewheel with twin decks travels a 90-minute route taken by trappers, traders, and settlers of the 19th century. | 1700 N. River Rd. | 701/255–4233 | www.lewisandclarkriverboat.com | $10.95 | Memorial Day–Labor Day, 3 cruises daily 2 PM–10 PM.

OTHER POINTS OF INTEREST

Dakota Zoo. In Seratoma Park along the Missouri River, this zoo has more than 125 species. | Sertoma Park Rd., 2 miles southwest of Bismarck | 701/223–7543 | fax 701/258–8350 | $4.50 | May–Sept., daily 10–8; Oct., Fri.–Sun. 10–sunset, closed Mon.–Thurs.

ON THE CALENDAR

JUNE: _Expo._ An annual event, there are entertainment, carnival rides, exhibits, and concessions to fill a weekend with festivities at the Civic Center downtown. | 701/222–6487 or 701/222–4308.

JULY: _Fourth of July Spectacular._ The Bismarck-Mandan Symphony presents a dramatic musical show, concluding with a fireworks display on the Capitol grounds. | 701/222–4308.

AUG.: _Capitol A'fair._ This arts and crafts fair attracts artists from across the Midwest to the Capitol grounds. Stroll among more than 150 food and entertainment booths. | 701/223–5986 or 701/222–4308.

SEPT.: _United Tribes Technical College International Powwow._ One of the largest powwows in North America, United Tribes International Powwow draws contestants in Native American dancing and singing. Traditional garb, Indian foods, and handmade crafts add to the colorful festivities, held the first weekend after Labor Day on campus at 3315 University Dr. | 701/255–3285 or 701/222–4308.

SEPT.: _Folkfest._ Modeled after Oktoberfest, this week-long downtown festival has a parade, dances, a huge street fair with arts, crafts, and ethnic food. | 701/223–5660.

OCT.: _Edge of the West Rodeo._ Many of the nation's cowboys compete at the Bismarck Civic Center in the grand finale of more than 20 circuit rodeos in North Dakota and South Dakota. | 701/222–6487 or 701/222–4308.

Dining

INEXPENSIVE

China Garden. Chinese. Pastel colors with dashes of red add serenity to this small restaurant. The cuisine blends the best of north and south China. Known for sweet and sour dishes. No alcohol. | 1929 N. Washington St. | 701/224–0698 | $7–$16 | AE, MC, V.

Drumstick Café. American. This tiny café serves generous portions of two sauces: syrup and gravy. You can choose homemade potatoes and coleslaw, pancakes that fill platters from edge to edge, and homemade caramel rolls and angel food cake. Try the sour cream and raisin pie. Kids' menu. No alcohol. | 307 N. 3rd St. | 701/223–8449 | Closed Sun. | $5–$12 | No credit cards.

83 Diner. American. On the south side of the junction of U.S. 83 and I–94, this diner has chrome barstools and photos of 1950s movie stars. Chocolate malts and the James Dean burger—with mushrooms and Swiss—are local favorites. Kids' menu. No alcohol. | 1307 E. Interchange Ave. | 701/258–3470 | $8–$15 | AE, D, MC, V.

Green Earth Café and One World Coffeehouse. Vegetarian. This tiny downtown eatery has homemade vegetarian soups and sandwiches, and exotic breads. Order from the counter and see exhibits by local artists while you wait. Soups change daily. Try the gazpacho or carrot-ginger soup. Afternoons and evenings, the coffeehouse has live entertainment. No alcohol. | 208 E. Broadway Ave. | 701/223–8646 | No dinner Sun. | $4–$10 | No credit cards.

North American Steak Buffet. Steak. This is truly all-you-can-eat dining, with a salad bar, hot-foods bar, and desserts. Known for its grilled steak and chicken, the chocolate and banana pie and cheesecake goes quickly here, too. No alcohol. | 2000 N. 12th St. | 701/223–1107 | $8.29 | AE, D, MC, V.

Schlotzsky's. American/Casual. Get your deli sandwich with choices of breads, spreads, meats, and veggies, and order a soup or a giant cookie. Try the Original Sandwich, with ham, two kinds of salami, three cheeses, mustard, tomato, and other garnishes on a sourdough bun. Kids' menu. | 1329 E. Interstate Ave. | 701/221–2446 | $4–$6 | AE, D, MC, V.

The Woodhouse. American/Casual. You can place your order from the phone at your booth here. The menu says "no tipping necessary." Known for hamburgers, egg salad, and homemade lemon meringue pie. Kids' menu. No alcohol. | 1825 N. 13th St. | 701/255–3654 | $5–$10 | AE, D, DC, MC, V.

MODERATE

Bistro 1100, An American Café. Eclectic. You can try a little of everything at this relaxed eatery, including ostrich, wood-fired burgers, and Greek pizza (with prosciutto, artichoke, and feta). In nice weather, you can eat outside on a deck overlooking downtown and the railroad tracks. | 1103 E. Front Ave. | 701/224–8800 | Closed Sun. | $9.95–$26.95 | AE, MC, V.

Caspar's East 40. Eclectic. The interior is dark and intimate, with working fireplaces and antiques. Try the South American steak. For dessert, there's meringue glacé—French vanilla ice cream surrounded by meringue with raspberry or chocolate sauce and whipped cream. | 1401 E. Interchange Ave. | 701/258–7222 | Closed Sun. | $11–$36 | AE, MC, V.

Fiesta Villa. Mexican. In this old mission-style depot now famous for its margaritas, you can choose beef or chicken fajitas inside or, in nice weather, on a long patio filled with fountains and trees. | 411 E. Main Ave. | 701/222–8075 | No lunch Sun. | $9–$13 | AE, D, MC, V.

Los Amigos. Mexican. Authentic and homemade food—such as traditional tamales and chile relleno—with mouth-watering hot sauce and the right dash of cilantro. Kids' menu. | 431 S. 3rd St. | 701/223–7580 | Closed Sun. | $5–$10 | AE, D, DC, MC, V.

Minervas Restaurant and Bar. American/Casual. The best bet at lunch is the popular soup, salad, and sandwich bar. Dinner favorites include the hunter's steak—a rib eye with burgundy sauce—and Cajun chicken with linguine. | 1800 N. 12th St. | 701/222–1402 | Breakfast also served | $9–$16 | AE, D, DC, MC, V.

Space Aliens Grill and Bar. American/Casual. Look for the marquee topped with an alien spaceship announcing that earthlings are welcome at this out-of-this-world restaurant. Inside, an alien occasionally wanders through the crowd, giving kids tokens to enjoy the arcade. The French fries, served in a space cone, come with a choice of sauces. Known for barbecue ribs and fire-roasted pizza. Kids' menu. | 1304 E. Century Ave. | 701/223–6220 | $6–$15 | AE, D, MC, V.

EXPENSIVE

Captain Meriwether's. American. This restaurant is in an old train depot that was moved to the banks of the Missouri River. The interior has photographs of North Dakota, Native American artwork, and stuffed game. On the menu, beef, buffalo, and fresh catfish are

BISMARCK

INTRO
ATTRACTIONS
DINING
LODGING

favorites. You can eat on a deck overlooking the river. Kids' menu, Sun. brunch. | 1700 River Rd. | 701/224–0455 | $12–$25 | AE, D, DC, MC, V.

★ **Peacock Alley Bar and Grill.** American/Casual. In what was once the historic Patterson Hotel, this restaurant was the scene of countless political deals, captured in period photographs. The bar serves inexpensive lunches with pasta salads, soups, and sandwiches. There's also Cajun firecracker shrimp and pan-blackened prime rib. Kids' menu. Sun. brunch. | 422 E. Main Ave. | 701/255–7917 | No lunch or dinner Sun. | $12.95–$17 | AE, D, DC, MC, V.

Lodging

INEXPENSIVE

Comfort Suites. A 92-ft water slide at its pool makes this hotel, 2 mi from downtown, popular with families. Complimentary Continental breakfast. In-room data ports, some in-room hot tubs. Cable TV. Indoor pool. Hot tub. Exercise equipment, gym. Laundry service. Business services, airport shuttle, free parking. Some pets allowed. | 929 Gateway Ave. | 701/223–4009 or 800/228–5150 | fax 701/223–9119 | www.comfortsuites.com | 60 suites | $50–$90 | AE, D, MC, V.

Select Inn of Bismarck. At I–94 in a service strip, this two-story motel, built in 1976, is 3 mi from Kirkwood Mall and 1 mi from Heritage Center at the State Capitol. Complimentary Continental breakfast. In-room data ports, in-room safes, some kitchenettes, some microwaves, some refrigerators, some in-room hot tubs. Cable TV. Laundry facilities. | 1505 Interchange Ave. | 701/223–8060 or 800/641–1000 | fax 701/223–8293 | www.selectinn.com | 99 rooms, 1 suite | $41–$43, $63 suite | AE, D, DC, MC, V.

Super 8. This three-story hotel is at Exit 159 off I–94, a mile from the Capitol building. Room service. Cable TV. Laundry service. Business services, free parking. Some pets allowed. | 1124 E. Capitol Ave. | 701/255–1314 or 800/800–8000 | fax 701/255–1314 | www.super8.com | 61 rooms | $30–$55 | AE, D, DC, MC, V.

MODERATE

Best Western Doublewood Inn. At I–94 and Hwy. 83, this two-story motel is ¼ mi from the State Capitol. Restaurant, bar, room service. In-room data ports, microwaves, refrigerators. Cable TV, some in-room VCRs. Indoor pool. Hot tub, sauna. Video games. Playground. Laundry services. Business services, airport shuttle, free parking. Pets allowed (fee). | 1400 E. Interchange Ave. | 701/258–7000 or 800/554–7077 | fax 701/258–2001 | www.bestwestern.com | 143 rooms | $73 | AE, D, DC, MC, V.

Comfort Inn. Poolside rooms have direct access to the courtyard in this hotel 2 mi north of downtown. The lounge and casino have a nightly happy hour. Complimentary Continental breakfast. Cable TV. Indoor pool. Hot tub. Game room. Laundry service. Business services, airport shuttle. Some pets allowed. | 1030 Interstate Ave. | 701/223–1911 or 800/228–5150 | fax 701/223–6977 | www.comfortinn.com | 148 rooms, 5 suites | $45–$50, $55 suites | AE, D, DC, MC, V.

Expressway Suites. Close to Kirkwood Mall, this hotel is at Expressway and Washington Sts., within 3 blocks of the Civic Center. Bar, complimentary Continental breakfast. In-room data ports, microwaves, refrigerators. Cable TV. Indoor pool. Hot tub. Gym. Laundry facilities, laundry service. Business services, airport shuttle. | 180 E. Expressway | 701/222–3311 or 888/774–5566 | fax 701/222–3311 | www.fargoweb.com/ expressway | 64 suites | $59–$66, $105–$115 suites | AE, D, DC, MC, V.

Fairfield Inn by Marriott–North. If you're a golfer you might want to stay here: There are four courses within 6 mi. It's also near a small shopping center and U.S. 83. Complimentary Continental breakfast, room service. In-room data ports. Cable TV. Indoor pool. Hot tub. Laundry service. Business services. Free parking. | 1120 Century Ave. E | 701/223–9077 or 800/228–2800 | fax 701/223–9077 | www.fairfieldinn.com | 47 rooms, 16 suites | $60–$85; $70–$90 suites | AE, D, DC, MC, V.

Fairfield Inn by Marriott–South. This 3-story hotel is two blocks from Kirkwood Mall. Complimentary Continental breakfast, room service. In-room data ports. Cable TV. Indoor pool. Hot tub. Laundry service. Business services. | 135 Ivy Ave. | 701/223–9293 or 800/228–2800 | fax 701/223–9293 | www.fairfieldinn.com | 63 rooms, 16 suites | $60–$85, $70–$90 suites | AE, D, DC, MC, V.

Holiday Inn. The hotel's downtown location makes it the base for many concert artists and performers at the Bismarck Civic Center, 1 mi away. Restaurant, bar, room service. In-room data ports. Cable TV, in-room VCRs (and movies). Indoor pool. Beauty salon, hot tub. Gym. Laundry service. Business services, airport shuttle. | 605 E. Broadway | 701/255–6000 or 800/465–4329 | fax 701/223–0400 | www.basshotels.com/holiday-inn | 215 rooms, 35 suites | $64–$85, $89 suites | AE, D, DC, MC, V.

Kelly Inn. This two-story motel is one block from the north edge of the Capitol grounds. Restaurant, bar, room service. In-room data ports. Cable TV. Indoor pool. Hot tub, sauna. Exercise equipment. Laundry service. Airport shuttle. | 1800 N. 12th St. | 701/223–8001 or 800/635–3559 | fax 701/223–8001 | 97 rooms, 4 suites | $61, $65–$95 suites | AE, D, DC, MC, V.

Ramada Suites. At Exit 161 off I–94, this all-suites 1996 Ramada is between two shopping areas, 2 and 5 mi away. A truck stop and restaurant are next door. Complimentary Continental breakfast. In-room data ports, microwaves, refrigerators. Cable TV, some in-room VCRs. Indoor pool. Hot tub. Exercise equipment. Video games. | 3808 E. Divide Ave. | 701/221–3030 | fax 701/221–3030 | www.ramada.com | 67 suites | $63–$68 | AE, D, DC, MC, V.

EXPENSIVE

Country Suites. A water slide in the pool area highlights this three-story hotel built in 1998. It's 3 mi north of downtown, 6 blocks north of I–94. Complimentary Continental breakfast. In-room data ports, microwaves, refrigerators, some in-room hot tubs. Cable TV. Indoor pool, wading pool. Hot tub, sauna. Exercise equipment. Laundry facilities, laundry service. Business services, airport shuttle. No pets. | 3205 North 14th St. | 701/258–4300 or 800/456–4000 | fax 701/258–4300 | 76 rooms | $95 | AE, D, DC, MC, V.

Radisson Inn. Many of the rooms here have large work areas and private patios overlooking the indoor pool. The hotel is across from Kirkwood Mall, 4 mi from the airport. Restaurant, bar, room service. In-room data ports, some in-room hot tubs. Cable TV. Indoor pool. Hot tub, sauna. Gym. Laundry service. Business services, airport shuttle. Some pets allowed. | 800 S. 3rd St. | 701/258–7700 or 800/333–3333 | fax 701/224–8212 | www.radisson.com | 298 rooms, 8 suites | $75–$90, $180–$195 suites | AE, D, DC, MC, V.

BOTTINEAU

MAP 7, E1

(Nearby towns also listed: Kenmare, Minot, Rugby)

In 1884 the Great Northern Railroad established Bottineau, population 2,500, and named after Pierre Bottineau, a well-known local frontiersman. The community is the largest near the Turtle Mountains, which are 150 square mi of hills left by glaciers. When European traders and trappers first explored the hills in the mid-1700s, they found them inhabited by the Chippewa. The blending of cultures created a new people, called the Metis. Lake Metigoshe is the main community of the Turtle Mountains, just 12 mi northeast of Bottineau. The name Metigoshe comes from the Chippewa language meaning "clear lake surrounded by oak trees." The lake, straddling the U.S.–Canada border, has become one of North Dakota's premier resort areas. There are about 850 cabins on the U.S side and 200 in Canada. Public access areas and private businesses line the 38 mi of lake shore.

BOTTINEAU

INTRO
ATTRACTIONS
DINING
LODGING

Information: **Greater Bottineau Area Chamber of Commerce and Convention and Visitors Bureau** | Rte. 5E 58318 | 701/228–3849 or 800/735–6932 | www.bottineau.com.

Attractions

Bottineau Winter Park Ski Area. Nine 225-ft slopes attract skiers and snowboarders here; the length of the longest slope is 1400 feet, and there's also a toboggan chute. Conditions are usually good, thanks to snowmaking. | At Rte. 43, 3 mi west of County Rd. 49 | 701/263–4556 or 800/305–8079 | fax 701/263–4446 | www.bottineau.com | $15 | Thanksgiving weekend–mid-March.

Homen State Forest. More than 4,000 acres, with two small lakes, are home to 100 species of nesting birds. Hunting, canoeing, picnicking, and primitive camping are allowed. | 307 1st St. E | 701/228–5422 | fax 701/228–5448 | www.state.nd.us/forest | Free | Daily.

★ **International Peace Garden.** Established in 1934, this 2,300-acre garden is flowering testimony to peace between Canada and the U.S. There are 100,000 flowers planted here annually. The garden has an 18-ft floral clock, the Peace Tower, and the Peace Chapel, with picnic areas, gift shops, and playgrounds. In winter, you can cross-country ski and showshoe 12 mi of groomed trails. On U.S. 281, 12 mi north of Dunseith. | 701/263–4390 or 204/534–2510 | www.peacegarden.com | $10 per vehicle, free mid-Sept.–Apr. | May–Aug., daily 8 AM–10 PM; early Sept.–mid-Sept., daily 8–8; mid-Sep.–Apr., daily 9–5.

J. Clark Salyer National Wildlife Refuge. Some of the largest freshwater marshes in America distinguish this 58,700-acre preserve in the Souris River basin, inhabited by great blue herons, muskrat, ducks, geese, and other wildlife. A 22-mi driving tour winds through marshlands, grasslands, sandy hills, and forests. You can canoe on a 13-mi stretch of the Souris River. | U.S. 2, at Rte. 14 NW | 701/768–2548 | May–Oct., daily 5 AM–11 PM.

Lake Metigoshe State Park. Named by the Chippewa Native Americans, this 1,551-acre park has a lake, boat ramp, and forest in the Turtle Mountains. The park is on the 250-mi Peace Garden snowmobile trail. There's cross-country skiing as well. From Bottineau, go north on Main St. 14 mi. to Rte. 43; turn left, the follow signs. | Off Rte. 43 | 701/263–4651 | $4 per vehicle | Daily.

Turtle Mountain Chippewa Casino. Blackjack, poker, simulcast racing, and bingo compete with 325 slot machines for your attention at this site 30 mi east of Bottineau. The snack bar and Blue Lagoon Bar serve a buffet daily. | Rte. 5 | 701/477–3281, 701/477–3340, or 800/477–3497 | Free | Sun.–Wed. 7 AM–3 AM, Thurs.–Sat. open 24 hours.

Turtle Mountain Chippewa Heritage Center. An art gallery and museum, the center has sculptures by internationally recognized artists. Exhibits concentrate on local history. The gift shop sells authentic Native American crafts. To get here, take U.S. 281 through Belcourt; go 1 block past the first light in Belcourt; then follow signs. | Box 257, Belcourt | 701/477–6140 or 701/477–6451, ext. 180 | Free | Mid-May–mid-Sept., weekdays 9–4:30, weekends 1–5; mid-Sept.–mid-May, weekdays 10–4, closed weekends.

Turtle Mountain State Forest. Oak, aspen, green ash, balsam poplar, and willow are among the trees in this 7,000-acre forest. Trails are marked for hiking, horseback riding, mountain biking, cross-country skiing, and snowmobiling. You can canoe on the small lake, see white-tailed deer and moose, and camp. | 307 1st St. E | 701/228–5422 | fax 701/228–5448 | www.state.nd.us/forest | Free. | Daily.

W'eel Turtle. This mammoth outdoor sculpture of a turtle was built from discarded tire rims. Set 18 mi, west of Bottineau, it greets you as you approach Dunseith from the south. | Main St., downtown Dunseith | 701/244–5491.

ON THE CALENDAR

JUNE: *Old-Time Fiddlers' Contest.* Fiddlers show their talent at this competition at the International Peace Garden. The show attracts the best fiddlers from 15 states and Canadian provinces. | 701/838–8472 or 701/838–4579.

JUNE–JULY: *International Music Camp.* Music students of all ages and from all parts of the world gather at the International Peace Garden to camp and take classes. At the end of each week, musicians perform outdoor concerts in amphitheaters in the park. | 701/838–8472 or 701/263–4211 (summer) | www.musiccamp.minot.com.

Dining

Birchwood Steakhouse and Northern Lights Lounge. Steak. Locals favor this lakeside restaurant near the Canadian border. On the menu are pepper steak, or the captain's choice, a selection of scallops, shrimp, and northern pike. Sunday brunch. | 2 Birchwood Heights Rd. | 701/263–4283 | No dinner Sun. | $7–$27 | MC, V.

Loveland's Steak Cove. Steak. This supper club has a "steak pit" where you choose your steak, place it on the grill, and cook it to your exact liking. | 345 11th St. W | 701/228–2296 | Closed Sun. | $10–$24 | AE, D, MC, V.

Norway House Restaurant. American. In the Norway House motel, the restaurant serves prime rib, boiled shrimp, and fish fry, and sundaes and cheesecakes for dessert. | 1255 Rte. 5 NE | 701/228–3737 | No dinner Sun.–Mon. | $7–$19 | MC, V.

Tommy Turtle Lanes and Restaurant. American/Casual. This relaxed restaurant is known for its generous portions, with a menu of burgers with onion rings and homemade desserts like sour cream raisin bars and Special K bars. Kids' menu. | 403 11th St. W | 701/228–2132 | $6–$13. | No credit cards.

Lodging

Lake Metigoshe State Park Cabins. Three log cabins in this wooded 1,551-acre park are close to the lake, with paved and wooded trails for biking and hiking. The one- and two-bedroom cabins sleep up to 8 and have queen-size beds, futons, propane fireplaces, decks, and an outside fire ring. Bring your own bath and bed linens. Lake Metigoshe is 15 mi north of Bottineau on Highway 43. No air-conditioning, kitchenettes, no room phones, no TV. Lake. Hiking. Beach, dock, boating, fishing. Cross-country skiing, tobogganing. Kids' programs (ages 6 and up), playground. No smoking. | Lake Metigoshe State Park # 2, 13 mi, NE of Bottineau | 701/263–4651 | fax 701/263–4648 | www.state.nd.us/ndparks | 3 cabins (showers only) | $52–$72 | D, MC, V.

Norway House. This large one-story motel is on the east edge of town, 1 block from the Tommy Turtle Park. Liquor store adjacent. Restaurant, bar, room service. Cable TV. Airport shuttle. Some pets allowed. | 1255 Rte. 5 NE | 701/228–3737 | fax 701/228–3740 | 46 rooms | $35–$41 | AE, D, MC, V.

BOWMAN

MAP 7, B5

(Nearby towns also listed: Amidon, Dickinson, Medora)

Deep in ranching and farming country, Bowman has a population of 1,700. Originally named Twin Buttes when it was founded in 1907, the town's name quickly changed to honor either a territorial legislator or an official of the Milwaukee Road Railroad, depending on which source you choose to believe. Tourists come to Bowman to scour the nearby fields for dinosaur treasures. At the Hell Creek formation around Bowman a complete triceratops skeleton was unearthed. Near Rhame (12 mi west) there's an ongoing excavation of a T-Rex skeleton, one of only 12 known in the world.

Information: Bowman Chamber of Commerce | Box 1143 58623 | 701/523–5880 or 701/523–3805 during summer | www.bowmannd.com.

Dakota Buttes Visitors Council | Box 1323, Hettinger, ND 58639 | 701/567–2531 | www.hettingernd.com.

Attractions

Bowman–Haley Dam and Lake. Maintained by local interest groups, this recreation area has camping, fishing, and hiking trails. Reservations are not accepted. It's about 15 mi southeast of Bowman, accessible via gravel road. | Off Rte. 85 | 701/252–7666 | Free | Daily.

Butte View State Campground. The campground is a popular halfway point between Medora and the Black Hills. It's 1½ mi east of town. | Rte. 12 | 701/523–3896 | Free, camping fees | Mid-May–mid-Sept., daily.

Cedar River National Grassland. This 6,700-acre, mixed-grass prairie straddles the North Dakota and South Dakota border. Primitive camping is allowed. | Grand River/Cedar River Ranger District, Lemmon, SD; 1005 W. 5th Ave. | 605/374–3592 | Free | Daily.

Mystic Theater. This restored 1914 silent movie and vaudeville theater is on the National Register of Historic Places and currently hosts local productions. You can't miss it; there's only one real street in town. | 103 N Main St., Box 93, Marmarth | 701/279–6996 | Free | By appointment.

Pioneer Trails Regional Museum. The museum has a working fossil lab and tour, and exhibits on local culture and history. The fossil tours are on weekends from April to August. | 12 1st Ave. NE | 701/523–3600 | fax 701/523–3600 | www.bowmannd.com | $2 | Apr.–Oct., Mon.–Sat. 9–6, Sun. 1–6; Nov.–Mar., Mon.–Sat. 10–4, Sun. 1–4.

Western Way Depot. You can shop for Western and boutique clothing, local art, and antiques here in the 1908 Gascoyne train station. | 410 1st Ave. SW | 701/523–3145 or 800/294–4402 | Free | Mon.–Sat. 10–6, closed Sun.

ON THE CALENDAR

JUNE: *North Dakota State High School Rodeo Finals.* The best young cowboys and cowgirls compete for state honors here on Father's Day weekend at the 4 Winds Arena. The rodeo has bareback, saddle bronco, and bull riding, steer wrestling, breakaway roping, calf roping, goat tying, pole bending, and barrel racing. | 701/523–5880.

Dining

Long Pines Steakhouse and Lounge. Steak. The lodge-style restaurant's interior has a huge stone fireplace and early 1900s lamps from a Pullman railroad car. The king cut prime rib is mammoth. Or try a buffalo rib eye steak or burger. | 13 1st Ave. NW | 701/523–5201 | Closed Sun. | $7–$23 | AE, D, DC, MC, V.

Pastime Club and Steakhouse. Steak. Waiters are dressed in tuxedos here in tiny Marmarth (population 147). The menu has prime rib and South American rib eye, or try the lemon chicken or shrimp caprice. | 14 Main St., Marmarth | 701/279–9843 | No supper Mon. | $7.50–$17 | MC, V.

Lodging

Budget Host 4U Motel. A 1960s brick motel four blocks west of downtown, with ample parking for trucks, this hostelry has a few rooms with their own steam baths and saunas. There's in-room coffee, and the Gateway Family Restaurant is next door. Microwaves, refrigerators. Cable TV. | 704 Highway 12W | 701/523–3242 or 800/BUDHOST | www.budgethost.com | 35 rooms, 5 suites | $40, $80 suites | AE, D, DC, MC, V.

Historic Jacobson Mansion Bed and Breakfast. On the road between Scranton and Gascoyne, 30 mi NW from Bowman, this three-story, 1895 Queen Anne-style home has a peaceful country backdrop. Complimentary breakfast. | Route 67, Scranton | 701/275–8291 | fax 701/275–8299 | 3 rooms | $60 | No credit cards.

North Winds Lodge. Oak trim, brass, and soft color schemes distinguish the handful of newer rooms at this hostelry is on the edge of town, with views of the countryside. Some refrigerators. Cable TV. Pool. Laundry service. Business services. Some pets allowed. | 503 Rte. 85S | 701/523–5641 or 888/684–9463 | fax 701/528–5641 | 10 rooms | $40–$47 | AE, D, MC, V.

CARRINGTON

(Nearby towns also listed: Devils Lake, Jamestown, New Rockford)

One of the larger towns in the center of the state, Carrington is at the junction of U.S. 281 and U.S. 200, the busiest rural intersection in North Dakota. Carrington was an unnamed prairie settlement in 1883, which later developed along the route of the Northern Pacific Railroad. Pioneers, undaunted by frigid winters without wood for fuel or construction, made homes of sod, known as "soddies." Today Carrington, population 2,200, has become synonymous with agriculture processing. The town attracted the cooperatives that formed the AgGrow Oils processing plant and Dakota Growers Pasta. Fields of durum wheat in Carrington are harvested and processed into semolina and various pasta shapes.

Information: Convention and Visitors Bureau | Box 439, 58421 | 701/652–2524 or 800/699–2524.

Attractions

Arrowwood National Wildlife Refuge. One of North Dakota's 63 wildlife refuges, 15,000-acre Arrowwood has three natural lakes, one man-made marsh, and a 5½-mi driving tour route. You can see migrating waterfowl, swans, canvasbacks, and bald eagles in the spring and fall. | 7745 11th St. SE, Pingree | 701/285–3341 | fax 701/285–3350 | Free | Daily dawn to dusk.

Dakota Growers Pasta Plant. With the finest durum wheat in the world grown in North Dakota, farmers formed their own cooperative in 1992 to make semolina and process it into pasta products. Here you can see the massive production line from a balcony. | One Pasta Ave. | 701/652–2855 or 800/280–2855 | fax 701/652–3552 | www.dakotagrowers.com | Free | Weekdays 8–noon.

Foster County Museum. You can see old military items, pioneer memorabilia, and pioneer wedding dresses are at this museum. | 175 16th Ave. S | 701/652–3363 or 701/652–2477 | Free | Late May–Aug., Sun. 2–5, or by appointment.

McHenry Railroad Loop and Museum. The only railroad loop preserved on the North American continent is on display here. The depot and museum have Great Northern Railway memorabilia and a 1938 Russell snowplow. Take a train ride. | Main St. N, McHenry | 701/785–2333 | Free | First and third Sun. of June, July, Aug., 1–3:30; first Sun. in Sept.; special rides by appointment.

Pipestem Flowers. You can buy Anne Hoffert bird feeders and wreaths here. She grows native flora, gathers traditional grains, and then dries and crafts them into her creations. | 7060 Rte. 9 | 701/652–2623 or 800/446–1986 | fax 701/652–1441 | www.pipestemcreek.com | Free | Weekdays 8:30–4, weekends by appointment.

Posey's Old-Time Tractor Museum. If you enjoy threshing shows, don't miss this large collection of antique tractors. | 1397 U.S. 281, Pingree | 701/285–3536 | Free | Daily 9–6, or by appointment.

ON THE CALENDAR
JUNE: *Foster County Fair and Roughrider Rodeo.* This old-fashioned county fair has a midway with games and rides, livestock, and agriculture exhibits, a petting zoo, pig racing, live music, and a "dance in the dirt" event. | 701/652–2581 or 701/652–2524.

Dining
Chieftain Conference Center. American. A 20-ft-tall wooden Big Chief stands outside the front of this restaurant, which is almost like mini-museum with its displays of Native Amer-

ican artifacts inside. Try the beer cheese soup or, for dessert, the homemade sour cream rhubarb or sour cream raisin pie. No alcohol. | 60 4th Ave. S | 701/652–3131 | fax 701/652–2151 | Breakfast also served | $7–$17 | AE, D, DC, MC, V.

Jackie's Corner Grill. American. Good home cooking attracts repeat customers to this family-oriented café. One of the biggest draws is the homemade rhubarb pie. No alcohol. | 730 4th Ave. S | 701/652–3699 | No dinner past 5 PM; breakfast also served | $5–$15 | No credit cards.

Prairie Inn Restaurant. American. The hot beef sandwich, with mashed potatoes and gravy inside, is a local favorite here, along with caramel rolls, steaks, homemade pastries, and homemade soups. No alcohol. | Intersection of U.S. 281 N and U.S. 200 | 701/652–3976 | Breakfast also available | $7–$25 | AE, D, MC, V.

Lodging

Blue Swan Bed and Breakfast. This 1900 home, four blocks from the courthouse, has original chandeliers and lighting fixtures. A wide central staircase leads to the two guest rooms, one with duck stamp prints, duck wallpaper, and a king-sized water bed. The oak room has a hand-crocheted bedspread. Complimentary breakfast. No room phones. No smoking. | 629 2nd St. N | 701/652–3978 | fax 701/652–3978 | 2 rooms (with shared bath) | $60 | No credit cards.

Chieftain Motor Lodge. A tall wooden Native American sculpture stands outside this two-story property. Inside, you can see Native American artifacts. The rooms are burgundy and dark green and there's a sports bar. Restaurant, bar, room service. In-room data ports, some microwaves, some refrigerators. Cable TV. Hot tub. Gym. Laundry facilities. Business services. Some pets allowed. | 60 Fourth Ave. S | 701/652–3131 | fax 701/652–2151 | 47 rooms, 1 suite | $47–$52, $86 suites | AE, D, MC, V.

Super 8. At Rte. 281/52, this two-story motel is three blocks from Main Street. Complimentary Continental breakfast. In-room data ports. Cable TV. Laundry facilities. Some pets allowed. | 101 4th Ave. S | 701/652–3982 or 800/800–8000 | fax 701/652–3984 | www.super8.com | 36 rooms, 4 suites | $34–$52, $80 suites | AE, D, MC, V.

CAVALIER

(Nearby towns also listed: Grafton, Pembina)

In the northeast corner of the state, Cavalier, population 1,500, is one of four towns that anchor the Rendezvous Region (the others are Langdon, Pembina, and Walhalla). During the 1800s, the area was inhabited by French fur trappers, Chippewa Native Americans, and Scandinavian settlers. The largest Icelandic settlement in America is here. Besides breathtaking landscape with blooming fields, pine forests, and river-gouged valleys, the geologic formations display rocks considered among the oldest on the planet. And just a hint about dining: This area has a long-standing tradition of all-you-can-eat feeds, so ask around for whose "night" it is and enjoy a feast.

Information: **Cavalier Area Chamber of Commerce** | Box 271, 58220 | 701/265–8188 | cacc@polarcomm.com.

Attractions

Cavalier County Museum. This museum at Dresden has a Catholic church made of native rock, a log cabin, a one-room country schoolhouse, and a caboose in this tiny community of five. | 1213 12th Ave., Langdon | 701/256–3940 or 701/256–5957 | Free | Memorial Day–Labor Day; varying hours.

Icelandic State Park. At the park and adjacent Gunlogson Nature Preserve, you can see great blue herons, ruffed grouse, beaver, and many more small animals. Also, the Gunlogson Homestead and the Pioneer Heritage Center have exhibits of the region's ethnic diversity. | 13571 Rte. 5 | 701/265–4561 | fax 701/265–4443 | www.state.nd.us/ndparks | $4 per vehicle | Mid-May–Labor Day, Mon.–Thurs. 9–8, Fri.–Sun. 9–6; Labor Day–mid-May, weekdays 9–5, Sun. 1–5.

ON THE CALENDAR
JUNE: *Rendezvous Festival.* On the second weekend of June at Icelandic State Park, this festival has a buck skinner's encampment, a reenactment of Custer's 7th Cavalry, and an ethnic art show. | 701/265–4561.

AUG.: *Kids' Weekend.* The "Iron Kid" contest, a treasure hunt, and other outdoor programs make this event popular among visiting campers and locals, the first weekend in August at Icelandic State Park. | 701/265–4561.

Dining
Cedar Inn Family Steakhouse and Lounge. Steak. This eatery has a prime rib sandwich, double bacon cheeseburgers, and barbecue ribs. Lunch is served in the lounge only. Kids' menu. | 502 Division Ave. S | 701/265–8341 | fax 701/265–4706 | Closed Sun. | $7–$20 | AE, MC, V.

Gracie's. American. Homecooked fried chicken, twice-baked potatoes, and fruit pies highlight the menu at this downtown Langdon restaurant. Kids' menu. Sun. brunch. No alcohol. | 1021 12th St, Langdon 30 mi W of Cavalier | 701/256–2750 | $5–$9 | No credit cards.

Northern Lights Grill. American. A bird house collection fills this restaurant 35 mi west of town; photos by local artists hang on the walls. The shrimp and broccoli fettucine Alfredo is popular. | Rte. 5 | 701/256–3131 | No dinner Sun. | $7–$18 | MC, V.

Stables Restaurant. American/Casual. Harnesses and other antiques decorate this big red barn of a place. The menu offers pizza made with homemade dough, as well as hamburgers and steak, and there's an all-you-can-eat chicken dinner on Tuesdays and all-you-can-eat walleye on Wednesdays. Kids' menu. | 112 1st St. Lot 3, Langdon, 30 mi W of Cavalier | 701/256–3377 | Closed Sun. | $10–$18 | MC, V.

Lodging
Cedar Inn. A dining room, lounge, and shop on the property here make this a convenient stopover point. It's 5 mi from Icelandic State Park. Dining room. In-room data ports, some microwaves, some refrigerators. Cable TV. Laundry facilities. Some pets allowed. | 502 Division Ave. S | 701/265–8341 or 800/338–7440 | fax 701/265–4706 | 39 rooms, 1 suite | $46, $55 suite | AE, MC, V.

221 Melsted Place Bed & Breakfast. A preserved farmstead, this 1910 Victorian three-story block house is surrounded by wheat fields, 13 miles southwest of Cavalier. The President of Iceland stayed here in 1999. The house has hardwood floors and pastel walls, and rooms with antiques. One room has a gold leaf headboard with lace canopy. Outside, a Victorian gazebo has an all-season spa with fireplace. Complimentary breakfast. No air-conditioning. Some room phones. No TV in some rooms. TV in common area. Spa. No pets. No kids under 12. No smoking. | 221 Melsted Pl., Mountain | 701/993–8257 | fax 701/993–8257 | www.melstedplace.com | 5 rooms (with shared bath) | $80–$120 | D, MC, V.

DEVILS LAKE

(Nearby towns also listed: Carrington, New Rockford, Rugby)

The waters and wetlands south of Devils Lake, population 7,800, are one of the biggest natural draws in the state, with bird watching, hunting, and fishing. The town is situated on the largest natural body of water in North Dakota. It was established in 1882 by Lieutenant H. M. Creel, who settled on the north shore of Devils Lake after retiring from the Army. The town was named Creelsburgh, then Creel City, and finally Devils Lake when railway officials decided they wanted to change the name before building a station. The community joins Rugby, Minot, and others that grew along the St. Paul, Minneapolis, and Manitoba Railway. Today, U.S. 2 follows much the same route. Just south of Devils Lake you'll find the 137,000-acre reservation of the Spirit Lake Sioux. The reservation was formerly known as Fort Totten Sioux Indian Reservation, named for a tiny village that grew around Fort Totten itself. Today, the fort and the Spirit Lake Casino are the main attractions on the reservation.

Information: Devils Lake Area Tourism Office | Box 879, 58301 | 701/662–4903 or 800/233–8048 | www.devilslakend.com. **Spirit Lake Sioux Tribe** | Box 359, Fort Totten 58335 | 701/766–4221.

Attractions

Belle Isle Indian Gallery and Gift Shop. You can find a collection of old handiwork by Native Americans, beadwork, pipes, and cradle boards here in this building with a small grocery store and gas station. A museum downstairs has a diorama of the area landscape, and a craft shop in the back sells beads, needles, and local artwork. | 120 Main St. | 701/766–4555 | Free | Mon.–Sat. 8–6, Sun. 11–5.

Devils Lake. With 100,000 acres and 300 mi of shoreline, this is the largest natural body of water in North Dakota. The lake—and the nearby community—derived its name from a Native American word that meant "bad water," because warriors drowned in it. Known for its whopper walleye, perch, and northern pike, the lake has no natural outlet and has been rising constantly, consuming lakeside homes, farmland, and pastures; roads are constantly being raised to stay above the water levels. | 1525 Duncan Rd. | 701/662–4903 or 800/233–8048 | fax 701/662–2147 | www.devilslakend.com.

Devils Lake State Parks. Sprawling Devils Lake is the attraction for a state park with four subsections: Graham's Island, Shelver's Grove, Black Tiger Bay, and The Narrows. | 1525 Duncan Rd. | 701/766–4015 | www.state.nd.us/ndparks. | $4 per vehicle.
Graham's Island is the most popular and most developed of the state park's recreation areas, with 1,122 acres of picnicking, hiking trails, camping with hot showers, boat ramps, and designated swimming areas. Go west out of Devils Lake on Rte. 14, then 6 mi south. | 701/766–4015 | $4 per vehicle | Daily.
Shelver's Grove is a small 20-acre version of Graham's Island. There's no boat ramp or designated swimming area here, however. Head east out of Devils Lake on Rte. 2 for 3 mi. | 701/662–7106 or 800/807–4723 | $4 per vehicle | Mid-May–mid-Sept., daily.
Black Tiger Bay is used exclusively for boat access to Devils Lake. | 701/766–4015 | $4 per vehicle | Mid-May–mid-Sept., daily.
The Narrows is also a boat access to Devils Lake. | 701/766–4015 | $4 per vehicle | Mid-May–mid-Sept., daily.

Fort Totten State Historic Site. Fort Totten began as a military installation in 1867, then it was a Native American boarding school until it closed in 1959. Today, it's the largest and best preserved fort of its kind west of the Mississippi River. At the Pioneer Daughters Museum you can see military, Native American, and pioneer artifacts. The commissary storehouse is an interpretive center with exhibits. Colors indicate specific areas: Gray with red trim

INDIAN RESERVATIONS

Within the borders of North Dakota are four sovereign nations: Indian reservations. One of these reservations extends to South Dakota.

Fort Berthold Indian Reservation. In 1851, one million acres were set aside in west-central North Dakota for the Mandan, Hidatsa, and Arikara tribes, who eventually banded their dwindling numbers together to form the Three Affiliated Tribes. Today, Lake Sakakawea (created out of the Missouri River with 600 mi of shoreline) divides the reservation into four sections connected by few roads and fewer bridges. The great lake flooded bottomlands on the reservation, forcing whole villages to relocate. About 8,500 people are enrolled tribal members; about 5,400 live on the reservation. Major enterprises on the reservation are Four Bears Casino and Lodge, LCM corporation specializing in highway construction and maintenance, and Northrop Dakota Plant, specializing in electronic circuit board manufacturing for defense contracts. A seven-member tribal government is elected by popular vote.

Spirit Lake Nation. The 245,000 acres of this reservation for the Sisseton-Wahpeton band of Sioux, established in 1867, are just south of Devils Lake. At one time, the reservation was called Devils Lake Sioux Indian Reservation. About 4,400 people are enrolled members of the Spirit Lake Nation tribe, and about 3,800 live on the reservation, governed by a six-member tribal council. The community of Fort Totten includes the tribal office and Little Hoop Community College, an accredited, two-year institution. Major enterprises on the reservation are Spirit Lake Casino and two manufacturing companies specializing in defense contracts. Sioux Manufacturing products include laminated ballistic helmets and protective panels; Dakota Tribal Industries makes cargo slings, camouflage screen cases, and multipurpose netting for military field use.

Standing Rock Indian Reservation. More than 2.3 million acres were set aside in 1868 for the Yanktonai, Hunkpapa, and Blackfoot Sioux tribes. Straddling the North and South Dakota border, with the Missouri River forming the eastern boundary, the sparsely populated reservation has 8,000 enrolled members governed by a 15-member tribal council. Fort Yates hosts the tribal offices and Sitting Bull Community College, an accredited two-year institution. Fort Yates was also the original burial site for Sitting Bull. Ranching is the main occupation on the wide open prairie of the reservation. The main enterprise on the North Dakota side of the reservation is Prairie Knights Casino and Lodge.

Turtle Mountain Chippewa Reservation. In 1882, 150,000 acres were set aside for the Turtle Mountain Band of Chippewa in the mountainous area along the Canadian border. Today, a nine-member tribal council governs 11,000 of 25,500 enrolled members living here. Enterprises on the reservation include the Turtle Mountain Chippewa Casino, Turtle Mountain Manufacturing specializing in cargo trailers and truck boxes for defense contracts, and Uniband Data Entry offering data entry services for both government and private corporation contracts. The tribe also manages a bison herd. Belcourt, seat of tribal government, is home to KEYA, the nation's oldest Native American–owned radio station, and Turtle Mountain Community College, an accredited two-year institution moving to a beautiful brand-new campus.

© Artville

are military colors, and white with green trim are school colors. The company barracks and main school building later became Fort Totten Little Theater, with annual musical productions by the local community. Fort Totten is listed on the National Register of Historic Places. To get there from Devils Lake, go 15 mi on Rte. 57 and follow signs. | Off Rte. 57 | 701/766–4441 or 800/233–8048 | fax 701/766–4882 | www.state.nd.us./hist | $4 | Mid-May–mid-Sept., daily 8–5; mid-Sept.–mid-May by appointment.

Lake Region Heritage Center. Also known as the Old Post Office Museum, this center shows early life in the Devils Lake region with the area's first fire engine, a restored courtroom, and Native American artifacts. | 502 4th St. | 701/662–3701 | Free | Daily 8:30–5.

Lake Region Museum (Sheriff's House). In a two-story 1910 Greek Revival house, you can browse through many rooms fitted with antiques. | 416 6th St. | 701/662–3701 | Free | Memorial Day–Labor Day, daily noon–5 or by appointment.

Spirit Lake Casino and Resort. With 500 slot machines, craps, blackjack and poker tables, simulcast racing, keno, and bingo, this casino attracts a steady stream of patrons. At nighttime, you can see the bright neon lights that trim the casino's roofline. Buffet dining is available, and the hotel has a great view of Devils Lake. RV parking is nearby. There's a marina, built in 1999, at the lake. | 7889 Rte. 57, Spirit Lake | 701/766–4747 or 800/946–8238 | fax 701/766–1507 | Free | Daily.

Sully's Hill National Game Preserve. One of four fenced refuges for bison and elk, 900-acre Sully's Hill also protects waterfowl, white-tailed deer, fox, raccoons, mink, and songbirds. The visitor center has wildlife exhibits and summer programs in an outdoor amphitheater. Auto and hiking tours are self-guided, with a great view of the area and nearby city as your reward for making it to the top of the observation tower. From Devils Lake, go south at the junction of Rte. 2 and Rte. 57; go 15 mi on Rte. 57; follow signs to Sully's Hill. | Box 286, Fort Totten | 701/766–4272 | fax 701/766–4272 | www.r6.fws.gov/refuges/Sullys | Free; car tour $2 | Jun.–Aug. 8–9; auto tour May–Oct. 8–9.

ON THE CALENDAR

JULY: *Akicita Honoring Powwow.* The North American Indian Dance Championship at Fort Totten's town center highlights this powwow, which also has Native American art displays, a parade, and a rodeo. | 701/766–4211 (afternoons).

JULY: *Fort Totten Little Theater.* You can see Broadway musicals here performed by professional and local performers in the fort's amphitheater. | 701/662–8888.

Dining

The Cove. American. Grilled walleye and Juneberry pie, made from local fruit, top the menu at this restaurant with Devil's Lake views. Or, you can choose from 5-oz burgers to steaks, pasta, and seafood. A fieldstone fireplace dominates the room, and elk antler chandeliers hang from the cathedral ceiling. | 1012 Woodland Dr. | 701/662–5996 | fax 701/662–7280 | www.woodlandresort.com | Breakfast also served June–Aug. | $7–$19 | D, MC, V.

Dakota Buffet. American/Casual. Popular with locals, this buffet in the Spirit Lake Casino has a nightly all-you-can-eat special. Try Friday night's prime rib. Sun. brunch. | 7889 Rte. 57, Spirit Lake | 701/766–4747 or 800/946–8238 | fax 701/766–1507 | No dinner Sun. | $9.95 | AE, D, DC, MC, V.

Mr. and Mrs. J's. American/Casual. When you walk in, you hang your coat on a pitchfork here. Try an omelette or the salad bar. Kids' menu. Sun. brunch. Beer and wine only. | Rte. 2 and 5th Ave. | 701/662–8815 | $7–$18 | AE, MC, V.

Lodging

Comfort Inn. One mi outside of central Devils Lake, this hotel is on U.S. 2. Complimentary Continental breakfast. Microwaves, refrigerators. Cable TV. Indoor pool. Hot tub. Laundry facilities. Business services. Some pets allowed. | 215 U.S. 2E | 701/662–6760 or 800/266–3948 | fax 701/662–6760 | www.comfortinn.com | 82 rooms, 5 suites | $55–$76 | AE, D, MC, V.

Dakota Motor Inn. There's a small casino in the lounge at this two-story property with pastel rooms and local art. Restaurant, bar, complimentary Continental breakfast, room service. Cable TV. Indoor pool. Video games. Pets allowed. | Rte. 2E | 701/662–4001 or 888/662–7748 | fax 701/662–4003 | 80 rooms | $28–$54 | AE, D, MC, V.

Days Inn. Four mi from Devils Lake, this hotel attracts quite a few watersport enthusiasts. Complimentary Continental breakfast. Some microwaves, some refrigerators, some in-room hot tubs. Cable TV. Business services. Some pets allowed. | Junction of Rte. 2 and Rte. 20 | 701/662–5381 or 800/329–7466 | fax 701/662–3578 | www.daysinn.com | 44 rooms | $55–$65 | AE, D, MC, V.

Spirit Lake Casino and Resort. The hotel overlooks Devils Lake and is next to the casino. RV parking is nearby, and there's a marina. Rooms are pink and blue with floral patterns. Restaurant, complimentary Continental breakfast. Some refrigerators, some in-room hot tubs. Cable TV. Indoor pool, wading pool. Sauna. Gym. Business services. | 7889 Rte. 57, Spirit Lake | 701/766–4747 or 800/946–8238 | fax 701/766–1507 | www.spiritlakecasino.com | 45 rooms, 18 suites | $65; $80–$125 suites | AE, D, DC, MC, V.

Super 8 Motel. Built in the 1980s and remodeled in 1998, this motel is on Hwy. 2, 8 mi northeast of downtown. Complimentary Continental breakfast. Cable TV. Indoor pool, hot tub. Pets allowed. | 1001 Hwy 2E | 701/662–8656 or 800/800–8000 | fax 701/662–8656 | www.super8.com | 39 rooms | $65 | AE, D, DC, MC, V.

Woodland Resort. The lodge, cabins, and motel overlook the lake, 5 mi southwest of Devil's Lake on the scenic shoreline at Creel Bay. The lodge was built in 1997, the motel in 2000, with units of log siding outside and wood-paneling inside. The resort has a restaurant and a store that sells bait, tackle, and limited groceries. Restaurant, bar, picnic area. Some kitchenettes, some microwaves, some refrigerators. Lake. Hiking. Beach, dock, water sports, boating, fishing. Ice-skating, cross-country skiing, snowmobiling. Playground. Laundry facilities. | 1012 Woodland Dr. | 701/662–5996 | fax 701/662–7280 | www.woodlandresort.com | 15 rooms, 6 cabins, 5 lodge units (all with showers only) | $40 motel, $60 lodge, $75 cabins | D, MC, V.

DICKINSON

MAP 7, B4

(Nearby towns also listed: Amidon, Bowman, Killdeer, Medora)

Cattle, dairy, and grain established Dickinson as an agricultural trade center in the southwestern corner of the state soon after it was founded in 1880 as Pleasant Valley Siding. The name changed to Dickinson in 1881 in recognition of a land agent and New York politician who visited in 1880, and whose brother stayed to oversee development. With the 1950s discovery of oil here, the economy boomed, only to bust with the oil price crisis in the 1970s and '80s. Today, the Queen of the Prairies—a longtime nickname acknowledging the beauty of the area—is one of the state's 10 largest communities with manufacturing, agriculture, and oil contributing to its revived economy.

Dickinson, population 16,000, also reflects the strong ranching culture with its numerous pickups and polite cowboys. Dickinson State University is the only North Dakota institution of higher learning with a national collegiate rodeo team.

Information: Dickinson Convention and Visitors Bureau | Box 181, 58601 | 701/483–4988 or 800/279–7391 | www.dickinsonnd.com.

Attractions
Assumption Abbey. Thirty Benedictine monks live here. The property has a 1909 Bavarian Romanesque church, with an interior of lofty arches, 24 paintings of saints, and 52 stained-

glass windows. The twin church spires can be seen for miles down the highway. Browse the woodcrafts, pottery, honey, and wine in the gift shop. | 418 3rd Ave. W | 701/974-3315 | fax 701/974-3317 | www.assumptionabbey.com | Free | Grounds open daily; tours available; gift shop open weekdays 8 AM-11 AM and 1 PM-4 PM.

Dakota Dinosaur Museum. A huge triceratops greets you at the entrance of this museum, which has 12 full-scale dinosaur skeletons. You can also see local rocks, minerals, mammals, and fossilized plants and seashells. | 200 Museum Dr. | 701/255-3466 | www.dakotadino.com | $5 | Call for hours, closed Jan.-Feb.

Enchanted Highway. This self-guided driving tour takes you past metal sculptures of a pheasant family, a grasshopper family, a 51-ft Teddy Roosevelt, and a tin family with a 45-ft father, 44-ft mother, and 23-ft son. Organizers hope to eventually build 10 metal roadside sculptures. Go 10 mi from Dickinson, in Leffert off of Exit 72 (of I-94). Go south 20 mi to Leffert and it ends in the town of Regent. | Box 181 | 701/483-4988 or 800/279-7391 | Free.

Hettinger County Museum. A drugstore, schoolhouse, and blacksmith shop here are filled with Native American artifacts, local and regional memorabilia, and an art and medical collection. A separate building has farm machinery. | Main St., Regent | 701/563-4547 | Free | Mid-Apr.-Oct., Wed. 1-3 or by appointment; closed Thurs.-Tues.

Joachim Regional Museum. Rotating exhibits explore the history of southwestern North Dakota. | 200 Museum Dr. | 701/225-4409 | www.dickinsoncvb.com. | Free | Memorial Day-Labor Day, daily 9-5.

Little Missouri National Grasslands. This is the largest and most diverse of 19 grasslands in the western United States, covering a 140 mi of prairie by the Forest Service and area grazing associations. You can see wildlife, paleontological digs, and oil exploration. You need 3 hours to complete a self-guided driving tour, beginning and ending in Medora, and covering 58 mi. There are no hiking trails. From Dickinson, go west on I-94 for 30 mi.; the Badlands run north and south along I-94. | RR 6, Dickinson | 701/225-5151 or 800/279-7391 | www.fs.fed.us/r1/dakotaprairie/ | Free | Daily.

Patterson Lake Recreation Area. The campground here is 10 minutes from downtown. Take Rte. 10 West, 3 mi outside of Dickinson; follow signs 1 mi south. | 701/225-2074 | Memorial Day-Labor Day, $1 per vehicle | Daily; Memorial Day-Labor Day, camping.

Prairie Outpost Park. This outdoor museum has a stone house built by Germans from Russia, a *stabbur* (a tiny wooden house built in traditional Norwegian style), and a rural school. | 200 Museum Dr. | 701/225-3466 | Free | Memorial Day-Labor Day, weekdays 10-4; call for weekend hours.

ON THE CALENDAR
JULY: *Roughrider Days.* A classic Western-style downtown celebration, this weekend event has a rodeo, parade, tractor pull, demolition derby, concerts, and fireworks display. | 800/279-7391 or 701/483-4988.
JULY: *Taylor Horsefest*. Horse lovers can watch a parade of horse-drawn rigs, horseback riders, and breed displays on the last Saturday in July. There are also cowboy movies, poetry, and arts and crafts in Taylor, 10 mi east of Dickinson, and one mile north of I-94. | 701/483-4988, 701/974-2355 or 800/279-7391.
JULY: *Ukrainian Festival*. The Ukraine culture is celebrated downtown on a weekend of music, art, dance, food, traditional regalia, and church services. | 701/255-1286.
SEPT.: *Northern Plains Heritage Festival*. This weekend event downtown at the Museum Complex, 200 Museum Dr., has a parade, food and crafts fair, and entertainment. | 701/483-4988 or 800/279-7391.

Dining
Dakota Rose Restaurant. American/Casual. Try the Monte Cristo sandwich here, next door to the Travelodge motel. Kids' menu. | 532 15th St. W | 701/227-1853 | $9-$15 | AE, D, DC, MC, V.

Elks Lodge #1137. Steak. Evening meals and the Saturday lunch buffet are local favorites. The 1137 rib eye and homemade caramel nut sundaes are house specialties. It's in North Dickinson, at the interstate. Kids' menu. | 501 Elks Dr. | 701/438–1137 | Closed Sun. No lunch Sat. | $7.50–$18 | AE, D, DC, MC, V.

Knights of Columbus Club. American. The K of C Club has a noon buffet with soup, salad, homemade filled breads (apple, poppy) and caramel rolls. Pork prime rib is another special. | 1531 W. Villard St. | 701/483–0186 | Closed Sun. | $6–$27 | AE, D, MC, V.

Rattlesnake Creek Brewery and Grill. American. Try microbrewed beer, the Killdeer Mountain fiery scalloped potatoes, and Teddy's raspberry chicken, a favorite here. Kids' menu. | 2 W. Villard St. | 701/438–9518 | $10–$15 | AE, D, DC, MC, V.

Lodging

Americinn. The lobby here has a fireplace, and the hotel is close to shopping and museums. Complimentary Continental breakfast. In-room data ports, some microwaves, some refrigerators, some in-room hot tubs. Cable TV. Indoor pool. Hot tub. Laundry facilities. Business services. | 229 15th St. W | 701/225–1400 or 800/634–3444 | fax 701/225–5230 | www.americinn.com | 40 rooms, 6 suites | $59–$99 | AE, D, MC, V.

Comfort Inn. The indoor pool has a spiral waterslide. The hotel is on the north side of I–94, across from Prairie Hills Mall, 1½ mi outside downtown. Complimentary Continental breakfast. In-room data ports, kitchenettes. Cable TV. Indoor pool. Hot tub. Laundry facilities. Business services, airport shuttle. Some pets allowed. | 493 Elk Dr. | 701/264–7300 or 800/221–2222 | fax 701/264–7300 | www.comfortinn.com | 107 rooms, 10 suites | $72; $85–$105 suites | AE, D, MC, V.

Hartfiel Inn B&B. The suite in this 1980 downtown home has white furniture, navy walls, and wall-to-wall carpeting. French, German, and English rooms have hardwood floors with area rugs, black iron four poster or brass beds, and desks. The Common living room has a working fireplace. Breakfast, chosen from a menu, is from 5:30–11:30 in the formal dining room or on the tile terrace overlooking the lavish gardens with a waterfall, arbor, private hot tub cottage with stereo and a life-size statue of the goddess Hebe. Complimentary breakfast. Some in-room VCRs. Hot tub. Library. Some pets allowed. No smoking. | 509 3rd Ave. W | 701/225–6701 | fax 701/225–1184 | hartfielinn@goesp.com | 3 rooms (2 with shower only), 1 suite | $59–$68, $89 suite | MC, V.

Oasis Motel. This two-story brick and concrete motel is less than a block from the bus station and 1½ blocks from Dickinson State University. Furnishings are dark wood. For breakfast you'll receive a complimentary card for the Donut Hole, 1½ away. Some microwaves, some refrigerators. Cable TV. Outdoor pool. Some pets allowed. | 1000 W. Villard St. | 701/225–6703 or 888/225–6703 | fax 701/225–6703 | 34 rooms | $46 | AE, D, DC, MC, V.

Travelodge. The huge lobby of this three-story motel, across from the Prairie Hills Mall, has a fireplace. A mezzanine overlooks the pool. Restaurant (*see* Dakota Rose Restaurant, *above*), bar, room service. Some refrigerators. Cable TV. Indoor pool. Hot tub, Sauna, Video games. Laundry facilities. Business services, airport shuttle. Some pets allowed. | 532 15th St. W | 701/227–1853 or 800/422–0949 | fax 701/225–0090 | www.travelodge.com | 149 rooms | $60–$64 | AE, D, DC, MC, V.

FARGO

MAP 7, H4

(Nearby towns also listed: Valley City, Wahpeton; Moorhead, Minnesota)

The largest of North Dakota's cities with a population of about 75,000, Fargo is at a crossroads between Minneapolis and Seattle, and St. Louis and Winnipeg. Less than

10,000 years ago, it was the bottom of Lake Agassiz, a massive glacial lake that left incredibly rich, fertile soil in the Red River Valley.

As the homesteaders brought farming to the area, the Red River Valley earned its reputation as the Breadbasket of the World. Under the Homestead Act, settlers were deeded 160 acres in exchange for living on the land and farming part of it for at least five years. Pioneers, largely from Scandinavia, began arriving by the thousands in the 1870s. Founded in 1871, Fargo was named for one of the owners of the Wells-Fargo Express Co., William G. Fargo. Moorhead, its sister city across the river, is named for an executive of the Northern Pacific Railway, which cuts through the area.

The combined population of Fargo, adjacent West Fargo, and Moorhead is more than 100,000 and generates nearly a quarter of North Dakota's taxable sales. College students have a notable influence through their sizeable presence at North Dakota State University, Moorhead State University, and Concordia College, all in the area. Fargo is also headquarters to Great Plains Software, a business and accounting software development firm. More than just a major commerce, education and health-care center, Fargo is a destination as well. Fargo's visitors center resembles a grain elevator. Visible from I–94, this white building is the place for information, help, and a friendly chat.

Information: **Fargo/Moorhead Convention and Visitors Bureau** | 2001 44th St. SW, 58103 | 701/282–3653 or 800/235–7654 | fax 701/282–4366 | www.fargomoorhead.org.

Attractions

Bonanzaville USA. Bonanzaville's 15-acre site uses 42 original and re-created buildings, from a sod house to a country store, to depict life here in the 1880s. The museums have farm equipment, antique cars, and airplanes. | 1351 W Main Ave., West Fargo | 701/282–2822 or 800/700–5317 | fax 701/282–7606 | www.fargocity.com/bonanzaville | $6 | Memorial Day–late Sept., daily 9–5; May and Oct., weekdays 9–5.

Children's Museum at Yunker Farm. A bright red barn is just one of the attractions at this hands-on learning museum for children. Check out the live bee hive. | 1201 28th Ave. N | 701/232–6102 | www.childrensmuseum-yunker.org | $3 | School year Tues., Wed., Fri., Sat. 10–5, Thurs. 1–8, Sun. 1–5.

Edgewood Golf Course. Established in 1951, this wooded 18-hole course is well maintained. | 3218 2nd St. N | 701/232–2824 | Apr.–late Oct.

Fargodome. On the campus of North Dakota State, this is the largest indoor facility in the state. It hosts more than 125 events annually, including sports, crafts, concerts, festivals, and fairs. | 1800 University Dr. | 701/241–9100 or 701/298–2777 (event line) or 701/235–7171 (tickets) | fax 701/237–0987 | www.fargodome.com | Varies.

Fargo-Moorhead Beez. The F-M Beez is one of eight professional basketball teams that make up the International Basketball Association. Home games are played at Fargo Civic Center. | 5½ 8th St. S | 701/232–4242 | fmbeez@fmbeez.com | $7–$25 | Call for schedule.

Fargo-Moorhead Community Theatre. This community theater stages seven productions yearly between September and June. | 333 Fourth St. S | 701/235–6778 | www.fargoweb.com/fmct | $10–$15 | Call for schedule.

Fargo Theatre. Once a vaudeville movie palace, this 1926 downtown landmark has been restored to its original Art Moderne look. The Wurlitzer pipe organ still plays for silent movie nights, and today the theater hosts live performances, films, and conferences. | 314 Broadway | 701/235–4152 and 701/235–8385 | www.fargotheatre.org | $6 | Call for performance times.

I–29 Amusement Park. Attractions include a 440-ft water slide, go-carts, miniature golf, batting cages, kiddie rides, and an arcade. | 1625 35th St. SW | 701/235–5236 | www.fargo-moorhead.org | $7 | May–Sept., daily noon–10:45.

North Dakota State University. Home of the "Bison" and the Fargodome, NDSU educates nearly 10,000 students each year. Established in 1890 as an agriculture college, today it is well regarded for its agricultural sciences department and leadership in crop research. | 1301 12th Ave. N | 701/231–8643 | www.ndsu.nodak.edu | Free | Daily.

Plains Art Museum. One of the largest fine arts museums between Minneapolis and Seattle, this center has three galleries of traditional and contemporary art by regional and national artists. Housed in a renovated open-beamed, 19th-century warehouse, it includes a café and gift shop. | 701 1st Ave. N | 701/232–3821 or 800/333–0903 | fax 701/293–1082 | www.plainsart.org | $3 | Mon. 10–5, Tues., Thurs. 10–8, Wed., Fri., Sat. 10–6, Sun. noon–6.

RedHawks. A professional baseball team in Fargo since 1996, the team is among 16 teams in the Independent Northern League. Games are played at the Newman Outdoor Field. | 1515 15th Ave. N | 701/235–6161 or 800/303–6161 | fax 701/297–9247 | www.fmredhawks.com | $4–$8 | Call for schedule.

Red River Zoo. New in 1998, the zoo has 45 species of animals on 25 acres. Children enjoy the petting zoo. | 4220 21st Ave. SW | 701/277–9240 | fax 701/277–9238 | www.redriver-zoo.org | $5 | May–mid-Sept., daily 10–8; mid-Sept.–mid-Oct., daily 10–5.

Roger Maris Baseball Museum. In the West Acres Shopping Center, the museum honors the Fargo native whose 61 home runs in 1961 was a record until Mark McGwire and Sammy Sosa bested it in 1998. | 13th Ave. S exit, off I-29 | 701/282–2222 or 701/235–9679 | www.ndroger-maris.com | Free | Mon.–Sat. 10–9, Sun. noon–6.

Sports Bubble. Golfers get their winter fix at this all-season driving range. Lessons and a PGA golf simulator are also available. | 2761 12th Ave. SW | 701/280–0824 | $5–$10 | Mon.–Sat. 7 AM–9 PM, Sun. 10–9.

Trollwood Park. More an outdoor activity center than just a park, Trollwood has concerts, cultural events, food vendors, and arts and crafts displays. And it's a great place for a stroll. The Trollwood Performing Arts School also performs here on summer weekends. | Broadway at 37th Avenue N | 701/241–8160 | Free | June–Aug.

West Acres Shopping Center. A gigantic one-story shopping center, West Acres has more than 100 shops, restaurants, and offices. Strip malls and free-standing stores are near the mall, making 13th Avenue South a major shopping district. Take the 13th Ave. S exit, off I-29. | 3902 13th Ave. S | 701/282–2222 | fax 701/282–2229 | www.westacres.com | Mon.–Sat. 10–9, Sun. noon–6.

ON THE CALENDAR

JAN.: *Fargo Farm Show.* One of the area's largest farm shows has more than 700 farm- and ranch-related exhibits in the Fargodome. | 1800 University Dr. | 701/241–9100 or 701/298–2777 (event line).

JUNE: *Red River Valley Fair.* For 10 days in June you can see livestock, plants and flowers, crafts, antiques, and art. Nightly grandstand entertainment at the Red River Valley Fairgrounds in West Fargo has top names in country and rock music. | Last week of June | 701/282–2200 or 800/456–6408.

JUNE: *Scandinavian Hjemkomst Festival.* This citywide event, usually the last week in June, draws people of Scandinavian descent from all over the world. Events are held at Trollwood Park in Fargo, the Heritage-Hjemkomst Interpretive Center in Moorhead, and Concordia College in Moorhead. There's authentic food, storytelling, dancing, music, a style show with Scandinavian costumes, and a dinner and concert. | 218/233–5604 or 800/235–7654 | http://hometown.aol.com/arlans/myhomepage/festival.html.

JULY: *Red River Downtown Street Fair.* Hundreds of browsers converge on eight city blocks downtown to browse more than 300 exhibits of crafts—both traditional and trendy—and original artworks, food booths, and see live entertainment. | 701/241–1570.

AUG.: *Pioneer Days at Bonanzaville USA.* Homespun arts and the everyday skills of the pioneers highlight this two-day celebration during the third week in August in

West Fargo. Costumed demonstrators dip candles, spin cloth, and thresh wheat. | 701/282–2822.

SEPT.: *Big Iron.* Named for gargantuan tractors and combines, this agricultural show at River Valley Fairgrounds attracts more than 300 exhibitors and thousands of visitors. | 701/282–4444.

Dining

Basie's on 42nd Street. Continental. This restaurant in the Ramada Plaza Suites has elegant dining in a jazzy environment. Try pan-blackened walleye or sauteed Atlantic salmon with béarnaise sauce, and top it off with the crème brûlée. On Friday and Saturday nights you can hear live piano music. Kids' menu. Sunday brunch. | 1635 42nd St. SW | 701/277-9000 | Reservations essential | $16–$34 | AE, D, DC, MC, V.

Chili's Southwestern Grill. Southwestern. This restaurant is known for chili, fajitas and its spicy chicken pasta. For dessert, there's the paradise pie—a chocolate chip bar topped with vanilla ice cream and served on a skillet with melted cinnamon butter. Kids' menu. | 4000 13th Ave. S | 701/282–2669 | $6.50–$15 | AE, D, DC, MC, V.

Chuck E. Cheese. American. This is a chain restaurant with pizza, rides, entertainment, and video games. | 1202 Nodak Dr. | 701/232–7967 | $7–$25 | AE, D, MC, V.

Doublewood Grill. American/Casual. Blackened salmon and rotisserie chicken are served up in the mission-style dining room here. Popovers are always on the menu. Kids' menu. | 3333 13th Ave. S | 701/235–3333 | $6.50–$23 | AE, D, MC, V.

Fargo Cinema Grill. American/Casual. Watch an old movie while you munch on popcorn, burgers, or sandwiches. Get a free movie and meal on your birthday. Kids' menu. | 630 1st Ave. N | 701/239–4716 | No lunch weekdays | $9–$20 | MC, V.

Fargo Cork. American/Casual. Dark wood and brick decorate the dining room at this Fargo mainstay. Try the prime rib or crab legs. Salad bar. Kids' menu. | 3301 S. University Dr. | 701/237–6790 | No lunch | $10–$25 | AE, D, DC, MC, V.

The Grainery. American. With rustic woodwork throughout, this restaurant's dining areas are on several levels, requiring a few steps up or down. Peppercorn steak and beer cheese soup top the menu. Salad bar. Kids' menu. | 13th Ave. S exit, off I–29 | 701/282–6262 | No dinner Sun. | $9–$27 | AE, D, DC, MC, V.

Grandma's Saloon and Deli. American/Casual. This regional chain restaurant has chicken tetrazzini, center cut steak, and chicken fettucine. | 4201 13th Ave. SW | 701/282–5439 | $10–$22 | AE, D, DC, MC, V.

Juano's Mexican Restaurant. Mexican. Try the carne asada Juano's chimichanga (a deep-fried, burrito filled with thinly sliced steak), and, of course, the margaritas. | 402 N. Broadway | 701/232–3123 | Closed Sun. | $7–$15 | AE, MC, V.

Kroll's Diner. American. This 1950s-style diner has shakes and malts, some German specialties, and homemade strawberry rhubarb pie. Breakfast is served 24 hours. Kids' menu. | 1570 32nd Ave. S | 701/297–5936 | $5–$16 | AE, D, DC, MC, V.

Lone Star Steakhouse. Steak. The servers perform line dances at this Western-theme eatery with Cajun Texas rib eye. You can wash it down with a beer or a Pecos Peach—a margarita with Peach Schnapps. Kids' menu. | 4328 13th Ave. SW | 701/282–6642 | $10–$25 | AE, D, DC, MC, V.

Luigi's. Italian. The favorites here are the amaretto chicken and filet prosciutto—filet mignon sauteed in a Madeira demi-glacé, topped with prosciutto and provolone. The restaurant resembles a villa. Kids' menu. | 1501 42nd. St. SW | 701/241–4200 | $6–$19 | AE, D, MC, V.

Mexican Village. Mexican. In downtown, this regional chain restaurant is known for chimichangas and pollo fundito (a deep-fried chicken burrito). Try the hot sauce. Kids eat free on Sundays. | 814 Main Ave. | 701/293–0120 | $7–$9 | AE, D, DC, MC, V.

Olive Garden Italian Restaurant. Italian. This is the only Olive Garden in North Dakota. Known for its predictably competent service, house salad, fettuccine Alfredo, and lasagna. Kids' menu. | 4339 13th Ave. SW | 701/277–1241 | $11–$25 | AE, D, DC, MC, V.

Outback Steakhouse. Steak. Sirloin is the most popular cut of meat here, across from West Acres Mall. Try the filet, with a pepper-based seasoning. You can eat outside on the patio. Kids' menu. | 401 38th St. SW | 701/277–5698 | Reservations not accepted | No lunch | $10–$23 | AE, D, DC, MC, V.

Pepper's American Café. American/Casual. Casual fare is what you'll find at this South Fargo restaurant and sports bar, popular for smoked ribs, steaks, and burgers. Kids' menu. Breakfast available on weekends. | 2510 S. University Dr. | 701/232–2366 | $6–$15 | AE, D, DC, MC, V.

Playmakers. American. This sports bar and restaurant in a cavernous building has a volleyball sandlot in back. You can also find a sportswear shop and an arcade and entertainment center here. The menu has lots of sandwich-and-fries combos. | 2525 9th Ave. SW | 701/232–6767 | $6–$18 | D, MC, V.

Sammy's Pizza. Pizza. In downtown, this place is popular for its pizza, lasagna, and home-style dishes. | 301 Broadway | 701/235–5331 | $7–$18 | MC, V.

Santa Lucia. Greek. The chicken and lamb souvlaki reign supreme here, with seafood specials and gyros popular, too. There's a fountain inside. Kids' menu. | 505 40th St. SW | 701/281–8656 | Closed Mon. | $12–$15 | AE, D, DC, MC, V.

TGI Friday's. American/Casual. You'll find a little of everything on the menu: burgers, fries, Cajun chicken, and sandwiches. It's a fun place with lots of American trinkets on the walls. Kids' menu. Right next door to the West Acres Mall. | 4100 13th Ave. SW | 701/281–3030 | $9–$23 | AE, D, DC, MC, V.

Valley Kitchen. American. The pancakes here are crowd pleasers. After eating, check out the table in the back with a diorama of the Fargo area imbedded in it. Salad bar. Kids' menu. No alcohol. | 3601 W. Main Ave. | 701/237–0731 | $7–$12 | D, MC, V.

Lodging

AmericInn. This two-story motel is two blocks from West Acres Mall and 5 mi southwest of Fargo just off I–29. Built in 1992, it's in a commercial strip with entertainment and shopping. Complimentary Continental breakfast. In-room data ports, some microwaves, some refrigerators, some in-room hot tubs. Cable TV. Indoor pool. Hot tub, sauna. Video games. Laundry facilities, laundry service. Business services. | 1423 35th St. SW | 701/234–9946 or 800/634–3444 | fax 701/234–9946 | www.americinn.com | 54 rooms, 7 suites | $75, $120 suites | AE, D, DC, MC, V.

Best Western Doublewood Inn. The hotel is 3 mi from downtown Fargo and two blocks from West Acres Mall. Restaurant, bar, room service. Microwaves, refrigerators, some in-room hot tubs. Cable TV. Indoor pool. Beauty salon, hot tub, sauna. Business services, airport shuttle. Some pets allowed. | 3333 13th Ave. S | 701/235–3333 or 800/528–1234 | fax 701/280–9482 | www.bestwestern.com | 162 rooms, 11 suites | $79–93, $115 suites | AE, D, DC, MC, V.

Best Western Kelly Inn. The kelly green exterior of this two-story hotel gives a splash of color to the neighborhood. In warm months, lounge around the hourglass-shaped outdoor pool. The property is next to a bingo parlor. North Dakota University, West Acres Mall, and Bonanzaville are less than 3 mi. Restaurant, bar. Microwaves, refrigerators, some in-room hot tubs. Cable TV. 2 pools (1 indoor). Hot tub, sauna. Laundry facilities. Business services, airport shuttle, free parking. Some pets allowed. | 3800 Main Ave. | 701/282–2143 or 800/635–3559 | fax 701/281–0243 | www.bestwestern.com | 117 rooms, 16 suites | $69–$84, $108–$164 suites | AE, D, DC, MC, V.

Bohlig's Bed and Breakfast. Fargo's first B&B, opened in 1989, is a two-story architect-designed 1911 Prairie-Georgian style house with oak crown moldings and beams and beveled leaded glass windows, eight blocks west of downtown. There's a big veranda out front and two screened porches overlook flower gardens in back. Complimentary breakfast. No air-conditioning, no room phones, no TV in some rooms, TV in common area. No pets. No kids under 16. No smoking. | 1418 3rd Ave. S | 701/235–7867 | 3 rooms (2 with shared bath) | $45–$50 | No credit cards.

C'mon Inn. A soaring peaked roof with natural wood and fieldstone exterior walls and interior exposed beams distinguish this 1996 motel. There are tropical trees, five hot tubs, and a pool in the atrium, and a stone fireplace in the library. Rooms are done in pastels with blond furniture and quilted spreads. Five miles southwest of downtown Fargo off I-94. Complimentary Continental breakfast. In-room data ports, some refrigerators, some in-room hot tubs. Cable TV. Indoor pool, wading pool. Exercise equipment. Video games. No pets. | 4338 20th Ave. SW | 701/277–9944 or 800/334–1570 | fax 701/277–9117 | www.cmoninn.com | 72 rooms, 8 suites | $75, $106 suites | AE, D, MC, V.

Comfort Inn–East. This hotel is at the interstate, ½ mi from the Fargo Waterslide. Complimentary Continental breakfast. In-room data ports, microwaves, refrigerators. Cable TV. Indoor pool. Hot tub. Business services, free parking. Some pets allowed. | 1407 35th St. S | 701/280–9666 or 800/221–2222 | fax 701/280–9666 | www.comfortinn.com | 64 rooms | $72–$82 | AE, D, DC, MC, V.

Comfort Inn–West. Within ½ mi of West Acres shopping center, this hotel is within walking distance of restaurants, stores, and a movie theater, and is 5 mi from a miniature golf course. Complimentary Continental breakfast. In-room data ports, some microwaves, some refrigerators. Cable TV, some in-room VCRs. Indoor pool. Hot tub. Business services, free parking. Some pets allowed. | 3825 9th Ave. SW | 701/282–9596 or 800/221–2222 | fax 701/292–9596 | www.comfortinn.com | 42 rooms, 14 suites | $72–$82 | AE, D, DC, MC, V.

Comfort Suites. A maroon and emerald green is the outside color of this hotel next door to the Fargo Waterslide and 1 mi from a golf course and casino. Complimentary Continental breakfast. In-room data ports, microwaves, refrigerators. Cable TV. Indoor pool. Hot tub. Laundry service. Some pets allowed. | 1415 35th St. S | 701/237–5911 or 800/221–2222 | fax 701/237–5911 | www.comfortsuites.com | 66 rooms | $85–$100 | AE, D, DC, MC, V.

Country Suites by Carlson. West Acres Mall is four blocks from this two-story motel, with blonde wood in the lobby and rooms of pink and blue. Bar, complimentary Continental breakfast. In-room data ports, kitchenettes. Cable TV. Indoor pool. Hot tub. Exercise equipment. Business services, airport shuttle. Some pets allowed. | 3316 13th Ave. S | 701/234–0565 or 800/456–4000 | fax 701/234–0565 | www.fargoweb.com/countrysuites/ | 99 suites | $77–$160 | AE, D, DC, MC, V.

Expressway Inn. The inn's large cobblestone courtyard with patio furniture has become a popular site for weddings and receptions. Rooms are blues and greens. The property is adjacent to I-94, next door to a Kmart. Restaurant, room service. In-room data ports, some in-room hot tubs. Cable TV. Hot tub. Gym. Pool. Laundry facilities, laundry service. Business services, airport shuttle. | 1340 21st Ave. S | 701/235–3141 or 800/437–0044 | fax 701/234–0474 | www.fargoweb.com/expressway | 105 rooms, 11 suites | $59–$64, $129–$140 suites | AE, D, MC, V.

Fairfield Inn by Marriott. When you stay here, you can get passes for a local gym. It's 4 mi west of downtown and just off I-29. Complimentary Continental breakfast. In-room data ports, some microwaves, some refrigerators. Cable TV. Indoor pool. Hot tub. Laundry service. Business services. No pets. | 3902 9th Ave. S | 701/281–0494 or 800/228–2800 | fax 701/281–0494 | www.fairfieldinn.com | 47 rooms, 16 suites | $80, $90 suites | AE, D, DC, MC, V.

Hampton Inn. While sitting by the pool, you can see the artwork supplied by a local gallery. You can walk to West Acres Mall, and many small casinos are in the area. Complimentary

Continental breakfast. In-room data ports, Cable TV, some in-room VCRs. Indoor pool. Hot tub. Gym. Laundry services. Business services. | 3431 14th Ave. SW | 701/235–5566 or 800/426–7866 | fax 701/235–7382 | www.hamptoninn.com | 75 rooms | $70 | AE, D, DC, MC, V.

Holiday Inn. A pirate ship in the pool area has turned this hotel into a hot spot for families. Rooms have large desks for business travelers. It's at I–29 and I–94 and 4 mi from downtown. Restaurant, bar, room service. In-room data ports. Cable TV. Indoor and outdoor pools. Hot tub. Gym. Laundry facilities. Business services, airport shuttle. Some pets allowed. | 3803 13th Ave. S | 701/282–2700 or 800/465–4329 | fax 701/281–1240 | www.basshotels.com/holiday-inn | 302 rooms, 7 suites | $105–$130, $139–$159 suites | AE, D, DC, MC, V.

Holiday Inn Express. At West Acres Shopping, this four-story hotel is in the middle of a busy commercial strip. It's 4 mi from downtown. Complimentary Continental breakfast. In-room data ports. Cable TV. Indoor pool. Hot tub. Laundry facilities. Business services. Some pets allowed. | 1040 40th St. SW | 701/282–2000 or 800/465–4329 | fax 701/282–4721 | www.basshotels.com/holiday-inn | 71 rooms, 6 suites | $69–$80, $95–$115 suites | AE, D, DC, MC, V.

Kelly Inn–13th Avenue. A small pool gives kids and adults a chance to unwind at this hotel in the heart of the major shopping district. Complimentary Continental breakfast. Cable TV. Indoor pool. Hot tub, sauna. Laundry facilities. Business services, airport shuttle. Some pets allowed. | 4207 13th Ave. SW | 701/277–8821 or 800/635–3559 | fax 701/277–0208 | www.fargomoorhead.org | 46 rooms, 13 suites | $61–$69 | AE, D, DC, MC, V.

La Maison des Papillons. Oak parquet sunburst design floors greet you at this 1899 house with pineapple and acorn cornices and antiques, collectibles, and family heirlooms. The pillared porches overlook butterfly bushes, and rooms are named after butterflies. The Swallowtail is blue, with a stained-glass window above the four-poster brass bed. There's ample on-street parking. Complimentary breakfast. No room phones. TV in common area. No pets. No smoking. | 423 8th St. S | 701/232–2041 | 4 rooms (with shared bath) | $50–$70 | AE, D, MC, V.

Microtel Inn & Suites. This 1999 budget hotel is 2½ mi west of downtown Fargo off I–29, 1 mi from North Dakota State University, and 1½ from the Fargo dome. Complimentary Continental breakfast. Some in-room data ports, some kitchenettes, some microwaves, some refrigerators, some in-room hot tubs. Cable TV. Indoor pool. Hot tub. No pets. | 1108 38th St. NW | 701/281–2109 or 888/771–7171 | fax 701/281–2149 | www.microtelinn.com | 83 rooms, 23 suites | $52–$62, $62–$72 suites | AE, D, DC, MC, V.

Radisson Hotel. From the restaurant on the second floor, you can see the city. The lobby's atrium extends to the third floor, with balconies overlooking it. A golf course and Yunker Children's Museum is 10 mi away. Restaurant, bar, room service. In-room data ports, some minibars, some in-room hot tubs. Cable TV. Hot tub, sauna. Exercise equipment. Business services, airport shuttle, free parking. Some pets allowed. | 201 N. 5th St. | 701/232–7363 or 800/333–3333 | fax 701/298–9134 | www.radisson.com | 151 rooms, 6 suites | $75–$115, $130–$155 suites | AE, D, DC, MC, V.

Ramada Plaza Suites. Families enjoy the 150-ft water slide at this six-story hotel, while locals prefer the hotel's restaurant, Basie's. The suites are furnished in mahogany and cherry wood. It's across the street from the West Acres Mall. Restaurant (see Basie's on 42nd Street), bar, room service. In-room data ports, some in-room hot tubs. Cable TV. Indoor pool. Hot tub, sauna. Gym. Laundry services. Business services, free parking. Some pets allowed. | 1635 42nd St. SW | 701/277–9000 or 800/272–6232 | fax 701/281–7145 | www.ramadafargo.com | 67 rooms, 118 suites | $80–$105, $120–$315 suites | AE, D, DC, MC, V.

Sleep Inn. Cookies are offered each evening here, across the street from Fargo-Moorhead visitor center, and 1½ mi from the Roger Maris Museum. Complimentary Continental breakfast. In-room data ports. Cable TV. Indoor pool. Hot tub. Exercise equipment. Laundry services. Business services, free parking. Some pets allowed. | 1921 44th St. SW | 701/

281–8240 or 800/905–7533 | fax 701/281–2041 | www.sleepinnfargo.com | 61 rooms | $62–$72 | AE, D, DC, MC, V.

Super 8 Motel and Suites. The Fargodome and the airport are within 5 mi of this two-story hotel. The suites have recliners. Complimentary Continental breakfast. In-room data ports. Cable TV. Indoor pool. Hot tub. Laundry facilities, laundry services. Business services, free parking. Some pets allowed. | 3518 Interstate Blvd. | 701/232–9202 or 800/800–8000 | fax 701/232–4543 | www.super8.com | 84 rooms, 25 suites | $34–$57; $47–$117 suites | AE, D, DC, MC, V.

FORT YATES

MAP 7, D5

(Nearby towns also listed: Bismarck, Linton, Mandan)

Fort Yates, population 183, is the headquarters of Standing Rock Indian Reservation, home to 4,500 Sioux. The community grew around the military post founded in 1875. The fort was abandoned officially in 1903, and the community continued in this ranching area. The reservation itself—880,000 acres in North Dakota and South Dakota—is a tableau of huge hills, occasional clumps of trees, and fantastic roadside views of the Missouri River. The reservation's eastern border is on Lake Oahe. Fort Yates is home to Sitting Bull Community College and is the original burial site of the great chief and medicine man. Another interesting site is Standing Rock, the stone from which the reservation takes its name. In certain light, the stone resembles a seated woman with a shawl. Legend says that an Arikara woman married a Dakota man, who then took a second wife. Jealous, the first wife refused to leave when the band broke camp. When a search party returned to retrieve her, she had turned to stone.

Information: Standing Rock Sioux Tribe | Box D, 58538 | 701/854–7201 or 701/854–7226 | www.state.sd.us/tourism/sioux/srock.htm.

Attractions

Lake Oahe and Dam. The 231-mi-long Lake Oahe reservoir on the Missouri River spans from Pierre, South Dakota, to Bismarck. It's one of six main projects by the U.S. Army Corps of Engineers on the upper Missouri River. Completed in 1962, the dam created the fourth-largest man-made reservoir in the U.S. and a major recreation area. If you're an angler you can hook northern pike, Chinook salmon, perch, smallmouth bass, and, of course, walleye, the fresh-tasting delicacy of the northern states. | U.S. Army Corps of Engineers, 28563 Powerhouse Rd., 6 mi north of Pierre, SD, via Rte. 1806 | 605/224–5862 | cenwo.nwo. usace.army.mil/html/Lake_Proj/oahe.htm.

Marina at Prairie Knights. This docking area is on Lake Oahe, right in the backyard of the state's most elegant casino. There's water access and 12 boat slips with 24-hour security, a picnic area, swimming area, 30 RV sites, a fish-cleaning station, and showers. A Coast Guard–approved fishing guide is available with at least 30 days' notice. Technically in Fort Yates, but it's on Standing Rock Sioux reservation. | 46 mi S of Bismarck on Hwy. 1806 (or Rte. 24); 15 mi N of Fort Yates on Hwy. 1806 (or Rte. 24), Fort Yates | 701/854–7777 or 800/ 425–8277 (within ND) | fax 701/854–3795 | www.prairieknights.com | Free | Daily.

Prairie Knights Casino and Lodge. This Vegas-style casino has blackjack, slots, video poker, keno, and poker tables. The fanciest of five reservation casinos, Prairie Knights' has wall murals and a large outdoor sculpture of horses. No tipping is allowed in the casino and restaurants. A 69-room lodge is adjacent to the casino. Nearby, the Marina at Prairie Nights on Lake Oahe has ramps, slips, a picnic area, and RV sites. | 3932 Rte. 24, Bismarck | 701/854–7777 or 800/425–8277 (within ND) | fax 701/854–3795 | www.prairieknights.com | Free | Daily.

Sitting Bull Burial State Historic Site. A marker sits on the original burial ground of Hunkpapa Sioux leader Sitting Bull. A powerful and revered spiritual leader of the Teton Sioux, Sitting Bull fought at the Battle of Little Bighorn in 1876. He was killed by Native American police at his home on December 15, 1890. Today he is interred near Mobridge, SD. | State Historical Society of North Dakota, 612 E Boulevard Ave., Bismarck | 701/328–2666 | fax 701/328–3710 | www.state.nd.us/hist | Free | Daily.

Sitting Bull Community College. Chartered in 1973, the college has about 230 students in associate degree programs ranging from bison management to business administration. Numerous vocational and continuing education programs also are available. The college is in the process of building a new campus just south of the existing building. | 1341 92nd St. | 701/854–3861 | fax 701/854–3403 | Free | Weekdays, call ahead for tours.

ON THE CALENDAR

JUNE–AUG.: *Powwows.* Just about any weekend throughout the summer you can find a powwow on the Standing Rock Indian Reservation. These powwows follow the traditional format with Grand Entry, giftings, dance competitions, and concessions. | 701/854–7201 or 701/854–7226.

Dining

Feast of the Rock Buffet. American/Casual. This is a popular all-you-can-eat buffet. The real treat is that all items are chef-prepared and elegantly presented. The buffet is inside Prairie Knights Casino. | 3932 Rte. 24, Bismarck | 701/854–7777 or 800/425–8277 | $9 | AE, D, DC, MC, V.

Hunter's Club Steakhouse. Steak. Elegant dining in a quiet environment contrasts with the casino noise beyond the restaurant doors. Although steaks are the main fare, the menu also has a selection of seafood and pasta, with a few vegetarian dishes. Also try the potato-crusted walleye served with red wine syrup and grilled onions. | 7932 Rte. 24 | 701/854–7777 or 800/425–8277 | Closed Mon. | $17–$20 | AE, D, DC, MC, V.

Lodging

Lodge at Prairie Knights. This hotel, next to a casino and near a marina, has original art by Native Americans, and a stone fireplace. Bar. In-room data ports, in-room safes, some in-room hot tubs. Cable TV. Video games. | 3932 Hwy. 24, Bismarck | 701/854–7777 or 800/425–8277. | fax 701/854–3795 | www.prairieknights.com | 67 rooms, 2 suites | $60–$75, $85–$130 suites | AE, D, DC, MC, V.

GARRISON

MAP 7, C3

(Nearby towns also listed: Minot, New Town, Washburn)

Garrison, population 1,500, sits on the north shore of Lake Sakakawea. The Garrison Dam, fifth largest in the United States, is on the south side of the lake. Town officials like to do things in a big way. So in addition to a pair of red-topped water towers labeled "Hot" and "Cold," Garrison has a neon-signed City Hall and a 26-ft fiberglass statue of a walleye. Established in 1903, the town was originally 5 mi away. In 1905, the city was moved closer to the new Soo Line railroad.

Information: **Chamber of Commerce** | Box 459, 58540 | 701/463–2600 or 800/799–4242 | fax 701/463–7400.

Attractions

Audubon National Wildlife Refuge. More than 200 bird species are here in this 14,300-acre refuge. On a 7½-mi driving tour you can see Canada geese and other waterfowl, and white-tailed deer. Stop by the visitors center to check out the exhibits and collect information. | 3275 11th St. NW, Coleharbor | 701/442–5474 | www.fws.gov | Free | Daily dawn to dusk.

Fort Stevenson State Park. A favorite spot for fishing and camping enthusiasts, the park is on the north shore of Lake Sakakawea and has a full-service marina with 70 slips. The park also hosts numerous summer events, from fishing tournaments to frontier reenactments. It's named for a frontier fort that served as a supply depot for Dakota Territory military posts. | 1252A 41st Ave. NW | 701/337–5576 | www.state.nd.us/ndparks | $4 per vehicle | Daily dawn to dusk; campgrounds mid-May–mid-Oct.

Garrison Dam. Fifth largest in the United States, the mile-long structure controls flooding on the Missouri River and generates electricity. Finished in 1954, the dam also created Lake Sakakawea and a recreation industry. The powerhouse includes a vast network of power stanchions, high-voltage lines, and transformers. Tours of the power plant are conducted by the U.S. Army Corps of Engineers. From Garrison, go 6 mi east on Rte. 37 to Rte. 83; go 10 mi south on 83 to junction 48; go west on Rte. 200 for 14 mi; follow signs to Garrison Dam. | Box 517, Riverdale | 701/654–7411 | Free | Memorial Day–Labor Day, noon–4.

Heritage Park Foundation Museum. This outdoor museum is a pioneer park with a railroad depot, church, telephone office, and homestead house–with original furnishings. One block west of Main St. on 1st. Ave. NW. | 701/463–2631 | Free | Memorial Day–Labor Day, Fri. 11–5 or by appointment; closed Sat.–Thurs.

Indian Hills Resort. For lakeside fun, stay a day or two here on Good Bear Bay. There are cabins, tent camping sites, RV sites, a boat ramp, guide service, and concessions. Go 31 mi west of Garrison on Rte. 37. | Box 700, Garrison | 701/743–4122 | www.sportsmansweb.com/indianhills | Camping $6.50, cabins $50 | Mid-May–mid-Oct.

Lake Sakakawea. The third largest man-made lake in the United States starts just south of Williston and extends more than 10 mi to the southeast, where it stops at the Garrison Dam. Access to the lake is fairly easy, with more than 1,600 mi of publicly owned shoreline. Walleye, northern pike, and salmon create exceptional sport fishing. From Garrison, go 25 mi south on Rte. 200; 1 mi north of Pick City; follow signs. | U.S. Army Corps of Engineers, Garrison Project, Box 527, Riverdale | 701/654–7411 | cenwo.nwo.usace.army.mil/html/Lake_Proj/garrison.htm.

Lake Sakakawea State Park. Next to the Garrison Dam, this park has a full-service marina with 80 slips, two large boat ramps, and camp sites. About 220,000 visitors a year visit this park. From Garrison, 25 mi south on Rte. 200; 1 mi north of Pick City; follow signs. | Box 732, Riverdale | 701/487–3315 | www.state.nd.us/ndparks | $4 per vehicle | Daily; campgrounds mid-May–early Oct.

North Dakota Fishing Hall of Fame. In the city park beside a sculpture named Wally the Walleye, this log house museum documents anglers and whoppers of North Dakota. | N. Main St. | 701/463–2600 or 800/799–4242 | Free | Memorial Day–Labor Day, Fri.–Sun., closed Mon.–Thurs.

Wally The Walleye. This 26-ft, 820-lb fiberglass outdoor sculpture honors Lake Sakakawea for its trophy walleye fishing. | N. Main St. | 701/463–2600 or 800/799–4242 | Free.

ON THE CALENDAR

MAY: *Block Long Event. Skydance Sakakawea.* On Memorial Day weekend, the Chamber of Commerce creates a 300-ft-long food item—a pizza, sandwich, or cake—for everyone to snack on. The event is free and held on Main Street in Garrison. Participants compete, demonstrate, and entertain with their airborne creations at the Skydance at

Fort Stevenson State Park, a sanctioned kite-flying event. | 701/463–2600 or 800/799–4242.

AUG.: *CANDISC.* The seven-day, 424-mi Cycling Around North Dakota in Sakakawea Country attracts up to 300 cyclists who pedal their way through historic areas and scenic highways. The race begins and ends at Fort Stevenson State Park. | 701/463–2600 or 800/799–4242.

AUG.: *North American Walleye Anglers Tournament.* Top walleye fishing pros compete for prize money and tour standings here on Lake Sakakawea at Fort Stevenson State Park. | 701/463–2600 or 800/799–4242.

NOV.–DEC.: *Dickens Village Festival.* The entire city of Garrison returns to Victorian times recalled in Charles Dickens's *A Christmas Carol,* complete with street vendors, an English market, and street urchins. Each night, enjoy a lighted evening parade and performances by "Scrooge" at the Kota Theater. | 701/463–2600 or 800/799–4242.

Dining

Four Seasons Restaurant and Ice Cream Parlor. American/Casual. In a plain concrete block building you can find an assortment of sandwiches such as chili cheeseburgers and turkey clubs, and buffalo steak. Try the grilled chicken bacon melt. Kids' menu. Sunday brunch. No alcohol. | 182 N. Main St. | 701/463–2044 | $6–$13 | No credit cards.

Lake Road Restaurant. American/Casual. The restaurant completely refurbished its interior in 1998. It's known for hamburgers and a few German dishes such as *knoephle* soup. Kids' menu. Sun. brunch. On Rte. 37, 6 mi west off Rte. 83. | Rte. 37 | 701/463–2569 | $9–$12 | MC, V.

Stoney End. Steak. Originally built as a WPA project in the 1930s, the restaurant has field-stone inside and out, two stone fireplaces—one in the dining room and one in the Cabin Fever lounge—and original art throughout the building. The menu has certified Black Angus beef, prime rib (only on Saturday) with secret seasoning. On the last weekend of every month there's ethnic cuisine. Kids' menu. | On Rte. 37, 1 mi east of Garrison | 701/337–5590 | Closed Sun. No lunch | $10–$22 | DC, MC, V.

Totten Trail Lounge. American/Casual. Stuffed and mounted hunting trophies—from fish to deer—adorn the walls at this roadside café and lounge. The supreme pizza—with sausage, pepperoni, onions, peas, and mushrooms—and the burgers are popular. | 1412A U.S. 83 NW, Coleharbor | 701/337–5513 | $6–$13 | AE, MC, V.

KODAK'S TIPS FOR USING LIGHTING

Daylight
- Use the changing color of daylight to establish mood
- Use light direction to enhance subjects' properties
- Match light quality to specific subjects

Dramatic Lighting
- Anticipate dramatic lighting events
- Explore before and after storms

Sunrise, Sunset, and Afterglow
- Include a simple foreground
- Exclude the sun when setting your exposure
- After sunset, wait for the afterglow to color the sky

From *Kodak Guide to Shooting Great Travel Pictures* © 2000 by Fodor's Travel Publications

Lodging

Garrison Motel. Remodeled in 1997, this property, on the Lewis and Clark Trail, is 4 mi from Lake Sakakawea. Some microwaves, some refrigerators. Cable TV. Some pets allowed. | 539 4th Ave. SE | 701/463–2858 | 30 rooms | $41 | AE, D, MC, V.

Indian Hills Resort. Good Bear Bay at Lake Sakakawea resort is the site of this 1980s resort with four two-bedroom condos with two double beds and a rollaway in each unit. Walleye fishing here is prime, so paddle boats and kayaks are available. A two-night minimum is required. Primitive cabins and camping are also available. The resort is 31 mi west of Garrison off Hwy. 1804. No air-conditioning, kitchenettes, no phones, no TV. Lake. Hiking. Beach, water sports, boating, fishing. | 7302 14th St. NW | 701/743–4122 | fax 701/743–4490 | www.sportsmansweb.com | 4 condos (with shower only) | $60 | Nov.–Apr. | AE, D, DC, MC, V.

Robin's Nest Bed and Breakfast. In a restored 1906 farmhouse, there are two rooms with antiques and collectibles. A third-floor hunting loft with its own shower sleeps five. One room has a TV. Complimentary breakfast. | 101 E. Central Ave. | 701/463–2465 or 701/463–2003 | 3 rooms | $50 | No credit cards.

GRAFTON

MAP 7, H2

(Nearby towns also listed: Cavalier, Grand Forks, Pembina)

Grafton, with 4,800 residents, is just off I–29 and in the middle of prime soil for growing sugar beets, potatoes, beans, and small grains. The ag-based community has diversified, attracting a window manufacturer and potato chip maker. You can tour local farms by calling ahead to the local Chamber of Commerce. The community dates to 1879 and was named by its first postmaster in honor of his wife's home county in New Hampshire.

Information: Grafton Chamber of Commerce | 432 Hill Ave., 58237 | 701/352–0781.

Attractions

Elmwood House. This 1895 Victorian mansion has fine art glass, a maple staircase, oak woodwork, and 20 acres of native flora and fauna along the Park River. The mansion is listed on the National Register of Historic Places. | Stephen Ave. and 2nd St.; street dead-ends at Elmwood House | 701/352–0152 (house) or 701/352–1338 (tour) | Free | June–Aug., Sun. 2–4 or by appointment.

St. Joseph's Chapel. Just large enough for a priest and two altar servers, this quaint roadside chapel is one of the smallest in the United States. Mass is held once a year here. On private land, the tiny chapel is cared for by the landowners. Built in 1907, it is listed on the National Register of Historic Places. | 6207 County Rd. 2 | 701/352–0781 | Free | Daily.

St. Stanislaus Bishop and Martyr Church. Dedicated in 1901, this Gothic Revival church reflects the Polish heritage of the surrounding community, where homilies were spoken in Polish until 1959. In 1911, German artisans paid for their voyage to America by decorating the interior with four huge oil paintings and extensive, elaborate stenciling. With 19 stained-glass windows, a canopied pulpit, and twin carved confessionals, the church is reminiscent of grand cathedrals in Europe. St. Stanislaus is listed on the National Register of Historic Places. | 6098 Rte. 4, Warsaw | 701/248–3981 | Free | Daily 8–5.

Walsh County Heritage Village. More than 20 19th-century buildings (including a log cabin and millinery store) and an old caboose make up in this outdoor museum. Also, there's a working carousel built in 1918. | 695 W. 12th St. | 701/352–3280 | fax 701/352–1597 | Free | Memorial Day–Labor Day, Sun. 1–5 or by appointment.

JUNE: *Summerfest.* The whole community turns out for this extended weekend event that used to be the Sugar Beet Festival. Street dances, school reunions, and a parade are just some

GRAND FORKS

(Nearby town also listed: Grafton)

Grand Forks, the state's third-largest city with 52,500 people, gained a place in national headlines during the terrible floods that devastated the city April 1997. On the North Dakota–Minnesota border and bounded on the east by the Red River of the North, Grand Forks is subject to occasional river rising, but 1997 was extraordinary. Following one of the worst winters on record—more than 8 ft of snow and ice—the docile Red River crested at more than twice its usual peak, over 54 ft (flood stage is 28 ft). The entire population was evacuated, and more than 75% of homes and buildings were flooded. Downtown Grand Forks suffered the worst when electrical short circuits set off fires in the midst of the flood destroying many city blocks. Today, signs of the flood and fire are still visible, but the community was devoted to rebuilding and regaining its reputation as a regional center; reconstructed homes, businesses, and schools gave the community a well-deserved rejuvenation.

Indomitable Grand Forks owes its existence to the river as an early trade and transportation route between Winnipeg, Manitoba, and Minneapolis, Minnesota. Wayfarers rested at Les Grandes Fourches—named by early French explorers for the nearby confluence of the Red Lake River and Red River—as early as the 1850s. In 1870 the name changed to English Grand Forks, and the city gained its first year-round occupants. The oldest of the state's major cities, Grand Forks is the second oldest permanent white settlement in North Dakota. After Scandinavian immigrants arrived en masse in the 1870s and 1880s, Grand Forks became a major agricultural and educational center. Today, it's home to the nation's only state-owned mill and elevator and the state's oldest university.

Information: Greater Grand Forks Convention and Visitors Bureau | 4251 Gateway Dr., 58206 | 701/746–0444 or 800/866–4566 | www.grandforkscvb.org.

Attractions

Grand Forks Air Force Base. Home to the 319th Air Refueling Wing, you can take a group tour of the base, a KC-135 aircraft, and the air traffic control center—the second tallest structure in North Dakota. The community population on base is more than 10,500. The base needs two weeks' notice for tours. | GFAFB Public Affairs Office, 450 G St., Grand Forks Air Force Base | 701/747–5019 | fax 701/747–5022 | www.grandforks.af.mil | Free | Weekdays 7:30–4:30.

Hatton–Eielson Museum. Aviator Carl Ben Eielson, the first person to fly over the North Pole, grew up in Hatton. A restored Queen Anne house, the museum was his boyhood home and celebrates his brief aviator life and local history. There's a memorial arch dedicated to Eielson in the town cemetery. | 405 Eielson St., Hatton | 701/543–3726 | fax 701/543–4013 | $3 | Memorial Day–Sept., Sun. 1–4:30 or by appointment.

Myra Museum. Many exhibits in several buildings depict the history of Grand Forks County. The white clapboard home of Thomas Campbell, America's self-styled Wheat King during the early 1900s, is here. Exhibits focus on the premier efforts of pioneer women. You can explore an 1870s post office, a 1920s one-room schoolhouse, and the Myra Museum, built in 1976 in a prairie style to blend in with its surroundings. This building has exhibits on the area's settlement history and the Grand Forks County Historical Society's archives. | 2405 Belmont Rd. | 701/775–2216 | $3 | Mid-May–mid-Sept., daily 1–5 or by appointment.

North Dakota Mill And Elevator. This flour manufacturer, with products under the Dakota Maid label, is the only state-owned mill and elevator in the nation, although it receives no state financial assistance. The Mill cleans, processes, and mills 5,000 bushels of wheat daily. Constructed in 1922, the mill is listed on the National Register of Historic Places. | 1823 Mill Rd. | 701/795–7000 or 800/538–7721 | www.ndmill.com | Free.

Turtle River State Park. West of Grand Forks 19 mi on Hwy. 2, this park showcases the Turtle River wooded valley and grasslands. The park also has several log and stone structures built by the 1934–1941 Civilian Conservation Corps. | 3084 Park Ave., Arvilla | 701/594–4445 or 800/807–4723 (campsite reservations) | www.state.nd.us/ndparks | $4 per vehicle | Daily.

University of North Dakota. Founded in 1883, the university educates more than 10,000 students in 160 diverse programs, such as law, medicine, engineering, fine arts, and aerospace studies. The Chester Fritz Library here has rare genealogy and manuscript collections. The English Coulee, meandering through campus, was a contributing culprit in the devastating 1997 flood, which abruptly ended the university's semester. The hockey team has won the national NCAA Division I title six times. | University Ave. | 701/777–2011 or 800/225–5863 | www.und.nodak.edu | Free | Daily; tours by appointment only.

Often rated as one of the finest facilities in the upper Midwest, the **Chester Fritz Auditorium** carries the name of the international investment banker whose second million-dollar contribution to the university made the auditorium possible (the first million enabled the construction of the Chester Fritz Library). The 2,300-seat auditorium, at the corner of University Avenue and Yale Drive, has three seating levels. | 701/777–3076 | www.und.nodak.edu/tour/6.htm | Free; show prices vary | Weekdays 8–4:30; appointments appreciated.

Built in 1902, the **J. Lloyd Stone Alumni Center/Oxford House,** a Colonial Revival mansion on the corner of Centennial Drive and University Avenue, was home for UND presidents until 1954, and also housed the art department for a while. Rescued from demolition in the 1970s, the home now has 1902-vintage collectibles, along with offices for the alumni association, and is listed on the National Register of Historic Places. | Box 8157, Grand Forks | 701/777–2611 | www.nodak.edu/tour/13.htm | Free | Weekdays 8–4:30, and by appointment.

Formerly the campus gym, this light and airy 1907 building on Centennial Drive and Campus Road is now the **North Dakota Museum of Art,** with permanent and traveling exhibits of contemporary art. A coffee bar on the lower level is open weekdays and also serves lunch. | 701/777–4195 | www.ndmoa.com | Free | Weekdays 9–5, weekends 1–5.

A jewel in the University's crown, the **Odegard School of Aerospace Sciences** has aviation, meteorology, and space studies programs housed in futuristic buildings. | 4125 University Ave. | 701/777–2791 | www.aero.und.edu | Free | Weekdays by appointment.

Waterworld. You can cruise down one of two 320-ft water tubes to get a good soaking on a hot day or play miniature golf at the largest water park in North Dakota. | 3651 S. Washington St. | 701/746–2795 | $4.50 1 PM–4 PM, $3.50 4 PM–7 PM; $2 for miniature golf | Memorial Day–Aug., daily 1–7.

Widmans. Indulge your passion for chocolate with these gourmet, handmade chocolate confections. A Widmans original called the "chipper" (a chocolate-covered potato chip) is widely imitated by other chocolatiers. | 106 3rd St. S | 701/775–3480 | Free. | Weekdays 9:30–5:30, Sat. 9:30–5.

ON THE CALENDAR

APR.: *Time Out And Wacipi Native American Days.* Time Out is a week-long series of workshops, seminars, and exploration of Native American cultures, while the Wacipi celebrates with the multi-tribe powwow over the weekend, with singing and dancing competition. The powwow takes place on the UND campus in the Hyslop Sports Center. | University of North Dakota | 701/777–4291.

JULY: *Greater Grand Forks Fair and Exhibition.* For about 10 days in the mid-July, the speedway and grounds around it become an entertainment center with a carnival, 4-H exhibits, petting zoo, and concerts. | County fairgrounds | 701/343–2862 or 800/866–4566.

JULY: *Summerthing Kids Days.* Your kids at any age can enjoy hands-on art projects and entertainment at this summer festival. | University Park | 701/746–2750.

SEPT.: *University of North Dakota Potato Bowl Week.* Celebrating one of Red River Valley's most abundant crops, this week-long event has a parade, an annual UND football game and bonfire, a pancake breakfast, and the world's largest French fry feed. | Around town | 701/777–4321 or 800/866–4566.

DEC.: *First Night Greater Grand Forks.* You can celebrate New Year's Eve at a huge non-alcoholic party with music and fireworks. | Downtown | 701/746–0444, 800/866–4566 or 701/746–2750.

Dining

Bonzer's. American. Paintings from the 1800s hang on the oak wood walls and above the bar. The menu has a Ruben and the Meatless Monster, along with 40 varieties of sandwiches and soups. The Empire movie theater is across the street from this downtown restaurant. | 420 DeMers Ave. | 701/775–0365 | Closed Sun. | $7–$11 | MC, V.

Jeannie's Restaurant. American. Here you can find hamburgers and breakfast served 24 hours. The restaurant has carpeted floors, dark-wood tables, and some booths for privacy. Try one of the several delicious roast beef dinners or the chicken-fried steak. Kids' menu. No alcohol. | 1106 S. Washington St. | 701/772–6966 | Open 24 hours | $4–$19 | MC, V.

John Barley-Corn. American. This popular steak restaurant has woodwork and a maze of rooms with 19th-century pictures and knickknacks on the walls. Lavosh, a wafer-thin cracker bread crust prepared with melted Havarti cheese, and the prime rib are favorites. A model airplane hangs from the ceiling in the pub area. Kids' menu. | 2800 Columbia Rd. | 701/775–0501 | No dinner Sun. | $13–$31 | AE, D, DC, MC, V.

Lola's Northern Italian Restaurant. Northern Italian. In a 1897 building, the restaurant has 18-ft ceilings, original hardwood floors, a wood-fired oven made of pounded copper, and a wine cellar. Known for spaghetti, lasagna, grilled salmon, fusilli with scallops, and Shrimp Diablo. | 124 N. 3rd St. | 701/775–5454 | No lunch. Closed Sun. | $13–$30 | MC, V.

Mexican Village. Mexican. The interior is dark with Mexican colors and accents. Try the enchiladas and burritos. Kids' menu. Beer and wine only. | 1218 S. Washington St. | 701/775–3653 | $8–$15 | MC, V.

Players Sports Grill and Bar. American. Along with 26 TVs, there's sports memorabilia and equipment, and pictures of University of North Dakota athletes on the walls. Buffalo wings, hamburger pasta, and chicken Caesar salad are a few of the favorites. Kids' menu. | 2120 S. Washington St. | 701/780–9201 | Breakfast also available | $8–$14 | AE, D, DC, MC, V.

Sanders 1997, The Millennium Café. American Continental. The owner/chef here rescued the rosemaling painted booths during the 1997 flood and opened seven weeks later in a temporary location. Specials are: Tuesday–Italian; Wednesday–French; and Thursday–German. The Swiss *eider* beef (prime rib cooked with garlic, basil, rosemary, and olive oil) and authentic Maryland crab cakes made with blue crab from Chesapeake Bay are unique treats. | 22 S. 3rd St. | 701/746–8970 | Closed Sun., Mon. | $24–$35 | AE, DC, MC, V.

Shangri-La Restaurant. Chinese. The dark red fabrics and dark wood furnishings give this restaurant a richness that reflects its Chinese sauces. The menu is mostly Cantonese with barbecued duck and beef with broccoli. Known for its *chow fun* (rice noodle) dishes. Sun. brunch. | 4220 5th Ave. N | 701/775–5549 | $7–$17 | D, MC, V.

Speedway Restaurant. American. Inside you can see racing and automotive items everywhere, from car hoods to road signs. The restaurant has sirloin T-bone steaks and barbecue, and jumbo shrimp. Kids' menu. | 805 42nd St. N | 701/772–8548 | $5–$14 | AE, D, MC, V.

Lodging

Best Western Town House. Built in 1976, this downtown two-story inn with all-around parking is two blocks from the Corporate Center and Federal Building and four blocks from the courthouse. You can get a complimentary pass to the YMCA across the street. Restaurant, bar, room service. Some kitchenettes, some minibars, some microwaves, some refrigerators. Cable TV. Indoor pool. Hot tub, sauna. Miniature golf. Video games. Laundry service. Airport shuttle. | 710 1st Ave. N | 701/746–5411 or 800/528–1234 | fax 701/746–1407 | www.bestwestern.com | 97 rooms, 4 suites | $74, $89–$139 suites | AE, D, DC, MC, V.

C'mon Inn. The two-story, wood hotel, built in 1993, has a local-field stone foundation and exterior accents to the soaring wood beams. Rooms have king- or queen-size beds. In a commercial area 3 mi from downtown, the hotel is near the city's major shopping district. Complimentary Continental breakfast. In-room data ports. Cable TV, in-room VCRs. Indoor pool. Hot tub. Gym. Video games. Laundry service. Business services. | 3051 32nd Ave. S | 701/775–3320 or 800/255–2323 | fax 701/780–8411 | www.cmoninn.com/grand-forks.htm | 72 rooms, 8 suites | $50–$66; $89 suites | AE, D, MC, V.

Comfort Inn. Built in the 1980s, the exterior of the hotel is a neutral stucco. It's in a commercial area 3 mi from downtown. Restaurants, shopping malls, and theaters are within five blocks. Complimentary Continental breakfast. Cable TV. Indoor pool. Hot tub. Laundry service. Business services. Some pets allowed. | 3251 30th Ave. S | 701/775–7503 or 800/228–5150 | fax 701/775–7503 | www.comfortinn.com | 58 rooms, 7 suites | $70; $80 suites | AE, D, DC, MC, V.

Country Inn and Suites By Carlson. This three-story inn is at Business Route 81, 10 minutes from downtown. Suites have fireplaces. A few blocks away, east and west, are Columbia Mall and Waterworld Waterslide Park. Complimentary Continental breakfast. In-room data ports. Cable TV, some in-room VCRs (and movie rentals). Indoor pool. Hot tub, sauna. Laundry facilities, laundry service. Business services. Some pets allowed. | 3350 32nd Ave. S | 701/775–5000 or 800/456–4000 | fax 701/775–9073 | 64 rooms, 25 suites | $60; $70 suites | AE, D, DC, MC, V.

Days Inn. This two-story inn, remodeled in 1999, is central to downtown and 2 mi from UND. Complimentary Continental breakfast. In-room data ports. Cable TV. Indoor pool. Hot tub, spa. Small pets allowed. Laundry service. Business services. | 3101 34th St. S | 701/775–0060 or 800/329–7466 | fax 701/775–0060 | www.daysinn.com | 52 rooms, 5 suites | $64, $74 suites | AE, D, DC, MC, V.

Econo Lodge. Built in 1982, this two-story hotel is 2 mi from downtown at the intersection of I–29 and Highway 2. You'll find an entrance to Turtle River State Park to the west. Complimentary Continental breakfast. In-room data ports. Cable TV. Business services. Some pets allowed. | 900 N. 43rd St. | 701/746–6666 or 800/553–2666 | fax 701/746–6666 | www.econolodge.com | 38 rooms, 6 suites | $47–$49, $52 suites | AE, D, DC, MC, V.

Fabulous Westward Ho Motel. Built in 1953, the two-story, wood-structured motel is part of a complex that has an entertainment center with with wagon wheels, red flocked wallpaper, and dark wood trim. Fast-food restaurants and car dealerships surround the motel, 3 mi from downtown. 3 restaurants, bar. In-room data ports. Cable TV. Outdoor Pool. Sauna. Business services. Some pets allowed. | 3400 Gateway Dr. | 701/775–5341 or 800/437–9562 | fax 701/775–3703 | 104 rooms, 4 suites | $50, $69 suites | AE, D, DC, MC, V.

Fairfield Inn by Marriott. The three-story hotel, built in 1990, has a white stucco exterior. In a commercial district 3 mi from downtown, it borders the Columbia Mall and the city's major shopping district. Complimentary Continental breakfast. In-room data ports. Cable TV. Indoor pool. Hot tub. Laundry service. Business services. | 3051 34th St. S | 701/775–7910 or 800/228–2800 | fax 701/775–7910 | www.fairfieldinn.com/GFKGF | 58 rooms, 4 suites | $65, $85 suites | AE, D, DC, MC, V.

511 Reeves Bed and Breakfast. This 1901 Queen Anne home, on a landscaped half-acre, has formal English gardens. The front porch, with wicker furniture, overlooks the rose garden. Rooms have polished cotton bishop-sleeve curtains, antiques, and 19th-century furniture with wall-to-wall navy blue carpeting. There's a business line for Internet access. In a quiet residential area and historic district, it's ½ south of downtown. Complimentary breakfast. No room phones, TV in common area. No pets. No kids under 9. No smoking. | 511 Reeves Dr. | 701/775–3585 | fax 701/780–0290 | www.bbonline.com/nd/511reeves | 3 rooms (2 with shared bath) | $75–$85 | AE, MC, V.

Happy Host Inn. Just east of shopping malls and chain restaurants, this 1970s motel has rooms with parking front and rear. It is 5 mi south of downtown. Complimentary Continental breakfast. Some microwaves, some refrigerators. Cable TV. No pets. | 3101 S. 17th St. | 701/746–4411 or 800/489–4411 | fax 701/746–4755 | 62 rooms | $34 | D, DC, MC, V.

Holiday Inn. A large block south of the University of North Dakota and across the railroad tracks, this 1950 hotel has shuttle services to UND, the medical park, and the airport. Restaurant, bar, room service. In-room data ports. Cable TV. Indoor pool, wading pool. Hot tub, sauna. Putting green. Gym. Video Games. Laundry facilities. Business services, airport shuttle. Some pets allowed. | 1210 N. 43rd St. | 701/772–7131 or 888/249–1464 | fax 701/780–9112 | www.basshotels.com/holiday-inn | 149 rooms, 1 suite | $76–$79, $135 suite | AE, D, DC, MC, V.

Prairie Inn. Two theme suites, the Jungle Safari and Caesar's Court, come with champagne, wet bar, two color TVs, and VCR at this 1970s brick motel on the northwest outskirts of the town center. There's a gas station and a Perkin's Restaurant next door. Complimentary Continental breakfast. Some kitchenettes, some minibars, some microwaves, some refrigerators, some in-room hot tubs, some in-room VCRs. Indoor pool. Video games. No pets. | 1211 N. 47th St. | 701/775–9901 or 800/571–1115 | fax 701/775–9936 | 94 rooms, 2 suites | $43, $109–$179 suites | AE, D, DC, MC, V.

Ramada Inn. Built in 1973, this two-story, brick motel sits just north of Hwy. 2 and east of I–29, 4 mi east of the airport, with complimentary van service to the bus depot and train depot. Pool-side rooms have direct access through large sliding glass doors to the courtyard and pool. The hotel is ½ mi from the University and 2 mi from downtown Grand Forks. The lobby area has some games for kids. Restaurant, bar, room service. In-room data ports. Cable TV. Indoor pool, wading pool. Hot tub, sauna. Laundry facilities. Business services, airport shuttle. | 1205 N. 43rd St. | 701/775–3951 or 800/272–6232 | fax 701/775–9774 | www.ramada.com | 100 rooms | $68–$82 | AE, D, DC, MC, V.

Roadking Inn–Columbia Mall. The hotel is so close to Columbia Mall that it's almost in the parking lot. The two-story motel built in the 1970s and has a brick exterior. In a commercial area with several neighboring hotels, a restaurant is six blocks away and downtown is 3 mi north. Complimentary Continental breakfast. In-room data ports. Cable TV. Indoor pool. Hot tub. Video games. Laundry facilities, laundry services. Business services. | 3300 30th Ave. S | 701/746–1391 or 800/707–1391 | fax 701/746–8586 | 81 rooms, 4 suites | $56–$68, $99 suites | AE, D, MC, V.

Select Inn. The hotel has three buildings, two are no smoking. Off I–29 at Exit 141, then east on Gateway Drive (Hwy. 2) and south on W. 42nd Street, the hotel is on the west side of the road, about 2 mi from the University and 3 mi from downtown. Complimentary Continental breakfast. In-room data ports. Cable TV. Laundry facilities. Business services. Pets allowed (fee). | 1000 N. 42nd St. | 701/775–0555 or 800/641–1000 | fax 701/775–9967 | www.selectinn.com | 119 rooms, 1 suite | $35–$45, $40 suite | AE, D, DC, MC, V.

JAMESTOWN

(Nearby towns also listed: Carrington, Valley City)

Known as "The Buffalo City," a concrete sculptured buffalo sits on a hill, visible from almost everywhere in Jamestown. The city is halfway between Bismarck and Fargo, making it an attractive place to stop, stretch your legs, and visit. Jamestown, population 15,500, grew up in the valley where the James and Pipestem Rivers meet, a lush area with outdoor recreation and agriculture. The community, founded in 1871, expanded in later years to include manufacturing in its economic profile. Jamestown also has the distinction of being the hometown of Louis L'Amour, the famous author of westerns.

Information: Jamestown Promotion and Tourism Center | 212 3rd Ave. NE, 58401 | 701/252–4835 or 800/222–4766 | www.jamestownnd.com.

Attractions

1883 Stutsman County Courthouse. Constructed in the Gothic Revival tradition in 1883, this courthouse dates back to Dakota Territory days. A brick building with stone arches rising above the front entrance, a tower rises above it all giving the impression of a church rather than a courthouse. | 511 2nd Ave. SE | 701/251–1855 | Free | Weekdays 9–5, tours by appointment.

Fort Seward Military Post and Interpretive Center. The fort was built between 1872 and 1877 to protect Northern Pacific railroad workers. Today the foundations and basements are all that remain of the original structure. An ongoing archeological dig continues on the site. | 601 10th Ave. NW | 701/252–6844 | Free | Apr.–Oct., daily.

Frontier Village. A re-created frontier town, this village has the oldest general store in the state, a one-room school house, a barbershop, a church, and other buildings. A giant buffalo statue overshadows the village, next to the National Buffalo Museum and the Live Buffalo Herd. | Louis L'Amour St., at 17th St. SE | 701/252–6307 | Free | Memorial Day–Labor Day, daily 9–9.

At 26-ft high, the 60-ton steel-and-concrete **Frontier Village Buffalo Statue** is visible from the highway. Erected in the 1950s, the gigantic beast dwarfs the herd of real bison that roam the enclosed grounds next door. | Free | Daily.

Gifts Dakota Style. You can buy North Dakota products here. All items in the store and catalog—from soup mixes to compact discs—are grown or produced in the state. | Hwy. 281 and 25th St. SW, Buffalo Mall | 701/251–2400 or 800/447–6564 | fax 701/252–6774 | www.shopnd.com | Weekdays 10–9, Sat. 10–6, Sun. noon–5.

National Buffalo Museum. With more than $1.5 million in artifacts and original art, the museum showcases the history of the American bison. A live buffalo herd visible from the museum includes White Cloud, a rare Albino buffalo, born in 1996. | 500 17th St. SE | 701/252–8648 | www.ndtourism.com | $3 | Memorial Day–Labor Day, daily 9–8; winter hours, daily 10–5.

Stutsman County Memorial Museum. You can see a treasure of memorabilia reflecting the culture of early North Dakotan pioneers in this brick home with Native American artifacts, 1800s clothing, and military uniforms. | 321 3rd Ave. SE | 701/252–6741 | $5 | June–early Oct., daily 1–5; Sun., Wed. also open 7 PM–9 PM.

Whitestone Hill Battlefield State Historic Site. A 20-year war between the Sioux and U.S. Cavalry began with a battle here on September 3, 1863, ending as the sun set beyond the prairie. Today there is a granite marker commemorating the Sioux lives lost, a small museum, and a picnic area. About 45 mi south of Jamestown, off Route 281 and west on Route 2, this site is worth the effort. | State Historical Society of North Dakota, 612 E Boule-

vard Ave., Bismarck | 701/328–2666 | www.state.nd.us/hist | Free | Mid-May–mid-Sept.,
Thurs.–Mon. dawn to dusk.

ON THE CALENDAR

JUNE: *Fort Seward Wagon Train.* Canvas-topped box wagons can jostle you about re-
creating the life of the traveling pioneer. Teams of draft horses or mules pull the wagons, with an experienced "teamster" at the helm, so you just have to hang on. The
wagon train has a "chuck wagon" to carry victuals and cooking utensils. The week-long
working trail ride covers about 15 mi a day, starting at Jamestown and following a different route each year. Camp activities include history talks, skits, singing, and arts and
crafts. | Fort Seward Wagon Train, Box 244, Jamestown | 701/252–6844.

JULY: *White Cloud Days/Tatanka Festival.* White Cloud is the name of the world's only
living albino buffalo. The community celebrates this unique buffalo with a parade, cultural presentations, birthday cake, pony rides, stagecoach rides, kids games, and a street
dance. You can join in the fun at the Frontier Village and National Buffalo Museum. |
701/252–4835 or 800/222–4766 or 701/252–8648.

Dining

Depot Cafe. American. Hot roast beef sandwiches highlight the menu here, along with
homemade soups and a salad bar. No alcohol.| 2nd Ave. and 3rd St. NE | 701/252–1003 | Break-
fast also available. Closes at 7 PM | $5–$10 | MC, V.

Gladstone Restaurant and Time Out Sports Café. American. Gladstone is popular for
shrimp scampi and seasoned chicken Alfredo. Dim lighting, candle light, and pictures of
the Gladstone from the 1930s and 1940s set the tone. The café serves lighter meals. Kids'
menu. Sun. brunch.| 111 2nd St. NE | 701/252–0700 | Breakfast also available. No dinner Sun.
| $11–$26 | AE, D, DC, MC, V.

Great Dragon Chinese Restaurant. Chinese. The extensive menu has more than 120 choices,
with teriyaki chicken, General Tso's chicken, and a daily lunch buffet. There's wood panel-
ing with oriental paintings, and lamps on each table. Kids' menu. | 509 10th St. SE | 701/
251–2533 | $7–$11 | AE, D, MC, V.

Perkins Family Restaurant and Bakery. American. This chain restaurant serves omelettes,
pancakes and waffles, burgers and sandwiches, soup and salad bread bowls, dinner
entrées, and pastries and desserts. There are wildlife pictures and etched glass windows
are unique to this restaurant. No alcohol. | I–94 and Hwy. 281S | 701/252–1370 | Open 6 AM–
midnight | $7–$11 | AE, D, DC, MC, V.

Ponderosa Steakhouse. American. With a dark clapboard exterior, the interior has antique
pots and pans hanging from the old white, wood walls. A stuffed deer mounted on the
wall and antique guns add to the local pioneer spirit. The restaurant has sirloin steaks and
prime rib. Salad bar. No alcohol. | 611 25th St. SW | 701/252–1848 | $7–$15 | D, MC, V.

Wagon Masters Restaurant and Lounge. American. The restaurant could pass as a large
pioneer kitchen with antiques, artifacts, and other western and pioneer artworks scattered
about the dining area. The salad bar is a covered wagon and the soup pots are wooden
barrels. Cajun dishes and prime rib are the local specialties. Salad bar. Kids' menu. | 805
S.W. 20th St. | 701/252–4243 | $8–$18 | AE, D, DC, MC, V.

Lodging

Comfort Inn. Built in the 1990s in a commercial area, the two-story, brick hotel is 1 mi from
downtown and across the street from the National Buffalo Museum and its accompany-
ing giant buffalo sculpture. Just north of I–94, off Hwy. 281 at Exit 258, this hotel has interior corridors. Restaurant, bar, complimentary Continental breakfast. In-room data ports.
Cable TV. Indoor pool. Hot tub. Business services. Pets allowed (fee). | 811 20th St. SW | 701/
252–7125 or 800/228–5150 | fax 701/252–7125 | www.comfortinn.com | 43 rooms, 9 suites |
$64, $74 suites | AE, D, DC, MC, V.

Dakota Inn. With a gas station next door and the Buffalo Mall across the street, this 1970s motel is 1½ mi south of Jamestown. A go cart track is out back. Restaurant, bar. Some mini-bars, some in-room hot tubs. Cable TV. Indoor pool. Hot tub. Video games. Laundry facilities. No pets. | Hwy. 281S and I–94 | 701/252–3611 or 800/726–7924 | fax 701/251–1212 | 118 rooms, 1 suite | $55, $115 suite | AE, D, MC, V.

Gladstone Select Hotel. In downtown, attached to the Gladstone Restaurant and one block from the Jamestown Mall and a few blocks from several local restaurants, the two-story hotel has nine theme suites. The Stadium Club room is surrounded with a grand-stand mural and sports memorabilia, a large screen TV, and a grid-iron painted ceiling. You can enjoy a hearty breakfast, lunch and dinner at the Prairie Rose restaurant on site. If you venture north in the winter, the Gladstone has winter plug-ins for your vehicle. 2 Restaurants (see Gladstone Restaurant, above), bar (see Time Out Sports Café, above), room service. In-room data ports. Cable TV. Indoor pool. Hot tub. Laundry facilities, laundry service. Business services, airport shuttle. Some pets allowed. | 111 2nd St. NE | 701/252–0700 or 800/641–1000 | www.selectinn.com | fax 701/252–0700 | 108 rooms, 9 suites | $54–$57, $86 suites | AE, D, DC, MC, V.

Holiday Inn Express. Built in 1995 off I–94, the three-story motel has a drive-up stucco exterior. In a commercial area, only 2 mi from downtown and just a few yards away from restaurants and shopping centers, the motel is also 1 mi from the National Buffalo Museum and the gigantic buffalo sculpture. Rooms have blonde-colored furniture and southwestern wallpaper. It's also across the street from the Sinclair gas station with the green dinosaur statue mounted in front. Complimentary Continental breakfast. In-room data ports. Cable TV. Indoor pool. Hot tub. Gym. Business services, parking fee. | 803 20th St. SW | 701/251–2131 or 800/465–4329 | fax 701/251–2599 | www.basshotels.com/holiday-inn | 52 rooms | $51–59 | AE, D, DC, MC, V.

KENMARE

MAP 7, C2

(Nearby town also listed: Minot)

In the early 1890s, clusters of families put down roots near lignite mines in the area which eventually became the community of Kenmare in 1897. Today, the mines are closed and agriculture and hunting-related tourism provide the economic mainstays for the small community of 1,200 people. Officially designated the Snow Goose capital of North Dakota, Kenmare and the numerous small wetlands in this region provide a home to more waterfowl than anywhere in the country, making this a popular area for wildlife observation. Approach Kenmare from the south and you'll see the efforts of exuberant graduating high school seniors who used white rocks to form the last two digits of their graduation year on the side of a hill where class numbers have been displayed proudly for over 20 years.

Information: Association of Commerce | 320 Central Ave., 58746 | 701/385–4038 | www.tradecorridor.com/kenmare.

Attractions

Danish Mill. Built in 1902 by a Danish immigrant, this windmill processed 200 sacks of grain a day and operated around the clock in its heyday. After WWI, the mill shut down, and today it is one of the few remaining Danish mills in the country. You can't enter the windmill, but you can see the red structure from outside. In the center of town, this structure anchors the city park. | 324 City Park | 701/385–4857 | tradecorridor.com/kenmare | Free | Daily.

Des Lacs National Wildlife Refuge. A bird-watcher's paradise, the refuge spans a 25-mi-long corridor straddling the Des Lacs River, 1 mi west of Kenmare. An 11 mi gravel road accesses great viewing areas of nearly 300 species of birds. You need special permits to hunt or trap here. | Refuge Manager, Box 578 | 701/385-4046 | Free | Weekdays 7:30-4.

Scenic Lake Road. Access for bird watching, observing wildlife, biking, or hiking abound on this 12 mi stretch of road paralleling Des Lacs Lake. Along this North Dakota Scenic Backway you can stop to read 13 interpretive panels at pullouts and scenic overlooks along the route. Begin at the Baden overpass at U.S. Hwy. 52. | Free | Daily.

Taskers Coulee Picnic Area. You can try for a glimpse of vireos, black and white warblers, ovenbirds, and veery here. At this lighted full-service picnic area in the heavily wooded coulee, you can hike or participate in organized sports on the playground, sand volleyball court, and baseball diamonds. Just south of the Des Lacs Wild Life Refuge you can access the Coulee via Ward County Road #1A. | Kenmare Association of Commerce, Box 324 | 701/385-4857 | tradecorridor.com/kenmare | Free | May–Sept., daily.

ON THE CALENDAR

OCT.: *Goosefest.* Half a million geese stop over at the refuges and wetlands around Kenmare during their annual migration south. Goosefest, an annual hunting festival, celebrates sportsmanship, camaraderie, and the pleasure of a good hunt. A week of events has contests with $32,000 in prizes awarded, wild game feeds, and a banquet. | 701/385-4857.

Dining

Cindy's Café. American. You can indulge in great homemade food at this plain, old-fashioned small town café. Pictures of ducks and geese, local icons, hang on the wall. Try the Cindy Burger, with bacon and cheese and a side of fries or onion rings, or for breakfast. No alcohol. | 27 W. Division St. | 701/385-4861 | Breakfast also available. No dinner Sun. | $5–$7 | No credit cards.

Pizza Hub. American. The Hub is fully carpeted with wooden tables and chairs and pictures mounted on the walls. Along with Hub Special Pizza and the local favorite, white pizza, they also serve a loaded all-meat pizza with several kinds of cheese. Homemade pies. Kids' menu. Beer only. | N. Broadway (no street number) | 701/385-4896 | $5–$14 | No credit cards.

Ying Bin Chinese Restaurant. Chinese. The restaurant seats 70 and has Cantonese sweet and sour dishes. Buffet. | 118 Central Ave. | 701/385-4447 | $6–$21 | No credit cards.

Lodging

Farm Comfort Bed & Breakfast. In a 1960s ranch house, on a 360-acre farm where durum wheat and canola grow, the rooms here have modern furnishings, painted walls, and coordinated bedroom sets. Tours of the farm are available. Common areas include the basement family room with such antiques as cream separators, bun warmers, and butter churns. Limited Swedish is spoken. Pets are allowed, but not inside. This B&B is 7½ mi southwest of Kenmare. Complimentary breakfast. No air-conditioning. TV in common area. No kids under 10. No smoking. | 58200 394th Ave. NW | 701/848-2433 | 2 rooms (with shared bath) | | $45 | No credit cards.

KILLDEER

MAP 7, B4

(Nearby towns also listed: Dickinson, Theodore Roosevelt National Park)

A ranching and cowboy town, Killdeer, in 1914, became the terminus for the Northern Pacific Railway branch out of Mandan. The annual rodeo, the state's oldest continuous rodeo since 1923, can give you a thrill, as the grounds are small and intimate for the sporting events. You can park your RV near the rodeo grounds for free. Killdeer, population 700, is a great place to gas up, as there isn't another gas station around for 40 mi. The National Grasslands wave off to the west, and the Little Missouri River meanders its way through badlands and a state park just a few miles north of town.

Information: **Killdeer City Hall** | 214 Railroad St., 58640 | 701/764–5295 | www.killdeer.com. **McKenzie County Tourism Bureau** | 201 5th Street NW, Watford City 58854 | 701/842–2804 or 800/701–2804 | www.4eyes.net/tourism.htm.

Attractions

Dunn County Museum. This small museum has an exhibit on translucent Knife River flint, highly prized by Native Americans for spear points, arrowheads, and tools. Local quarries mined the flint for at least 11,000 years. | 153 Museum Trail, Dunn Center | 701/548–8057 or 701/548–8111 | Free | Memorial Day–Labor Day, Mon.–Sat. 9–5, Sun. 1–5.

Old Sod Post Office. Built in 1912 of cedar logs and sod, and listed on the National Register, this structure served Grassy Butte as a Post Office from 1914 to 1964. It's now a museum with antiques and relics from the 1800s and early 1900s. | Box 124 Maine St., Grassy Butte | 701/863–6769 | Free | Memorial Day–June, weekends 9–4; July–Labor Day, daily 9–4.

Killdeer Mountain Battlefield State Historic Site. A marker commemorates a July 28, 1864 battle between 2,200 troops commanded by General Alfred Sully and 6,000 Sioux Indians, 10½ mi northwest off Hwy. 22. With the aid of artillery batteries, Sully scattered the encamped village reported to have 6,000 warriors, with losses of 5 soldiers and perhaps 100–150 Indians. | State Historical Society of North Dakota, 612 E. Boulevard Ave., Bismarck | 701/328–2666 | fax 701/328–3710 | www.state.nd.us./hist | Free | Daily.

Little Missouri State Park. You may have second thoughts as you head in the gravel road off Hwy. 22, at least until you catch your first glimpse of the rugged badlands. Called "Mako Shika" or "where the land breaks" by the Sioux, these unusual land formations create the state's most awe-inspiring scenery. The beehive-shape rock formations resulted from the erosion of sedimentary rock deposited millions of years ago by streams flowing from the Rocky Mountains. Undeveloped and rugged, this wilderness area has primitive camping and 75 mi of horseback trails. If you want to explore the park's extensive trail system and almost 5,800 acres of park land, several horse rentals and guide services can accommodate you. | C/o Cross Ranch State Park, 1403 River Rd., Center | 701/764–5256 summers, 701/794–3731 winters | www.state.nd.us/ndparks | $4 per vehicle | Daily.

Lost Bridge. In the 1930s the government built a bridge across the Little Missouri 22 mi north of Killdeer, but a road to the bridge wasn't built until 20 years later. Dismantled in 1994, a piece of the Lost Bridge, with a plaque, is mounted next to the "new" bridge on Route 22.

Medicine Hole. On top of one of the Killdeer Mountains northwest of Killdeer, Medicine Hole is one of the state's few caves. Native American legend says that the first people and animals emerged from here. Although the cave is on private land, you can follow the signs posted by the landowners. Drive, park where designated, and then hike the last 30 minutes. | 701/764–5805 | Free | Daily.

Route 22 Scenic Byway. Hills and sky roll on forever along this scenic route between Killdeer and New Town to the north. Gas up in Killdeer (gas stations are few in this area) and drive north. The 64 mi scenic stretch takes you past the Killdeer battlefield, mountains, the Little Missouri State Park, Lost Bridge, and on through Fort Berthold Indian Reservation, where the road connects with Route 23. Turn east and you see another park, a museum, and a casino before crossing the narrow Four Bears Bridge over the Missouri River. Then turn left at the sign for Crow Flies High Butte, and end this jaunt through time with a remarkable view of Lake Sakakawea. | Free | Daily.

Kings Elk Ranch. Some of the elk here are so docile they'll eat apples from your hand. | Kings Elk Ranch, 10831 3rd street NW | 701/764–5419 | Free | Daily, by appointment.

Knife River Ranch Vacations. Ranching activities include branding, trailing cattle, bull runs, roundup, and guided trail rides. You can rent a horse from the Ranch or bring and board your own in separate corrals. | 1700 County 5, Golden Valley | 701/983–4290 | fax 701/983–4295 | www.kniferiverranch.com | $55 for cabins; extra fee for trail rides | Daily.

ON THE CALENDAR
JULY: *Killdeer Mountain Roundup Rodeo.* Begun in 1923, this is North Dakota's oldest Professional Rodeo Cowboy Association–sanctioned rodeo. The community goes all out, hosting a Native American and frontier encampment, classic car show, parade, fireworks, and street dance. | Killdeer rodeo grounds | July 4 | 701/225–8216.

Dining
Alice's Restaurant. American. Baskets on the walls and an antique cookstove in the corner are in this 50-seat restaurant in downtown Dunn Center, about 6 mi east of Killdeer on Rte. 200. Dark green linens, flowers, and candles cover the tables. All the food here is homemade. Daily specials might be cabbage rolls or stuffed peppers, home-baked pies such as sour cream raisin. | 12 Main St., Dunn Center | 701/548–8058 | Closed Monday. Breakfast also served | $6–$13 | No credit cards.

Buckskin Bar & Grill. Steak. In the center of town, this steak house, saloon, and dance hall seats 350 in various dining rooms. Built in 1915, the building has rough wood walls, original wood floors, and tin ceilings. Stuffed, mounted critters adorn the walls in one room. Other rooms have photographs of local cowboy celebrities who often dine here. Steak and seafood is the focus, with prime rib a specialty. They're famous for the homemade apple cobbler. Kids' menu. | 416 Central Ave. | 701/764–5321 | fax 701/764–5057 | $7–$15 | AE, MC, V.

Ginny's Burger Ranch. American. Specials are the sunrise hash browns and hamburger steak. Twenty miles west of Killdeer and 35 mi north on Hwy. 85, you can take a scenic drive through the National Grasslands on your way to dinner. Kids' menu. Sun. brunch. No alcohol. | Hwy. 85, Watford City | 701/842–6315 | Breakfast also available | $10–$19 | MC, V.

Lodging
Badlands Eastview Campground and Trail Rides. When you're staying in one of the four hand-crafted theme cabins here, it's hard to tear yourself away to take a horseback ride through the wilds of the Little Missouri State Park. Campers and RVs are welcome. | 10460 Ken Street NW | 701/764–5219 | www.badlandstrailrides.com | $20 2-hr ride; $30–$75 per 2 adults for cabins | Daily.

Naard Creek Ranch. Built in 1999, this secluded log cabin in the badlands about 21 mi northwest of Killdeer is set on 340 acres and sleeps up to 10 people in a bedroom, bunkroom, loft, and futon in the living room. The interior is knotty pine. The main property is a working cattle ranch. Microwave, refrigerator. No room phones, no TV. Hiking. No smoking. | 11580 6th St. NW | 800/511–0434 | www.naardcreek.com | 1 cabin | $75 | No credit cards.

LINTON

(Nearby towns also listed: Bismarck, Fort Yates, Mandan)

This agricultural community was named for a local attorney who didn't want the recognition; a compromise was reached, and as a result, his true name was altered to an extent he found acceptable, ending up with Linton. Today Linton, population 1,410, hosts a remarkable retreat center called the Rivery, which caters to national businesses looking for a rustic getaway in which to conduct meetings.

Just south of Linton is Strasburg, where you'll find the Ludwig and Christina Welk Homestead, boyhood home of bandleader Lawrence Welk. The journey south along U.S. 83 includes terrain of undulating hills and brilliant bursts of yellow sunflower fields in the summer. Most of the population of this part of North Dakota is still made up of descendants of the original wave of European immigrants—Scandinavians, German-Russians, Czechs—who homesteaded the region in the 1890s.

Information: Chamber of Commerce | 101 1st St. NE, 58552 | 701/254–4267.

Attractions

Ludwig and Christina Welk Homestead. The original clapboard-sided sod house is the birthplace of accordion-playing bandleader Lawrence Welk. The house and outlying buildings have been restored as a memorial to the hardy German-Russian immigrants who fled the Ukraine during the 1870s and 1880s. You can see genuine Welk family furniture and memorabilia inside the buildings, and as you stroll the grounds you'll hear broadcasts of recordings of Welk's music. This site, 10 mi south of Linton, is listed on the National Register of Historic Places. | 845 88th St. SE (Box 52), Strasburg | 701/336–7470 | www.tradecorridor.com/strasburg | $3 | Mid-May–mid-Sept., daily 10–5, rest of the year by appointment only.

Sts. Peter and Paul Catholic Church. Completed in 1911, this church is now listed on the National Register of Historic Places. It has an 85-ft steeple, huge Romanesque arches, and cruciform layout. | 106 N. 7th St., Wilton | 701/774–6464 | Free | Daily 8–8.

ON THE CALENDAR

JUNE: *Dairy and Ag Day.* This day-long community event celebrates dairy and agriculture on the first Friday in June with the dairy princess crowning, a parade, and games for kids and adults, including "Messy Bessy" in which a live cow participates. Free-will donations are accepted for the noon meal, and free ice cream is available in the afternoon. | 701/254–4460.

Lodging

Hideaway Creek Lodge. You get privacy and open space at this 1900s farmhouse on ten acres, 25 mi southwest of Linton. You rent the entire four-bedroom house. The kitchen is fully equipped. No air-conditioning. Refrigerator. Laundry facilities. | 752 87th St. SW | 701/336–7709 | 4 rooms (with shared bath) | $50 | Nov.–May | No credit cards.

MANDAN

MAP 7, D4

(Nearby towns also listed: Bismarck, Fort Yates, Linton, Washburn)

Mandan, population 15,200, came into existence in 1872 in response to Northern Pacific railroad plans. The area went through several names until 1878, when a railroad official chose to recognize the Mandan tribe that lived near the riverbank. Mandan is a shipping and warehousing center, and it grew swiftly in the years after 1882, when the Northern Pacific railroad completed a bridge from Bismarck across the Missouri River. An 1890s law left on the books until recently required state government officials to reside in Bismarck, because the treacherous river lacked adequate bridges. In fact, the first bridge for nonrailroad traffic was constructed in 1922. Mandan is distinct from Bismarck in scale and atmosphere, with an emphasis on relaxed small-town ideals. John Steinbeck once described Mandan as the Gateway to the West. Main St. is still lined with tall false-front stores, a few bars, and western-wear shops.

Information: Convention and Visitors Bureau | 1600 Burntboat Dr., 58503 | 701/222–4308 or 800/767–3555 | www.bismarck-mandancvb.org.

Attractions

Five Nations Arts. This shop, set up in an old railroad depot, sells traditional and contemporary arts and crafts from 200 regional Native American artists. Several weekends every year, Native American artists come and work in-house. | 401 W. Main St. | 701/663–4663 | fax 701/663–4751 | www.5nationsarts.com | Free | May–Sept. Mon.–Sat. 9–7, Sun. 12–5, Oct.–Dec. Mon.–Sat. 10–6, Sun. 12–5, Jan.–Apr. Mon.–Sat. 10–5.

Fort Abraham Lincoln State Park. Rich in Native American and military history, this 1870s fort began as a fur-trading post in the 1780s. By 1872 it had been renamed for Lincoln, and it soon became the home of the 7th Cavalry and General George Custer. The officers' quarters that Custer shared with his wife, Libby, have been reconstructed to their appearance of 1876, when the doomed general left on his fateful expedition to the Little Big Horn. Also in the 75-acre park are reconstructed barracks, a commissary store with gift shop, infantry blockhouses, a soldiers' cemetery, and On-A-Slant Indian Village. The park museum has an exhibit on the Mandan Native Americans in a Civilian Conservation Corps–era fieldstone building. Overlooking the Missouri River, the park also has campgrounds and trails, and is listed on the National Register of Historic Places. | 4480 Fort Lincoln Rd. | 701/663–9571 or 701/663–1464 | fax 701/663–4751 | www.state.nd.us/ndparks | $4 | Memorial Day–Labor Day, daily dawn to dusk.

On-A-Slant Indian Village was inhabited by Mandan Native Americans between 1650 and 1750. About 1,000 people lived in the village, but by the early 1800s, most had been wiped out by smallpox. Four reconstructed earth lodges give a sense of the Mandan people's world. The village is listed on the National Register of Historic Places.

Huff Hills Ski Area. Snowmaking machines and daily grooming keep the 80-acre ski area with 20 runs in consistently good shape. Two chairlifts, ski and snowboard rentals, and a small restaurant are available. | 5554 Rte. 80 | 701/663–8390 | Lift tickets $18 | Thanksgiving–Mar., Thurs.–Sun. 10–5.

New Salem Sue. Built in 1974, the world's largest (concrete) Holstein cow stands on a bluff overlooking I–94. A full 38 ft in height and 50 ft in length, she's easily visible at least 5 mi away. She's there to honor the dairy farmers in the New Salem area. A road winds up to the cow, giving you an up-close view. | 704 Main Ave., New Salem | 701/843–8159 | Free | Daily.

North Dakota State Railroad Museum. Photographs, artifacts, uniforms, and model hopper cars fill the museum devoted to iron-horse history. Outside you can see a 1913 Soo caboose and a 1954 Burlington Northern caboose. While you're there, enjoy a free ride on the mini-train. | 3102 37th St. NW | 701/663–9322 or 701/663–6779 | Free | May–Sept., daily 1–5.

ON THE CALENDAR

JUNE: *Frontier Army Days.* Relive the days of the 7th Cavalry with displays, drills, Custer House tours, and entertainment during a weekend encampment. Custer buffs abound; you may run into several George and Libby Custers. | Fort Abraham Lincoln State Park | 701/663–4758.

JULY: *Jaycees Rodeo Days.* Rodeos, a carnival, parade, art-in-the-park festival, and a huge fireworks display attract thousands during this Independence Day event. | Mandan rodeo grounds and downtown | July 4 | 701/663–1136.

JULY–AUG.: *Nu'eda Corn and Buffalo Festival.* The Mandan culture comes alive on this weekend of life-style demonstrations. | Fort Abraham Lincoln State Park | 701/663–4758.

Dining

Captain's Table Dining Room. American. This restaurant with nautical decor and low lighting has inspired many romantic dinners and marriage proposals. A cozy little bar/jazz club is adjacent. The restaurant is in the Best Western Seven Seas Motor Inn. Known for South American steak, although many come for the prime rib–lobster combination. Kids' menu. Sun. brunch. | 2611 Old Red Trail | 701/663–3773 | Breakfast also available | $18–$39 | AE, D, DC, MC, V.

Dakota Farms. Steak. Breakfast is on the menu all day in this bright, family-style restaurant known for its friendly service. Try the Dakota Stuffed Omelet, or go for one of their steak dinners, such as the chicken-fried steak covered with sausage sauce or the 6-oz Dakota steak with peppers and onions. Kids' menu. No alcohol. | 1120 E. Main St. | 701/663–7322 | Breakfast also available | $7–$10 | D, MC, V.

Kroll's Diner. American. You can spot this bright, shiny 1950s-style diner from the street. Kroll's has three locations in Bismarck and Mandan, but only one diner like this. Inside, the bebop decor complements the '50s-style menu. You can try the *knoephle* soup—German chicken and dumplings. Then there's the country-fried steak with gravy, or the Love-Me Tenders, which consist of chicken strips and a choice of a baked potato or salad. Kids' menu. No alcohol. | 4401 Memorial Hwy. | 701/667–0940 | Tues.–Sat. open 24 hours; Sun.–Mon. closes at 10 | $5–$7 | AE, D, MC, V.

★ **Mandan Drug.** American. You can see that this restaurant was once a pharmacy because it still has a pharmacy section and other features of the original drugstore, including stools, a jukebox filled with 60s songs, and a player-piano. Try the Sakakawea sandwich with turkey breast, cream cheese, and cranberry sauce. Follow a sandwich or homemade soup for lunch with an old-fashioned cherry soda or a brown cow—that's a root beer float with chocolate syrup—and then take home some delicious hand-made candy. No alcohol. | 316 W. Main St. | 701/663–5900 | Closed Sun. No dinner | $4–$7 | MC, V.

Speedway Restaurant and Lounge. American. This is a casual restaurant with a bar and lounge, with a menu of 4-oz sirloin served with shrimp, and prime rib. Kids' menu. | 2815 Memorial Hwy. | 701/663–2833 | Closed Sun. | $9–$23 | DC, MC, V.

Lodging

Best Western Seven Seas Motor Inn. This three-story hotel sits on the top of a hill, with views of Mandan and beyond. It was built in the 1970s and is in a commercial zone 2 mi from downtown and 4 mi from the region's largest shopping mall. There's nautical decor throughout, and also a casino. Restaurant, bar, room service. In-room data ports, kitchenettes. Cable TV. Indoor pool. Hot tub. Business services, free parking. Some pets allowed. | 2611 Old Red Trail | 701/663–7401 or 800/597–7327 | fax 701/663–0025 | www.bestwestern.com | 103 rooms, 4 suites | $67, $99 suites | AE, D, DC, MC, V.

North Country Inn & Suites. This 1998, one-story wood and brick motel has lots of parking in front. Rooms have modern oak furnishings, including a desk and matching green carpet, curtains, and bedspreads. Two bridal suites are booked far ahead. Complimentary Continental breakfast. In-room data ports, some microwaves, some refrigerators, some in-room hot tubs. Cable TV. No pets. | 1200 E. Main St. | 701/663–6497 or 800/464–0158 | fax 701/667–0158 | 15 rooms, 4 suites | $55, $155 suites | AE, D, MC, V.

MEDORA

MAP 7, A4

(Nearby towns also listed: Amidon, Dickinson, Theodore Roosevelt National Park)

The romantic history of the Wild West flavors everything in historic Medora, a walkable frontier town with museums, tiny shops, a nightly musical, and other attractions. Founded in 1883 before North Dakota was a state, Medora is named for the American-born wife of the French Marquis de Mores, who dreamed of building a slaughterhouse empire on the prairie. The venture collapsed—leaving behind a 26-room mansion—and the cowtown faded until the 1960s, when its tourism potential was spotted by Harold Schafer, a North Dakota native whose fortunes were built on his company's Gold Seal products such as Mr. Bubble. (Schafer's son, Ed, was elected governor of North Dakota in 1992 and re-elected in 1996.) Today Medora thrives as a popular summer tourist destination. Among its attractions is the Pitchfork Steak Fondue, a sumptuous feast with 11-oz rib-eye steaks cooked the cowboy way in the outdoors on Jaden Terrace overlooking the river and the town ($19.50). The best time to see Medora in its full cowboy glory is Memorial Day to Labor Day. Off season, most shops and museums close, and the population dwindles to about 100. In the fall, however, you can savor the silence and take off on hikes without meeting another soul.

Information: **Medora Foundation** | 500 Pacific Ave., 58645 | 701/623–4444 or 800/633–6721 | www.medora.org.

Attractions

Billings County Courthouse Museum. The story of early Medora is told through an extensive collection of military and western firearms, regional and Ukrainian art, and Native American artifacts. The building is listed on the National Register of Historic Places. | 475 4th St. | 701/623–4829 | $2 | Memorial Day–Labor Day, daily 9–5.

Burning Hills Amphitheatre. Built into a bluff, the seven-story amphitheater hosts nightly performances of the Medora Musical every summer. If you sit near the top, you can enjoy a panoramic view of the Badlands, with an occasional bison grazing in the distance. The amphitheater was renovated in 1992 at a cost of $4 million and seats almost 3,000 people. | Box 198 | 701/623–4444 or 800/633–6721 | fax 701/623–4494 | www.medora.org | Medora Musical $17–$19 | Memorial Day–Labor Day.

Chateau De Mores State Historic Site. A French nobleman and his wife, Medora, with dreams of a slaughterhouse empire constructed this 26-room mansion in 1883. The couple entertained Theodore Roosevelt during his Dakota ranching days, hosted extravagant hunting parties, but never realized their cattle empire. The chateau is restored to its glory days and offers interpretive tours during the summer. About 1 mi from the chateau is the De Mores Memorial Park, the spot indicated by a lone-standing brick chimney, all that remains of the beef-packing plant. | 1 Chateau La. (Box 106) | 701/623–4355 | fax 701/623–4921 | www.state.nd.us/hist | $5 | Mid-May–mid-Sept., daily 8:30–6, rest of year by appointment only.

Chateau Nuts. Nuts of every imaginable variety are stocked here in huge quantities. | 350 Main St. | 701/623–4825 | Memorial Day–Labor Day, daily 9–8.

Golden Valley County Museum. Dioramas showcase a country bedroom, kitchen, and parlor. You can also see Native American artifacts, a horse-drawn hearse, tractors and other machinery, and a one-room country schoolhouse. Unique to the museum are the family display cases, purchased by individual families to show heirlooms and other memorabilia. | 180 1st Ave. SE, Beach | 701/872–3908 or 701/872–3938 | Free | Apr.–Oct., weekdays 11–3, or by appointment.

Harold Schafer Heritage Center. Besides housing a modern art gallery, this center salutes the man who saved Medora from obscurity, using the wealth he earned through his Gold Seal Co., manufacturer of Mr. Bubble and other products. | 335 4th St. | 701/623–4444 or 800/633–6721 | fax 701/623–4494 | www.medora.org | Free | Memorial Day–Labor Day, daily 10–6.

Medora Doll House. Antique dolls and toys fill almost every inch of this small house, built by the Marquis de Mores in 1884. Also known as the von Hoffman House, it's listed on the National Register of Historic Places. | 485 Broadway | 701/623–4444 or 800/633–6721 | fax 701/623–4494 | www.medora.org | $3 | Memorial Day–Labor Day, daily 10–6.

Museum of the Badlands. This collection has one of the region's most extensive exhibits of Plains Native American artifacts along with personal items of the Apache chief Geronimo. | 195 3rd Ave. | 701/623–4444 or 800/633–6721 | fax 701/623–4494 | www.medora.org | $3 | Memorial Day–Labor Day, daily 10–6.

Prairie Fire Pottery. Handmade stoneware pottery and terra-cotta tiles with wildlife tracks are displayed in a studio and showroom. Blue glaze created by the sculptor fires into a smokey hue with highlights that suggest the northern lights. The studio supplies 27 different animal-track tiles to zoos and parks worldwide. | 127 Main St. E | 701/872–3855 | Free | Mon.–Sat. 9–6, or by appointment.

ON THE CALENDAR
MAY: *Dakota Cowboy Poetry Gathering.* Local and national cowboy poets read their works on a weekend at the Medora Community Center that includes a Western art show and crafts display. | 701/623–4444 or 800/633–6721.
JUNE–SEPT.: *Medora Musical.* The Badlands are the backdrop for this nightly Grand Ole Opry–style musical, with singing, dancing, and a patriotic salute to Theodore Roosevelt, former area resident. Hosted at the Burning Hills Amphitheatre—which seats almost 3,000 people—the musical is a sell-out most nights. | 701/623–4444 or 800/633–6721.

Dining
Chuckwagon Cafeteria. American. Known for ribs, chicken, and steaks, this restaurant also has a sandwich shop and bakery. Come here to eat and see photographs of early days of Medora and an extensive collection of Indian arrowheads. Umbrellas shade the patio outdoors. Sun. brunch. No alcohol. | 250 3rd Ave. | 701/623–4444 | Closed Labor Day–Memorial Day | $6–$10 | AE, D, MC, V.

Little Missouri Saloon and Dining. The restaurant has hardwood floors and wooden tables, heavy red curtains with gold tassels, and an oak-back bar. The walleye, trout, and steaks are popular. Or try the buffalo burgers and buffalo rib-eye. Kids' menu. | 440 3rd St. | 701/623–4404 | Closed Labor Day–Memorial Day | $7–$40 | No credit cards.

Rough Rider Hotel Dining Room. American. Barbecued buffalo ribs, prime rib, and huge hamburgers are the big draw here, but you can also see photos of Theodore Roosevelt hanging on the rustic walls, with modern pictures of wildlife. The building is itself an original and the restored walls and ceiling are made of lumber from the exterior of the building. | 301 3rd Ave. at Main St. | 701/623–4444 | No lunch or dinner on Sun. | $16–$26 | AE, D, MC, V.

Trapper's Kettle. American. The decor is traps, kettles, newspaper clippings, and stuffed animals, and a canoe is the salad bar. The chili topped with cheese is a favorite with locals; also popular are the frontier-style hearty scones. Salad bar. | 83 U.S. 85 N, Hwy. 94, Belfield | 701/575–8585 | Breakfast also available | $9–$19 | AE, D, DC, MC, V.

Lodging
AmericInn Motel and Suites. Glowing wood, stuffed animals, and western themes dominate this motel, the newest (1997) of Medora's lodgings. The two-story cement-block building is in a commercial area three blocks from downtown; restaurants and stores are nearby. Complimentary Continental breakfast. Cable TV. Indoor pool. Hot tub, sauna. Laundry facilities. Business services, free parking. Some pets allowed. | 75 E. River Rd. S | 701/623–4800 or 800/634–3444 | fax 701/623–4890 | www.americinn.com | 56 rooms, 8 suites | $60, $89–$120 suites | AE, D, DC, MC, V.

Badlands Motel. This single-story motel with wood siding, built in the 1980s, is in a commercial area near Medora Community Center and two blocks from downtown restaurants and stores. In-room data ports. Cable TV. Pool. Business services, free parking. | 501 Pacific Ave. (Box 198) | 701/623–4422 or 800/633–6721 | fax 701/623–4494 | 116 rooms | $67–$79 | Closed Oct.–Apr. | AE, D, MC, V.

Dahkotah Lodge and Guest Ranch. A real working cattle ranch, the Dahkotah offers you a true life-style change, if only for a few days. Located in a residential area 19 mi outside of town, the single-story cedar-sided ranch was built in 1991. No room phones, no TV in rooms. Horseback riding. Free parking. | 4456 W. River Rd. | 701/623–4897 or 800/508–4897 (in ND) | www.dahkotahlodge.com | 4 cabins | $360 (2–night minimum stay) | AP | AE, D, MC, V.

★ **Rough Riders Hotel.** Built in 1883, this downtown hotel is operated by the Theodore Roosevelt Medora Foundation, a nonprofit organization that restores historic qualities of Medora. Rooms on the second floor have country-western antiques, brass beds, patchwork quilts, and red velvet drapes. There's a restaurant on the first floor. Parking is on the street. You have pool privileges at Badlands Hotel, four blocks away. Cable TV. No pets. No smoking. | 301 3rd Ave. | 701 623–4444 or 800/633–6721 | fax 701/623–4494 | www.medora.com | 9 rooms (7 with shower only) | $82–$92 | AE, D, MC, V.

Sully Inn and Book Corral. This downtown motel, built in the 1970s, has a bookstore in the reception area called Book Corral. You can get a 10% discount on bookstore purchases. Rooms have oak furnishings, with shades of brown and beige and colorful quilts on each bed. There is plenty of parking. Some kitchenettes, some microwaves, some refrigerators. Cable TV. Laundry facilities. No smoking. | 425 Broadway | 701/623–4455 or 877/800–4992 | fax 701/623–4992 | ellison@medora.midstate.net | 19 rooms (showers only) | $60 | AE, D, MC, V.

MINOT

MAP 7, D2

MINOT

INTRO
ATTRACTIONS
DINING
LODGING

(Nearby towns also listed: Garrison, Kenmare)

Situated among rolling hills, Minot (rhymes with "why not") has a population of 34,500 and is a unique blend of various cultures. Cowboys came from the Dakota frontier, Scandinavians settled the area, and the Air Force base brings a fluctuating population of diverse experiences and backgrounds. Established in 1886, Minot was named for a Great Northern Railway director killed in a train wreck. The city grew so rapidly after the arrival of the railroad that it was nicknamed "Magic City," a name it's still known by today. The city still "grows" rapidly twice a year, when thousands of people arrive for the huge State Fair in July, and the Norsk Hostfest in October. Tourism, the Air Force base, and education supplement the agricultural-based economy.

Information: Convention and Visitors Bureau | 1020 S. Broadway, 58702 | 701/857–8206 or 800/264–2626 | www.visitminot.org.

Attractions

Big Sky Buffalo Ranch. This bison ranch has free tours that will take you into the middle of a herd of 350 head. Lean and low in cholesterol, bison steaks and other cuts can be bought from the ranch, which also ships meat and jerky products nationwide. | 204 S. Main St. (Box 224), Granville | 701/728–6505 or 800/570–7220 | fax 701/728–6505 | bigskybuffalo.com/bigskybu | Free | May–Sept., weekdays 9–6, Sat. 9–4, Sun. noon–4.

Granville/McGillicuddy City USA. For four years, Granville, population 250, will be known as McGillicuddy City USA. Winners of a contest sponsored by the Schnapps corporation, the town was chosen over other small communities nationwide willing to change its name for four years in return for $100,000. Check out the buffalo meat and western store on Main St. for interesting gifts. | 701/728–6505 | fax 701/728–6505 | www.bigskybuffalo/granville.

Minot Air Force Base. A city in its own right, with a population of almost 13,000, the base is home to the 5th Bomb Wing, which flies B-52 bombers, and the 91st Missile Wing, one of three Minuteman missile wings in the Air Force Space Command. A "windshield" tour lasts 20 minutes. Make reservations for group tours two weeks in advance. | 201 Summit Dr., Suite 105, Minot AFB | 701/723–2170 | www.minot.af.mil | Free | Weekdays 7:30–4:30.

Oak Park. This secluded wooded park, perfect for picnicking or relaxation, is also the home for farmers markets during the summer. | 1305 4th Ave. NW | 701/857–4136 | Free | 7 AM–11 PM.

Roosevelt Park and Zoo. The 20-acre zoo has more than 200 mammals, birds, and reptiles. Cross the bridge to Yonker's Farm, and you can pet farm animals. Near the end of summer, the park showcases the Horticulture Club's beautiful displays of native and exotic flowers. In the northwest corner of the park there's a swimming pool with waterslide, and a miniature train will take you on a tour of the park. | 1219 Burdick Expressway E | 701/857–4166 | $4; special rate for children | May–Sept., daily 10–7.

Scandinavian Heritage Center and Park. You can see a 220-year-old house shipped directly from Norway, a Scandinavian storehouse, a Danish windmill, an international flag display, and an eternal flame. | 1020 S. Broadway (Box 972) | 701/852–9161 | Free | Weekdays 10–4, or by appointment.

Souris Valley Golf Club. Founded in 1967, this challenging 18-hole course is in excellent condition. | 2400 14th Ave. SW | 701/838–4112 | Apr.–Oct.

Upper Souris National Wildlife Refuge. A favorite refuge for migratory waterfowl, the refuge attracts tundra swans to its marshlands. An auto route along the crests of hills shows off the refuge and you can view the Souris River valley. At the south end of the refuge, an earthen dam creates a lake named for J. N. "Ding" Darling, a conservationist and cartoonist. | 17705 212 Ave. NW, Berthold | 701/468–5467 | Free | Daily; information center: weekdays 8–4:30.

Ward County Historical Society Museum and Pioneer Village. A collection of preserved and restored historic buildings, automobiles, artifacts, and curios includes a log cabin and one-room schoolhouse. The grounds and buildings are used for family reunions, meetings, and weddings. | 2005 Burdick Expressway E (Box 994) | 701/839–0785 | $2 | May–Sept., Tues.–Sun. 10–6, or by appointment.

ON THE CALENDAR

JAN.: *KMOT Ag Expo.* Almost 40,000 people congregate at this gigantic indoor farm show that includes seminars, exhibits, and a living ag classroom. For a quick look, check out the Web site for KMOT TV, the expo's sponsor. | North Dakota State Fair Center, Minot | 701/852–4101 or 800/472–2917 or 701/852–5254 | www.kmot.com.

JULY: *North Dakota State Fair.* This traditional fair shows off the best in agriculture, from 4-H projects to the latest in farm equipment. The nine-day event attracts 250,000 annually, with more than 600 commercial exhibitors and 20,000 4-H and Future Farmers of America exhibits. There are 11 stages of free small shows, major concerts, a carnival, rodeos, and livestock and horse shows, and also a frontier encampment. | All Seasons Arena, 2005 Burdick Expressway E | 701/852–3247 or 701/857–7620 | 3rd–4th weeks of July.

JULY: *Prairie Rose State Games.* A multi-sport festival for North Dakota's amateur athletes, these Olympic-style games began in 1987. Hosted every odd-numbered year in Bismarck and moving to other major cities in even-numbered years—the events are held in venues throughout town—the games may include baseball, bowling, fencing, mountain biking, skateboarding, swimming, track, and wrestling. | Minot | 701/328–5357.

SEPT.: *Motor Mania.* The largest motor-sport event in North Dakota, more than 30,000 fans come here to see all types of racing, a classic car show, a rod run, and a bike rally. | All Seasons Arena, 2005 Burdick Expressway E | 701/857–8206 or 800/264–2626.

OCT.: *Norsk Hostfest.* Simply the largest (and still growing) Scandinavian festival this side of the Atlantic, this event attracts big names in entertainment (such as Bob Hope, Barbara Mandrell, and the Oak Ridge Boys) while showcasing foods, costumes, dance, music, and Scandinavian celebrities. Tens of thousands attend this event at the 200,000-square-ft All Seasons Arena. | All Seasons Arena, 2005 Burdick Expressway E | www.hostfest.com | Mid-Oct. | 701/852–2368.

Dining

Applebee's Neighborhood Grill and Bar. American. Town memorabilia and pictures of local athletic teams line the walls at this chain restaurant. The best-known dishes are the Bourbon St. steak and the smothered chicken, but the locals also favor the vegetable pizza. Kids' menu. Sun. brunch. | 2302 15th St. SW | 701/839–2130 | $9–$15 | AE, D, DC, MC, V.

Field and Stream Restaurant. American. This 220-seat restaurant has goldfish in a little running stream inside, and is decorated with linens. There's a trophied 80-lb king salmon up on the wall. Choose from filet mignon and Canadian walleye. | Hwy. 83 N | 701/852–3663 | Closed Sun. | $12–$40 | AE, D, DC, MC, V.

Grand Hunan Chinese Restaurant. Chinese. The portions of soup are so generous at this restaurant that they make a good meal by themselves, but try the almond chicken or the shrimp with garden vegetables. The restaurant is in an Oriental-style building with high, vaulted ceilings. Kids' menu. | 1631 S. Broadway | 701/852–1471 | Closed Mon. | $8–$16 | AE, D, DC, MC, V.

Ground Round Bar and Grill. American. This local franchise of a national chain has a few "extras" on the menu, such as Mexican and pasta dishes. Try the lemon-pepper chicken, chicken Alfredo, or the 6-oz steak and half-rack-of-ribs combo. The restaurant has antiques and artifacts on the walls along with graphic pictures of World War I and II and stained-glass lighting. Kids' menu. Sun. brunch. | 2110 Burdick Expressway E | 701/838–3500 | fax 701/838–3860 | $6–$17 | AE, D, DC, MC, V.

Perkins Family Restaurant and Bakery. American. This chain restaurant with its bakery counter has televisions all around and an indoor porch with views of the road. The menu has chicken fajitas, and granny's country omelet and bread bowl salads. Kids' menu. No alcohol. | 405 20th Ave. SW | 701/838–2020 | Breakfast also available | $9–$19 | AE, D, MC, V.

Sammy's Pizza, Pasta and Chicken. American/Casual. The building is gray and rather plain looking, but inside the restaurant is set up like a little Italian marketplace, or piazza, with a lot of Italian paintings on the walls. Try any of the pizzas. | 126 4th Ave. NW | 701/852–4486 | $9–$12 | MC, V.

Schatz Crossroads Cafe. Café. Come here for home-style cooking and excellent breakfasts. Most popular are breakfasts Number 1 (two eggs, hash browns, and bacon or ham) and Number 99 (hash browns, ham, onion, and eggs scrambled together and served with cheese melted on top). Kids' menu. | 1305 20th Ave. SE | 701/838–5588 | Breakfast also available | $5–$12 | AE, D, MC, V.

Lodging

★ **Best Western International Inn.** On a hilltop near the airport, this large, five-story hotel is within walking distance of several restaurants and 2 mi from downtown. The rooms are large, with contemporary furnishings. The hotel's restaurant has window seating overlooking the city. Restaurant, room service. Cable TV. Indoor pool. Beauty salon, hot tub. Some pets allowed. | 1505 N. Broadway | 701/852–3161 or 800/735–4493 | fax 701/838–5538 | www.bestwestern.com | 266 rooms, 4 suites | $62–$75, $125 suites | AE, D, DC, MC, V.

Best Western Kelly Inn. This two-story stucco hotel was built in 1992 in a commercial area. It's within walking distance of the Dakota Square Mall, the town's major shopping district, and restaurants, and is 3 mi from downtown. Complimentary Continental breakfast, bar. In-room data ports. Cable TV. Indoor pool. Hot tub. Video games. Business services, free parking. Some pets allowed. | 1510 26th Ave. SW | 701/852–4300 or 800/735–5868 | fax 701/838–1234 | www.bestwestern.com | 80 rooms, 20 suites | $59, $80–$125 suites | AE, D, DC, MC, V.

Comfort Inn. The hotel was built in 1989 in a commercial area next to the Dakota Square Mall, the major shopping mall of Minot, and near theaters and restaurants. Complimentary Continental breakfast. In-room data ports. Cable TV. Indoor pool. Hot tub. Video games. Laundry facilities, laundry service. Business services, free parking. Some pets allowed. | 1515 22nd Ave. SW | 701/852–2201 or 800/228–5150 | fax 701/852–2201 | www.comfortinn.com | 140 rooms, 12 suites | $58–$75, $70–$95 suites | AE, D, DC, MC, V.

Dakotah Rose Bed & Breakfast. This downtown Victorian, built in 1906, has first and second floor verandas. The third floor has a balcony and a ballroom common area. The Victorian room has a high-rise brass bed with a leaded-glass window above it and large tapestry rugs covering the hardwood floors. Grandma's attic has antique dolls and old-fashioned quilts. A rock garden with flowers and weeping willows dot the landscaped acre on the Souris river. There are 14 clear or stained-glass leaded windows including some Tiffany. Complimentary breakfast. Some room phones. TV in common area. No pets. No smoking. | 510 4th Ave. NW | 701/838–3548 | 5 rooms (with shared bath), 2 suites | $55, $75 suites | AE, MC, V.

Days Inn. One of several hotels near the city's main shopping area, Dakota Square Mall, this is also near U.S. 2 and U.S. 83. The two-story brick hotel was built in 1982. Complimentary Continental breakfast. Cable TV. Indoor pool. Hot tub, sauna. Video games. Laundry facilities. Business services, free parking. Some pets allowed. | 2100 4th St. SW | 701/852–3646 or 800/329–7466 | fax 701/852–0501 | www.daysinn.com | 81 rooms, 1 suite | $40–$59, $75 suite | AE, D, DC, MC, V.

Fairfield Inn by Marriott. This three-story stucco hotel was built in 1991. It's near the Dakota Square Mall and 2 mi from downtown. Complimentary Continental breakfast. In-room data ports. Cable TV. Indoor pool. Hot tub. Business services, free parking. | 900 24th Ave. SW | 701/838–2424 or 800/228–2800 | fax 701/838–2424 | www.fairfieldinn.com | 58 rooms, 4 suites | $60–$65, $75 suites | AE, D, DC, MC, V.

Hillside House Bed & Breakfast. A picket fence and flower gardens front this small, 1902 Victorian on a residential hillside overlooking downtown. The English Rose room has a garden theme, feather bed comforters, antiques, a brass bed, and wall-to-wall carpeting. There's an enclosed wraparound sun porch and a tea room for your afternoon tea. Complimentary breakfast. TV in common area. No room phones. No pets. No smoking. | 425 S. Main St. | 701/839–8492 | 4 rooms (with shared bath) | $50 | MC, V.

Holiday Inn Riverside. This huge, seven-story hotel, built in 1983, is 15 blocks from downtown. The hotel is in a commercial neighborhood, but nearby houses give it a residential look. Within 1 mi there's a mall and zoo, and the state fairgrounds are right across the street. In the center of the hotel is an enormous atrium that overlooks a lounge and seating area. Restaurant (*see* Ground Round Bar and Grill), bar, room service. In-room data ports. Cable TV. Indoor pool. Beauty salon, hot tub, sauna. Video games. Laundry service. Business services, airport shuttle. Some pets allowed. | 2200 Burdick Expressway E | 701/852–2504 or 800/468–9968 | fax 701/852–2630 | www.basshotels.com/holiday-inn | 170 rooms, 3 suites | $89, $200 suite | AE, D, DC, MC, V.

Select Inn. Across the street from Minot International Airport and only three blocks from Minot State University, this motel caters to senior citizens with a Select Senior Club that offers 15% discounts. Canadian cash is accepted at par. A park and fly program lets you leave your car here for up to 14 days. Complimentary Continental breakfast. In-room safes, some kitchenettes, some microwaves, some refrigerators. Cable TV. Laundry facilities. | 225 N. Broadway | 701/852–3411 or 800/641–1000 | fax 701/852–3450 | www.selectinn.com | 97 rooms, 1 suite | $40, $51 suite | AE, D, DC, MC, V.

Super 8. This hotel is two blocks from the airport on the north end of town, is close to Minot University and 1 mi from downtown. Cable TV. Laundry facilities. Business services, free parking. Some pets allowed. | 1315 N. Broadway | 701/852–1817 or 800/800–8000 | fax 701/852–1817 | www.super8.com | 60 rooms | $30–$35 | AE, D, DC, MC, V.

NEW ROCKFORD

(Nearby towns also listed: Carrington, Devils Lake)

In between North Dakota's four largest cities, New Rockford, population 1,600, is a bustling rural community with several small businesses, including a nursing home and a movie theater. The construction of a bison-processing plant was an economic boon to the area, providing jobs and a market for farms with bison herds. Like many North Dakota towns, New Rockford started with the arrival of the railroad in 1882.

Information: New Rockford Chamber of Commerce | Box 67, 58356 | 701/947–5626 | tradecorridor.com/newrockford.

Attractions

Ken-Mar Buffalo Ranch. You can take a coach tour for a glimpse of a working buffalo ranch. | 1397 65th Ave. NE | 701/947–5951 | fax 701/947–5951 | Free | Weekdays, tours by appointment.

North American Bison Cooperative. Built in 1993, this is the world's first processing plant devoted exclusively to bison meat. Marketed worldwide, frozen bison products can be purchased and shipped from here. | 1658 Hwy. 281 | 701/947–5951 | fax 701/947–5951 | www.nabison-coop.com | Free | Weekdays 8–5, tours by appointment.

ON THE CALENDAR

SEPT.: *Central North Dakota Steam Threshers Show.* This event has a parade of antique and current farm machinery, a pancake breakfast, fiddlers' jamboree, dance, and crafts. | County Fair grounds | Third weekend of Sept. | 701/947–2461.

Dining

Rockford Cafe. American. Plain and simple describes the restaurant and its home-style cooking. Try the homemade tomato macaroni, or the turkey dressing. The dining area has wood tables and chairs and paintings on the walls. Kids' menu. No alcohol. | 1 Ave. N | 701/947–5624 | Breakfast also available | $4–$6 | No credit cards.

Lodging

Beiseker Mansion. This 15-room, three-story Queen Anne–style mansion with twin turrets was built in 1899. The mansion is operated by Dr. Jerome Tweton, a retired professor of North Dakota history, whose 3,000-volume library is sure to offer you something interesting to read. There's a fireplace in the common room. The inn is in a residential area, ½ block from a pizza restaurant, three blocks from downtown, and 25 mi west of New Rockford. Complimentary breakfast. In-room VCRs. In-room hot tub (in suite). | 1001 NE 2nd St., Fessenden | 701/547–3411 or 888/626–0207 | 4 rooms (3 with shared bath), 1 suite | $58–$68, $98 suite | AE, D, MC, V.

Bison Lodge. Built in 1959 and remodeled in 1994, this motel is on the south end of the strip, about eight blocks east of New Rockford center, off Hwy. 281. A small motel with parking out front and restaurants and gas stations nearby, the furnishings are sturdy oak, with rooms in mauve and teal colors. There are five additional units in a hunter's lodge with kitchenettes and game cleaning facilities. Complimentary Continental breakfast. Cable TV. Some pets allowed. | 222 First St. S | 701/947–5947 | fax 701/947–5059 | 13 rooms | $34 | AE, D, MC, V.

NEW TOWN

MAP 7, C3

(Nearby town also listed: Theodore Roosevelt National Park)

New Town, a community of 1,300, is the seat of tribal government for the Three Affil-iated Tribes, a formal association of the three Indian nations—Mandan, Arikara, and Hidatsa—that reside on the nearly 1 million-acre Fort Berthold Reservation. New Town is aptly named, as it was created in 1950 by developers to replace three tiny villages now at the bottom of Lake Sakakawea. Elbowoods (founded in 1889), Sanish (1914), and Van Hook (1914) were all flooded with the damming of the Missouri River. Besides lake recreation, the sparsely populated reservation hosts ranching and farming ventures, construction businesses, and a casino.

© Corbis

POWWOWS: DANCING TO THE BEAT OF THE HEART

North Dakota's native people are descendants of Chippewa, Mandan, Hidatsa, Arikara, Sioux-Yanktonai, Hunkpapa, Sisseton, Wahpeton, and other Dakota tribes. For all these tribes, powwows have served as a traditional festival that celebrates tribal heritage. Today, powwows continue to be important expressions of Native American culture.

The smaller, community-based powwows are often the most fun because they are family oriented. You can recognize most powwow grounds by the circular arbor providing shade. Bring a lawn chair, stake your place, and prepare for a day-long experience. Although the Grand Entry—the official opening ceremony in which all dancers participate—usually occurs at 1 PM and 7 PM, don't trust your watch; speeches and other events often take longer than planned, and preempt the prompt start of anything. Once the dancing starts, prepare to sit and watch a while. The costumes are designed especially for the particular dance performed. Most fun, perhaps, are the tiny tots—some barely able to walk—who are proudly dressed in their very best dance costumes and twirling and tapping to the beat of the drum groups. When the announcer calls an "intertribal" dance, this is your cue to try it yourself, and you'll be welcomed in your street clothes.

Come late morning to the powwow and sample the fry bread sold by vendors. Listen to the announcers, whose words follow a style of speaking and cadence established generations ago. Before, during, and after the dancing, there usually will be a gifting or two or three. A gifting is a ceremony at which an individual or family presents gifts—often star quilts—in honor of a loved one's memory, to cele-brate the homecoming of a soldier, or to acknowledge a new family member. In some cases, a new family member can be someone adopted into the clan. Family is important in this culture. Clan families often call someone a sister or grandson or cousin who actually may be a distant relative, if related at all.

Two of the nicest, small powwows that are easy to find are at White Shield (the second weekend of July) and Little Shell at New Town (the second weekend in August). The United Tribes Technical College powwow (the second weekend in Sep-tember in Bismarck) is one of the largest in the United States, with hundreds of dancers and thousands of spectators. While this event is more organized than typi-cal powwows, it doesn't have quite the same family atmosphere.

Information: **Convention and Visitors Bureau** | 100 Soo Place, 58763 | 701/627–3500 | marcia@djcnt.com.

Attractions

Crow Flies High Observation Point. This spot overlooking Lake Sakakawea has a spectacular view of sparkling water and rolling hills. Three miles west of New Town. | 701/627–4477.

Four Bears Bridge. This narrow bridge, named for Mandan Indian Chief Four Bears, spans a mile of Lake Sakakawea, making this the longest bridge in the state. It is also one of the few bridges across Lake Sakakawea. It was dedicated in 1955 after the old bridge had to be relocated when the Garrison Dam project was finished. Four miles west of New Town. | 701/627–4477.

Four Bears Casino and Lodge. An economic force for the reservation, this Las Vegas–style casino has 400 slots, blackjack, poker, bingo, craps, and more. It also has 85 full-service hookups for RVs and many special events, including concerts, rodeos, car shows, and boxing. This spot is four miles west of New Town, off Hwy. 23 just across the Four Bears Bridge. | HC3 Box 2A | 701/627–4018 or 800/294–5454 | fax 701/627–4012 | Free | Sun.–Thurs. 8 AM–2 AM, Fri.–Sat. 24 hours.

Four Bears Memorial Park. Four Bears was a Mandan Indian Chief and hero who died from smallpox in 1837. In 1834 Karl Bodmer painted his portrait, and the artist George Catlin also knew Four Bears. The memorial park honors the chief and all local Native Americans who died in conflicts from World War I to Vietnam. Four miles west of New Town. | 701/627–4477 | Free | Daily.

Old Scouts Cemetery. This small cemetery has headstones memorializing some of Custer's Arikara scouts, although they aren't buried here. Instead, many later warriors—all veterans and military personnel—are buried here. Note that all headstones face east into the rising sun. | 701/627–4477 | Free | Daily.

Paul Broste Rock Museum. Natural granite from the area was used to create the stone building with a private collection of 5,000 rocks, agates, minerals, and crystals. Specimens from around the world have been cut, ground, and polished to enhance their beauty. | N. Main St., Parshall | 701/862–3264 | tradecorridor.com/parshall/rockmuseum | Free | Mid-Apr.–mid-Oct., daily 10–6, or by appointment.

Three Affiliated Tribes Museum. This diverse museum explores the history of the Mandan, Hidatsa, and Arikara cultures through artifacts and arts and crafts. You can see dresses with elk teeth. Four miles west of New Town next to Four Bears Casino, off Hwy. 23. | New Town | 701/627–4477 | $3 | Memorial Day–Labor Day, daily 10–6.

Van Hook Marina. This little resort area is known locally as "fisherman's paradise" for its walleye. Campgrounds, fish cleaning, a bait shop, a boat ramp, and guide services are all here. The bait shop owners are world-class walleye anglers. | 1801 Van Hook | 701/627–3811 | Free | May–Aug., daily 6:30 AM–10 PM; Sept.–early Oct., daily 6:30 AM–8 PM.

ON THE CALENDAR

AUG.: *Little Shell Powwow.* This powwow is easy to visit because the exceptional accommodations of Four Bears Casino and Lodge are nearby. | Powwow grounds | 2nd weekend in Aug. | 701/627–4768.

OCT.: *Makoti Threshing Bee.* More than 10,000 people gather to see reenactments and demonstrations of an older farm era. Antique threshing machines run by steam engines and kerosene tractors kick-start into life again for this weekend event. You can also take in the fiddlers' contest, dance, giant flea market, parade, and slow races for old two-cylinder John Deere tractors. | 701/726–5693 or 701/726–5656.

Dining

Lucky's Café at Four Bears Casino. American. This "sit-down" restaurant is within the Four Bears Casino. Try the walleye dinner or the T-bone steak. There are paintings of Native American tribes hanging on the walls. Four miles west of New Town, off Hwy. 23. | 701/627–4018 | Breakfast also available | $8–$14 | AE, D, MC, V.

Riverside. American. The restaurant is popular for its prime rib feasts on weekends. Kids' menu. | 358 Main St. | 701/627–4403 | No lunch Sat., Sun. | $8–$14 | AE, MC, V.

Scenic 23. American. This is a great place for family dining—the walls are decorated with paintings of home interiors. It's also popular during the summer months with anglers, who come in after spending the day on the water to eat steak, lobster, and prime rib. Kids' menu. | 1803 Van Hook | 701/627–3949 | Closed Sun. No lunch | $7–$20 | AE, D, MC, V.

Lodging

Four Bears Casino and Lodge. This small, two-story brick motel is next to the casino and has a great view of Lake Sakakawea. It was built in 1996 and is 4 mi west of downtown, off Hwy 23. You can go fishing in a nearby park. Restaurant, bar. In-room data ports. Cable TV. Video games. Laundry facilities. Business services, free parking. Some pets allowed. | HC3 Box 2A | 701/627–4018 or 800/294–5454 | fax 701/627–4012 | 40 rooms | $55 | AE, D, MC, V.

PEMBINA

MAP 7, G1

(Nearby towns also listed: Cavalier, Grafton)

At Canada's border, Pembina was a meeting place for French fur trappers, Chippewa Native Americans, and Scandinavian settlers during the mid-1800s. Their children and grandchildren, the Metis, carried on the fur trade well into the 19th century. Now a town of 600 residents, Pembina boasts an outstanding state museum where you can see a panoramic view of the Pembina valley from the tower. Thirty miles south of town is Walhalla (population 1,130), also established in the mid-1800s. Walhalla is known as the Moose Capital of North Dakota because of the many moose in the area.

Information: Pembina City Office | 152 W. Rollette St., 58271 | 701/825–6819. **Walhalla Economic Development Office** | 1103 Central Ave, Walhalla 58282 | 701/549–2707 | www.tradecorridor.com./walhalla/.

Attractions

Frost Fire Mountain Ski and Summer Resort. Carved into the heavily wooded Pembina Hills, 7 mi west of town, this popular ski area has 10 ski runs, a 2,600-ft drop and double and triple chair lifts. There's a lounge, a lodge, and dining area, too. | County Rd. 55 | 701/549–3600 | fax 701/549–3602 | Ski season mid-Nov.–Mar.

Gingras Trading Post State Historic Site. Now a museum, these hand-hewn log buildings held fur trade exchanges in the 19th century. One Saturday each August, you can see living history reenactments here, 1½ mi northeast of Walhalla. The restored site is on the National Register of Historic Places. | 10534 129th Ave. NE | 701/549–2775 or 701/328–2666 (winters) | fax 701/328–3710 | www.state.nd.us./hist | Free | Mid-May–mid-Sept., daily 10–5.

Pembina Gorge. Glaciers and the winding Pembina River created the forested valley here on 12,500 acres, where elk roam free in the Tetrault Woods State Forest. | 101 5th Street, Walhalla | Free | Daily.

At **Tetrault Woods State Forest,** you can see spectacular views of the Pembina Gorge. The 431 acres of the forest are home to an elk herd. Trails are maintained for hiking, horseback riding, and snowmobiling. | 101 5th St., Walhalla | 701/549–2441 | fax 701/228–5448 | www.state.nd.us/forest | Free | Daily.

Pembina State Museum. The only regional museum mandated by North Dakota's Century Code, the building's seven-story tower has a glass observation deck. As you enter, walk around the river graphic carved in the sidewalk. Inside, exhibits cover 100 million years of local history. | 805 Hwy. 59 | 701/825–6840 | fax 701/825–6383 | www.state.nd.us/hist | Free, tower $2 | Mid-May–mid-Sept., Mon.–Sat. 9–6, Sun. 1–6; mid-Sept.–mid-May, Mon–Sat. 8–5, Sun. 1–5.

ON THE CALENDAR

JULY–AUG.: *Frost Fire Summer Theatre.* Broadway musicals fill a roofed amphitheater on summer nights, 7 mi west of town. | County Rd. 55 | 701/549–3600.

Dining

The Depot. American. Trains are on the wallpaper and in photos on the walls of this restaurant. Choose from a menu of cheese burgers and hot pork, and homemade pies. Kids' menu. Sunday brunch. | 623 W Stutsman St. | 701/825–6773 | Breakfast also available | $5–$10 | No credit cards.

Walhalla Inn Supper Club. American. Chainsaw-carved wood statues of North Dakotans such as Sakakawea, Teddy Roosevelt, and Sitting Bull stand outside this steakhouse and lounge. Prime rib and deep fried shrimp top the menu. On Fridays, try the all-you-can-eat fish platters. Kids' menu. | 508 Sunset Ave., Walhalla | 701/549–2700 | Breakfast also available. No lunch Mon.–Sat., no dinner Sun. | $12–$20 | D, MC, V.

Lodging

Forestwood Inn. This 1984 two-story wood and brick hotel is five blocks from downtown. Rooms are furnished in deep earth tones. In-room data ports. Cable TV. Hot tub. Some pets allowed. | 504 Sunset Ave., Walhalla | 701/549–2651 | 28 rooms, 1 suite | $33–$44, $71 suite | AE, D, DC, MC, V.

Red Roost Motel. You can spot this 1960s motel downtown by its bright red exterior, trimmed with white. Cable TV. Some pets allowed. | 203 Stutsman | 701/825–6254 | 9 rooms | $33 | No credit cards.

RUGBY

MAP 7, E2

(Nearby town also listed: Bottineau)

Midway between Devils Lake and Minot, Rugby (population 2,900) is an agricultural town with a unique claim to fame: it's at the geographical center of North America. A two-story stone cairn along the south side of U.S. 2 marks the center, although the real geographical center is a few miles south, in a pond off Route 3. The Great Northern Railroad built a station here, creating the town in 1886. A railroad official named it for Rugby, England.

Information: Greater Rugby Area Convention and Visitors Bureau | 224 Highway 2 SW, 58368 | 701/776–5846 | rugbynorthdakota.com.

Attractions

Dale and Martha Hawk Museum. More than 300 antiques, including farm tractors that still run, are displayed in the five buildings here, just south of town, ⅛ mi east of the intersection of Routes 2 and 3. There's a one-room schoolhouse and a general store, and locals get married in the country church. | HCR 1 Box 19B, Wolford | 701/583–2381 | tradecorridor.com/rugby | $3 | By appointment only, Oct. 15–Apr. 1.

Geographical Center of North America. An outdoor two-story rock cairn with a plaque notes the center. The actual heart of the continent is 6 mi west of Balta, about 18 mi south of Rugby on Route 3, on the southeast corner of intersection with Hwy. 2. | tradecorridor.com/rugby | Free | Daily.

Geographical Center Pioneer Village and Museum. Thousands of 19th- and 20th-century farming tools, Native American and Eskimo artifacts, and antique classic cars occupy 27 buildings. There's an 1886 Great Northern depot, a blacksmith shop, and the story of North Dakotan Clifford Thompson, who at 8'7" was the world's tallest man during his lifetime, 1904–1955. | 104 Hwy. 2E | 701/776–6414 | tradecorridor.com/rugby | $5 | May–Sept., Mon.–Sat. 8–7, Sun. 1–7.

Northern Lights Tower. You can see a simulated northern lights display reflected into the night sky from a 110-ft tower here. | ⅛ mi east of intersection of Hwy. 3 on the south side of Hwy. 2 | 701/776–5846 | Free | Daily after sundown.

ON THE CALENDAR

AUG.: *Village Fair.* At the Prairie Village Museum, this one-day event held the second Sunday in August from 8 AM to 7 PM has pioneer demonstrations with meal preparation in a wooden cook cart, blacksmithing, buttermaking, and laundering with old-time washboards. Or listen to music in the church and saloon. The Sandven building, usually housing machinery and farm equipment, becomes the dance site for cloggers, square dancers, and polka and waltz dancers. Booths have regional foods and crafts. | 701/776–6414.

Dining

Bob's Pizza and Restaurant and Lounge. American. You can play video games at the back of this diner look-alike while you wait for your pizza, roasted chicken, or steak. Salad bar. Buffet lunch. Kids' menu. | Hwy. 2 | 701/776–5657 | $4–$13 | D, MC, V.

Hub Restaurant and Lounge. American. Wilderness scenes and stuffed trophies surround you at the Hub, named for Rugby's location at the center of the continent. Try the Hub Stew, the restaurant's signature dish. Salad bar. Sat. buffet brunch. Kids' menu. Sun. brunch. | 215 Hwy. 2 SW | 701/776–5807 | $5–$16 | AE, D, MC, V.

Lodging

Econo Lodge. There are gas stations, a store, and restaurants within a mile of this two-story brick hotel on Highway 2. Restaurant, bar. Cable TV. Indoor pool. Hot tub. Video games. Business service. Some pets allowed. | Hwy. 2E south of the intersection with Hwy. 3 | 701/776–5776 or 800/424–4777 | fax 701/776–5156 | www.econolodge.com | 59 rooms, 1 suite | $40–$55, $90 suite | AE, D, DC, MC, V.

Hillman Inn & Campground. A 1960s motel at U.S. 2 and Route 3, built of cement block with brown and beige colors. Complimentary Continental breakfast. Some refrigerators. Cable TV. Laundry facilities. Pets allowed. | U.S. 2 and Rte. 3 | 701/776–5272 | fax 701/776–2300 | 39 rooms in 2 buildings (showers only) | $44 | D, MC, V.

THEODORE ROOSEVELT NATIONAL PARK

MAP 7, B3

(Nearby towns also listed: Amidon, Dickinson, Killdeer, Medora, New Town, Williston)

★ Gorges, tablelands, and craggy ravines define the Badlands that make up much of this 70,000-acre park. Theodore Roosevelt came here to hunt in 1883 and the next year started the Maltese Cross and Elkhorn open-range cattle ranches. About these adventures he later said, "I never would have been President if it had not been for my experiences in North Dakota." The park, dedicated in 1947, is divided into South and North Units. The Little Missouri River winds its way through the South Unit. The North Unit is more rugged and heavily forested in places. Both units offer outstanding views of buffalo, deer, antelope, coyote, prairie dogs, wild horses, and bald eagles. The park is at its best in summer and fall, when the roads aren't blocked by ice and snow.

Information: Theodore Roosevelt National Park | 315 2nd Ave., Medora, 58645 | 701/623–4466 | www.nps.gov/thro.

Attractions

Maah Daah Hey Trail. You can hike and ride horses or mountain bikes on this 120-mi trail. Its name means "grandfather" or "be here long" in the Mandan language. The trail passes through the rugged Badlands and the Little Missouri National Grasslands. Maps are available through the U.S. Forest Service. | USDA Forest Service, 1511 E Interstate Ave., Bismarck | 701/225–5151 | Free | Daily.

North Unit. More rugged than the South Unit, the North Unit has spectacular views and chance meetings with bison, mule deer, and elk. You can take a 14-mi loop trail to the Oxbow Overlook, or other self-guided trails that wind in and out of ravines. At the Visitor Center, 15 mi south of Watford on Route 85, you can see a slide show about the park before making your visit. | HC02 Box 35 Watford | 701/842–2333 | fax 701/842–3101 | www.nps.gov/thro | $5 per person, $10 per vehicle | Daily. Visitor Center: Memorial Day–Sept., daily 9–5:30.

Painted Canyon Scenic Overlook. Catch your first glimpse of Badlands majesty here and get a taste of what the Grand Canyon looks like. You can learn more about the Badlands from the wildlife and geology exhibits in the Visitor Interpretive Center. | 201 E Riverroad, Medora | 701/623–4466 | fax 701/623–4840 | www.nps.gov/thro | Free | Daily. Visitor Center: mid-June–Labor Day, daily 8–6; Apr.–mid-June, daily 8:30–4:30; Sept.–mid-Nov., daily 8:30–4:30.

South Unit. A 36-mi scenic loop takes you by prairie dog towns, coal veins, and panoramic views of the Badlands. Self-guided trails, most under 1 mi long, introduce you to the area's geology, ecology, and history. At the Visitor Center, a 13-minute film describes the park. | 315 2nd Ave., Medora | 701/623–4466 | fax 701/623–4840 | www.nps.gov/thro | $5 per person, $10 maximum per vehicle | Daily. Visitor Center: mid-June–Labor Day, daily 8–8; Labor Day–mid-June, daily 8–4:30.

When Theodore Roosevelt came to the Badlands in the 1880s, he became a cattle rancher. The **Elkhorn Ranch Site** was one of his ventures and is in the National Register of Historic Places. Today there are no buildings or signs here. Make sure to check at the South Unit Visitor's Center for road and river fording conditions. The ranch is 35 mi north of the Visitor Center on gravel roads. | Off Route 94 at Medora | 701/623–4466 | fax 701/623–4840 | www.nps.gov/thro | Daily.

Next door to the Visitor Center in the South Unit is Theodore Roosevelt's **Maltese Cross Ranch Cabin,** which was moved from its original site in Roosevelt's lifetime.

The **Peaceful Valley Ranch Horse Rides** are one way to see the South Unit the way cowboys and frontiersmen did a century ago. Guides lead you on some of the park's 80 mi of marked horse trails. | 7 mi north from South Unit Visitor Center | 701/623–4568 | $16 for 90 minutes; longer rides available | Memorial Day–Labor Day, daily.

Trail Rides by Little Knife Outfitters. Test your spirit of the West with this horseback adventure in the North Unit's Badlands. You can be an inexperienced rider to go on the guided one- and two-day tours. Fifteen miles south of Watford City, look for signs off U.S. 85, just north of the North Unit of Theodore Roosevelt National Park. | Box 82, Watford City | 701/842–2631 | $100 1 day, $180 2 days, including meals, horse, and equipment | Memorial Day–Labor Day, daily.

THEODORE
ROOSEVELT
NATIONAL PARK

INTRO
ATTRACTIONS
DINING
LODGING

ON THE CALENDAR

AUG.: *Founder's Day.* You can enter the park for free to commemorate the establishment of the National Park Service on August 25, 1916. Cookies and lemonade are served in the visitor center, and special programs on the National Park system run throughout the park all day. | 701/623–4466.

VALLEY CITY

MAP 7, G4

(Nearby towns also listed: Fargo, Jamestown)

This farming community of 7,100, on the banks of the Sheyenne river, is a gateway to the region. You can take scenic road trips along the valley and see the abundant wildlife, or join in the local historical reenactments. Downtown, the antiques shops are full of bargains, and in fall, the valley's lush vegetation is breathtakingly colorful. First established as a station by the Northern Pacific Railroad in 1872, the community tried several names until it settled on Valley City in 1878.

Information: **Valley City Chamber of Commerce** | 205 N.E. 2nd St., 58072 | 701/845–1891.

Attractions

Baldhill Dam and Lake Ashtabula. Ashtabula is a Native American word that means "fish river." The dam, completed in the 1950s, created a 27-mi lake just north of town where you can fish, camp, and watch the wildlife. | 2630 114 Ave. SE | 701/845–2970 | Free; camping fees | May–Oct., daily.

Fort Ransom State Park. Named for a military fort that protected trade from 1867 to 1872, the park is 40 mi south of town and has scenic views on the Sheyenne River. On the fort's site, the Bjone Visitor Center has local history exhibits, and in summer the Sodbuster Days recreate settlement life. | 5981 Walt Hjelle Parkway, Fort Ransom | 701/973–4331 | $4 per vehicle | May–Oct., daily dawn–dusk.

PACKING IDEAS FOR COLD WEATHER

- ❑ Driving gloves
- ❑ Earmuffs
- ❑ Fanny pack
- ❑ Fleece neck gaiter
- ❑ Fleece parka
- ❑ Hats
- ❑ Lip balm
- ❑ Long underwear
- ❑ Scarf
- ❑ Shoes to wear indoors
- ❑ Ski gloves or mittens

- ❑ Ski hat
- ❑ Ski parka
- ❑ Snow boots
- ❑ Snow goggles
- ❑ Snow pants
- ❑ Sweaters
- ❑ Thermal socks
- ❑ Tissues, handkerchief
- ❑ Turtlenecks
- ❑ Wool or corduroy pants

*Excerpted from *Fodor's: How to Pack: Experts Share Their Secrets*
© 1997, by Fodor's Travel Publications

Highline Bridge. This 1907 bridge across the Sheyenne River is 3,838 ft long and is the longest and one of the tallest bridges of the Northern Pacific System. Still used by trains, the bridge now is part of Burlington Northern Rail System. On the north edge of Valley City on County Rd. 21. | 701/845–1891.

Kathryn Road/Scenic Byway. Here's one of the most pastoral stretches of road in North Dakota along Routes 21 and 58. It winds along the Sheyenne River south of Valley City, and takes you past Clausen Springs park, the tiny community of Kathryn, and Fort Ransom State Historic Site before reaching Fort Ransom State Park.

Little Yellowstone Park. You can camp and bring your kids to this 26-acre forest with play-grounds. From Valley City, go south on the Cathryn Rd. until it dead-ends. Turn left; follow signs. | 701/796–8381 | Free | May–Oct., daily.

Sheyenne National Grasslands. One of the few remaining in the United States, this 70,000-acre tall-grass prairie is a haven for prairie chickens, butterflies, and the threatened white-fringed orchid. The 80 mi of trails are designed for hiking, horseback riding, and mountain biking, and primitive camping is allowed. Turn off Cathryn Road, 40 mi south of town, to enter the prairie. | 701 Main St., Lisbon | 701/683–4342 | www.fs.fed.us/grasslands | Free | Daily.

Valley City State University. Students bring their laptop computers to class at this technology-oriented university on one of the town's steepest hills. Visit the hilltop Equinox Calendar and see a circle of stones that tells the time. | 101 S.W. College St. | 701/845–7101 or 701/845–7452 | fax 701/845–7464 | www.vcsu.nodak.edu | Free | Daily.
A circle of stones arranged on a hilltop with radiating rock arms, the **Medicine Wheel** solar calendar provides a glimpse into North American Indian history. | 101 S.W. College St. | 701/845–7101 or 701/845–7452 | fax 701/845–7464 | www.vcsu.nodak.edu | Daily.

ON THE CALENDAR

MAR.: *North Dakota Winter Show.* Horse and livestock shows, rodeos, and farm exhibits attract thousands during the first ten days of March here in the Winter Show Arena. | 701/845–1401.
JULY, SEPT.: *Fort Ransom Sodbuster Days.* You can witness the day-to-day life of a heritage farm in these week-end historic recreations of the pioneer era at Fort Ransom State Park. | 701/973–4331.
SEPT.: *Sheyenne Valley Arts And Crafts Festival and 7th Cavalry Reenactment.* Fort Ransom becomes an arts center while the park hosts a cavalry charge during this week-end event. | 701/973–4461.

Dining

Another Time. American/Casual. Antique tables and chairs and paintings on the walls create a cozy retreat at this converted home. Lunch on grilled chicken with French dip, or drop by for coffee and a homemade pastry. No alcohol. | 106 5th Ave. SW | 701/845–3171 | Breakfast also available. Closed Sun. No dinner | $5–$9 | No credit cards.

Broken Spoke Family Restaurant. American. Log sculptures and war bonnets showcase the area's history in this local hot spot famous for barbecued pork ribs, steaks, and burgers. Buffet. Sun. brunch. No alcohol. | 100 Main St. W | 701/845–5968 | Breakfast also available | $6–$8 | MC, V.

Chinese Palace. Chinese. Mongolian vegetarian dishes add a special twist to the Chinese menu. But don't plan on late nights, because this café-style eatery closes at 9 PM. Kids' menu. Beer and wine only. | 849 Main St. W | 701/845–4169 | Closed Sun. | $5–$14 | D, MC, V.

City Lights Supper Club. American. On a hill overlooking the city, this steakhouse has three dining rooms with views. Specialties are hamburger steaks, and fresh fish on Fridays and Saturdays. Try the lobster. | 2369 Elm St. | 701/845–9733 | Closed Sun. No lunch | $8–$31 | AE, D, DC, MC, V.

Kenny's Restaurant. American. You can eat breakfast any time at this family-friendly restaurant with diner-style booths. Other menu choices are light grilled chicken breasts and chopped steak dinners. No alcohol. | 225 Main St. W | 701/845–4442 | $4–$6 | AE, D, DC, MC, V.

Roby's. American. An ice cream bar and homemade pastries satisfy sweet tooths in this family gathering place, where old pictures of town line the walls. For more substantial fare, try the beef and chicken enchiladas. Salad bar. Sun. brunch. No alcohol. | 1066 Main St. W | 701/845–4284 | Breakfast also available | $5–$14 | MC, V.

Sabir's Supper Club. American. Soccer memorabilia fills the lounge here, or eat in the candlelit dining room filled with art and flowers. Known for steaks and stir-fry. Kids' menu. | Winter Show Dr. | 701/845–0274 | No lunch | $10–$30 | AE, D, DC, MC, V.

Lodging

Super 8. The Winter Show Arena, Baldhill Dam, and downtown are all within one mile of this two-story 1977 motel. In-room data ports. Cable TV. Business services. Some pets allowed. | 822 11th St. SW | 701/845–1140 or 800/800–8000 | fax 701/845–1145 | www.super8.com | 30 rooms | $35–$41, $41–$51 deluxe rooms | AE, D, DC, MC, V.

Valley Bed and Breakfast. You may see deer in the backyard of this white brick residence, 2 mi south of I–94 and 3 mi south of downtown. A large recreation room has a fireplace. Grounds are landscaped with flower beds, and there's a pond with wild ducks. Although built in 1987, rooms are furnished with antiques, including a sleigh bed. Complimentary breakfast. Some room phones, no TV in some rooms, TV in common area. Indoor pool. Hot tub, sauna. Video games. Laundry facilities. No pets. No smoking. | 3611-117 R Ave. SE | 701/845–5893 | fax 701/845–1847 | 6 rooms (with shared baths), 1 suite | $59, $89 suite | D, MC, V.

Victorian Charm Guest Inn. You can rest at the tables and chairs in the gardens of this 1898 Victorian home, or use the three-season sun porch, outdoor porch with swing, living room, dining room, and piano room with baby grand, as well as the library. Rooms have antiques, brass beds, lace curtains, and hardwood floors with area rugs. Walk two blocks south to the business district. Complimentary breakfast. No room phones. No TV in some rooms. TV in common area. Library. Laundry facilities. No pets. No smoking. | 535 N. Central Ave. | 701/845–0887 | fax 701/845–1847 | 5 rooms (4 with shared baths) | $59 | D, MC, V.

Volden Farm Bed and Breakfast. Antiques from around the world furnish the rooms here, 30 mi north of Valley City. You can linger over a book in the library or idle out on the porch. The cottage has Norwegian sleigh beds. Complimentary breakfast. No TV in rooms. | 11943 County Rd. 26, Luverne | 701/769–2275 | fax 701/769–2610 | 2 rooms with shared bath, 1 cottage | $60, $95 cottage | No credit cards.

Wagon Wheel Inn. At I–94, and 2½ mi from downtown, this two-story motel was built in the 1980s. Complimentary Continental breakfast. Cable TV. Pool. Hot tub. Business services. | 455 Winter Show Rd. | 701/845–5333 or 800/319–5333 | fax 701/845–2335 | 83 rooms, 5 suites | $40, $69–$105 suites | AE, D, MC, V.

WAHPETON

MAP 7, H5

(Nearby town also listed: Fargo)

Wahpeton, on the Red River, across from Breckenridge, Minnesota, gets its name from a Native American word that means "leaf village." The city is in the middle of a fertile region where farmers grow wheat, sunflowers, sugar beets, and corn. But the 8,700 residents of Wahpeton also have a manufacturing history: the delicate and colorful Rosemeade Pottery, now sought after by collectors, was made here from 1940 to 1956. In the early 1870s the city was known as Chahinkapa ("end of the woods" in Sioux), a name that the park and zoo bear today.

Information: Wahpeton Chamber of Commerce | 118 6th St. N, 58075 | 701/642–8744 or 800/892–6673 | www.wahpchamber.com/visitors.

Attractions

Bagg Bonanza Farm. Nine of the remaining 12 (originally there were about 21) buildings have been restored on this, the only intact bonanza farm in the U.S., 13 mi west of town on Route 13. Now a National Historic Site, the farm dates from the 1860s, when The Great Northern Railroad went bankrupt and sold off 5,000-acre lots to buyers. | Box 702, Mooreton | 701/274–8989 | $3.50 | Memorial Day–Labor Day, Fri. noon–5, weekends noon–6.

Chahinkapa Zoo. Otters, snow leopards, zebras, and camels are some of the exotic animals you can see here. And at Grandpa's Little Petting Zoo you can touch the goats, sheep, pigs, and miniature horses. | 1004 Hughes Dr. | 701/642–8709 | fax 701/642–1428 | www.wahpchamber.com | $4 | Memorial Day–Sept., daily 10–8.

Prairie Rose Carousel. Try a nostalgic ride on this restored 1926 Spillman antique, housed in a climate-controlled building. | 120 N. 4th St. | 701/642–8709 or 800/892–6673 | www.wahpchamber.com | $1 per ride | Memorial Day–Labor Day, daily 11–8; Sept., weekends 11–8.

Dakota Magic Casino. In this Las Vegas–style casino you can choose from almost 600 slots, live-action keno, poker tables, and craps. The restaurant is open 24 hours. On the border between North and South Dakota, 20 mi south of Wahpeton, the casino is owned and operated by the Sisseton-Wahpeton Sioux Tribe. | 16849 102 St. SE, Hankinson | 800/325–6825 | www.dakotamagic.com | Free to enter | Daily 24 hours.

Fort Abercrombie State Historic Site. The first permanent military post in North Dakota, the 1858 fort was built to protect wagon trails and steamboats traveling on the Red River. The fort withstood a siege by the Sioux in 1862. Today, you can see the blockade houses and visit the museum on this site, 10 mi north of town off I–29. | 816 Broadway St., Abercrombie | 701/553–8513 or 701/328–2666 | fax 701/328–3710 | www.state.nd.us/hist | Fort, free; museum $3 | Mid-May–mid-Sept., Wed.–Sun. 8–5.

Kidder Recreation Area. You can catch walleye, Northern Pike, and the world's largest catfish here, and camping is allowed. | 1600 4th St. N | 701/642–2811 or 701/221–6300 for fishing license | $10 per night camping; $15–25 fishing permits | May–Oct., daily.

Richland County Historical Museum. Native American and settlement artifacts fill this museum, but it's best known for its collection of precious Rosemeade Pottery. You can see vases, and bird and dog sculptures. | 11 7th Ave. N | 701/642–3075 | www.wahpchamber.com | Free | Apr.–Nov., Tues., Thurs., weekends 1–4.

ON THE CALENDAR

JUNE: *Carousel Days.* This festival has arts, a parade, carnival, music, dance, and even a parachute show. | 701/642–8744 or 800/892–6673.

Dining

Fry'n Pan Family Restaurant. American. You can have breakfast any time of the day or night here. The bacon cheeseburgers and the ribs are favorites with the locals. Salad bar. Kids' menu. No alcohol. | 1008 Dakota Ave. | 701/642–4351 | Open 24 hours | $6–$14 | AE, MC, V.

Prante's. Continental. Patrons drive for miles to come here for the pasta entrées and steak. Velvet drapes, paintings, and soft carpets fill the dining room. | 1605 N. 11th St. | 701/642–1135 | Buffet on Sun. | $10–$18 | AE, D, MC, V.

Lodging

Fairview Bed and Breakfast. The 1800s craftsman-style two-story bungalow is on the National Register of Historic Places, 12 mi west on Highway 13. This 40-acre hobby farm has horses, rabbits, and chickens. Rooms have antiques, lace-curtained windows, and chenille spreads with wool comforters. The suite has a working fireplace. The brass light fixtures are originals. Complimentary breakfast. No air-conditioning, some refrigerators. Some in-room VCRs, some room phones, no TV in some rooms, TV in common area. | 17170 82nd St. SE | 701/274–8262 | fairview@rrt.net | 3 rooms (with shared bath), 1 suite | $50–$60, $70 suite | Nov.–Apr. | No credit cards.

Super 8. At the north end, this 1976 two-story motel is at Route 210 as soon as you get into town. You can play video games in the pool area. Restaurant, bar, complimentary Continental breakfast, room service. In-room data ports. Cable TV. Indoor pool. Hot tub. Video games. Laundry facilities. Business services. | 995 21st Ave. N | 701/642–8731 or 800/800–8000 | fax 701/642–8733 | www.super8.com | 56 rooms, 2 suites | $48–$52, $54–$65 suites | AE, D, DC, MC, V.

WASHBURN

MAP 7, D4

(Nearby towns also listed: Bismarck, Garrison, Mandan)

Explorers Lewis and Clark spent the winter of 1804–05 at Fort Mandan, just 2 mi west of town. Washburn itself was founded in 1882 by "King John" Satterlund, an ambitious entrepreneur who named the new town after his friend, Cadwaller Washburn, governor of Wisconsin. Today, this tranquil community about 40 mi north of the state's capital is home to 1,500 people who are very proud of their Lewis and Clark connections. Washburn is the site of one of the rare bridges in the state that crosses the Missouri River.

Travel north and you'll reach Stanton, a tiny community where arrowheads and other Native American Artifacts are on view in the courthouse. Further on, still on Route 200, are Hazen and Beulah, coal country centers and friendly competitors for just about everything, even high school athletic titles. Coal power and the region's farmland drive the economy of the towns.

Information: Lewis and Clark Interpretive Center | 2576 8th Street SW, 58577 | 701/462–8535 | www.ndlewisandclark.com. **Mercer County Visitor Bureau** | 120 Central Ave., Beulah 58523 | 701/873–4585 or 800/441–2649 | tradecorridor.com/beulah. **Hazen Community Development** | 801 Highway Dr., Hazen 58545 | 701/748–6886 | www.hazennd.org.

Attractions

Antelope Valley Station. You can see a two-story-high model of the plant on your tour of this coal-fired power station with about $270 million invested in equipment and controls to protect the environment. It consistently meets or surpasses state and federal air quality standards. | 294 County Rd. 15, Beulah | 701/873–4545 or 701/223–0441 | www.basin-electric.com/avs | Free | Weekdays 8–4:30.

Coal Creek Station. Coal Creek is the country's largest lignite-powered electric generating plant. Tours are available by calling ahead. Between Washburn and Underwood in McLean County. | 8 mi north on Hwy. 83; follow signs | 701/442–3211 | Free | Weekdays by appointment.

Cross Ranch Centennial State Park. Towering cottonwood trees fringe the last free-flowing, undeveloped stretch of the Missouri River. You can camp here or rent a log cabin from the Visitor Center 20 mi southwest of Washburn. In September you can dance to the rhythms of a bluegrass festival. | 1403 River Rd., Center | 701/794–3731 | fax 701/794–3262 |

www.state.nd.us/ndparks | $4 per vehicle | Daily dawn to dusk; campgrounds mid-May–mid-Sept.

Cross Ranch Nature Conservancy Preserve. Next door to Cross Ranch Centennial State Park is this 5,000-acre nature preserve with interconnected hiking trails and a pasture for bison 20 mi southwest of Washburn. Bring binoculars so you don't miss the great wildlife viewing. | 1401 River Rd., Center | 701/794–8741 | fax 701/794–3544 | Free | Daily dawn–dusk.

Fort Clark State Historic Site. A fur-trading post built in 1830 near the Missouri River, 15 mi west of Washburn off Hwy. 83, the fort burned down in 1860. Today, you can reconstruct its history with the help of markers along a walking trail. The site is on the National Register of Historic Places. | State Historical Society of North Dakota, 612 E Boulevard Ave., Bismarck | 701/328–2666 | fax 701/328–3710 | www.state.nd.us/hist | Free | Daily.

Fort Mandan. Built in the shape of a triangle on the banks of the Missouri River just west of Washburn, this fort was Lewis and Clark's home through the winter of 1804–05. It's fully restored and on the National Register of Historic Places. | Lewis and Clark Interpretive Center, 2576 8th St. SW | 701/462–8535 | www.ndlewisandclark.com | Free | Daily dawn–dusk.

Freedom Mine. Freedom Mine is one of the 10 largest coal mines in the United States. Its lignite feeds three power stations and a gas plant within an hour of the mine. You can arrange a tour by calling 24 hours ahead. | 204 County Rd. 15, Beulah | 701/873–2281 | Free | Weekdays by appointment.

Great Plains Synfuels Plant. The plant began turning coal into gas in 1984. Each year, it uses about 6.3 million tons of coal to produce more than 54 billion cubic ft of natural gas. Tours are available by calling ahead. | 420 County Rd. 26, Beulah | 701/873–6667 or 701/223–0441 | www.basinelectric.com/dgc | Free | Weekdays by appointment.

Knife River Indian Villages National Historic Site. Sakakawea met Lewis and Clark here and became their guide and translator in the early 1800s. But community life at this site goes back at least 8,000 years, and flourished until the mid-19th century, when disease started taking its toll on the Native American people in the region. At the interpretive center you can see artifacts as old as 9,000 years, and visit a reconstructed earthlodge, 50 ft across by 12 ft high. | County Rd. 37, Stanton | 701/745–3309 | fax 701/745–3708 | www.nps.gov/knri | Free | Mid-May–Labor Day, daily 7:30–6; Labor Day–mid-May, daily 8–4.

POWER TRIP

In a compact section between U.S. 83 at Washburn and Route 200 to Hazen and Beulah, you can see the smokestacks and open mining that indicate one of the state's great resources: lignite coal. The abundant coal is largely surface mined, and the land later reclaimed to near-original condition.

The lignite reserves in the western two-thirds of North Dakota represent one of the world's largest deposits and about 80 percent of the recoverable lignite in the United States. Nearly all the lignite mined in North Dakota is consumed in the state to generate electric power, which makes electricity from lignite-fired power plants one of the state's leading exports.

Seven power plants, one coal gasification plant, and one hydroelectric dam all operate within an hour of each other. Private companies operate seven large strip mines, including Freedom Mine—one of the 10 largest coal mines in the nation. Freedom Mine is adjacent to the Antelope Valley Station power plant and the Great Plains Synfuel Plant, the nation's first and largest commercial coal gasification plant. Their proximity to each other (north of Beulah and west of Washburn), make an ideal tour package. Call ahead for a tour Monday through Friday.

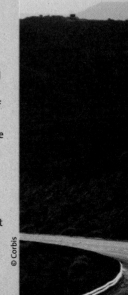

Knife River Mine. This mine supplies lignite to the Coyote and Heskett electric-generating stations. Tours are available by calling ahead. | Highway 49 S, Beulah | 701/873–4333 | fax 701/530–1451 | www.kniferiver.com | Free | Weekdays by appointment.

Lewis and Clark Interpretive Center. Lewis and Clark's voyage of discovery to this area in 1804–06 is the focus of this center, where you can see a hand-carved replica of the four-ton canoes the explorers used. All the Native American groups Lewis and Clark met are represented by objects and artifacts, and there are 1830s illustrations by Karl Bodmer. | 2576 8th St. SW, Washburn | 701/462–8535 | www.ndlewisandclark.com | $2 | Memorial Day–Labor Day, daily 9–7; Labor Day–Memorial Day, daily 9–5.

McLean County Historical Society Museum. You'll know you've found the building because of the huge mural of Lewis and Clark next door. Inside are Native American, settlement, and military collections, as well as Lewis and Clark information. | Corner of 6th and Maine, Washburn | 701/462–3660 and 701/462–3744 | www.vmerkel@westriv.com | Free | Memorial Day–Labor Day, Tues.–Sat. 2–5, or by appointment.

ON THE CALENDAR

JUNE: *Lewis and Clark Days.* Join the growing crowds who come to the Lewis and Clark Interpretive Center every year to celebrate the famous expedition with historical reenactments, living history performances, a parade, a carnival, and an arts fair. | 701/462–8535.

JULY: *Northern Plains Indian Culture Fest.* At this weekend event in the Knife River Indian Villages, you can experience Native American culture through flint knapping, bead working, porcupine quill work, and teepee raising. | 701/746–3309.

SEPT.: *Missouri River Bluegrass and Ol' Time Music Festival.* Started in 1991, this Labor Day weekend festival at Cross Ranch State Park attracts up to 1,500 fans with six to eight music groups including nationally known bluegrass acts. | 701/794–3731.

Dining

Dakota Farms Family Restaurant. American. Sit at a booth by the front window and you can watch the highway traffic while breakfasting on ham and eggs. Or retire to the dining area in the back to enjoy a rib steak. Kids' menu. No alcohol. | 1317 Border La. | 701/462–8175 | $6–$9 | D, DC, MC, V.

Lewis and Clark Café. American. Antique wagon wheels and old photos help this small-town café serve up history with its meals. Try the burger or steak named for Lewis and Clark. Kids' menu. No alcohol. | 602 Main St.; Between 6th and Maine | 701/462–3668 | Breakfast also available. No dinner Sun. | $3–$7 | No credit cards.

Lodging

Scot Wood Motel. On the Lewis and Clark trail, this 1970s two-story brick motel is six blocks from downtown, three blocks from the Lewis and Clark Center, and 3 mi from Fort Mandan. There's coffee all day and a microwave in the lobby. A Dakota Farms Restaurant is next door. Cable TV. Pets allowed (fee). | 1323 Frontage Rd. | 701/462–8191 | fax 701/462–3795 | 24 rooms | $35–$48 | AE, D, DC, MC, V.

WILLISTON

MAP 7, A2

(Nearby towns also listed: New Town, Theodore Roosevelt National Park)

In 1887 the Great Northern Railroad built a station here and called it Little Muddy. Visiting a year later, the president of the company renamed it in honor of a friend. The town grew quickly, turned to wheat farming instead of ranching, and was able to survive the droughts of the 1930s. Economic life took an abrupt turn from agriculture to industry when oil was discovered in 1951. Williston is only a few miles from the oil-rich geological formation known as Williston Basin, and the city's population of 12,100 now fluctuates with the price of oil.

Information: Williston Convention and Visitors Bureau | 10 Main St., 58801 | 701/774–9041 or 800/615–9041.

Attractions

Buffalo Trails Museum. Epping, 22 mi northeast, is a small town with a big museum. In seven buildings you will find antiques, geospheres, and fossils, but the most unusual items are the recreated dentist's office, sickroom, and parlor with lifesize papier-mâché figures. From Williston, head east on Hwy 2. Turn right on County Hwy 42; follow signs to the museum. | Epping, ND | 701/859–4361 | $2 | June–Aug., Mon.–Sat. 9–5, Sun. 1:30–5:30; Sept.–Oct., Sun. 1:30–5:30, or by appointment.

Fort Buford State Historic Site. Built in 1866 near the concourse of the Missouri and Yellowstone rivers, this military post was the site of Sitting Bull's surrender in 1881. The officers' quarters are now a museum, and in the soldiers' cemetery you can hunt for unusual, humorous headstones. | 15349 39th La. NW | 701/572–9034 | $4 | Mid-May–mid-Sept., daily 9–6; mid-Sept.–mid-May by appointment only.

Fort Union Trading Post National Historic Site. You can admire the impressive palisade and three-story bastions of Fort Union from the highway. John Jacob Astor's American Fur Company built the fort, which dominated trade on the upper Missouri River from 1828 to 1867. | 15550 Hwy. 1804 | 701/572–9083 | www.nps.gov/fous | Free | Memorial Day–Labor Day, daily 8–8; Labor Day–Memorial Day, daily 9–5:30.

Lake Park Drive-In. See a movie at one of the few drive-in theaters still running in the country. The show goes on at dusk, but come early so the kids can enjoy the outdoor playground. | Hwy. 2N | 701/572–9137 | $6 | Apr.–Sept., Fri., Sat. 9 PM.

Lewis and Clark State Park. Lewis and Clark camped here in the early 1800s. Today, there's a marina and boat ramp, campgrounds, and a self-guided nature trail at this spot 20 mi southeast of Williston. | 4904 119th Rd. NW, Epping | 701/859–3071 | $4 per vehicle | Daily; full services mid-May–mid-Sept.

Lewis and Clark Trail Museum. Each room of this school house, 35 mi south of Williston, is devoted to one facet of local history. | Hwy. 85, north of Alexander | 701/828–3595 | $2 | Memorial Day–Labor Day, Mon.–Sat. 9–5, Sun. 1–5.

Links of North Dakota. Seasoned players fly in from around the country to golf at this championship 18-hole course 28 mi east of Williston. You will understand why when you see the spectacular Lake Sakakawea views. Facilities include a driving range, two nine-hole putting greens, a chipping green, and two practice bunkers. | 5153 109th NW, Ray | 701/568–2600 | fax 701/568–2603 | $30–$35 greens fees | Mid-Apr.–mid-Oct.

Spring Lake Park. You can fish in the trout pond or ride an old-fashioned merry-go-round in this city park. Drive up the hill to see a nice view of Williston. | Hwy. 2N, Williston | 701/572–5141 | Free | Daily.

Writing Rock State Historic Site. On top of a hill with a sweeping view of ranch lands, you can see two boulders inscribed with Indian petroglyphs. From Williston, go 30 mi. north on Hwy. 85, then 20 mi. on Hwy. 50 to Grenora; go north 10½ mi. to Fortuna; east 1 mi. on a gravel road; follow signs to Writing Rock. | State Historical Society of North Dakota, 612 E Boulevard Ave., Bismarck | 701/328–2666 | fax 701/328–3710 | www.state.nd.us./hist | Free | Daily.

ON THE CALENDAR

MAY: *Roughrider International Art Show.* More than 75 artists from Canada to New Mexico enter this juried art show hosted by the Airport International Inn at 3601 2nd Ave. W. You can select your favorites on Mother's Day weekend. | 701/774–9041.

MAY: *Williston Band Day.* A tradition for over half a century, Band Day and its parade attracts 40 bands from Montana, North Dakota, and Canada. Head to Harmon Park in the town center after the parade to stake out a comfortable place to eat cotton candy or a picnic while listening to the 3½-hour concert in the park. | Sat. of Mother's Day weekend | 701/774–9041 or 800/615–9041.

JUNE: *Buffalo Trails Days.* Epping, 22 mi northeast, hosts this old-timer's celebration where you can follow the four-block parade to go back in time on the crowded dirt streets. To get away from the heat, slip into the Buffalo Trails Museum. | 701/859–4361.

JUNE: *Fort Union Trading Post Rendezvous.* You can see a Native American encampment and over 20 reenactments of a fur-trade rendezvous here at the Trading Post grounds on the third weekend in June at Fort Union 23 mi west of town on Hwy. 1804. Witness beaver skinning and examine antique weapons, all to the sound of bagpipes and fiddles. | 701/572–9083.

JULY: *Fort Buford 6th Infantry State Historical Encampment.* Fort Buford's most spirited years, 1866 to 1895, are evoked with military ceremonies, drills, and black powder firing demonstrations. | 701/572–9034.

JULY: *Wildrose Fireworks Extravaganza!* A local pyro-technician shows his talent in this old-fashioned fireworks display. | 701/774–9041 or 800/615–9041.

Dining

Airport International Inn. American. The soft lighting, candles, and carpet invite romantic dinners. Try the steamed Tork, a fish entrée served with salad or baked potato. Or try the steak. Kids' menu. Sun. brunch. | 3601 2nd Ave. W | 701/774–0241 | Breakfast also available | $11–$24 | AE, D, DC, MC, V.

Dakota Farms Family Restaurant. American. The Dakota Farms serves breakfast all day, and has a local reputation for fair prices and good service. Come in for all-you-can eat fish on Fridays. Kids' menu. No alcohol. | 1906 2nd Ave. W | 701/572–4480 | Breakfast also available | $8–$15 | D, MC, V.

El Rancho Restaurant. Eclectic. With American, Mexican, and Asian foods on the menu, there's something for everyone. Favorites are the prime rib dinner and the chicken stir fry. Kids' menu. Sun. brunch. | 1623 2nd Ave. W | 701/572–6321 | No lunch Sun. | $14–$25 | AE, D, DC, MC, V.

Gramma Sharon's Cafe. American. For home-cooked, inexpensive meals, try Gramma's, but don't come here for the atmosphere: it's attached to a gas station. Known for omelets. Kids' menu. No alcohol. | Hwy. 2 and Hwy. 85 N intersection | 701/572–1412 | Open 24 hours | $5–$12 | No credit cards.

Lunch Box. American/Casual. New and old lunch boxes are everywhere in this café where the menu lists soups, salads, and unusual sandwiches. Try the almond chicken salad or the roast beef on a fresh pita, homemade chili, and pies. No alcohol. | 20 W. Broadway | 701/572–8559 | Closed Sun. Closes at 6:30 | $3–$8 | No credit cards.

Lund's Landing/Anilene's Kitchen. American. On the shore of Lake Sakakawea, this mom-and-pop shop at the Ray marina has pan-fried walleye. Sit by the fireplace and ask to hear the owners' fishing stories. Kids' menu. | 11350 Hwy. 1804 | 701/568–3474 | Breakfast also available. Closed Nov.–Apr. | $7–$20 | No credit cards.

Trapper's Kettle. American. You can see traps of all kinds, stuffed animals, and a canoe that holds the salad bar here. Dishes include cheese-topped chili, beef ribs, and shrimp dinners. Kids' menu. Sun. brunch. | 3901 2nd Ave. W | 701/774–2831 | Breakfast also available | $9–$15 | AE, D, MC, V.

Lodging

Airport International Inn. Six blocks from the airport and 4 mi from downtown, this two-story hotel also has a conference center. Restaurant, bar. Indoor pool. Hot tub. | 3601 2nd Ave. W | 701/774–0241 | fax 701/774–0318 | 140 rooms, 4 suites | $41, $59–$61 suites | AE, D, DC, MC, V.

El Rancho Motor Hotel. This Southwestern-style motel is six blocks from downtown and is well known for its restaurant. Restaurant, bar. In-room data ports. Cable TV. Laundry service. Some pets allowed. | 1623 2nd Ave. W | 701/572–6321 or 800/433–8529 | fax 701/572–6321 | 91 rooms | $52–$58 | AE, D, DC, MC, V.

Lund's Landing Marina Resort. There are cedar camping cabins here built between 1998 and 2000 that have knotty pine interior and camp furniture with bunk beds. The cabins have no running water; shower and toilets are in the main building. This resort is 22 mi east in Ray on Highway 1804. You can rent kayaks, pontoons, and fishing boats, and there's a kids' fishing dock here. The restaurant serves breakfast, lunch, and dinner. Picnic area. Refrigerators. Lake. Dock, boating, fishing. No smoking. | 11350 Hwy. 1804, Ray | 701/568–3474 | www.lundslanding.com | 6 cabins (shared shower only) | $65 | Dec.–Apr. | MAP and AP | MC, V.

South Dakota

South Dakota may rank as one of the nation's youngest and least populated states, but its history is as robust and exciting as that of any state in the union. South Dakota's rich past encompasses woolly mammoths, prairie homesteaders, French fur traders, the culture and history of the Lakota (Sioux) people, gold rushes, and mountain memorials.

The vast majority of South Dakota's rolling plains are used for growing crops and grazing cattle, and for more than a century agriculture has ranked as the state's leading industry. Most of the state's residents live east of the Missouri River, where prairie potholes and rolling river breaks share the land with well-kept farms and rural communities.

The central portion of the state is dominated by the "mighty Mo," where a series of huge dams backs up water well into North Dakota and creates the "Great Lakes of South Dakota." The Missouri River is also roughly the defining line between the Central and Mountain time zones, as well as a subtle topographic boundary between farm land and ranch land.

Western South Dakota is truly the starting point for America's Wild West. Marked by windswept prairie, rugged badlands, and an emerald oasis known as the Black Hills, this is the South Dakota most travelers come to see. Within its depths are dark, cool caves and shaded brooks, but it also has mountain memorials carved in stone and scenic vistas that stir the soul.

Thanks to the four presidents at Mount Rushmore, the legendary Lakota leader at Crazy Horse, and year-round gaming action at an old gold-dust camp named Deadwood, the Black Hills are the state's main tourist draw, generating about 3 million visitors annually and adding $1.5 billion to the state's economy.

Of the state's five largest cities, however, four lie east of the Missouri River. The largest—Sioux Falls—has a population of 110,000, followed by Aberdeen, Watertown,

CAPITAL: PIERRE	POPULATION: 732,405	AREA: 77,116 SQUARE MI
BORDERS: MT, WY, NE, ND, IA, MN	TIME ZONES: CENTRAL AND MOUNTAIN	POSTAL ABBREVIATION: SD
WEB SITE: WWW.TRAVELSD.COM		

and Brookings, each with less than a fourth of that number. The only truly "large" town in western South Dakota—a relative term in a rural state—is Rapid City, on the eastern slopes of the Black Hills. It claims about 60,000 residents.

Over succeeding centuries, the land that is South Dakota has been home to enormous dinosaurs, woolly mammoths, giant short-faced bears, paleolithic peoples, herds of buffalo so vast they darkened the prairie to the horizon, more than a half-dozen Native American nations, European emissaries, entrepreneurs, and explorers, U.S. cavalry units, gunslingers, mule-skinners, and madams. And despite its size, any step taken on South Dakota turf probably matches a footprint left by some fascinating historical figure of this great state's history.

In its short life as a state, South Dakota has spawned leaders in art, literature, sports, warfare, publishing, politics, and entertainment. Among the greats: Sitting Bull, Crazy Horse, Tom Brokaw, Sparky Anderson, Billy Mills, Oscar Howe, Mary Hart, Cheryl Ladd, George McGovern, and Tom Daschle.

Others who have passed through this diverse state have not left unaffected by it. Explorers Lewis and Clark first encountered Native Americans in what later became South Dakota. General George Armstrong Custer built on his Civil War fame by leading an 1874 expedition into the Black Hills, confirming the presence of gold and setting off the last great gold rush in America.

Famed lawman and gunfighter Wild Bill Hickok also found the Black Hills charming—right up to the moment he was shot dead while playing poker in a Deadwood saloon. Author L. Frank Baum gathered material from life while living in Aberdeen, then went on to write his best-selling *Wonderful Wizard of Oz*. And Al Neuharth, who spent his early childhood retrieving cow "chips" for the family stove on an eastern South Dakota farmstead, established *USA Today* and became a media mogul and multimillionaire.

Although the population of many U.S. metropolitan areas is greater than that of all of South Dakota, the state's strength and attraction may well come from those who chose to settle here, and from the countless myths, legends, and stories that together form its enduring history.

History

By the time European explorers reached what would become South Dakota, thousands of years of human history had already taken place on the Great Plains. The state's prehistory is marked by changing climatic zones, alterations in the course of the Missouri River, which slices through it, and the evolution of its flora and fauna.

The first humans followed vast herds of buffalo onto the Plains, and by the time Europeans arrived in the 1600s the state was peopled by Arikara, Cheyenne, and Sioux Indians, whose descendants are here still. In 1803, Lewis and Clark mapped the Missouri, and during the remainder of the century, immigrants and miners invaded the state, leading to an inevitable clash with indigenous culture.

In the 20th century, South Dakota's history marched on with the rest of the nation's, and as more people settled the state they suffered through dustbowls and the Depres-

SD Timeline

7,000 BC	500 BC	AD 500–800	
Paleo-Indians arrive on the prairies of the Great Plains and what is present-day South Dakota in pursuit of massive herds of buffalo.	Indian tribes build tepees, using buffalo hides.	Semi-nomadic Mound Builders flourish in the northeast part of the state. Tribes are known for burial rituals, which included wrapping the body and the departed's most precious pos	sessions, and interring them in large earthen mounds.

sion and two world wars. But faith in the future and recognition of the heroes of the past (and a suitable mass of granite) created expressions of admiration on a colossal scale in the Black Hills.

INTRODUCTION
HISTORY
REGIONS
WHEN TO VISIT
STATE'S GREATS
RULES OF THE ROAD
DRIVING TOURS

From 1927 to 1941, sculptor Gutzon Borglum and a dusty crew of unemployed miners transformed a pine-clad cliff into the Shrine of Democracy, leaving behind giant likenesses of George Washington, Thomas Jefferson, Abraham Lincoln, and Theodore Roosevelt and one of America's most-recognized icons—Mount Rushmore National Memorial.

In 1948, sculptor Korczak Ziolkowski, who had briefly assisted Borglum at Rushmore, began a monumental tribute to Native Americans after Sioux chief Henry Standing Bear told him that the Sioux "would like the white man to know the red man has great heroes too." Crazy Horse Memorial, which celebrated a half-century of progress in 1998, is carried on today by Korczak's wife, Ruth, and seven of their ten children.

As the new century got off to a start, South Dakotans were optimistic and confident that the values and work ethic ingrained in them from a pioneer past would carry them through an uncertain future, and that the vastness and beauty of South Dakota would continue to provide a livelihood and attract millions of visitors.

Regions

1. DAKOTA HERITAGE AND LAKES

The settlement of South Dakota began in the southeastern corner of the state, where explorers Lewis and Clark were followed by a giant wave of Norwegian pioneers who dropped anchor and began farming a sea of prairie that stretched to the horizon. This region continues to be the most heavily populated area of the state. Anchored by Sioux Falls, Vermillion, and Yankton, southeast South Dakota is also filled with thousands of farms, feedlots, and rural communities tucked in among vast cornfields, river valleys, state parks, and recreation areas.

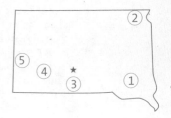

Seven miles north of Vermillion, visible from Route 19, is Spirit Mound, a brown hump on the prairie that was visited by Lewis and Clark in 1804. The pair were joined by members of their expedition on a walk to the mound after being told it was inhabited by feisty midget warriors. Although they viewed a flock of swallows and the surrounding grasslands from the mound's summit, they did not discover any militant pygmies.

Towns listed: Madison, Mitchell, Sioux Falls, Vermillion, Yankton.

2. GLACIAL LAKES AND PRAIRIES

Prairie potholes, pristine glacial lakes, and gently rolling hills define the landscape of northeast South Dakota, an area that still echoes with the saga of the Plains Indians and the pioneer settlers who first inhabited this region. Home to several succeeding

900		1325	1500	1700
Plains Villagers establish communities along the banks of the Missouri River and other South Dakota rivers. Both hunters and gardeners, they plant maize, craft earthenware ceram-	ics, and construct large earth-lodge towns encircled by ditches and dirt walls to fend off their enemies.	Near present-day Crow Creek, 500 Arikara men, women, and children are massacred in a rare incident of pre-Columbian tribal violence.	The Arikara (also known as Ree) inhabit the state.	The Sioux (also known as Lakota) begin migration into South Dakota from Minnesota, driving the Arikara north and west. Organized into 33 major tribes (Teton, Yankton, and San-

Indian cultures and, more recently, frontier forts, it offers city museums and many historic sites filled with artifacts from its fabled past.

The South Dakota Art Museum on the SDSU campus at Brookings displays the work of two of the state's finest painters—Harvey Dunn, a sodbuster's son who captured the romantic side of prairie life, and Oscar Howe, a Sioux artist whose powerful, modernistic paintings tell of his people's spirit and culture.

Of particular interest for those attracted to the history and settlement of the West is Fort Sisseton State Park, where you can still roam the barracks, officers' quarters, and guardhouses of this 1864 outpost. Its historical festival the first weekend of June brings back the bluecoats, bugles, and bayonets for a superb re-creation of pioneer life in the 1860s.

Towns listed: Aberdeen, Brookings, Huron, Milbank, Miller, Redfield, Sisseton, Watertown, Webster.

3. GREAT LAKES

The sweeping landscape of central South Dakota is dominated by the Missouri River. For centuries before and many years after pioneers arrived on the scene, this mighty river was as unpredictable as the weather, changing course and flooding its banks with virtually every spring thaw. Fortunately, the Missouri has been tamed by four earthen dams, which store enough water to cover 900 square mi of the state.

The Missouri runs through the heart of South Dakota for 435 mi. Its waters and those of its two great lakes—Oahe and Sharp—wash more than 3,000 mi of shoreline and lap at the sites of frontier forts and the ruins of traders' outposts.

On the east bank of the "Mighty Mo," smack dab in the middle of South Dakota, stands Pierre (pronounced "pier"), the state capital. Selected for its central location, Pierre is probably the most isolated capital in the nation. It has no interstate highways nearby and is serviced only by commuter airlines. Nonetheless, it is home to one of the most beautiful capital buildings in the United States, as well as exceptional museums, and extraordinary outdoor recreation options.

Towns listed: Chamberlain, Mobridge, Pierre, Platte, Winner.

4. SOUTH-CENTRAL AND BADLANDS

High buttes, deep canyons, and badlands mark the south-central region of South Dakota. Save for a few state highways and rural electric lines, the topography of this region has changed little since humans first arrived here millennia ago.

Of the estimated 70,000 Lakota who call South Dakota home, about three-fourths live on reservations. Two reservations in this region—Rosebud and Pine Ridge—cover well over 2 million acres.

Just south of the tiny town and tourist mecca called Wall, you encounter one of the eeriest, most hostile landscapes imaginable, the chiseled spires, ragged ridges, and

tee), the Sioux rule the Dakotas for 150 years.

1743
Frenchmen François and Joseph La Verendrye leave an inscribed lead plate on a Missouri River bluff near present-day Fort Pierre, claiming the surrounding region for their king, Louis XV.

The plate would be discovered in 1913 by children playing on a hillside.

1775
French Canadian mountain man Pierre Dorion paddles up the Missouri River from St. Louis, and marries into the Yankton Sioux tribe.

1790
Jacques d'Église and Joseph Garreau, French Canadians in the employ of the Spanish, venture into Dakota territory to trade furs.

steep-sided canyons of Badlands National Park. This terrain ravaged by the forces of nature has been supporting human inhabitants for more than 12,000 years. All told, the park covers 244,000 acres.

Towns listed: Badlands National Park, Wall.

INTRODUCTION
HISTORY
REGIONS
WHEN TO VISIT
STATE'S GREATS
RULES OF THE ROAD
DRIVING TOURS

5. BLACK HILLS

The Black Hills, capped by 18 peaks more than 7,000 ft high, cover an area roughly 50 mi wide and 120 mi long—about the size of the state of Delaware. Two-thirds of the Black Hills are in extreme western South Dakota, the rest in eastern Wyoming.

Within this region are four areas administered by the National Park Service: Mount Rushmore National Memorial, Wind Cave National Park, Jewel Cave National Monument, and Devils Tower National Monument. The last is over the border in northeastern Wyoming. In addition, visitors will find hundreds of campsites, hotel and motel rooms, bed-and-breakfasts, and mountain resorts in which to relax. Dozens of private attractions offer everything from drive-through wildlife parks and reptile gardens to buffalo jeep safaris and hot springs.

What captures the imagination of most road-weary travelers is the magnificent scenery of this ancient, pine-covered mountain range. Accessible by car, horse, bike, or on foot, the Black Hills are at once intimate and inviting. You can trace the history of the major gold rush that played out here, gaze at two massive mountain memorials, or opt for 24-hour gaming action and excellent arts fairs, concerts, celebrations of Native American culture, and the largest motorcycle rally in the world.

Towns listed: Belle Fourche, Custer, Deadwood, Hill City, Hot Springs, Keystone, Lead, Rapid City, Spearfish, Sturgis.

When to Visit

South Dakota's weather tends to be as diverse as its geography, and its climate ranks as one of the most extreme in the world. Over the past century, recorded temperatures have ranged from -58°F at McIntosh on February 16, 1936, to 120°F at Gannvalley on July 5, 1936. South Dakota's record snowfall of 38.9 inches fell in Lead on October 26, 1996; its record rainfall was 8 inches in Elk Point on September 10, 1900. With the exception of hurricanes, the state has witnessed virtually every type of extreme weather condition imaginable, yet, for the most part, its climate is extremely pleasant.

The vast majority of visitors descend on South Dakota in the summer months, and the state and national parks, monuments, memorials, and private attractions are packed. Visitors during shoulder seasons (Apr.–May and Sept.–Oct.) and off-season convention business account for an increasing percentage of the state's traffic, particularly in Sioux Falls and Rapid City.

1794
The Spanish Missouri Company sends out an expedition, led by Jean Baptiste Truteau, with orders to stop d'Église and Garreau from representing them in the territory. Truteau and his company spend the winter of 1795 and the following spring with the Arikara, until attacked by the Sioux in May 1796. Not yet considered a threat to Indians, the white men are released.

1803
The French-owned Louisiana Territory is purchased by President Thomas Jefferson, adding to the U.S. an 828,000-square-mi swath west of the Mississippi extending from New Orleans in the south to the Rocky Mountains and Canada on the west and north.

1804
Armed with orders from President Jefferson, Meriwether Lewis, William Clark, and a crew of 29 set out to follow the Missouri River to its headwaters, hop the divide to the Columbia River, and

CLIMATE CHART

Average High/Low Temperatures (°F) and Monthly Precipitation (in inches).

	JAN.	FEB.	MAR.	APR.	MAY	JUNE
ABERDEEN	20/-2	26.9/6.5	39.8/19.8	57.3/33	69.7/44.5	78.8/54.3
	0.37	0.47	1.34	1.95	2.41	3.15

	JULY	AUG.	SEPT.	OCT.	NOV.	DEC.
	83/61	84.4/56.8	72.9/46.1	60.4/34.2	40.5/19.9	25.4/5.3
	2.75	2.13	2.13	1.12	0.59	0.41

	JAN.	FEB.	MAR.	APR.	MAY	JUNE
RAPID CITY	32/9	38.2/15.2	45.9/22.2	57.9/32.2	68.1/42.3	77.8/51.7
	0.39	0.52	1.03	1.89	2.68	3.06

	JULY	AUG.	SEPT.	OCT.	NOV.	DEC.
	87/59	85.1/56.1	74.4/45.5	62.5/34.9	46.7/22.8	35.6/12.7
	2.04	1.67	1.23	1.10	0.56	0.47

	JAN.	FEB.	MAR.	APR.	MAY	JUNE
SIOUX FALLS	23/2	29.6/9.7	42.3/22.6	59/34.8	70.7/45.9	80.5/56.1
	0.51	0.64	1.64	2.52	3.03	3.40

	JULY	AUG.	SEPT.	OCT.	NOV.	DEC.
	86/62	83.3/59.4	73.1/48.7	61.2/36.0	43.4/22.6	32.3/12.5
	2.68	2.85	3.02	1.78	1.09	0.70

FESTIVALS AND SEASONAL EVENTS

WINTER

Jan. **Frozen Foot Rendezvous.** The pre-1840s fur trade is re-created by costumed actors, including the setting up of an outdoor encampment. Activities at Oakwood Lakes State Park, near Brookings, include a wild-game cooking contest, a treasure hunt, snowshoe races, and muzzleloader shoots. | 605/693–4589.

Jan.–Feb. **Black Hills Stock Show and Rodeo.** This Rapid City event held the last weekend of January through the first week of February is one of America's great indoor stock shows and rodeos, with sales ranging from buffalo to bucking horses. Includes a stockman's ball, wild-horse races, and commercial exhibits. | 605/355–3861.

Feb. **Chinese New Year.** Lion dancers, a parade, a yellow doll contest, martial arts demonstrations, Chinese artifacts, and revelry mark this festive annual celebration on the historic streets of Deadwood. | 800/999–1876 or 605/578–1876.

1807

observe the developing British presence in the Pacific Northwest. Between Vermillion and Yankton, they meet their first Sioux and gain Pierre Dorion as an interpreter.

Armed with the accounts of the Lewis and Clark expedition, Spanish explorer and entrepreneur Manuel Lisa leaves for the upper Missouri valley to trade with the Indians. Within 2

years, Lisa has organized the fur trade along the entire Missouri River, opening the way for frontier forts and pioneer settlements.

1822

The Rocky Mountain Fur Company begins organizing trading parties into present-day South Dakota. Among its core group are Wild West legends Jedediah Smith, Jim

Bridger, and Hugh Glass.

SPRING

Mar. **St. Patrick's Day Celebration.** Live music, Irish food, fun, and a comical parade are part of this annual Deadwood celebration. Food and drink specials and entertainment are offered city-wide. | 800/999–1876 or 605/578–1876.

St. Patrick's Day Parade. Sioux Falls celebrates a day of family fun with a parade that begins at 4 and winds through the downtown area. | 605/338–4009.

May **Crazy Horse Memorial Day Weekend Open House.** Crazy Horse Memorial, near Custer. You can mix with guest artists and craftspeople interact at the memorial's Native American Education/Cultural Center. | 605/673–4681.

Custer State Park Open House. This two-day open house celebrates the start of a new visitor season with free admission and fishing and a variety of good-time entertainment for the whole family. | 605/255–4515.

SUMMER

June **Aberdeen Arts Festival.** A quarter-century old, this event has established itself as one of the most successful arts exhibitions in the state. The two-day festival of arts and crafts, food, children's activities, and entertainment is held on Father's Day weekend. | 605/226–1557.

Wild Bill Days. Memorializing one of Deadwood's gold rush–era characters, this popular event keeps evolving, but most often includes big-name entertainment, a battle of the bands, and free street dances on historic Main St. | 800/999–1876 or 605/578–1876.

Crazy Horse Volksmarch. At the Crazy Horse Memorial, near Custer, this 10K hike is the largest event of its kind in the world and also a rare opportunity to hike up the mountain carving in progress. | 605/673–4681.

Czech Days. An ethnic festival in Tabor celebrates the region's Czech heritage. Polka music and traditional dances feature 130 performers in Czech costumes. Ethnic foods and demonstrations are also on tap. | 605/463–2476.

Fort Sisseton Historical Festival. Cavalry and infantry drills, living history demonstrations, arts and crafts, old-time fiddlers, a military costume ball, exhibits of Native American culture, a

1831
The *Yellowstone* becomes the first steamboat to paddle its way up the Missouri River, reaching Fort Tecumseh (later Fort Pierre). The first permanent white settlement in South

Dakota is established at Fort Pierre Chouteau.

1848
Father Pierre-Jean De Smet visits the Black Hills and an Indian chief presents him with a bag of glittering powder. Immediately recognizing it as gold, he quickly proclaims, "Put it

away and show it to nobody."

1851
In an attempt to ease tensions between Indians and immigrant settlers, the Laramie Treaty allots 60 million acres to the Sioux and establishes tribal borders. Land speculators

fur-trader camp, cowboy poets, and more. Held the first week-
end in June. | 605/448–5701.

Sturgis Cavalry Days. Historical reenactments, a parade, an
art show, a military ball, a buffalo feed, a period fashion show,
and art shows in Sturgis. Many events are held at Fort Meade,
an 1878 military outpost. | 605/347–2556.

June–July   **Laura Ingalls Wilder Pageant.** Held the last weekend of June
and the first two weekends in July, this event commemorates
the pioneer era and the long-ago days of *The Little House on
the Prairie* in De Smet (*see* Huron), where the popular author
lived. The annual pageant is based on Wilder's life and work
with reenactments presented nightly. | 605/692–2108.

July   **Black Hills Heritage Festival.** This Rapid City event includes
free entertainment, arts in the park, crafts and food vendors,
and a carnival. | 605/394–4115.

Black Hills Roundup. Belle Fourche's three-day pro rodeo
includes a free barbecue, a carnival, and a parade. | 888/345–
JULY.

Brookings Summer Arts Festival. Brookings puts on an outdoor extravaganza of art, antiques, kids' activities, food, and
entertainment. | 605/693–4589.

Sitting Bull Stampede Rodeo and Celebration. In Mobridge
you can experience three days of professional rodeo, two
Main St. parades, a carnival, and a fireworks display. | 605/
845–2387.

July–Aug.   **Days of '76.** This Black Hills classic staged in Deadwood has
been around for over 75 years and has pro rodeo, free street
dances, a carnival, western arts and crafts, and two exquisite
3-mi-long parades. | 800/999–1876 or 605/578–1876.

Aug.   **Central States Fair.** Top-name entertainment, rodeo performances, cattle shows, a carnival, a German tent, and live
music make this Rapid City blowout one of the longest-run-
ning fairs in the region. | 605/355–3861.

Kool Deadwood Nites. This Deadwood event held the last full
weekend in August includes classic and street rod competi-
tions, a parade, a barbecue, a sock hop and street dance with
big-name entertainment, poker runs, and a show and shine,
in which all the cars are parked along Main St. and the public

	1858		**1860**	**1861**
arrive and settle in the Sioux Falls and Yankton areas.	Capt. J. B. S. Todd, a cousin of Mary Todd Lincoln and orga-nizer of the Upper Missouri Land Co., takes part in negoti-ating a treaty with the Yankton Sioux for the purchase of 14 million acres	between the Big Sioux and Missouri rivers for 12 cents an acre. Norwegians begin to establish claims near the Ver-million and James rivers.	Irish immigrants begin to arrive in the area.	Congress recognizes the area's growth and establishes the Dakota Territory. Yankton, in extreme southeastern South Dakota, is named territorial capital.

INTRODUCTION
HISTORY
REGIONS
WHEN TO VISIT
STATE'S GREATS
RULES OF THE ROAD
DRIVING TOURS

is allowed to get an up-close view of them. | 800/999–1876 or 605/578–1876.

Sioux Empire Fair. The fair in Sioux Falls includes grandstand entertainment, a carnival, food vendors, and many 4-H, livestock, domestic arts, horticultural, and commercial exhibits. | 605/367–7178.

Sturgis Rally and Races. The world-famous annual motorcycle rally draws tens of thousands of bikers and spectators. Includes unique motorcycle shows, concerts, touring activities throughout the Black Hills, and national racing events. | 605/347–9190.

Yankton Riverboat Days. PRCA rodeo action, concerts, more than 150 arts and crafts booths, ethnic food, a parade, a waterskiing show, and many entertainment options make this among the most popular events in the southeast part of the state. | 605/665–3636.

Aug.–Sept.   **South Dakota State Fair.** One of the nation's last true agricultural expositions, this Huron classic includes unlimited entertainment on 10 free stages, a carnival midway, grandstand shows, rodeos, and car racing. | 605/353–7340 and 800/529–0900.

AUTUMN

Sept.   **Deadwood Jam.** Held on Main St. in Deadwood, the Black Hills' premier music event has the tops in country, rock, and blues music. | 800/999–1876 or 605/578–1876.

Oct.   **Custer State Park Buffalo Roundup.** One of the country's largest buffalo roundups is a sight to be remembered. Cowboys and park staff use horses, pickups, and helicopters to herd 1,400 head of bison into the park's corrals. | 605/255–4515.

State's Greats

From the windswept plains and glacial lakes of eastern South Dakota, past the moonscape of the Badlands, to the majesty and grandeur of Mount Rushmore, Crazy Horse, and the fabled Black Hills, this is a state known for its natural wonder and scenic diversity.

Adventure tourism abounds, whether camping on a quiet lakefront, hunting pheasant, deer, or wild turkeys, fly-fishing a rippling brook, or stealing away for a scenic excur-

1862	**1868**		**1870**	**1873**
U.S. Congress passes the Homestead Act, opening up millions of acres to hearty immigrants. In the Dakota Territory, 160-acre parcels sell for about $18 each.	New Fort Laramie Treaty establishes the Great Sioux Reservation, granting the tribes all rights to land in the Dakota Territory west of the Missouri River to the	Bighorns of western Wyoming.	The Northern Pacific Railroad begins laying tracks through the Powder River country west of the Black Hills, in obvious violation of the 1868 Fort Laramie Treaty.	The Dakota Territorial Legislature asks Congress to provide soldiers to drive "hostile" Indians from the Black Hills.

sion aboard your favorite mountain bike. Hiking and rock-climbing are popular pastimes in summer, while downhill skiing, cross-country skiing, and snowmobiling fill up the winter enthusiast's calendar.

Beaches, Forests, Parks, and Trails

The best beaches in South Dakota tend to be on man-made reservoirs throughout the state, where provisions have been made for visitor-friendly facilities. Among the best are **Angostura Reservoir State Recreation Area, Pactola,** and **Sheridan** in the Black Hills, **Oahe Dam and Reservoir** in the central region, and numerous smaller lakes in the southeast and northeast. Angostura and Pactola reservoirs are favorite spots for pleasure boaters, while Sheridan is primarily used as a fishing reservoir, although its beaches generally attract good summer crowds. The exceptional size of Oahe Reservoir and its status as one of the nation's prime spots for trophy walleye fishing put it a notch above other reservoirs and lakes in the state. Boats are much larger on Oahe, and many guide services cater to amateur and professional fishermen.

Within the confines of the million-acre **Black Hills National Forest,** teeming with wildlife, are granite peaks, ponderosa pine forests, alpine meadows, and gurgling streams rippling with trout.

South Dakota is proud of its parks, and virtually every small and large town in the state offers a shady preserve and a well-tended lawn perfect for a picnic or a nap. State parks and recreation areas dot the South Dakota map. Among the most impressive are **Custer State Park,** considered the crown jewel in the system, and **Lewis and Clark Recreation Area,** which attracts more than 40,000 visitors a week in peak season. Visitors are drawn to the scenic grandeur, granite spires, wildlife viewing, and outstanding hiking trails of Custer State Park, while water sports are the chief attraction of Lewis and Clark Recreation Area.

The state also is home to several branches of the national park system, including **Mount Rushmore National Memorial,** visited by more than 2.5 million people a year, **Wind Cave National Park, Badlands National Park,** and **Jewel Cave National Monument.** They are close enough together to fill a week-long vacation itinerary. The primary interests at Rushmore, of course, are the presidential portraits, although a recent $60 million improvement program has created new walking trails, concessions, an amphitheater, and a museum. At Wind Cave you can tour the "underground wilderness" as well as an aboveground preserve with free-roaming wildlife, including bison, elk, deer, and antelope. Jewel Cave is a much smaller park, and its focal point remains its cave, which ranks as the fourth-longest in the world. Both caves are excellent choices on both warmer summer days and chilly winter days, as they maintain a stable interior temperature in the high 50s (F). Scenic drives and easy hiking trails make the Badlands an excellent choice for vehicle tours or simply getting out of the car and exploring.

1874

Lt. Col. George A. Custer, whom the Sioux called "Yellow Hair," leads 10 cavalry and 2 infantry companies on the first white expedition into the Black Hills. In short order, he confirms the existence of gold, which he casually mentions in his correspondence. A Chicago newspaper prints Custer's account, and the gold rush is on.

1875

Late in the year, the Commissioner of Indian Affairs orders all Sioux bands to report to reservation agencies by January 31, 1876. All Sioux failing to do so will be considered "hostile."

1876

In March, Gen. George Crook leads his command into the field against the Sioux bands. Custer commands one of the forces. Crook's troops retreat in a June 17 battle against Sioux, Cheyenne, and Arapaho warriors. Hunkpapa Sioux leader Sitting Bull and other chiefs move their encampment into the valley of the Little Bighorn River. On June 25, Custer and his 7th

Culture, History, and the Arts

Prairie pioneer culture and history are everywhere in South Dakota, particularly in the eastern and central portions of the state, where immigrant homesteaders came to put down roots and begin anew. The finest exhibits, interpretive offerings, and art reflecting the state's history can be found at the **South Dakota Cultural Heritage Center** in Pierre, the **South Dakota Art Museum** on the campus of South Dakota State University in Brookings, the **Siouxland Heritage Museums** in Sioux Falls, and **The Journey** in Rapid City. Each of these museums provides history lovers with an opportunity to revisit the state's colorful past. Pierre's Cultural Heritage Center provides an excellent overview of South Dakota's Native American culture and pioneer heritage, while the Siouxland Heritage Museums and The Journey offer a glimpse into the regional distinctions within the state.

Native American culture and history are explored at many other venues as well, including the **Akta Lakota Museum and Lakota Visitors Center** in Chamberlain, the **Indian Museum of North America** at Crazy Horse Memorial, and the **Center for Western Studies** at Augustana College in Sioux Falls. The first two are dedicated to preserving the history of the Lakota Indians, while the Crazy Horse facility exhibits artifacts from all Plains Indian nations. The Center for Western Studies has historic photographs and manuscripts, Sioux artifacts, Norwegian rosemaling, and prairie art, as well as an invaluable collection of documents and books for scholarly study.

Sports

South Dakotans tend to characterize themselves as sports lovers. Most were raised with a fishing pole or hunting rifle in their hands and prefer the outdoor activities that help them fend off cabin fever, particularly in the off-season months.

The best walleye fishing in the world can be found on **Lake Oahe,** and guides with well-equipped boats and fish-finders are readily available. In the Black Hills, wading creeks in search of elusive brook and brown trout is the favored activity, while trophy lake trout are found in the deep reservoirs.

The 111-mi-long **Centennial Trail** extends across the entire Black Hills region from north to south, and the new **George S. Mickelson Trail,** dedicated in 1998, also offers mountain bikers and hikers a 114-mi rails-to-trails trek through the Black Hills backcountry. With an additional 6,000 mi of fire trails, logging roads, and abandoned railroad grades, it's easy to understand why the Black Hills are a top spot for pleasure biking.

Deadwood, Pierre, Rapid City, and Sioux Falls all offer impressive walking trails and bike paths following greenbelts, parkways, or streams in their respective communities. In winter, the Black Hills have more than 310 mi of groomed snowmobile trails, consistently ranked among the best in the nation by snowmobiling clubs and publications.

INTRODUCTION
HISTORY
REGIONS
WHEN TO VISIT
STATE'S GREATS
RULES OF THE ROAD
DRIVING TOURS

1877

Cavalry discover the camp and attack. Pinned down by more than 4,000 Indian warriors, Custer and more than 200 soldiers under his command are annihilated. By August, Congress

begins punishing peaceful agency Indians by cutting off food rations until they agree to cede the Black Hills.

After the Manypenny Commission forces the Sioux to relinquish the Black Hills, Congress ratifies the agreement on February 28, sending a wave of fortune-seekers on their way

to the Black Hills. Crazy Horse and his band of 1,100 men, women, and children surrender to authorities at the Red Cloud Agency on May 6. Four months later, Crazy Horse dies after

receiving a fatal wound from a soldier's bayonet.

Other Points of Interest

A visit to South Dakota gives you the rare opportunity to view two monumental mountain carvings, one completed and one in progress. Following a 10-year fundraising campaign, Mount Rushmore unveiled almost $60 million in facility improvements in 1998, greatly enhancing the interpretive offerings and visitor amenities at the memorial. Also in 1998, **Crazy Horse Memorial** celebrated a half-century of progress on the largest sculptural undertaking in the world with the dedication of the completed face of the Lakota leader's likeness.

Another family favorite in the Black Hills is **Reptile Gardens,** an unusual but strangely fascinating attraction that started with a sackful of rattlesnakes six decades ago and just kept growing. Today, you can enjoy hundreds of colorful orchids and 40,000 other flowers, a walk-through aviary, a giant tortoise habitat, four funny shows, and the world's largest collection of reptiles.

Rules of the Road

License Requirements: To drive in South Dakota, you must be at least 14 years old and have a valid driver's license. Residents of other states, Canada, and most other countries may drive as long as they possess a valid license.

Right Turn on Red: Everywhere in the state, unless otherwise posted, you may make a right turn on red *after* a full stop. Exceptions include one-way streets in downtown Rapid City, which are posted.

Seatbelt and Helmet Laws: All drivers and front-seat passengers under 18 years of age must wear a seatbelt. Children under age 5 may only ride in a federally approved child safety seat, or if they exceed 40 pounds, the child may be secured with a seatbelt. Motorcyclists 18 and older are not required to wear a helmet in South Dakota. Minors riding or driving a motorcycle must wear a helmet. Eye protection is required for all motorcyclists. It is recommended that all motorcyclists have headlights and taillights on at all times.

Speed Limits: In 1995, South Dakota raised its speed limit to 75 mph on its two interstates, except as noted near Rapid City and Sioux Falls. Posted limits on state and secondary highways are usually 65 mph, although most Black Hills scenic roadways are set at 55 mph. While South Dakota Highway Patrol officers are sometimes tolerant of those who moderately surpass speed limits during the daylight hours, they have little patience for nighttime speeders, and none at all for drunk drivers.

For More Information: Contact the South Dakota Highway Patrol at 605/773-3105. | 500 E. Capitol Ave., Pierre .

1880	1889	1890		1919
The "Great Dakota Boom" begins in earnest with the influx of Bohemians, Germans, Swedes, Finns, Poles, and Swiss.	South Dakota becomes the nation's 40th state on November 2, with open ground, settlers descending on the state, and hammers pounding.	On December 15, 39 Indian policemen and four special agents attempt to arrest Sitting Bull at his encampment. In the melee that follows, 5 policemen and 9 Indians are killed, including Sit-	ting Bull, arguably the most famous Indian ever.	Custer State Park is established, setting aside 73,000 acres as a preserve. The park is home to one of the nation's largest buffalo herds.

Black Hills and Badlands Driving Tour

FROM BADLANDS NATIONAL PARK TO MOUNT RUSHMORE NATIONAL MEMORIAL

INTRODUCTION
HISTORY
REGIONS
WHEN TO VISIT
STATE'S GREATS
RULES OF THE ROAD
DRIVING TOURS

Distance: 250 mi   Time: 3 days

Breaks: This tour begins with the stark beauty of the Badlands, then travels to Rapid City—gateway to the breathtaking scenery of the Black Hills. You will experience the exquisitely restored gold-rush town of Deadwood, then retreat to the vast wildlife preserve of Custer State Park. Along the way, you'll visit South Dakota's best-known memorials. There is ample opportunity for breaks on this excursion. Overnight stays are planned in Rapid City and Custer State Park. Avoid this tour at the height of winter, when heavy snowfalls sometimes make roads impassable.

❶ **Badlands National Park** is a 244,000-acre geologic wonderland. Rte. 240 wiggles through this moonlike landscape on its 32-mi loop off I–90. The Ben Reifel Visitor Center at Cedar Pass, 9 mi south of the interstate, and the White River Visitor Center, in the southern Stronghold Unit off BIA 27, will help acquaint you with the remote area and its wildlife. The roadless 64,250-acre Sage Creek Wilderness Area inside the park is protected from development and is open only to hikers, backpackers, and other outdoor enthusiasts. The only trails within the wilderness area have been created by the hooves of bison.

❷ The town of **Wall** is home to the **Wall Drug Store**; just follow the signs. From the beginning, the internationally known emporium of galleries and unique attractions provided free ice-water to road-weary travelers. It now stocks Black Hills gold jewelry, Native American pottery and moccasins, western clothing, books, art, postcards, curios, and 6,000 pairs of cowboy boots. It also owns the **Western Art Gallery Restaurant,** with 210 original oil paintings and seating for 530 diners. Check out the 5¢ coffee and homemade pies, rolls, and donuts.

❸ **Rapid City,** just 55 mi west of Wall on I–90, is the gateway to the Black Hills and a pleasant stop in its own right. From here it is possible to visit five national parks, memorials, and monuments on simple day trips, returning to the comfort of your established home away from home at night. You can stop at the free **Dinosaur Park,** with its commanding views, **Storybook Island** (1301 Sheridan Lake Rd., off Jackson Blvd., 605/342–6357), a free children's fantasyland park, and the **Stavkirke Chapel in the Hills,** a replica of the 850-yr-old Borgund Church in Norway. You'll also discover more than 80 hotels and motels with over 4,000 guest rooms, numerous restaurants, and a 13-mi bike and walking path through the center of town. The **Journey Museum** examines Black Hills history and culture. For outstanding shopping head downtown or visit the 12-store Rushmore Mall off I–90 on the city's north side. This concludes the first day of your tour.

1927		1941	1948	1962
Work begins on Mount Rushmore, a mountain carving symbolizing the birth, growth, preservation, and development of the United States with colossal likenesses of Washington, Jef-	ferson, Lincoln, and Theodore Roosevelt. President Calvin Coolidge visits the Black Hills for a 3-week vacation. He likes it so much he stays for 3 months.	The construction at Mount Rushmore ends with the death of sculptor Gutzon Borglum and imminent U.S. involvement in World War II.	Work begins on Crazy Horse Memorial, which honors Native Americans through the carved visage of the legendary Lakota leader.	President John F. Kennedy travels to Pierre to dedicate Oahe Dam, the second largest earthrolled dam in the world.

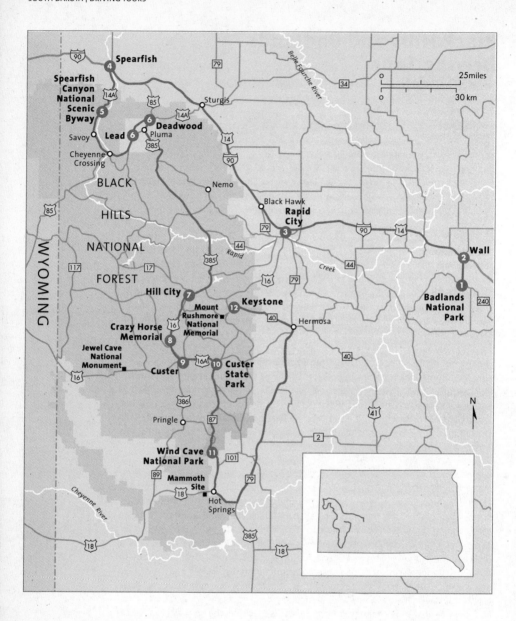

1978
Remains of 1325 massacre of Arikara tribal members are found during an archaeological dig.

1989
South Dakota's voters approve limited-stakes gaming for Deadwood, setting in motion the largest restoration and preservation project in the nation. South Dakota celebrates a century of statehood.

1991
President George Bush dedicates Mount Rushmore in a star-filled program at the mountain memorial.

INTRODUCTION
HISTORY
REGIONS
WHEN TO VISIT
STATE'S GREATS
RULES OF THE ROAD
DRIVING TOURS

❹ Begin day two with the 46-mi drive west on I–90 to **Spearfish,** one of the state's prettiest towns. Set in a broad valley at the mouth of Spearfish Canyon, the town's main attractions are a new convention center, historic sandstone buildings, the **Black Hills Passion Play,** presented on an outdoor stage since 1938, and the **Matthews Opera House,** a restored 1906 theater. You might also want to stop by the **D. C. Booth Historic Fish Hatchery,** which offers a century of history and free admission to its museum, historic home, fish ponds, and underwater viewing windows, or the **High Plains Heritage Center and Museum,** which has western art and artifacts, as well as cowboy music and poetry on certain nights.

❺ **Spearfish Canyon National Scenic Byway** greets motorists with 1,000-ft-high limestone palisades that tower to the right and left of U.S. 14A as it winds through the 19-mi gorge. The actual entrance to the canyon is in town, on the southwest side of Spearfish. Spearfish Creek splashes along the canyon floor as towering Black Hills spruce scent the air. Several canyon waterfalls, including Bridal Veil and Roughlock, are popular roadside stops. Summertime hikers enjoy donning "creek shoes" and exploring the side canyons, including Squaw Creek, Iron Creek, and Eleventh Hour Gulch. An excellent lunch spot can be found at Latchstring Village, where the **Spearfish Canyon Resort** offers accommodations and the **Latchstring Restaurant** provides appetite-pleasing entrées made from scratch.

❻ The twin cities of **Lead/Deadwood,** a bit farther on U.S. 14A, provide the ideal spot to stretch your legs. Visit Lead's **Black Hills Mining Museum** or the Homestake Visitor Center to learn more about mining's impact on the hills. In Deadwood, the **Adams Memorial Museum** displays rare artifacts from the town's colorful past. The **Old Style Saloon No. 10** bills itself as "the only museum in the world with a bar" and offers music, blackjack, poker, and slots. Upstairs, at the **Deadwood Social Club,** you'll discover outstanding food at reasonable prices.

❼ **Hill City,** approximately 40 mi south on U.S. 385, is another mining town turned tourist mecca. Its Main St. has fascinating shops and galleries, as well as the **Mount Rushmore Brewing Company,** with good pub fare and a wide selection of microbrews.

❽ **Crazy Horse Memorial,** the colossal mountain carving of the legendary Lakota leader, is just south of Hill City on U.S. 16/385. The memorial's complex includes the **Indian Museum of North America,** which displays beautiful bead and quillwork representing many of the continent's Native nations.

❾ **Custer,** 5 mi south of Crazy Horse Memorial on U.S. 385, is a friendly community surrounded by some of the most incredible scenery in the Black Hills, including Custer State Park, the Needles Highway, Harney Peak, Wind Cave National Park, and **Jewel Cave National Monument.** Jewel Cave was named for the nailhead and dogtooth spar crystals that line its more than 100 mi of passageways. It is currently ranked as the second-longest cave in the United States (after Kentucky's Mammoth Cave). You can take an elevator down 234 ft, and various tours are offered at different times of the year.

❿ **Custer State Park,** 5 mi east of Custer on U.S. 16A, has 73,000 acres of scenic beauty, exceptional drives, close-up views of wildlife, and fingerlike granite spires rising from the forest floor. Stay in one of four enchanting mountain lodges, relax through a hayride and chuckwagon supper, or take a Jeep tour into the buffalo herds. You won't want to leave. This concludes day two of your tour.

⓫ Begin day three with a visit to **Wind Cave National Park,** south of Custer State Park via Rte. 87 and U.S. 385. The park has 28,000 acres of wildlife habitat above ground and the world's seventh-longest cave below, with 76 mi of mapped passageways. Six mi farther south on U.S. 385 you come to **Hot Springs** (605/745–4140 or 800/325–6991). Here are still more historic sandstone buildings, the amazing **Mammoth Site,** where some 50 of the giant beasts have been unearthed, and **Evans Plunge,** with the world's largest naturally heated indoor swimming pool.

⑫ Take U.S. 18 east, then Rte. 79 north, then Rte. 40 west to **Keystone** to visit nearby **Mount Rushmore National Memorial,** where you can view the huge carved busts of four U.S. presidents.

Return to Rapid City via U.S. 16A and 16, then follow I–90 east approximately 50 mi to Badlands National Park, your point of origin.

Southeast South Dakota Driving Tour
FROM SIOUX FALLS TO MITCHELL

Distance: 250 mi   Time: 2 days

Breaks: This tour starts in Sioux Falls—South Dakota's largest city—exploring its highlights, then takes in several surrounding attractions before ending in Mitchell, home of the world's only Corn Palace.

❶ **Sioux Falls** has more than 400 restaurants and the best shopping in the state. Its downtown area has shops, galleries, and natural attractions. Both the **Old Courthouse**

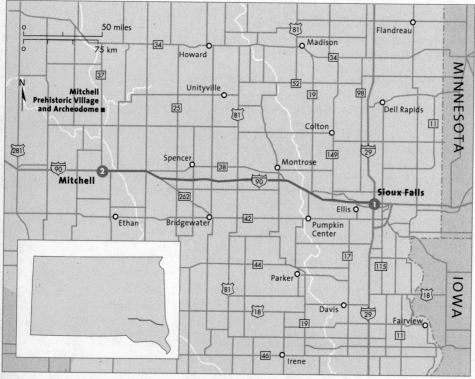

Museum and the **Pettigrew Home and Museum** have exhibits exploring the culture and heritage of the Siouxland region. The **Jim Savage Western Art and Gift Gallery** displays Native American and western art, as well as pottery, antiques, and collectibles. **Falls Park,** near the city center, lets you see how the city got its name, after the falls of the Big Sioux River. You can picnic there or explore the park's walking trails. The **Great Plains Zoo** has 400 live animals, a children's zoo, and a train, and the **Delbridge Museum of Natural History** has one of the largest collections of mounted animals in the world, each displayed in its natural habitat. **Empire Mall** is the state's largest shopping center, with 180 stores. After a day of taking in Sioux Falls' attractions, plan to spend the night and resume your tour in the morning.

❷ Begin day two with a drive to **Mitchell,** about an hour west of Sioux Falls on I–90. Mitchell's livelihood comes from the cornfields that cover this region. You'll find friendly residents and ample opportunities for lodging, dining, and sightseeing. The **Corn Palace** is a must-see. Built in 1892 to encourage settlement and prove the richness of eastern South Dakota soil, this unusual and colorful building has massive interior and exterior murals made of specially grown corn. The **Oscar Howe Art Center** houses a permanent collection of paintings and a dome mural by the celebrated Yankton Sioux artist Oscar Howe. The art center offers free admission and a gift shop. The **Middle Border Museum of American Indian and Pioneer Life** has seven buildings, including an art gallery, an 1885 schoolhouse, a 1909 country church, a 1900 train depot, and a restored 1886 Italianate home. The **Mitchell Prehistoric Village and Archeodome,** just north of town off Rte. 37, is the site of a settlement dating back to 900 BC. It includes a full-scale reconstruction of a prehistoric earth lodge and offers year-round archaeological digs. **Enchanted World Doll Museum** displays 4,000 antique and modern dolls from around the world, posed in 400 different scenes reminiscent of nursery rhymes, fairy tales, and everyday life of the 1800s and 1900s.

Return to I–90 and drive east 70 mi to return to Sioux Falls.

ABERDEEN

INTRO
ATTRACTIONS
DINING
LODGING

ABERDEEN

MAP 8, G2

(Nearby town also listed: Redfield)

Established by the Milwaukee Railroad in the fertile valley of the James River in 1880, Aberdeen is named after the town in the Scottish Highlands. The settlement quickly became known as "Hub City" for the network of rail lines extending out from it like the spokes of a wheel. Aberdeen continues to be a retail, healthcare, and cultural center for the northeast region of the state. Among its features are Storybook Land, a children's fantasy park, and Northern State University, which stands on 52 tree-shaded acres in the center of town.

Information: Aberdeen Chamber of Commerce and Aberdeen Convention and Visitors Bureau | 516 S. Main St. (Chamber), and 514½ S. Main St. (Visitors Bureau) 57402-1179 | 605/225–2860 or 800/645–3851 | www.aberdeencvb.com.

Attractions
Dacotah Prairie Museum. This is a museum of local history with displays and artifacts from eastern South Dakota as well as a wildlife gallery with 50 mounts and an art gallery featuring the work of South Dakota artists. | 21 S. Main St. | 605/626–7117 | www.brown.sd.us/museum | Free | Tues.–Fri. 9–5, weekends 1–4.

Family National Wildlife Refuge. A hike, bike, or car tour meanders along the James River; there are views of the local wildlife. It is 30 mi northeast of Aberdeen. | 39650 Sand Lake Dr., Columbia | 605/885-6320 | Free | May–Sept.

Mina State Recreation Area. The park has a campground, a boat ramp, and swimming and picnic areas. You can rent a modern, three-bedroom cabin year-round on the wooded shore of man-made Mina Lake. If you want, you can make the reservations for the cabin over the Internet. | 37908 Youth Camp Rd. | 800/710-2267 | www.sdcamp.com | $3 per person, $5 per vehicle, $20 annually.

Richmond Lake State Recreation Area. Three park areas cater to the needs of campers, swimmers, boaters, and anglers. You can find a place to camp or rent a three-bedroom cabin at nearby Mina Recreation Area. | R.R. 2, Box 500 | 800/710-2267 | www.state.sd.us/sdparks | $3 per person, $5 per vehicle, $20 annually.

Wylie Park. Wylie Park has more than 175 acres of grassland filled with wildlife, a campground, picnic areas, and a swimming complex. The animal compound has bison, deer, elk, sheep, goats, and ducks. Nearby is Storybook Land, a children's fantasy park. | North Highway 281 | 605/626-3512 and 888/326-9693 | www.aberdeen.sd.us | Free | Mid-Apr.–mid-Oct., daily 10 AM–11 PM.

ON THE CALENDAR

FEB.: *Winter Carnival.* You can find ice skating, cross-country skiing, bobsledding, and other winter activities. | 605/626-7015.
MAY: *Pari-mutuel Horse Racing.* This event includes horse racing at its best and children's activities. | 605/226-3464 | Last three weekends in May.
JUNE: *L. Frank Baum Oz Festival—The Dakota Heritage.* You can explore the town that Oz-creator Frank Baum lived in from 1888 to 1891, and meet Dorothy, the Scarecrow, the Tin Man, and the Lion. There are vendors, live theater, games, crafts, and music. | 800/645-3851.

Dining

The Flame. American. Here you'll find casual, relaxed dining with family-style service. The steak is a popular menu choice, as are the pastas. | 2 S. Main St. | 605/225-2082 | Closed Sun. | $7–15 | AE, D, DC, MC, V.

Maverick's Steak and Cocktail. American. Buffalo rib-eye steak is the signature dish at this restaurant where everything is served outdoors. Also on the menu are BBQ ribs and prime rib. There are weekly specials and a decent winelist. | 1702 6th Ave. SE | 605/225-1314 | $8–$18 | DC, MC, V.

Millstone Family Restaurant. American, Continental. Millstone serves chicken and steak and has an extensive soup and salad bar. You can eat breakfast any time or have a slice of homemade pie. | 2210 6th Ave. SE | 605/229-4105 | Open 24 hours | $4–$8 | DC, MC, V.

Minerva's. American. At this restaurant in the Ramkota Hotel, you can eat surrounded by dark oak woodwork by a crackling fire. The Cajun chicken linguine or the bacon-wrapped Montreal pork chop are good, and you can top it all off with the tiramisu. | 1400 8th Ave. NW | 605/226-2988 | Breakfast is also available | $7–$15 | AE, D, DC, MC, V.

Lodging

AmericInn. Spacious guest rooms are a mainstay in this brick hostelry. Two guest suites have fireplaces of their own. This location, next to Lakewood Mall on Hwy. 12, is 1 mi from the airport and the Swisher Field Sport Complex. Complimentary Continental breakfast. In-room data ports, some kitchenettes, some microwaves, some refrigerators, in-room hot tubs. Cable TV. Indoor pool. Spa, steam room. Airport shuttle. Pets allowed (fee). | 310 Centennial St. | 605/225-4565 or 800/634-3444 | fax 605/229-3792 | www.americinn.com | 64 rooms | $54–$156 | AE, D, MC, V.

Best Western Ramkota. This hotel off Hwy. 281 is set between two golf courses on the northeast edge of town. It is also convenient to bowling. Restaurant (*see* Minerva's), bar, picnic area, room service. Cable TV. Indoor pool, wading pool. Hot tub, sauna. Video games. Laundry service. Business services, airport shuttle. Pets allowed. | 1400 8th Ave. NW | 605/229–4040 | fax 605/229–0480 | ramkotaabr@dtgnet.com | 154 rooms | $69 | AE, D, DC, MC, V.

Ramada Inn. At this hotel just 1½ mi from the airport you will find clean, comfortable rooms and a relaxing whirlpool tub. Restaurant, bar, complimentary Continental breakfast, room service. Cable TV. Indoor pool. Hot tub. Exercise equipment. Video games. Business services, airport shuttle. Pets allowed. | 2727 6th Ave. SE | 605/225–3600 | fax 605/225–6704 | 152 rooms | $69 | AE, D, DC, MC, V.

Super 8. This motel on the east side of town has standard chain rooms, but this is the original, first-ever Super 8. A mall and dining are nearby. Complimentary Continental breakfast. In-room data ports, some microwaves, some refrigerators. Cable TV. Indoor pool. Sauna. Exercise equipment. Laundry facilities. Airport shuttle. Pets allowed. | 2405 6th Ave. SE | 605/229–5005 | 108 rooms | $51–$53 | AE, D, DC, MC, V.

Ward Hotel. This nicely maintained hotel has been a fixture of downtown Aberdeen since 1928. The lobby lounge, bar, and restaurant are a sometime local destination. Restaurant, bar. No air-conditioning in some rooms. Laundry facilities. | 104 S. Main | 605/225–6100 | fax 605/229–5185 | 70 rooms | $30–$50 | AE, D, MC V.

White House Inn. A distinctive landmark in the area and just 5 blocks from Main St., this modern concrete-and-steel inn has quiet, spacious rooms. Complimentary Continental breakfast. In-room data ports. Cable TV. Laundry facilities. Business services. Pets allowed. | 500 6th Ave. SW | 605/225–5000 or 800/225–6000 | fax 605/225–6730 | 96 rooms | $42–$44 | AE, D, MC, V.

BADLANDS
NATIONAL PARK

INTRO
ATTRACTIONS
DINING
LODGING

BADLANDS NATIONAL PARK

MAP 8, C4

(Nearby towns also listed: Pine Ridge, Wall)

Badlands National Park, 160 square mi in the southwest region of the state, is best viewed in early morning and at dusk, when deep shadows define the eerie forms. The fossil-laden soils hold the remains of huge beasts that once roamed the region. For the best overview of this massive park, stop by the Ben Reifel Visitor Center at Cedar Pass, 9 mi south of I–90 on Rte. 240.

Information: Badlands National Park | Box 6, Interior, 57750 | 605/433–5361 | www.nps.gov/badl.

Attractions

Badlands National Park. (*See* Wall.) The 244,000-acre park has 64,000 acres of wilderness, eight marked hiking trails that stretch over 11 mi, and two visitor centers (Ben Reifel Visitor Center at Cedar Pass and the White River Visitor Center). Towering spires, ragged ridgelines, and deep canyons are some of the memorable sights. | Hwy. 240, Interior | 605/433–5361 | fax 605/433–5404 | www.nps.gov/badl | $5 per person, $10 per vehicle.

White River Visitor Center Museum. Artifacts from the parklands and educational maps are worth a visit. | Off Hwy. 27 | 605/455–2878 | $10 per vehicle, $5 per horse and bicycle | Call for hours.

ON THE CALENDAR

MAY–SEPT.: *Interpretive Park Programs.* For daily visitors, park rangers lead informative guided walks covering the natural and ecological history of the region. | 605/433–5361.

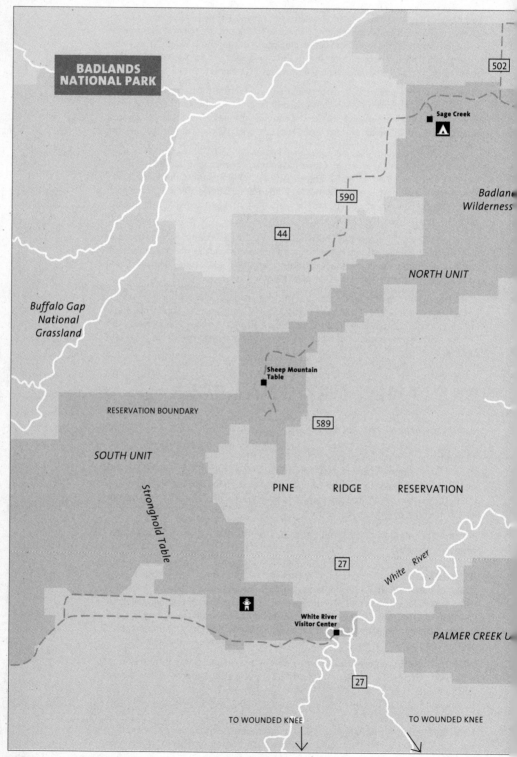

BADLANDS
NATIONAL PARK

502

Sage Creek

590

Badlan
Wilderness

44

NORTH UNIT

Buffalo Gap
National
Grassland

Sheep Mountain
Table

RESERVATION BOUNDARY

589

SOUTH UNIT

PINE   RIDGE   RESERVATION

Stronghold Table

27

White River

White River
Visitor Center

PALMER CREEK U

27

TO WOUNDED KNEE

TO WOUNDED KNEE

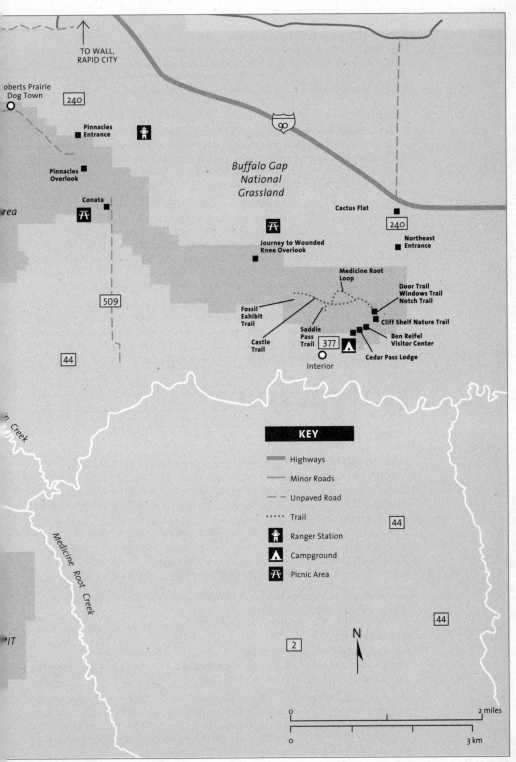

TO WALL,
RAPID CITY

240

oberts Prairie
Dog Town

Pinnacles
Entrance

Pinnacles
Overlook

Conata

rea

509

44

Buffalo Gap
National
Grassland

90

Cactus Flat

240

Northeast
Entrance

Journey to Wounded
Knee Overlook

Medicine Root
Loop

Door Trail
Windows Trail
Notch Trail

Fossil
Exhibit
Trail

Cliff Shelf Nature Trail

Castle
Trail

Saddle
Pass
Trail

377

Ben Reifel
Visitor Center

Cedar Pass Lodge

Interior

n Creek

Medicine Root Creek

IT

KEY

━━━ Highways

─── Minor Roads

─ ─ ─ Unpaved Road

· · · · Trail

Ranger Station

Campground

Picnic Area

44

44

2

N

2

0   2 miles

0   3 km

Dining

★ **Cedar Pass Lodge and Restaurant.** American, Southwestern. The atmosphere is rustic in this open-air full-service restaurant with its exposed beam ceiling and knotty pine walls. Enjoy steak and trout or Indian tacos and fried bread, accompanied by a cold beer or a glass of wine after a refreshing walk in the Badlands National Forest nearby. | Badlands Loop Rd. | 605/433–5460 | Breakfast is also available. Closed Nov.–Apr. 1 | $8–$16 | AE, D, DC, MC, V.

Lodging

Badlands Budget Host Motel. Every room in this motel has views of the Badlands National Forest, which is 1 mi away. You can have breakfast and dinner on the premises or walk over to a nearby restaurant. Restaurant, room service. Outdoor pool, wading pool. Video games. Playground. Laundry facilities. Pets allowed. | Rte. 377, Interior | 605/433–5335 or 800/388–4643 | 21 rooms | $50 | Closed Oct.–Apr. | MC, V.

Badlands Ranch RV Resort and B&B. This 2,000-acre ranch is set right in the middle of Badlands National Park. The property was developed several years ago with a mix of cabins and motel accommodations; a log-construction ranch house has Jacuzzi tubs with decks overlooking the park. The setting—complete with gazebo, duck ponds, picnic areas, and a bonfire site—makes it ideal for summer family reunions. Hunting guides are provided in season. Picnic area. Hot tub. | HCR 53, Interior | 605/433–5599 | fax 605/433–5598 | www.badlandsranchandresort.com | 7 cabins, 4 rooms, 1 lodge | $48–$88 | AE, D, MC, V.

★ **Cedar Pass Lodge and Restaurant.** Cedar Pass has spacious individual log cabins with views of the Badlands peaks, each with two beds. There's a gift shop with local crafts, including turquoise and beadwork. You'll find hiking trails that run next to the cabins. Restaurant, picnic area. Hiking. Some pets allowed. | 1 Cedar St., Interior | 605/433–5460 | fax 605/433–5560 | 24 cabins | $45 | Closed Nov. 1–Apr. 14 | AE, DC, MC, V.

BELLE FOURCHE

MAP 8, A3

(Nearby towns also listed: Deadwood, Lead, Spearfish, Sturgis)

Just 30 mi southwest of the geographic center of the United States, Belle Fourche is definitely the dead center of the cattle and sheep industries of northwest South Dakota. Belle Fourche was founded in 1890 by Seth Bullock, one of Theodore Roosevelt's close friends. Bullock was a Rough Rider and the first sheriff of Deadwood, where he built the impressive Bullock Hotel, which still greets visitors today. You'll find a string of shops, taverns, and offices in the narrow downtown business district of Belle Fourche and some new sports bars and chain restaurants along the bypass. Among the town's highlights are the Tri-State Museum, the nearby Belle Fourche Reservoir, and the annual Black Hills Roundup, one of the nation's oldest and best rodeos.

Information: **Belle Fourche Chamber of Commerce** | 415 5th Ave. 57717-1435 | 605/892–2676 or 888/345–5859 | www.bellefouche.org.

Attractions

Belle Fourche Reservoir and Orman Dam. This popular, rustic boating and fishing destination 8 mi east of Belle Fourche is also the site of one of the state's best Fourth of July fireworks displays. | Hwy. 212 | 605/892–2676 | Free.

Dream Maker Buffalo Ranch. Just 18 mi west out of Belle Fourche you can climb on board a wagon and ride out to the buffalo herds. The region is home to the unique great white buffalo (1 out of every 60 million buffalos are white). Dream Maker has tentative plans for a move to Custer in spring 2001; call the toll-free number for more information. | HCR 69 | 307/896–2906 or 877/292–8777 | $8 | Daily, 9 AM–dusk.

Johnny Spaulding Cabin. The was the first building in Butte County, circa 1876. | 801 State St. | 605/892–2676 | Free | June–Aug., Mon.–Sat. 8–8.

Tri-State Museum. The three states are South Dakota, Wyoming, and Montana, and their history is presented in exhibits and memorabilia. | 831 State St. | 605/892–3705 | Free | June–Aug., Mon.–Sat. 8–8.

ON THE CALENDAR

JUNE: *All Car Rally.* This car show with all makes and models takes place downtown. | 888/345–JULY.

JULY: *Black Hills Roundup.* This three-day professional rodeo includes a free barbecue, carnival, parade, and fireworks. | Roundup Rodeo Grounds, Roundup St. | 605/892–2676 or 888/345–JULY | July 2–4.

AUG.: *Butte Lawrence County Fair.* You'll find agricultural exhibits and displays, entertainment, and food vendors. | 888/345–JULY.

SEPT.: *Sanctioned Chili Cook-Off.* Entrants in this free, annual competition dress up in costumes. The International Chili Society sponsors this event. | 605/892–2676 or 888/345–5859.

Dining

Belle Inn Restaurant. American. This family owned establishment known for steaks, sirloin tips, buffalo burgers, and homemade hash browns is just 1 mi from the center of town. | Hwy. 85S and 34 | 605/892–4430 | Breakfast is always available | $4–$8 | No credit cards.

Prime Time Sports Grill. American. A relaxed, full-service restaurant with full lunch and dinner menus. Sports fans can catch events on one of the many televisions. Known for Philly steak sandwiches, wrap sandwiches, and generous portions on every order. The Rancher tenderloin tips are worth a try. | 818 5th Ave. | 605/892–6666 | $6–$16 | AE, D, MC, V.

Lodging

Ace Motel. Economical rooms one block off the highway in a quiet location are what you'll find here. Children under 12 stay free. Some microwaves, some refrigerators. Cable TV. Some pets allowed. | 109 6th Ave. | 605/892–2612 | 15 rooms | $28–$48 | D, MC, V.

Candlelight B&B. This spot is only minutes away from Devils Tower and other Black Hills area attractions. Complimentary Continental breakfast. No pets. No smoking. | 819 5th Ave. | 605/892–4568 | 5 rooms | $45–$65 | MC, V.

Motel 6. This chain motel's rooms have blue decor and tiled bathrooms. The motel is 10 blocks from downtown and next door to a family-style restaurant. It's also convenient to many attractions, such as Mount Rushmore (about 1 hr), a golf course, the Black Hills Passion Play (a summer event similar to the European Passion plays), and gaming and skiing in Deadwood (about ½ hr). Kids 17 and under stay free. Cable TV. Indoor pool. Hot tub. Laundry facilities. Some pets allowed. | 1815 5th Ave. | 605/892–6663 | fax 605/892–6638 | 51 rooms | $66 | AE, D, MC, V.

BERESFORD

INTRO
ATTRACTIONS
DINING
LODGING

BERESFORD

MAP 8, H5

(Nearby towns also listed: Sioux Falls, Vermillion)

This town was known as Paris in 1873, but in 1884, when the Northwestern Railroad was built, the name was changed to honor Admiral Lord Charles Beresford of England, who had a financial interest in the railroad. Today, Beresford's economic base is decidedly agricultural, although the community also keeps busy servicing motorists on nearby I–29.

Information: **Beresford Chamber of Commerce** | Box 167, 57004 | 605/763–2021.

Attractions

Golf Club. An 9-hole miniature golf course. | 510 W. Elm St. | 605/763–2202 | $9–$14 | Mid. Apr.–Mid. Oct., daily 7–dusk.

Union County State Park. This quiet park located 12 mi south of Beresford has a playground, hiking and horseback trails, camping areas, rest rooms, and showers. | Highway #1C | 605/987–2263 | $3 per person, $5 per vehicle, $20 annually.

ON THE CALENDAR

JUNE: *Beresford Chamber of Commerce Old-Fashioned Saturday Night.* Show and shine car, tractor, and motorcycle display with plenty of family activities: pony rides, petting zoo, miniature train rides, and food booths. | 605/763–2021.

Dining

Emily's Family Restaurant. American. Emily's specializes in hamburger steaks and pork chops. There is a salad bar. A light menu and lunch specials can also be found here. | I–29 and Hwy. 46 | 605/763–5300 | Breakfast is always available. Daily 6 AM–10 PM | $5–$10 | D, MC, V.

Lodging

Crossroads. The rooms are large and on the ground floor, with individual parking spaces outside. Truck parking is available. The town of Beresford is small but has all essential facilities, and there is a restaurant within walking distance. Children under 12 stay free. Cable TV. Some pets allowed (fee). | I–29 and Rte. 46 | 605/763–2020 | fax 605/763–2504 | 20 rooms | $34–$38 | AE, D, DC, MC, V.

Super 8 Motel. This single-story motel built in 1998 is near downtown and I–29. Complimentary Continental breakfast, room service. In-room data ports, some refrigerators, some microwaves. Cable TV. Indoor pool. Spa. Exercise equipment. Laundry facilities. Pets allowed (fee). | 1410 W. Cedar | 605/763–2001 or 800/800–8000 | fax 605/763–2001 | www.super8.com | 35 rooms. 3 whirlpool suites | $60–$110 | AE, D, DC, MC, V.

BROOKINGS

MAP 8, H3

(Nearby town also listed: Madison)

Brookings was founded in 1881 and named for Wilmot W. Brookings, a pioneer settler who was born in Woolwich, Maine, and moved to Dakota Territory in August 1857. During his half-century of service to the state, Brookings was among the first members of the Squatter Legislature, was named governor of Dakota Territory, served as an associate justice, published the Sioux Falls *Leader*, organized a railroad, served as a member of the state constitutional convention, and worked variously as promoter, owner, and director of six major banks and companies in the state. Brookings accomplished all of this, even though he had lost both his legs below the knees after being caught in a severe blizzard in February 1858. He was the first recorded amputee in South Dakota. This quaint community is dominated by the beautiful campus of South Dakota State University, with 8,500 undergraduate students. SDSU's botanical gardens, museums, sports program, and cultural and social organizations keep the town hopping. Among the highlights in Brookings are the South Dakota Art Museum, displaying works by artists Oscar Howe and Harvey Dunn, and the McCrory Gardens, billed as the "prettiest 70 acres in South Dakota."

Information: Brookings Chamber of Commerce, and Brookings Convention and Visitors Bureau | 2308 6th St. E, 57006-0431 | 605/692–6125 or 800/699–6125 | chamber@brookings.com | www.brookings.com/chamber.

Attractions

Agricultural Heritage Museum. The museum is dedicated to the preservation and interpretation of objects related to South Dakota's agricultural history and rural heritage from 1860 to the present. | South Dakota State University, Medary Ave. and 11th St. | 605/688–6226 | www.agmuseum.com | Free | Mon.–Sat. 10–5, Sun. 1–5.

Brookings Area MultiPlex. This is an event and convention center that hosts rodeos, concerts, and conventions year-round. The largest of the MultiPlex facility's venues is the Arena, with 53,000 square ft of unobstructed clear space. The Multiplex is the winner of the American Building Company, 1999 Building of the Year Award. | 824 32nd Ave. (intersection of Hwy. 29 and I–29) | 605/692–7539 | fax 605/697–6393 | plex@brookings.net | www.brookingsareamultiplex.com | Call ahead for events.

Oakwood Lakes State Park. Three burial grounds remain as a reminder that this was once an annual gathering spot for Native American tribes. Today the park is popular with boaters, fishermen, hikers, and campers. Canoe rentals and camping cabins are available. | 46109 202ndSt., Bruce (20 mi north of Brookings) | 605/627–5441 or 800/710–2267 | www.state.sd.us/gsp | $3 per person, $5 per vehicle, $20 annually.

South Dakota Art Museum. The museum houses extensive collections by prairie painter Harvey Dunn, Sioux artist Oscar Howe, and others. Collections include Sioux craftwork and embroidery from the island of Madeira. | Medary Ave. at Harvey Dunn St. | 605/688–5423 | Free.

South Dakota State University. The state's largest educational institution was founded in 1881 and offers programs in more than 200 disciplines. | Medary Ave. and 11th St. | 605/688–4541 | www.sdstate.edu | Free.
The **McCrory Gardens** are a fragrant escape, often described as "the prettiest 70 acres in South Dakota" and one of the top 10 small botanical gardens in the United States. On the grounds are 14 formal theme gardens, including the Centennial Prairie Garden, the Children's Maze, and the Rock Garden. | 6th St. and 20th Ave. | 605/692–6125 or 800/699–6125 | Free.

ON THE CALENDAR

JAN.: *Frozen Foot Rendezvous.* The pre-1840s fur trade era is re-created by costumed players in an outdoor encampment. Activities include a wild-game cooking contest, a treasure hunt, snowshoe races, and muzzleloader shoots. | 605/693–4589 | Jan. 1–3.
JAN.: *Kool Kids Klassic Fishing Derby.* This ice-fishing event for kids includes free fishing poles, snacks, and beverages. | 605/627–5441.
FEB.: *Annual SDSU Wacipi.* This traditional powwow includes arts and crafts displays. | 605/688–6236.
JULY: *Summer Artsfestival.* This outdoor extravaganza of art, antiques, children's activities, food, and entertainment includes artisans, craftspeople, and entertainers from across the United States. | 605/693–4589.

Dining

Kenny's Embers America. American. Kenny's serves Sunday buffet and full-service family style dining with steak, hamburgers, and seafood; there's also a full bar with a lounge. | 2515 E. 6th St. | 605/692–5078 | Breakfast is always available | $4–$11 | AE, D, MC, V.

Pheasant Restaurant. Contemporary. You can choose from steaks, stir fry, and a multitude of salads. There are daily specials and you can indulge yourself with homemade cheesecake. There's a cocktail lounge and bar, as well. | 726 Main Ave. S | 605/692–4723 | Closed Sun. | $6–$13 | D, MC, V.

The Ram. American. This three-story restaurant is in a 1920s bank building with granite pillars on its facade. The Ram has a full menu that includes steaks, sandwiches, burgers, pastas, and prime rib. Inside you'll find sure proof that this was once a bank: the original safe and framed newspapers telling of a bank robbery. | 327 Main Ave. | 605/692–2485 | Closed Sun. | $10–$25 | AE, D, DC, MC, V.

Lodging

Brookings Inn. This clean and quiet facility is 1 mi from a golf course and South Dakota State University. Restaurant, bar (with entertainment), picnic area, room service. Cable TV. Indoor pool. Hot tub, sauna. Miniature golf. Exercise equipment. Video games. Laundry facilities. Business services, airport shuttle. Some pets allowed. | 2500 E. 6th St. | 605/692–9471 | fax 605/692–5807 | 125 rooms | $62 | AE, D, DC, MC, V.

Comfort Inn. This chain hotel is at exit 132 off I–29, 2 mi from South Dakota State University. The McCrory Gardens are mi away. Complimentary breakfast. In-room data ports, microwaves, refrigerators. Cable TV. Business services. No pets. | 514 Sunrise Ridge Rd. | 605/692–9566 | 51 rooms | $59–$125 | AE, D, DC, MC, V.

Fairfield Inn. This 3-story hotel, which is downtown less than 1 mi from Hwy. 14 and I–29, has standard rooms for business travelers and tourists. The inn is also close to stores and restaurants. Complimentary Continental breakfast. Some in-room hot tubs. Cable TV. Indoor pool. Hot tub. Exercise equipment. Video games. Laundry facilities. Business services. | 3000 LeFevre Dr. | 605/692–3500 or 800/228–2800 | fax 605/692–3500 | 76 rooms, 6 suites | $59–$65, $89–$115 suites | AE, D, DC, MC, V.

Staurolite Inn and Suites. Staurolite is less than 1mi from South Dakota State University and 2 blocks from McCrory Gardens. The rooms are spacious, and some have private patios or balconies, or outside entrances. The restaurant is self-service. Children under 18 stay free. Restaurant, bar (with entertainment), room service. In-room data ports, some microwaves, some refrigerators. Cable TV. Indoor pool, wading pool. Hot tub. Video games. Laundry facilities. Business services, airport shuttle. Some pets allowed. | 2515 E. 6th St. | 605/692–9421 | 102 rooms | $55–$67 | AE, D, DC, MC, V.

Super 8 Motel. This motel built in 1995 is just 2 mi from South Dakota State University. It's at Exit 132 off I–29 east on Hwy. 14. Three rooms with whirlpool are available. Complimentary Continental breakfast. Some microwaves, some refrigerators. Cable TV. Outdoor pool. Video games. Laundry facilities. Pets allowed. | 3034 LeFevre Dr. | 605/692–6920 or 800/800–8000 | fax 605/692–6920, Ext. 401 | www.super8.com | 67 rooms | $40–$80 | AE, D, DC, MC, V.

CHAMBERLAIN

MAP 8, F4

(Nearby towns also listed: Mitchell, Pierre, Platte, Winner)

At the spot where I–90 crosses the Missouri River, Chamberlain is a popular destination for sport fishermen and pheasant and game hunters. Situated on the eastern shore of Lake Francis Case, the town has motels, hotels, and restaurants. Lewis and Clark camped just south of present-day Chamberlain on Sept. 15, 1804. The town was founded in 1880 and named for Selah Chamberlain, the director of the Milwaukee Railroad, which helped attract settlers to the region. Chamberlain's economic strength comes from the fertile soils of the surrounding farmland and from the thousands of visiting sportsmen who stalk pheasants, grouse, prairie chickens, turkeys, geese, ducks, antelope, mule, and whitetail deer and fish in 107-mi-long Lake Francis Case.

Information: Chamberlain Area Chamber of Commerce | 115 W. Lawler St., 57325 | 605/734–6541 | chamberlain.sd.org.

Attractions

Akta Lakota Museum and Lakota Visitors Center. A moving look at Sioux life on the Great Plains prior to the arrival of European settlers. | St. Joseph's Indian School, N. Main St. | 605/734–3452 | Free | Memorial Day–Labor Day, Mon.–Sat. 8–6, Sun. 1–5; Labor Day–Memorial Day, Mon.–Sat. 8–5 or by appointment.

American Creek Recreational Area. This federally operated recreation area on the east bank of the Missouri River has a campground, great fishing, a playground, beach, boat ramp, and showers. | Hwy. 50 and G St. | 605/734–0522 or 877/444–6777 | www.reserveusa.com | Free; campsites $12, $15 with hookup | May–Sept. 30.

Big Bend Dam–Lake Sharpe. This is one of a series of Missouri River dams that create South Dakota's "Great Lakes." It's on the Lower Brule and Crow Creek reservations 25 mi north of Chamberlain. Picnicking and campsites are available. | Hwy. 47 N, off I–90 | 605/245–2255 or 877/444–6777 (reservations) | $14 campsites | June–Aug., daily; Sept.–May by appointment only.

ON THE CALENDAR

JUNE: *South Dakota Street Rod Association Annual Rod Run.* Rod run, cruise, poker run, and show and shine. | 605/734–5047.

Dining

Al's Oasis. American. This large restaurant has a country theme, as you'll gather from the cowboy murals. You can come here for prime rib, country-fried steak, buffalo burgers, and a full-service salad bar. For dessert the hot apple pie with cinnamon ice cream is a good choice. Kids' menu. | 605/734–6054 | Breakfast also available | $5.75–$16 | AE, D, MC, V.

Casey's Drug, Jewelry and Cafe. American. This café with an Irish theme shares space with a drugstore and jewelry store. It's popular for its "Perfect Cheeseburger" and homemade pies, and offers a spectacular view over the Missouri River. A salad bar and kids' menu are available. | Welcome West Plaza | 605/734–6530 | Reservations not accepted | Open daily 7 AM–9 PM | $7–12 | AE, D, MC, V.

Charley's. American. There's a full bar serving New York strips and fresh walleye trout; there's also a full salad bar. | 606 E. King Ave. | 605/734–6238 | Closed Sunday | $8–$15 | DC, MC, V.

Lodging

Best Western Lee's Motor Inn. This standard Best Western accommodation is near the river and downtown. Family suites are available. Complimentary Continental breakfast. Cable TV. Indoor pool. Hot tub, sauna. Video games. | 220 W. King St. | 605/734–5575 | 52 rooms, 8 suites | $56–$80, $90 suites | AE, D, DC, MC, V.

Cedar Shore Resort. This independent resort and campground built in 1995 is 2 mi from downtown right along the Missouri River. All rooms have decks or balconies. The lobby and atrium have a contemporary design, with 30 ft ceilings and original South Dakota artwork. Conference center. Restaurant, bar, dining room, room service. In-room data ports, some microwaves, some refrigerators. Cable TV. Indoor pool. Hot tub, sauna. Tennis court. Basketball, exercise equipment, hiking, horseback riding, volleyball. Water sports, fishing. Laundry facilities. Pets allowed (fee). | 3.5 mi from Exit 260 off I–90; 1500 Shoreline Dr., Ocoma | 605/734–6376, 888/697–6363 | fax 605/734–6854 | info@cedarshore.com | www.cedarshore.com | 99 rooms, 8 suites | $89–$99 | AE, D, DC, MC, V.

Comfort Inn. Built in 1976, this Comfort Inn is on service road I–92 between Crowcreek and Loperool casinos. Hunting, fishing, and boating are available nearby. Cable TV. Hot tub. Pets allowed (fee). | 203 E. Hwy. 16 | 605/734–4222 or 800/228–5151 | fax 605/734–4222 | www.comfortinn.com | 35 rooms | $59–$159 | AE, D, DC, MC, V.

Oasis Inn. The rooms are standard, but some of them come with views of the Missouri River. In fact, this hotel is well located for fishing and water sports and is within walking distance of several restaurants. Bar, picnic area, complimentary Continental breakfast. In-room data ports. Cable TV. Outdoor hot tub, sauna. Playground. Laundry facilities. Pets allowed. | Rte. 16 | 605/734–6061 or 800/635–3559 (in SD) | fax 605/734–4161 | 68 rooms | $70–$79 | AE, D, DC, MC, V.

River View Inn. The rooms are standard but they overlook the river. The inn is near fishing and water activities. From here you can visit the Indian museum, just 1 mi away. Cable TV. Indoor pool. Hot tub, sauna. Laundry facilities. Pets allowed (fee). | 128 N. Front St. | 605/734–6057 | 29 rooms | $50–$72 | Usually closed Nov.–Mar. | AE, D, MC, V.

Riverview Ridge B&B. A little over 3 mi from the town center, these 30 acres on the Missouri River are right on the Lewis and Clark Trail. The story is that Lewis and Clark actually slept under the house. Complimentary breakfast. Laundry service. No pets. No smoking. | HC 69 | 605/734–6084 | www.bbonline.com/sd/riverviewridge/ | 3 rooms (2 with shared bath) | $60–$75 | MC, V.

Super 8. This standard Super 8 accommodation has clean, economical rooms and sits on a hill overlooking the Missouri River. A deck with tables and chairs makes a nice spot to enjoy the view. Complimentary Continental breakfast. Cable TV. Pool. Hot tub, sauna. Video games. Laundry facilities. Pets allowed. | Lakeview Heights and Main St. | 605/734–6548 | 56 rooms | $61 | AE, D, MC, V.

CUSTER

MAP 8, A4

(Nearby towns also listed: Hill City, Hot Springs, Keystone, Rapid City)

This is where George Armstrong Custer's expedition discovered gold in 1874, leading to the gold rush of 1875–76. Situated amid pine-clad cliffs and some of the state's most magnificent scenery, Custer is among the most inviting communities in the state. Just minutes from Mount Rushmore, Crazy Horse, Custer State Park, and the best scenic drives in the region, the community is the ideal headquarters for a Black Hills adventure. Custer's economic mainstay continues to be tourism.

Information: Custer County Chamber of Commerce | 615 Washington St., 57730 | 605/673–2244 or 800/992–9818 | www.custersd.com.

Attractions

★ **Black Hills National Forest.** Custer is the headquarters for the Black Hills National Forest, on the western edge of South Dakota. The forest covers more than 1 million acres and makes up almost half of the entire Black Hills region. Teeming with wildlife and natural beauty, it offers fishing, camping, hiking, mountain biking, and horseback riding. Other entry points are Deadwood, Hill City, Hot Springs, Lead, Rapid City, Spearfish, and Sturgis. | 605/343–8755 | www.fs.fed.us/r2/blackhills | Free.

Cathedral Spires. Granite towers reach above the top of the trees toward the heavens. This registered National Landmark lies on Needles Highway in Custer State Park. | Custer Needles Hwy. | 605/673–2251 | www.state.sd.us/gfp/sdparks | Free.

Centennial Trail. This 111-mi trail crosses the prairie grasslands near Bear Butte State Park and climbs into the Black Hills high country, skirting lakes and streams, monuments, memorials, and campgrounds until it reaches Wind Cave National Park. Hikers are welcome on the entire trail, which is accessible from 22 trailheads. Portions are open to horseback riding and mountain bikers. | 605/673–2251 | Free.

★ **Crazy Horse Memorial.** The colossal mountain carving still in progress depicts Lakota leader Crazy Horse atop his steed. At the memorial's base are a restaurant and gift shop, as well as legendary work by Crazy Horse sculptor Korczak Ziolkowski. | Ave. of the Chiefs | 605/673–4681 | $8 per person, $19 per carload, kids under 6 free.

At the base of the memorial is also one of the most impressive collections of Plains Indian artifacts in the country. The collection is presented in an airy setting of ponderosa pine and skylights at the **Indian Museum of North America.**

Custer County Courthouse Museum. There are 3 floors of artifacts and the region's premier exhibit on General George A. Custer's 1874 Black Hills expedition. Also found here is the first log cabin built in the Black Hills in 1875. | 411 Mt. Rushmore Rd. | 605/673–2443 | Free | June–Aug., Mon.–Sat. 9–9, Sun. 1–9; Sept., call for hours.

★ **Custer State Park.** This is one of the region's true treasures and South Dakota's crown jewel. You'll find 83 square mi of preserve alternating between alpine meadows, rolling foothills, pine forests, and fingerlike granite spires that jut up from the surrounding landscape; as well as accessible wildlife, forest trails, gurgling brooks, and one of the nation's largest bison herds. There's camping, summer theater, and 4 rustic mountain retreats. | HC 83 | 605/255–4515 | www.state.sd.us | May–Oct. $4 per person, $10 per vehicle (good for seven days); Nov.–Apr. $3 per person, $8 per vehicle (good for seven days) | Daily.
The **Peter Norbeck Visitor Center Museum** includes park history exhibits and mounts in a rugged granite and wood structure. | 605/255–4464 | Mid-May–Memorial Day, daily 9–5; Memorial Day–Labor Day, daily 8–8; Labor Day–Oct., daily 9–5.

Flintstones Bedrock City. Step into Bedrock at this Stone Age fun park with rides on the Flintmobile and the Iron Horse train. Play areas, a theater, camping, gifts, and brontoburgers and dinodogs at the drive-in round out the Flintstone experience. | U.S. 16/385 | 605/673–4079 | $6 | Mid-May–mid-Sept., daily 8:30–8.

Jewel Cave National Monument. This is the world's third-longest cave, with over 120 mi of known passages. The cave was formed as water dissolved minerals out of the limestone. Exploration is hampered by the fact that the caves are still prone to flooding. Rare and unusual boxwork, frostwork, and popcorn formations, as well as stalactites, stalagmites, and crystals are here. An elevator takes you 234 ft underground to view this incredible maze. Tours are available. | 605/673–2288 | $8; special rate for children, kids under 6 free | Memorial Day–Labor Day, daily 8–7:30; Labor Day–Memorial Day, daily 8–4; call for tour hours.

National Museum of Woodcarving. The work of an original Disneyland animator and works by prominent caricature carvers are displayed here alongside works by more than 70 artists. | 605/673–4404 | $6 | May–Oct., daily; call for hours.

SIGHTSEEING TOURS/TOUR COMPANIES

Golden Circle Tours. You can enjoy motorcoach, mountain-bike, or customized tours with advice from people who know the trails. | 1 mi east of Custer on U.S. 16A | 605/673–4349 | Tour prices vary | May–Sept., daily; call to arrange tours.

ON THE CALENDAR

MAY: *Crazy Horse Memorial Day Weekend Open House.* The open house, with guest artists and craftspeople, is free for residents of South Dakota, North Dakota, Wyoming, and the Nebraska Panhandle. | 605/673–4681 | Memorial Day weekend.
MAY: *Spring Open House.* Free park admission, free fishing, and a variety of special events suitable for the entire family can be found during this open house. | 605/255–4515.
JUNE: *Crazy Horse Stampede and Gifts from Mother Earth Celebration.* PRCA and Great Plains Indian Rodeo Association action are combined with a Native American and western arts and crafts show and sale. The celebration includes a Native American fashion show and sale. | 605/673–4681.
JUNE: *Crazy Horse Volksmarch.* This 10K volksmarch is a rare opportunity to hike up the mountain carving in progress. | 605/673–4681 | First weekend in June.

JULY: *Gold Discovery Days.* You can take in the pageant of the Paha Sapa, a parade, carnival, balloon rally, festival in the park, arts and crafts fair, bed races, fun run/walk, firemen's ball, and more. | 800/992–9818.

OCT.: *Custer State Park Buffalo Roundup.* This is one of the nation's largest buffalo roundups, and one of South Dakota's most exciting events. Watch as cowboys and park crews saddle up and corral the park's 1,400 head of bison. Check out the Buffalo Roundup Arts Festival and Buffalo Wallow Chili Cook-off. | 605/255–4515.

Dining

Bavarian Restaurant. German. Set in a German-style building with murals of German country scenes on the walls of its dining room, this family-style restaurant and lounge offers buffets, as well as German and American meals at reasonable prices. The popular dish here is *rouladen* (thinly sliced sirloin wrapped with mustard, bacon, and a dill pickle and seared then baked for several hours until wonderfully tender). Of course, you may prefer one of the standbys such as prime rib. A fine selection of German beers and liqueurs is available. Buffet dining is available. Kids' menu. | U.S. 16/385 N | 605/673–4412 | Breakfast also available (May–Sept.) Closed Feb. | $10–$16 | D, MC, V.

Blue Bell Lodge and Resort. American. After feasting in a rustic log dining room, you can try a hayride capped with a chuckwagon cookout. Blue Bell is known for fresh trout and buffalo, which you can have as a steak or as stew. Kids' menu. | Rte. 87 S | 605/255–4531 or 800/658–3530 | Breakfast also available. Closed mid-Oct.–Mother's Day | $19–$20 | AE, D, MC, V.

Chief Restaurant. American. One of Custer's 30 restaurants, the Chief has family-style dining and a broad menu. You can dine on buffalo steaks and burgers, a Philly steak sandwich, or the "Cochise buffalo steak" (a tender sirloin filet with herb butter), as well as prime rib. Many of the tables are set up around a large indoor fountain. There is a salad bar and the service is family-style. Kids' menu. | 140 Mt. Rushmore Rd. | 605/673–4402 | Breakfast also available. Closed Nov.–mid-Apr. | $10–$20 | AE, D, MC, V.

Heritage Village. American. Four main courses, including buffalo stew and great burgers, are accompanied by a foot-stomping music show. Set in a renovated barn, the restaurant has a rustic theme with exposed wood and western art. There is also a rodeo clown museum here. A salad bar is available. The music show begins at 8 PM. Kids' menu. | 1 Village Ave., Crazy Horse | 605/673–4761 | Breakfast also available. Closed mid-Oct.–mid-May | $10 | AE, D, MC, V.

Laughing Water Restaurant. Native American. This airy pine restaurant with windows facing the Crazy Horse Memorial is noted for its fry bread and buffalo burgers. There's a soup and salad bar, but you'd do well to stick to the Native American offerings—try the Indian taco and Buffaloski (a Polish sausage made with Dakota buffalo). Kids' menu. | Ave. of the Chiefs. | 605/673–4681 | Closed Nov.–Apr. | $8–$16 | AE, D, MC, V.

Skyway. American. This easygoing family restaurant serves chicken-fried steak, liver and onions, buffalo ground round, and several Mexican dishes. | 511 Mt. Rushmore Rd. | 605/673–4477 | Breakfast also available | $6–$15 | AE, D, DC, MC, V.

State Game Lodge and Resort. American. You can eat in the historic Pheasant Dining Room, an upscale, impressive setting once frequented by President Calvin Coolidge, who made it his summer White House in 1927. The menu is varied, and the place is known for pheasant and buffalo specialties. There is a salad bar and a lunch buffet. Kids' menu. | HCR 83 | 605/255–4541 or 800/658–3530 | Breakfast also available. Closed mid-Oct.–Mother's Day | Reservations required | $15–$28 | AE, D, MC, V.

Sylvan Lake Resort. American. The Lakota Dining Room has an exceptional view of Sylvan Lake and Harney Peak, the highest point between the Rockies and the Swiss Alps. On the menu are buffalo selections, including steaks. You can enjoy your cocktail or tea out on the veranda. The rainbow trout is also good. There is a salad bar and a lunch buffet. Kids' menu. | 605/574–2561 | Breakfast also available. Closed Oct.–Mother's Day | $10–$20 | AE, D, MC, V.

Lodging

American President's Resort (Cabins and Camp). This resort specializes in family reunions. The individual cabins come complete with kitchens. Camping with full hookups is available. Picnic areas. Some kitchenettes. Pool. Spa. Miniature golf. Horseback riding. Playground. Laundry facilities. | U.S. 16A | 605/673–3373 | www.presidentsresort.com | 45 cabins, 15 rooms, 70 campsites | $65–$99, $70–$100 cabins, $19–$27 campsites | D, MC, V.

Bavarian Inn. This looks just like a traditional German resort nestled in the pines; some rooms have views of the Black Hills, and all upstairs rooms open onto balconies with seating areas. The inn is less than 1 mi from downtown. Special rates are available for families with children under 12. Restaurant, bar. Cable TV. 2 pools (1 indoor). Hot tub, sauna. Tennis. Video games. Playground. Some pets allowed. | U.S. 16/385 N | 605/673–2802 or 800/657–4312 | fax 605/673–4777 | www.custer-sd.com/bavariansd/bavarian | 64 rooms | $80–$83 | AE, D, DC, MC, V.

Blue Bell Lodge and Resort. This hideaway retreat in Custer State Park has a western flavor. The modern hand-crafted log cabins have fireplaces, a lodge, and a conference center. There is a campground on the premises, and hayrides and cookouts are part of the entertainment. A stable offers trail rides and overnight pack trips on old Indian trails. Restaurant, bar, picnic area. No air-conditioning, some kitchenettes, some refrigerators. Cable TV, some room phones. Hiking, horseback riding. Playground. Laundry facilities. Some pets allowed. | 605/255–4531 or 800/658–3530 | fax 605/255–4706 | e-mail@custerresorts.com | www.custerresorts.com | 29 cabins | $87–$170 (2–8 people) | Closed Oct.–Mother's Day | AE, D, MC, V.

Custer Mansion. This antiques-furnished B&B is a Victorian Gothic mansion listed on the National Register of Historic Places. The mansion, which is 5 mi from Crazy Horse and 17 mi from Mount Rushmore, sits on 1/4 acres of gardens and aspen trees that you're free to wander. One of the six guest rooms has a TV and VCR. Picnic area, complimentary breakfast. No air-conditioning. TV and VCR in common area, no room phones. Some in-room hot tubs. Outdoor hot tub. No smoking. | 35 Centennial Dr. | 605/673–3333 | fax 605/673–6696 | 6 rooms | $74–$124 | MC, V.

Fobaire Ranch. Two separate rustic log cabins each sit on 4 acres of a 225-acre cattle ranch, with a porch and full kitchen. For outdoor eating there are BBQ grills, an old time jack pump for water, and picnic tables surrounded by a pond and forest. The ranch is 2 mi west of Custer. The Crazy Horse Monument is within hiking distance. Picnic area. Hiking. Fishing. Laundry service. No pets. | Rt. 1 | 605/673–5592 | 2 cabins | $75–$150 | MC, V.

French Creek Guest Ranch B&B. You can soak up views of the Needles formation while porch-sitting at this luxurious "bed-and-barn" on a 25-acre working horse ranch. French Creek is designed to meet the needs of the traveling horse owner: the stable has eight wooden box stalls each with its own run, and four large corrals with wooden fencing. Horses may be boarded for an additional fee. Facilities are also available for a horse trailer or camper hookup. The ranch is 1 1/2 mi from Custer State Park. Restaurant, complimentary Continental breakfast. Refrigerators in rooms. Sauna. Tennis court. Basketball, hiking, horseback riding, volleyball. Fishing. No kids under 13. | 605/673–4790 or 877/673–4790 | fax 605/673–4767 | mikebb@frenchcreekranch.com | www.frenchcreekranch.com | 2 rooms | $115 | MC, V.

Legion Lake Resort. This is a family-oriented rustic lakeside lodge with cabins surrounded by a pine forest in Custer State Park (which has an entrance fee). Restaurant. No air-conditioning. Some kitchenettes. No room phones. Hiking. Beach, boating, bicycles. Playground. Pets allowed. | HC 83 | 605/255–4521 or 800/658–3530 | fax 605/255–4753 | e-mail@custerresorts.com | www.custerresorts.com | 25 cabins | $75–$120 | Closed Oct.–Mother's Day | AE, D, MC, V.

Raspberry and Lace B&B This historic B&B 8 mi north of Custer, 6 mi south of Hill City, and 4 mi from the Crazy Horse monument is next to the Mickleson Trail, an old railroad path. There's a trout stream on the property. Refrigerators. Hot tub. Hiking, fishing. No pets. | 12175 White Horse Rd. | 605/574–4920 | rasplacebb@aol.com | www.raspberryandlace.com | 4 rooms | $85–$95 | AE, D, MC, V.

State Game Lodge and Resort. Once the summer White House for Presidents Coolidge and Eisenhower, this stately stone-and-wood lodge has well-appointed rooms and pine-shaded cabins. There are also Jeep rides into the buffalo area. Restaurant, bar, picnic area. No air-conditioning in some rooms, kitchenettes (in some cabins). Cable TV, some room phones. Hiking. Some pets allowed. | HC 83 | 605/255–4541 or 800/658–3530 | fax 605/255–4706 | e-mail@custerresorts.com | www.custerresorts.com | 7 lodge rooms, 40 motel rooms, 33 cabins | $75–$215 lodge rooms, $89–$132 motel rooms, $75–$315 cabins | Closed Oct.–Mother's Day | AE, D, MC, V.

Strutton Inn B&B. This luxurious 3-story Victorian home with king-size rooms sits on 4 acres. It's in the heart of the Black Hills, which can be enjoyed from the 140 ft veranda with a gazebo on each corner looking out over a lovely garden. Inside this well-furnished retreat there are an antique doll and crystal collection and a 46-inch big screen TV. The inn is within 20 mi of Mt. Rushmore and Crazy Horse Monument; Custer Park is 2 mi from downtown. Complimentary breakfast. Microwaves, refrigerators. Airport shuttle. No pets. No smoking. | 605/673–4808 or 800/226–2611 | fax 605/673–2395 | strutton@gwtc.net | www.strutton-inn.cc | 9 rooms | $70–$135 | MC, V.

Super 8. This typical Super 8 motel is 20 mi south of Mount Rushmore and within walking distance of several restaurants. Some rooms have views of the Black Hills. Complimentary Continental breakfast. Cable TV. Pool. Laundry facilities. | 415 W. Mt. Rushmore Rd. (U.S. 16) | 605/673–2200 | fax 605/673–2201 | 54 rooms | $96 | AE, D, DC, MC, V.

Sylvan Lake Resort. The spacious stone-and-wood lodge overlooks pristine Sylvan Lake. Rustic cabins, some with fireplaces, are scattered along the cliff and in the forest. Numerous hiking trails make this a great choice for active families. Restaurant, bar, dining room, picnic area. No air-conditioning in some rooms, kitchenettes (in many cabins). Lake. Hiking. Beach, boating. | HC 83 | 605/574–2561 or 800/658–3530 | fax 605/574–4943 | e-mail@custerresorts.com | www.custerresorts.com | 35 rooms in lodge, 31 cabins | $85–$130 lodge rooms, $82–$215 cabins | Closed Oct.–Mother's Day | AE, D, MC, V.

DEADWOOD

MAP 8, A3

(Nearby towns also listed: Belle Fourche, Lead, Rapid City, Spearfish, Sturgis)

Once known as the wildest and woolliest gold camp in the West, Deadwood has been tamed a bit since it was founded in the 1870s by a wave of miners, muleskinners, and madams who sought the new El Dorado in gold-filled Deadwood Gulch. In fact, over the last decade more than $85 million has been invested in restoration and preservation projects in the mile-high community, earning the whole town a designation as a National Historic Landmark. As you enter the town you'll find yourself greeted by ornate Victorian facades, brick streets, and period lighting that echo Deadwood's past. The real fun is found in nearly 80 gaming halls that grace downtown, many with restaurants and live entertainment.

Information: Deadwood Area Chamber of Commerce, and Visitors Bureau | 735 Main St., 57732 | 605/578–1876 or 800/999–1876 | www.deadwood.org.

Attractions

Adams Memorial Museum. The oldest history museum in the Black Hills is an exceptional repository of historic memorabilia from Deadwood's past. There are frequent special exhibits and events. | 54 Sherman St. | 605/578–1714 | Free | May–Sept., Mon.–Sat. 9–6, Sun. noon–5; Oct.–Apr., Mon.–Sat. 10–5.

Broken Boot Gold Mine. Join guides on a journey into an authentic underground gold mine and pan for gold. If nothing else, you'll receive a souvenir stock certificate. | Upper Main Street, Hwy. 14A | 605/578–9997 | $4.50; gold panning $4.50 extra | May–Aug., daily 8–5:30; Sept., daily 9–4:30.

Casino Gambling. Deadwood has offered casino-style gaming for more than a decade; just don't expect the glitz of Las Vegas or Atlantic City. In Deadwood, you can check out nearly 80 small gaming halls in the downtown area, many with elaborate century-old Victorian facades. The town is listed as a National Historic Landmark. Each gaming hall has its own charm and ambience, but check out the **Franklin Hotel** (700 Main St. | 605/578–2241 or 800/688–1876), the town's oldest building and gaming hall, and the **Midnight Star** (677 Main St. | 605/578–1555), the town's tallest building and owned by none other than actor Kevin Costner.

Ghosts of Deadwood Gulch Wax Museum. This is a western heritage wax museum with scenes depicting Deadwood's most turbulent years. Included is a progressive audio-visual presentation with 19 episodes. | Old Town Hall, 12 Lee Street | 605/578–3583 | $5; special rate for children | Memorial Day–Labor Day, daily 9–5.

Mickelson Trail. This 114-mi trail, named for the late Governor George S. Mickelson, is one of the most recent additions to Black Hills outdoor recreation opportunities. Thirteen trail-heads, most with parking, toilets, and tables, provide access to this rails-to-trails project extending across the back-country from Deadwood to Edgemont. Bicycles and horses are allowed on the trail. A trail pass (required for users aged 12 and up) can be purchased at self-service trail stations at most trailheads. | HC 37, Lead | 605/584–3896 | $2 trail pass required for hikers 12 and up.

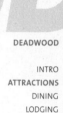

DEADWOOD

INTRO
ATTRACTIONS
DINING
LODGING

INDIANS, SODBUSTERS, AND GOLD SEEKERS

An ample exploration of South Dakota's history will yield one inevitable conclusion: a great deal of blood, sweat, and tears has flowed through the prairie grasses and past the ponderosa pines of this rough and tumble state.

With virtually every step, today's visitor will retrace the footprints of a thousand faceless Indians, madams, muleskinners, sodbusters, and gold seekers who variously sought their fortune, fame, or mere subsistence in this often unforgiving land.

In South Dakota, a traveler can see 100 mi to the horizon and retrace 100 years in a day. At Bear Butte, Wounded Knee, and a hundred other sites revered by Native Americans, visitors can come to understand the plight of the region's first inhabitants. Indeed, from the frontier forts and simple sod shanties that followed pioneers across the vast grasslands of eastern South Dakota to the Victorian architecture so exquisitely preserved on the brick-lined streets of Deadwood, the smell of history permeates this place.

In a relatively young state such as South Dakota, residents have striven to preserve a rich and colorful past, perhaps because their history is so recent. In so doing, they have captured the spark of individuality that helped settle the West, tame the raging rivers, and harness the land with horse, pick, and plow.

© Artville

Mount Moriah Cemetery. This cemetery is the final resting place for such notables as Wild Bill Hickok and Calamity Jane along with lesser lights like Potato Creek Johnny. You can pick up a walking map with tombsite locations and some interesting tales. | 1 Smith Rd. | 605/578–1087 | $1 | Memorial Day–Labor Day, daily 7–8; Labor Day–end of Sept., daily 9–5.

Old Style Saloon #10. The Saloon is billed as the only museum in the world with a bar. Thousands of artifacts, vintage photos, and even a 2-headed calf can be found in this hangout, where you can go to party. You'll find live entertainment nightly, gaming, and excellent food upstairs at the Deadwood Social Club. A reenactment of "The Shooting of Wild Bill Hickok" is featured 4 times a day in the summer months. | 657 Main St. | 605/578–3346 | www.salon10.com | Free | Memorial Day–Labor Day, Sun.–Mon. 8 AM–2 AM, Tues.–Sat. 8 AM–3 AM; Labor Day–Memorial Day, daily 8 AM–2 AM.

SIGHTSEEING TOURS/TOUR COMPANIES

Boot Hill Tours. You can take a narrated 1-hour bus tour of Deadwood and Mount Moriah. The starting point is on Main St. near the Bodega Bar. | 662 Main St. | 605/578–3758 | $6 | June–early Oct., daily 9:30, 11, 1, and 5.

Original Deadwood Tour. This is an entertaining and informative hour-long bus tour of Deadwood and Mount Moriah Cemetery. | 677 Main St. | 605/578–2091 | $6.75 | May–late Sept., daily 10:30, 11:30, 1:30, and 3:30.

ON THE CALENDAR

FEB.: _Chinese New Year._ Included in this free celebration are lion dancers, a parade, a yellow doll contest, martial arts demonstrations, and citywide drink, food, and entertainment specials. | 800/999–1876.
FEB.: _Mardi Gras._ You'll find a Cajun cook-off with free tastings, costumes, decorations, a parade of lights, and food and drink specials citywide. | 800/999–1876.
MAR.: _St. Patrick's Day Celebration._ This is one of the zaniest nights of the year in the Black Hills. There's a parade, live music, Irish food, and more. | 800/999–1876.
JUNE: _Wild Bill Days._ Battle of the bands, kids' games, vendors, and big-name entertainment can all be found at this event on Main St. | 800/999–1876.
JUNE–AUG.: _Trial of Jack McCall._ You can watch a reenactment on Main St. of the shoot-out and capture of Jack McCall, murderer of famed lawman and scout Wild Bill Hickok, at 8 PM, except Sun. After the "capture," McCall is escorted to Town Hall where he is placed on trial in a historic Miner's Court. | 605/578–3583 or 605/578–2510.
JULY: _Days of '76._ This event has a beautiful Black Hills backdrop, the finest setting for a rodeo in the world. A PRCA rodeo, two 3-mi parades with vintage carriages and coaches, free street dances, and a western arts and crafts festival make this one of the best events in South Dakota. | 800/999–1876.
SEPT.: _Deadwood Jam._ This is the Black Hills' premier music event, with top names in country, rock, and blues music. It's held on Main St. | 800/999–1876 or 605/578–1876.
OCT.: _Deadweird._ This Halloween celebration includes a citywide costume contest with cash prizes, a haunted house that will make you scream, and one of the rowdiest nights in a town known for being wild and woolly. | 800/999–1876 | Oct. 31.
OCT.: _Octoberfest._ Here's some traditional German fun with polka music and a home-brew contest, a German food cook-off, and free concerts on Main St. | 800/999–1876.

Dining

Bully's Bullock Hotel (Bully's Restaurant). American. Sit back and relax by the fireplace while you enjoy a steak or hamburger at this casual, relaxed spot. | 633 Main St. | 605/578–1745 or 800/336–1876 | Dinner only | $8–$18 | AE, MC, V.

Creekside Restaurant. American. Part of the Deadwood Gulch Resort, this restaurant is decorated like an old saloon, complete with a bar from the 1880s. You'll find yourself greeted with hearty breakfasts and plate-size steaks. The rib-eye steak is considered by some to be the best steak in town, and the apple-almond chicken is a crowd pleaser as well. | Hwy. 85 S | 605/578–1294 or 800/695–1876 | Breakfast also available | $10–$20 | AE, D, MC, V.

★ **Deadwood Social Club.** Northern Italian. You'll find a homey, relaxed setting with light jazz and blues playing in the background, historic photos on the walls, and one of South Dakota's best wine selections in the cellar. The restaurant is known for Black Angus beef and chicken, seafood, and pasta dishes. | 657 Main St. | 605/578–3346 or 800/952–9398 | Closed Mon. | $7.95–$17.95 | AE, MC, V.

Diamond Lil's. American. Serving burgers and chicken sandwiches, this sports bar has Kevin Costner memorabilia. | 677 Main St. | 605/578–3550 | No breakfast | $4–$15 | DC, MC, V.

Franklin Hotel Dining Room. American. Charbroiled steaks, buffalo, pasta, and vegetarian dishes are served in a Victorian dining room with a bar in this downtown restaurant. | 700 Main St. | 605/578–2241 | $8–$18 | AE, DC, MC, V.

Jake's. Contemporary. Owned by actor Kevin Costner, this may well be South Dakota's premier dining experience. You can enjoy elegant dining in an atrium setting. Cherry wood, fireplaces, and special lighting enhance the experience. Some interesting choices are the buffalo roulade, Cajun seafood tortellini, filet mignon, or fresh fish. You can listen to a pianist while you eat. | Midnight Star Casino, 677 Main St. | 605/578–1555 | Closed Sun. No lunch | $19–$29 | Reservations required | AE, D, DC, MC, V.

Lodging

Best Western Hickok House. This two-story motel with a casino on-site is eight blocks from downtown, Exit 17 off I–90, Hwy. 85 S Restaurant, bar, dining room. Cable TV. Hot tub. Laundry service. No pets. | 137 Charles St. | 605/578–1611 or 800/837–8174 | fax 605/578–1855 | www.bestwestern.com | 45 rooms | $50–$100 | AE, D, MC, V.

Branch House. This two-story redbrick hotel with skylights is in downtown Deadwood. Restaurant. Complimentary Continental breakfast. No air-conditioning in some rooms, in-room data ports, some microwaves, some refrigerators. Cable TV. Business services. Laundry service. No pets. | 37 Sherman St. | 605/578–1745 or 800/336–1876 | fax 605/578–1382 | www.bullockhotel.com/branch.htm | 8 rooms | $69–$89 | AE, D, DC, MC, V.

★ **Bullock Hotel.** A casino occupies the main floor of this meticulously restored hotel, which was built by Deadwood's first sheriff, Seth Bullock, in 1895. You can spot the hotel's pink granite facade right away. Reproductions of the original furniture complement the hospitality bars, and hot tubs are offered in the suites. The rooms are furnished in a Victorian style. Restaurant, bar, room service. Some in-room hot tubs. Cable TV. Business services. | 633 Main St. | 605/578–1745 or 800/336–1876 | fax 605/578–1382 | hub@mato.com | www.bullockhotel.com | 28 rooms | $75–$155 | AE, D, MC, V.

Calamity Rose. This exquisite 3-story Victorian B&B built in 1896 is furnished lavishly with antiques, yet designed with understated elegance. You can stay in one of four suites and one single queen room. Calamity Rose is within 5 blocks of casinos and downtown, with some 60 attractions within an hour's drive. Complimentary breakfast. Cable TV. Laundry service. No pets. No smoking. | 21 Lincoln Ave. | 605/578–1151 or 877/518–1151 | fax 605/578–3193 | calamity@mato.com | www.calamityrose.com | 1 room, 4 suites | $64–$99 | AE, MC, V.

Days Inn Deadwood Gulch Resort. Pine-clad hills and a creek await you at this family-style resort, which also has a casino and a deck with a view of the mountains. It's about 1 mi from town, and a trolley stops in front of the hotel to take you to various sites in Deadwood. There is nearby hiking, horseback riding, fly-fishing, biking, and snowmobiling on the Mickelson Trail. Restaurant (see Creekside Restaurant), bar. Cable TV. Pool. Hot tub. Hiking. Bicycles. Some pets allowed (fee). | Hwy. 85 S | 605/578–1294 or 800/695–1876 | fax 605/578–2505 | www.deadwoodgulch.com | 98 rooms | $109 | AE, D, DC, MC, V.

Franklin Hotel. Built in 1903, the imposing Franklin Hotel in the heart of Deadwood has housed many famous guests, including John Wayne, Teddy Roosevelt, and Kevin Costner. The original banisters, ceilings, and fireplace add character. A casino is in the hotel. Restaurant, bar (with entertainment). Room service. Cable TV. Business services. Some pets allowed. | 700 Main St. | 605/578–2241 or 800/688–1876 | fax 605/578–3452 | franklin@deadwood.net | www.deadwood.net/franklin | 81 rooms | $92 | AE, D, DC, MC, V.

Holiday Inn Express. This 4-story chain hotel has fireplaces and 3 whirlpool rooms, as well as a meeting room and banquet facilities. There is also an on-site casino. Skiing at Terry Peak and Deer Mountain are within 6 mi. Complimentary Continental breakfast. In-room data ports, kitchenettes. Heated pool. Hot tub. Exercise equipment. No pets. | 22 Lee St. | 605/578–3330 or 888/777–4465 | fax 605/578–3335 | www.hiexpress.com/deadwoodsd | 78 rooms, 22 suites | $129–$199 | AE, D, DC, MC, V.

Mineral Palace. A recent addition to Main St., the Mineral Palace was built to blend in with historic Deadwood. This full-service hotel has a king suite with a hot tub and fireplace. A casino and cappuccino bar are in the hotel. Restaurant, bar, room service. Some refrigerators, some in-room hot tubs. Cable TV. Videogames. Business services. | 601 Main St. | 605/578–2036 or 800/847–2522 | fax 605/578–2037 | mpalace@deadwood.com | 63 rooms | $99, suites $125–$195 | AE, D, MC, V.

KODAK'S TIPS FOR PHOTOGRAPHING PEOPLE

Friends' Faces
- Pose subjects informally to keep the mood relaxed
- Try to work in shady areas to avoid squints
- Let kids pick their own poses

Strangers' Faces
- In crowds, work from a distance with a telephoto lens
- Try posing cooperative subjects
- Stick with gentle lighting—it's most flattering to faces

Group Portraits
- Keep the mood informal
- Use soft, diffuse lighting
- Try using a panoramic camera

People at Work
- Capture destination-specific occupations
- Use tools for props
- Avoid flash if possible

Sports
- Fill the frame with action
- Include identifying background
- Use fast shutter speeds to stop action

Silly Pictures
- Look for or create light-hearted situations
- Don't be inhibited
- Try a funny prop

Parades and Ceremonies
- Stake out a shooting spot early
- Show distinctive costumes
- Isolate crowd reactions
- Be flexible: content first, technique second

HILL CITY

(Nearby towns also listed: Custer, Keystone, Rapid City)

With 400 sleeping rooms, a dozen restaurants, 19 campgrounds, and 8 service stations, Hill City is well equipped to take advantage of its proximity to Mount Rushmore and Crazy Horse by offering quality guest conveniences. The town was founded in 1876 by gold miners, and today Hill City's art galleries and restaurants are among the best in the Black Hills. The bank robbery and shoot-out staged on Main St. in the summer months is a kick. For an authentic ride aboard a steam-powered train, check out the Black Hills Central Railroad. Tourism is what drives Hill City's economy, although the pine forests surrounding the community have also become a popular haven for retirees.

Information: **Hill City Area Chamber of Commerce** | Box 253, 57745 | 605/574–2368 or 800/888–1798 | www.hillcitysd.com.

Attractions

Pactola Reservoir. This reservoir in the Black Hills National Forest is surrounded by ponderosa pine forests and has a public beach, three picnic areas, two scenic overlooks, two campgrounds, two boat-launch facilities, hiking trails, and the Pactola Pines Marina, a full-service facility with pontoon rentals, gasoline, and a convenience store with supplies. | Hwy. 385, 15 mi north of Hill City | 605/343–8755 | www.fs.fed.us/bhnf | Free | Mid-May–Oct. 1, daily 8:30–6.

Sheridan Lake. The lake has 400 surface acres and is surrounded by ponderosa pine forests, picnic areas, and hiking trails. The facilities include two public beaches and a full-service marina with slip rental, boat rental, convenience store, gasoline, and supplies. Group and individual campsites are available. It costs $3 for a National Forest Service day-use permit. The marina is closed when ice is too thick to boat or too thin to ice fish. | 16451 Sheridan Lake Rd., 9 mi north of Hill City | 605/574–2169 | www.sheridanlakemarina.com | Memorial Day–Labor Day, $3; Labor Day–Memorial Day, free.

Sylvan Rocks Climbing Lessons and Adventures. You can try rock climbing at Sylvan Rocks. Classes range from beginner to advanced and the maximum number of climbers per guide is 3. | 301 Main St., Hill City | 605/574–2425 | fax 605/342–1487 | $125–$425 | Call ahead for hours.

SIGHTSEEING TOURS/TOUR COMPANIES

Black Hills Central Railroad. You step back in time when you board this train. The antique steam locomotive takes you through the Black Hills back-country from Hill City to Keystone. | Hill City Depot, Railroad Ave. | 605/574–2222 | $16 | Mid-May–early Oct., four daily departures; call for schedule; reservations required.

Wade's Gold Mill. You can take an educational tour of a historic mining museum with gold panning, a modern placer mill, a stamp mill powered by a steam engine, and an extensive historic photo collection. | 12401 Deerfield Rd. | 605/574–2680 or 605/574–2279 | $8; panning $5 extra | Memorial Day–Labor Day, daily 9–6.

ON THE CALENDAR

MAY–SEPT.: *Bank Robbery and Shoot Out.* Weeknights from 7–7:30, western characters stroll Main St. Following a demonstration in front of City Hall, a shoot-out takes place with desperadoes. | 605/574–2368.

JULY: *Heart of the Hills Celebration and Parade.* An annual parade of more than 80 entries is held in conjunction with the Heart of the Hills Logging Show, which features tree felling, ax throwing, log bucking, and a hot saw competition. | 605/574–2368 or 605/574–4417.

SEPT.: *Hill City 10K Volksmarch.* This 10K walk threads along the Mickelson Trail in Black Hills National Forest. A daily trail pass ($2.00) is required. | 605/388–0611.

Dining

Alpine Inn. American. Here you'll find European charm in the Old West. The lunchtime menu changes daily but always includes an array of healthy selections from sandwiches to salads (with no fried food). The dinner menu includes only one item: filet mignon. Lunch is offered on the veranda overlooking Main St. Beer and wine only are served. | 225 Main St. | 605/574–2749 | Reservations not accepted | Closed Sun. | $5–$10 | No credit cards.

Mount Rushmore Brewing Company. American. Spacious dining is on tap in one of the Black Hills' newest microbreweries, set up in a building listed on the National Historic Register. Exposed brick, wood walls, antiques, a baby grand piano with entertainment weekly, and the visible brewing equipment add to the atmosphere. There is a large selection of wine, microbeers, imports, and espresso. Mount Rushmore is known for super steaks, seafood, pizza, and hearty pub fare, including the popular "white chili" made from great northern beans and chicken and spices. Beer and wine only are served. | 349 Main St. | 605/574–2400 | $6–$15 | May 1–Labor Day | D, MC, V.

Lodging

Best Western Golden Spike Inn. Only minutes from Mount Rushmore and Crazy Horse and 1½ blocks from the Mickelson Trail, the Golden Spike offers comfortable lodging and several rooms with views of the mountains. The pool is the ideal place to relax—it's in a room with wood walls and pine pillars. A garden with scattered tables, an espresso bar, and a gift shop are part of the hotel complex. Restaurant. Cable TV. Indoor pool. Hot tub. Exercise equipment. Bicycles. Video games. Laundry facilities. Some pets allowed. | 106 Main St. | 605/574–2577 or 800/528–1234 | fax 605/574–4719 | 62 rooms | $117 | Closed Nov. 21–Mar. | AE, D, DC, MC, V.

Comfort Inn Hill City. This two-story inn built in 1996 lies only 10 mi northwest of Mt. Rushmore, and 8 mi north of Crazy Horse Monument on the Mickelson Trail. Complimentary breakfast. Cable TV, room phones. Indoor pool. Hot tub. Baby-sitting. No pets. | 678 Main St. | 605/574–2100 or 800/228–5150 | fax 605/574–4936 | www.comfortinn.com | 55 rooms | $59–$119 | Nov. 15–Apr. 15 | AE, D, MC, V.

Coyote Blues Village B&B. This European-style lodge on 30 acres in the midst of the Black Hills (10 mi north of Hill City) displays a unique mix of antique furnishings and contemporary art. The on-site bakery serves up fresh fruit and Swiss muesli with a hearty breakfast on an outdoor deck. Each room has a private deck with a hot tub. A creek runs through the property, which is ideal for hiking. Refrigerators, in-room hot tubs. Cable TV. Gym, hiking. No pets. No smoking. | Hill City | 605/574–4477 or 888/253–4477 | fax 605/574–2101 | coyotebb@dtgnet.com | www.coyotebluesvillage.com | 6 rooms | $60–$125 | D, MC, V.

Deerview Bed and Breakfast. This stone-faced B&B 5 mi west of town and central to the Black Hills is in a private setting of about 3 acres with gardens in a pine forest. The rooms are beautifully decorated and have private baths. You can eat breakfast in your room or take it on the outdoor patio. Hunting and snowmobile trails are available nearby. Complimentary breakfast. Microwaves, refrigerators. Cable TV. Hot tubs. No kids. No smoking. | 12110 Deerfield Rd. | 605/574–4204 | 3 rooms | $105 | D, MC, V.

High Country Guest Ranch. The 16 log cabins at this ranch are on 40 acres surrounded by the Black Hills National Forest 4 mi west of Hill City and 30 min from Mt. Rushmore and Crazy Horse Monument. Cabins can sleep up to 12 and some include a Jacuzzi, a deck porch, and fireplaces. Complimentary breakfast. Some kitchenettes. Heated outdoor pool. Hot tub. Hiking, horseback riding. Fishing. Bicycles. Ice-skating, sleigh rides, snowmobiling. No smoking. | 12172 Deerfield Rd. | 605/574–9003 or 888/222–4628 | fax 605/574–4732 | hcranch@rapidnet.com | www.highcountryranch.com | 16 cabins with 1, 2, or 3 bedrooms | $59–$199 | AE, D, MC, V.

Lodge at Palmer Gulch. In an idyllic mountain valley near Mount Rushmore, the lodge is shadowed by the massive granite ramparts of Harney Peak. With its pools, waterslide, outdoor activities, and children's programs of movies and other entertainment, this is a great place for families. A free shuttle takes you to Mount Rushmore and Crazy Horse. Camping is allowed on the premises. Restaurant, picnic area. No air-conditioning in some rooms. Some kitchenettes. Cable TV, some room phones. 2 outdoor pools. Hot tub, sauna. Miniature golf. Basketball, horseback riding, volleyball. Video games. Children's programs, playground. Pets allowed. | 12620 Hwy. 244 | 605/574–2525 or 800/562–8503 | fax 605/574–2574 | palmerkoa@aol.com | www.travelsd.com | 62 rooms, 30 cabins | $113 | Closed Oct. 15–Apr. 15 | AE, D, MC, V.

HOT SPRINGS

(Nearby town also listed: Custer)

Founded in 1879 by farmers and ranchers who followed gold miners to the Black Hills, Hot Springs is among the oldest tourist destinations in the Black Hills. With tourism as its economic base, Hot Springs continues to draw visitors with such quality attractions as Evans Plunge, a large indoor-outdoor naturally heated pool, the Mammoth Site, where nearly 50 woolly and Columbian mammoths have been unearthed to date, and the nearby Black Hills Wild Horse Sanctuary, home to herds of wild mustangs. When combined with adjacent national parks, this qualifies as a "don't miss" on any vacation itinerary.

Information: Hot Springs Area Chamber of Commerce | 801 S. 6th St. 57747-2962 | 605/745–4140 or 800/325–6991 | www.hotspringssd.com.

Attractions

Angostura Reservoir State Recreation Area. Water-based recreation is the main draw at this area. Four campgrounds and modern facilities complement the park's marina, beachside restaurant, floating convenience store, and modern cabins. Boat and Wave-Runner rentals are available. | Hwy. 385, 10 mi south of Hot Springs | 605/745–6996 | www.state.sd.us/sdparks | $3 per person, $5 per vehicle, $20 annually | Daily dawn to dusk.

Beaver Creek Bridge. Approximately 2 mi north of the Wind Cave Visitors Center is this bridge, built in 1929. The bridge architecture, which incorporates the rock forms at this site, is the only one of its kind in the state. | Hwy. 87 | 605/745–4600 | Free | During park hours.

Black Hills Wild Horse Sanctuary. Hundreds of wild mustangs inhabit this 11,000-acre preserve of rugged canyons, forests, and grasslands nestled along the lazy Cheyenne River. Guided tours and hikes are available, as are chuckwagon dinners and Indian tepees. | Hwy. 71, 10 mi south of Hot Springs | 605/745–5955 or 800/252–6652 | $15 | Memorial Day–Labor Day, Mon.–Sat. 9:30–5; tours at 10, 1, and 3.

Chautauqua Park. Red rock walls form the background as springs cascade and ripple through the ground around picnic tables and fireplaces. | Battle Mountain Ave. and N. River Rd. | 605/745–4140 | Free.

Evans Plunge. Get ready to splash in the world's largest natural warm-water indoor swimming pool. Includes indoor-outdoor pools, waterslides, pool games, traveling rings, a sauna, a steam room, and a fitness center. | 1145 N. River St. | 605/745–5165 | $8 | Memorial Day–Labor Day, weekdays 5:30 AM–10 PM, weekends 8 AM–10 PM.

Fall River County Museum. Set up in a turn-of-the-20th-century schoolhouse, this museum has artifacts and displays relevant to the history of Hot Springs. | 300 N. Chicago St. | 605/745–5147 | Free | May–Oct. 1, Mon.—Sat. 9–5.

Historic District. In 1890, a group of ambitious entrepreneurs decided to make use of the "healing waters" of the town's natural springs and transform them into a health spa. Aided by the arrival of the railroad in 1891 and the construction of many beautiful sandstone buildings, they succeeded, and the town thrived as a spa for two decades. Today, buildings from that era form the community's Historic District, which includes homes, resort hotels, sanatoriums, and commercial buildings erected between 1890 and 1915. | 800/325–6991 | www.hotsprings-sd.com | Free.

★ **Mammoth Site of Hot Springs.** Nearly 50 giant mammoths have already been unearthed from a prehistoric sinkhole where they came to drink 26,000 years ago. You can watch the excavation in progress and take guided tours of this unique discovery. | Southern city limits on U.S. 18 truck bypass | 605/745–6017 or 800/325–6991 | www.mammothsite.com | $5; special rates for senior citizens and children; kids 5 and under free | Daily, call for hours.

Southern Hills Golf Course. This 9-hole course opened in 1979 and was recently listed as the number-one 9-hole course by *Golf Digest*. | 605/745–6400 | Mar.–Oct. | D, MC, V.

Wind Cave National Park. The park is about 7 mi north of Hot Springs. This is the world's seventh-longest cave, and you can explore 92 mi of known passageways. Above ground, discover a 28,000-acre wildlife preserve that is home to bison, pronghorns, and prairie dogs. | Hwy. 385 | 605/745–4600 | Free, tours $6–$20 | Daily 8–6.

ON THE CALENDAR

JUNE: *Mammoth Days.* Includes mammoth games for children, artifacts, demonstrations and displays, a picnic, a social, and more. | 605/745–6017.

SEPT.–OCT.: *Badger Clark Hometown Cowboy Poetry Gathering.* Cowboy musicians and poets join for jam sessions and cowboy show. Admission is $8, special rates for children. | 800/325–6991.

Dining

Elk Horn Cafe. American. Your choices here range from burgers to steaks that are hand cut on the premises. There are also homemade soup, chicken-fried steak, and "death by chocolate" cake. You can eat breakfast on one of the two decks outside with a view of town. | 310 S. Chicago St. | 605/745–6556 | Breakfast also available | $5–$10 | AE, MC, V.

Lodging

Best Western Inn. This two-story inn is three blocks from downtown. Complimentary Continental breakfast. Cable TV. Outdoor pool. | 602 W. River | 605/745–4292 or 888/605–4292 | fax 605/745–3584 | www.bestwestern.com | 32 rooms | $49–$104 | AE, D, DC, MC, V.

Comfort Inn. Near the main highway, U.S. 385, and three blocks from downtown, this hotel offers easy access to the Mueller Civic Center. Family suites are available, and some rooms have views of a small river. Complimentary Continental breakfast. Microwaves, refrigerators. Some in-room hot tubs. Cable TV. Indoor pool. Hot tub. Gym. Laundry facilities. Business services. Pets allowed. | 737 S. 6th St. | 605/745–7378 or 800/228–5150 | fax 605/745–3240 | 51 rooms, 9 suites | $109, $129 suites | AE, D, MC, V.

Dakota Prairie Ranch B&B. This ranch house B&B with country and antique furnishings is just 20 min southeast of Hot Springs, and a short 15 min from the Black Hills, Pine Ridge Indian Reservation, and the Wild Horse Sanctuary. On this fourth-generation cattle ranch you can tag along and help with the chores, go on wagon and trail rides, and visit a prairie dog town. There's a hearty ranch style breakfast; lunch and dinner are provided by prior arrangement. Hunting is available in season. Complimentary breakfast. TV/VCR in common area. Hot tub. Fishing. | Oelrichs | 605/535–2001 or 888/535–2001 | cnlseger@gwtc.net

| www.bbonline.com/sd/dakotaranch | 3 rooms with shared bath, 2 suites | $60–$80 | D, MC, V.

Rocking G Bed and Breakfast. This log-cabin home, approximately 2 mi from the Wind Cave Visitors Center, overlooks the Minnekahta Valley. Complimentary breakfast. TV in common area. Library. | 605/745–3698 | fax 605/745–5527 | rockingg@gwtc.net | 3 rooms | $65–$70 | D, MC, V.

Super 8 Motel. This typical Super 8 accommodation is next to the Mammoth Site and about 1 mi from the Hot Springs restaurants. Many rooms have a view of the Black Hills, and several large family-size rooms are available. Complimentary Continental breakfast. Some microwaves, some refrigerators. Cable TV. Video games. Laundry facilities. Pets allowed. | 800 Mammoth St. | 605/745–3888 or 800/800–8000 | fax 605/745–3385 | www.super8.com | 48 rooms | $92 | AE, D, MC, V.

HURON

MAP 8, G3

(Nearby town also listed: Redfield)

Founded in 1879 by surveyors for the Chicago and Northwestern Railroad, Huron is today a regional hub for manufacturing, shopping, and health facilities, as well as home to the South Dakota State Fair. With its Crossroads Convention Center, Huron has become a favorite for state meetings and conventions. Its Campbell Park Historic District has many preserved buildings from the turn of the 20th century.

Information: Huron Chamber of Commerce and Convention and Visitors Center | 15 4th St. SW 57350-2404 | 605/352–0000 (visitor center) and 605/352–8775 (chamber) or 800/487–6673 | www.huroncvb.com.

Attractions

Campbell Park Historic District. This section of town preserves 89 turn-of-the-20th-century structures, including many residences in the Queen Anne and colonial styles. | Between 5th and 7th streets | 605/352–0000 or 800/487–6673 | Free.

Centennial Center. Often referred to as the Old Stone Church, the 1887 structure, which is listed on the National Register of Historic Places, is now used for weddings, special events, and gatherings. | 48 4th St. SE | 605/352–7255 or 800/487–6673 | Free | Weekdays, afternoons by appointment only.

Dakotaland Museum. You can examine more than 5,000 artifacts and historical documents, maps, and photos related to the settlement of the Huron area with a special emphasis on exhibits related to agricultural development. | 3rd St. on State Fairgrounds | 605/352–4626 or 605/352–2633 | $1 | Memorial Day–Labor Day, daily 9:30–4.

Gladys Pyle Historic Home. The 1894 Queen Anne home of the first woman elected to the U.S. Senate includes original oak woodwork, fixtures, and stained-glass windows. | 376 Idaho Ave. SE | 605/352–2528 | $1.50, children 10 and under free | Daily 1–3:30.

Hubert H. Humphrey Drugstore. Once owned by the father of the former vice president, the drugstore is still home to a variety of mementos from the Humphrey family. Hubert worked in the store during the Depression. | 233 Dakota Ave. S | 605/352–4064 | Free | Mon.–Sat. 9–5.

Laura Ingalls Wilder Memorial. Tours include the memorial to the Ingalls family, familiar from the *Little House on the Prairie* series. In town, you can visit the site of the original home the family lived in during their first year in the Dakotas as well as the gift shop. In the gift shop you can get a road map that details 16 sites mentioned in the books. Free horse-drawn wagon tours on additional acreage that Pa Ingalls farmed are given Friday through Sunday once a month, June to August; call for details. | Homestead Rd. (Memorial); 105 Olivet Ave. (original home and gift shop); 20812 Homestead Rd. (wagon rides); about 32 mi west of Huron | 605/854–3383 or 800/880–3383; for wagon rides, 605/854–3984 | $5; special rate for children | June–Aug., daily 9–6; Sept., Mon.–Sat. 9–4, Sun. noon–4; Oct., Apr., May, Mon.–Sat. 9–4; Nov.–Mar., weekdays 9–4.

ON THE CALENDAR

JUNE: *Laura Ingalls Wilder Pageant.* Held the last weekend of June and the first two weekends of July; actors re-create scenes from the pioneering days of De Smet, where Laura Ingalls Wilder grew up. A pageant based on Laura's life and books is presented outdoors nightly at 9. | 605/692–2108.

JULY: *Heartland Rodeo.* This all 4-H rodeo is a weekend event. | 605/352–8775.

AUG.: *South Dakota State Fair.* Held the first week of August, this is one of the nation's last true agricultural expositions. The main showcases are agriculture, livestock, machinery, education, home arts, and horticultural exhibits. Included is entertainment on 10 free stages, a carnival midway, grandstand shows, a rodeo, and car racing. | State Fairgrounds | 605/353–7340 and 800/529–0900.

NOV.: *Holiday Parade of Lights.* This night parade with floats, vehicles, and marchers decorated with Christmas lights includes hot chocolate, cider, carolers, and more. | 605/352–8775.

Dining

Festivals. American. One of the town's top restaurants, this casual steak house with oak walls, brass trim, and ivory-topped tables is in the Crossroads Convention Center. Popular menu selections include seafood fettuccine, prime rib sandwich, and the mud pie. If you come on Sunday, you can try the Super Sunday Breakfast Buffet. | 100 4th St. SW | 605/352–3204 | Breakfast also available | $9–$18 | AE, D, DC, MC, V.

Library. American. One of the Crossroads Convention Center's two restaurants, this is more formal than Festivals, and also one of the town's best. With its three walls of books and leather chairs, the dining room looks like the library in a well-appointed mansion. Linen tablecloths and stemware add to the appeal. Lobster is a popular choice, as are the T-bone steak and the tomato-basil capellini. | 100 4th St. SW | 605/352–3204 | $15–$31 | AE, D, DC, MC, V.

The Oxbow. American. There's a little of everything—burgers, steaks, fish–on the menu at this homey restaurant run by the Myers family in DeSmet. | Hwy. 14, DeSmet | 605/854–9988 | No credit cards | $4–$13

Lodging

Cottage Inn Motel. Across the street from the Oxbow and also run by the Myers family, this motel has spacious rooms 33 mi from Huron. | Hwy. 14, DeSmet | 605/854–3896 | 37 rooms | $40 | AE, D, DC, MC, V.

Crossroads Hotel and Convention Center. Within walking distance of Huron's business district, the hotel proudly displays the locally sculpted *Spirit of Dakota* on its front lawn. 2 restaurants, bar, room service. In-room data ports, some refrigerators. Cable TV. Indoor pool. Hot tub, sauna. Business services, airport shuttle. Pets allowed. | 100 4th St. | 605/352–3204 | fax 605/352–3204 | 100 rooms | $57–$75 | AE, D, DC, MC, V.

Dakota Inn. Totally remodeled in 1997, this inn stands next to the city park and a scenic bike path. A restaurant is within walking distance. Guide services for pheasant hunting are available. Complimentary Continental breakfast. In-room data ports. Cable TV. Pool. Bowling. Business services. Pets allowed. | 924 4th St. and Hwy. 14E | 605/352–1400 or 800/933–6626 | fax 605/352–1400 | $65 | AE, D, MC, V.

Holiday Inn Express. This facility on the south end of Huron offers clean, comfortable rooms at a moderate price; all the rooms come equipped with irons, ironing boards, and hairdryers. Several restaurants are within walking distance. Huron is known as the "Pheasant Capital of the World," and this hotel fills up a year in advance for the hunting season. Complimentary Continental breakfast. In-room data ports, in-room safes. Some in-room hot tubs. Cable TV. Sauna. Exercise room. Laundry facilities. Pets allowed. | 100 21st St. SW | 605/352–6655 or 800/465–4329 | fax 605/353–1213 | 60 rooms, 8 suites | $70, $89–$125 suites | AE, D, DC, MC, V.

Marie's B&B. This vintage B&B in downtown Huron dates from 1905. There's a collection of Norman Rockwell pictures on the premises. Free Continental breakfast. Cable TV, some room phones. Laundry facilities. | 870 Dakota St. | 605/352–0929 or 877/484–4281 | fax 605/849–3597 | 6 rooms | $35 per person | MC, V.

KEYSTONE

MAP 8, B4

(Nearby towns also listed: Custer, Hill City, Rapid City)

Keystone's 600 motel and hotel rooms, 10 restaurants, 5 campgrounds, 40 gift shops, and proximity to Mount Rushmore make it one of the busiest towns in the Black Hills. Keystone was founded by prospectors, has been sustained by the carving of Mount Rushmore, and is supported today by more than 2.5 million annual visitors who pass through on their way to view the presidential portraits. Among Keystone's key attractions are the Rushmore-Borglum Story (at the Borglum Historical Center), an excellent preamble to any visit to the mountain memorial, and Beautiful Rushmore Cave, which lives up to its name.

Information: Keystone Chamber of Commerce | 110 Swanzey St., 57751-0653 | 605/666–4896 or 800/456–3345 | www.keystonechamber.com.

Attractions

Beautiful Rushmore Cave. Stalagmites, stalactites, flowstone, ribbons, columns, helectites, and the "Big Room" are all part of a worthwhile tour into the depths of the Black Hills. In 1876, miners found the opening to the cave while digging a flume into the mountainside to carry water to the gold mines below. The cave was opened to the public in 1927, just before the carving of Mount Rushmore began. | 13622 Hwy. 40 | 605/255–4384 and 605/255–4634 | www.beautifulrushmorecave.com | $7, special rates for children 7–12 | May 1–Memorial Day and Labor Day–Oct. 31, daily 9–5; Memorial Day–Labor Day, daily 8–8.

Big Thunder Gold Mine. You can take a guided tour through an underground gold mine, get some free gold ore samples, and do a little gold panning. | Route 40 | 605/666–4847 or 800/314–3917 | $6.95 | May–mid-Oct., daily 9–5.

Borglum Historical Center. Here you can study paintings and sculptures by Gutzon Borglum, the creator of Mount Rushmore, and see a collection of the artist's mementos. | 342 Winter St. | 605/666–4448 | $7 | May and Oct., daily 8:30–4; June–Aug., daily 8–7.

Cosmos Mystery Area. This is an unusual and entertaining attraction, where no one stands straight and balls roll uphill. | Hwy. 16, 4 mi north of Keystone | 605/343–9802 | $6 | Apr.–Oct., daily 9:45–4.

Keystone Historical Society Museum. There's a celebration each August 3rd for Carrie Ingall's Day in the old Keystone School Building, with an open house and birthday cake. | Main St. | 605/666–4494 | Free | June 1–Labor Day, Mon.–Sat. 10–4.

★ **Mount Rushmore National Memorial.** One of the nation's most popular attractions is just 3 mi from Keystone. You can now enjoy almost $60 million worth of new visitor facilities, as well as the giant likenesses of Washington, Jefferson, Lincoln, and Theodore Roosevelt. | Hwy. 244 | 605/574–2523 | www.nps.gov/moru | Free, parking $8 annually.

Wildcat Valley Resort and Campground. Here you'll find an exotic wildcat exhibit, a camp store, animal prints, and a chance to pan for gold. | 999 Front St. | 605/255–4059 | $5; special rates for children | Call for hours.

SIGHTSEEING TOURS/TOUR COMPANIES

Rushmore Aerial Tramway. Take this tramway for spectacular views of the surrounding mountains and forests, as well as the famous sculptures from about a mile away. The circuit takes about 20 minutes and you can step out into parkland at the far end to stretch your legs. | 605/666–4478 | $8 | May–mid-Sept., daily 9–6.

Rushmore Helicopter Sightseeing Tours. Choose from among four different trips in this memorable excursion above the fabled Black Hills. One flight offers a close-up view (from 300 ft) of the face of George Washington. | U.S. 16A, in Keystone | 605/666–4461 | Starts at $20 | Mid-May–Sept.; call for days and hours.

ON THE CALENDAR

JULY: *Independence Day Celebration.* The state's largest and most spectacular fireworks display takes place each year under Mount Rushmore accompanied by music and dancing. | 605/574–2523.

SEPT.–OCT.: *Black Hills Autumn Expedition.* Twenty-four days of events celebrate the season throughout the Black Hills region. | 800/456–3345.

Dining

Buffalo Dining Room. American. The building is made of glass and has views of Mount Rushmore; the menu offers a wide range of choices for breakfast, lunch, and dinner, including such standard fare as burgers and pasta but also the very popular buffalo stew. You can choose to end your meal with a "monumental bowl of ice cream." | Hwy. 24 | 605/574–2515 | Breakfast is also available. No dinner mid-Oct.–early Mar. | $6–$11 | AE, D, MC, V.

Ruby House Restaurant and Red Garter Saloon. American. This quiet hideaway with Victorian decor is just a few miles from Mount Rushmore. Popular menu items include buffalo steak, prime rib, and a homemade bread pudding with caramel sauce. | Main St. | 605/666–4404 | Breakfast also available. Closed Nov.–Apr. | $10–$20 | Reservations required | D, MC, V.

Rushmore Supper Club and Lounge. American. This family-owned and -operated restaurant serves steaks, seafood, and homemade Mexican food. You can eat out on the deck or have cocktails down in the basement sports bar. | Main St. | 605/734–6238 | No lunch in winter | $10–$20 | DC, MC, V.

Spokcane Creek Resort. American. You can eat pizza and subs for lunch and dinner and homemade biscuits and gravy for breakfast. | Box 927, Hwy. 16A, Keystone | 605/666–4430 | Closed Labor Day–Memorial Day | $4–$7 | DC, MC, V.

Lodging

Best Western Four Presidents. In the shadow of Mount Rushmore in downtown Keystone, this hotel's rooms have been remodeled. You can walk to the city park and dining. Complimentary Continental breakfast. Some in-room hot tubs. Cable TV. Pets allowed. | 250 Winter St. | 605/666–4472 | fax 605/666–4574 | 33 rooms, 1 suite | $84–$94, $135 suite | All but 3 rooms closed Nov.–Apr. | AE, D, DC, MC, V.

Buffalo Rock Lodge B&B. A large, native rock fireplace surrounded by hefty logs adds to the rustic quality of this lodge decorated with Western artifacts. There's an extensive view of Mt. Rushmore from an oversize deck surrounded by plush pine forests filled with wildflowers. Complimentary Continental breakfast. In-room hot tubs. Hiking. Fishing. Pets allowed. | On Playhouse Rd., 5 mi east of Keystone | 605/666–4781 or 888/564–5634 | 3 rooms | $125–$150 | DC, MC, V.

Holy Smoke Resort. The log cabins and the historic Nugget Lodge are set in what was once the largest mining (gold, silver, copper) camp in the area. You are 4 mi from Mount Rushmore and horse trails. There's an RV park with full hookups. Hot tub, spa. No smoking. | U.S. 16A | 605/855–6918 | www.blackhills.com/holysmoke | 12 cabins, 1 lodge room | $70–$120 cabins, $50 lodge room | Closed Oct.–Apr. | AE, D, MC, V.

Kelly Inn. This family favorite 2½ mi from downtown has extra large guest rooms, including family rooms with bunk beds and rooms for people with disabilities. Complimentary Continental breakfast. Some microwaves, some refrigerators. Cable TV. Hot tub. Exercise equipment. Laundry facilities. Business services. Pets allowed. | 320 Old Cemetery Rd. | 605/666–4483 or 800/635–3559 | fax 605/666–4883 | www.blackhills.com/kellyinn | 44 rooms | $90–$100 | Closed Nov.–Mar. | AE, D, DC, MC, V.

Mt. Rushmore White House Resort This independent, two-story motel built around 1985 is near downtown, 30 mi off of I–90. You're minutes from Crazy Horse Memorial, 1880 Train, cave touring, amusement parks, helicopter rides, and recreational activities. Some kitchenettes, some refrigerators. Cable TV. Outdoor heated pool. Pets allowed (fee). | 115 Swanzey St. | 605/666–4929 or 800/456–1878, 800/504–3210 | fax 605/666–4805 | info@mtrushmoreresorts.com | www.mtrushmoreresorts.com | 70 rooms | $59–$99 | DC, MC, V.

Powder House Lodge. In the pines off U.S. 16A, this rustic lodge has cabins and a friendly staff. The lodge caters to family vacations with its outdoor heated pool, access to hiking trails, nearby stables, playground, and proximity to Mount Rushmore. Restaurant. Cable TV. Outdoor pool. Playground. Pets allowed. | 24127 Hwy. 16A | 605/666–4646 or 800/321–0692 | 37 rooms, 12 cabins | $80–$90 | Closed Sept.–mid-May | AE, D, MC, V.

Roosevelt Inn. This mid-size inn, less than 1 mi from the east entrance of Mount Rushmore National Memorial, is one of the closest hotels to the "Faces" (though you cannot see them from the inn itself). Mountain view rooms are especially inviting during autumn. Some suites have balconies. Cable TV. Outdoor pool. | 206 Old Cemetery Rd. | 605/666–4599 or 800/257–8923 | fax 605/666–4535 | info@rosyinn.com | www.rosyinn.com | 21, including one handicap accessible room | $45–$110 off-season, $90–$190 peak season | No breakfast | AE, MC, V.

LEAD

MAP 8, A3

(Nearby towns also listed: Belle Fourche, Deadwood, Rapid City, Spearfish, Sturgis)

Lead was founded in 1876 by a wave of miners who had rushed across the Dakota prairie in search of Black Hills gold following the Custer Expedition's discovery in 1874. (Although the discovery of gold was confirmed in 1874, the army didn't allow prospectors into the Black Hills until two years later.) The onetime mining town is now in the process of reinventing itself. Major restoration projects are under way on Main St., and the town has come back to life even as the scope of mining has decreased. Ideally situated for year-round recreation and retirement homes, Lead's future is actually brighter than its past.

Information: Lead Area Chamber of Commerce | 640 W. Main St., Suite A, 57754 | 605/584–1100 | www.leadmethere.org.

Attractions
Andy's Trail Rides. Adventures in the Black Hills include buggy and wagon rides, cattle drives, overnight camping, and fishing trips. | 5 mi southwest of Lead on Hwy. 14 | 605/584–1100 | Call for prices.

Black Hills Mining Museum. Displays explore the history of mining in the Black Hills. There are guided tours through simulated tunnels and stopes, a video theater, and gold panning. | 323 W. Main St. | 605/584–1605 and 888/410–3337 | $4.25, panning $4.25 extra | May–Sept., daily 9–5; Oct.–Apr., Tues.–Sat. 9–4.

Deer Mountain. Ski lessons, rentals, and cross-country trails are available here, as well as three lifts and 32 downhill trails with a 700-ft vertical drop. Includes lodge facilities. | 1000 Deer Mt. Rd. | 605/584–3230 | www.skideermountain.com | $24; $72 4-day pass | Nov.–Mar., Wed., Thurs., Sun. 9–4, Fri., Sat. 9–9.

Terry Peak. A 1,100-ft vertical drop, 20 trails, and loads of snow make this 400-acre ski area in the Black Hills popular. Includes five chairlifts, a rental shop, lessons, and day lodge facilities. | Hwy. 85, 3 mi west of Lead | 605/584–2165 or 800/456–0524 | www.terrypeak.com | $32 | Nov.–Mar., daily 9–4.

SIGHTSEEING TOURS/TOUR COMPANIES

Homestake Gold Mine Surface Tours. You can tour the surface workings of one of the oldest continuously operating mines in the world. You'll view giant hoists, ore crushing and processing, and the huge Open Cut surface mine. | 160 W. Main St. | 605/584–3110 | $5.25 | Visitor center open weekdays 9–5, weekends 10–5; tours May–Sept., daily 8:30–3:30.

ON THE CALENDAR

JAN.: *Winterfest*. Dogsled rides, ice skating, entertainment, a parade, a snowmobile competition, dinner, and a dance are all part of this annual event held along Main St. in downtown Lead. | 605/584–1100.

JULY: *Gold Camp Jubilee*. Included in this midsummer event are a parade, food and craft vendors, mining contests, kids' games, a carnival, an art festival, entertainment, and the area's largest fireworks display. | 605/584–1100 | July 3–4.

Dining

Stampmill Restaurant and Saloon. American. The dark-wood and brickwork interior make this 1892 building special and intimate. Photos trace the history of Lead and the mines. Two suites are available for overnight accommodations. Food is available in the saloon. You might try the Black Angus steaks or the French onion soup. | 305 W. Main St. | 605/584–1984 | $8–$15 | D, MC, V.

Lodging

Barefoot Resort. Two separate, three-story building phases are planned for this condo resort overlooking the top of the Black Hills. You can stay in cozy apartment-style villas, each with its own terrace, fireplace, and kitchen 6 mi from Deadwood, casinos and numerous sites. You can enjoy both winter sports and summer excursions. Indoor pool. Hot tub, sauna, spa. Basketball, horseback riding. volleyball. Skiing, snowmobiling. Laundry facilities. | HC 37 | 605/584–1577 or 800/424–0225 | barefoot@mato.com | www.barefootresort.com | 32 rooms | $150–$275 | AE, MC, V.

Best Western Golden Hills Resort. Gold-tinted windows on this high-rise hotel in downtown Lead recall the area's roots and the hotel's original owner, the Homestake Mining Co. Restaurant, bar. Some refrigerators, some in-room hot tubs. Gym. Business facilities. | 900 Miners Ave. | 605/584–1800 or 888/465–3080 | fax 605/584–3933 | www.bestwestern.com | 96 rooms, 4 suites | $99–$109, $135–$185 suites | AE, D, MC, V.

Deer Mountain B&B. This is a log home B&B with a ski resort right next door. You can relax by the fireplace or enjoy a game of pool in the billiards room. After complimentary hors d'oeuvres or dessert at night you can rest your muscles in the indoor hot tub. Deer Mountain is 3 mi south of Lead next to Deer Mountain Ski Resort and 5 minutes away from skiing, snowmobiles, and sleigh rides. Complimentary breakfast. TV in common area. Hot tub. Hiking. Pets allowed (fee). | HC 37 | 605/584–2473 | fax 605/584–3045 | vonackerman@dtgnet.com | www.bbonline.com/sd/deermtn/ | 4 rooms (2 with shared bath) | $65–$85 | D, MC, V.

White House Inn. This white hotel, more than a decade old, offers economy lodging with direct access to snowmobile and hiking trails and close proximity to ski resorts. There's free transportation to Deadwood's main street and the casinos. Complimentary Continental breakfast. Some microwaves, some refrigerators, some in-room hot tubs. Cable TV. Hot tub. Snowmobiling. Business services. Pets allowed (fee). | 395 Glendale Dr. | 605/584–2000 or 800/654–5323 | 71 rooms, 17 suites | $75–$90, $75–$120 suites | AE, D, DC, MC, V.

LEMMON

(Nearby town also listed: Mobridge)

Near the North Dakota border, Lemmon serves as a healthcare, shopping, and recreational center for much of northwest South Dakota. In addition to a hospital, four motels, and five restaurants, the town also has the world's largest park dedicated solely to petrified wood and fossils. The free Lemmon Petrified Wood Park has more than 400 specimens, all found within 25 mi of town.

Information: Lemmon Chamber of Commerce | 100 3rd St. W, 57638-1523 | 605/374–5716.

Attractions
Lemmon Petrified Wood Park. This park has more than 400 unusual structures made up of specimens found within a 25-mi radius of Lemmon. Nearly all the finds have been arranged to form spires, castles, pyramids, or other whimsical shapes. Created in 1930–32, the park was the pet project of O. S. Quammen, who hoped to learn more about petrified wood, create a public display of the fossils, and provide work for men unemployed during the Depression. | 500 Main Ave. | 605/374–5716 | Free.

ON THE CALENDAR
NOV.: *Christmas Craft Fair.* You can buy handcrafted artwork and gifts for the holiday season. | 605/374–5716.

Dining
Busted T Cafe. American. The café serves steaks and seafood; there's also a full salad bar. Wednesday and Saturday there's an open buffet. | Main St. | 605/374–3680 | $4–$10 | No credit cards.

Lodging
Lemmon Country Inn. This is a two-story split-level inn, 1 mi east of Lead on U.S. 12; a restaurant is nearby. You can visit the petrified wood park, which is 1 mi away, or the Shayhill Reservoir, which is 12 mi away. Complimentary Continental breakfast. Cable TV. | 19405 U.S. 12 | 800/591–3711, 605/374–3711 | fax 605/374–5936 | 30 rooms | $39–$53 | AE, MC, V.

Prairie Motel. This motel off U.S. 12 is within 15 min of the petrified wood park, fishing on Shade Hill Lake, and a restaurant. Some microwaves, refrigerators. Cable TV. Pets allowed. | 115 10 St. E | 605/374–3304 | 13 rooms | $30–$60 | AE, D, MC, V.

MADISON

MAP, H4

(Nearby towns also listed: Brookings and Sioux Falls)

Madison was created by the merger of the villages of Herman and Madison in 1875. Home to Dakota State University (the state's first normal school, founded in 1881), Madison is a lively town of 6,200 residents northwest of Sioux Falls. DSU employs approximately 200 people, and a dozen manufacturing companies provide economic stability for the town. Among Madison's offerings are the Smith-Zimmerman State Museum, nearby Lake Herman State Park, and Prairie Village, with more than 40 historic buildings brimming with antiques.

Information: Madison Chamber of Commerce | 315 S. Egan Ave., 57042-0467 | 605/256–2454 | www.madison.sd.us/chamber.

Attractions

Dakota State University. Founded in 1881 as the state's first normal school, this institution has evolved into a four-year state-supported university. | Egan Ave. and 8th St. NE | 605/256–5111 | Free.

Smith-Zimmermann State Museum. This museum explores the history and development of the prairie as it traces the ethnic backgrounds of the mostly Norwegian and German settlers to the Eastern Dakota prairies. Collections include farm implements and household items from 19th-century settlements. | 221 N. 8th St. | 605/256–5308 | www.smith-zimmermann.dsu.edu | Free | Tues.–Sat. 1–4.

Lake Herman State Park. Herman Luce and his son William were the first white settlers in this vicinity when they claimed squatter's rights on the eastern shore of the lake in June 1870. Their snug and sturdy oak cabin still stands. The park hosts an annual event in June with activities such as log-cabin building, rope and candle making, and cooking. Camping cabins are available year-round, and a groomed cross-country ski trail is ready when snow flies at this popular lakeside park. Within the park are also wooded hiking trails. Camping is found here and at nearby Walkers Point Recreation Area. | 605/256–5003 or 605/256–2454 | $3 per person, $5 per vehicle, $20 annually.

Prairie Village. South Dakota's pioneer heritage comes to life in this authentic turn-of-the-20th-century prairie town. A steam locomotive makes its way around a 2-mi track, and train rides are available every Sunday May through Sept. You can tour nearly 50 buildings furnished with original decor. | W. Hwy. 34 | 605/256–3644 or 800/693-3644 | $5 | May–Sept., daily 9–6.

ON THE CALENDAR

JUNE: *Golden Railroad Days.* Dinner train, train rides, model railroad displays, steam locomotives, and carousel rides are included in this festival. | 605/256–3644.

AUG.: *Steam Threshing Jamboree.* More than 300 antique tractors and cars are on view. Included are examples of steam- and horse-powered threshing, a plowing contest, antique machinery, car and horse parades, and musical entertainment. | Late Aug. | 605/256–3644.

Dining

F and M Cafe. American. Homemade soups, homestyle breakfast, steaks, and country fixings. The café is right outside of town on Highway 34W. | Hwy. 34W, West Havens | 605/256–2051 | Breakfast also available | $3–$12 | AE, MC, V.

Moonlight. American. This family-style steak house 2½ mi west of Madison offers intimate dining with some antique tables. Popular menu items include steaks, king crab, and prime rib finished with a hearty dessert of cheesecake. | Hwy. 34W, 2 mi west of the junction of Rte. 34 and U.S. 81 | 605/256–0551 | Closed Mon., Tues. No lunch | $8–$15 | D, MC, V.

KODAK'S TIPS FOR PHOTOGRAPHING LANDSCAPES AND SCENERY

Landscape
- Tell a story
- Isolate the essence of a place
- Exploit mood, weather, and lighting

Panoramas
- Use panoramic cameras for sweeping vistas
- Don't restrict yourself to horizontal shots
- Keep the horizon level

Panorama Assemblage
- Use a wide-angle or normal lens
- Let edges of pictures overlap
- Keep exposure even
- Use a tripod

Placing the Horizon
- Use low horizon placement to accent sky or clouds
- Use high placement to emphasize distance and accent foreground elements
- Try eliminating the horizon

Mountain Scenery: Scale
- Include objects of known size
- Frame distant peaks with nearby objects
- Compress space with long lenses

Mountain Scenery: Lighting
- Shoot early or late; avoid midday
- Watch for dramatic color changes
- Use exposure compensation

Tropical Beaches
- Capture expansive views
- Don't let bright sand fool your meter
- Include people

Rocky Shorelines
- Vary shutter speeds to freeze or blur wave action
- Don't overlook sea life in tidal pools
- Protect your gear from sand and sea

In the Desert
- Look for shapes and textures
- Try visiting during peak bloom periods
- Don't forget safety

Canyons
- Research the natural and social history of a locale
- Focus on a theme or geologic feature
- Budget your shooting time

Rain Forests and the Tropics
- Go for mystique with close-ups and detail shots
- Battle low light with fast films and camera supports
- Protect cameras and film from moisture and humidity

Rivers and Waterfalls
- Use slow film and long shutter speeds to blur water
- When needed, use a neutral-density filter over the lens
- Shoot from water level to heighten drama

Autumn Colors
- Plan trips for peak foliage periods
- Mix wide and close views for visual variety
- Use lighting that accents colors or creates moods

Moonlit Landscapes
- Include the moon or use only its illumination
- Exaggerate the moon's relative size with long telephoto lenses
- Expose landscapes several seconds or longer

Close-Ups
- Look for interesting details
- Use macro lenses or close-up filters
- Minimize camera shake with fast films and high shutter speeds

Caves and Caverns
- Shoot with ISO 1000+ films
- Use existing light in tourist caves
- Paint with flash in wilderness caves

From *Kodak Guide to Shooting Great Travel Pictures* © 2000 by Fodor's Travel Publications

Lodging

Katharine's Mysterious House B&B. This is the oldest Victorian house in town, built in the late 1800s. Storybook theme rooms with flower gardens surround the porches. It's across from Memorial Park, one block from South Dakota State University, and 4 mi from Prairie Village. Restaurants are a short walking distance away. Complimentary Continental breakfast. Microwaves. refrigerators. Laundry service. No pets. No smoking. | 518 N. Egan Ave. | 605/256–4118 | 5 rooms | $60–$90 | No credit cards.

Lake Park. Only minutes from pheasant hunting, lake recreation, and gambling, this all-ground-level motel offers trailer and camper parking and hookups. Some rooms have views of a garden, and one has an in-room hot tub. There is a restaurant behind the hotel. Refrigerators. Cable TV. Pool. Hot tub. Pets allowed. | 1515 N.W. 2nd St. | 605/256–3524 | 37 rooms | $40–$50 | AE, D, MC, V.

Super 8. This motel is about 1 mi from Prairie Village, an outdoor campground, and outdoor museum, and five blocks from Dakota State College. It's also next to the city park, which has a pool and tennis court that you're welcome to use as a hotel guest. A restaurant is next door. Complimentary Continental breakfast. Cable TV. Pets allowed (fee). | Junction Hwy. 34 and 81 | 605/256–6931. | www.super8.com | 34 rooms | $47 | AE, D, DC, MC, V.

MILBANK

MAP 8, H2

(Nearby towns also listed: Sisseton, Watertown)

Railroading played a major role in the founding and growth of the small town of Milbank. It was established by a railroad in 1878 as Milbank Junction, then in October 1881 its residents voted to incorporate as the Village of Milbank. Named for Jeremiah Milbank, a railroad official, the town revolved for many years around the regular arrival and departure of the train. Today Milbank is best known for its historic mill and its August Arts in the Park celebration. Agriculture serves as its current economic base.

Information: Milbank Chamber of Commerce | 401 S. Main St., 57252 | 605/432–6656 or 800/675–6656.

Attractions

Blue Cloud Abbey. Blue Cloud is a Catholic community of 45 Benedictine monks, disciples of St. Benedict of Nursia, Italy. The order dates back to AD 480–547. Mass is said Sundays and holy days at 10 AM. The abbey is 15 mi west of Milbank along Hwy. 12. | Box 98 | 605/432–5528 | fax 605/432–4754 | Tours by appointment | Daily, 8–4:30.

Hartford Beach State Park. Walleyes are the big draw at this quiet park on the shore of Big Stone Lake, which offers mature trees, hiking trails, swimming, a boat ramp, and a campground with a handicapped-accessible campsite. Fall colors are beautiful here. The park is 15 mi northwest of Milbank. | Corona | 605/432–6374 | $3 per person, $5 per vehicle, $20 annually.

ON THE CALENDAR

JAN.: *Grant County Farm and Home Show.* Over 100 booths display the latest farm and home products; there's lively entertainment and seminars. | 800/675–6656.

Dining

Lantern Inn. American. This casual supper club serves up steaks, seafood, and ribs accompanied by a full salad and potato bar. A cocktail bar and full-catering staff are also on hand. | Hwy. 15 S | 605/432–4421 | Closed Sun. | $6–$12 | AE, MC, V.

Millstone. American. This country-theme casual spot offers burgers, pasta, and homemade desserts. The skillet breakfast is very popular. There are also a kids' menu and Sunday brunch. | 1107 E. 4th Ave. | 605/432–6866 | Breakfast also available | $6–$10 | Reservations not accepted | MC, V.

Lodging

Lantern Motel and Supper Club. All rooms are ground level at this clean, quiet motel with soft water, winter hookups, and truck parking. The motel is 5 blocks from downtown. Restaurant, complimentary Continental breakfast. Cable TV. Sauna. Pets allowed. | 1010 S. Dakota St. | 605/432–4591 or 800/627–6075 | fax 605/432–4986 | 30 rooms | $40 | AE, D, MC, V.

Manor Motel. This 30-room motel is across from a grinding mill and 12 mi south of Big Stone Lake. Restaurant. Microwaves, refrigerators. Cable TV. Indoor pool, sauna. Laundry service. | Hwy. 13 E | 605/432–4527 | fax 605/432–4529 | manor-motel-sd@hotmail.com | www.glpta.org/manormotel/htm | 30 rooms | $36–$44 | AE, MC, V.

Super 8. This motel offers comfortable rooms with truck parking and outdoor winter hookups on the east side of town, 1 mi from the business district. Complimentary Continental breakfast. Some microwaves, some refrigerators. Cable TV. Hot tub, sauna. Business services. | Rte. 12 E | 605/432–9288 or 800/800–8000 | 39 rooms | $44–$50 | AE, D, MC, V.

MILLER

MAP 8, F3

(Nearby town also listed: Redfield)

Miller was named for Henry Miller, an Iowa farmer who settled in the area in 1881. More than a century later, its economic mainstay continues to be agriculture, although the area attracts its share of pheasant hunters for the fall season. Fifty miles north of I–90, Miller is home to nearly 1,700 residents, 43 sleeping rooms, 14 food establishments, 2 campgrounds, 6 service stations, 5 museums, a 9-hole golf course, and a pool with a 141-ft waterslide. Two sparkling fountains greet you as you enter Crystal Park.

Information: Miller Civic and Commerce Center | 224 N. Broadway, Miller, 57362 | 605/853–3098 | www.millersd.org.

Attractions

McWhorter Museum. The museum houses artifacts illustrative of the area's pioneer history, as well as objects from the office of the turn-of-the-century physician for whom it was named and the old Miller Train Depot. | 426 N. Broadway | 605/853–3098 | Free | By appointment only.

MISSION

MAP 8, E5

(Nearby towns also listed: Murdo, Winner)

Mission was founded in 1915 by S. J. Kimmel, and was so called because of the number of church missions in the vicinity. Today, the majority of its residents are employed either by federal and tribal government and schools or on area ranches.

Information: Rosebud Sioux Tribal Office | Box 430 and 11 Legion Ave., Rosebud, 57570 | 605/747–2381.

Attractions

Buechel Memorial Lakota Museum. You can see Teton Sioux artifacts and other exhibits, such as photographs of Spotted Tail, a Teton leader and uncle of Crazy Horse. Also included is a 300-plant herbarium. | 350 S. Oak St. | 605/747–2745 | Free | June–Aug., daily 9–5.

Ghost Hawk Park. Here are nearly 50,000 acres of stark, barren beauty in the middle of Crazy Horse Canyon. | BIA Rd. No. 7 | 605/856–2538 | Free.

Oyate Trail. "Oyate" is the Lakota word for "the people" or "the nation." This 388-mi stretch of highway—from I–29 on the east, to the southern foothills of the Black Hills—provides a natural way to delve into the rich history of the local Native-American (Yankton, Rosebud, and Oglala Lakota) culture and its influence on the land, its people, and the immigrant Northern European settlers. Important cultural and historical sites are visited along the way in a manageable and well-paced tour. | Harrich | 605/775–2903 | www.oyate-trail.org | Free.

Rosebud. The heart of the 950,000-acre Rosebud Indian Reservation has tribal offices, schools, stores, a medical center, and Sinte Gleska University, the only such institution on any of the state's Indian reservations. The tribal membership population is 32,499. | 11 Legion Ave. | 605/747–2381 | Free | Headquarters building open weekdays 8–5.

ON THE CALENDAR

FEB.: *Sinte Gleska University Founders Day Celebration.* This event celebrates the founding of the state's only university on an Indian reservation. A traditional powwow is held on Friday, contest powwows on Saturday and Sunday. Included are arts and crafts vendors. | 605/856–2413.

JUNE: *Ring Thunder Traditional Powwow.* You'll find traditional naming and honoring ceremonies, Father's Day tributes, and recognition of veterans and youth. | 605/856–2159.

AUG.: *Rosebud Fair and All Indian Rodeo.* Includes traditional wacipi (dance), drum money, tiny tots day money, veteran tributes, a carnival, a parade, a road run, a Miss Rosebud pageant, dances, and free meals. | 605/747–2381.

Dining

Starlite Snack Shop. American. This is a casual sandwich and burger restaurant with such items as Philly cheese steaks and cheeseburgers. | Main St. | 605/856–4360 | $4–$10 | No credit cards.

Lodging

Antelope Country Inn. This inn at the I–83 and 1883 junction is within 3 mi of the Prairie Hills Golf Club. Restaurant. Cable TV. Laundry facilities. Pets allowed. | 175 Adam St. | 605/856–2371 | 12 rooms | $35–$60 | AE, MC, V.

Quality Inn Rosebud Casino. This 2-story casino hotel is almost midway between Mission and Valentine, Nebraska, on Hwy. 83. There's an adjoining casino with 116 slots, table games, bingo hall, and nightly prime rib buffet. You can visit a 500-seat entertainment center on the beautiful Rosebud Sioux Reservation about 140 mi away. Restaurant, bar. Complimentary breakfast. Cable TV. Indoor pool. Hot tub. Exercise equipment. | Hwy. 83 | 877/521–9913 or 605/378–3800 | fax 605/378–3367 | www.qualityinn.com | 60 rooms | $55–$60 | AE, D, MC, V.

MITCHELL

MAP 8, G4

(Nearby towns also listed: Chamberlain, Huron, Sioux Falls)

As is the case with virtually every South Dakota town east of the Black Hills, Mitchell was founded by a railroad (in 1879) and peopled with immigrant sodbusters enticed by overly optimistic promotional materials spawned by railroads and land companies. Today its economic vitality can be traced to those same agrarian roots. Mitchell also benefits from a seasonal tourist industry and offers an eclectic collection of attractions. It is home to the world's only Corn Palace, a colorful structure with portions of its interior and its entire exterior covered with corn murals and decorations. This quiet town of 14,000 is also home to the Oscar Howe Art Center, Prehistoric Indian Village and Archeodome (the nation's first), the International Balloon and Airship Museum, the Enchanted World Doll Museum, the Friends of the Middle Border Museum of American Indian and Pioneer Life, and Case Art Gallery.

Information: Mitchell Convention and Visitors Bureau | 601 N. Main St., 57301-1026 | 605/996–6223 or 800/257–2676 | www.cornpalace.org.

Attractions

Corn Palace. This is one of South Dakota's most recognizable attractions. Dating back to 1892, the colorful building is adorned inside and out with thousands of bushels of native corn, grains, and grasses incorporated into beautiful murals. The building is redecorated each year. | 604 N. Main St. | 605/996–7311 and 800/257–2676 | www.cornpalace.org | Free | Memorial Day–Labor Day, daily 8–9; May and Sept., daily 8–5; Oct.–Apr., weekdays 8–5.

Dakota Wesleyan University. "Sacrifice or Service" is the motto of this university, founded in 1885. The 40-acre campus includes a KOKA House which is affiliated with the KOKA Women's Institute in Kyoto, Japan. | 1200 W. University Ave. | 605/995–2600 | Free.

Enchanted World Doll Museum. The museum houses 4,000 antique and contemporary dolls from around the world, all posed in 400 enchanting scenes. | 615 N. Main St. | 605/996–9896 | $3.50; special rate for children | Memorial Day–Labor Day, daily 8–8; Mar., Apr., Oct., Nov., Mon.–Sat. 9–5 and Sun. 1–5.

Lake Mitchell Park and Recreation Center. Public parks, beaches, and a great spot for picnicking are good reasons for visiting; there are also opportunities for camping, fishing, and boating. | 1300 N. Main St. | 605/995–8457 (Apr.–Nov. 1, camping) or 605/995–8450 and 605/996–7180 (Nov.–Mar.) | $11 per site; water and sewer $1 extra, electricity $2.50 extra. Cable TV $1 extra.

Middle Border Museum of American Indian and Pioneer Life. The 7 buildings that form this museum include an art gallery, an 1885 schoolhouse, a 1909 country church, a 1900 train depot, and a restored 1886 Italianate home. More than 100,000 artifacts are on display relating details of Native American and pioneer life. | 1311 S. Duff St. | 605/996–2122 | $3 | May, Sept., daily 9–5; June–Aug., Mon.–Sat. 8–6, Sun. 10–6; Oct.–Apr. by appointment only.

Mitchell Prehistoric Indian Village and Archeodome. The nation's first archeodome encloses a portion of the 1,100-year-old prehistoric Indian village. Guided tours take you through the structure, as well as a full-scale reconstruction of an earth lodge in the Boehnen Memorial Museum. | Indian Village Rd. (2 mi north of Mitchell) | 605/996–5473 | $5; special rate for children | Memorial Day–Labor Day, daily 8–6; May, Sept., Oct., daily 9–4; Nov.–Apr. by appointment only.

Oscar Howe Art Center. Throughout his life, and through his powerful work, this Sioux artist inspired fellowship and understanding between Native Americans and whites. The center, a National Historic Site, houses the permanent collection of his abstract art, each piece of which tells a tale of Indian life and spirituality. | 119 W. 3rd | 605/996–4111 | Donations accepted | Memorial Day–Labor Day, Mon.–Sat. 9–5, Sun. 10–5; Labor Day Day–Memorial Day, Tue.–Sat. 10–5.

State Theater. This community theater started life as a vaudeville house in the early part of the 20th century. At press time the building was undergoing a new restoration. | Main St. | 605/996–6223 or 800/257–2676 | Call for prices | Weekends.

JULY: *Corn Palace Stampede Rodeo.* Includes 4 professional rodeos, a Main St. parade, and dances both nights. | 605/996–8299.

SEPT.: *Corn Palace Polka Festival.* You can have 3 days of polka fun with 2 hardwood dance floors and nearly a half-dozen bands. | 605/995–8427.

Dining

Asiana Oriental Cuisine. Pan-Asian. Here you'll find an array of Asian cuisine—Vietnamese, Cambodian, Thai, and Chinese—all with spicy variations. You can try one of the 8 different soups for starters before tasting from the evening's buffet, a regular feature. | 322 E. Havens St. | 605/996–7729 | $6–$10 | D, MC, V.

Brig Restaurant and Lounge. American, Seafood. A quintessential ship's brig sets the mood for handcut aged beef, prepared on the premises, or local seafood. Pasta dishes are also available. You can have cocktails by the fireplace down in the beamed lounge, or dance in the reception area. | 2700 N. Main | 605/996–7444 | Closed Mon. No lunch | $10–$17 | AE, DC, MC, V.

Chef Louie's. Steak. Chef Louie's serves good food in a relaxed atmosphere; this white-table-top restaurant has 3 dining rooms and offers a hearty portion of prime rib or barbecued ribs, among other choices. Chicken and seafood are also available. | 601 E. Havens St. | 605/996–7565 | Closed Sun. | $15–$20 | AE, D, DC, MC, V.

Country Kitchen. American. Everything from steaks to spaghetti and sandwiches is served up here. Breakfast always served, and there's a breakfast buffet on weekends. | 1101 S. Burr St. | 605/996–9391 | $4–$11 | DC, MC, V.

Dakota Road House. American. Chain restaurant specializing in casual service and good steak burgers, chicken, pasta, and seafood. | I–90 at Exit 330 | 605/996–6501 or 800/888–4702 | $4–$15 | DC, MC, V.

Happy Chef. American. Offerings from the summer salad bar complement other menu choices such as T-bone and sirloin steak. Sunday there's a breakfast buffet. Banquet room available. | Junction of I–90 and Hwy. 37 | 605/996–2800 | 24 hours Fri. and Sat. | $4–$8 | AE, DC, MC, V.

Lodging

AmericInn. This 2-story chain motel with 8 suites is 1½ mi from downtown and near I–90 across from Cabela's Outlet Store. There are a few fast food eateries 1 block away. Complimentary Continental breakfast. Some minibars, some microwaves, some refrigerators. Cable TV. Indoor pool. Hot tub, sauna. | 1421 S. Burr St. | 800/634–3444 or 605/996–9700 | 54 rooms | $60–$80 | AE, D, DC, MC, V.

Anthony. This family-style single-story motel on the south end of town has a friendly staff and clean rooms; in the fall it caters to hunters. Picnic area. Some microwaves, some refrigerators. Cable TV. Outdoor pool. Miniature golf. Basketball. Laundry facilities. Airport shuttle. | 1518 W. Havens St. | 605/996–7518 or 800/477–2235 | fax 605/996–7251 | 34 rooms | $60 | AE, D, MC, V.

Corn Palace Motel. This single-story motel has efficiencies and cabins; it's just a block off I–90, Exit 332. It's near the famous Corn Palace—the world's biggest bird feeder, built to celebrate the area's fertile farmland. Complimentary Continental breakfast. Some kitchenettes. Cable TV. Laundry facilities. Pets allowed. | 902 S. Burr St. | 605/996–5559 | 50 rooms | $45–$95 | AE, MC, V.

Days Inn. This motel has quiet, comfortable rooms near I–90. You can find dining and shopping nearby. A 24-hour Internet café is on the site. Complimentary Continental breakfast. In-room data ports, some microwaves, some refrigerators. Cable TV. Indoor pool. Hot tub. Laundry facilities. | 1506 S. Burr St., I–90 and Rte. 37 | 605/996–6208 | fax 605/996–5220 | 65 rooms | $65–$80 | AE, D, DC, MC, V.

Der Rumboly Platz Country B&B Hunting and Horse Camp. This is a fourth-generation working horse farm 10 mi outside of town. You can take a horseback ride or a stroll in the countryside. Der Rumboly, which was built in the late 1800s, has 7 bedrooms. In the informal kitchen/dining room that overlooks the property, you can sample German pancakes and Belgian waffles. Horseback riding. Laundry facilities. Pets allowed. | 40732 266th St., Ethan | 605/227–4385 | 7 rooms | $50 | No credit cards.

EconoLodge. This standard chain motel is just ½ mi from I–90. Complimentary Continental breakfast. Cable TV. Business services. Some pets allowed (fee). | 1313 S. Ohlman St. | 605/996–6647 | fax 605/996–7339 | 44 rooms | $58–$77 | AE, D, MC, V.

Flavia's Place B&B. This Italian Revival–style house, 2 blocks from downtown Mitchell, dates from 1882. The private baths all have the original red clawfoot bath tubs. Flavia's caters to hunters. Lunch and dinner are served by prior arrangement. Full complimentary breakfast. Pets allowed. No smoking. | 515 E. 3rd St. | 605/995–1562 | 4 rooms (3 with shared bath) | $60–$90 | AE, DC, MC, V.

Holiday Inn. This is the largest hotel in the area and a convenient and quiet location not far from I–90, close to gasoline and retail services. An 18-hole miniature golf course is on the premises, and there is a patio off the bar. Restaurant, bar, room service. In-room data ports. Cable TV. Indoor pool, wading pool. 2 hot tubs, sauna. Miniature golf. Laundry facilities. Business services, airport shuttle. Some pets allowed (fee). | 1525 W. Havens St. | 605/996–6501 | fax 605/996–3228 | 153 rooms | $80–$100 | AE, D, DC, MC, V.

Motel 6. Economy rooms near I–90 with coffee available in the morning. Several restaurants are just a short drive away. Pool. Pets allowed. | 1309 S. Ohlman St. | 605/996–0530 | fax 605/995–2019 | 96 rooms | $40 | AE, D, DC, MC, V.

Siesta. An economy motel with clean rooms and complimentary coffee near a restaurant and small shopping center and about 1 mi from downtown Mitchell. In-room data ports. Cable TV. Pool. Pets allowed. | 1210 W. Havens St. | 605/996–5544 or 800/424–0537 | fax 605/996–4946 | www.siestamotel.com | 22 rooms | $38–$58 | AE, D, MC, V.

Super 8. This chain hotel has comfortable rooms convenient to I–90 and about 1½ mi from downtown Mitchell. Complimentary Continental breakfast. Some in-room hot tubs. Cable TV. Indoor pool. Hot tub. Laundry facilities. Business services. | 177 S. Burr St. | 605/996–9678 | fax 605/996–5339 | www.super8.com | 107 rooms | $53–$70 | AE, D, DC, MC, V.

Thunderbird Lodge. This moderately priced motel caters to hunters and tourists. Complimentary Continental breakfast. Cable TV. Hot tub, sauna. Laundry facilities. | 1601 S. Burr St. | 605/996–6645 or 800/341–8000 | fax 605/995–5883 | 48 rooms | $68 | AE, D, DC, MC, V.

MOBRIDGE

MAP 8, E1

(Nearby town also listed: Lemmon)

Mobridge was founded in 1906 by the remnants of the Milwaukee Railroad crew that constructed a bridge over a horseshoe bend in the Missouri River. An unknown telegrapher sent word of their location as succinctly as possible, and his dots and dashes, intended to signal "Missouri Bridge," gave Mobridge its name. Billed as the "Oasis of Oahe," Mobridge capitalizes on the best walleye fishing in the nation. Nearby are the Lewis and Clark Trail, the Sitting Bull Monument, and excellent fishing, boating, camping, and hunting opportunities. The Sitting Bull Stampede each July 2–4 has a top-notch pro rodeo. Today Mobridge serves as a retail, medical, social, and commercial hub for north-central South Dakota, drawing rural ranch families and residents of the nearby Standing Rock and Cheyenne River Indian Reservations, as well as sport fishermen who savor the offerings of the upper Missouri River.

Information: **Mobridge Chamber of Commerce** | 212 Main St., 57601-2533 | 605/845–2387 and 888/614–FISH | www.mobridge.org.

Attractions

Indian Creek Recreation Area. Included are camping, 2 boat ramps, a fish-cleaning station, and a marina on the shore of Lake Oahe. Indian Memorial Campground, with full facilities, is 2 mi west. | Indian Creek Rd. (2 mi east and 1 mi south of Mobridge) | 605/845–2252 | cenwo.nwo.usace.army.mil | $14 per site; Golden Age and Golden Access cards accepted | Memorial Day–Sept.

Klein Museum. Included are local pioneer and Sioux artifacts, as well as a restored schoolhouse from the early 1900s and changing art exhibits. | 1820 W. Grand Crossing | 605/845–7243 | $2; special rate for children | Apr.–Oct., Mon., Wed.–Fri. 9–noon, 1–5, weekends 1–5.

Scherr Howe Arena. The arena hosts local school activities, such as high-school basketball and volleyball games. Murals by Sioux artist Oscar Howe adorn the walls. | 212 Main St. | 605/845–3700 or 605/845–2387 | Free | Mon.–Fri. 9–5.

Sitting Bull Monument. Alone on a windswept bluff above a horseshoe bend of the Missouri River stands a 7-ton granite bust of Sitting Bull, arguably the most famous Native American. Sculpted by Crazy Horse artist Korczak Ziolkowski, this enduring work captures the quiet pride of the legendary Sioux warrior. | State Hwy. 1806 (4 mi west of Mobridge) | 605/845–2387 | Free.

ON THE CALENDAR

JULY: *Sitting Bull Stampede Rodeo and Celebration.* Included are daily professional rodeos and 2 big Main St. parades, a carnival, and fireworks. | 605/845–2387 | July 2–4.

Dining

Windjammer Lounge and Captain's Table Supper Club. American. Overlooking beautiful Lake Oahe, this restaurant offers hearty meals and scenic vistas in a nautical-theme atmosphere. The prime rib and steak are popular choices. | Wrangler Motor Inn, 820 W. Grand Crossing | 605/845–3641 or 800/341–8000 | Closed Sun. No lunch | $10–$20 | AE, D, DC, MC, V.

Lodging

Best Value Wrangler Motor Inn. Just 5 mi from the Sitting Bull Monument, very near the Klein Museum, and alongside the Lewis and Clark trails, this is a convenient spot to stay. The motel caters to hunters and fishermen. Many of the rooms have balconies overlooking the Missouri River and Lake Oahe. Restaurant, bar, room service. Some microwaves, some refrigerators. Cable TV. Indoor pool. Hot tub. Exercise equipment. Video games. Business services, airport shuttle. Pets allowed. | 820 W. Grand Crossing | 605/845–3641 or 800/341–8000 | fax 605/845–3641 | 61 rooms | $56–$61 | AE, D, DC, MC, V.

Super 8. This standard chain is on the banks of the Missouri River, convenient to Lake Oahe and about 1 mi from downtown Mobridge. Some rooms have river views. Cable TV. Pets allowed. | 1301 W. Grand Crossing | 605/845–7215 | fax 605/845–5270 | 30 rooms | $51 | AE, D, DC, MC, V.

MURDO

MAP 8, D4

(Nearby towns also listed: Mission, Pierre)

Founded in 1906, Murdo was named for Murdo McKenzie, an early-day cattleman and manager of the Matador Cattle Company, which ran 20,000 head on the ranges of western South Dakota. The town supports 10 motels capable of accommodating 2,500 guests, as well as 2 campgrounds, 8 restaurants, and 5 service stations. Among its top attractions is the Pioneer Auto Museum and Antique Town, with classic cars and massive collections of Americana. Ranching continues to be the most important component of Murdo's economy.

Information: Murdo Chamber of Commerce | Box 242, 57559 | 605/669–3333.

Attractions

Pioneer Auto Museum and Antique Town. More than 250 rare, classic vehicles, ranging from a 1902 Oldsmobile to Elvis Presley's personal motorcycle, are housed with fine china, hand organs, and nickelodeons in a 10-acre, 39-building antique town. | 503 E. 5th St. | 605/669–2691 | $7.00 | Mar. 1–Nov. 1, daily 8:30–8.

ON THE CALENDAR

MAY: *Pioneer Auto Swap Meet, Car & Antique Auction.* Car lovers from several states come to wheel and deal at the Pioneer Auto Museum. | 503 E. 5th St. | 605/669–2691.

Dining

Star Family Restaurant American. An old soda fountain is a highlight of this eatery, ornamented with memorabilia from the '60s. Meatloaf made from scratch, steaks, and pies are some representative samples of the home-style fare. | 103 E. 5th St. (U.S. 16) | 605/669–2411 | Closed Oct.–early May. Breakfast also available | $8–$15 | MC, V.

Triple H Truck Stop and Restaurant. American. Biscuits and gravy, buffalo burgers, and omelettes stand out among the other traditional items at this no-frills highway eatery. Kids' menu. | 601 E 5th St. | 605/669–2465 | Reservations not accepted | Open 24 hours | $6–$10 | AE, D, MC, V.

Lodging

Best Western Graham's. At this single-story chain, just off I–90 (between Exits 191 and 192), a parking lot separates the rooms from the outdoor pool. Cable TV. Pool. Basketball. Playground. Business services. | 301 W. 5th St. | 605/669–2441 | fax 605/669–3139 | www.best-western.com | 45 rooms | $85 | AE, D, DC, MC, V.

Landmark Country Inn. Less than 1 mi south of I–90, on 30 acres, this inn has 2 buildings (2 floors each). Some of the individually appointed rooms have waterbeds. Some in-room hot tubs. Cable TV. Indoor Pool. Hot tub. Video games. | HC 77, Box 2 | 605/669–2846 | Nov.–Mar. | 24 rooms | $25 | AE, D, MC, V.

Murdo Days Inn–Range Country. Knotty pine accents and minimalist Western flair make this chain motel, opened in 1999, feel more like a bed and breakfast. The sunny lobby doubles as a breakfast room, and rooms on the second floor feel especially spacious thanks to vaulted ceilings. Complimentary Continental breakfast. In-room data ports. Cable TV. Indoor pool. Hot tub. Laundry facilities. | 302 W. 5th St. | 605/669–2425 or 800/329–7466 | fax 605/669–2235 | www.daysinn.com | 41 | $43–$56 | AE, D, DC, MC, V.

PIERRE

MAP 8, E3

(Nearby towns also listed: Chamberlain, Murdo)

Commanding the central location in the state and graced with one of the nation's prettiest capitol buildings, Pierre may well be the country's most isolated state capital. Arikara villages once lined the shores of the Missouri River near present-day Pierre. Later, tribes of the Sioux nation migrated to the area. The first record of white men dates from 1743, when two brothers claimed the region for their French king. Sixty-one years later, fabled explorers Lewis and Clark and their Corps of Discovery had their first encounter with the Teton Sioux here, and shortly afterward fur traders established a frontier fort. In 1889 (9 years after its official founding), Pierre was named the state's first capital after a long and vocal battle, chiefly because of its central location. Among its attractions are massive Oahe Dam, the South Dakota Cultural Heritage Center, and the South Dakota Discovery Center and Aquarium. Originally a laid-back cow town turned state capital, Pierre now thrives as a regional commercial and medical hub. It also attracts numerous conventions owing to its central location.

Information: Pierre Area Chamber of Commerce, and Pierre Convention and Visitors Bureau | 800 W. Dakota 57501-0548 | 605/224–7361 or 800/962–2034.

Driving Around Town: Quirky Pierre is so small that it's easy to get around on foot. Leave your car in one of the free parking lots. There are only a few meters, which are in front of the federal building, and usually only post-office patrons use them. You can park in front of any of the shops for free on Pierre Street, the main drag, or anywhere else for that matter, without a problem. There are no real rush hours, but you may have a little more trouble crossing the street, or you might be a minute later getting to your destination between 7:30 and 8 in the morning, around lunchtime, and again between 5 and 6 in the evening. The whole place goes to sleep after 5:30, except for restaurants and theaters. There is only one one-way street in town, and that's Pierre Street. You can make a right turn on red down the one-way street.

TRANSPORTATION INFORMATION

Airports: Commuter air service is provided by Mesaba/Northwest Airlink and United Express from the **Pierre Municipal Airport.** | 4000 Airport Rd, Pierre | 605/224–9000, 605/224–1722 [Mesaba/Northwest Airlink], or 605/224–2949 [United Express]. **Bus Lines: Jack Rabbit Lines** (605/224–7651).

NEIGHBORHOODS

Downtown Pierre. Like many South Dakota towns, Pierre is small and spans only four or five square blocks, though the commercial strip stretches for a mile or so. Petunias brighten the sidewalks in the warmer months. Visit the beautiful State Capitol building, which was modeled after Montana's capitol building. Inside this marquette sandstone building, take a look at the Greek and Roman designs and stenciling, as well as impressive murals telling the story of the state's beginnings. Stroll around the man-made lake on the Capitol grounds, where you will see several sculptures, an eternal flame, and the governor's official residence. The South Dakota Cultural and Heritage Center has exhibits on the state's history. You can also visit the three giant aquariums housed in the Discovery Center and Aquarium, which displays native species of fish.

Attractions

ART AND ARCHITECTURE

State Capitol. Marble wainscotting, Ionic columns, and a terrazzo tile floor are some of the classical details that adorn the interior of this building, constructed between 1905 and 1910 at a cost of just under $1 million, and modeled on Montana's capitol. A copper dome and marble and bronze statues ornament the exterior. | 500 E. Capitol Ave. | 605/773–3765 | Free | Weekdays 8 AM–10 PM.

BEACHES, PARKS, AND NATURAL SIGHTS

Capitol Lake. Despite central South Dakota's extreme winter temperatures, this lake never completely freezes, making it a haven for Canada geese, wood ducks, mallards, and other migratory waterfowl. | 500 E. Capitol Ave. | 605/224–7361 or 800/962–2034 | Free.

Capitol Lake is fed by a natural spring whose waters contain an unusually high concentration of natural gas, which in turn fuels what's called the **Flaming Fountain** on the northwest shore of the lake. The fountain's perpetual glow serves as a memorial to all veterans.

Hilger's Gulch and Governor's Grove. A 1¹/₁₀-mi walking/jogging/bicycle path meanders through this beautiful city park, which contains hundreds of new trees, 28 monuments dedicated to former South Dakota governors, and Gates of the Counties, built of native stone from each of the state's counties. | 500 E. Capitol Ave. | 605/224–7361 or 800/962–2034 | Free.

Lake Oahe. Walleye fishing, swimming, boating, and windsurfing draw many to the largest of South Dakota's "Great Lakes" reservoirs where winds can be stiff and waters rough. Tours of the Oahe Dam and Powerhouse, which extends 231 mi from Pierre to Bismarck, North Dakota, and which is visible from space, are given regularly. | 28563 Powerhouse Rd. | 605/224–5862 or 605/224–5864 | Free | Tours available Memorial Day–Labor Day, daily 8:30–3:30; Labor Day–Memorial Day, appointments must be made 24 hrs in advance.

Steamboat Park. A playground, tennis and basketball courts, softball diamonds, a swimming pool, a beach, and an ice-skating rink in this park are next door to Hilger's Gulch and Governor's Grove. | 500 E. Capitol Ave. | 605/224–7361 or 800/962–2034 | Free.

CULTURE, EDUCATION, AND HISTORY

Fighting Stallions Memorial. Dedicated to the memory of the late Gov. George S. Mickelson and 7 other state residents who died in a plane crash in April 1993, this exceptional bronze memorial was a gift from the people of South Dakota. It is a replica of a carving created by the late Korczak Ziolkowski, sculptor of Crazy Horse Memorial in the Black Hills. | 500 E. Capitol Ave. | Free.

MUSEUMS

South Dakota Cultural Heritage Center. Early Native American cultures, the arrival of white settlers, riverboats, and railroads are some of the subjects of the museum's exhibits, though the most popular display is a walk-through sod shanty, where you can listen to stories told by a pioneer woman, visit a Lakota tepee, and explore an old-time gold-mining operation. | 900 Governor's Dr. | 605/773–3458 | Free | Weekdays 9–4:30, weekends 1–4:30.

South Dakota National Guard Museum. Civil War and vintage guns, World War I machine guns, a World War II Sherman tank, General Custer's dress sword, and an A-7D aircraft fill this museum. | 303 E. Dakota Ave. | 605/224–9991 | Free | Mon., Wed., Fri. 8–5; Tues., Thurs., weekends by appointment only.

SPORTS AND RECREATION

Farm Island State Recreation Area. First noted in the journals of Lewis and Clark, this site now has a modern campground with cabins, a nature area, and boat-launching facilities. | Hwy. 34 E | 605/224–5605 | farmisland@gfp.state.sd.us | $3 per person, $5 per vehicle, $20 annually | May–Sept., daily dawn to dusk.

OTHER POINTS OF INTEREST

South Dakota Discovery Center and Aquarium. Missouri River fish are among the many varieties that fill the aquariums at this science playground, which also includes more than 50 self-guided hands-on science activities. On weekends, you can explore the center's planetarium shows. | 805 W. Sioux Ave. | 605/224–8295 | $4 | May–Aug., daily 1–5; Sept.–Apr., daily 1–5.

ON THE CALENDAR

AUG.: *Riverfest.* A rodeo and an air show are some of the highlights at this festival, which also includes a free picnic, an outdoor concert, raft races, and a kid's carnival. | 605/224–7361.

WALKING TOUR

Capital City Walk (Approximately four hours)

Begin your walking tour of the capital on Sioux Avenue, at the **Best Western Ramkota Inn RiverCentre,** one of the community's favored gathering spots. The restaurant in this spacious hotel and convention center is perfect for a pre-walk breakfast or lunch. Just across the street is the **South Dakota Discovery Center and Aquarium,** a fun, hands-on science and technology center enjoyed by both adults and children. Try the gyrochair or the anti-gravity mirrors. Next to the Discovery Center is the Pierre Area Chamber of Commerce, and Pierre Convention and Visitors Bureau, which provides a wide variety of visitor guides, maps, and attractions and lodging listings, as well as personal assistance to travelers. Across the street, on the banks of the Missouri River, **Steamboat Park** has a walking/jogging/bicycle path, playground equipment, and picnic shelters in a beautiful riverside landscape. Walk southeast on Dakota Avenue to Poplar Avenue, turn right, and walk 1 block to Missouri Avenue. Follow Missouri Avenue for a 7-block stroll along the Missouri River, past flocks of Canada geese, to Chapelle Street, then make a left. One block northeast, at the intersection with Dakota Avenue, is the **South Dakota National Guard Museum,** whose eclectic collection includes one of Lt. Col. George Armstrong Custer's swords, a Civil War–era horse-drawn gun, and an A-7D jet fighter, among other military memorabilia. After visiting the museum, continue 1 block northeast on Chapelle Street, turn right on Sioux Avenue, walk 3 blocks to Ree Street, then turn left and continue 2 blocks uphill to Wells Avenue. As you crest the hill, **Capitol Lake** and the dome of the South Dakota State Capitol will greet you. Capitol Lake, on the east side of the Capitol building, is fed by a warm artesian well, so that despite central South Dakota's extreme winter temperatures it never completely freezes. The lake has accordingly become a winter haven for Canada geese, wood ducks, mallards, and many other species of migratory waterfowl. The lake's **Flaming Fountain** is also fed by an artesian well, this one with a natural-gas content so high it can be lit. Firefighters and lawmen who perished in the line of duty are remembered at the Fallen Fire Fighters and Law Enforcement memorials on the Capitol grounds, while Korean and Vietnam War memorials honor and recognize South Dakotans who lost their lives in those conflicts. Also overlooking Capitol Lake is a more recent addition—the impressive bronze **Fighting Stallions Memorial,** erected as a lasting tribute to the late Gov. George S. Mickelson and 7 other South Dakotans who lost their lives in a plane crash on April 19, 1993. At the east end of the lake, you'll find the Governor's home, an 18-room private residence, which is not open to the public. The South Dakota Visitor Center, on the shore of Capitol Lake, is open from 8 AM to 10 PM daily and provides a complete selection of visitor information. Widely regarded as one of the most beautiful capitol buildings in the United States, South Dakota's **State Capitol** was modeled after the Montana State Capitol in Helena. Restored for the state's centennial in 1989, the building has mosaic floors, marble staircases, scagliola columns, stained-glass skylights, and early 19th-century artwork. Self-guided tour brochures and other travel information are available at the Tour Guide/Security Office near the back door of the Capitol Annex. After touring the Capitol building, exit from the rear of the Capitol Annex and follow Broadway Avenue east to Governor's Drive. Take a left and walk approximately 7 blocks, past the Kneip Building, the State Library, and Church Street, to the **South Dakota Cultural Heritage Center.** Among the state's top cultural attractions, this museum provides the finest in interpretive exhibits examining South Dakota's Native American and pioneer heritage. Then head south on Governor's Drive and turn right on Church Street. **Hilger's Gulch and Governor's Grove** will be on your left. This enticing city park includes a 1¹⁄₁₀-mi walking/jogging/bicycle path, as well as hundreds of newly planted trees and 28 monuments dedicated to former governors of South Dakota. The park also includes the Gates of the Counties, built of stone native to each county in the state. Continue west on Church Street and turn left on Nicollet Avenue. Two blocks farther, the State Capitol building will be on your left. Turn right on Capitol Avenue, then left on Highland Street. Proceed 2 blocks, then turn right on Sioux Avenue and continue 10 blocks to return to the Best Western Ramkota Inn RiverCentre, where you began.

Dining

Best Western Ramkota Inn RiverCentre. American. Steaks, prime ribs, and walleye are the dinner favorites at this airy restaurant with high ceilings and views of the Missouri River. Kids' menu. | 920 W. Sioux Ave. | 605/224–6877 | Breakfast also available. Sun. brunch | $9–$16 | AE, D, DC, MC, V.

Cattleman's Club. Steak. This is an Old West steakhouse that you can trust to serve you a T-bone without the frills. Piles of sawdust on the floor and an impressive view of the Missouri River add to the cowboy flavor. | 29608 SD Hwy. 34 | 605/224–9774 | $10–$19 | AE, D, MC, V.

La Minestra. Italian. Authentic—and fresh—Italian fare and one of the best wine lists in the region are the hallmarks of this trattoria. You can indulge in pasta with roasted vegetables, or pork tenderloins with a black mission fig, brandy, and butter sauce. | 106 E. Dakota Ave. | 605/224–8090 | $8–$14 | D, MC, V.

Southside Bakery and Pizzeria. Pizza. Convenient to downtown and the Capitol Building, this establishment will lure you with its freshly baked pastries and rolls and its Chicago-style pizza. | 200 E. Dakota Ave. | 605/224–6761 | $7–$12 | MC, V.

Lodging

INEXPENSIVE

Capitol Inn. On one of the city's main thoroughfares, this 2-story hotel is 2 blocks east of the capitol and surrounded by restaurants and shopping. Some refrigerators. Cable TV. Pool. Business services. Pets allowed. | 815 E. Wells Ave. | 605/224–6387 or 800/658–3055 | fax 605/224–8083 | 86 rooms | $33–$39 | AE, D, DC, MC, V.

Super 8. Near the convention center and the Discovery Museum, this 3-story motor lodge sits on U.S. 14. Complimentary Continental breakfast. Some in-room data ports. Cable TV. Laundry facilities. Business services. Pets allowed. | 320 W. Sioux Ave. | 605/224–1617 | www.super8.com | 78 rooms | $32–$65 | AE, D, DC, MC, V.

MODERATE

Best Western Kings Inn. Two blocks from the Missouri River and the capitol building, the 2-floor chain stands in the heart of the downtown area. Restaurant, bar, room service. Some refrigerators. Cable TV. Hot tub, sauna. Business services. Pets allowed. | 220 S. Pierre St. | 605/224–5951 | fax 605/224–5301 | 104 rooms | $55–$58 | AE, D, MC, V.

Best Western Ramkota Inn RiverCentre. Next to the RiverCentre convention complex, this hotel overlooks the Missouri River. Some rooms open onto the indoor pool. Restaurant, bar, room service. Some refrigerators. Cable TV. Indoor pool, wading pool. Hot tub. Laundry facilities. Business services, airport shuttle. Pets allowed. | 920 W. Sioux Ave. | 605/224–6877 | fax 605/224–1042 | ramkota@dtgnet.com | www.bestwestern.com | 151 rooms | $69–$200 | AE, D, DC, MC, V.

Days Inn. The 3-floor hotel sits 3 blocks from the Missouri River on U.S. 14. Complimentary coffee and fresh cookies are provided each afternoon in the lobby. Complimentary Continental breakfast. Cable TV. Business services. Pets allowed. | 520 W. Sioux Ave. | 605/224–0411 | fax 605/224–0411 | www.daysinn.com | 81 rooms | $55–$80 | AE, D, DC, MC, V.

Governor's Inn. This motel greets you with fresh-baked cookies daily, and many of the spacious rooms and suites are furnished with recliners. Even your trusty sidekick is welcome—hunting dogs are permitted for a small fee. Complimentary Continental breakfast. Some microwaves, some refrigerators, some in-room hot tubs. Cable TV. Indoor pool. Hot tub. Exercise equipment. | 700 W. Sioux Ave. | 605/224–4200 | fax 605/224–4200 | www.govinn.com | 82 rooms | $59–$105 | AE, D, MC, V.

River Place Inn Bed & Breakfast. The backdrop for this contemporary, 3-story home is the majestic Missouri River. Floor-to-ceiling windows and large balconies provide a light, fresh atmosphere and great views of the river and the surrounding prairie. Two rooms have private baths. Complimentary breakfast. Cable TV. Hot tub. | 109 River Pl. | 605/224–8589 | fax 605/945–2216 | www.bbonline.com | 4 | $50–$150 | MC, V.

PINE RIDGE

MAP 8, B5

(Nearby town also listed: Badlands National Park)

Pine Ridge is home to the headquarters of the Oglala Sioux tribe and the Pine Ridge Indian Reservation, south of Badlands National Park. With 1,783,741 acres, the home of the Oglala Sioux is second in size only to Arizona's Navajo Reservation. The town of Pine Ridge, which sits on the reservation's extreme southern edge, is home to the Oglala Nation Powwow and Rodeo, held the first weekend in August. Founded in 1877 as an Indian agency for Chief Red Cloud and his band of followers, Pine Ridge thrives today from government jobs. The majority of its residents work for the Bureau of Indian Affairs, the tribe, or the schools.

Information: **Oglala Sioux Tribe.** | Box 87, Oglala, 57764 | 605/867–1024.

Attractions
Red Cloud Indian School Heritage Art Museum. Exquisite star quilts and works by artists representing 30 tribes fill the galleries. | 100 Mission Dr. | 605/867–5491 | Free | Jun.–Aug., daily 8–5; Sept.–May, weekdays 8–5.

Wounded Knee Historical Site. A solitary stone obelisk commemorates the site of the December 29, 1890, massacre at Wounded Knee. It is 12 mi northwest of Pine Ridge, along Hwy. 18. | Free.

ON THE CALENDAR
JUNE: *Red Cloud Indian Art Show.* Native American artists' paintings and sculptures are the focus of this 6-week long exhibition, beginning on the first Sunday of the month, at the Red Cloud Indian School. | 605/867–5491.
AUG.: *Oglala Nation Powwow and Rodeo.* This traditional powwow and rodeo is hosted by the Oglala Sioux tribe at the Powwow Grounds on the west side of town. | 605/867–5821.

Dining
Martin Livestock Cafe. Steak. A modest, but welcoming meat and potatoes restaurant, approximately 10 mi from the Wakpamni Bed and Breakfast. | E. Hwy. 18, Martin | 605/685–6716 | $7–$16.

Lodging
Wakpamni Pine Ridge Indian Reservation. This contemporary B&B on a working wheat farm specializes in Oglala Lakota arts and culture (you can opt to stay in one of 2 tepees). No private baths. Gift shop on premises. Complimentary breakfast. Hot tub. Horseback riding. Library. No kids under 12. | HC 64, Batesland | 605/288–1800 | fax 605/288–1868 | bswick@gpcom.net | 6 rooms, 2 tepees | $60–$100 | AE, MC, V.

PLATTE

(Nearby town also listed: Chamberlain)

This small community sits at the junction of Rtes. 44 and 45, south of Chamberlain and just 14 mi from the Missouri River. Settled in 1882 by immigrants from the Netherlands, Platte is home to 2 motels, a bed-and-breakfast, and Dyke's Gardens. The majority of Platte's visitors come for the excellent walleye and bass fishing at nearby Lake Francis Case, as well as some of the best pheasant hunting in the state. Agriculture is what supports the town, a shopping hub for the area.

Information: **Platte Chamber of Commerce.** | 500 Main St., Platte, 57369 | 605/337–3921.

Attractions

Ft. Randall Dam—Lake Francis Case. At the base of the massive earthen dam is the Ft. Randall Historic Site, commemorating a military outpost established in 1856. Among the fort's early visitors were William Tecumseh Sherman, George Custer, and Sioux leader Sitting Bull. | U.S. 281/18 | 605/487–7847 | Free | May–Oct., daily.

Platte Creek State Recreation Area. The well-protected natural cove where Platte Creek flows into Lake Francis Case has a beach, a boat launch, boat rentals, fish-cleaning stations, and camping sites. | Hwy. 44 | 605/337–2587 | $3 per person, $5 per vehicle, $20 annually.

Snake Creek State Recreation Area. Wooded ravines and scenic Missouri River bluffs form the backdrop for this area, a favorite with walleye fishermen who make use of the marina, campgrounds, and cabins. | Hwy. 44 | 605/337–2587 | $3 per person, $5 per vehicle, $20 annually.

ON THE CALENDAR
JULY: *Crazy Days.* This annual community event includes food booths, arts and crafts exhibits, and fun and games. | 605/337–2275 or 800/510–3272.

Dining
Pizza Ranch Restaurant. American. This is the original restaurant of the Midwestern chain, specializing in pizzas and wraps. Other menu items include taco salad, pastas, buffet, and sandwiches. | 801 E. 7th St. | 605/337–3250 | Closed Sun. | $5–$10 | No credit cards.

Lodging
King's Inn. The single-story, exterior corridor motel sits in the heart of town, on the main thoroughfare. If you catch a fish or pheasant, you can freeze it for free. Complimentary Continental breakfast. Cable TV. Hot tub. Playground. Pets allowed. | 221 E. 7th St. | 605/337–3385 or 800/337–7756 | ben@kingsinnmotel.com | www.kingsinnmotel.com | 36 rooms | $41–$62 | AE, D, MC, V.

Prairie Skies Country Inn. Innkeepers Tom and Barb Travis converted an old barn into a contemporary B&B decorated with local arts and crafts. You can rent out the entire house for a family get-together or a hunting or fishing vacation. A full kitchen is available to guests. Special hunting packages are available. Complimentary Continental breakfast. Cable TV. Hot tub. | 26949 360th Ave. | 605/337–3764 | fax 605/337–2614 | www.prairieskies.com | 5 rooms | $80–$200 | MC, V.

RAPID CITY

MAP 8, B3

(Nearby towns also listed: Custer, Deadwood, Hill City, Keystone, Lead, Sturgis)

Western South Dakota's largest city and the gateway to the Black Hills, Rapid City is nestled among the eastern foothills of the ancient mountain range. Rapid City was founded in 1876 by pioneer settlers hoping to capitalize on trade with Deadwood and Lead, the gold-mining centers of the Black Hills in the 1870s. Today Rapid City is a tourist center, as well as a retail, healthcare, and entertainment hub for residents of the region. Among its premier attractions are the Rushmore Plaza Civic Center (the arena of which was christened by Elvis Presley in one of his final concerts); the new $12.5-million Journey Museum, which combines 5 outstanding public and private collections; Storybook Island, a free fantasyland fun park; and the recently redeveloped Canyon Lake and its surrounding parklands. In addition, Rapid City is serviced by a modern regional airport and has a 120-store mall on its northern edge.

Information: **Rapid City Chamber of Commerce, and Convention & Visitors Bureau |** 444 Mt. Rushmore Rd. N, 57701 | 605/343–1744 or 800/333–2072.

NEIGHBORHOODS

Historic Downtown. The downtown commercial and historic area includes 38 buildings constructed in pueblo-style, with flat roofs and stucco walls. Basically a square, abutted on the east by 5th Street, on the south by Joseph Street, with Mt. Rushmore Road to the west and Main Street to the north, this area has a concentration of historic buildings. Here you'll find the heart of Rapid City, including the hand-chiseled Gambrel Building (1930s), the First National Bank Building (1914), the Sweeney Building (1886), and the Pennington County Bank Building. Most now house shops, restaurants, and businesses.
West Boulevard Historic District. Wide, shady streets and vintage homes in the Colonial and Queen Anne Victorian styles fill this peaceful 18-block residential area southwest of downtown.

TRANSPORTATION INFORMATION

Air Travel: The **Rapid City Regional Airport** (605/393–9924) is 10 mi southeast of town on Route 44. Northwest Airlines, Skywest (a Delta subsidary), and United Express have regularly scheduled flights into Rapid City.
Bus: For interstate travel, **Jackrabbit** (605/348–3300) runs buses throughout the state and has links with **Greyhound** to get you elsewhere (Greyhound does not have service within the state of South Dakota). There are no passenger trains in Rapid City.
Driving Around Town: A slow tractor causes the worst traffic in town, at least outside tourist season. In summer, legions of RVs meandering through the streets choke things up, and the road to Mt. Rushmore can be pretty slow going. Use care if you're traveling in winter: snow and ice can make for treacherous driving; call the **South Dakota Department of Transportation** (605/773–3571) for road-construction reports in summer and weather updates in winter.

Attractions

Bear Country U.S.A. Bears, wolves, elk, bighorns, and other North American wildlife roam free in their natural habitat here. Bear cubs, wolf pups, and other park offspring are housed in a walk-through area. Allow at least 1½ hrs for your visit. | 13820 Hwy. 16 S | 605/343–2290 | www.bearcountryusa.com | $8.50 | May–Oct., daily 8–6, or during daylight hours.

Black Hills Caverns. Frost crystal, amethyst, logomites, calcite crystals, and other specimens fill the cave, first discovered by pioneers in the late 1800s. Half-hour and hour tours are available. | 2600 Cavern Rd. | 605/343–0542 | $8 per hour, $7 per half-hour | May 1–Oct. 15, daily 8:30–5:30.

Black Hills Flea Market. This is one of the largest flea markets on the plains, selling everything from art, jewelry, and furniture to used clothing, books, and knickknacks. | 5500 Mt. Rushmore Rd. | 605/343–6477 | Free | May–Sept., Sat.–Sun., and national holidays that fall on Fri. or Mon., 7–dusk.

Black Hills National Forest. Hundreds of miles of hiking, mountain biking, and horseback riding trails crisscross this million-acre forest on the western edge of the state. Other entry points are Custer, Deadwood, Hill City, Hot Springs, Lead, Spearfish, and Sturgis. | Black Hills National Forest Visitor Center, 803 Soo San Dr. | 605/343–8755 | www.fs.fed.us/bhnf | Free | Daily, visitor center mid-May–Sept.

Canyon Lake. You can rent a paddleboat, fish, or feed the ducks and Canada geese along the banks of this small lake. | 4111 Jackson Blvd. | 605/394–4175 | Free.

Children's Science Center. A great rainy-day alternative if you have young children, the Center offers interactive learning programs about wild animals, the universe, and the planet under our feet. Programs change with the season. Call ahead for information. | 515 West Blvd. | 605/394–6996 | www.hpcnet.org/sdsmt/childrens_science_center | $3, under 3 years old free | Tues.–Fri. 9–5, Sat. 10–4.

Cosmos of the Black Hills. No one knows what makes the world seem out-of-whack at this fun center, but everyone comes out believing that they can climb on walls, stand at an angle, and defy the laws of physics. | 4021 W. Chicago | 605/343–9802 | $2, under 12 free | Jun. 1st–Labor Day, daily 7–dusk; Labor Day–Nov. 1st, Mon.–Fri. 9–5.

Crystal Cave Park. A trout pond and the bones of a hapless explorer are two of the sights on the 45-minute, non-strenuous tours of this crystal-lined cavern. | 7770 Nameless Cave Rd. | 605/342–8008 | $7.50 | May 1–Oct. 15, daily 9–6.

Dahl Fine Arts Center. A 180-ft panorama, enhanced by a sound and light presentation, brings 200 years of American history to life. The Dahl also has a sales gallery of original work by regional artists. | 713 7th St. | 605/394–4101 | Free | Mon.–Sat. 9–5, Sun. 1–5.

Dinosaur Park. Seven life-size replicas of colossal prehistoric reptiles guard the crest of Skyline Drive where you have a view of the entire city. | 940 Skyline Dr. | 605/348–0462 | Free.

Flying T BBQ Supper and Show. Foot-stompin' fiddle, steel guitar, and song mix with clean family comedy at this Rapid City mainstay where meals are all-you-can-eat. | 8971 S Hwy. 16 | 605/342–1905 | $12, includes food and show | Mid-May–mid-Sept., daily.

The Journey Museum. Interactive exhibits explore the history of the Black Hills from the age of the dinosaurs through Native American history to the days of the pioneers. | 222 New York St. | 605/394–6923 | www.journeymuseum.com | $6 | Memorial Day–Labor Day, daily 8–7; Labor Day–Memorial Day, Mon.–Sat. 1–4, Sun. 11–5.

Reptile Gardens. The world's largest reptile collection and one of the Black Hills' premier family attractions has snakes, gators, crocs, and 4 entertaining shows. There are stunning botanical gardens as well. | U.S. 16 | 605/342–5873 or 800/335–0275 | www.state.sd.us/state/executive/tourism/adds/reptile.htm | $7 | Apr.–Oct., daily 9–3.

Sitting Bull Crystal Caverns. Crystalline chambers, reflecting pools, and limestone fill these underground caverns, through which tours are led. | 13745 Hwy. 16S | 605/342–2777 | $7 | June–Aug., daily 7–7; May, Sept., Oct., daily 8–6.

South Dakota School of Mines and Technology. Established in 1885, this 4-year university excels in engineering programs. | 501 E. St. Joseph St. | 605/394–6999 | www.sdsmt.edu/ | Free | Weekdays 7:30–3:30.

The **Museum of Geology.** Arguably the finest collection of fossilized bones, from giant dinosaurs, marine reptiles, and prehistoric mammals, is housed in this museum, which also contains extensive collections of agates, fossilized cycads, rocks, gems, and minerals. | O'Harra Memorial Building, 501 E. St. Joseph St. | 605/394–2467 or 800/544–8162 | Free | Memorial Day–Labor Day, Mon.–Sat. 8–6, Sun. 12–6; rest of the year, weekdays 8–5, Sat. 9–4, Sun. 1–4.

Stavkirke Chapel in the Hills. Norse dragon heads mix with Christian symbols in this chapel, held together with pegs. Scandinavian immigrant artifacts are contained in a log-cabin museum next door. | 3788 Chapel La. | 605/342–3880 | Free | May 1–Sept. 30, 7 AM–sunset.

Storybook Island. Nursery rhymes come to life in animated and real-life scenes at this children's fantasy theme park, which also includes summer children's theater. | 1301 Sheridan Lake Rd. | 605/342–6357 | Donations accepted | Memorial Day–Labor Day, daily 8–8.

Thunderhead Underground Falls. Six hundred feet within a mountain, along a deserted mineshaft, you'll find a spectacular waterfall, first discovered by miners while blasting for gold. | 10940 W. Hwy. 44 | 605/343–0081 | $4.75 | May–Oct., daily 9:30–6:30, or during daylight hours.

SIGHTSEEING TOURS/TOUR COMPANIES

Black Hills Petrified Forest. This tour, including an audio-visual presentation and a 5-block nature walk, details the geologic evolution of western South Dakota from the earth's beginning to the present. Allow 45 minutes to an hour for your visit. | 8228 Elk Creek Rd. | 605/787–4560 | www.elkcreek.org | $7 | Memorial Day–Labor Day, daily 8–7; May and Sept., daily 9–5.

Gray Line Sightseeing Tours. Customized sightseeing tours of the Black Hills and surrounding areas are available for groups or individuals, as well as charters and convention services. | 1600 E. St. Patrick St. | 605/342–4461 or 800/456–4461 | www.blackhillsgrayline.com | $34 | Mid-May–mid-Oct., daily 8–5.

Mount Rushmore Tours/Stagecoach West. Sightseeing tours of the Black Hills and its attractions are given daily. | Ft. Hayes Chuckwagon | 605/343–3113 | $35–$49 (includes meals) | June–Sept., daily; call for reservations.

ON THE CALENDAR

YEAR-ROUND: *Moonwalk.* Guided walks, on the Friday night closest to the full moon, have a different topic each month. The walks are held in a number of towns in the Black Hills area, including Custer, Hill City, and Spearfish. | 605/673–2251.

JAN.–FEB.: *Black Hills Stock Show and Rodeo.* World-champion wild horse races, bucking horses, timed sheepdog trials, draft horse competitions, and a stockmans' banquet and ball are some of the events you'll witness at this professional rodeo at the Rushmore Plaza Civic Center. | 605/342–8325.

FEB.: *Black Hills Sport Show and Sale.* The newest recreational vehicles, motorcycles, boats, bicycles, campers, and fishing and hunting equipment, are all displayed at the Rushmore Plaza Civic Center. | 605/343–4279.

JUNE: *West Boulevard Summer Festival.* Arts and crafts booths, children's activities, ethnic and traditional food vendors, and live entertainment fill the West Boulevard Historic District during Fathers' Day Weekend. | 605/348–9439.

JULY: *Black Hills Heritage Festival.* Free entertainment from big-name acts and exceptional food make this festival, held in Memorial Park around Independence Day, one of the region's most popular arts-in-the-park events. | 605/341–5714.

AUG.: *Central States Fair.* Top-name grandstand entertainment, professional rodeos, cattle shows, 4-H days, a carnival, a petting zoo, and a German tent make up this classic regional fair, held at Central States Fairgrounds. | 605/355–3861.

Dining

Botticelli Ristorante Italiano. Italian. Statuary and columns give this Northern Italian eatery a classical appearance. Veal and chicken dishes as well as creamy pastas complement daily specials such as the seafood on Wednesday night. Live jazz is heard on Friday and Saturday nights. | 523 Main St. | 605/348–0089 | No lunch Sun. | $7–$20 | AE, MC, V.

Carini's. Italian. Authentic southern Italian cuisine is served in a sparse setting. You'll get enormous portions of all the traditional dishes. | 324 St. Joseph's St. | 605/348–3704 | $9–$15.95 | AE, MC, V.

Circle B Ranch Chuck Wagon Supper & Music Show. American. Chuckwagon suppers include tender roast beef and chicken, biscuits, and all the trimmings. The ranch also offers western music shows, miniature golf, gold panning, and trail and wagon rides. Dinner with a show is $14. | 22735 Hwy. 385 | 605/348–7358 | Reservations essential | Closed Oct.–Apr. No lunch | $14 | MC, V.

Firehouse Brewing Co. American. Occupying an historic 1915 firehouse, the state's first brew pub is ornamented throughout with brass fixtures and fire-fighting equipment. The 5 house-brewed beers are the highlight of the menu, which also includes a variety of hearty pub dishes such as pastas, salads, and gumbo. Thursday nights buffalo prime rib is the specialty. Kids' menu. | 610 Main St. | 605/348–1915 | Reservations not accepted | No lunch Sun. | $10–$25 | AE, D, DC, MC, V.

Fireside Inn. Steak. A warm fireside setting complements some of the best beef in the Dakotas. A spacious new patio is ideal for cocktails before dinner. Try the bean soup, New York steak, or the 20-oz Cattlemen's Cut. | Hwy. 44 W | 605/342–3900 | No lunch | $11–$17 | AE, D, MC, V.

Flying T Chuckwagon. Barbecue. Ranch-style meals of barbecued beef, potatoes, and baked beans are served on tin plates in this converted barn. Dinner is followed by a western show featuring music and cowboy comedy, and there's now a western breakfast show from 7–9 AM. | 8971 Hwy. 16 S | 605/342–1905 | Reservations essential | Closed mid-Sept.–late May. No lunch | $12 | D, MC, V.

Golden Phoenix. Chinese. Relaxed, friendly, and quick service together with convenient parking make this one of South Dakota's best Chinese restaurants. Try the Mongolian beef, sesame chicken, or Hunan shrimp. | 2421 W. Main St. | 605/348–4195 | $8–$10 | AE, D, DC, MC, V.

Landmark Restaurant and Lounge. American. This hotel restaurant is popular for its lunch buffet, and for dinner specialties that include prime rib, beef Wellington, freshwater fish, and wild game. | 523 6th St. | 605/342–1210 | $22–$36 | AE, D, DC, MC, V.

Lodging

Abend Haus Cottages and Audrie's Bed and Breakfast. Log cabins and suites, each with a private hot tub and appointed with Old World antiques, sit among ponderosa pines, 7 mi west of Rapid City. Desserts and homemade breakfasts are provided. Complimentary breakfast. Kitchenettes, microwaves, refrigerators, in-room hot tubs. Cable TV, in-room VCRs. No kids under 18. No smoking. | 23029 Thunderhead Falls Rd. | 605/342–7788 | www.audriesbb.com | 4 suites, 6 cabins | $95–$130 suites, $145–$175 cabins | No credit cards.

★ **Alex Johnson Hotel.** Period furnishings recreate the air of the '20s in this 9-floor 1928 hotel surrounded by shops and restaurants in downtown Rapid City. Restaurant, bar (with entertainment). Some refrigerators, some in-room hot tubs. Cable TV. Airport shuttle. No pets. | 523 6th St. | 605/342–1210 or 800/888–2539 | fax 605/342–7436 | www.alexjohnson.com | 141 rooms, 2 suites | $98–$145 | AE, D, DC, MC, V.

Audrie's Bed & Breakfast. Victorian antiques and an air of romance greet you at this out-of-the-way inn, 6 mi west of Rapid City on U.S. 44 in the heart of the Black Hills. You can stay in comfortable suites, cottages, and creekside cabins, most with fireplaces and private baths. Complimentary Continental breakfast. Cable TV. Hot tub. No smoking. | 23029 Thunderhead Falls Rd. | 605/342–7788 | 6 suites, 4 cottages/cabins | $135 | MC, V.

Best Western Ramkota. This 2-story hotel and convention facility sits just north of I–90 at exit 59, next door to the Rushmore Mall. Restaurant, bar (with entertainment), room service. In-room data ports, some refrigerators. Cable TV. Indoor-outdoor pool. Hot tub. Exercise equipment. Playground. Laundry facilities. Business services, airport shuttle. No pets. | 2111 LaCrosse St. | 605/343–8550 | fax 605/343–9107 | www.bestwestern.com | 272 rooms | $79–$119 | AE, D, DC, MC, V.

Best Western Town 'N Country Inn. The five, 2-story buildings of this chain motel sit 1 mi from downtown on the road to Mount Rushmore and near Rapid City Regional Hospital. Restaurant. Some refrigerators. Cable TV. 2 pools, 1 indoor. Playground. Airport shuttle. No pets. | 2505 Mt. Rushmore Rd. | 605/343–5383 or 877/666–5383 | fax 605/343–9670 | www.bestwestern.com | 100 rooms | $89–$99 | AE, D, DC, MC, V.

Brandsted's Timber Ridge Lodge. On 12 private acres in Black Hills National Forest, Brandsted's 5,000-square-ft main lodge and adjacent guest house are ideal for families or groups of up to 24 persons. Rough hewn logs, stone fireplaces, a fully equipped kitchen,

BLACK HILLS: AN EMERALD OASIS IN A SEA OF PRAIRIE

Creek-carved canyons. Sky-high granite spires. Mountain meadows and meandering brooks watering fragrant wildflowers and wandering wildlife. All in an afternoon in South Dakota's fabled Black Hills.

With 17 peaks exceeding 7,000 ft, "hills" is a misnomer. But, unlike the nearby Rocky Mountains, the Black Hills are accessible and intimate. National parks, monuments, memorials, scenic highways, and hundreds of miles of developed hiking, biking, horseback riding, and snowmobiling trails make this one of America's most popular vacation destinations.

In addition to outstanding outdoor recreation opportunities, the Black Hills are home to Mount Rushmore National Memorial and Crazy Horse Memorial, two enduring icons carved from the ageless granite of this ancient mountain range. Travelers explore a dozen quaint communities whose colorful characters and rich past fill the annals of Western lore.

Roughly the size of Delaware, the Black Hills stand as an emerald oasis in a vast sea of prairie. A century ago, pioneers sailed their prairie schooners across the grasslands until they reached this secluded and mysterious preserve. Most never went home. And still today, the Black Hills beckon newcomers with their promise of the discovery of natural wonders and unmatched beauty.

Towns listed: Belle Fourche, Custer, Deadwood, Hill City, Hot Springs, Keystone, Lead, Rapid City, Spearfish, Sturgis.

and a Chickering piano are among the amenities. Picnic area. Cable TV. Basketball, hiking, volleyball. Cross-country skiing. Playground. Laundry facilities. | 151 Kings Rd. | 605/343–2115 or 605/348–0676 | www.blackhills.com/timberridge | 6 rooms in two cabins | $115–$200 | AE, D, MC, V.

Carriage House Bed & Breakfast. Four-poster beds, a heart-shaped hot tub, a porch swing, and lace curtains reflect the romantic style of this restored, turn-of-the-century home. Carriage House is just a few blocks from the center of downtown Rapid City. Complimentary breakfast. Cable TV. | 721 West Blvd. | 605/343–6415 or 888/343–6415 | www.carriagehouse-bb.com | 4 rooms | $95–$160 | AE, MC, V.

Comfort Inn. Just south of I–90 at exit 59, this interior corridor hotel sits less than 1 mi from Rushmore Mall and about 2 mi from the civic center. Complimentary Continental breakfast. Cable TV. Indoor pool. Hot tub. Business services. No pets. | 1550 N. LaCrosse St. | 605/348–2221 | fax 605/348–3110 | www.choicehotels.com | 73 rooms | $99–$130 | AE, D, DC, MC, V.

Days Inn. This 2-story chain sits south of I–90 at exit 59. Complimentary Continental breakfast. In-room data ports, some refrigerators. Cable TV. Indoor pool. Hot tub. Laundry facilities. Business services. No pets. | 1570 Rapp St. | 605/348–8410 | fax 605/348–3392 | www.daysinn.com | 77 rooms, 16 suites | $79–$109 | AE, D, MC, V.

Fair Value Inn. One mile north of downtown, this 2-story motel sits just south of I–90 at exit 59. Cable TV. Pets allowed. | 1607 LaCrosse St. | 605/342–8118 | 25 rooms | $45–$65 | AE, D, DC, MC, V.

Hayloft Bed & Breakfast. This Victorian farmhouse has antique furnishings, gingham and floral print linens, and nature at its doorstep. Some rooms have private baths and entrances, and young children are welcome. Complimentary breakfast. Some in-room hot tubs. Cable TV. | 9356 Neck Yoke Rd. | 605/343–5351 or 800/317–6784 | hayloft4bb@aol.com | 8 rooms | $85–$115 | MC, V.

Holiday Inn Express. On the south side, near Rapid City Regional Hospital, this 3-story hotel, built in 1995, is just off U.S. 16. Complimentary Continental breakfast. In-room data ports, some refrigerators, some in-room hot tubs. Cable TV. Indoor pool. Hot tub. Laundry facilities. Business services. No pets. | 750 Cathedral Dr. | 605/341–9300 | fax 605/341–9333 | 63 rooms, 7 suites | $80–$100, $100–$120 suites | AE, D, DC, MC, V.

Holiday Inn–Rushmore Plaza. Within the 8-story atrium of this hotel, glass elevators ascend and descend beside a waterfall and lush trees. Built in 1990, it is next to the civic center. Restaurant, bar. In-room data ports, in-room safes, some refrigerators. Cable TV. Indoor pool. Hot tub. Exercise equipment. Laundry facilities. Business services, airport shuttle. No pets. | 505 N. 5th St. | 605/348–4000 | fax 605/348–9777 | www.basshotels.com | 205 rooms, 48 suites | $111–$121, $138 suites | AE, D, DC, MC, V.

Radisson Hotel Rapid City/Mt Rushmore. Murals and a large Mt. Rushmore rendering in the marble floor distinguish the lobby of this 9-floor hotel, in the heart of Rapid City. Restaurant, bar with entertainment, room service. In-room data ports, some in-room hot tubs. Cable TV. Indoor pool. Beauty salon. Business services, airport shuttle. No pets. | 445 Mt. Rushmore Rd. | 605/348–8300 | fax 605/348–3833 | radisson@rapidcity.com | www.radissonrapidcity.com | 176 rooms, 5 suites | $209–$279 | AE, D, DC, MC, V.

Ramada Inn. This 4-floor hotel sits just south of I–90 at exit 59. Bar. Some refrigerators. Cable TV. Indoor pool. Business services. Pets allowed. | 1721 LaCrosse St. | 605/342–1300 | fax 605/342–1300 | www.ramada.com | 139 rooms | $109–$179 | AE, D, DC, MC, V.

Super 8. This 3-story brick and stucco hotel is just north of I–90 at exit 59, about ½ mi from the Rushmore Mall. Complimentary Continental breakfast. Cable TV. Laundry facilities. Business services. Pets allowed. | 2124 LaCrosse St. | 605/348–8070 | fax 605/348–0833 | 119 rooms | $66–$76 | AE, D, DC, MC, V.

Whispering Pines Campground and Lodging. Whispering Pines has full RV hook-ups, nightly block party–style cookouts, and accessibility to Mount Rushmore. Cabins and camping grounds are also available at a reasonable price. There is an on-site café, general store, and gift store. Basketball. Shops, video games. Playground. Laundry facilities. | 22700 Silver City Rd. | 605/341–3667 | fax 605/341–3667 | www.blackhillscampresort.com | $21.95 for full RV hook–ups; $30–$40 cabins; $150 vacation home rentals | D, MC, V.

REDFIELD

MAP 8, F2

(Nearby towns also listed: Aberdeen, Huron, Miller)

Redfield was the first place in South Dakota to successfully introduce the Chinese ring-necked pheasant, which quickly outnumbered state residents and eventually became the official state bird. The town was established by pioneer settlers in 1880, under the name Stennett Junction. Its name was changed to Redfield the following year in honor of Joseph Barlow Redfield, an auditor for the Chicago and Northwestern Railroad. Redfield served as a commercial hub for surrounding farmsteads, much as it does today. This friendly, central South Dakota community has a beautiful city park with a great swimming pool and water slide. Redfield also has a historical museum, a Carnegie Library, a llama ranch, and free camping. Fisher Grove State Park, 7 mi east on U.S. 212, has a restored 1880 schoolhouse, a modern campground, picnic facilities, a hiking trail, and an adjacent 9-hole golf course.

Information: Redfield Chamber of Commerce | 626 N. Main St., 57469 | 605/472–0965.

Attractions

Fisher Grove State Park. Once a popular gathering place for Native American tribes, who conducted annual councils and trade fairs at its famous council stone site, the 277-acre park (10 mi east of Redfield) now has hiking trails, campsites, and a restored 19th-century schoolhouse. | 17290 Fishers La., Frankfort | 605/472–1212 | $3 per person, $5 per vehicle, $20 annually.

Two Bridges Llama Farm. A breeding farm more than 60 llamas strong is unexpected in this small town. Tours are available. | 605/472–1548.

ON THE CALENDAR

DEC.: *Good Neighbor Day.* An annual event that encourages locals (and travelers) to get to know each other through refreshments, games, and prize drawings. | 605/472–0965.

Dining

Sak's Family Restaurant. American. Meatloaf like mom used to make. Locals come to Sak's, near the old rail station, for lunch and gossip. | 17531 Hwy. 281 | 605/472–1626 | $7–$12 | D, MC, V.

Lodging

Arctic Swan Bed & Breakfast Inn and Hunting Lodge. This restored 19th-century hunting lodge accommodates hunters, executives, and families. Pheasant-hunting packages are available, a meeting room for 20 persons is on-site, and the entire third floor can be converted into a family suite. Complimentary breakfast. TV in common area. | 515 E. 16th Ave. | 605/472–4123 or 877/472–4123 | innkeeper@arcticswan.com | www.arcticswan.com | 7 rooms | $57–$80 rooms, $95–$115 suites | MC, V.

Super 8. On the western edge of town, this 2-story hotel is at the junction of U.S. 281 and 212. Cable TV. No pets. | 826 W. 4th St. | 605/472–0720 | fax 605/472–0855 | www.super8.com | 27 rooms | $40–$60 | AE, D, DC, MC, V.

Wilson Motor Inn. Just off Highway 212E, this single-story hotel sits in a commercial area on the east side of town. Cable TV. No pets. | 1109 E. 7th Ave. | 605/472–0550 or 800/690–0551 | fax 605/472–2019 | 24 rooms | $30–$50 | D, MC, V.

SIOUX FALLS

(Nearby towns also listed: Beresford, Madison, Mitchell)

Founded in 1856 by the Western Town Site Company on a strip of land near the falls of the Big Sioux River, Sioux Falls was abandoned in 1862 for fear of attack by Santee Indian raiders, who burned the settlement after pioneers fled to Yankton. Following the Civil War, with the protection of the U.S. Cavalry, the rebuilding of Sioux Falls began, and by 1873 the town claimed 573 residents. Situated at the junction of I–90 and I–29, Sioux Falls is the only city in the state with more than 100,000 residents. It has maintained steady growth through a diversified mix of agriculture, manufacturing, banking, medical services, transportation, communications, and wholesale and retail trade. Private and college-affiliated art galleries abound in Sioux Falls, and it has imposing museums, a symphony orchestra, playhouses, and dance companies.

Information: Sioux Falls Chamber of Commerce, and Convention and Visitors Bureau | 200 N. Phillips Ave., Ste. 102, 57104-1425 | 605/336–1620 or 800/333–2072.

SIOUX FALLS

INTRO
ATTRACTIONS
DINING
LODGING

Attractions

Augustana College. This 4-year private school, with nearly 1,700 students, 44 majors, 37 minors, and 14 pre-professional programs, is also home to the Center for Western Studies and a full-scale bronze casting of Michelangelo's *Moses*. Campus tours, lasting about 2 hours, are available. | 2001 S. Summit Ave. | 605/336–5516 | www.augie.edu | Free | Weekdays 8–5, Sat. 9–11.

Empire Mall. South Dakota's largest shopping center contains 180 stores and 32 movie theaters. | I–29 and 41st St. | 605/361–3301 | Free.

EROS (Earth Resources Observation Systems) Data Center. Audio-visual exhibits, including photographs of the Earth taken from aircraft and satellites, are on display at the Department of the Interior's data center. Tours last 1 to 2 hours. | 47914 252 St. | 605/594–6511 | edcwww.cr.usgs.gov | Free | Weekdays 8–5.

Falls Park. On the banks of the Big Sioux River, next to the falls that gave the town its name, pink quartzite is visible through cascading water. | Falls Park Dr. | 605/336–1620 or 800/333–2072 | Free | Daily 9–9.

Sherman Park. Home to the Great Plains Zoo and the Delbridge Museum of Natural History, this 32-acre park is a great place for a picnic or a relaxing afternoon in the shade of giant cottonwoods. | 805 S. Kiwanis Ave. | Free.
The **Delbridge Museum of Natural History** has a large collection of mounted game animals from around the globe, all displayed in naturalistic habitats. | 805 S. Kiwanis Ave. | 605/367–7059 | $6 for both museum and zoo | Apr.–Oct., daily 9–7; Nov.–Mar., daily 10–5. Modeled after the San Diego Zoo, the **Great Plains Zoo** has birds of prey, grizzly bears, Siberian tigers, and black-footed penguins. Exhibits approximate the natural habitat of a variety of species from 5 continents. | 805 S. Kiwanis Ave. | 605/367–7003 | $6 for both museum and zoo | Apr.–Oct., daily 9–7; Nov.–Mar., daily 10–5.

Siouxland Heritage Museums. This organization is made up of the Old Courthouse Museum and the Pettigrew Home and Museum. | 200 W. 6th St. | 605/367–4210 | Free | Mon.–Wed. 9–5, Thurs. 9–9, Fri.–Sat. 9–5, Sun. 12–5.

The **Old Courthouse Museum** is a restored 1890 quartzite courthouse, where exhibits illustrate the culture and heritage of the Siouxland region, from Native American habitation through the pioneer period. | 200 W. 6th St. | 605/367–4210 | Free | Mon.–Wed., Fri.–Sat. 9–5, Thurs. 9–9, Sun. 1–5.

The **Pettigrew Home and Museum** is an 1889 Queen Anne house, once home to U.S. Senator Richard F. Pettigrew. The natural history of the local area is displayed in galleries among many period antiques. | 131 N. Duluth Ave. | 605/367–4210 | Free | Mon.–Sun. 12–5.

University of Sioux Falls. This 4-year Christian university with 1,200 students provides courses in 30 majors, as well as 2 master's programs. | 1101 W. 22nd St. | 605/331–6608 | www.the-coo.edu | Free.

USS *South Dakota* Battleship Memorial. World War II mementos and original artifacts such as anchors, main mast, and gun barrels, make up this memorial honoring the highly decorated ship and the men who served on board. The USS *South Dakota* helped defend the aircraft carrier *Enterprise* in the Pacific theater. | W. 12th St. and Kiwanis Ave. | 605/367–7060 | Free | Memorial Day–Labor Day, Mon.–Thurs. 11–5:30, Fri. 11–6, Sat.–Sun. 11–6:30.

ON THE CALENDAR

JAN.: *Greater Sioux Falls Outdoor Show.* Fishing, hunting, camping, and boating demonstrations are the focus of this weekend event, held at the Sioux Empire Arena and Expo Hall.; | 605/336–2988.

JAN.: *Sioux Empire/Sioux Falls Farm Show.* Horse pulls, livestock competitions, and kids' activities make up this winter farm festival held at the Sioux Empire Arena and Expo Hall. | 605/373–2016.

FEB.: *Artists of the Plains Art Show and Sale.* Artwork of regional artists is on view and for sale at this silent auction at the Radisson Encore Inn. | 605/336–4007.

MAR.: *Schmeckfest.* Swiss, German, and Hutterite meals mix with craft displays, bake sales, and musical performances at this festival on Freeman Academy Campus. | 605/648–3290.

MAR.: *Sioux Empire Sportsmen's Show.* Hunting and fishing seminars are held at the Sioux Empire Arena and Expo Hall in conjunction with the boat and RV shows. | 612/755–8111.

JUNE: *Great Plains Balloon Race.* Balloons are launched on Saturday and Sunday mornings from Tea airport, 4 mi southwest of Sioux Falls. Where the race ends depends on wind and weather. | 605/332–6161.

Dining

Canton Café. Chinese. Big portions and reasonable prices make this a popular destination for local families. The menu offers non-Asian choices in addition to traditional Cantonese fare. | 311 S. Garfield Ave. | 605/332–2851 | $6–$10.95 | MC, V.

Champ's Sports Café. American. Sports memorabilia decorate the walls at this bar, which specializes in barbecued ribs, burgers, and onion rings. | 2101 W. 41st St. | 605/331–4386 | $5–$15 | AE, D, DC, MC, V.

Grain Bin. American. This is a do-it-yourself kind of restaurant where a sandwich bar has all the fixin's. Special all-you-can-eat nights let you get your fill of steak, ribs, or seafood. | 5015 N. Cliff Ave. | 605/373–0214 | $3.95–$16.95 | D, MC, V.

Minerva's. American. Dark cherry woods and cozy booths complement a menu filled with fresh seafood, aged steak, and pastas. A particular favorite are the pork medallions. Kids' menu. | 301 S. Phillips | 605/334–0386 | Closed Sun. | $10–$20 | AE, D, DC, MC, V.

Rio Bravo Cantina. Mexican. This lively Mexican restaurant is known for its happy hour, taco bar, and Sunday buffet. On Thursday night there is live entertainment. | 2801 S. Louise Ave. | 605/362–2610 | $5–$8.95 | D, MC, V.

Sioux Falls Brewing Co. American. Unique deli sandwiches, bratwurst, and burgers complement the restaurant's wide selection of original ales and stouts. | 431 N Phillips Ave. | 605/332–4847 | $5.95–$7.95 | AE, D, MC, V.

Spezia. Italian. Nearly forgotten old recipes vie with newly adapted favorites from the wood burning pizza oven on the menu of this spacious, bright eatery. | 1716 S. Western Ave. | 605/334–7491 | $7–$12 | AE, D, MC, V.

Theo's Great Food. Mediterranean. Marble floors augment the glass and ceramic-tile walls at this restaurant where flowers and candles top the tables. The rack of lamb is a highlight of the menu, which also includes pastas, wood-roasted pizzas, seafood, and chicken dishes. Kids' menu. | 601 W. 33rd St. | 605/338–6801 | Sun. brunch | $15–$25 | AE, D, DC, MC, V.

Tomacelli's Pizza. Pizza. You can pile into a booth, watch the big screen TV, and build your own pie or choose from Tomacelli's thick-crust specialties in this informal pizzeria. | 2309 W. 12th St. | 605/335–8500 | $8–$12 | MC, V.

West Winds Restaurant. American. The house favorite is a prime melt sandwich, with strips of steak, cheese, bacon, and barbecue sauce. Other comfort foods such as pot pies and pasta dishes are also available. | 4603 W Homefield Dr. | 605/361–5300 | $4.95–$9.95 | D, MC, V.

Lodging

AmericInn. A fireplace warms the lobby of this 2-floor hotel, just west of I–29 at exit 77. Complimentary Continental breakfast. Cable TV. Indoor pool. Hot tub. Business services. No pets. | 3508 S. Gateway Blvd. | 605/361–3538 or 800/634–3444 | fax 605/361–3538 | www.americinn.com | 65 rooms | $60–$70 | AE, D, DC, MC, V.

Baymont Motel. Just west of I–29 at exit 77, this 3-floor hotel sits 3 blocks from the Empire Mall. Complimentary Continental breakfast. Some refrigerators. Cable TV. Indoor pool. Hot tub. Some pets allowed. | 3200 Meadow Ave. | 605/362–0835 | budgetel.com | 82 rooms | $74–$84 | AE, D, DC, MC, V.

Best Western Ramkota Inn. The Dakotas' largest convention center, this 2-story hotel sits just east of I–29 at exit 81, next to the Sioux Falls Regional Airport. Restaurant, bar. Room service. Cable TV. 2 pools, wading pool. Hot tub, sauna. Playground. Laundry facilities. Business services, airport shuttle. Some pets allowed. | 2400 N. Louise Ave. | 605/336–0650 | fax 605/336–1687 | www.bestwestern.com | 226 rooms | $89–$99 | AE, D, DC, MC, V.

Budget Host Plaza Inn. Three mi north of downtown, this single-story hotel is off I–229 at exit 6. Cable TV. Pool. Pets allowed. | 2620 E. 10th St. | 605/336–1550 or 800/283–4678 | fax 605/339–0616 | 38 rooms | $39–$41 | AE, D, DC, MC, V.

Comfort Inn. This 2-story chain hotel, east of I–29 at exit 77, stands ½ mi north of the Empire Mall. Complimentary Continental breakfast. Some refrigerators. Cable TV. Indoor pool. Hot tub. Some pets allowed. | 3216 S. Carolyn Ave. | 605/361–2822 | www.choicehotels.com | 65 rooms | $49–$99 | AE, D, DC, MC, V.

Comfort Suites. Across from the Empire Mall, this 3-floor chain hotel sits just south of the Comfort Inn, off I–29 at exit 77. Complimentary Continental breakfast. Cable TV. Indoor pool. Hot tub. Business services. Pets allowed. | 3208 S. Carolyn Ave. | 605/362–9711 | www.choice-hotels.com | 61 rooms | $75 | AE, D, DC, MC, V.

Days Inn—Airport. On the north side of town, this 2-floor chain sits just south of I–90 at exit 399, less than 1 mi from the Sioux Falls Regional Airport. Complimentary Continental breakfast. Cable TV. Business services, airport shuttle. No pets. | 5001 N. Cliff Ave. | 605/331–5959 | www.daysinn.com | 87 rooms | $59–$64 | AE, D, DC, MC, V.

Days Inn Empire. This 2-floor hotel sits 2 blocks west of I–29 at exit 77, less than 1 mi from the Empire Mall. Complimentary Continental breakfast. In-room data ports. Cable TV. Business services. No pets. | 3401 Gateway Blvd. | 605/361–9240 | fax 605/361–5419 | www.daysinn.com | 80 rooms | $44–$58 | AE, D, DC, MC, V.

Empire Inn. This locally owned motel is across the street from the Empire Mall and reasonably priced. Complimentary Continental breakfast. Cable TV. Indoor pool. Hot tub, sauna. | 4208 W. 41st St. | 605/361–2345 | 84 rooms | $31.95–$55.95 | AE, D, MC, V.

Encore Inn. Connected to a TGI Fridays and next to the Empire Mall, this 3-floor hotel is east of I–29 at exit 77. Restaurant, room service. In-room data ports, some refrigerators. Cable TV. Indoor pool. Hot tub. Business services, airport shuttle. No pets. | 4300 Empire Pl | 605/361–6684 | fax 605/362–0916 | 98 rooms, 7 suites | $99–$129; $179–$279 suites | AE, D, DC, MC, V.

Exel Inn. Near the Sioux Falls Arena, a sports and concert venue, this 2-floor hotel is 2 mi west of downtown. Complimentary Continental breakfast. Some in-room hot tubs. Cable TV. Laundry facilities. Some pets allowed. | 1300 W. Russell St. | 605/331–5800 | fax 605/331–4074 | 104 rooms | $39–$59 | AE, D, DC, MC, V.

Hampton Inn Sioux Falls. Location is a bonus at this exceptionally well-maintained hotel directly off I–29 at exit 78, adjacent to restaurants and movie theaters and within 1 mi of the Empire Shopping Mall. Some in-room hot tubs. Cable TV. Indoor pool. Hot tub. Gym. | 2417 S. Carolyn Ave. | 605/362–1700 | fax 605/362–1800 | www.hamptoninn.com | 100 rooms | $54–$84 | AE, D, MC, V.

Holiday Inn—City Centre. The only high-rise hotel in downtown Sioux Falls, this 10-floor chain, built in 1972, is the state's largest. Complimentary cocktails and hors d'oeuvres are served in the evenings. Restaurant, bar, room service. In-room data ports. Cable TV. Indoor pool. Hot tub. Exercise equipment. Business services, airport shuttle. No pets. | 100 W. 8th St. | 605/339–2000 | fax 605/339–3724 | www.basshotels.com | 302 rooms | $99–$124 | AE, D, DC, MC, V.

Kelly Inn. East of I–29 (at exit 81), this 2-floor chain is 4 mi from the Sioux Falls Regional Airport. Cable TV. Hot tub, sauna. Laundry facilities. Airport shuttle. Some pets allowed. | 3101 W. Russell St. | 605/338–6242 or 800/635–3559 | fax 605/338–5453 | 43 rooms | $62–$75 | AE, D, DC, MC, V.

Motel 6. Less than 1 mi from the Sioux Empire Arena, this 2-story motel sits east of I–29 at exit 81. Cable TV. Pool. Business services. Some pets allowed. | 3009 W. Russell St. | 605/336–7800 | fax 605/330–9273 | www.motel6.com | 87 rooms | $40–$48 | AE, D, DC, MC, V.

Oaks Hotel and Convention Center. Large rooms with plush wall-to-wall carpeting and lots of storage space make this attractive for families. The University of Sioux Falls, the Great Plains Zoo, and Minerva's restaurant are all less than 3 mi away. Restaurant, bar, complimentary Continental breakfast. Cable TV. Indoor-outdoor pools. Hot tub, sauna. Playground. | 3300 W. Russell St. | 605/ or 800/326–4656 | 200 rooms | $56–$85 | AE, D, MC, V.

Ramada Inn Convention Center. This 2-floor hotel, sitting just south of the Sioux Falls Regional Airport, has a large indoor recreation center, including a video casino and a comedy club. Restaurant, bar (with entertainment), room service. In-room data ports. Cable TV. Indoor pool. Hot tub, sauna. Putting green. Laundry facilities. Business services, airport shuttle. Some pets allowed. | 1301 W. Russell St. | 605/336–1020 | fax 605/336–3030 | www.ramada.com | 200 rooms | $80–$90 | AE, D, DC, MC, V.

Rose Stone Inn Bed & Breakfast. Approximately 8 mi from downtown Sioux Falls, this quiet, Victorian retreat offers a soothing English garden in the back, and guest rooms with names like Ivy and Violets and Peach Blossoms and Lace. Complimentary breakfast. TV in common area. | 504 East 4th St., Dell Rapids | 605/330–0534 | fax 605/428–3698 | Rostoninbb@aol.com | 5 rooms | $65–$85 | D, MC, V.

Select Inn. This 2-story chain hotel is just west of I–29 at exit 77. Complimentary Continental breakfast. Cable TV. Pets allowed. | 3500 S. Gateway Blvd. | 605/361–1864 | fax 605/361–9287 | www.selectinn.com | 100 rooms | $42–$45 | AE, D, DC, MC, V.

Sioux Falls Residence Inn. Larger rooms designed for extended stays—1- and 2-bedroom suites are available—make this newer motel attractive, as does its location adjacent to the Empire Shopping Mall. Some kitchenettes. Cable TV. Indoor pool. Tennis. Gym. Laundry service. | 4509 W. Empire Pl. | 605/361–2202 | www.marriott.com | 66 rooms | $91–$149 | AE, D, DC, MC, V.

Sioux Falls Sheraton Hotel. This 6-story downtown hotel is attached to the Sioux Falls Convention Center by a walkway. The glass and steel atrium is softened with greenery and waterfalls. Complimentary Continental breakfast, room service. In-room data ports. Cable TV, some kitchenettes. Indoor pool. Exercise equipment. Business services. | 1211 N. West Ave. | 605/331–0100 | fax 605/339–7852 | www.sheraton.com | 184 rooms | $65–$120 | AE, D, DC, MC, V.

Super 8. The 3-story hotel sits just south of the Sioux Falls Regional Airport. Restaurant. In-room data ports. Cable TV. Business services. Pets allowed. | 1508 W. Russell St. | 605/339–9330 | www.super8.com | 95 rooms | $39–$50 | AE, D, DC, MC, V.

SISSETON

MAP 8, H1

(Nearby towns also listed: Milbank, Webster)

Founded at the base of the "Coteau des Prairies" (hills of the prairie), Sisseton takes its name from a frontier fort that still stands today. Sisseton is ideally situated for exploration of northeast South Dakota, with several nearby fishing lakes, Fort Sisseton State Park, Sica Hollow State Park, trail rides, powwows, and the Joseph N. Nicollet Tower and Interpretive Center. The pioneer fort was built in 1864 in response to the Minnesota Uprising of 1862, which left 800 white men, women, and children dead in southern Minnesota, Dakota Territory, and northern Iowa. Thanks to reconstruction work by the Works Progress Administration in the 1930s, the fort remains one of the best-preserved military posts in the United States. The town of Sisseton has 3 motels, a campground, a dozen restaurants, shopping, a new swimming pool, and a scenic golf course.

Information: Sisseton Chamber of Commerce | Box 221, 57262 | 605/698–7261.

Attractions

Ft. Sisseton State Park. Seventeen original and reconstructed buildings fill the grounds of this Civil War–era fort, previously called Fort Wadsworth. It is 30 mi west and 5 mi south of Sisseton. | 11907 434th Ave., Lake City | 605/448–5701 | www.state.sd.us/sdparks/ftsiseton/ft_siss.htm | $3 per person, $5 per vehicle, $20 annually.

Joseph N. Nicollet Tower and Interpretive Center. This interpretive center 3½ mi west of Sisseton is dominated by a 75-ft-tall observation tower that overlooks 3 states and a dozen communities. The center houses the great map created by the French cartographer Joseph N. Nicollet in 1839, as well as original works of art depicting the history of the area and an interpretive film that explores the region's plains and prairies. | Hwy. 10 | 605/698–7672 | Free | Memorial Day–Labor Day, daily 10–5.

Roy Lake State Park. You'll find a 100-unit campground and full-service resort on the shore of this popular boating and fishing lake 22 mi west and 2 mi south of Sisseton. Walleye, bass, and panfish are plentiful in Roy Lake. | 11545 Northside Dr., Lake City | 605/448–5701 | roylakestp@gfp.state.sd.us | $3 per person, $5 per vehicle, $20 annually. | Daily.

Sica Hollow State Park. This park 15 mi northwest of Sisseton preserves the favored camp-sites of the Dakota bands that once roamed the Great Plains and hosts great numbers of whitetail deer, wild turkeys, marmots, beavers, minks, raccoons, and songbirds. A 3-mi road winds through ravines and along wooded hillsides, and the Trail of Spirits, a National Recreational Trail, is available for hiking. | 11545 Northside Dr., Lake City | 605/698–7261 | www.state.sd.us/sdparks/sica/sica.htm | $3 per person, $5 per vehicle, $20 annually.

ON THE CALENDAR
JUNE: *Ft. Sisseton Historical Festival.* Cavalry and infantry drills, arts and crafts, old-time fiddlers, a military costume ball, Indian cultural demonstrations, muzzleloader shoots, square dancing, and cowboy poetry combine for this event in Ft. Sisseton State Park. | 605/448–5701.

Dining
American Hearth. American. You can try a grilled chicken or Reuben sandwich at this casual spot popular with families. Kids' menu. | 6 Hickory St. SE | 605/698–3077 | Breakfast also available | $5–$10 | No credit cards.

Jack Sons. American. This sports bar has sloppy burgers and filling 1-dish meals. | Hwy. 10 E | 605/698–7826 | $5.95–$9.95 | AE, D, MC, V.

Lodging
Holiday Motel. On the eastern edge of town, this single-story hotel is 1 block from a restaurant. Cable TV. Some pets allowed. | Hwy. 10 E | 605/698–7644 or 800/460–9548 | 19 rooms | $37–$40 | AE, D, DC, MC, V.

Viking Motel. This family-run hotel is 20 mi from Roy Lake and Sica Hollow state parks. Cable TV. Some pets allowed. | Hwy. 10 W | 605/698–7663 | 24 rooms | $37–$43 | MC, V.

SPEARFISH

MAP 8, A3

(Nearby towns also listed: Belle Fourche, Deadwood, Lead, Sturgis)

One of the prettiest communities in the state, Spearfish is a thriving town of 8,000 on the northern tier of the Black Hills. With excellent lodging, restaurants, and shopping, you'll find things to do here year-round. Among the favored attractions are nearby Spearfish Canyon, a National Scenic Byway, the Black Hills Passion Play, one of America's longest-running stage productions (already viewed by an estimated 10 million people), the High Plains Heritage Center, Matthews Opera House, and the century-old D. C. Booth Historic Fish Hatchery.

The first settlers came to Spearfish Valley in 1876, to take advantage of the steady streams of clear water flowing from the hills and the rich, black soils. The first store opened the following year, and students began attending the town's first school in 1878. In 1887, Spearfish Normal School, now Black Hills State University, graduated its first class, and in 1898 the D. C. Booth Fish Hatchery, one of the oldest in the West, was established. Today Spearfish is among the fastest-growing communities in the state, attracting new residents with its beautiful neighborhoods, revitalized Main Street, and ideal setting.

Information:Spearfish Chamber of Commerce, and Convention and Visitors Bureau | 106 W. Kansas, 57783-0550 | 605/642–2626 or 800/626–8013.

Attractions
Black Hills State University. Founded in 1883, this 4-year, state-sponsored university commands a near-idyllic small-town setting, with 3,600 students, and courses offered in 42

majors and 40 minors. Call for campus tour information | 1200 University Ave. | 605/642–6343 | www.bhsu.edu | Free | Mon.–Fri. 7–4.

Spearfish Canyon Scenic Byway. The byway is a 20-mi trip up the steep sides of the northernmost canyon in the Spearfish zone. Travel along winding pigtail-shape bridges and horseshoe curves that hug canyon walls. | Hwy. 14 E, Spearfish | 605/673–2251 | www.fs.fed.us/r2/blackhills | Free.

D. C. Booth Historic Fish Hatchery. This century-old hatchery, which was once owned by Dewitt Clinton Booth, contains a museum, a historic home, fish ponds, and underwater viewing windows. The museum displays fishery artifacts such as the fearnow pails. | 423 Hatchery Circle | 605/642–7730 | www.fws.gov/r6dcbth/dcbooth.html | Free | Museum and Home, Memorial Day–Labor Day, daily 9–6; Grounds open year-round, daily dawn to dusk.

High Plains Heritage Center and Museum. Western art and artifacts, including bronze sculptures and paintings, are displayed in this modern facility. Outdoors, you can view antique implements, a sod dugout, a 1-room school, a log cabin, live buffalo, longhorns, and minihorses. Cowboy poetry and music is performed in the theater on Wednesday evenings from Memorial Day to Labor Day. | 825 Heritage Dr. | 605/642–9378 | $4 | Memorial Day–Labor Day, daily 9–8; Labor Day–Memorial Day, daily 9–5.

Matthews Opera House. When it was opened in 1906, this opera house was the only cultural establishment in this region of the country. Refurbished and reopened in the late 1980s, the opera house continues its tradition with a mix of music, vaudeville, comedy, and drama. | 614½ Main St. | 605/642–7973 | $10, special rates for children.

Spearfish Canyon. Southwest of Spearfish, this canyon is home to more than 1,000 species of plants. The road that winds through the canyon is designated a National Scenic Byway, and meanders along the banks of Spearfish Creek past waterfalls and towering trees. The upper reaches of the canyon provided the backdrop for the closing scenes of Kevin Costner's epic *Dances With Wolves*. | U.S. 14A | 605/642–2626 or 800/626–8013 | Free.

SIGHTSEEING TOURS/TOUR COMPANIES

Star Aviation Air Tours. Air tours in airplanes highlight local landmarks, including Mount Rushmore and Devil's Tower. A minimum of 2 people are required for all tours. | 310 Aviation Pl | 605/642–4112 or 800/843–8010 | www.aviation@mato.com | $19.50 for 20 minutes, $96 for 2-hr tour | Daily 8–dusk.

ON THE CALENDAR

FEB.: *Hot Chocolate Days.* A variety of snow-related events, including a winter fashion show and dance, a kids' carnival, an art show, and winter sports along Main St., brings the whole town together. | 605/642–2626.

JULY: *Black Hills Corvette Classic.* Corvettes from across the country descend on Spearfish for a week of show, shine, and socializing. | 605/334–4134.

JUNE–AUG.: *Black Hills Passion Play.* Performed for 6 decades, this is one of America's longest-running stage productions. The performance is held in an outdoor amphitheater, with 22 scenes and a cast of 200, depicting the life of Christ and the Passion. | 605/642–2646 or 800/457–0160 | June–Aug., Tues., Thurs., Sun. 8 PM.

JUNE–AUG.: *Summer Season at Matthews Opera House.* This community arts center is set in a restored 1906 opera house with ceiling murals. Summer is its performance season. | 605/642–7973 | Mon., Wed., Fri., Sat. evenings; Sun. matinees.

SEPT.: *Taste of Spearfish.* This annual food fest lets you sample delectable dishes from area restaurants. Music and children's activities are also featured. | 605/642–2626.

Dining

Eleventh Hour Bistro. American. Flowers and linen tablecloths adorn the tables at this casual spot. You can try one of the wild game items, such as pheasant, or a sirloin steak. Outdoor

SPEARFISH

INTRO
ATTRACTIONS
DINING
LODGING

dining is available on a covered patio. Kids' menu. | 447 Main St. | 605/642–5701 | $10–$20 | D, MC, V.

Latchstring Restaurant. American. A wonderful view of Spearfish Canyon will accompany your meal at this casual spot. For breakfast try the sourdough pancakes. Popular dinner entrées include the fresh trout and steaks. Kids' menu. | Spearfish Canyon, U.S. 14A | 605/584–3333 | Breakfast also available | $11–$17 | D, MC, V.

Mad Mary's. Steak. Guns, saddles, and ropes scattered throughout this eatery combine to give it a Western feel. Popular dishes include the filet mignon and prime rib. Kids' menu. | 539 W. Jackson Blvd. | 605/642–2848 | No lunch | $10–$24 | AE, D, DC, MC, V.

Lodging

All American Inn. In a commercial area, this 2-story hotel is 1 mi east of downtown. Spearfish Canyon is 1½ mi away. Complimentary Continental breakfast. Cable TV. Indoor

THE ULTIMATE RIDE

Sturgis, as any motorcycle enthusiast will tell you, is all about the ride. To a biker, this small town is known as "Motorcycle Mecca," and with good reason. It's the home of the Sturgis Motorcycle Rally, and bikers from all over the world flock here to be part of the greatest motorcycle event anywhere.

For 10 days each August, this peaceful Black Hills region reverberates with the steady rumble of 2-wheeled (and occasionally 3-wheeled) machines, winding their way through pine-forested mountains and across sprawling prairies from all directions, heading for Sturgis. The visitors set up camp, sometimes literally, anywhere they can find within a 100-mi radius, and little Sturgis bursts at the seams with crowds of bikers and spectators.

The first Sturgis Rally and Races in 1938 was a small event, hosted by a local motorcycle club called the Jackpine Gypsies. A handful of spectators gathered to watch 9 racers compete. But that was then. In 2000, an estimated 650,000 participants attended, nearly doubling the population of the entire state and making the rally the largest outdoor event in the United States. The races at the rally are still sponsored by the Jackpine Gypsies, but today it takes a stadium to hold the crowd, and around 200 racers compete in hill-climbing, dragster, motocross, and track events.

Apart from the motorcycle shops, exhibits, museums, races, shows, and breathtaking Black Hills scenery, there's a warm camaraderie at Sturgis among people from all walks of life who share a passion for the kind of freedom found only on the open road. At Sturgis these free spirits meet, mingle, and give their all to the celebration of the motorcycle lifestyle.

Mechanics to moguls, they all show up at the rally, some wearing leather from head to toe, some in designer clothes, and some dressed in little more than tattoos. But that's all part of the fun. The great thing about Sturgis, says one veteran, is that "you've got everything from Neanderthals to Yuppies going there, but everybody gets along for 10 days—no matter whether you have spit-polished boots, or your boots are falling apart!"

pool. Hot tub. | 2275 E. Colorado Blvd. | 605/642–2350 or 800/606–2350 (in SD) | fax 605/642–9312 | 40 rooms | $39–$89 | AE, D, DC, MC, V.

City Campground. This campground offers full hookups and tent sites along Spearfish Creek. All-level sites are well shaded. | 404 S. Canyon St. | 605/642–1340 or 605/642–1333 | Non-hookup is $12–$14 for up to 4 people, $1 for each additional person; hookup is $21 for up to 4 people, $1 for each additional person | May–mid-Oct., daily.

Comfort Inn. Built in 1997, this 2-story hotel is right off exit 14 on I–90. There is a restaurant next door. Complimentary Continental breakfast. Cable TV. Indoor pool. Hot tub. Laundry facilities. Some pets allowed. | 2725 1st Ave. | 605/642–2337 | fax 605/642–0866 | 40 rooms | $75–$99 | AE, D, DC, MC, V.

Days Inn. A movie theater and restaurant are across the street from this 2-story hotel. The downtown area is ½ mi away. Complimentary Continental breakfast. Cable TV. Laundry facilities. | 240 Ryan Rd. | 605/642–7101 | fax 605/642–7120 | 50 rooms | $80–$85 | AE, D, DC, MC, V.

Eighth Street Inn Bed & Breakfast. Listed on the National Historic Register, this home (circa 1900) has a large porch, a lovely parlor, and beautiful grounds. Complimentary breakfast. | 735 8th St. | 605/642–9812 | 4 rooms | $60–$120 | No credit cards.

Fairfield Inn By Marriott. There is a restaurant across the street from this 3-story hotel. The downtown area is 3 mi to the west and High Plains Heritage Museum is ½ mi away. Complimentary Continental breakfast. Some refrigerators, some in-room hot tubs. Cable TV. Indoor pool. Hot tub. Cross-country skiing, downhill skiing. No pets. | 2720 1st Ave. E | 605/642–3500 or 800/228–2800 | fax 605/642–3500 | 50 rooms, 7 suites | $88; $95–$150 suites | AE, D, DC, MC, V.

Kelly Inn. I–90 is 1 block away and downtown's main strip is 4 blocks to the west. There is a restaurant next door. Some in-room hot tubs. Cable TV. Hot tub, sauna. Laundry facilities. Pets allowed. | 540 E. Jackson | 605/642–7795 or 800/635–3559 | fax 605/642–7751 | 50 rooms | $70–$85 | AE, D, DC, MC, V.

Spearfish Canyon Resort. All rooms at this lodge offer scenic views of the canyon and the suites contain fireplaces. You can go trout fishing in Spearfish Creek, which is within walking distance. Bar. Minibars, some refrigerators. Cable TV. Hot tub. Fishing. Cross-country skiing, downhill skiing. Laundry facilities. Business services. | Spearfish Canyon, U.S. 14A | 605/584–3435 or 800/439–8544 | fax 605/584–3990 | tms@spfcanyon.com | www.black-hills.com/comm/spfcanyonresort | 44 rooms, 10 suites | $79–$109, $190–$205 suites | AE, D, MC, V.

Spearfish Creek Inn. This inn is alongside a creek but is still in the heart of town. Pool. Fishing. | 430 W. Kansas St. | 605/642–9941 | 24 rooms | $45–$55 | MC, V.

STURGIS

MAP 8, B3

(Nearby towns also listed: Belle Fourche, Deadwood, Lead, Rapid City, Spearfish)

Fort Meade opened as a peacekeeping fort in 1878, 2 years after the 7th Cavalry's disastrous defeat by the Sioux at the Battle of the Little Bighorn. Its first commander was Col. Samuel Sturgis, who had lost his son in the infamous battle. The town that sprang up around the fort became known as Sturgis. This Black Hills border town is normally as sleepy as it looks, except for 10 days each August when it hosts the world's largest motorcycle rally and some 250,000 enthusiasts from around the world flood the town and fill every motel for 100 mi around. Sturgis is also home to Bear Butte State Park, the Black Hills National Cemetery, the Fort Meade Cavalry Museum, and the National Motorcycle Museum and Hall of Fame. Sturgis is content to sustain itself as a small trading center for surrounding ranchers and host to tourists who visit the Black Hills.

Information: Sturgis Area Chamber of Commerce | 606 Anna St., 57785-0504 | 605/347–2556.

Attractions

Bear Butte State Park. Rising from the surrounding prairie like a lone sentinel, Bear Butte has been sacred to the Cheyenne and Sioux, who still make regular pilgrimages here. The park, which is 4 mi northeast of Sturgis, is home to a bison herd, and there are hiking trails that lead to the butte's summit. | Hwy. 79 | 605/347–5240 | www.state.sd.us/gfp/sdparks/bearbutt/bearbutt.htm | $3 per person, $5 per vehicle, $20 annually | Daily, dawn to dusk.

Black Hills National Cemetery. Billed as the "Arlington of the West," this massive cemetery is the final resting place of more than 15,000 veterans. | I–90, Exit 34 | 605/347–3830 | Free | Daily 8:30–4.

Fort Meade Cavalry Museum. Old cavalry quarters, historic documents (including letters written by Gen. George Armstrong Custer), and numerous photographs, including shots of the all-Sioux Troop L, highlight the collection of artifacts at this museum, which is 1½ mi east of Sturgis. | Hwy. 34 | 605/347–9822 | $3 | May–Sept. 15, daily 9–5.

National Motorcycle Museum and Hall of Fame. Nearly 100 antique motorcycles, including Steve McQueen's 1915 Cyclone Racer and a 1907 Harley-Davidson, are on display. | 1650 Lazelle St. | 605/347–4875 | www.museum.sturgis-rally.com | $4 | Mon.–Sat. 9–5, Sun. 11–4.

Wonderland Cave. This 300-million-year-old cavern is full of crystal formations and contains an icicle fence. | Alpine and Vanocker Canyon Rds | 605/578–1728 | $8.00, special rates children | May–Oct., daily 8–8.

ON THE CALENDAR

JUNE: *Sturgis Cavalry Days.* Living history reenactments at Fort Meade, a downtown parade, and a period fashion show are among the highlights of this weekend event. | 605/347–2556.

JUNE: *Sturgis Regional High School Rodeo.* Held at the Sturgis Fairgrounds, this is a full rodeo. Winners qualify for the State High School Rodeo Finals. | 605/347–2556.

AUG.: *Sturgis Rally and Races.* This world-famous motorcycle rally is attended by tens of thousands of bikers and spectators. It includes unique motorcycle shows, concerts, touring activities throughout the Black Hills, and national racing events. | 605/347–6570.

Dining

Mom's Restaurant. American. This mom-and-pop joint has some of the best burgers and shakes in town. Their breakfast menu is short but sweet. | 2214 Junction Ave. | 605/347–3709.

World Famous Roadkill Cafe. American. Started by 2 bike-rally enthusiasts, the café promises to bring food "from your grill to ours!" including the "Chicken That Didn't Quite Cross the Road," "Smidgen of Pigeon," and the daily special, "Guess That Mess!" These clever monikers hide the fact that the café offers fairly standard stuff—breakfast, tuna melts, buffalo, and beef burgers—as well as a car-filling collection of roadkill cookbooks, T-shirts, and novelty items. | 1333 Main St. | 605/347–4502 | Reservations not accepted | Closed Sept.–May | $9–$18 | MC, V.

Lodging

Bear Butte Bed & Breakfast. This 1890 farmhouse is a working ranch where you can observe daily chores. Lots of surrounding land gives you, and the farm animals, plenty of room to roam, and you'll find plenty of hiking trails to follow. You have to share the bathroom, and the entertainment includes a player piano. Complimentary breakfast. | Hwy. 79, Box 366 | 605/347–2137 | House rents as one unit | $60–$85 | Credit cards not accepted.

Best Western Phil-Town Inn. A favorite among bikers during the annual motorcycle rally in August, this 2-story motel is ½ mi south of the downtown area. Restaurant. Cable TV. Pool. Hot tub. Laundry facilities. Business services. | 2431 S. Junction | 605/347–3604 | 56 rooms | $64–$94 | AE, D, MC, V.

Days Inn. Built in 1993, this 2-story motel is in a commercial area. I–90 is 1 block away. Complimentary Continental breakfast. Cable TV. Hot tub, sauna. Laundry facilities. Business services. | U.S. 14A | 605/347–3027 | fax 605/347–0291 | 53 rooms | $65–$110 | AE, D, DC, MC, V.

Poker Alice House/National 9 Junction Inn. You can stay in one of the Junction Inn's 28 rooms or next door in the Poker Alice House, named for the notorious former proprietress who smoked cigars, played cards, and ran a brothel. Complimentary Continental breakfast. | 1802 S. Junction Ave. | 605/347–5675 or 800/658–3695 | 32 rooms | $45–$70, full house rents from $120 | AE, D, MC, V.

Super 8. Off exit 30 on I–90, this 3-story motel is ½ mi east of downtown. Cable TV. Hot tub. Exercise equipment. Laundry facilities. Pets allowed. | I–90 | 605/347–4447 | fax 605/347–2334 | 59 rooms | $37–$77 | AE, D, DC, MC, V.

VERMILLION

MAP 8, H5

(Nearby towns also listed: Beresford, Yankton)

Fort Vermillion, established by the American Fur Company in 1835, was the earliest settlement in the area. The town of Vermillion, named for the red clay on which it was built, was founded in 1859 on the banks of the Missouri and Vermillion rivers 1 mi south of the fort, but a major flood in 1881 swept away most of its structures. Following the flood, most new homes were built higher up on the bluffs and farther from the river. Vermillion's history is interwoven with both the pioneer heritage and Native American culture. With a population of 10,000 including the students, Vermillion still feels like an unpretentious small town. It continues to serve as a commercial hub, but its economy is mostly dependent on the University of South Dakota, which was founded in Vermillion in 1862 and has a student population of 7,000.

Information: Vermillion Chamber of Commerce | 906 E. Cherry St., 57069-1602 | 605/624–5571 or 800/809–2071.

Attractions

Spirit Mound. As you approach you'll see this brown mound slowly rise above the prairie and break the horizon line. In 1804 Lewis and Clark made a pilgrimage to the site, as local Indian lore held that the natural mound had mystical origins. | Hwy. 19, 7 mi north of Vermillion | Free.

University of South Dakota. This 4-year state university offers academic programs in more than 100 areas. Although it was founded in 1862, classes didn't begin until 1882. USD's Dakotadome is the only multipurpose dome in the region. | 414 E. Clark St. | 605/677–5326 or 877/COYOTES (toll–free) | www.usd.edu | Free.
A world-class exhibition of more than 5,000 rare, antique musical instruments, including former President Clinton's saxophone, Civil War band instruments, South Pacific drums, Elizabethan ivory lutes, and 1 of only 2 surviving Stradivari guitars, is at the **Shrine to Music Museum.** | 414 E. Clark St. | 605/677–5306 | Free | Weekdays 9–4:30, Sat. 10–4:30, Sun. 2–4:30.
Included among the numerous historical exhibits at the **W. H. Over State Museum** is a life-size diorama of a Teton village. | 1110 Ratingen St. | 605/677–5228 | Free | Weekdays 9–5, weekends 2–5.

Dining

Recuerdo's Italian/Mexican Restaurant. Eclectic. Nothing too fancy here, but the selections of traditional tacos and burritos, as well as basic red-sauce pastas, are satisfying enough. | 112 E. Main St. | 605/624–6445 | $6.95–$11.95 | D, MC, V.

Silver Dollar. American. Random sports memorabilia and dozens of screens for event viewing line this sports-theme restaurant. One good choice is the slow-cooked prime rib. | 1216 E. Cherry | 605/624–4830 | $10–$20 | AE, D, DC, MC, V.

Lodging

Budget Host Tomahawk. Down the road from the University of South Dakota, this single-story motel is 1 mi from restaurants. Complimentary Continental breakfast. Cable TV. Pool. Business services. | 1313 W. Cherry | 605/624–2601 or 605/624–2449 for reservations | 20 rooms | $37–$39 | AE, D, DC, MC, V.

Comfort Inn. The meeting rooms and business services, such as the wet bars and recliners in the rooms, all tell you this place is designed for business travelers. But it's equally comfortable for anyone just passing through. Complimentary Continental breakfast. Cable TV. Pool. Exercise equipment. Business services. | 701 W. Cherry St. | 605/624–8333 or 800/228–5150 | www.comfortinn.com | 46 rooms | $43–$60 | AE, D, MC, V.

WALL

MAP 8, C4

(Nearby town also listed: Badlands National Park)

Built on the "wall" of the South Dakota Badlands, this town of 834 residents was founded in 1907 as a railroad station for the Chicago and Northwestern Railroad. Today Wall is home to the world-famous Wall Drug Store, which got its real boost when its owners decided to hand out free ice-water to passing motorists en route to the

YOUR FIRST-AID TRAVEL KIT

- ❏ Allergy medication
- ❏ Antacid tablets
- ❏ Antibacterial soap
- ❏ Antiseptic cream
- ❏ Aspirin or acetaminophen
- ❏ Assorted adhesive bandages
- ❏ Athletic or elastic bandages for sprains
- ❏ Bug repellent
- ❏ Face cloth
- ❏ First-aid book
- ❏ Gauze pads and tape
- ❏ Needle and tweezers for splinters or removing ticks
- ❏ Petroleum jelly
- ❏ Prescription drugs
- ❏ Suntan lotion with an SPF rating of at least 15
- ❏ Thermometer

* Excerpted from *Fodor's: How to Pack: Experts Share Their Secrets*
© 1997, by Fodor's Travel Publications

Black Hills. Other attractions include a Wild West wax museum and the National Grasslands Visitor Center. Wall's prosperity is inseparably tied to the fortunes of the Hustead family, which founded the Wall Drug Store and whose third generation manages it today. The store is the town's largest employer.

Information: **Wall–Badlands Area Chamber of Commerce** | 501 Main St., 57790-0527 | 605/279–2665 or 888/852–9255.

Attractions

Badlands National Park. (*See* Badlands National Park.) Approximately 6 mi south of Wall, this 244,000-acre moonscape holds vast wilderness areas and 8 marked hiking trails that stretch over 11 mi. The Ben Reifel Visitor Center at Cedar Pass (9 mi south of I–90 on Rte. 240) and the White River Visitor Center (in the southern Stronghold Unit off BIA Hwy. 27) acquaint visitors with the area. For a scenic drive, try Rte. 240, which wiggles past towering spires, ragged ridgelines, and deep canyons. | Rte. 240 | 605/433–5361 | fax 605/433–5404 | www.nps.gov/badl | $5 per person, $10 per vehicle.

National Grasslands Visitor Center. Managed by the U.S. Forest Service, this visitor center focuses on interpreting and providing information about the national grasslands with more than 20 exhibits highlighting a variety of subjects, including prairie plants and animals, recreation opportunities, and management activities. Three national grasslands are found in western South Dakota: Grand River, Fort Pierre, and Buffalo Gap. | 708 Main St. | 605/279–2125 | Free | Jun.–Aug., daily 7 AM–8 PM; Sept.–May, daily 8–4:30.

Wall Drug Store. This South Dakota original got its start by offering free ice-water to road-weary travelers. Today its 4 art-gallery dining rooms seat 520 visitors, and its Western Mall has 14 shops. The store also boasts a life-size mechanical Cowboy Band and Chuckwagon Quartet. | 510 Main St. | 605/279–2175 | Free | Memorial Day–Labor Day, daily 6 AM–10 PM; Labor Day–Memorial Day, daily 6:30 AM–6 PM.

ON THE CALENDAR

DEC.: *Parade of Trees.* Gather downtown to see local businesses in their Christmas finery. Refreshments, games, and caroling are all part of the fun. | 605/279–2665.

Dining

Cactus Family Restaurant and Lounge. American. This all-day restaurant in downtown Wall specializes in hotcakes and made-from-scratch pies. A giant roast-beef buffet is offered in summer. | 519 Main St. | 605/279–2561 | $6–$19 | D, MC, V.

★ **Elkton House Restaurant.** American. This comfortable restaurant with wood paneling and a sunroom has fast service and a terrific hot roast-beef sandwich, served on white bread with gravy and mashed potatoes. | 203 South Blvd. | 605/279–2152 | $7–$15 | D, MC, V.

Western Art Gallery Restaurant. American. In the Wall Drug Store and capable of sitting more than 500 patrons, this restaurant displays more than 200 original oil paintings, all with a Western theme. Try a hot beef sandwich or a buffalo burger. Kids' menu. | 510 Main St. | 605/279–2175 | Breakfast also available | $5–$15.

Lodging

Ann's Motel. Just 1 block from Wall Drug, this motel offers small but clean rooms equipped with televisions, phone, in-room coffee, and full-size bathtubs. Cable TV, room phones. | 114 4th Ave. | 605/279–2501 | 12 rooms | $27–$43 | MC, V.

Best Western Plains. This hotel is 7 mi from Badlands National Park and 4 blocks from downtown. There is a restaurant 1½ blocks away. Cable TV. Pool. Pets allowed. Business services. | 712 Glenn St. | 605/279–2145 or 800/528–1234 | fax 605/279–2977 | 74 rooms, 8 suites | $69–$105, $120–$145 suites | AE, D, DC, MC, V.

Circle View Guest Ranch. This cozy bed and breakfast has spectacular views of the Bad-lands, and is 30 mi from downtown Wall. Despite the fireplaces, the guest rooms lack the usual B&B charm and look more like hotel rooms, but the location is unbeatable. Kitch-enettes. Cable TV. | 20055 E. Hwy. 44, Scenic | 605/433–5581 | www.circleviewranch.com | 7 rooms | $50–$75 | No credit cards.

Days Inn. Built in 1993, this 2-story hotel is 3 blocks from the Wall Drug Store. Cable TV. Hot tub, sauna. | 10th Ave. and Norris St. | 605/279–2000 or 800/329–7466 | fax 605/279–2004 | 32 rooms | $85 | AE, D, MC, V.

Knights Inn. There is a restaurant across the street from this 2-story motel. It is 3 blocks from downtown. Restaurant. Cable TV. Pool. Hot tub. Laundry facilities. Business services. | 110 S. Boulevard | 605/279–2127 or 800/782–9402 | fax 605/279–2599 | 47 rooms | $85 | AE, D, MC, V.

Super 8. This 2-story motel is 8 mi from Badlands National Park. There are 2 restaurants within 4 blocks of the motel. Cable TV. | 711 Glenn St. | 605/279–2688 | fax 605/279–2396 | 29 rooms | $72–$76 | AE, D, DC, MC, V.

WATERTOWN

(Nearby towns also listed: Milbank, Webster)

Watertown dates back to 1871, and was established after the Winona and St. Peter Rail-road Co. completed a line from Minnesota to the eastern shore of Lake Kampeska, which proved to be the ideal site for a township. It was first called Kampeska, but later was changed at the urging of two brothers who happened to come from Watertown, New York. Near Lake Kampeska and Lake Pelican, Watertown is a pleasant community of 18,000 residents, many of whom are the descendants of the first settlers in the area. Among Watertown's major attractions is the new $10-million Redlin Art Center, which has a planetarium and 100 original works by South Dakota native Terry Redlin. Other highlights are the Bramble Park Zoo and the 1883 Mellette House, commemorating the life of the Dakota Territory's last governor and the state of South Dakota's first gover-nor, Arthur C. Mellette. Watertown is the commercial hub of northeastern South Dakota and also profits from its medical services industry and outdoor recreation.

Information: Watertown Chamber of Commerce, and Convention & Visitors Bureau | 1200 33rd St. SE, 57201-6113 | 605/886–5814 or 800/658–4505.

Attractions

Bramble Park Zoo. From colorful peacocks to shaggy bison, this zoo is home to more than 300 mammals, reptiles, and birds. Live animal demonstrations are held on weekends. | 901 6th Ave. NW (Hwy. 20) | 605/882–6269 | www.watertownsd.com | $4 | May–mid-Sept., daily 10–8, mid-Sept.–May, daily 10–4.

Historic Uptown Watertown. Stroll among more than 40 turn-of-the-century homes of noteworthy South Dakotans, including Curt DeGraff and Benjamin Cortland. This is only a walk-by tour; the homes are not open to the public. | Between Maple and Park Sts. | 605/886–7335 | Free.

Kampeska Heritage Museum. The focus of this museum is the development of Watertown and the surrounding region from homesteading to World War II. Among the numerous exhibits are two that display what a dentist's office and general store looked like in the early 1900s. | 27 1st Ave. SE | 605/886–7335 | www.watertownsd.com | Free | Sept.–Apr., week-days 1–5, May–Aug., weekdays 8–5.

Lake Kampeska. Three city parks with campgrounds can be found on the shores of this lake. You can go fishing, swimming, or waterskiing in it. | Hwy. 20 NW | 605/882–6260 | Free.

Mellette House. Family heirlooms and portraits fill this Italianate villa built in 1883 by Arthur C. Mellette, South Dakota's first governor. | 421 5th Ave. NW | 605/886–4730 | www.water-townsd.com | May–Sept., Tues.–Sun. 1–5.

Redlin Art Center. Situated in a sea of wildflowers, the Redlin Art Center is visible for miles from the surrounding prairie. Named after one of America's foremost artists, Terry Redlin, the center houses 100 original paintings and a high-tech planetarium. | U.S. 212 and I–29 | 605/882–3877 | www.watertownsd.com | Free; planetarium $2 | Weekdays 8–5, Sat. 10–4, Sun. 12–4.

ON THE CALENDAR

FEB.: *Dakota Territory Shoot-Out Snowmobile Ice Drags.* Snowmobile races and radar runs featuring pro racers from across the country are the focus of this weekend event. Other activities include kitty-kat races, which are snowmobile races for the kids, and a poker run, in which competitors snowmobile to various businesses in town and collect cards. | 605/886–8496.

FEB.: *Watertown Winter Farm Show.* More than 120 farm and home exhibitors displaying equipment and demonstrating new techniques converge upon the Codington County Expo Building. There is also a livestock show. | 605/886–5814.

JUNE: *Artwalk.* This fine arts festival on the first weekend of the month includes kids' art activities, strolling musicians, and food vendors. | 605/882–8900.

Dining

Lakeshore. American. On the quiet shore of Lake Kampeska, you can look out at the serene waters as you dine. Try the prime rib or a juicy steak. There is live piano music nightly. | 100 N. Lake Dr. | 605/882–3422 | Closed Sun.–Mon. No lunch | $15–$25 | AE, D, MC, V.

MacGregor's Restaurant. American. Unexpected first-class dining in a small-town setting. You'll find gourmet selections of steaks, seafood, and desserts. | 1712 9th Ave. SW | 605/882–5922 | Jacket required | $10–$22 | AE, D, MC, V.

Senor Max's. Mexican. A friendly family joint where chimichangas are the house specialty. If you're not in the mood, there's also a full Mexican menu along with hamburgers and chicken sandwiches. | 1300 9th Ave. SE | 605/882–3252 | $6–$10 | MC, V.

Lodging

Best Western Ramkota Inn. In a commercial area, this 2-story hotel is 2 mi southwest of the downtown area and 3 mi west of the Redlin Art Center. Restaurant, bar. In-room data ports, room service, some in-door hot tubs. Cable TV. Indoor pool. Hot tub, sauna. Business services, airport shuttle. | 1901 9th Ave. SW | 605/886–8011 or 800/528–1234 | fax 605/886–3667 | 98 rooms, 3 suites | $61, $95–$130 suites | AE, D, DC, MC, V.

Comfort Inn. This chain has typical amenities in a central location near the Redlin Arts Center and less than 4 mi from the zoo. Complimentary Continental breakfast. Some kitchenettes. Cable TV. Indoor pool. Business services. | 800 35th St. Circle | 605/886–3010 | www.comfortinn.com | 60 rooms | $49–$100 | AE, D, DC, MC, V.

Days Inn Watertown. This Days Inn has a downtown location with spacious rooms and family-size suites. Complimentary Continental breakfast. Cable TV. Hot tub. Laundry service. Business services. | 2900 9th Ave. SE | 605/886–3500 | fax 605/886–0820 | www.daysinn.com | 56 rooms, 2 suites | $45–$77, $92 suites | AE, D, MC, V.

Super 8. There is a movie theater and shopping center 6 blocks from this 3-story motel. Lake Kampeska is 5 mi away. Cable TV. Indoor pool. Hot tub, sauna. Cross-country skiing. | 503 14th Ave. SE | 605/882–1900 | 58 rooms | $63 | AE, D, DC, MC, V.

Travel Host. This 2-story motel is 1 mi south of downtown. There is a supper-only restaurant across the street and a 24-hour cafe 3 blocks away. Complimentary Continental breakfast. Cable TV. Pets allowed. | 1714 9th Ave. SW | 605/886–6120 or 800/658–5512 | fax 605/886–5352 | 29 rooms | $39–$45 | AE, D, DC, MC, V.

WEBSTER

MAP 8, H2

(Nearby towns also listed: Sisseton, Watertown)

The gateway to some of the state's best fishing lakes and pheasant hunting, Webster also houses the largest collection of tractors in South Dakota. Founded in 1881 and named for J. P. Webster, a Minnesota settler who came to the area in 1880 and helped found the community, Webster is only minutes from Blue Dog, Waubay, Enemy Swim, Minnewasta, and Pickerel lakes; the town offers great opportunities for anglers year-round. The Museum of Wildlife, Science and Industry is west of town on Hwy. 12.

Information: Webster Chamber of Commerce | 702 Main St., 57274 | 605/345–4668 or 888/571–7582 | www.webstersd.com.

Attractions

Day County Museum. This museum in the basement of the county courthouse has a collection of early guns, Dakota Indian artifacts, and hundreds of historical documents. | R.R. 2, Box 141A | 605/345–3765 | Free | Mon., Wed., Fri. 2–5.

Museum of Wildlife, Science and Industry. This museum has an extensive tractor collection, as well as the nation's only "shoe house," a building shaped like a shoe that houses a massive shoe collection. You can also visit a small village consisting of a livery stable, a church, a blacksmith's shop, a railroad depot, pioneer houses, a post office, and a general store. | Hwy. 12 | 605/345–4751 | Donations accepted | May–Oct. weekdays 9–5, weekends 1–5.

Waubay National Wildlife Refuge. Surrounded by 3 lakes and 14 mi east of Webster, this refuge is made up of more than 4,600 acres of prairie potholes and 700 acres of oak forest and is the nesting place for more than 100 species of birds. A variety of migratory waterfowl, including Canada geese, blue-winged teal, and mallards, as well as rare white pelicans and Western grebes, make their home here. | County Rd. 1 | 605/947–4521 | Free | Daily dawn to dusk.

ON THE CALENDAR

JAN.: *Day County Farm and Home Show.* Exhibits at this show are geared to the farm community and those interested in home improvement. | 888/571–7582.

Dining

A&W Family Restaurant. American. Everyone from teenagers to families eats at this casual spot, which has been a community fixture since 1957. You might want to try the roasted chicken. Outdoor dining on picnic tables is available. | 10 Hwy. 12 E | 605/345–4140 | Closed last week in Dec.–third week in Jan. | $4–$5 | No credit cards.

Lakeside Farm Bed & Breakfast. You can sample farm life—as well as homemade cinnamon buns and hand-churned ice cream. This is a B&B with shared bathrooms. Children are welcome. Complimentary breakfast. | 605/486–4430 | gjhagen@sullybuttes.net | 2 rooms | $35–$50 | No credit cards.

Lodging

Holiday Motel. Less than 1 mi from the Museum of Wildlife, Science and Industry, this single-story hotel is just off the intersection of Hwy. 12 and Rte. 25. There is a restaurant next door. Cable TV. | Hwy. 12 | 605/345–3323 | 20 rooms | $30–$38 | MC, V.

Super 8. Built in 1982, this 2-story motel is in a rural area and across the street from the Museum of Wildlife, Science and Industry. Cable TV. | Hwy. 12 | 605/345–4701 | fax 605/345–4701 | 27 rooms | $33–$53 | AE, D, DC, MC, V.

WINNER

MAP 8, E4

(Nearby towns also listed: Chamberlain, Mission)

Tripp County was opened to homesteading in 1909, and the first county seat was established at Lamro. Two years later, the Chicago Railroad extended its line through the territory, missing Lamro by 2 mi and making it necessary to establish a new town site along the railroad. When the town was chosen by popular vote to be the new county seat, it was appropriately named "Winner." Today this service center for the hearty farmers and ranchers of the region may also be South Dakota's friendliest town. Winner also lays claim to the best pheasant hunting in the state.

Information: Winner Chamber of Commerce | 220 E. 3rd St. 57580-0268 | 605/842–1533 or 800/658–3079.

WINNER

INTRO
ATTRACTIONS
DINING
LODGING

ON THE CALENDAR

JUNE: *Regional High School Rodeo.* High school students compete in a full range of rodeo events, including calf roping, steer wrestling, and bull riding at the Winner Rodeo Grounds. Winners advance to the State High School Rodeo Finals. | 605/842–3666.
AUG.: *Mid Dakota Fair.* Demonstrations and workshops at the Tripp County 4-H grounds teach kids basic farming and homemaking skills, including how to care for livestock and sewing. The Agricultural Olympics, featuring events like bale tossing and fence jumping, is a crowd favorite. | 605/842–1533.

Dining

OutWest Bar Grill and Cafe. American. You can come for a cold one and stay for piles of nachos, juicy ribs, and satisfying sandwiches. | 865 W. 2nd St. | 605/842–2324 | $6–$10 | MC, V.

Lodging

Buffalo Trail. This single-story motel on the Oyate Trail is in the heart of South Dakota's prime pheasant hunting area. Downtown is 1 mi away. Picnic area, complimentary Continental breakfast. In-room data ports. Cable TV. Pool. Driving range, putting green. Pets allowed. | 1030 W. 2nd St. | 605/842–2212 | fax 605/842–3199 | 31 rooms | $44–$99 | AE, D, DC, MC, V.

Tobin House Bed & Breakfast. This stone house is furnished with cherrywood antiques and has a fireplace frame of petrified wood. The bathrooms are shared. Complimentary breakfast. | 605/842–2502 | tdtobin@gwtc.net | 4 rooms | $65–$120 | MC, V.

Warrior Inn. There are a handful of restaurants 1 block from this single-story motel on the eastern edge of Winner. Bar, complimentary Continental breakfast. Cable TV. Indoor pool. Hot tub. | 845 E. Hwy. 44 | 605/842–3121 or 800/658–4705 | 39 rooms | $90 | AE, D, DC, MC, V.

YANKTON

MAP 8, H5

(Nearby town also listed: Vermillion)

Founded in 1859 by fur trappers and traders plying the Missouri River, the original capital of the Dakota Territory retains a frontier charm on the banks of the Missouri River. Historic homes hint of a heritage steeped in riverboats and railroads, frontier forts and the fur trade. Visitors to Yankton will find self-guided tours, great festivals, and a gateway to the Lewis and Clark Recreation Area, which is 5 mi west of town on Rte. 52. The shores of popular 22-mi-long Lewis and Clark Lake are lined with rolling golf courses, cabin sites, campgrounds, beaches, and marinas. Yankton is a commercial center with numerous small businesses and some large ones, including Gurney Seed and Nursery, which has been in business since 1894.

Information: **Yankton Chamber of Commerce** | 218 W. 4th St. 57078-0588 | 605/665–3636 | www.yanktonsd.com.

Attractions

Bede Art Gallery/Mt. Marty College. Located in Mt. Marty's Roncalli Center, the gallery displays arts and crafts from local Native Americans and university students. | 1105 W. 8th St. | 605/668–1011 | www.mtmc.edu | Free | Sept.–May, daily 10–4.

Dakota Territorial Capitol. Built in 1989 and housed in Riverside Park, this structure is a replica of the original Dakota Territory Capitol building, which was built in 1862. Great detail was placed upon the doors, windows, and woodwork in order to mimic the construction of the original building. | Levy and Douglas Sts. | 605/668–5231 | www.yanktonsd.com | Free | Tours by appointment only.

Dakota Territorial Museum. Sioux artifacts and steamboat displays trace the history of the region and the first settlement in Dakota Territory. Historic buildings on the museum grounds include the Great Northern Depot, the Territorial Council building, and a working blacksmith shop, all of which date back to the late 1800s–early 1900s. | 610 Summit Ave. | 605/665–3898 | $2, free Wed. for individuals and groups under 10 people; special rates for children | Memorial Day–Labor Day, Tues.–Sat. 10–5, Sun. 1–5; Labor Day–Memorial Day, Tues.–Sat. 10–5, Sun. by appointment.

Lewis and Clark Recreation Area. This park is home to both Gavins Point Dam and Lewis and Clark Lake, which is one of the most popular recreational lakes in the state and home to many species of fish, including catfish, whitebass, and bluegills. There are also campgrounds, cabins, a restaurant, and a marina on the grounds. | 43349 Rte. 52 | 605/668–2985 | www.lewisandclarkpark.com | Free.

ON THE CALENDAR

JUNE: *Tabor Czech Days.* The town's Czech heritage is celebrated with polka music, traditional dance featuring 130 performers in native costume, and a parade. You can also watch how a popular Czech pastry, the kolache, is made. | 605/463–2476.

AUG.: *Riverboat Days.* More than 150 arts and crafts booths, 2 concerts, ethnic food, a parade, a waterskiing show, a car show, a tractor pull, a poker run, beach volleyball, and entertainment attract more than 100,000 visitors to this event each year. | 605/665–3636.

Dining

Happy Chef. American. This 24-hour favorite of truckers and insomniacs serves stick-to-your-ribs burgers, meatloaf, and fried chicken. Lighter fare is also available. | E. Hwy. 50 | 605/665–3944 | $5–$12 | MC, V.

Jodean's Steakhouse and Lounge. American. American antiques decorate this casual steakhouse. You might try the filet mignon or the buffet, which includes items such as baked chicken and barbecued ribs. | Hwy. 81N | 605/665–9884 | No lunch | $7–$15 | AE, D, MC, V.

Lewis and Clark Marina. Seafood. The house restaurant for the Lewis and Clark Resort serves up fresh local trout and catfish as well as other delights. | Rte. 52 W | 605/665–5650 | $8.95–$13.00 | AE, D, MC, V.

Pancho's Villa. Mexican. This restaurant has south-of-the-border favorites on the spicier side. The steak fajitas are good. | 1512 Broadway St. | 605/665–7452 | $6.95–$11.95 | AE, D, MC, V.

Yesterday's Café. American. You can get fresh soups, salads, and sandwiches here, and most are available for carry-out if you're heading to the lake. | 2216 Broadway St. | 605/665–4383 | $4.95–$8.50 | MC, V.

Lodging

Best Western Kelly Inn. This 2-story hotel on the east side of town is 2 mi from the Dakota Territorial Capitol. Complimentary Continental breakfast. Some refrigerators. Cable TV. Indoor pool, wading pool. Hot tub. Exercise equipment. Cross-country skiing. Video games. Business services. Pets allowed. | 1607 Hwy. 50 E | 605/665–2906 | fax 605/665–4318 | 119 rooms, 4 suites | $69–$89, $150–$250 suites | AE, D, DC, MC, V.

Broadway Inn. A fast food eatery is across the street from this 2-story motel. It is 1 mi from downtown. Bar. Complimentary Continental breakfast. Cable TV. Pool. Cross-country skiing. | 1210 Broadway | 605/665–7805 | fax 605/668–9519 | 37 rooms | $61 | AE, D, MC, V.

Comfort Inn. The Yankton Mall is across the street from this 2-story motel on the north side of town. There are many places to eat within a 3-block radius. Complimentary Continental breakfast. In-room data ports. Cable TV. Hot tub. Business services. Some pets allowed. | 2118 Broadway | 605/665–8053 | fax 605/665–8165 | 45 rooms | $56 | AE, D, DC, MC, V.

Days Inn. Built in 1992, this 2-story motel is on the northern edge of town. It is across the street from a fast food eatery and a family restaurant. Complimentary Continental breakfast. In-room data ports. Cable TV. Hot tub. Business services. | 2410 Broadway | 605/665–8717 | fax 605/665–8841 | 45 rooms | $43–$63 | AE, D, DC, MC, V.

Gavins Point Bed & Breakfast. These are family-style accommodations overlooking Lewis and Clark Lake. Complimentary breakfast. TV in common area. Hot tub. | 252 Gavins Point Rd. | 605/665–7163 | rwgpbb@byelectic.com | 5 rooms | $70–$80 | MC, V.

Lewis and Clark Resort. On the grounds of the Lewis and Clark State Recreation Area, some of the rooms at this resort offer views of the lake. Lewis and Clark Marina, where you can dock your boat, is a short stroll away. Restaurant. Cable TV. Pool. Marina, boating. Laundry facilities. Business services. | 43349 Rte. 52 | 605/665–2680 | fax 605/665–8613 | 24 rooms, 10 cabins | $79, $184 cabins | Closed Oct.–Apr. | AE, D, MC, V.

Star Lite Inn Motel. This locally owned motel is near the historic downtown district and the Dakota Territorial Museum. The rooms are sparse, but microwaves and kitchenettes are available if you plan an extended stay. The motel offers free parking to trucks. Cable TV. | 500 Park St. | 605/665–7828 | 14 rooms | $30–$40 | MC, V.

Super 8. There is a restaurant next door to this 3-story motel. Lewis and Clark State Recreational Area is 6 mi away. Bar. Cable TV. Cross-country skiing. | 1705 Hwy. 50E | 605/665–6510 | 58 rooms | $45 | AE, D, DC, MC, V.

Index

Atlas

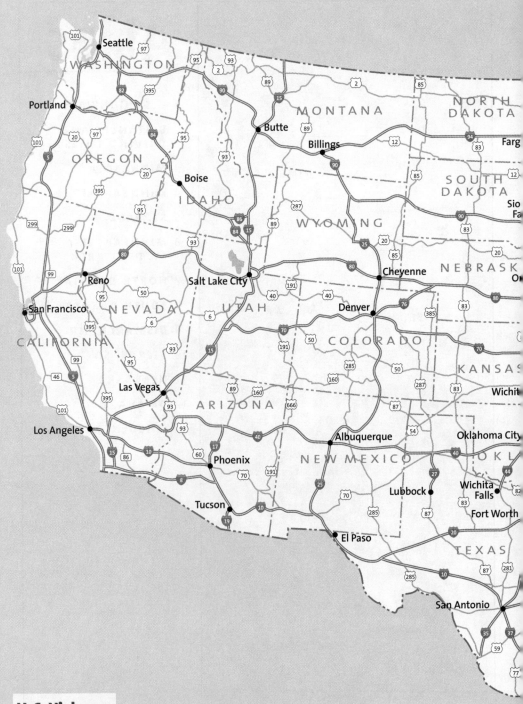

1

U. S. Highways

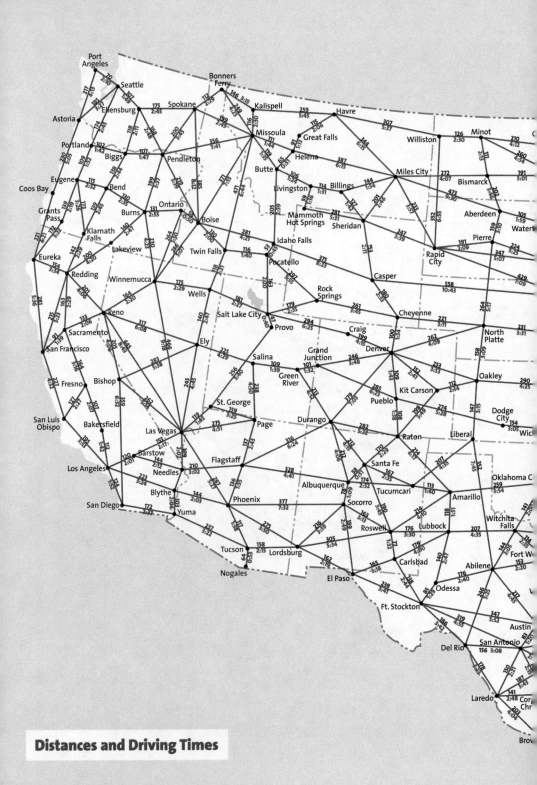

Port Angeles
Seattle
Bonners Ferry
Ellensburg
Spokane
Kalispell
Havre
Astoria
Williston
Minot
Portland
Biggs
Pendleton
Butte
Great Falls
Helena
Miles City
Bismarck
Coos Bay
Eugene
Bend
Ontario
Boise
Livingston
Billings
Aberdeen
Water
Grants Pass
Burns
Klamath Falls
Mammoth Hot Springs
Sheridan
Pierre
Eureka
Lakeview
Twin Falls
Idaho Falls
Rapid City
Redding
Winnemucca
Wells
Pocatello
Casper
Reno
Salt Lake City
Rock Springs
Cheyenne
North Platte
Sacramento
Provo
Craig
Denver
Oakley
San Francisco
Ely
Salina
Grand Junction
Kit Carson
Dodge City
Fresno
Bishop
Green River
Pueblo
Liberal
Wic
San Luis Obispo
St. George
Page
Durango
Raton
Bakersfield
Las Vegas
Oklahoma C
Los Angeles
Barstow
Flagstaff
Santa Fe
Tucumcari
Amarillo
Witchita Falls
Needles
Albuquerque
Fort W
San Diego
Blythe
Phoenix
Socorro
Roswell
Lubbock
Abilene
Yuma
Tucson
Lordsburg
Carlsbad
Odessa
Nogales
El Paso
Ft. Stockton
Austin
Del Rio
San Antonio
Laredo
Cor
Chr
Brow

Distances and Driving Times

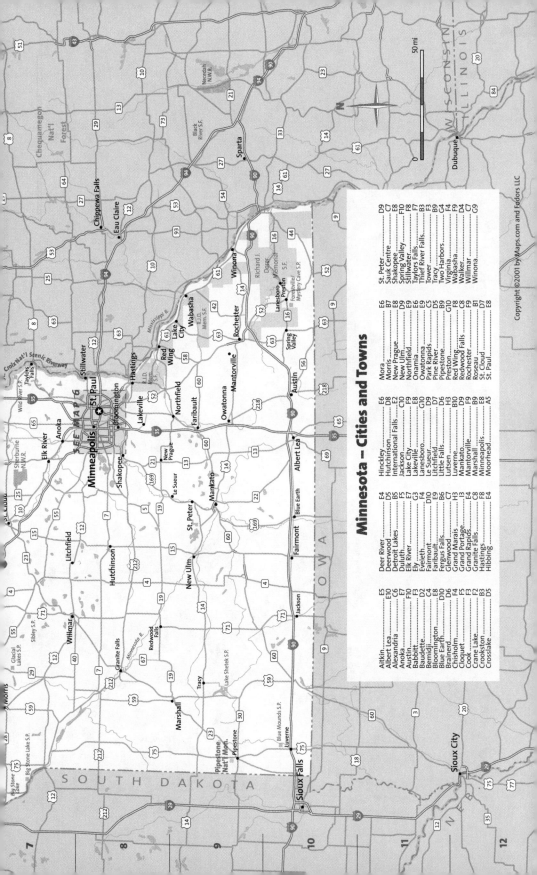

Minneapolis, MN

Mpls. Sculpture Garden

Loring Park

Riverside Park

Riverside Park

St. Anthony Falls

Nicollet Island

Mississippi River

University of Minnesota

Williams Arena

Mariucci Arena

Bell Mus. of Natural History

HHH Metrodome

Elliot Park

Stevens Square

Morrison

Gateway Center

Planetarium

IDS Center

Nicollet Mall

Target Center

Orchestra Hall

Convention Center

Como Ave SE

Van Cleve Park

Washington Ave SE

Delaware Ave SE

E River Rd

Pleasant St

E River Rd

9th St SE

8th St SE

7th St SE

6th St SE

5th St SE

4th Ave SE

3rd Ave SE

2nd Ave SE

Main St SE

Central Ave

Hennepin Ave

1st Ave NE

University Ave SE

15th Ave SE

14th Ave SE

13th Ave SE

6th Ave SE

7th St SE

7th Ave SE

8th Ave SE

10th Ave SE

11th Ave SE

5th Ave SE

4th Ave SE

2nd St S

1st St S

1st Ave S

2nd Ave S

3rd Ave S

4th Ave S

5th Ave S

6th Ave S

7th Ave S

Chicago Ave S

Park Ave S

Portland Ave S

Washington Ave S

2nd St S

3rd St S

4th St S

5th St S

6th St S

7th St S

8th St S

9th St S

10th St S

11th St S

12th St S

Grant St

E 14th St

E 15th St

E 16th St

E 17th St

E 18th St

E 19th St

E 21st St

E 22nd St

Columbus Ave S

Park Ave S

Portland Ave S

Chicago Ave S

Elliot Ave S

10th Ave S

11th Ave S

13th Ave S

14th Ave S

15th Ave S

Bloomington Ave

Minnehaha Ave

Cedar Ave S

Riverside Ave

19th Ave S

20th Ave S

6th Ave S

22nd Ave S

25th Ave S

27th Ave S

E Franklin Ave

5th St S

4th St S

7th Ave S

2nd St S

3rd St S

1st St S

Ave S

Willow St

Harmon Pl

Yale Pl

Hennepin Ave

Lasalle Ave

LaSalle Ave

Nicollet Ave

Marquette Ave

2nd Ave S

Hennepin Ave

1st Ave N

2nd Ave N

3rd Ave N

4th Ave N

Washington Ave N

2nd St N

4th St N

5th St N

6th Ave N

7th St N

1st St N

W River Rd

W. Island Ave

W. Island Ave

W 14th St

W 15th St

15th St

16th St

Royalston Ave

Glenwood Ave

Lakeside Ave

Border Ave

Oak Grove St

Clifton Ave

Groveland Ave

Ridgewood Ave

W. Franklin Ave

Lyndale Ave S

W 22nd St

Clinton

Nicollet

1st Ave S

2nd Ave S

3rd Ave S

4th Ave S

4th Ave S

E 14th St

35W

94

94

52

12

12

52

94

52

47

65

55

55

55

55

55

394

122

35W

N

0   0.5 mi

Copyright ©2001 by Maps.com and Fodors LLC

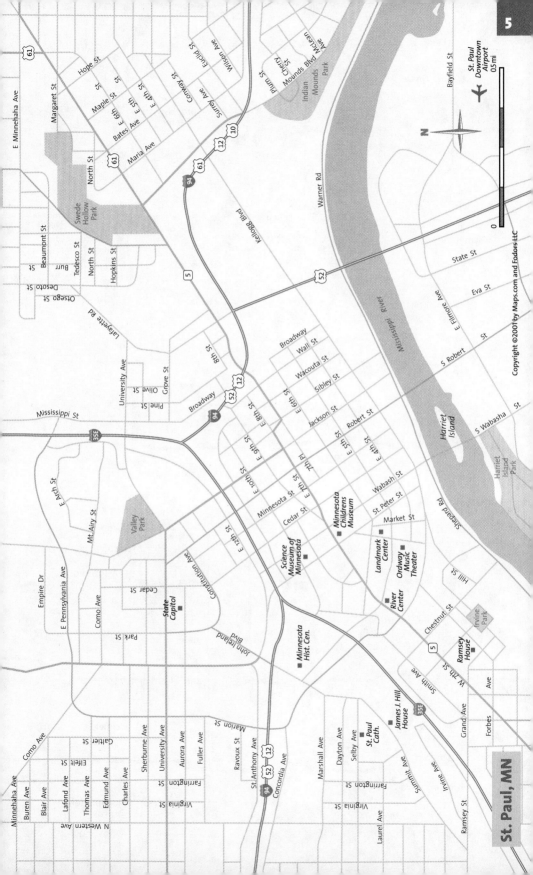

Minneapolis/St. Paul Area

Copyright ©2001 by Maps.com and Fodors LLC

0   2 mi

North Dakota – Cities and Towns

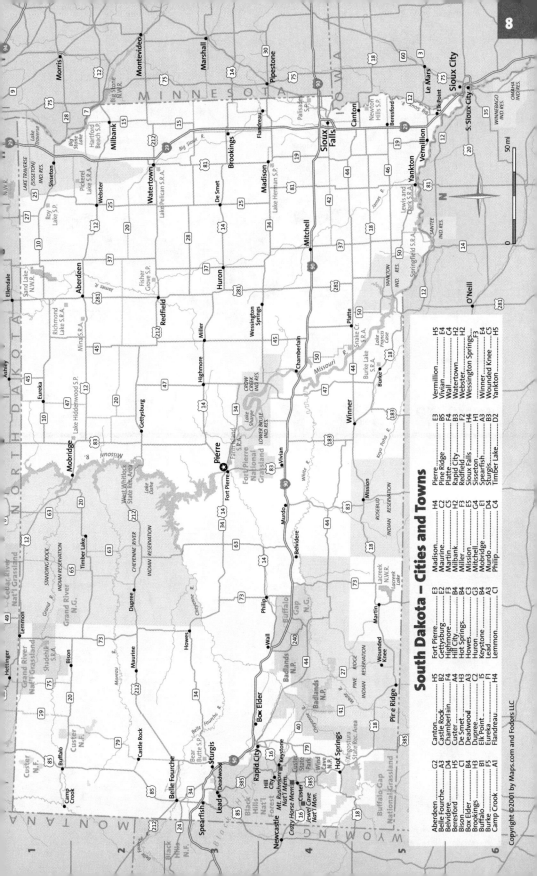

South Dakota – Cities and Towns

Aberdeen	G2	Canton	H5	Madison	E3	Pierre	H5	Vermillion	E3
Belle Fourche	A3	Castle Rock	B2	Maurine	E2	Pine Ridge	C2	Vivian	B5
Belvidere	C4	Chamberlain	F4	Martin	F3	Platte	G5	Wall	C4
Beresford	H5	De Smet	A4	Milbank	B4	Rapid City	H2	Watertown	E4
Box Elder	B4	Deadwood	H3	Miller	E5	Redfield	F3	Webster	H2
Brookings	B1	Dupree	A3	Mitchell	G3	Sioux Falls	H4	Wessington Springs	F3
Buffalo	A1	Elk Point	I5	Mobridge	B4	Sisseton	G4	Winner	F3
Burke	B1	Eureka	F1	Murdo	B3	Sioux Falls	H1	Winner	E4
Camp Crook	A1	Flandreau	H4	Philip	C1	Spearfish	A3	Wounded Knee	C5
				Keystone	I5	Sturgis	D4	Yankton	H5
Fort Pierre	H5	Lead	F1			Lemmon	A3	Timber Lake	D2
Gettysburg	B2								
Highmore	F4								
Hot Springs	H2								
Howes	A4								
Huron	G2								

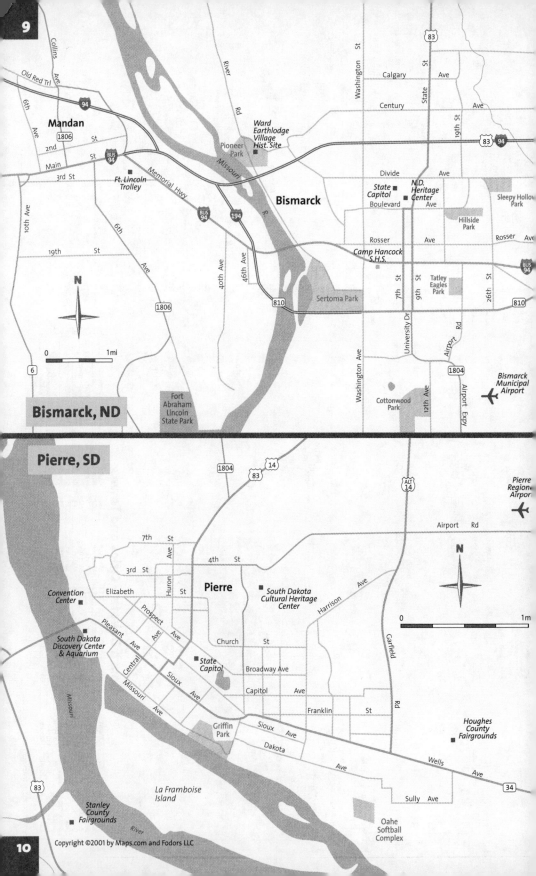

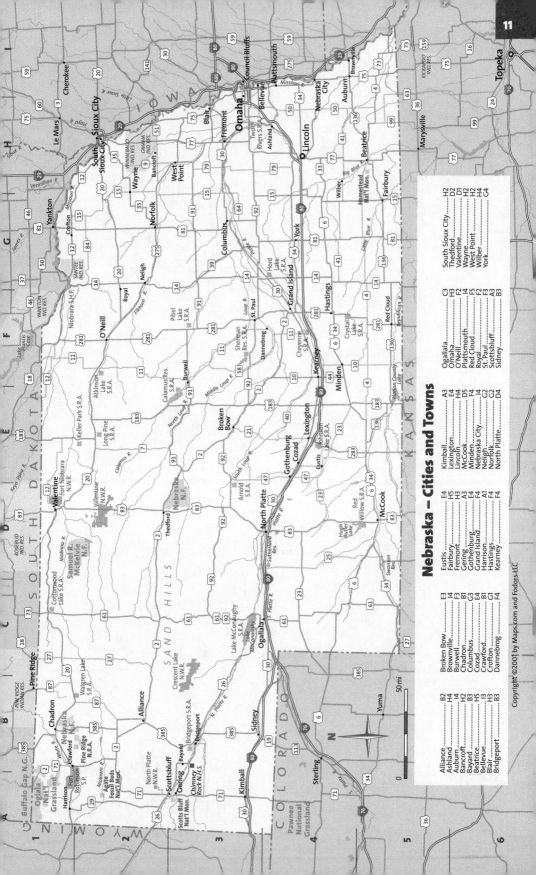

Nebraska – Cities and Towns

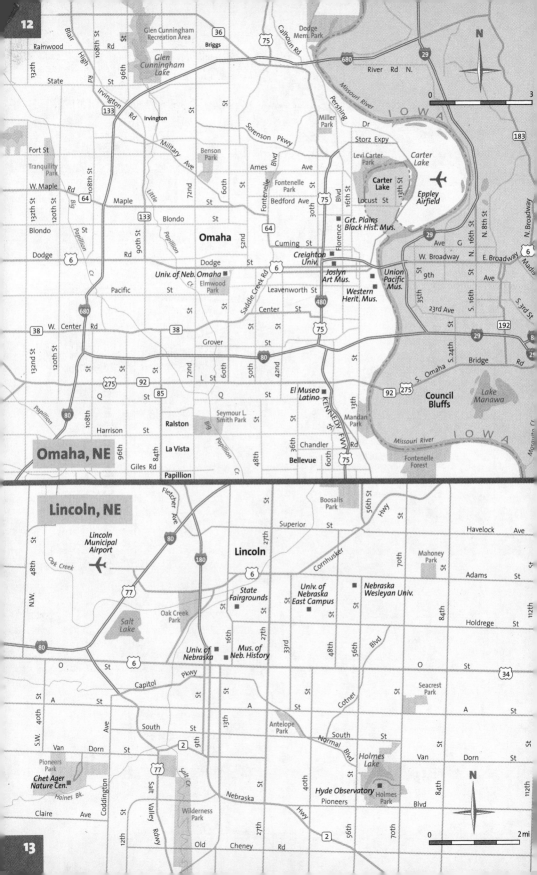